lonely planet

South
Italy

**Naples &
Campania**
p36

**Puglia,
Basilicata &
Calabria**
p102

Sicily
p161

THIS EDITION WRITTEN AND RESEARCHED BY

Cristian Bonetto,
Gregor Clark, Helena Smith

Contents

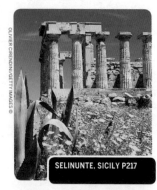
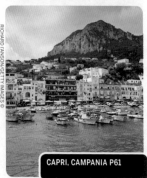
OLIVIER CIRENDINI/GETTY IMAGES ©

RICHARD l'ANSON/GETTY IMAGES ©

Contents

SPAGHETTI ALLE VONGOLE

UNDERSTAND

SURVIVAL GUIDE

SPECIAL FEATURES

Welcome to Southern Italy

Italy's north may have the euros, but the south has the soul. Beautifully sun-bleached, weathered and worn, this is Italy at its most ancient, complex and seductive.

Cultural Riches

For millennia the crossroads of civilisations, southern Italy is littered with the legacies of grand cultures, from the Greeks and Romans to the Saracens, Normans and Spanish. Channel the classics at the Greek temples of Segesta and Paestum, or on the chariot-grooved streets of Pompeii and Herculaneum. Even older are the prehistoric *sassi* (cave dwellings) of Matera, yet another of the south's wonders. Compare the Byzantine glitter of Sicily's cathedrals to the darkness of Caravaggio's *Flagellazione* in Naples, then watch the region outdo itself with some of the country's finest baroque.

Endless Feasting

Italy's south is a never-ending feast: bubbling, wood-fired pizza and potent espresso in Naples; long, lazy lunches at vine-framed Pugliese farmhouses; freshly caught sardines on Tyrrhenian islands; lavish, luscious pastries in chintzy *pasticcerie* (pastry shops). Go mushroom hunting in the wilds of Calabria, taste-test your first red aubergine (eggplant) at an heirloom trattoria in Basilicata, feast on fresh sea urchin on an Adriatic beach, or just kick back with a glass of crisp local Falanghina as you debate who has the creamiest buffalo mozzarella – Caserta, Paestum or Foggia?

A Warm Benvenuto

You'll rarely be short of a conversation south of Rome. Southern Italians are naturally curious, famously affable, and quick to share their opinion. Family and friends are sacred, and time spent laughing, arguing or gossiping is as integral to southern life as lavish Sunday lunches and long, hot summers. Here, simple questions will quickly turn into earnest conversations, while casual chats can easily transform into budding friendships. So pick up a few local words, polish that smile, and don't be surprised if you head home with a string of new life-long *amici* (friends).

Natural Highs

With rugged mountains, fiery volcanoes and glittering coastal grottoes, southern Italy feels like one giant playground waiting to be tackled. Crank up the heart rate white-water rafting down Calabria's river Lao; scaling Europe's most active volcano, Stromboli; or diving into prehistoric sea caves on Puglia's Promontorio del Gargano. If you need to bring it down a notch, consider slow pedalling across Puglia's gentle countryside, sailing along the Amalfi Coast, or simply stripping down and soaking in Vulcano's healing geothermal mud. The options may be many, but there is one constant – a landscape that is beautiful, diverse and just a little magic.

Why I Love Southern Italy

By Cristian Bonetto, Author

Southern Italy is like the Slow Food of travel. While much of Europe marches to an increasingly homogenised beat, this raffish corner of the continent dances to its own hypnotic tune. Here, melancholy folk songs still fill the air; eyeshadow is applied thick and bright; and hearts are proudly worn on sleeves. Many of my fondest travel memories have been formed here: epic Sunday lunches with new-found friends; hot winds whistling through ancient temples; quiet swims in milky-blue Tyrrhenian waters. I might hail from the north, but my heart belongs to the Mezzogiorno.

For more about our authors, see page 304

Above: Palermo p165

Southern Italy

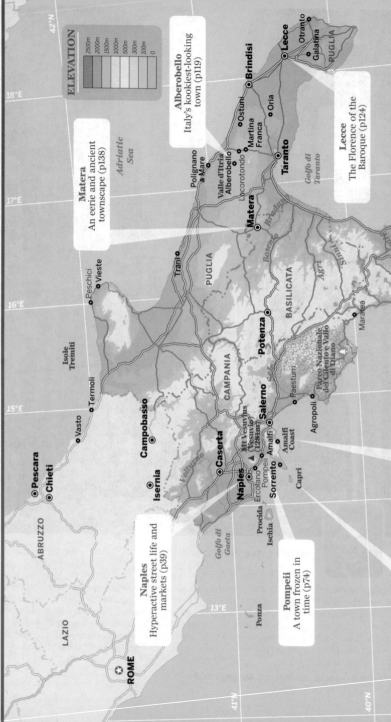

Naples
Hyperactive street life and markets (p39)

Pompeii
A town frozen in time (p74)

Matera
An eerie and ancient townscape (p138)

Alberobello
Italy's kookiest-looking town (p119)

Leece
The Florence of the Baroque (p124)

ELEVATION
2500m
2000m
1500m
1000m
500m
300m
100m
0

0   50 miles
0   100 km

ROME

LAZIO

ABRUZZO

Pescara
Chieti

Isole
Tremiti

Vasto

Termoli

Peschici
Vieste

Trani

Campobasso

Isernia

Caserta

Naples
Mt Vesuvius
Vesuvio
(1281m)
Pompeii
Ercolano
Sorrento
Amalfi
Amalfi
Coast
Capri

Procida
Ischia

Ponza

Golfo di
Gaeta

CAMPANIA

Salerno

Paestum

Agropoli

Maratea

Parco Nazionale
del Cilento e Vallo
di Diano

BASILICATA

Potenza

PUGLIA

Matera

Polignano
a-Mare

Valle d'Itria
Alberobello
Locorotondo
Martina
Franca

Ostuni

Oria

Taranto

Golfo di
Taranto

Brindisi

Lecce

Otranto
Galatina

PUGLIA

Adriatic
Sea

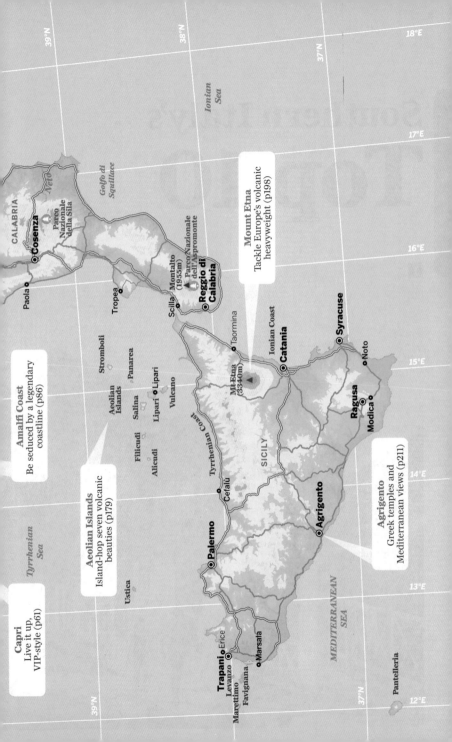

Capri
Live it up, VIP-style (p61)

Aeolian Islands
Island-hop seven volcanic beauties (p179)

Amalfi Coast
Be seduced by a legendary coastline (p86)

Mount Etna
Tackle Europe's volcanic heavyweight (p198)

Agrigento
Greek temples and Mediterranean views (p211)

CALABRIA

Cosenza

Parco Nazionale della Sila

Neto

Golfo di Squillace

Ionian Sea

Paola

Tropea

Scilla Montalto (1955m)

Parco Nazionale dell'Aspromonte

Reggio di Calabria

Taormina

Ionian Coast

Catania

Syracuse

Noto

Mt Etna (3340m)

Stromboli

Panarea

Aeolian Islands

Salina

Lipari Lipari

Vulcano

Tyrrhenian Coast

Ragusa

Modica

SICILY

Filicudi

Alicudi

Ustica

Cefalù

Palermo

Agrigento

Tyrrhenian Sea

MEDITERRANEAN SEA

Trapani Erice

Levanzo

Marettimo

Favignana

Marsala

Pantelleria

Ionian Sea

39°N

38°N

37°N

39°N

37°N

18°E

17°E

16°E

15°E

14°E

13°E

12°E

Southern Italy's
Top 10

1

Ghostly Pompeii

1 Nothing piques human curiosity quite like a mass catastrophe, and few have left a mark like Pompeii (p74), a once-thriving Roman town frozen in its death throes for all time. Wander Roman streets, the grassy, column-lined forum, the city brothel, the 5000-seat theatre and the frescoed Villa dei Misteri while you ponder Pliny the Younger's terrifying account of the tragedy: 'Darkness came on again, again ashes, thick and heavy. We got up repeatedly to shake these off; otherwise we would have been buried and crushed by the weight'.

Naples

2 Both rough and refined, tender and tough, Naples (p39) thrives on contradiction and complexity. Gritty alleyways meet palm-fringed boulevards; crumbling facades mask baroque ballrooms; and cultish shrines flank fashionable bars. Intensity underlines the details, from the muscle of Neapolitan espresso to the high-octane rush of the city's markets and streets. Add to this a jumble of castles, royal palaces and superlative art, and you have yourself one of southern Italy's most unexpected highlights.

MICHELE FALZONE/GETTY IMAGES ©

LONELY PLANET/GETTY IMAGES ©

Temples in Agrigento

3 Few archaeological sites evoke the past like Agrigento's Valley of the Temples (p211). Located on a ridge overlooking the Mediterranean, the stoic temples belonged to Akragas, a once-great city settled by the Greeks. The scars of ancient battles endure in the 5th-century-BC Tempio di Hera, while the Tempio della Concordia inspired Unesco's own logo. To conjure the ghosts of the past, roam the ruins late in the afternoon, when the crowds have thinned and the wind whistles between the columns.
Below: Tempio della Concordia

Matera

4 The best time to explore Matera (p138) is before it gets up, when the town is tinged gold by the morning sun and the scent of the day's first coffee lingers in the air. Matera is an extraordinary place: its World Heritage–listed *sassi* (former cave dwellings) were developed from caves that pock a dizzying ravine. In no other place do you come face to face with such powerful images of Italy's lost peasant culture; these cavernous dwellings echo a level of poverty difficult to fathom in a wealthy G8 country.

Capri

5 Even the summer hordes can't quite dilute the ethereal magic of Capri (p61). Described as 'one of the magnetic points of the earth' by the writer and painter Alberto Savinio, Italy's most fabled island has been seducing mere mortals for millennia. Emperor Tiberius reputedly threw his lovers off its dizzying cliffs, travellers on the Grand Tour waxed lyrical about its electric-blue grotto, and celebrities continue to moor their yachts in its turquoise waters. For a view you won't forget, head to the summit of Monte Solaro (think bath-time boats and sugar-cube houses).

Alberobello

6 Imagination runs riot in Alberobello (p119), famed for its kooky, one-of-a-kind architecture. We're talking *trulli* – whitewashed circular dwellings with cone-shaped roofs. Looking like they're straight out of a Disney cartoon, these sunbaked dwellings tumble down the slopes like armies of hatted dwarves. You can dine in some of them and sleep in others. Just don't be surprised if you need to pinch yourself... Was that Snow White? Are you on Earth? Unesco seems to thinks so; they've made the *trulli* World Heritage treasures. Top right: *Trulli*

Aeolian Island–Hopping

7 The Greeks don't have a monopoly on Mediterranean island-hopping. Sicily's Aeolian Islands (p179) might be a little less famous than their Aegean Sea rivals, but they are no less stunning. Mix and match from seven volcanic outcrops, among them thermal hot-spot Vulcano (p182), vine-laced Salina (p183) and lava-oozing Stromboli (p185). But don't just take our word for it. The islands are one of only four Italian natural landscapes on Unesco's World Heritage list (the others being Sicily's Mt Etna, the Dolomites and Monte San Giorgio). Above right: Aerial view of Stromboli

Scaling Mt Etna

8 Known to the Greeks as the 'column that holds up the sky', Mt Etna (p198) is Europe's largest volcano and one of the world's most active. It's also the highest mountain south of the Alps. The ancients believed the giant Tifone (Typhoon) lived in its crater and lit up the sky with regular, spectacular pyrotechnics. At 3330m it towers above Sicily's Ionian coast, and since 1987 its slopes have been part of the Parco dell'Etna, an area that encompasses both alpine forests and the forbiddingly black summit.

Amalfi Coast

9 The world-famous Amalfi Coast (p86) bewitches with its astounding beauty and gripping geology: coastal mountains plunge into crystal-blue sea in a prime-time vertical scene of precipitous crags, sun-bleached villages and lush forest. While some may argue that the Italy's most beautiful coast is Liguria's Cinque Terre or Calabria's Costa Viola, it was the Amalfi Coast that prompted American writer John Steinbeck to describe it as a 'dream place that isn't quite real when you are there and beckoningly real after you have gone'.

Right: Positano (p87)

Baroque Lecce

10 The extravagant architectural character of many Puglian towns is down to the local style of *barocco leccese* (Lecce baroque). The local stone was so soft, art critic Cesare Brandi once claimed 'it can be carved with a penknife'. Local craftsmen vied for ever-greater heights of creativity, crowding facades with swirling vegetal designs, gargoyles and strange zoomorphic figures. Lecce's Basilica di Santa Croce (p126) is the high point of the style, so outrageously busy the Marchese Grimaldi said it made him think a lunatic was having a nightmare. Above: Facade of the Basilica di Santa Croce

Need to Know

For more information, see Survival Guide (p261)

Currency
Euro (€)

Language
Italian

Visas
Generally not required for stays of up to 90 days (or at all for EU nationals); some nationalities will need a Schengen visa.

Money
ATMs at every airport, most train stations and widely available in towns and cities. Credit cards accepted in most hotels and restaurants.

Mobile Phones
European and Australian phones work, other phones should be set to roaming. Use a local SIM card for cheaper rates on local calls.

Time
Central European Time (GMT/UTC plus one hour)

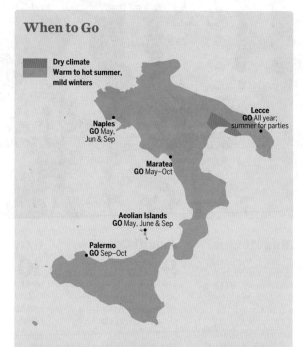

When to Go

Dry climate
Warm to hot summer, mild winters

Lecce
GO All year; summer for parties

Naples
GO May, Jun & Sep

Maratea
GO May–Oct

Aeolian Islands
GO May, June & Sep

Palermo
GO Sep–Oct

High Season
(Jul & Aug)
➡ Queues and crowds at big sights, beaches and on the road, especially in August.
➡ A good period for cultural events in tourist areas.

Shoulder Season (Apr–Jun & Sep–Oct)
➡ Good deals on accommodation.
➡ Spring is best for festivals, flowers and local produce.
➡ Autumn is best for warm weather and the grape harvest.

Low Season
(Nov–Mar)
➡ Prices can be 30% lower than high season (except Christmas, New Year and Easter).
➡ Many sights, hotels and restaurants close in coastal and mountainous areas.
➡ Dont miss Christmas feasts and colourful Carnevale.

Websites

Lonely Planet (www.lonely
planet.com/italy) Destination
information, hotel bookings,
traveller forum and more.

Trenitalia (www.trenitalia.com)
Italian railway website.

Agriturismi (www.agriturismi.
it) Guide to farm accommodation options.

Slow Food (www.slowfood.com)
For the best local producers,
restaurants and markets.

Enit Italia (www.italiantourism.
com) Italian government tourism website.

Italia Kids (www.italiakids.com)
Fantastic family resource.

Important Numbers

To dial listings in the book
from outside Italy, dial your
international access code, Italy's
country code, and then the
number (including the '0').

Country code	☏39
International access code	☏00
Ambulance	☏118
Police	☏113
Fire	☏115

Exchange Rates

Australia	A$1	€0.70
Canada	C$1	€0.71
Japan	¥100	€0.75
New Zealand	NZ$1	€0.62
Switzerland	Sfr1	€0.81
UK	UK£1	€1.18
US	US$1	€0.74

For current exchange rates see
www.xe.com

Daily Costs

**Budget:
Less than €100**

➡ Dorm bed: €15–€30

➡ Double room in a budget
hotel: €50–€110

➡ Pizza or pasta: €6–€12

➡ Excellent markets and delis
for self-catering

**Midrange:
€100–€250**

➡ Double room in a hotel:
€100–€220

➡ Lunch and dinner in local
restaurants: €25–€50

**Top End:
More than €250**

➡ Double room in a four- or
five-star hotel: €200–€450

➡ Top restaurant dinner:
€50–€150

Opening Hours

Opening hours vary throughout
the year. We've provided high-
season opening hours; hours
will generally decrease in the
shoulder and low seasons. In
this guide, 'summer' times generally refer to the period from
April to September or October,
while 'winter' times generally
run from October or November
to March.

Banks 8.30am–1.30pm &
3.30–4.30pm Monday to Friday

Restaurants Noon–2.30pm &
7.30–11pm or midnight

Cafes 7.30am–8pm

Bars & Clubs 10pm–4am

Shops 9am–1pm & 4–8pm
Monday to Saturday

Arriving in Southern Italy

Capodichino Airport (Naples)
A shuttle bus to the centre of
Naples will cost €3; they run
every 20 minutes from 6.30am
to 11.40pm. Taxis have a €19 set
fare and take 30 minutes.

**Karol Wojtyła Airport (Palese
Airport; Bari)** A shuttle bus to
the centre of Bari will cost €4;
buses run hourly from 5.35am
to 12.10am. A taxi will cost about
€24 and will take 15 minutes.

**Falcone-Borsellino Airport
(Palermo)** A shuttle bus to
the centre of Palermo will cost
€6.10; buses run half hourly
from 5am to midnight. Trains
cost €5.80; they run every 20
to 40 minutes from 5.54am to
10.05pm. Taxis have a €35–€45
set fare and take 30 minutes.

Getting Around

Transport in southern Italy is
reasonably priced and usually
efficient.

Train Reasonably priced, with
extensive coverage and frequent
departures.

Car Handy for travelling at your
own pace, or for visiting areas
with minimal public transport.
Not a good idea for travelling
within major urban areas.

Bus Cheaper and slower than
trains. Useful for more remote
villages not serviced by trains.

Ferries & Hydrofoils Large
ferries *(navi)* service Campania
and Sicily. Smaller ferries
(traghetti) and hydrofoils
(aliscafi) service the Bay of
Naples islands, the Amalfi
Coast, Puglia's Isole Tremiti, and
Sicily's Aeolian Islands. Most
services are reduced in winter.

For much more on
getting around, see
p276

First Time

For more information, see Survival Guide (p261)

Checklist

➡ Ensure your passport is valid for at least six months past your arrival date

➡ Check airline baggage restrictions

➡ Organise travel insurance

➡ Make bookings (for accommodation and entertainment)

➡ Inform your credit/debit card company of your travels

➡ Check if you can use your mobile (cell) phone

➡ Check requirements for hiring a car

What to Pack

➡ Hat, sunglasses and sunscreen for a comfortable summer

➡ Electrical adapter to recharge gadgets

➡ An appetite for southern Italy's favourite sport: eating!

➡ Smart threads for the traditional evening *passeggiata* (stroll) and elegant posing in piazzas

➡ Patience for coping with inefficiency

➡ A detailed driving map

Top Tips for Your Trip

➡ Visit in the shoulder season (spring and autumn) – the weather is usually good and the crowds are thinner.

➡ If you're driving, get off the main roads when you can: some of the most stunning scenery is best enjoyed on secondary or tertiary roads.

➡ Make an effort to speak at least a few Italian words. A little effort can go a long way.

➡ Avoid restaurants with touts and the mediocre *menu turistico* (tourist menu).

What to Wear

Appearances matter in Italy. In general, trousers (pants), jeans, shirts and polo shirts for men and skirts or trousers for women will serve you well in the city. Shorts, T-shirts and sandals are fine in summer and at the beach, but long sleeves are required for dining out. Come evening, think smart casual. A light sweater or waterproof jacket is useful in spring and autumn, and sturdy shoes are good for visiting archaeological sites.

Sleeping

Book ahead if travelling in the high season, especially if visiting popular coastal areas. Also consider booking ahead if visiting cities or towns during major events. See p262 for more accommodation information.

➡ **Hotels** All levels of price and quality, from cheap-and-charmless to sleek-and-exclusive.

➡ **Farm-Stays** Perfect for families and for relaxation, *agriturismi* (farm stays) range from rustic farmhouses to luxe country estates.

➡ **B&Bs** Often great value, options span rooms in family houses to self-catering studio apartments.

➡ **Pensions** Similar to hotels, though *pensioni* are generally of one- to three-star quality and family-run.

➡ **Hostels** You'll find both official HI-affiliated and privately run *ostelli* (hostels), many also offering private rooms.

Money

Credit and debit cards can be used almost everywhere with the exception of some rural towns and villages.

Visa and MasterCard are widely recognised. American Express is only accepted by some major chains and big hotels, and very few places take Diners Club.

ATMs (known as Bancomats) are everywhere, but be aware of transaction fees. Some ATMs in Italy reject foreign cards. If this happens, try a few before assuming your card is the problem.

For more information, see p268.

Bargaining

Gentle haggling is common in markets. Haggling in stores is generally unacceptable, though good-humoured bargaining at smaller artisan or craft shops is not unusual if making multiple purchases.

Tipping

➡ **When to Tip** Tipping is customary in restaurants, optional elsewhere.

➡ **Taxis** Optional, but most people round up to the nearest euro.

➡ **Restaurants** Most restaurants have a *coperto* (cover charge; usually €2 to €3). Some also include a *servizio* (service charge) of 10% to 15%. If service isn't included, a small tip is appropriate.

➡ **Bars** Most locals usually leave small change on the bar when ordering coffee; if drinks are brought to your table, tip as you would in a restaurant.

Language

Unlike many other European countries, English is not widely spoken in Italy. Of course, you can get by in the main tourist centres, but in the countryside you'll need to master a few basic phrases. This will improve your experience no end, especially when ordering in restaurants, some of which have no written menu.

1 **What's the local speciality?**
Qual'è la specialità di questa regione?
kwa·le la spe·cha·lee·ta dee kwes·ta re·jo·ne

A bit like the rivalry between medieval Italian city-states, these days the country's regions compete in speciality foods and wines.

2 **Which combined tickets do you have?**
Quali biglietti cumulativi avete?
kwa·lee bee·lye·tee koo·moo·la·tee·vee a·ve·te

Make the most of your euro by getting combined tickets to various sights; they are available in all major Italian cities.

3 **Where can I buy discount designer items?**
C'è un outlet in zona? che oon owt·let in zo·na

Discount fashion outlets are big business in major cities – get bargain-priced seconds, samples and cast-offs for *la bella figura*.

4 **I'm here with my husband/boyfriend.**
Sono qui con il mio marito/ragazzo.
so·no kwee kon eel mee·o ma·ree·to/ra·ga·tso

Solo women travellers may receive unwanted attention in some parts of Italy; if ignoring fails have a polite rejection ready.

5 **Let's meet at 6pm for pre-dinner drinks.**
Ci vediamo alle sei per un aperitivo.
chee ve·dya·mo a·le say per oon a·pe·ree·tee·vo

At dusk, watch the main piazza get crowded with people sipping colourful cocktails and snacking the evening away: join your new friends for this authentic Italian ritual!

Etiquette

Italy is a surprisingly formal society; the following tips will help you avoid any awkward moments.

➡ **Greetings** Shake hands and say *buongiorno* (good day) or *buonasera* (good evening) to strangers; kiss both cheeks and say *come stai* (how are you) to friends. Use *lei* (you) in polite company; use *tu* (you) with friends and children. Only use first names if invited.

➡ **Asking for help** Say *mi scusi* (excuse me) to attract attention; use *permesso* (permission) to pass by in a crowded space.

➡ **Religion** Dress modestly (cover shoulders, torso and thighs) and show respect when visiting religious sites.

➡ **Eating & Drinking** When dining in an Italian home, bring a small gift of *dolci* (sweets) or wine and dress well. Let your host lead when sitting and starting the meal. When dining out, summon the waiter by saying *mi scusi* (excuse me).

➡ **Gestures** Maintain eye contact during conversation.

If You Like...

Food, Glorious Food

Southern Italy's rich soil, produce-packed hillsides and turquoise seas are a giant natural larder. Culinary traditions are fiercely protected and eating well is a given. Tuck in!

Pizza Feast on Italy's top export in its spiritual home, Naples. (p54)

Buffalo mozzarella Sink your teeth into Italy's silkiest cheese in Campania. (p37)

Seafood So fresh it's eaten *crudo* (raw) in Campania (p39), Puglia (p103) and Sicily (p161).

Street food From *pizza fritta* (deep-fried pizza) in Naples (p54) to *panelle* (chickpea fritters) in Palermo (p172), fast food comes with culinary cred.

Markets Lip-smacking produce and street life collide at markets like Porta Nolana (p45), Ballarò (p169) and La Pescheria (p193).

Medieval Towns

Cobbled streets snake up hillsides to sculpted fountains, the scent of *ragù* (meat and tomato sauce) wafts from shuttered windows and washing hangs like holiday bunting.

Ravello Romantic gardens, heavenly views, and a world-class music festival above the Amalfi Coast. (p93)

Taormina A chic summertime favourite, with secret gardens and an ancient panoramic amphitheatre. (p187)

Cefalù Arabesque streets, a Norman cathedral and lapping waves. (p177)

Maratea A 13th-century *borgo* (medieval town) with pint-sized piazzas and startling views across the Gulf of Policastro. (p146)

Erice Ancient walls, brooding castles, and views across to Africa. (p221)

Baroque Architecture

Southern Italy found its soulmate in the baroque period. Plunge into a world of outrageous palaces and bling-tastic churches.

Val di Noto A valley adorned with model baroque towns, including best-of-the-lot Noto. (p207)

Lecce This hallucinogenic city is to the baroque what Florence is to the Renaissance. (p124)

Palazzo Reale The Italian baroque's epic swansong. (p61)

Catania The Piazza del Duomo is a World Heritage pin-up. (p192)

The Great Outdoors

Saunter between sea and sky in Campania, slip into silent forests in Basilicata and Calabria, and come face to face with Mother Nature's wrath in lava-spewing Sicily.

Sentiero degli Dei Hit the 'Path of the Gods' for a different take on the Amalfi Coast. (p87)

Mt Etna Hike the picturesque slopes of Europe's tallest active volcano. (p198)

Parco Nazionale del Gargano Explore an enchanted world of pines, orchids and sacred pilgrimage sites. (p112)

IF YOU LIKE...HIDDEN TREASURES

Subterranean Naples is a thrilling, silent sprawl of ancient cisterns, wartime hideouts and royal escape routes. For a sneak peek, descend into the remarkably restored Tunnel Borbonico (p52).

Islands & Beaches

Northern Italy would sell its soul for a coastline this alluring. From bijou islands to crystal-clear grottoes, the south's offerings are as varied as they are beautiful.

Puglia The region's superlative beaches include Baia dei Turchi (p133) and the cliff-backed beaches of the Gargano (p112).

Aeolian Islands Island-hop Sicily's seven volcanic gems. (p179)

Capri Golden light and a mesmerising grotto lure A-list jet-setters. (p61)

Maratea This Basilicata beauty gives the Amalfi Coast a run for its money. (p146)

Vivid History

Southern Italy's cosmopolitan past comes to life in its glorious art and architecture. Lose yourself in frescoed scenes of classical mythology or ponder the glories of Constantinople in Byzantine mosaics.

Villa Romana del Casale Sicily's top Roman site is home to the finest Roman floor mosaics in existence. (p216)

Museo Archeologico Nazionale Showstopping sculptures, frescoes and mosaics from Pompeii, Herculaneum and beyond at Naples' top museum. (p41)

Herculaneum From frescoed homes to time-warped changing rooms, Roman life lives on in its original, ill-fated setting. (p72)

Cattedrale di Monreale Lavish 12th-century tile-work brings the Old Testament to life in this Arab-Norman wonder. (p176)

(Above) Pizza, Naples
(Below) Teatro Greco (p189), Taormina

Month by Month

February

Short and accursed is how Italians traditionaly describe February. It might still be chilly down south, but almond trees start to blossom and Carnevale season brightens things up with confetti, costumes and sugar-dusted treats.

✯✯ Carnevale

In the period leading up to Ash Wednesday, many southern towns stage pre-Lenten carnivals. One of the most flamboyant is the Carnevale di Acireale (p193), the elaborate and whimsical floats of which are famous throughout the country.

March

The weather in March is capricious: sunny, rainy and windy all at once. The official start of spring is 21 March, but the main holiday season starts with Easter week.

✯✯ Settimana Santa

Processions and passion plays mark Easter Holy Week across the south. On Good Friday and the Thursday preceding it, hooded penitents walk through the streets of Sorrento (p83). On Procida, Good Friday sees wooden statues and life-size tableaux carted across the island for the Procession of the Misteri (p70).

May

The month of roses and early summer produce makes May a perfect time to travel, especially for walkers. The weather is warm but not too hot and prices throughout the south are good value. It's also patron-saint season.

✯✯ Festa di San Gennaro

As patron-saint days go, Naples' Festa di San Gen-naro has a lot riding on it, namely securing the city from volcanic disaster. The faithful gather in the cathedral to see San Gennaro's blood liquefy. If it does, the city is safe. Repeat performances take place on 19 September and 16 December.

✯✯ Ciclo di Rappresentazioni Classiche

Classical intrigue in an evocative setting, the Festival of Greek Theatre (www.indafondazione.org) brings Syracuse's 5th-century-BC amphitheatre to life from mid-May to mid-June, with performances from Italy's acting greats.

June

The summer season kicks off in June. The temperature cranks up quickly, beach lidos start to open in earnest and some of the big summer festivals commence. There's a national holiday on 2 June, the Anniversary of the Republic.

✯✯ Ravello Festival

Perched high above the Amalfi Coast, Ravello draws world-renowned artists during its summer-long festival (www.ravello festival.com). Spanning everything from music and dance to film and art exhibitions, events take place in the exquisite Villa Rufolo gardens from June to mid-September.

★ Napoli Teatro Festival

For three weeks in June, Naples becomes a veritable stage, showcasing both local and international theatre and performance art in conventional and unconventional venues across the city.

July

School is out and Italians everywhere are heading out of the cities to the mountains or beaches for their summer holidays. Prices and temperatures rise. The beach is in full swing, but many cities host summer art festivals.

★ Taormina Arte

Ancient ruins and languid summer nights set a seductive scene for Taormina's arts festival (www.taormina-arte.com). Held between July and August, its program includes film, theatre, concerts and opera, from both Italy and beyond.

★ Festival della Valle d'Itria

Between mid-July and early August, the town of Martina Franca sets toes a-tapping with its music festival (www.festivaldellavalleditria.it). The focus is on classical music and opera, both obscure pieces and more famous works performed in their original form.

August

August in southern Italy is hot, expensive and crowded. Everyone is on holiday and while it may no longer be true that everything is shut, many businesses and restaurants do close for part of the month.

★ Ferragosto

After Christmas and Easter, Ferragosto is Italy's biggest holiday. While it now marks the Feast of the Assumption, even the ancient Romans once honoured their pagan gods on Feriae Augusti. Naples lets loose with particular fervour.

★ La Notte della Taranta

Puglia celebrates its hypnotic *pizzica* dance with the Night of the Taranta (www.lanottedellataranta.it), a two-week festival held in tiny Melpignano. Dancing aside, the event also showcases Salento's folk-music traditions.

September

This is a glorious month in the south. As summer wanes into autumn, the grape harvest begins. Adding to the culinary excitement are the many local *sagre* (food festivals), celebrating regional produce and traditions.

★ Couscous Fest

The Sicilian town of San Vito celebrates multiculturalism and its famous fish couscous at this six-day festival (www.couscousfest.it). Highlights include an international couscous cook-off, tastings and live world-music gigs.

November

The advent of winter creeps down the peninsula in November, but there's still plenty going on. Head south for the chestnut harvest, mushroom picking and All Saints Day.

★ Opera Season

Southern Italy is home to two of the world's great opera houses: Naples' Teatro San Carlo and Palermo's Teatro Massimo. The season traditionally runs from mid-October to March. Book tickets well in advance and don't forget to style up.

December

The days of alfresco living are at an end. Yet despite the cooler days and longer nights, looming Christmas festivities warm things up with festive street lights, nativity scenes and Yuletide specialities.

★ Natale

The weeks preceding Christmas are studded with religious events. Many churches set up nativity scenes known as *presepe*. While Naples is especially famous for these, you'll find impressive tableaux in many southern towns, including Erice in Sicily.

Itineraries

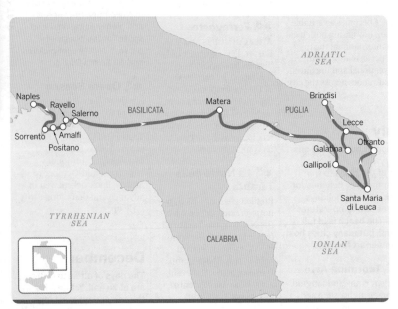

3 WEEKS Coast to Coast

Start on the Tyrrhenian Coast with three days in culture-packed **Naples**. On day four, time-travel in Pompeii before spending two relaxing nights in **Sorrento** shopping for artisan crafts, people-watching behind oversized sunglasses and sunning on its nearby beaches. Next up is the enigmatic Amalfi Coast. Lap up two days in romantic **Positano** and a further two days in **Amalfi** and panoramic **Ravello**, the latter home to breathtaking gardens and a summer-long arts fest. On day ten, continue east to **Salerno** for fabulous seafood and street life, then shoot inland to ancient **Matera**. Give yourself a couple of days to explore the town's extraordinary *sassi* (former cave dwellings) and to hike through the dramatic Matera Gravina gorge.

Continue on to the fortified port of **Gallipoli** for medieval architecture and the town's famed raw seafood. The following day, see Ionian and Adriatic seas meet in **Santa Maria di Leuca**, then take two days to lap up the sugar-soft, white sand beaches of the Baia dei Turchi in **Otranto**. Next stop: **Lecce**, home to some of Italy's most extraordinary baroque architecture. Spend three days here, making a side trip to **Galatina** to admire its astoundingly frescoed 14th-century basilica. From Lecce, it's an easy onward jump to transport hub **Brindisi**.

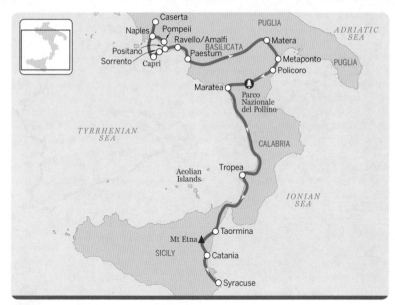

Grand Southern Tour

Grand *palazzi* (mansions), spectacular coastlines and World Heritage-listed towns and ruins – savour the best of southern Italy on this truly unforgettable route. Begin with four days in **Naples**, exploring its art-crammed palaces, secret cloisters and aqueducts. Take a day trip to **Caserta** to gape at its bigger-than-Versailles royal palace and another day trip to the haunting ruins of **Pompeii**. Treat yourself to two days on ethereal **Capri**, one of Italy's most spectacular islands, before jumping across to **Sorrento** for a day of shopping and ambling.

Come day eight, it's time to hit the hairpin turns of the Amalfi Coast. Indulge with two days in **Positano**, from where you can hike some of the breathtaking Sentiero degli Dei (Walk of the Gods), and another two nights in **Amalfi** or **Ravello**. Roam the stoic Greek temples of **Paestum** on day 12 before continuing east to fellow World-Heritage treasure **Matera**, taking two days to wine and dine in its arthritic laneways and extraordinary 'cave' buildings. Next up are the Greek ruins of **Metaponto**, the former hometown of Pythagoras and location of the incredible Tavole Paltine, one-time meeting point for medieval Crusaders. More ancient tales await in nearby **Policoro**, with archaeological artifacts spanning 9000 years. From here, slip into the sprawling wilderness of the **Parco Nazionale del Pollino**, Italy's largest national park. With Terranova di Pollino as your base, spend three days hiking through invigorating woods and exploring the curious Albanian villages of San Paolo Albanese and San Costantino Albanese.

Continue west to the superlative coastal jewel of **Maratea**. Allow two days to bathe in its turquoise waters, then continue south to Calabria's seaside showoff **Tropea** for two further days of seafood and sunsets. Further south in Villa San Giovanni, catch a ferry across to Sicily, spending two days in stylish, coastal **Taormina**, Sicily's former Byzantine capital and home to the world's most spectacularly located Greek amphitheatre. On day 25, scale mighty **Mt Etna**, then head back down for the architectural wonders of **Catania** on day 26. Wrap up in stunning **Syracuse**, a picture-perfect jumble of sun-bleached ruins, baroque piazzas, animated markets and irresistible blue sea.

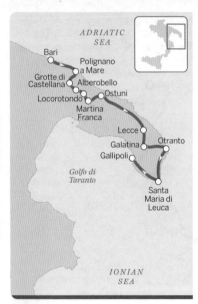

2 WEEKS Perfect Puglia

Puglia is one of Italy's most underrated regions. Start your revelation in dynamic **Bari**, exploring its ancient historic centre and huge Romanesque basilica. Strike out south, via **Polignano a Mare**, to the famous **Grotte di Castellana**, Italy's longest network of subterranean caves. From here, a two- to three-day drive south will take you through some of the finest Valle d'Itria towns, including **Alberobello**, with its hobbitlike *trulli* houses, wine-producing **Locorotondo**, beautiful baroque **Martina Franca** and chic, whitewashed **Ostuni**. Next up is **Lecce**, dubbed the 'Florence of the South' for its operatic architectural ensembles and scholarly bent. Hire a bike and spend at least three or four days here before moving on to **Galatina** to see its basilica, awash with astounding frescoes. Head east to the fortified port of **Otranto** and the inviting beaches of the Baia dei Turchi, then push south along the wild, vertiginous coastline to **Santa Maria di Leuca**, the very tip of the Italian stiletto. Conclude your adventure in the island city of **Gallipoli**, feasting on raw sea urchin and octopus in its elegant town centre.

3 WEEKS Best of Sicily

Sicily is sweet, spicy and intriguing. For a taste, fly into **Palermo** and take three days to savour its fusion architecture, mosaics and markets. Spend day four roaming the ruins at **Segesta** before continuing on to **Trapani** to sample its Arabesque cuisine. The next morning head up to **Erice**, one of Italy's most arresting medieval hilltop towns. Come back down to spend day six sipping sweet local wine in **Marsala** and day seven exploring ancient **Selinunte**. More archaeological marvels await on day eight at the Valle dei Templi in **Agrigento**, with its five Doric structures perched on a ridge overlooking the Mediterranean coast. On day nine, shoot southeast to the Val di Noto and spend a couple of days in its baroque, World Heritage-listed towns, especially **Ragusa**, **Modica** and **Noto**. Change gear on days 12 and 13 with a stay in youthful, worldly **Catania**, a city famed for its fish market and kicking nightlife. Tackle **Mt Etna** on day 14 before two days of wining and sunning in chic, coastal **Taormina**. From **Messina**, catch a hydrofoil to the **Aeolian Islands** for five days of island-hopping along this arresting volcanic ridge.

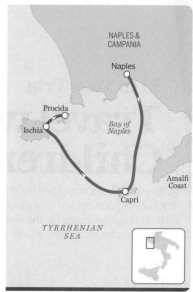

9 DAYS The Deep South

Start your soulful saunter in the cave city of **Matera**. Spend a couple of days exploring its famous *sassi,* as well as the *chiese rupestri* (cave churches), on a hike along the Gravina. From here, continue south to the Parco Nazionale del Pollino for a serious nature fix. Base yourself in **Terranova di Pollino** for four days, hiking through pine woods and beech forest to Basilicata's highest peak, Monte Pollino, and dancing to the *zampogne* (double-chantered pipes) in the Albanian villages of **San Paolo Albanese** and **San Costantino Albanese**. Don't leave the park without spotting the rare Bosnian pine tree, *pino loricato*. Lungs filled with mountain air, it's time to head west to the gorgeous coastal gem of **Maratea**. Pass a couple of days soothing your muscles in the town's crystalline Tyrrhenian waters, kicking back at local bars and feasting on fresh seafood. From here, head south to Calabria on the SS18 coastal road. If it's September, you might catch a chilli-eating competition in **Diamante**. Otherwise, keep moving until you reach Calabria's most arresting coastal town, **Tropea**, where your journey ends with piercing views and sunsets.

9 DAYS Campanian Island Hop

Three islands stud the Bay of Naples, and each has its own distinct feeling and appeal. Fly into **Naples** and soak up the city's heady jumble of hyperactive street life, frescoed churches and erudite palaces. On the third day catch a hydrofoil to **Capri**, your first island stop. Amble lazily through the chichi laneways of Capri Town and Anacapri, roam the ruins of an imperial Roman villa, and be rowed into the world's most arresting sea grotto. On day five, catch a ferry west to **Ischia**, the biggest of the bay islands. Spend your three days sauntering through luxurious gardens and soaking in the island's famous thermal waters. Swoon over the island's renowned white wine and tuck into its most celebrated dish, *coniglio all'ischitana* (Ischian-style rabbit). If you can manage to pull yourself away, catch a ferry across to pocket-sized **Procida** on day eight for two days of lo-fi bliss. Relive scenes from the film *Il Postino* in pastel-hued Marina Corricella, eat fresh fish by the beach and take a dive to explore the island's rich marine life. Refreshed and recharged, it's an easy hydrofoil trip back to Naples.

Plan Your Trip

Travel with Children

Italy is a dangerous place for children's cheeks. Italians adore *bambini* (children) and acts of face pinching are as prevalent as Ferragamo heels and handbags. On the flipside, the country has few special amenities for little ones, which makes a little planning go a long way.

The Regions

Naples & Campania Roam subterranean ruins, secret catacombs and cemeteries in Naples, a city famous for pizza and pastries. Get up close and personal with a slumbering Mt Vesuvius, play gladiators in Pompeii, Herculaneum and Pozzuoli, and splash happily on a picture-perfect bay island.

Puglia, Basilicata & Calabria Explore curious abodes in Puglia's Valle d'Itria and Basilicata's Matera, indulge in a little toilet humour in a medieval castle, or laze around on one of countless soft, sandy beaches. Puglia's relatively flat terrain makes for easy cycling adventures.

Sicily A wonderland of ancient temples and theatres, glittering Byzantine mosaics and gorgeous beaches. Catch a Sicilian puppet show, climb a volcano, or opt for some summertime island hopping. Whatever the season, give in to Italy's naughtiest, most colourful sweet treats.

Southern Italy for Kids

Southern Italy brims with world-famous archaeological sites, museums and other heritage treasures. But while Pompeian frescoes might thrill mum or dad, a youngster unversed in the wonders of history and art might not be quite as keen. Children's history books about the places you visit can help bring these sights to life. Suddenly, those old ruins become the scene of heroic battles, mythical creatures or a blockbuster apocalypse.

Remember to keep the pace low key, punctuating museum visits with plenty of gelato stops. Always make a point of asking staff members at tourist offices if they know of any special family activities, and get out into southern Italy's incredible countryside for some active fun.

Discounted admission for children is available at most Italian tourist attractions, though age limits can vary. Most government-run museums and archaeological sites offer free entry to EU citizens under the age of 18, though some staffers may extend this discount to all under 18s, despite the official 'EU-only' policy.

For more information and ideas, see Lonely Planet's *Travel with Children*, the superb website www.italiakids.com, or the more general www.travelwithyourkids.com.

Children's Highlights

History Was Here

➡ **Tunnel Borbonico** Secret escape routes, hideouts and vintage smugglers' cars bring wartime Naples to life on this subterranean walking tour. (p52)

➡ **Herculaneum** Smaller than nearby Pompeii, Herculaneum is easier to visit in a shorter time. It's also better preserved, complete with carbonised furniture. (p72)

➡ **Castel del Monte** This curious, octagonal 13th-century castle in Puglia is home to Europe's very first flush toilet. (p112)

➡ **Cappella Palatina** Golden, sparkly mosaics make for a dazzling introduction to Byzantine art in Palermo. (p169)

Alfresco Thrills

➡ **Aeolian Islands** Seven tiny volcanic islands off Sicily with everything from spewing lava to coastal trails and black-sand beaches. (p179)

➡ **Mt Vesuvius** It's an easy climb to the summit of this slumbering menace, from where the views are nothing short of spectacular. (p73)

➡ **Ischia** Catch a water taxi to a bubbling thermal beach or pool hop at a sprawling resort. (p68)

➡ **Maratea** Shallow, sandy beaches and a very walkable town centre make for summertime family bliss. (p146)

Kooky Kicks

➡ **Catacombe dei Cappuccini** These creepy Palermo catacombs are packed with mummies in their Sunday best. Not for the very young. (p169)

➡ **Cimitero delle Fontanelle** Take a tour of Naples' bizarre cemetery, stacked with skulls, shrines and some rather curious tales. (p52)

➡ **Alberobello** Was that Snow White? Imagination runs riot in this World Heritage–listed town, famous for its *trulli* (whitewashed circular dwellings with cone-shaped roofs). (p119)

➡ **Matera** Forget the Flintstones. Lose yourself in the surreal, storybook town of Matera, famed for its Unesco-protected *sassi* (stone houses carved out of caves and cliffs). (p138)

➡ **Museo Internazionale delle Marionette** Sicily is famous for its puppetry and this Palermo museum celebrates both local and international forms of the art. (p170)

Planning

Where to Stay

Hostels and apartments are sound options for families, offering multibed rooms, guest kitchens, lounge facilities and, in many cases, washing machines. In high season (July and August), camping grounds are buzzing, many offering activities for youngsters. Italy's *agriturismi* (farm stays) are great for fresh air, space and extra perks like animals or a swimming pool.

Book accommodation in advance when possible. In hotels, some double rooms can't accommodate an extra bed for kids, so check ahead. If the child is small enough to share your bed, some hoteliers will let you do this for free. The website www.booking.com specifies the 'kid policy' for every hotel listed and any extra charges incurred.

Getting Around

Arrange car rental before leaving home. Car seats for infants and children are available from most car-rental agencies, but should be booked in advance.

Public transport discounts are available for children (usually aged under 12). Intercity trains and buses are safe, convenient and relatively inexpensive.

MANGIA! MANGIA! (EAT! EAT!)

Food is a focus of life in Italy's south and kids are more than welcome at most eateries. Highchairs are often available and though kids' menus are rare, it's perfectly acceptable to order a *mezzo piatto* (half portion). *Arancini* (rice balls), *crocchè* (potato croquettes) and *pizza al taglio* (pizza by the slice) are great on-the-go snacks, as are panini from little grocery stores.

You can buy baby formula in powder or liquid form, as well as sterilising solutions such as Milton, at pharmacies. Fresh cow's milk is sold in cartons in supermarkets and in bars with a 'Latteria' sign. UHT milk is popular and in many out-of-the-way areas is the only kind available.

Plan Your Trip

Eat & Drink Like a Local

Italy is a gastronomic powerhouse and the country's south claims many of its most famous exports, from Gragnano pasta and San Marzano tomatoes, to buffalo mozzarella and cannoli (pastry shells with a sweet filling of ricotta or custard). Here, businesses still close for lunch and Sunday *pranzo* (lunch) remains a long, sacred family affair. Famished? You've come to the right place.

The Year in Food

While *sagre* (local food festivals) go into overdrive in autumn, there's never a bad time to raise your fork in southern Italy.

Spring (Mar–May)

Come for asparagus, artichokes and Easter specialities like Naples' *casatiello:* rustic-style bread stuffed with Neapolitan salami, pancetta and a variety of hard cheeses.

Summer (Jun–Aug)

This is the time for eggplants, peppers, berries and fresh seafood by the sea. Beat the heat with gelato and Sicilian *granite* (ices made with coffee, fresh fruit or locally grown pistachios and almonds).

Autumn (Sep–Nov)

Nibble on hearty chestnuts, mushrooms and game. In September, celebrate fish couscous at San Vito's famous Couscous Fest.

Winter (Dec–Feb)

Time for festive treats like Campania's *raffioli* (sponge and marzipan biscuits) and Sicily's *cobaita* (hard, sesame-seed confectionery).

Food Experiences

So much produce, so many specialities, so little time! Fine-tune your culinary radar with the following edible musts.

Meals of a Lifetime

➡ **Il Frantoio, Ostuni** Legendary eight-course feasts at an olive grove–fringed *masseria* (working farm). (p120)

➡ **Il Focolare, Ischia** A carnivorous, Slow Food stalwart, especially famous for its *coniglio all'ischitana* (Ischian-style rabbit). (p69)

➡ **Viva Lo Re, Ercolano** Local produce, contemporary tweaks and a sommelier's dream wine list, all close to the Ruins of Herculaneum. (p73)

➡ **Pizzeria Starita, Naples** Over 60 types of perfectly wood-fired pizza in a historic Neapolitan pizzeria. (p56)

➡ **Cucina Casareccia, Lecce** Savour the earthy, soulful flavours of *cucina povera* (poor man's cuisine) at this homely foodie destination. (p128)

➡ **Trattoria Ai Cascinari, Palermo** A traditional neighbourhood trattoria serving some of Palermo's best meals. (p173)

➡ **Osteria La Bettolaccia, Trapani** Sample Trapani's famous fish couscous and other Slow Food seafood classics. (p219)

Cheap Treats

➡ **Arancini** Deep-fried rice balls stuffed with *ragù* (meat sauce), tomato and vegetables.

➡ **Crocchè** Deep-fried, mozzarella-filled potato croquettes.

➡ **Pizza fritta** Neapolitan fried pizza dough stuffed with salami, dried lard cubes, smoked *provola* (provolone) cheese, ricotta and tomato.

➡ **Mozzarella di bufala** Silky, snow-white mozzarella made with buffalo milk.

➡ **Pane e panelle** Palermo chickpea fritters on a sesame roll.

➡ **Gelato** The best Italian gelato uses seasonal ingredients and natural colours.

Dare to Try

➡ **Pani ca meusa** A Palermo sandwich of beef spleen and lungs dipped in boiling lard.

➡ **Sanguinaccio** Hearty pig's blood sausage, particularly popular in Calabria and Basilicata.

➡ **Cavallo** Puglia's Salento region is famous for its horse meat. Taste it in dishes like *pezzetti di cavallo* (horse meat casserole with tomato, celery, carrot and bay leaves).

➡ **Stigghiola** A classic Sicilian dish of grilled sheep or goat intestine stuffed with onions and parsley, and then seasoned with salt or lemon.

➡ **'Mpanatigghiu** A traditional Sicilian pastry from Modica, filled with minced meat, almonds and the town's famous chocolate.

WHAT TO BOOK

Avoid disappointment with the following simple tips:

➡ Book high-end and popular restaurants, especially for Friday and Saturday evenings and Sunday lunch.

➡ In major tourist centres, always book restaurants in the summer high season and during Easter and Christmas.

➡ Book culinary and wine courses, such as Lecce's popular Awaiting Table (p127) cooking course, at least two months in advance.

Local Specialities

The Italian term for civic pride is *campanilismo* but a more accurate word would be *formaggismo:* loyalty to the local cheese. Clashes among medieval duchies and principalities involving castle sieges and boiling oil have been replaced by competition in speciality foods and wine. Keep reading for a gut-rumbling overview of southern Italy's culinary nuances, then turn to p248 to dig deeper into each region's culinary aces.

Naples & Campania

Explosions of flavour come with the territory in Campania, where intensely sweet tomatoes and superlative citrus thrive in volcanic soil. In Naples, tuck into Italy's best pizza, a wood-fired masterpiece of thin charred crust and slightly chewy dough. Its on-the-go sibling is the surprisingly light *pizza fritta:* fried pizza dough stuffed with salami, dried lard cubes, smoked *provola* cheese, ricotta and tomato.

Vegetarian decadence comes in the form of *parmigiana di melanzana* (fried aubergines layered with hard-boiled eggs, mozzarella, onion, tomato sauce and basil), while the city's signature *spaghetti alla puttanesca* (whore's spaghetti) blends tomatoes and black olives with capers, anchovies and (in some cases) a dash of red chilli. Altogether more virtuous is Campania's unique *friarielli,* a bitter, broccoli-like vegetable that is *saltata in padella* (pan-fried), spiked with *peperoncino* (red chilli) and often served with rustic *salsiccia di maiale* (pork sausage).

At the sweeter end of the spectrum are the *sfogliatella* (sweetened ricotta-filled pastry), *babà* (rum-soaked sponge cake) and *pastiera* (latticed tart filled with ricotta, cream, candied fruits and cereals flavoured with orange-blossom water).

Both Caserta and the Cilento region produce Italy's finest *mozzarella di bufala* (buffalo mozzarella), a star ingredient in Capri's refreshing *insalata caprese* (mozzarella, tomato and basil salad). The neighbouring island of Ischia is famed for its succulent *coniglio all'ischitana,* claypot-cooked local rabbit with garlic, chilli, tomato, basil, thyme and white wine.

Back on the mainland, Sorrento peddles sizzling *gnocchi alla sorrentina* (oven-baked gnocchi drizzled with mozzarella and *parmigiano reggiano* cheese) and ricotta-stuffed cannelloni, while the Amalfi Coast has no shortage of fish and seafood-based dishes. This fabled coast is also famous for two larger essentials: Cetara's *colatura di alici* (an intense anchovy essence) and Salerno's Colline Salernitane DOP olive oil.

Puglia, Basilicata & Calabria

Head southeast to Puglia for peppery olive oil, crunchy *pane* (bread), and honest *cucina povera*. Carbolicious snacks include *puccia* (bread with olives) and ring-shaped *taralli* (pretzel-like biscuits), while breadcrumbs lace everything from *strascinati con la mollica* (pasta with breadcrumbs and anchovies) to *tiella di verdure* (baked vegetable casserole). Vegetables play a leading role in Puglian cuisine, with herbivorous classics including *maritata,* a dish of boiled chicory, escarole, celery and fennel layered alternatively with *pecorino* (sheep's milk cheese) and pepper and covered in broth.

Puglia's coastline delivers spiky *ricci di mare* (sea urchins), caught south of Bari in spring and autumn. They might be a challenge to crack open, but once you've dipped your bread into the delicate, dark-red roe, chances are you'll be glad that you persisted. Easier to slurp is *zuppa di pesce* (fish soup), *riso cozze e patate* (baked rice, mussels and potatoes) and *polpo in umido* or *alla pignata* (steamed octopus teamed with garlic, onion, tomatoes, parsley, olive oil, black pepper, bay leaves and cinnamon).

Basilicata and Calabria are masters of salami and sausages – pigs here are prized and fed on natural foods such as acorns. Basilicata's *lucanica* or *lucanega* sausage is seasoned with fennel, pepper, *peperoncino* and salt, and eaten fresh – roasted on a coal fire – dried, or preserved in olive oil. The drooling continues with *soppressata,* the pork sausage from Rivello made from finely chopped, pasture-grazed pork that is dried, pressed and kept in extra-virgin olive oil; and *pezzenta* ('beggars' – probably a reference to their peasant origins) made from pork scraps and spicy Senise peppers. Across the border, the Calabrians turn pig's fat, offal and hot *peperoncino* into spicy, cured *'nduja* sausage.

In August, look out for red aubergines, unique to Rotonda, Basilicata, and originally from Africa. Spicy and bitter, they're often dried, pickled or preserved in oil and served as antipasti. Come autumn and the mountains yield delicious *funghi* (mushrooms) of all shapes and sizes. A favourite of the ancient Romans was the small, wild umbel oyster, eaten fried with garlic and parsley or accompanying lamb or vegetables. One of the best spots for a little mushroom hunting is Calabria's Parco Nazionale della Sila, which even hosts a *fungo*-focussed *sagra* (local festival).

Sicily

Sicily's history as a cultural crossroad shines through in its sweet and sour flavours. The Saracens brought the aubergine and spiced up dishes with saffron and sultanas. These ancient Arab influences live on in western Sicily's fragrant fish couscous, as well as the island's spectacular sweets. Sink your teeth into *cannoli, cuccia* (grain, honey and ricotta cake), and the queen of Sicilian desserts, the *cassata* (made with ricotta, sugar, vanilla, diced chocolate and candied fruits). Almonds are put to heavenly use in *pasta di mandorle* (almond cookies) and *frutti della Martorana,* marzipan sweets shaped to resemble fruits or vegetables. Both Arab and New World influences flavour Modica's lauded chocolate, spiked with anything from cinnamon to fiery red chilli.

Sicily's Norman invaders live on in *pasta alla Norma* (pasta with basil, eggplant, ricotta and tomato), while the island's bountiful seafood shines in staples like *pasta con le sarde* (pasta with sardines, pine nuts, raisins and wild fennel), Palermo's *sarde a beccafi co alla Palermitana* (sardines stuffed with anchovies, pine nuts, currants and parsley) and Messina's *agghiotta di pesce spada* (swordfish flavoured with pine nuts, sultanas, garlic, basil and tomatoes). Swordfish also gets top billing in *involtini di pesce spada* (thinly sliced swordfish fillets rolled up and filled with breadcrumbs, capers, tomatoes and olives).

Then there are Sicily's finger-licking *buffitieri* (hot street snacks), among them *sfincione* (spongy, oily pizza made with *caciocavallo* cheese, tomatoes, onions and occasionally anchovies) and Palermo's *pane e panelle* (fried chickpea-flour fritters, often served in a roll). Other doughy morsels include *calzone* (a pocket of pizza-like dough baked with ham, cheese or other stuffings), *impanata* (bread-dough snacks stuffed with meat, vegetables or cheese) and *scaccie* (discs of bread dough spread with a filling and rolled up into a crêpe). Queen of the street scene, however, is the ubiquitous *arancini* (rice balls stuffed with meat or cheese, coated with breadcrumbs and fried).

How to Eat & Drink Like a Local

Now that your appetite is piqued, it's time for the technicalities of eating *all'italiana*.

When to Eat

➡ **Colazione (breakfast)** A continental affair, often little more than a pre-work espresso, accompanied by a *cornetto* (Italian croissant) or *brioche* (breakfast pastry). In Sicily, your brioche might be filled with gelato or *granita* (flavoured crushed ice).

➡ **Pranzo (lunch)** A sacred time, with most businesses closing for the *la pausa* (afternoon break). Traditionally the main meal of the day, lunch usually consists of a *primo* (first course), *secondo* (second course) and *dolce* (dessert). Standard restaurant times are noon to 2.30pm, though most locals don't lunch before 1pm.

➡ **Aperitivo** Popular in cosmopolitan Naples, post-work drinks usually take place between 5pm and 8pm, when the price of your drink includes a buffet of tasty morsels.

➡ **Cena (dinner)** Traditionally a little lighter than lunch, though still a main meal. Standard restaurant times are 7.30pm to around 11pm, though many southern Italians don't sit down to dinner until 9pm or even later.

Where to Eat

➡ **Ristorante (restaurant)** Formal service and refined dishes.

➡ **Trattoria** Cheaper than a restaurant, with more-relaxed service and regional classics.

➡ **Osteria** Historically a tavern focused on wine, the modern version is often an intimate trattoria or wine bar offering a handful of dishes.

➡ **Enoteca** Wine bars often serve snacks to accompany your tipple.

➡ **Agriturismo** A working farmhouse offering food made with farm-grown produce.

➡ **Pizzeria** Cheap grub, cold beer and a convivial vibe. The best pizzerias are often crowded: be patient.

➡ **Tavola calda** Cafeteria-style spots serving cheap pre-made food like pasta and roast meats.

➡ **Friggitoria** Simple, take-away businesses specialising in deep-fried street snacks like *arancini*, *crocchè* and tempura-style vegetables.

➡ **Mercato** The market is an integral part of southern Italian life and a great place to pick up picnic provisions like fragrant bread, local cheeses, salami, antipasti, fruit and vegetables.

THE CAFFÈ LOWDOWN

Great *caffè* (coffee) in Italy is not a hipster novelty, it's an old-school tradition. Sip like a local with the following basics.

➡ Caffè latte and cappuccino are considered morning drinks, with espresso and macchiato the preferred post-lunch options.

➡ Baristas may offer a glass of water, either *liscia* (still) or *frizzante* (sparkling), with your espresso. Most southern Italians drink it before their coffee to cleanse the palate. If you are not offered a glass of water and would like one, simply say *Mi da un bicchiere di acqua, per piacere?* (Could I please have a glass of water?)

➡ Take the edge off with a *caffè corretto,* a shot of espresso spiked with liqueur (usually grappa).

➡ Coffee with dessert is fine, but ordering one with your main meal is a travesty.

TABLE MANNERS

➡ Cardinal sins: skipping or being late for lunch.

➡ *Buon appetito* is what you say before eating. *Salute!* (cheers!) is the toast used for alcoholic drinks – always make eye contact when toasting.

➡ Eat spaghetti with a fork, not a spoon.

➡ Don't eat bread with your pasta; using it to wipe any remaining sauce from your plate (called *fare la scarpetta*) is fine.

➡ Unless you have hollow legs, don't accept a second helping of that delicious *primo* – you might not have room for the *secondo*, *dolce*, *sopratavola* and *frutta*.

➡ Whoever invites usually pays. Splitting *il conto* (the bill) is common enough, itemising it is not.

➡ If invited to someone's house, bring flowers, wine or a tray of *dolcetti* from a local *pasticceria* (pastry shop).

Menu Decoder

For a translation of some of the words you'll find on Italian menus see p282.

➡ **Menù a la carte** Choose whatever you like from the menu.

➡ **Menù di degustazione** Degustation menu, usually consisting of six to eight 'bite size' courses.

➡ **Menù turistico** The 'tourist menu' usually signals mediocre fare – steer clear!

➡ **Piatto del giorno** Dish of the day.

➡ **Antipasto** A hot or cold appetiser. For a tasting plate of different appetisers, request an *antipasto misto* (mixed antipasto).

➡ **Primo** First course, usually a substantial pasta, rice or *zuppa* (soup) dish.

➡ **Secondo** Second course, often *carne* (meat) or *pesce* (fish).

➡ **Contorno** Side dish, usually *verdura* (vegetable).

➡ **Dolce** Dessert; including *torta* (cake).

➡ **Frutta** Fruit; usually the epilogue to a meal.

➡ **Nostra produzione** Made in-house.

➡ **Surgelato** Frozen; usually used to denote fish or seafood that's not freshly caught.

Regions at a Glance

Home to fairy-tale coastal hotspots like Capri and the Amalfi Coast, not to mention the cultural riches of Naples, it's not surprising that Campania has traditionally been southern Italy's blockbuster region.

In recent years Puglia and Basilicata have become the darlings of the in-the-know set, famed for their gorgeous beaches, fantastic food, architectural quirks and authentic festivals. While off-the-radar Calabria may lack big-hitter sights and cosmopolitan cities, it's well compensated by its rugged natural beauty, outdoor thrills and spicy rustic grub.

Like Campania, Sicily offers an enviable repertoire of landscapes, from volcanic peaks and vine-laced slopes to milky blue beaches. It's also home to some of Italy's greatest Graeco-Roman ruins, baroque architecture and culinary traditions.

Naples & Campania

Food
History
Coastline

Pizza & Pasta

Vying hard for Italy's culinary crown, Campania produces some of Italy's most famous flavours: coffee, pizza, tomatoes, pasta, *sfogliatella* and a panoply of seafood. Head into the hills for pit-reared *coniglio* (rabbit) slow-cooked with wild herbs.

Roman Ruins

Sitting beneath Mt Vesuvius, the Neapolitans abide by the motto carpe diem (seize the day). And why not? All around them – at Pompeii, Ercolano and the Campi Flegrei – they have reminders that life is short. Further afield, Paestum's glorious temples defy the test of time.

Cliffs & Coves

From the citrus-fringed panoramas of the Amalfi Coast to Ischia's tropical gardens and Capri's dramatic cliffs, the views from this coastline are as famous as the celebrities who holiday here. Add bubbling beaches and dazzling grottoes, and the appeal is as crystal clear as the sea itself.

p36

Puglia, Basilicata & Calabria

Beaches
Nature
Food

Seaside Savvy

Italy's northern shores may have all the drama, but the south has all the sand. Lounge beneath white cliffs in the Gargano, gaze at the violet sunsets in Tropea and spend summer on the golden beaches of Otranto and Gallipoli.

Wild Places

With its crush of spiky mountains, Basilicata and Calabria are where the wild things are. Burst through the clouds in mountaintop Pietrapertosa, pick bergamot in the Aspromonte and look out for Apennine wolves.

Culture & Cuisine

Puglia has turned its poverty into a fine art, both on and off the plate. Check out the renovated cave dwellings in Matera and then feast on creamy *burrata* (cheese made from mozzarella and cream) and turnip greens in Ostuni and Lecce.

p102

Sicily

Food
History
Nature

Seafood & Sweets

Sicilian cuisine will seduce seafood lovers and set that sweet tooth on edge. Tuna, sardines, swordfish and shellfish come grilled, fried or seasoned with mint or wild fennel. Desserts, laden with citrus, ricotta and nuts, include Arab-Italian dishes such as *cannoli* (pastry shells with a sweet filling of ricotta or custard), *cassata* (a concoction of sponge cake, ricotta, marzipan, chocolate and candied fruit) and marzipan fruits.

Cultural Hybrid

A Mediterranean crossroads for centuries, Sicily spoils history buffs with windswept Greek temples, Roman and Byzantine mosaics, Phoenician statues and sun-bleached Arab-Norman churches.

Volcanoes & Islands

Sicily's restless geology gives outdoor activities a thrilling kick. Pamper weary muscles in warm volcanic waters, hike the Aeolian Islands' dramatic coastlines or take in the thrill of the natural fireworks of Stromboli and Etna.

p161

On the Road

Naples & Campania

Includes ➡

Why Go?

Campania could be a multi-Academy Award winner, swooping everything from Best Cinematography to Best Original Screenplay. Strewn with three millennia worth of temples, castles and palaces, it heaves with legend – Icarus plunged to his death in the Campi Flegrei, sirens lured sailors off Sorrento, and Wagner put quill to paper in lofty Ravello. Campania's cast includes some of Europe's most fabled destinations, from haunting Pompeii and Herculaneum to Medchic Capri and Positano. At its heart thumps bad-boy Naples, a love-it-or-loathe-it sprawl of operatic *palazzi* (mansions) and churches, mouth-watering markets, and art-crammed museums. Home to Italy's top coffee and pizza, it's also one of the country's gastronomic superstars. Beyond its pounding streets lies a wonderland of lush bay islands, faded fishing villages and wild mountains. Seductive, vivacious and often contradictory: welcome to Italy at its nail-biting best.

Best Places to Eat

➡ L'Ebbrezza di Noè (p55)

➡ Il Focolare (p69)

➡ Da Gelsomina (p66)

➡ Viva Lo Re (p73)

Best Places to Stay

➡ La Minerva (p66)

➡ Hotel Piazza Bellini (p53)

➡ Hotel Luna Convento (p92)

➡ Casale Giancesare (p99)

When to Go
Naples

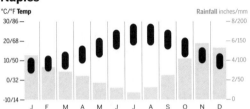

Easter Follow the faithful at Sorrento and Procida's mystical Easter processions.

May Naples celebrates culture with its event-packed Maggio dei Monumenti festival.

Sep Hit the coast for warm, languid days without the August crowds.

The Subterranean City

Mysterious shrines, secret passageways, forgotten burial crypts: it might sound like the set of an Indiana Jones film, but it's actually what lurks beneath Naples' loud and greasy streets. Subterranean Naples is one of the world's most thrilling urban wonderlands; a silent, mostly undiscovered sprawl of cathedral-like cisterns, pin-thin conduits, catacombs and ancient ruins.

Speleologists (cave specialists) estimate that about 60% of Neapolitans live and work above this network, known in Italian as the *sottosuolo* (underground). Since the end of WWII, some 700 cavities have been discovered, from original Greek-era grottoes to palaeo-Christian burial chambers and royal Bourbon escape routes. According to the experts, this is simply a prelude, with another 2 million sq metres of troglodytic treats to unfurl.

Naples' dedicated caving geeks are quick to tell you that their underworld is one of the largest and oldest on earth. Sure, Paris might claim a catacomb or two, but its subterranean offerings don't come close to this giant's 2500-year history.

And what a history it is. Naples' most famous saint, San Gennaro, was interred in the Catacomba di San Gennaro in the 5th century. A century later, in 536, Belisario and his troops caught Naples by surprise by storming the city through the city's ancient tunnels. According to legend, Alfonso of Aragon used the same trick in 1442, undermining the city walls by using an underground passageway leading into a tailor's shop and straight into town. Even the city's dreaded Camorra has got in on the act. In 1992 the notorious Stolder clan was busted for running a subterranean drug lab, with escape routes heading straight to the clan boss' pad.

CAMPANIA'S NATURAL WONDERS

→ **Grotta Azzurra** (p64) Nature outdazzles Disney in this magical coastal cave.

→ **Sentiero degli Dei** (p87) Experience the Amalfi Coast from a heavenly elevation.

→ **Parco Nazionale del Cilento e Vallo di Diano** (p100) A wild and rugged playground begging to be hiked.

→ **Mt Vesuvius** (p73) Peer into the crater of a panoramic time bomb.

→ **Capri Hiking Trails** (p65) Explore the island's bucolic side.

Don't Miss

Naples' Cappella Sansevero (p40) is home to the astounding *Cristo velato* (Veiled Christ), its marble veil so translucent it baffles to this day.

HOLD THE PRAWNS

Order a pizza marinara in Naples and you'll get a simple affair of tomato, garlic and olive oil. And the seafood? There is none. The pizza was named after fishers, who took it out to sea for lunch.

Best Places to Say 'Ti Amo'

→ Villa Cimbrone (p94)
→ Palazzo Petrucci (p55)
→ Monte Solaro (p64)
→ Teatro San Carlo (p50)
→ La Conchiglia (p71)

Naples' Top Museums

→ **Museo Archeologico Nazionale** (p41) A trove of ancient art and erotica.

→ **Museo di Capodimonte** (p51) From Caravaggio to Warhol.

→ **Novecento a Napoli** (p49) A stylish ode to Naples' 20th-century art scene.

Resources

→ **Turismo Regione Campania** (www.incampania.it) Up-to-date events, as well as articles and itineraries.

→ **Napoli Unplugged** (www.napoliunplugged.com) Smart, updated website covering sights, events, news and practicalities.

→ **Italy Traveller** (www.italytraveller.com) Boutique hotel listings, themed itineraries and travel ideas.

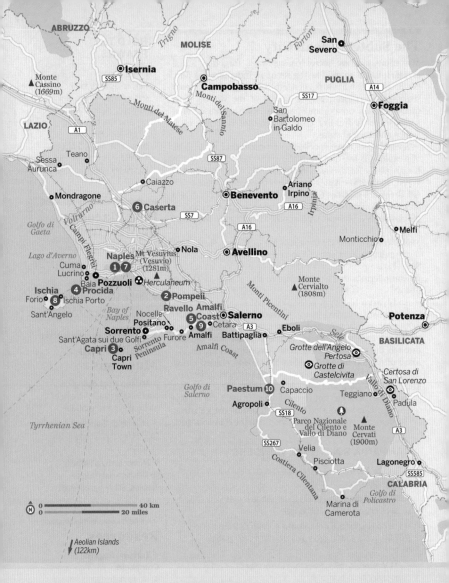

Naples & Campania Highlights

1 Exploring Naples' labyrinthine underworld on a **Tunnel Borbonico** (p52) tour.

2 Channelling the ancients on the ill-fated streets of **Pompeii** (p74).

3 Being bewitched by Capri's ethereal **Grotta Azzurra** (p64).

4 Lunching by lapping waves on pastel-hued **Procida** (p70).

5 Treating your senses to a concert at Ravello's dreamy **Villa Rufolo** (p93).

6 Pretending you're royalty at Caserta's **Palazzo Reale** (p61).

7 Re-evaluating artistic ingenuity in Naples' **Cappella Sansevero** (p40).

8 Indulging in a little thermal therapy on **Ischia** (p68).

9 Walking with the gods on the **Amalfi Coast** (p87).

10 Admiring Hellenic ingenuity at the World Heritage–listed temples of **Paestum** (p98).

NAPLES

POP 970,400

Italy's most misunderstood city is also one of its most intriguing – an exhilarating mess of bombastic baroque churches, cocky baristas and electrifying street life. Contradiction is the catchphrase here; a place where anarchy and pollution sidle up beside glorious churches, tranquil cloisters and story-book seaside castles. Naples' *centro storico* (historic centre) is a Unesco World Heritage Site, its museums lay claim to some of Europe's finest archaeology and art, and its gilded royal palaces make Rome look positively provincial. But what about the pickpockets? The Camorra? Certainly, Naples has its fair share of problems, yet the city is far safer than many imagine, its streets packed with some of Italy's warmest, kindest denizens. Expect to be caught in mafia gunfire and you'll be sorely disappointed. Expect a city packed with history, humanity and flavour and you'll be thoroughly satisfied.

History

According to legend, traders from Rhodes established the city on the island of Megaris (where Castel dell'Ovo now stands) in about 680 BC. Originally called Parthenope, in honour of the siren whose body had earlier washed up there (she drowned herself after failing to seduce Ulysses), it was eventually incorporated into a new city, Neapolis, founded by Greeks from Cumae (Cuma) in 474 BC. However, within 150 years it was in Roman hands, becoming something of a VIP resort favoured by emperors Pompey, Caesar and Tiberius.

After the fall of the Roman Empire, Naples became a duchy, originally under the Byzantines and later as an independent dukedom, until it was captured in 1139 by the Normans and absorbed into the Kingdom of the Two Sicilies. The Normans, in turn, were replaced by the German Swabians, whose charismatic leader Frederick II injected the city with new institutions, including its university.

The Swabian period came to a violent end with the victory of Charles I of Anjou at the 1266 battle of Benevento. The Angevins did much for Naples, promoting art and culture, building Castel Nuovo and enlarging the port, but they were unable to stop the Spanish Aragons taking the city in 1442. However, Naples continued to prosper. Alfonso I of Aragon, in particular, introduced new laws and encouraged the arts and sciences.

In 1503 Naples was absorbed by Spain, which sent viceroys to rule as virtual dictators. Despite Spain's heavy-handed rule,

Naples

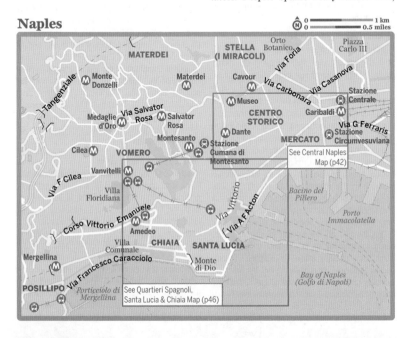

NAPLES IN...

Two Days

Start with a burst of colour in the cloister of the **Basilica di Santa Chiara** (p41), meditate on a Caravaggio masterpiece at **Pio Monte della Misericordia** (p44), and get dizzy under Lanfranco's dome fresco at the *duomo* (p44). After lunch, head underground on a **Napoli Sotterranea** (p52) tour, lose your breath over the astounding *Cristo velato* (Veiled Christ) in the **Cappella Sansevero** (p40), and kick back in bohemian Piazza Bellini. Next morning, explore ancient treasures at the **Museo Archeologico Nazionale** (p41), then head up to the **Certosa e Museo di San Martino** (p48) for extraordinary baroque interiors, Neapolitan art, and a sweeping panorama. Cap the night on the fashionable, bar-packed streets of **Chiaia** (p658).

Four Days

Spend the morning of day three cheek-to-crater with **Mt Vesuvius** (p73), then ponder its bone-chilling fury at **Herculaneum** (p72) or **Pompeii** (p74). Alternatively, spend the day at Caserta's mammoth, art-crammed **Palazzo Reale** (p61). On day four, grab some picnic provisions at the **Mercato di Porta Nolana** (p45) and devour them in the ground of **Palazzo Reale di Capodimonte** (p51). Nourished, eye up the bounty of artistic masterpieces inside, then spend a romantic evening shouting 'encore' at the luscious **Teatro San Carlo** (p50).

Naples flourished artistically and acquired much of its splendour. Indeed, it continued to bloom when the Spanish Bourbons re-established Naples as the capital of the Kingdom of the Two Sicilies in 1734. Aside from a Napoleonic interlude under Joachim Murat (1806–15), the Bourbons remained until unseated by Garibaldi and the Kingdom of Italy in 1860.

Modern Struggles & Hopes

Naples was heavily bombed in WWII, and the effects can still be seen on many monuments around the city. Since the war, Campania's capital has continued to suffer. Endemic corruption and the reemergence of the Camorra have plagued much of the city's postwar resurrection, reaching a nadir in the 1980s after a severe earthquake in 1980.

In 2011, the city's sporadic garbage-disposal crisis flared up again, leading frustrated residents to set fire to uncollected rubbish in the streets. In March 2013 it was the city's much-loved science museum, Città della Scienza, that went up in flames – an act of arson widely blamed on the Camorra.

Yet it's not all doom and gloom in a city often known for its trials and tribulations. The 2013 inauguration of Naples' Toledo metro station – partly designed by internationally renowned artists William Kentridge and Bob Wilson – made worldwide headlines for its stunning design. In the same year, the city welcomed the world as host of the Universal Forum of Cultures.

⊙ Sights

◎ Centro Storico

The three east–west *decumani* (main streets) of Naples' World Heritage-listed *centro storico* follow the original street plan of ancient Neapolis. Most of the major sights are grouped around the busiest two of these classical thoroughfares: 'Spaccanapoli' (consisting of Via Benedetto Croce, Via San Biagio dei Librai and Via Vicaria Vecchia) and Via dei Tribunali. North of Via dei Tribunali, Via della Sapienza, Via Anticaglia and Via Santissimi Apostoli make up the quieter third *decumanus*.

★ **Cappella Sansevero** CHAPEL
(Map p42; ☑ 081 551 84 70; www.museosansevero. it; Via Francesco de Sanctis 19; adult/reduced €7/5; ⊙ 10am-5.40pm Mon & Wed-Sat, to 1.10pm Sun; Ⓜ Dante) It's in this Masonic-inspired chapel that you'll find Giuseppe Sanmartino's incredible sculpture, *Cristo velato* (Veiled Christ), its marble veil so realistic that it's tempting to try to lift it and view Christ underneath. It's one of several artistic wonders, which also include Francesco Queirolo's sculpture *Disinganno* (Disillusion), Antonio Corradini's *Pudicizia* (Modesty) and riotously colourful frescoes by Francesco Maria

Russo, the latter untouched since their creation in 1749.

Downstairs, two meticulously preserved human arterial systems are a testament to the insatiable curiosity and geniality of alchemist Prince Raimondo di Sangro (1710–71), the man who commissioned the chapel's 18th-century makeover. According to Italian philosopher Benedetto Croce (1866–1952), di Sangro held a Faustian fascination for the *centro storico*'s masses, who accused him of everything from replicating the miracle of San Gennaro's blood to making furniture with the skin and bones of seven cardinals.

★**Basilica di
Santa Chiara**   BASILICA, CLOISTER
(Map p42; ☏ 081 797 12 31; www.monasterodisantachiara.eu; Via Benedetto Croce; cloisters adult/reduced €6/4.50; ☺ basilica 7.30am-1pm & 4.30-8pm, cloisters 9.30am-5pm Mon-Sat, 10am-2pm Sun; Ⓜ Dante) Vast, Gothic and cleverly deceptive, this mighty basilica is actually a 20th-century re-creation of Gagliardo Primario's 14th-century Angevin original, severely damaged by Allied bombing in August 1943. The pièce de résistance, however, is the basilica's adjoining majolica cloister.

Colourful 17th-century, Franciscan-themed frescoes adorn the 14th-century porticoes, while uplifting 18th-century ceramic tiles idealise country living in the cloister garden. Adjacent to the cloister, a small museum displays objects from the original 14th-century church, elaborate ecclesiastical props, as well as the excavated ruins of a 1st-century spa complex; look out for the remarkably well-preserved *laconicum* (sauna).

★**Museo Archeologico
Nazionale**   MUSEUM
(Map p42; ☏ 081 44 01 66; www.coopculture.it; Piazza Museo Nazionale 19; admission €8; ☺ 9am-7.30pm Wed-Mon; Ⓜ Museo, Piazza Cavour) Head

here for one of the world's finest collections of Graeco-Roman artefacts. Originally a cavalry barracks and later the seat of the city's university, the museum was established by the Bourbon king Charles VII in the late 18th century to house the rich collection of antiquities he had inherited from his mother, Elisabetta Farnese, as well as treasures looted from Pompeii and Herculaneum.

Before tackling the collection, consider investing in a copy of the *National Archaeological Museum of Naples*, published by Electa, or, if you want to concentrate on the highlights, audio guides are available in English. It's also worth calling ahead to ensure that the galleries you want to see are open, as staff shortages often mean that sections of the museum close for part of the day.

While the basement houses the Borgia collection of Egyptian relics and epigraphs, the ground-floor Farnese collection of colossal Greek and Roman sculptures includes the *Toro Farnese* (Farnese Bull) in Room XVI and the muscle-bound *Ercole* (Hercules) in Room XI. Sculpted in the early 3rd century AD and noted in the writings of Pliny, the *Toro Farnese*, probably a Roman copy of a Greek original, depicts the humiliating death of Dirce, Queen of Thebes. Carved from a single colossal block of marble, the sculpture was discovered in 1545 near the Baths of Caracalla in Rome and was restored by Michelangelo, before eventually being shipped to Naples in 1787. *Ercole* was discovered in the same Roman excavations, albeit without his legs. When they turned up at a later dig, the Bourbons had them fitted.

If you're short on time, take in both these masterpieces before heading straight to the mezzanine floor, home to an exquisite collection of mosaics, mostly from Pompeii. Of the series taken from the Casa del Fauno, it is *La battaglia di Alessandro contro Dario* (The Battle of Alexander against Darius) in Room LXI that stands out. The best-known

NAPLES & CAMPANIA NAPLES

ⓘ **BEFORE YOU EXPLORE**

If you're planning to blitz the sights, the Campania artecard (☏ 800 600601, 0639 96 76 50; www.campaniaartecard.it) is an excellent investment. A cumulative ticket that covers museum admission and transport, it comes in various forms. The Naples and Campi Flegrei three-day ticket (adult/reduced 18-25 yrs €16/10) gives free admission to three participating sites, a 50% discount on others and free transport in Naples and the Campi Flegrei. Other options range from €12 to €30 and cover sites as far afield as Pompeii and Paestum. The tickets can be bought at the Stazione Centrale (Central Station) tourist office, participating museums and archaeological sites, online, or through the call centre.

Central Naples

0.25 miles
500 m

Catacomba di Gennaro (1km);
Palazzo Reale di Capodimonte (2km)

Piazza Museo Nazionale

Museo Archeologico Nazionale

Piazza Principe Umberto

Corso Novara

Intercity Bus Station
Stazione Centrale
SITA Sud & CTS Bus Stop
ANM Bus Information Kiosk
Garibaldi

Via Firenze

Piazza Garibaldi

ANM Bus Station

Stazione Circumvesuviana

Via Amerigo Vespucci

Via della Marinella

Via Nuova Marina

SITA Sud Bus Stop (180m)

MERCATO

Piazza Masaniello
Santa Maria del Carmine
Chiesa di Carmine
Piazza G Pepe

Corso G Garibaldi
Via C Carmignano
Via Porta Nolana
Via Sopramuro
Fuori Porta Nolana

Via G Pica
Via S Cosmo
Via E Cosenz
Vico S Giovanni

Via Nolana
Via Lavinaio
Via A de Pace
Vico Barre

Via Mancini
Via Duchesca
Via Ranieri

Via Carbonara

Via P Colletta
Via S Nicola dei Caserti
Via dei Tribunali

Via dell'Annunziata

Corso Umberto I

Via Duca di San Donato

Via Sant'Eligio
Piazza del Mercato

Piazza Nicola Amore
Duomo (under construction)
Via Duomo

Via del Cimbri
Via della Zite
Vico Zuroli
Vico della Pace

CENTRO STORICO

Via Vicaria Vecchia
Via San Biagio dei Librai

Vicolo Sedil Capuano
Via Santissimi Apostoli

MADRE (50m)

Via Duomo

Cerasiello B&B (350m)

Vico Giganti
Via d'Anticaglia

Via San Gregorio Armeno

Vico S Severino
Vico S Nicola al Nilo
Via B Capasso
Via G Paladino

Vico Donnaromita
Via Mezzocannone

Corso Umberto I
Via Scialoja
Via Sapienza

Piazzetta Orefici

See Quartieri Spagnoli, Santa Lucia & Chiaia Map (p46)

Via del Porto
Via Donnalbina

Largo Giusso

Via San Geronimo
Vico San Domenico Maggiore

Cappella Sansevero

Piazza San Domenico Maggiore

Via San Paolo
Via San Sebastiano

Vico San Domenico Maggiore

Basilica di Santa Chiara
Santa Chiara
Via Santa Chiara

Piazza Luigi Miraglia
Piazza Bellini

Via Atri
Via F del Giudice
Via del Sole
Via S Gaudioso

Via Santa Maria di Constantinopoli
Via Broggia
Via Tommasi

Via Bellini

Via Enrico Pessina
Piazza Dante
Dante

Via Benedetto Croce
Via Port'Alba

Piazza del Gesù Nuovo

Via S Anna dei Lombardi
Via D Lioy
Piazza Carità
Piazza Dante

Via Toledo
Via Pignasecca

Via Brombeis

Central Naples

NAPLES & CAMPANIA NAPLES

depiction of Alexander the Great, the 20-sq-metre mosaic was probably made by Alexandrian craftsmen working in Italy around the end of the 2nd century BC.

Beyond the mosaics, the Gabinetto Segreto (Secret Chamber) contains a small but much-studied collection of ancient erotica. Guarding the entrance is a marble statue of a lascivious-looking Pan draped over a very coy Daphne. Pan is then caught in the act, this time with a nanny goat, in the collection's most famous piece – a small and surprisingly sophisticated statue taken from the Villa dei Papiri in Herculaneum. There is also a series of nine paintings depicting erotic positions – a menu of sorts for brothel clients.

Originally the royal library, the enormous Sala Meridiana (Great Hall of the Sundial) on the 1st floor is home to the Farnese Atlante, a statue of Atlas carrying a globe on his shoulders, as well as various paintings from the Farnese collection. Look up and you'll find Pietro Bardellino's riotously colourful 1781 fresco depicting the Triumph of Ferdinand IV of Bourbon and Marie Caroline of Austria.

The rest of the 1st floor is largely devoted to fascinating discoveries from Pompeii, Herculaneum, Boscoreale, Stabiae and Cuma. Among them are vivid wall frescoes from the Villa di Agrippa Postumus and the Casa di Meleagro, as well as ceramics, glassware, engraved coppers and Greek funerary vases.

Complesso Monumentale di San Lorenzo Maggiore
BASILICA

(Map p42; ☑ 081 211 08 60; www.sanlorenzomaggiorenapoli.it; Via dei Tribunali 316; church admission free, excavations & museum adult/reduced €9/7; ◎ 9.30am-5.30pm Mon-Sat, to 1.30pm Sun; ☑ C55 to Via Duomo) A masterpiece of French Gothic architecture, this late-13th-century basilica features the 14th-century, mosaic-covered tomb of Catherine of Austria, as well as splashes of frescoes by Giotto-collaborator Giovanni Barile in the ambulatory. According to legend, it was here that Boccaccio first fell for Mary of Anjou, the inspiration for his character Fiammetta, while the poet Petrarch called the adjoining convent home in 1345.

Beneath the complex are some remarkable *scavi* (excavations) of the original Graeco-Roman city, including the ruins of ancient bakeries, wineries and communal laundries. At the far end of the subterranean *cardo* (road) stands a *cryptoporticus* (covered market) with seven barrel-vaulted rooms.

THE ART OF THE NEAPOLITAN PRESEPE

Christmas nativity cribs may not be exclusive to Naples, but none match the artistic brilliance of the *presepe napoletano* (Neapolitan nativity crib). What sets the local version apart is its incredible attention to detail, from the lifelike miniature *prosciutti* (hams) in the tavern to the lavishly costumed *pastori* (crib figurines or sculptures) adoring the newborn Christ.

For the nobility and bourgeoisie of 18th-century Naples, the *presepe* provided a convenient marriage of faith and ego, becoming as much a symbol of wealth and good taste as a meditation on the Christmas miracle. The finest sculptors were commissioned and the finest fabrics used. Even the royals got involved: Charles III of Bourbon consulted the esteemed *presepe* expert, Dominican monk Padre Rocco, on the creation of his 5000-*pastore* spectacular, still on show at the Palazzo Reale (p50). Yet even this pales in comparison to the upsized Cuciniello crib on display at the Certosa e Museo di San Martino, considered the world's greatest.

Centuries on, the legacy continues. The craft's epicentre is the *centro storico* (historic centre) street of **Via San Gregorio Armeno** (Map p42), its clutter of shops and workshops selling everything from doting donkeys to kitsch celebrity caricatures. Serious connoisseurs, however, will point you towards the very few workshops that completely handcraft their *pastori* the old-fashioned way. Among the latter are **Ars Neapolitana** (Map p42; 392 537 71 16; Via dei Tribunali 303; 10am-6.30pm Mon-Fri, to 3pm Sat, also open 10am-6.30pm Sat & Sun late Oct-early Jan; C55 to Via Duomo) and **La Scarabattola** (Map p42; 081 29 17 35; www.lascarabattola.it; Via dei Tribunali 50; 10am-2pm & 3.30-7.30pm Mon-Sat; C55 to Via Duomo), both in the *centro storico*.

The religious complex is also home to the **Museo dell'Opera di San Lorenzo Maggiore** and its booty of local archaeological finds, including Graeco-Roman sarcophagi, ceramics and crockery from the digs below.

Pio Monte della Miséricordia   CHURCH, MUSEUM
(Map p42; 081 44 69 44; www.piomontedellamisericordia.it; Via dei Tribunali 253; admission €6; 9am-2pm Thu-Tue; C55 to Via Duomo) Caravaggio's masterpiece *Le sette opere di Miséricordia* (The Seven Acts of Mercy) is considered by many to be the single most important painting in Naples. And it's in this small, octagonal 17th-century church that you'll see it.

The 1st-floor museum is home to the *Declaratoria del 14 Ottobre 1607*, an original church document acknowledging payment of 400 ducats to Caravaggio for the masterpiece. The collection also includes a small, satisfying collection of Renaissance, baroque and 19th-century art, including works by Francesco de Mura and Giuseppe de Ribera.

Duomo   CATHEDRAL
(Map p42; 081 44 90 97; www.duomodinapoli.com/it/main.htm; Via Duomo; baptistry admission €1.50; cathedral & baptistry 8am-12.30pm & 4.30-7pm Mon-Sat, 8am-1.30pm & 5-7.30pm Sun; C55 to Via Duomo) Whether you go for Giovanni Lanfranco's fresco in the Cappella di San Gennaro (Chapel of St Janarius), the 4th-century mosaics in the baptistry, or the thrice-annual miracle of San Gennaro, don't miss Naples' spiritual centrepiece. Sitting on the site of an ancient temple to Neptune, the cathedral was initiated by Charles I of Anjou in 1272, consecrated in 1315 and largely destroyed in a 1456 earthquake. Copious alterations over the subsequent centuries have created a melange of styles and influences.

While the neo-Gothic facade was only added in the late 19th century, the high sections of the nave and the transept are the work of baroque overachiever Luca Giordano. Off the left aisle, the 17th-century **Cappella di San Gennaro** (Chapel of St Januarius, also known as the Chapel of the Treasury) was designed by Giovanni Cola di Franco and completed in 1637. The most celebrated artists of the period worked on the chapel – Giuseppe de Ribera painted the gripping canvas *St Gennaro Escaping the Furnace Unscathed* and Giovanni Lanfranco created the dizzying dome fresco. Hidden away in a strongbox behind the altar is a 14th-century silver bust in which sit the skull of San Gennaro and the two phials that hold his miraculously liquefying blood.

Below the high altar is the **Cappella Carafa**, a Renaissance chapel built to house yet more of the saint's remains.

Off the north aisle sits one of Naples' oldest basilicas, dating to the 4th century. Incorporated into the main cathedral, the **Basilica di Santa Restituta** was subject to an almost complete makeover after the earthquake of 1688. From it you can access Western Europe's oldest **baptistry**, pimped with glittering 4th-century mosaics. At the time of writing, the *duomo's* subterranean **archaeological zone** – featuring the remains of Greek and Roman buildings and roads – was closed indefinitely.

If you're intrigued by Naples' cultish love affair with San Gennaro, consider popping into the Duomo's adjacent **Museo del Tesoro di San Gennaro** (Map p42; ☑ 081 29 49 80; www.museosangennaro.com; Via Duomo 149; adult/reduced €7/5; ☺ 9am-5pm Fri-Tue, to 3pm Thu; ☐ C55 to Via Duomo); its glittering collection of precious ex-voto gifts includes bronze busts, silver ampullae, sumptuous paintings and a gilded 18th-century sedan chair used to shelter the saint's bust on rainy procession days.

★ **MADRE** ART GALLERY
(Museo d'Arte Contemporanea Donnaregina; ☑ 081 1931 3016; www.coopculture.it; Via Settembrini 79; admission €7, Mon free; ☺ 10am-7.30pm Mon & Wed-Sat, to 8pm Sun; Ⓜ Piazza Cavour) Seek refuge from the ancient at Naples' impressive contemporary-art museum. While the 1st floor is dedicated to specially commissioned installations (among them Rebecca Horn's eerie *Spirits* and Francesco Clemente's erotically charged Neapolitan fresco *Ave Ovo*), the 2nd floor's 'Historical Collection' of modern painting, photography, sculpture and installations includes blockbuster names like Damien Hirst, Cindy Sherman and Olafur Eliasson.

The museum also hosts top-notch temporary exhibitions spanning local to international artists.

Chiesa del Gesù Nuovo CHURCH
(Map p42; ☑ 081 551 86 13; Piazza del Gesù Nuovo; ☺ 7am-1pm & 4.15-8pm Mon-Sat, 7am-1.45pm Sun; Ⓜ Dante) In a case of architectural recycling, this 16th-century church actually sports the 15th-century, Giuseppe Valeriani–designed facade of Palazzo Sanseverino, converted to create the church. Inside, it's a baroque affair, with greats like Francesco Solimena, Luca Giordano and Cosimo Fanzago transforming the barrel-vaulted interior into the frescoed wonder that you see today. Puncturing the Piazza del Gesù Nuovo is Giuseppe Genuino's lavish **Guglia dell'Immacolata** (Map p42), an 18th-century obelisk.

Mercato di Porta Nolana MARKET
(Map p42; Porta Nolana; ☺ 8am-6pm Mon-Sat, to 2pm Sun; ☐ R2 to Corso Umberto I) Bellies rumble at this evocative street market, one of the city's best. The market's namesake is medieval city gate **Porta Nolana**, which stands at the head of Via Sopramuro. Its two cylindrical towers, optimistically named Faith and Hope, support an arch decorated with a basrelief of Ferdinand I of Aragon on horseback.

The *mercato* itself is an intoxicating place, where bellowing fishmongers and *frutti vendoli* (greengrocers) mix it with fragrant delis, bakeries and a growing number of ethnic food shops.

Chiesa e Chiostro di San Gregorio Armeno CHURCH, CLOISTER
(Map p42; ☑ 081 420 63 85; Via San Gregorio Armeno 44; ☺ 9am-noon Mon-Fri, to 1pm Sat & Sun; ☐ C55 to Via Duomo) Overstatement knows no bounds at this richly ornamented 16th-century monastic complex, its church featuring lavish wood and papier-mâché choir stalls, a sumptuous altar by Dionisio Lazzari, and Luca Giordano's masterpiece fresco *The Embarkation, Journey and Arrival of the Armenia Nuns with the Relics of St Gregory*.

Accessible by a gate on Vicolo Giuseppe Maffei is the complex's superb cloister. Here you'll find Matteo Bottigliero's whimsical baroque fountain and (at the southern end of the cloister) the convent's old bakery.

From a door at the southeast corner of the cloister you can access the beautiful *coro delle monache* (nuns' choir stall) that looks down on the church. The sneaky windows lining the oval cupola above belong to a second choir stall.

Chiesa di San Domenico Maggiore CHURCH
(Map p42; ☑ 081 45 91 88; Piazza San Domenico Maggiore 8a; ☺ 8.30am-noon & 4-7pm Mon-Sat, 9am-1pm & 4.30pm Sun; Ⓜ Dante) Completed in 1324 on the orders of Charles I of Anjou, this was the royal church of the Angevins. Of the few 14th-century remnants surviving the church's countless makeovers, the frescoes by Pietro Cavallini in the Cappella Brancaccio take the cake. The sacristy is equally noteworthy, featuring a beautiful ceiling fresco by Francesco Solimena and 45 coffins of Aragon princes and other nobles.

In the Cappellone del Crocifisso, the 13th-century *Crocifisso tra La Vergine e San Giovanni* is said to have spoken to St Thomas Aquinas, asking: *'Bene scripsisti*

Quartieri Spagnoli, Santa Lucia & Chiaia

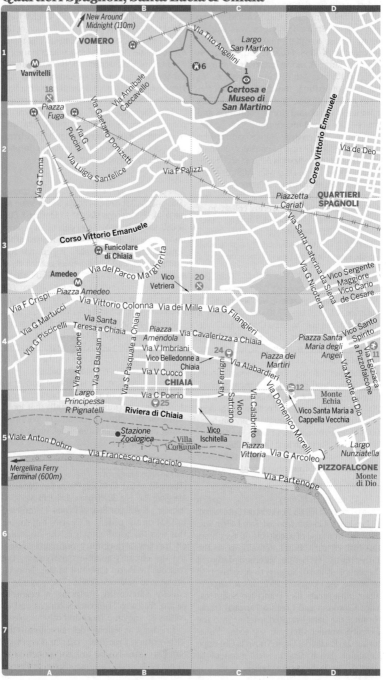

New Around Midnight (110m)

VOMERO

Vanvitelli

18

Piazza Fuga

Via Annibale Caccavello

Via Gaetano Donizetti

Via G Puccini

Via Luigia Sanfelice

Via G Toma

Via Tito Angelini

Largo San Martino

6

1

Certosa e Museo di San Martino

Via F Palizzi

Via de Deo

QUARTIERI SPAGNOLI

Piazzetta Cariati

Corso Vittorio Emanuele

Corso Vittorio Emanuele

Funicolare di Chiaia

Via del Parco Margherita

Vico Vetriera

20

Via Santa Caterina da Siena

Via G Nicotera

Vico Sergente Maggiore

Vico Cario de Cesare

Amedeo

Piazza Amedeo

Via F Crispi

Via G Martucci

Via G Piscicelli

Via Vittorio Colonna

Via dei Mille

Via G Filangieri

Via Santa Teresa a Chiaia

Via Ascensione

Via G Bausan

Via S Pasquale a Chiaia

Piazza Amendola

Via V Imbriani

Vico Belledonne a Chiaia

Via V Cuoco

Via Cavalerizza a Chiaia

24

Via Ferrigni

Via Alabardieri

Piazza dei Martiri

Piazza Santa Maria degli Angeli

Vico Santo Spirito

11

Via Egiziaca a Pizzofalcone

CHIAIA

Via C Poerio

25

Vico Satriano

Via Calabritto

Via Domenico Morelli

12

Monte Echia

Vico Santa Maria a Cappella Vecchia

Via Monte di Dio

Largo Principessa R Pignatelli

Riviera di Chiaia

Stazione Zoologica

Villa Comunale

Vico Ischitella

Piazza Vittoria

Via G Arcoleo

Largo Nunziatella

Viale Anton Dohrn

Via Francesco Caracciolo

PIZZOFALCONE

Monte di Dio

Mergellina Ferry Terminal (600m)

Via Partenope

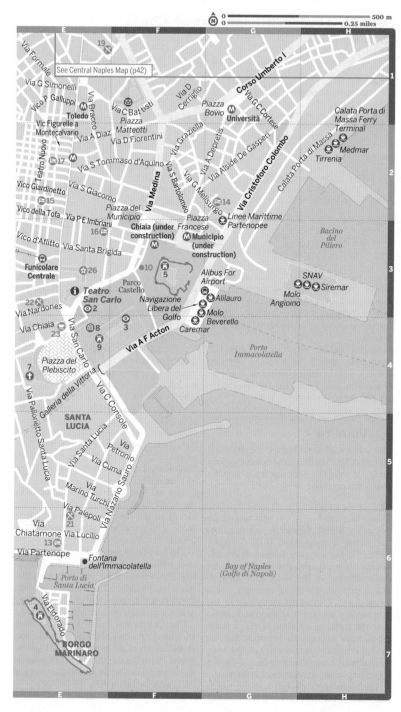

0   500 m
0   0.25 miles

See Central Naples Map (p42)

19

Via Formale
Via G Simonelli
Vico P Galluppi
Toledo
Vic Figurelle a
Montecalvario
Via Bracco
Via C Battisti
Piazza
Matteotti
Via A Diaz
Via D Fiorentini
Piazza
Bovio
Università
Corso Umberto I
Via G C Cortese
Via D Cerinnglio
Calata Porta di
Massa Ferry
Terminal
Teatro Nuovo
17
Via S Tommaso d'Aquino
Via Graziella
Via Alside De Gasperi
Via A Depretis
Via G Melisurgo
Via Cristoforo Colombo
Calata Porta di Massa
Medmar
Tirrenia
Vico Giardinetto
15
Via S Giacomo
Via Medina
Via S Bartolomeo
14
Linee Marittime
Partenopee
Bacino
del
Piliero
Vico della Tofa
Via P E Imbriani
Piazza del
Municipio
Piazza
Francese
Chiaia (under
construction)
Municipio
(under
construction)
Vico d'Aflitto
Via Santa Brigida
16
Funicolare
Centrale
26
Parco
Castello
10
5
Alibus For
Airport
SNAV
Siremar
Teatro
San Carlo
2
Navigazione
Libera del
Golfo
Alilauro
Molo
Angioino
22
Via Nardones
3
Molo
Beverello
Caremar
Porto
Immacolatella
Via Chiaia
23
8
9
Via A F Acton
7
Piazza del
Plebiscito
Galleria della Vittoria
Via C Console
SANTA
LUCIA
Via
Petronio
Via Santa Lucia
Via Curna
Via
Marino Turchi
Via Nazario Sauro
Porto
Immacolatella
Via Pallonetto Santa Lucia
Via
Palepoli
21
Via
Chiatamone   Via Lucilio
13
Via Partenope
Fontana
dell'Immacolatella
Porto di
Santa Lucia
Bay of Naples
(Golfo di Napoli)
4
Via Eldorado
BORGO
MARINARO

Quartieri Spagnoli, Santa Lucia & Chiaia

di me, Thoma; quam recipies a me pro tu labore mercedem?' (You've written good things about me, Thomas, what will you get in return?) Thomas' diplomatic reply? *'Domine, non aliam nisi te'* (Nothing if not you, O Lord).

Soaring outside on Piazza di San Domenico Maggiore is the Guglia di San Domenico, a 17th-century obelisk designed by Cosimo Fanzago, Francesco Antonio Picchiatti and Domenico Antonio Vaccaro.

◎ Vomero

Visible from all over Naples, the stunning Certosa di San Martino is the one compelling reason to take the funicular up to middle-class Vomero (*vom*-e-ro).

★Certosa e Museo
di San Martino   MONASTERY, MUSEUM
(Map p46; ☑ 848 800288; www.coopculture.it; Largo San Martino 5; adult/reduced €6/3; ⊙ 8.30am-7.30pm Thu-Tue, last entry 6.30pm; Ⓜ Vanvitelli, funicular Montesanto to Morghen) The high point (quite literally) of the Neapolitan baroque, this charterhouse-turned-museum was founded as a Carthusian monastery in the 14th century. Decorated, adorned and altered over the centuries by some of Italy's finest talent, most importantly Giovanni Antonio Dosio in the 16th century and baroque master Cosimo Fanzago a century later, it's now a superb repository of Neapolitan artistry.

The monastery's church and the rooms that flank it contain a feast of frescoes and paintings by some of Naples' greatest 17th-century artists, among them Francesco Solimena, Massimo Stanzione, Giuseppe de Ribera and Battista Caracciolo. In the nave, Cosimo Fanzago's inlaid marble-work is simply extraordinary.

Adjacent to the church, the Chiostro dei Procuratori is the smaller of the monastery's two cloisters. A grand corridor on the left leads to the larger Chiostro Grande (Great Cloister), considered one of Italy's finest. Originally designed by Dosio in the late 16th century and added to by Fanzago, it's a sublime composition of Tuscan-Doric porticoes, garden and marble statues. The sinister skulls mounted on the balustrade were a light-hearted reminder to the monks of their own mortality.

Just off the Chiostro dei Procuratori, the small Sezione Navale documents the history of the Bourbon navy from 1734 to 1860, and features a small collection of beautiful royal barges.

The Sezione Presepiale houses a whimsical collection of rare Neapolitan *presepi* (nativity scenes) from the 18th and 19th centuries, including the colossal Cuciniello creation, which covers one wall of what used to be the monastery's kitchen.

The Quarto del Priore in the southern wing houses the bulk of the picture collection, as well as one of the museum's most famous pieces, Pietro Bernini's tender *La vergine col bambino e San Giovannino* (Madonna and Child with the Infant John the Baptist).

A pictorial history of Naples is told in the section **Immagini e Memorie di Napoli** (Images and Memories of Naples). Here you'll find portraits of historic characters; antique maps, including a 35-panel copper map of 18th-century Naples in Room 45; and rooms dedicated to major historical events such as the Revolt of the Masaniello (Room 36) and the plague (Room 37). Room 32 boasts the beautiful Tavola Strozzi (Strozzi Table); its fabled depiction of 15th-century maritime Naples is one of the city's most celebrated historical records.

Castel Sant'Elmo CASTLE, MUSEUM
(Map p46; ☑081 558 77 08; www.coopculture.it; Via Tito Angelini 22; adult/reduced €5/2.50; ⊙castle 8.30am-7.30pm Wed-Mon, last entry 6.30pm; ⓜVanvitelli, funicular Montesanto to Morghen) Commanding spectacular city and bay views, this star-shaped castle was originally a church dedicated to St Erasmus. Some 400 years later, in 1349, Robert of Anjou turned it into a castle before Spanish viceroy Don Pedro de Toledo had it further fortified in 1538. Used as a military prison until the 1970s, it's now home to the satisfying **Novecento a Napoli** (☑081 558 77 08; ⊙9am-6pm

CAMPI FLEGREI

Stretching west of Posillipo Hill to the Tyrrhenian Sea, the Campi Flegrei (Phlegraean – or 'Fiery' – Fields) is home to some of Campania's most remarkable – and overlooked – Graeco-Roman ruins. Gateway to the area is the port town of Pozzuoli. Established by the Greeks around 530 BC, its most famous resident is the **Anfiteatro Flavio** (☑081 526 60 07; Via Terracciano 75; admission €4, incl entry to Parco Archeologico di Baia, Museo Archeologico dei Campi Flegrei & Scavi Archeologici di Cuma; ⊙varies, usually every hour from 9am-1pm Wed-Mon), Italy's third-largest ancient Roman amphitheatre.

A further 6km west, Baia was once a glamorous Roman holiday resort frequented by sun-seeking emperors. Fragments of this opulence linger among the 1st-century ruins of the **Parco Archeologico di Baia** (☑081 868 75 92; Via Sella di Baia; Sat & Sun adult/reduced €4/2, incl entry to Anfiteatro Flavio, Museo Archeologico dei Campi Flegrei & Scavi Archeologici di Cuma, Tue-Fri free; ⊙9am-1hr before sunset Tue-Sun; ⓐEAV BUS to Baia or ⓡCumana to Fusaro, then walk 900m), its mosaics, stuccoed *balneum* (bathroom) and imposing Tempio di Mercurio once part of a sprawling palace and spa complex. While the ruins are free on weekdays, weekend visitors need to purchase their tickets at the equally fascinating **Museo Archeologico dei Campi Flegrei** (Archaeological Museum of the Campi Flegrei; ☑081 523 37 97; http://museoarcheologicocampiflegrei.campaniabeniculturali.it; Via Castello 39; Sat & Sun €4, admission incl entry to Anfiteatro Flavio, Parco Archeoligico di Baia & Scavi Archeologici di Cuma, Tue-Fri free; ⊙varies, usually 9am-2.30pm Tue-Sun, last entry 1pm; ⓐEAV BUS to Baia), a further 2km south along the coast.

Yet another 2km south, in the sleepy town of Bacoli, lurks the magical **Piscina Mirabilis** (Marvellous Pool; ☑333 6853278; Via Piscina Mirabilis; donation appreciated; ⊙varies; ⓐEAV BUS to Bacoli then ⓡCumana to Fusaro), the world's largest Roman cistern. You'll need to call the custodian to access the site, but it's well worth the effort. Bathed in an eerie light and featuring 48 soaring pillars and a barrel-vaulted ceiling, the so-called 'Marvellous Pool' is more 'subterranean cathedral' than 'giant water tank'. While entrance is free, show your manners by offering the custodian a €2 or €3 tip.

Both the Ferrovia Cumana and the Naples metro (line 2) serve Pozzuoli, and the town is also connected to Ischia and Procida by frequent car and passenger ferries. To reach Baia, take the Ferrovia Cumana train to Fusaro station, walk 150m north, turning right into Via Carlo Vanvitelli (which eventually becomes Via Bellavista). The ruins are 750m to the east. To reach Bacoli, catch a Bacoli-bound EAV Bus from Fusaro.

Unfortunately, the Campi Flegrei's second-rate infrastructure and unreliable public transport, plus the fickle opening times of its sites make pretrip planning a good idea. Contact the **tourist office** (☑081 526 66 39; www.infocampiflegrei.it; Largo Matteotti 1a; ⊙9am-3pm Mon-Fri; ⓜPozzuoli, ⓡCumana to Pozzuoli) in Pozzuoli for updated information on the area's sights and opening times, or consider exploring the area with popular local tour outfit Yellow Submarine (p80).

Wed-Mon, entry on the hour, every hour), an art museum dedicated to 20th-century southern Italian art.

◉ Santa Lucia & Chiaia

★Teatro San Carlo THEATRE
(Map p46; ☑081 797 24 68; www.teatrosancarlo.it; Via San Carlo 98; guided tour adult/reduced €6/3; ⊙guided tours every hour from 10.30am-4.30pm Mon-Sat, to 12.30pm Sun, morning tours only Jan & Feb; ☑R2 to Via San Carlo) Even if you're not an opera fan, a guided tour of Italy's biggest and oldest opera house is worth an 'encore'. While the original 1737 theatre burnt down in 1816, Antonio Niccolini's 19th-century reconstruction is an extraordinary architectural gem, lavished with six gilded levels of boxes and a living testament to Naples' former status as Europe's music capital. Tickets for the guided tour are available at the theatre box office.

The adjoining Palazzo Reale is also home to the theatre's fascinating museum, Memus (Museum & Historical Archive of the Teatro San Carlo; Map p46; http://memus.squarespace.com; Piazza del Plebiscito, Palazzo Reale; adult/reduced incl Palazzo Reale €10/5; ⊙10am-5pm Mon, Tue, Thu & Fri, to 7pm Sat & Sun; ☑R2 to Piazza Trieste e Trento), and its collection of costumes, set designs and multimedia music features.

Standing opposite the theatre is the Galleria Umberto I, a breathtaking 19th-century arcade.

Palazzo Reale PALACE, MUSEUM
(Royal Palace; ☑081 40 04 54; www.coopculture.it; Piazza del Plebiscito; adult/reduced €4/3; ⊙9am-7pm Thu-Tue; ☑R2 to Via San Carlo) Envisaged as a 16th-century monument to Spanish glory (Naples was under Spanish rule at the time), the magnificent Palazzo Reale is home to the Museo del Palazzo Reale, a rich and eclectic collection of baroque and neoclassical furnishings, porcelain, tapestries, statues and paintings, spread across the palace's royal apartments.

Among the many highlights is the restored Teatrino di Corte, a lavish private theatre created by Ferdinando Fuga in 1768 to celebrate the marriage of Ferdinand IV and Marie Caroline of Austria. The Cappella Reale (Royal Chapel) houses a colossal 18th-century *presepe* (nativity scene) the *pastori* (crib figurines or sculptures) of which were crafted by

---

LOCAL KNOWLEDGE

NEAPOLITAN NUANCES

Local historian, architect and author Andrea Maglio says to keep an eye out for these easily missed musts.

Tunnel Borbonico

In this subterranean tunnel (p52) you can still see dusty old vehicles, graffiti and toilets from when it was used as a WWII air-raid shelter. It's a wonderful place to see Naples' stratified history.

Rival Obelisks

The impressive *guglie* (obelisks) that dot Spaccanapoli exemplify the collision of religion and politics in Naples. When a deputation of noblemen devout to San Gennaro erected the Guglia di San Gennaro (Map p42; Piazza Riario Sforza; ☑C55 to Via Duomo), the competing Dominicans quickly commissioned the Guglia di San Domenico (Map p42; Piazza San Domenico Maggiore), arguing that Naples' true patron saint was San Domenico. The bickering beckoned the mediation of the pope, who declared both saints patrons of the city.

Sacred Profanity

Naples is famous for blurring the boundary between the sacred and the profane. The Guglia di San Gennaro is built around an ancient Roman obelisk found under the city, while the Cimitero delle Fontanelle (p52) was home to a very cultish brand of Catholicism. In the paintings of Jusepe de Ribera, such as his *St Jerome and the Angel of Judgement* in the Palazzo Reale di Capodimonte the holy protagonists were often inspired by the city's poor. The result was a very human representation of the divine, reflecting the familiarity and irreverence that Neapolitans have always felt towards their much-loved saints.

a series of celebrated Neapolitan artists including Giuseppe Sanmartino, creator of the *Cristo velato* (Veiled Christ) inside the Cappella Sansevero (p40).

Designed by Domenico Fontana and completed two long centuries later in 1841, the palace also houses the Biblioteca Nazionale (National Library; Map p46; ☑ 081 781 92 31; www.bnnonline.it; Piazza del Plebiscito, Palazzo Reale; admission free; ☉ 8.30am-7.15pm Mon-Fri, to 1.15pm Sat, papyri exhibition closes 1pm; ☐ R2 to Piazza Trieste e Trento), which includes at least 2000 papyri discovered at Herculaneum and fragments of a 5th-century Coptic Bible. Entry to the library requires photo ID.

Facing the palace on Piazza del Plebiscito, the 19th-century Chiesa di San Francesco di Paola (Map p46; ☑081 74 51 33; Piazza del Plebiscito; ☉8.30am-noon & 4-7pm; ☐R2 to Via San Carlo) was inspired by Rome's ancient Pantheon.

Castel Nuovo   CASTLE, MUSEUM
(Map p46; ☑ 081 795 58 77; Piazza Municipio; admission €6; ☉ 9am-7pm Mon-Sat, last entry 6pm; ☐ R2 to Piazza Municipio) Dubbed the Maschio Angioino (Angevin Keep), this strapping castle was built in the late 13th century as part of Charles I of Anjou's ambitious urban expansion program. Christened the Castrum Novum (New Castle) to distinguish it from the older Castel dell'Ovo and Castel Capuano, the original structure's only survivor is the Cappella Palatina. The rest is the result of Aragonese renovations two centuries later, as well as a meticulous restoration effort prior to WWII.

The two-storey Renaissance triumphal arch at the entrance – the Torre della Guardia – commemorates the victorious entry of Alfonso I of Aragon into Naples in 1443, while the stark stone Sala dei Baroni (Hall of the Barons) is named after the barons slaughtered here in 1486 for plotting against King Ferdinand I of Aragon. Its striking ribbed vault fuses ancient Roman and Spanish late-Gothic influences.

Only fragments of Giotto's frescoes remain in the Cappella Palatina, on the splays of the Gothic windows. To the left of the chapel, the glass-floored Sala dell'Armeria (Armoury Hall) reveals Roman ruins discovered during restoration works on the Sala dei Baroni.

All this forms part of the Museo Civico, spread across several halls on three floors. The 14th- and 15th-century frescoes and sculptures are of the most interest, as is

Guglielmo Monaco's 15th-century bronze door, complete with embedded cannonball.

Castel dell'Ovo   CASTLE
(Map p46; ☑ 081 795 45 93; Borgo Marinaro; ☉ 9am-7.30pm Mon-Sat, to 2pm Sun; ☐ 154 to Via Santa Lucia) **FREE** Built by the Normans in the 12th century, Naples' oldest castle owes its name (Castle of the Egg) to Virgil. The Roman scribe reputedly buried an egg on the site where the castle now stands, warning that when the egg breaks, the castle (and Naples) will fall. Thankfully, both are still in one piece, and walking up to the castle's ramparts will reward you with a breathtaking panorama... and a steady string of lip-locked couples.

◉ Capodimonte & La Sanità

★ Palazzo Reale di Capodimonte   PALACE, MUSEUM, PARK
(☑ 081 749 91 11; www.coopculture.it; Parco di Capodimonte; museum adult/reduced €7.50/3.75, park admission free; ☉ museum 8.30am-7.30pm Thu-Tue, last entry 1hr before closing, park 7am-8pm daily; ☐ 2M or 178) On the northern edge of the city, this colossal palace took more than a century to build. It was originally intended as a hunting lodge for Charles VII of Bourbon, but as construction got under way in 1738, the plans kept on getting grander and grander. By its completion in 1759, Naples had a new palazzo. It's now home to the exceptional Museo Nazionale di Capodimonte.

It's spread over three floors and 160 rooms, you'll never see the whole art museum in one day. For most people, though, a full morning or afternoon is sufficient for an abridged best-of tour, and forking out €5 for the insightful audio guide is a worthy investment. Unfortunately, funding cutbacks have seen entire sections of the museum occasionally close for part of the day, so consider calling ahead if you're set on seeing a particular work.

On the 1st floor you'll find works by Bellini, Botticelli, Caravaggio, Masaccio and Titian. While the highlights are many, look out for Masaccio's *Crocifissione* (Crucifixion) and Parmigianino's *Antea*.

Upstairs, the 2nd-floor galleries display work by Neapolitan artists from the 13th to the 19th centuries, plus some spectacular 16th-century Belgian tapestries. The piece that many come to Capodimonte to see,

DON'T MISS

CATACOMBA DI SAN GENNARO

An evocative other-world of tombs, corridors and broad vestibules, the Catacomba di San Gennaro (☑081 744 37 14; www.catacombedinapoli.it; Via Tondo di Capodimonte 13; adult/reduced €8/5; ☉1hr tours every hour 10am-5pm Mon-Sat, to 1pm Sun) is Naples' oldest and most sacred catacomb. Not only home to 2nd-century Christian frescoes and 5th-century mosaics, it harbours the oldest known image of San Gennaro as the protector of Naples. Indeed, it was the interment of the saint's body here in the 5th century that turned this city of the dead into a Christian pilgrimage site.

Tours of the catacomb are run by the Cooperativa Sociale Onlus 'La Paranza' (☑081 744 37 14; www.catacombedinapoli.it; Via Tondo di Capodimonte 13; ☉info point 10am-5pm; ☐R4 to Via Capodimonte), the ticket office of which is to the left of the Chiesa di Madre di Buon Consiglio (☑081 741 00 06; Via Tondo di Capodimonte 13; ☉8am-12.30pm & 5-7pm Mon-Sat, 9am-1pm & 5-7pm Sun), a snack-sized replica of St Peter's in Rome completed in 1960. The co-operative also runs a fascinating walking tour called Il Miglio Sacro (The Holy Mile), which explores the neighbouring Sanità district. See its website for details.

Caravaggio's *Flagellazione* (Flagellation; 1607–10), hangs in reverential solitude in Room 78, at the end of a long corridor.

If you have any energy left, the small gallery of modern art on the 3rd floor is worth a quick look, if for nothing else than Andy Warhol's poptastic *Mt Vesuvius*.

Once you've finished in the museum, the Parco di Capodimonte – the palace's 130-hectare park – provides a much-needed breath of fresh air.

★ **Cimitero delle Fontanelle** CEMETERY
(☑081 744 37 14; Piazza Fontanelle alla Sanità 154; ☉10am-5pm; ☐C51 to Via Fontanelle) Currently holding an estimated eight million human bones, the ghoulish Fontanelle Cemetery was first used during the plague of 1656, before becoming the city's main burial site during the cholera epidemic of 1837. At the end of the 19th century it became a cult spot for the worship of the dead, which saw locals adopting skulls and praying for their souls.

It was hoped that once a soul was released from purgatory, it would bestow blessings in gratitude.

While you can visit the the cemetery independently, the lack of information makes joining a guided tour such as those organised by the Cooperativa Sociale Onlus 'La Paranza' much more rewarding. Avoid guides offering tours at the entrance.

☞ Tours

★ **Tunnel Borbonico** WALKING TOUR
(Map p46; ☑366 2484151, 081 764 58 08; www.tunnelborbonico.info; Vico del Grottone 4; 75min standard tour adult/reduced €10/5; ☉standard tour 10am, noon, 3.30pm & 5.30pm Fri-Sun; ☐R2 to Via San Carlo) Traverse five centuries of history along Naples' engrossing Bourbon Tunnel. Conceived by Ferdinand II in 1853 to link the Palazzo Reale to the barracks and the sea, the never-completed escape route is part of the 17th-century Carmignano Aqueduct system, itself incorporating 16th-century cisterns. An air-raid shelter and military hospital during WWII, this underground labyrinth rekindles the past with wartime artefacts.

Beyond the standard tour are an Adventure Tour (80 minutes,; adult/reduced €15/10) and an adults-only Speleo Tour (2½ hours; €40), both of which require pre-booking.

There is a second Tunnel Borbonico entrance, through the Parcheggio Morelli (Via Domenico Morelli 40) parking complex in Chiaia.

Napoli Sotterranea WALKING TOUR
(Underground Naples; Map p42; ☑081 29 69 44; www.napolisotterranea.org; Piazza San Gaetano 68; tours €9; ☉English tours 10am, noon, 2pm, 4pm & 6pm; ☐C55 to Via Duomo) This evocative 80-minute tour leads you 40m below street level to explore the historic centre's ancient labyrinth of aqueducts, passages and cisterns.

The passages were originally hewn by the Greeks to extract tufa stone used in construction and to channel water from Mt Vesuvius. Extended by the Romans, the network of conduits and cisterns was more recently used as an air-raid shelter in WWII.

Kayak Napoli BOAT TOUR
([☎] 331 9874271; www.kayaknapoli.com; three-hour tour €20) This popular kayaking tour along the Neapolitan coastline will have you gliding past ancient ruins, neoclassical villas and into grottoes. Tours cater to both rookie and experienced paddlers and depart from Villa Volpicelli on Via Ferdinando Russo, in the Posillipo district.

City Sightseeing Napoli BUS TOUR
(Map p46; [☎] 081 551 72 79; www.napoli.city-sightseeing.it; adult/reduced €22/11) City Sightseeing Napoli operates a hop-on, hop-off bus service with four routes across the city. All depart from Piazza Municipio–Largo Castello, and tickets are available on board. Tour commentaries are provided in eight languages, including English.

★ Festivals & Events

Festa di San Gennaro RELIGIOUS
([☉] Sat before 1st Sun May, 19 Sep, 16 Dec) The faithful flock to the *duomo* to witness the miraculous liquefaction of San Gennaro's blood on the Saturday before the first Sunday in May. Repeat performances take place on 19 September and 16 December.

Maggio dei Monumenti CULTURE
([☉] May) A month-long cultural feast, with a bounty of concerts, performances, exhibitions, guided tours and other events across the city; takes place throughout May.

Napoli Teatro Festival THEATRE
(www.napoliteatrofestival.it) Three weeks of local and international theatre and performance art, staged in conventional and unconventional venues across the city; June. A shorter, six-day edition takes place in September.

🛏 Sleeping

Spanning funky B&Bs and cheery hostels to old-school seafront luxury piles, slumber options in Naples are varied, plentiful and relatively cheap. For maximum atmosphere, consider the *centro storico,* where you'll have many of the city's sights on your doorstep.

🏙 Centro Storico & Port Area

Cerasiello B&B B&B €
([☎] 338 9264453, 081 033 09 77; www.cerasiello.it; Via Supportico Lopez 20; s €40-60, d €55-80, tr €70-95, q €85-110; [❄][✆]; [M] Piazza Cavour, Museo) This gorgeous B&B has four rooms with private bathroom, an enchanting communal terrace and decor melding Neapolitan art with North African furnishings. The stylish communal kitchen offers fabulous views of the Certosa di San Martino, a view shared by all rooms (or their bathroom) except room Fuoco (Fire), which looks out at a church cupola. Bring €0.10 for the lift.

DiLetto a Napoli B&B €
(Map p42; [☎] 338 9264453, 081 033 09 77; www.dilettoanapoli.it; Vicolo Sedil Capuano 16; s €35-55, d €50-75, tr €65-90, q €80-105; [P][❄][✆]; [M] Piazza Cavour) In a 15th-century *palazzo*, this savvy B&B features four rooms with vintage *cotto* floor tiles, organza curtains, local artisan lamps and handmade furniture designed by its architect owners. Bathrooms are equally stylish, while the urbane communal lounge comes with a kitchenette and dining table for convivial noshing and lounging.

★ Hotel Piazza Bellini BOUTIQUE HOTEL €€
(Map p42; [☎] 081 45 17 32; www.hotelpiazzabellini.com; Via Santa Maria di Costantinopoli 101; s €70-140, d €80-165; [❄][@][✆]; [M] Dante) This funky art hotel inhabits a 16th-century *palazzo*, its white spaces spiked with original maiolica tiles and the work of emerging artists. Rooms offer pared-back cool, with designer fittings, chic bathrooms and mirror frames drawn straight on the wall. Rooms on the 5th and 6th floors feature panoramic terraces.

Costantinopoli 104 BOUTIQUE HOTEL €€
(Map p42; [☎] 081 557 10 35; www.costantinopoli104.it; Via Santa Maria di Costantinopoli 104; s €140-170, d €160-280, ste €200-250; [❄][@][✆][▧]; [M] Dante) Chic and tranquil, Costantinopoli 104 is set in a neoclassical villa in the city's bohemian heartland. Although showing a bit of wear in places, rooms remain elegantly understated, comfortable and spotlessly clean – those on the 1st floor open onto a sun terrace, while ground-floor rooms face the small, palm-fringed pool.

Decumani Hotel de Charme BOUTIQUE HOTEL €€
(Map p42; [☎] 081 551 81 88; www.decumani.it; Via San Giovanni Maggiore Pignatelli 15; s €99-124, d €99-164; [❄][@][✆]; [▨] R2 to Via Mezzocannone) Slumber in the former *palazzo* of Cardinal Sisto Riario Sforza, the last bishop of the Bourbon Kingdom. The simple, stylish rooms feature high ceilings, parquet floors,

19th-century furniture and modern bathrooms with roomy showers and rustic wooden benchtops. Deluxe rooms boast a jacuzzi.

Toledo & Quartieri Spagnoli

Sui Tetti di Napoli
B&B €

(Map p46; ☑338 9264453, 081 033 09 77; www.suitettidinapoli.net; Vico Figuerelle a Montecalvario 6; s €35-65, d €45-80, tr €60-95, q €80-115; 🏵🛜; Ⓜ Toledo) This well-priced B&B is more like four compact apartments atop a thigh-toning stairwell. While two apartments share a terrace, the rooftop mini-apartment boasts its own, complete with mesmerising views. All include a kitchenette (the cheapest two share a kitchen), bright, simple furnishings and a homey vibe.

★ La Ciliegina Lifestyle Hotel
BOUTIQUE HOTEL €€

(Map p46; ☑081 1971 8800; www.cilieginahotel.it; Via PE Imbriani 30; d €170-230, junior ste €260-300; 🏵@🛜; ☐R2 to Piazza del Municipio) All 13 spacious, minimalist rooms at this chic, fashionista favourite include top-of-the-range Hästens beds, flat-screen TV and marble-clad bathrooms with water-jet jacuzzi showers (one junior suite has a jacuzzi tub). Breakfast in bed, or on the rooftop terrace, which comes complete with sunbeds, hot tub and a view of Vesuvius.

Hotel Il Convento
HOTEL €€

(Map p46; ☑081 40 39 77; www.hotelilconvento.com; Via Speranzella 137a; s €45-90, d €55-150, tr €65-140; 🏵🛜; ☐R2 to Via San Carlo) A soothing blend of antique Tuscan furniture, erudite bookshelves and candlelit stairs, this cosy hotel sits snugly in the atmospheric Quartieri Spagnoli. The elegant rooms combine creamy tones and dark woods with patches of 16th-century brickwork. For €80 to €180 you get a room with a private roof garden.

Santa Lucia & Chiaia

Hostel of the Sun
HOSTEL €

(Map p46; ☑081 420 63 93; www.hostelnapoli.com; Via G Melisurgo 15; dm €16-18, s €30-35, d €60-70; 🏵@🛜; ☐R2 to Via Depretis) HOTS is an ultrafriendly hostel near the ferry terminal. Located on the 7th floor (have €0.05 for the lift), it's a bright, sociable place with multicoloured dorms, a cute in-house bar,

and a few floors down a series of hotel-standard private rooms, seven with private bathroom.

B&B Cappella Vecchia
B&B €

(Map p46; ☑081 240 51 17; www.cappellavecchia11.it; Vico Santa Maria a Cappella Vecchia 11; s €60-65, d €80-90; 🏵@🛜; ☐C24 to Piazza dei Martiri) Run by a superhelpful young couple, this B&B is a first-rate choice. Six simple, comfy rooms feature funky bathrooms and different Neapolitan themes. There's a spacious communal area for breakfast, and free internet available 24/7. Check the website for monthly packages.

Grand Hotel Vesuvio
LUXURY HOTEL €€€

(Map p46; ☑081 764 00 44; www.vesuvio.it; Via Partenope 45; s €199-500, d €215-520; 🏵@🛜; ☐154 to Via Santa Lucia) Known for bedding legends (past guests include Rita Hayworth and Humphrey Bogart), this five-star heavyweight is a decadent wonderland of dripping chandeliers, period antiques and opulent rooms. Count your lucky stars while drinking a martini at the rooftop restaurant.

✖ Eating

Pizza and pasta are the staples of Neapolitan cuisine. Pizza was created here and nowhere will you eat it better. Seafood is another local speciality and you'll find mussels and clams served in many dishes.

Neapolitan street food is equally brilliant. *Misto di frittura* – zucchini flowers, deep-fried potato and aubergine – makes for a great snack, especially if eaten from paper outside a tiny streetside stall.

It's always sensible to book a table if dining at a restaurant on a Friday or Saturday night. Also note that many eateries close for two to four weeks in August, so check before heading out.

✖ Centro Storico

★ Pizzeria Gino Sorbillo
PIZZERIA €

(Map p42; ☑081 44 66 43; www.accademiadellapizza.it; Via dei Tribunali 32; pizzas €3-7.30; ⊙noon-3.30pm & 7-11.30pm Mon-Sat; Ⓜ Dante) Gino Sorbillo is king of the pizza pack. Head in for gigantic, wood-fired perfection, best followed by a velvety *semifreddo;* the chocolate and *torroncino* (almond nougat) combo is divine. Head in super early or expect to queue.

Trattoria Mangia e Bevi
CAMPANIAN €

(Map p42; ☑081 552 95 46; Via Sedile di Porto 92; meals €7; ☺12.30-3.30pm Mon-Fri; ⓜUniversità) Everyone from pierced students to bespectacled *professori* squeeze around the lively, communal tables for brilliant home cooking at rock-bottom prices. Scan the daily-changing menu (in Italian), jot down your choices and brace for gems like juicy *salsiccia* (pork sausage) and *peperoncino*-spiked *friarielli* (local broccoli).

Attanasio
BAKERY €

(Map p42; ☑081 28 56 75; Vico Ferrovia 1-4; snacks from €1.10; ☺6.30am-8pm Tue-Sun; ⓜGaribaldi) This retro pastry peddler makes one mighty *sfogliatella* (sweetened ricotta pastry), not to mention creamy *cannolli siciliani* (pastry shells stuffed with sweet ricotta) and runny, rummy *babà* (rum-soaked yeast cake). Savoury fiends shouldn't pass up the hearty *pasticcino rustico* (savoury bread), stuffed with *provola* (provolone) cheese, ricotta and salami.

La Campagnola
CAMPANIAN €€

(Map p42; ☑081 45 90 34; www.campagnolatribunali.com; Via dei Tribunali 47; meals €18; ☺12.30-4pm & 7-11.30pm Wed-Mon; ⓜDante) Boisterous and affable, this Neapolitan stalwart serves up soul-coaxing classics. Daily specials may include a killer *genovese* (pasta with a slow-cooked lamb, tomato and onion *ragù*) or a decadent *penne alla siciliana* (pasta with fried aubergine, *fior di latte* cheese, tomato and basil).

Palazzo Petrucci
MODERN ITALIAN €€€

(Map p42; ☑081 552 40 68; www.palazzopetrucci.it; Piazza San Domenico Maggiore 4; meals €50; ☺1-2.30pm & 7.30-10.30pm Tue-Sat, dinner only Mon, lunch only Sun; ⓜDante) Progressive Petrucci thrills with new-school creations like chickpea soup with prawns and concentrated coffee, or succulent lamb with dried apricots, *pecorino* (sheep's milk cheese) and mint. Polished service and a fine-dining air make it a perfect spot to celebrate something special.

🍴 Toledo, Quartieri Spagnoli & Vomero

Friggitoria Vomero
SNACKS €

(Map p46; ☑081 578 31 30; Via Cimarosa 44; snacks from €0.20; ☺9.30am-2.30pm & 5-9.30pm Mon-Fri, to 11pm Sat; 🚠Centrale to Fuga) Crunch blissfully at this spartan Vomero snack bar, famed for finger-licking *fritture* (fried snacks) like *frittatine di maccheroni* (fried pasta and egg) and *supplì di riso* (rice balls). Located opposite the funicular, it's a handy pit stop before legging it to the Certosa di San Martino.

Il Garum
ITALIAN €€

(Map p46; ☑081 542 32 28; Piazza Monteoliveto 2a; meals €35; ☺noon-3.30pm & 7-11.30pm ; ⓜToledo) One of the very few restaurants open on Sunday nights, softly lit Il Garum serves up delicately flavoured, revamped classics. Stand-out dishes include an exquisite grilled calamari stuffed with seasonal vegetables and cheese. Just leave room for desserts like *torta di ricotta e pera* (ricotta and pear cake), all made on-site.

Trattoria San Ferdinando
CAMPANIAN €€

(Map p46; ☑081 42 19 64; Via Nardones 117; meals €30; ☺12.30-3.30pm Mon-Sat, 7-11.30pm Tue-Fri; 🚌R2 to Piazza Trieste e Trento) Hung with theatre memorabilia, San Ferdinando pulls in well-spoken theatre types and intellectuals. Ask for a rundown of the day's antipasti and choose your favourites for an *antipasto misto* (mixed antipasto). The homemade desserts make for a satisfying dénouement.

🍴 Santa Lucia & Chiaia

★ L'Ebbrezza di Noè
CAMPANIAN €€

(Map p46; ☑081 40 01 04; www.lebbrezzadinoe.com; Vico Vetriera 9; meals €30; ☺8.30pm-midnight Tue-Sun; ⓜPiazza Amedeo) A wine shop by day, 'Noah's Drunkenness' transforms into a culinary hot spot by night. Slip inside for vino and conversation at the bar, or settle into one of the intimate, bottle-lined dining rooms for beautiful, creative dishes dictated by the morning's market finds. Adding X-factor are over 2000 wines, artfully selected by sommelier owner Luca Di Leva.

★ Ristorantino dell'Avvocato
CAMPANIAN €€

(Map p46; ☑081 032 00 47; www.ilristorantinodellavvocato.it; Via Santa Lucia 115-117; meals €37, degustation menus €35-40; ☺noon-3pm & 7.30-11pm, lunch only Mon & Sun; 📶; 🚌154 to Via Santa Lucia) This elegant nosh spot is home to affable chef and owner Raffaele Cardillo, whose passion for Campania's culinary heritage merges with a knack for subtle, refreshing twists – think gnocchi with fresh mussels, clams, crumbed pistachio, lemon, ginger and garlic.

The degustation menus are good value, as is the simpler three-course lunch menu (€15), available Monday to Friday.

✖ La Sanità

Pizzeria Starita
PIZZA €

(📞 081 557 46 82; Via Materdei 28; pizzas €3.50-13; ⊙ noon-3.30pm & 7.30pm-midnight Mon-Sat, dinner only Sun; Ⓜ Materdei) The giant fork and ladle hanging on the wall at this cultish pizzeria were used by Sophia Loren in *L'Oro di Napoli*, and the kitchen made the *pizze fritte* sold by the actress in the film. While the 60-plus pizza varieties include a tasty *fiorilli e zucchini* (zucchini, zucchini flowers and *provola*), our allegiance remains to its classic marinara.

Cantina del Gallo
CAMPANIAN €

(www.cantinadelgallo.com; Via Alessandro Telesino 21; pizzas €4-8, meals €15; ⊙ 11am-4pm & 7pm-midnight Mon-Sat, 12.30-4pm Sun; 🖀; 🚊 C51 to Via Fontanelle) Catholic kitsch and a bucket of feet-warming hot coals under the table. No, you're not at nonna's house, just at one of Naples' best-kept foodie secrets. Tuck into rarer specialities like *calzoncini* (wood-fired pizza dough with various fillings) or *A'Cafona*, a spicy, garlicky wood-fired pizza. The staff are sweet but speak little English.

🍷 Drinking & Nightlife

The city's student and alternative drinking scene is around the piazzas and alleyways of the *centro storico*. For a chicer vibe, hit the cobbled lanes of upmarket Chiaia. While some bars operate from 8am, most open from around 5.30pm and close around 2am.

Clubs usually open at 10.30pm or 11pm but don't fill up until after midnight. Many close in summer (July to September), some transferring to out-of-town beach locations. Admission charges vary, but expect to pay between €5 and €30, which may or may not include a drink.

Caffè Gambrinus
CAFE

(Map p46; 📞 081 41 75 82; www.grancaffegambrinus.com; Via Chiaia 12; ⊙ 7am-1am Sun-Thu, to 2am Fri, to 3am Sat; 🚊 R2 to Via San Carlo) Grand, chandeliered Gambrinus is Naples' oldest and most venerable cafe. Oscar Wilde knocked back a few here and Mussolini had some of the rooms shut down to keep out left-wing intellectuals. Sure, the prices may be steeper, but the coffee is superlative, the *aperitivo* (pre-dinner drinks with snacks)

and nibbles are decent and sipping a *spritz* (a type of cocktail made with *prosecco*) on Piazza Triesto e Trento is a moment worth savouring.

Intra Moenia
CAFE

(Map p42; 📞 081 29 07 20; Piazza Bellini 70; ⊙ 10am-2am; 🖀; Ⓜ Dante) This free-thinking cafe-bookshop-publishing house on Piazza Bellini is a good spot for chilling out. Browse limited-edition books on Neapolitan culture, pick up a vintage-style postcard, or simply sip a *prosecco* and act the intellectual. The house wine costs €4 a glass and there's a range of salads, snacks and classic Neapolitan grub for peckish bohemians.

Clu
BAR, RESTAURANT

(Map p46; www.clunapoli.com; Via Carlo Poerio 47; ⊙ 8am-1am Mon-Sun Sep-May, to 5pm Jun; 🚊 128 to Riviera di Chiaia) Überfashionable Clu is a huge hit with Chiaia's *aperitivo* crowd. Order a cumin-seed-infused Spice Vesper martini and snack on fab, free nibbles like oven-baked rice and pasta dishes, and ricotta and spinach pie. Sure there's a restaurant out the back (meals €25), but with so much free grub, why bother?

Chandelier
BAR

(Map p46; 📞 081 41 45 76; Vico Belledonne a Chiaia 34; ⊙ 6pm-late; 🚊 C25 to Piazza dei Martiri) A sleek, sexy combo of tinted glass, lipstick-red neon and ambient tunes, Chandelier draws a smart, after-work crowd with its crafty libations and fabulous *aperitivo* spread. Order a negroni *sbagliato* (the negroni's much smoother sibling) and schmooze over mini bruschettas, focaccias and pasta dishes – all free with your well-mixed drink.

☆ Entertainment

Options run the gamut from nail-biting football games to world-class opera. For cultural listings check www.incampania.it; for the latest club news check out the free minimag *Zero* (www.zero.eu, in Italian), available from many bars.

From May until September, al fresco concerts are common throughout the city. Tourist offices have details.

You can buy tickets for most cultural events at the box office inside Feltrinelli (📞 081 764 21 11; Piazza dei Martiri; ⊙ 4.30-8pm Mon-Sat).

Teatro San Carlo
OPERA, BALLET

(Map p46; 📞 081 797 23 31; www.teatrosancarlo.it; Via San Carlo 98; ⊙ box office 10am-7pm Mon-Sat, to 3.30pm Sun; 🚊 R2 to Via San Carlo) One of Italy's premier opera venues, the theatre stages a year-round program of opera, ballet and concerts, though tickets can be fiendishly difficult to come by.

Galleria 19
CLUB
(Map p42; www.galleria19.it; Via San Sebastiano 19; ⊙11pm-5am Tue-Sun; M Dante) Set in a long, cavernous cellar scattered with chesterfields and industrial lamps, this cool and edgy club draws a uni crowd early in the week and 20/30-somethings with its Friday live-music sets and Saturday electronica sessions. It's also home to one of the city's best mixologists, Gianluca Morziello, famed for his Cucumber Slumber.

New Around Midnight
LIVE MUSIC
(☑331 2326093; www.newaroundmidnight.it; Via Bonito 32a; admission €15; ⊙7.30pm-2am Thu-Sun mid-Sep–Jun; M Vanvitelli, funicular Montesanto to Morghen) This hybrid jazz club and eatery features mostly homegrown acts, with the occasional blues band putting in a performance. Check the website for upcoming gigs.

Football

Naples' football team, Napoli, is the third-most supported in the country after Juventus and Milan, and watching it play at the **Stadio San Paolo** (Piazzale Vincenzo Tecchio; M Napoli Campi Flegrei) is a highly charged rush. The season runs from late August to late May, with seats costing between €20 and €100. Book tickets at **Azzurro Service** (☑081 593 40 01; www.azzurroservice.net; Via Francesco Galeota 19; ⊙9am-1pm & 3.30-7pm Mon-Fri, also Sat & Sun match days; M Napoli Campi Flegrei), **Box Office** (Map p46; ☑081 551 91 88; www.boxofficenapoli.it; Galleria Umberto I 17; ⊙9.30am-8pm Mon-Fri, 9.30am-1.30pm & 4.30-8pm Sat; ⌕R2 to Piazza Trieste e Trento), as well as from some tobacconists, and don't forget your photo ID. On match days, tickets are also available at the stadium itself.

🛍 Shopping

Vico San Domenico Maggiore
ARTISANAL
Connecting Via dei Tribunali and Piazza San Domenico Maggiore, this skinny street is home to a fistful of artisan studios. Pop into tiny **Bottega 21** (Map p42; bottega21@ live.it; Vico San Domenico Maggiore 21; ⊙10.30am-1.30pm & 3-8pm Mon-Sat) for beautiful, hand-made leather goods, from boho-chic hand-bags and satchels to jewellery, belts and butter-soft notebook covers.

Laboratorio Galleria Pensatoio (Map p42; ☑339 1175276; Vico San Domenico Maggiore 2; ⊙11am-2pm & 5-8pm Fri & Sat, also open by prior appointment) is the studio of husband-and-wife art duo Sergio and Teresa Cervo. While Sergio is best known for his organic, industrial-style metal sculptures and furniture, Teresa cleverly recycles old materials into anything from funky lampshades to wire sculptures of Neapolitan espresso cups. Next door, heavenly scented **Kiphy** (Map p42; ☑393 8703280; www.kiphy.it; Vico San Domenico Maggiore 3; ⊙10.30am-2pm & 3-8pm Tue-Sat, open Mon & closed Sat & Sun Jun & Jul, closed Aug; M Dante) peddles pure, handmade slabs of soap, as well as freshly made shampoos, creams and oils using organic, fair-trade ingredients.

ℹ Information

I Naples (www.inaples.it) Naples' official tourist board site.

In Campania (www.incampania.com) Campania's official tourist website.

Loreto-Mare Hospital (Ospedale Loreto-Mare; ☑081 20 10 33; Via Amerigo Vespucci 26)

Napoli Unplugged (www.napoliunplugged.com) Smart, up-to-date website covering sights, events, news and practicalities.

Pharmacy (Stazione Centrale; ⊙7am-10pm Mon-Sat, 8am-9pm Sun)

Police station (☑081 794 11 11; Via Medina 75) For emergencies or to report a stolen car, call ☑113.

Post office (Piazza Matteotti; ⊙8am-6.30pm Mon-Sat)

Tourist offices For information and a map of the city visit one of these branches: Piazza del Gesù Nuovo 7 (Map p42; Piazza del Gesù Nuovo 7; ⊙9.30am-1.30pm & 2.30-6.30pm Mon-Sat, 9am-1.30pm Sun); Stazione Centrale (Map p42; Stazione Centrale; ⊙9am-6pm); Via San Carlo 9 (Map p46; Via San Carlo 9; ⊙9.30am-1.30pm & 2.30-6.30pm Mon-Sat, 9am-1.30pm Sun; ⌕R2 to Piazza Trieste e Trento)

ℹ Getting There & Away

AIR

Capodichino airport (NAP; ☑081 789 61 11; www.gesac.it), 7km northeast of the city centre, is southern Italy's main airport, linking Naples with most Italian and several major European cities. Budget carrier easyJet has several connections to/from Naples, including London (Gatwick and Stansted), Paris (Orly) and Berlin (Schönefeld).

BOAT

Naples, the bay islands and the Amalfi Coast are served by a comprehensive ferry network.

HYDROFOILS & HIGH-SPEED FERRIES

DESTINATION (FROM NAPLES – MOLO BEVERELLO)	FERRY COMPANY	PRICE (€)	DURATION (MINS)	DAILY FREQUENCY (HIGH SEASON)
Capri	Caremar / Navigazione Libera del Golfo / SNAV	16.30 / 20.50 / 20.10	50	4 / 9 / 24
Ischia (Casamicciola Terme & Forio)	Caremar / Alilauro / SNAV	16.40 / 17.60 / 18.60	50-65	6 / 10 / 8
Procida	Caremar / SNAV	13.20 / 15.90	40	8 / 4
Sorrento	Alilauro / Navigazione Libera del Golfo	12 / 12.30	35-40	6

There are several ferry and hydrofoil terminals in central Naples.

Molo Beverello (Map p46), right in front of Castel Nuovo, services fast ferries and hydrofoils for Capri, Sorrento, Ischia (both Ischia Porto and Forio) and Procida. Some hydrofoils for Capri, Ischia and Procida also leave from Mergellina, 5km further west.

Molo Angioino (Map p46), right beside Molo Beverello, services slow ferries for Sicily, the Aeolian Islands and Sardinia.

Calata Porta di Massa (Map p46), beside Molo Angioino, services slow ferries to Ischia, Procida and Capri.

Ferry services are pared back considerably in the winter, and adverse sea conditions may affect sailing schedules.

The tables list hydrofoil and ferry destinations from Naples. The fares, unless otherwise stated, are for a one-way, high-season, deck-class single.

Tickets for shorter journeys can be bought at the ticket booths on Molo Beverello, Calata Porta di Massa or at Mergellina. For longer journeys try the offices of the ferry companies or a travel agent.

The following is a list of hydrofoil and ferry companies:

Alilauro (Map p46; ☎ 081 497 22 01; www.alilauro.it)

Caremar (Map p46; ☎ 081 551 38 82; www.caremar.it)

Medmar (Map p46; ☎ 081 333 44 11; www.medmargroup.it)

Navigazione Libera del Golfo (NLG; Map p46; ☎ 081 552 07 63; www.navlib.it)

Siremar (Map p46; ☎ 081 497 2999; www.siremar.it)

SNAV (Map p46; ☎081 428 55 55; www.snav.it)

Tirrenia (Map p46; ☎ 892123; www.tirrenia.it)

BUS

Most national and international buses leave from Corso Meridionale, on the north side of Stazione Centrale.

On Piazza Garibaldi, **Biglietteria Vecchione** (☎ 081 563 03 20; Piazza Garibaldi; ☺ 6:30am-7.30pm Mon-Sat) displays timetables and sells tickets for most regional and inter-city buses. It also sells Unico Napoli bus and metro tickets.

Regional bus services are operated by numerous companies, the most useful of which is SITA Sud (p85). Connections from Naples include the following:

Amalfi €4.10, two hours, three daily Monday to Saturday

Salerno €4.10, 75 minutes, every 15 to 60 minutes Monday to Saturday

You can buy SITA Sud tickets and catch buses either from Porto Immacolatella, near Molo Angioino, or from outside Stazione Centrale. Tickets are also available from bars and tobacconists displaying the Unico Campania sign.

ATC (☎ 0823 96 90 57; www.atcbus.it) runs from Naples to:

Assisi 5¼ hours, twice daily

Perugia 4½ hours, twice daily

Miccolis (☎ 081 563 03 20; www.miccolis-spa.it) connects Naples to:

Brindisi €31, five hours, three daily

Lecce €34, 5½ to 6 hours, three daily

Taranto €23, four hours, three daily

Marino (☎ 080 311 23 35; www.marinobus.it) runs from Naples to:

Bari €17, three to 3¾ hours, three to five daily

Matera €20, four to 4½ hours, two daily

CAR & MOTORCYCLE

Naples is on the Autostrada del Sole, the A1 (north to Rome and Milan) and the A3 (south to Salerno and Reggio di Calabria). The A30 skirts Naples to the northeast, while the A16 heads across the Apennines to Bari.

On approaching the city, the motorways meet the Tangenziale di Napoli, a major ring road around the city. The ring road hugs the city's northern fringe, meeting the A1 for Rome in the east and continuing westwards towards the Campi Flegrei and Pozzuoli.

TRAIN

Naples is southern Italy's main rail hub. Most trains arrive at or depart from **Stazione Centrale** (⎅081 554 31 88; Piazza Garibaldi) or underneath the main station, from Stazione Garibaldi. Some services also stop at Mergellina station.

State-owned **Trenitalia** (⎅89 20 21; www. trenitalia.com) runs most intercity train services, including up to 42 trains daily to Rome. Travel times and prices vary. Options to/from Rome include the following:

Frecciarossa High Velocity; 2nd class one-way €43, 70 minutes

IC InterCity; 2nd class one way €24.50, two hours

Regionale Regional; one way €11.20, 2¾ hours

Privately owned **Italo** (⎅060708; www.ita-lotreno.it) runs high-velocity trains between Stazione Centrale in Naples and numerous major Italian cities, including Rome (2nd class one way €43, 70 minutes). Note that Italo trains from Naples to Rome stop at Roma-Tiburtina station and not at the main Roma-Termini station.

Tickets for high-velocity trains can work out much cheaper if booked even a few days in advance.

Circumvesuviana (p85) trains connect Naples to Sorrento (€4.10, 68 minutes, around 30 daily). Stops along the way include Ercolano (€2.20, 19 minutes) and Pompeii (€2.90, 38 minutes). Trains leave from **Stazione Circumvesuviana** (⎅800 211388; www.eavcampania.it; Corso Garibaldi), adjacent to Stazione Centrale (follow the signs from the main concourse).

Ferrovia Cumana (⎅800 211388; www.eav-campania.it) trains leave from Stazione Cumana di Montesanto on Piazza Montesanto, 500m southwest of Piazza Dante, running to Pozzuoli (€1.30, 22 minutes, every 20 minutes) and other Campi Flegrei towns beyond.

Ferrovia Circumflegrea, also based at Stazione Cumana di Montesanto, runs services to other Campi Flegrei towns, most of little interest to travellers.

❶ Getting Around

TO/FROM THE AIRPORT

By public transport you can catch the **Alibus** (⎅800 639525; www.unicocampania.it) airport shuttle (€3, 45 minutes, every 20 to 30 minutes) to/from Molo Beverello or Piazza Garibaldi. Tickets are available on board.

Official taxi fares to the airport are as follows: €23 from a seafront hotel or from the Mergellina hydrofoil terminal; €19 from Piazza del Municipio; and €15.50 from Stazione Centrale.

BUS

In Naples, buses are operated by the city transport company **ANM** (⎅800 639525; www.anm.it). There's no central bus station, but most buses pass through Piazza Garibaldi, the city's chaotic transport hub. To locate your bus stop you'll probably need to ask at the information kiosk in the centre of the square.

CAR & MOTORCYCLE

Vehicle theft and anarchic traffic make driving in Naples a bad option.

Officially much of the city centre is closed to nonresident traffic for much of the day. Daily restrictions are in place in the *centro storico,* in the area around Piazza del Municipio and Via Toledo, and in the Chiaia district. Hours vary but are typically from 7am to 6pm, possibly later.

FERRIES

DESTINATION (FROM NAPLES – CALATA PORTA DI MASSA & MOLO ANGIOINO)	COMPANY	PRICE (€)	DURATION	FREQUENCY (HIGH SEASON)
Aeolian Islands	Siremar / SNAV (summer only)	from 50 / from 65	9¾ / 4½ hr	2 weekly / 1 daily
Cagliari (Sardinia)	Tirrenia	from 49	16¼ hr	2 weekly
Capri	Caremar	12.70	80 min	3 daily
Ischia (Ischia Porto)	Caremar / Medmar	12.20 / 11.30	90 / 75 min	5 / 6 daily
Milazzo (Sicily)	Siremar	from 57	10½ hr	2 weekly
Palermo (Sicily)	SNAV / Tirrenia	from 57 / from 49	10¼-11¾ hr	1 to 2 / 1 daily
Procida	Caremar	12.20	65 min	5 daily

ℹ TICKETS PLEASE

Tickets for public transport in Naples and the surrounding Campania region are managed by Unico Campania (www.unicocampania.it) and sold at stations, ANM booths and tobacconists. There are various tickets, depending on where you plan to travel. The following is a rundown of the various tickets on offer:

⟶ **Unico Napoli** (90 minutes €1.30; daily €3.70 weekdays; €3.10 weekends) Unlimited travel by bus, tram, funicular, metro, Ferrovia Cumana or Circumflegrea.

⟶ **Unico 3T** (3 days €20) Unlimited travel throughout Campania, including the Alibus, EAV buses to Mt Vesuvius and transport on the islands of Ischia and Procida.

⟶ **Unico Ischia** (90 minutes €1.90; 1/2/3 days €6/10/13) Unlimited bus travel on Ischia.

⟶ **Unico Capri** (60 minutes €2.70; 24 hours €8.60) Unlimited bus travel on Capri. The 60-minute ticket also allows a single trip on the funicular connecting Marina Grande to Capri Town; the daily ticket allows for two funicular trips.

⟶ **Unico Costiera** (45 minutes €2.50; 90 minutes €3.80; 1/3 days €7.60/18) A money-saver if you plan on much travelling by SITA Sud or EAV bus and/or Circumvesuviana train in the Bay of Naples and Amalfi Coast area. The one- and three-day tickets also cover the City Sightseeing tourist bus between Amalfi and Ravello, and Amalfi and Maiori, which runs from April to October.

East of the city centre, there's a 24-hour car park at Via Brin (€1.30 for the first four hours, €7.20 for 24 hours).

If renting a car, expect to pay around €60 per day for an economy car or a scooter. The major car-hire firms are all represented in Naples.

Avis (☑ 081 28 40 41; www.avisautonoleggio.it; Corso Novara 5) Also at Capodichino airport.

Hertz (☑ 081 20 28 60; www.hertz.it; Corso Arnaldo Lucci 171) Also at Via Marina Varco Pisacane (beside the ferry terminal), at Capodichino airport and in Mergellina.

Maggiore (☑ 081 28 78 58; www.maggiore.it; Stazione Centrale) Also at Capodichino airport.

Rent Sprint (☑ 081 764 34 52; www.rentsprint.it; Via Santa Lucia 32) Scooter hire only.

FUNICULAR

Unico Napoli tickets are valid on the funiculars. Three of Naples' four funicular railways connect the centre with Vomero (the fourth, Funicolare di Mergellina, connects the waterfront at Via Mergellina with Via Manzoni).

Funicolare Centrale Ascends from Via Toledo to Piazza Fuga.

Funicolare di Chiaia From Via del Parco Margherita to Via Domenico Cimarosa.

Funicolare di Montesanto From Piazza Montesanto to Via Raffaele Morghen.

METRO

Naples' **Metropolitana** (☑ 800 568866; www.metro.na.it) metro system is covered by Unico Napoli tickets.

Line 1 Runs north from Università (Piazza Bovio), stopping at Toledo, Piazza Dante, Museo (for Piazza Cavour and Line 2), Materdei, Salvator Rosa, Cilea, Piazza Vanvitelli, Piazza Medaglie D'Oro and seven stops beyond. The expected 2014 completion of the Line 1 extension will see trains run to Garibaldi (Stazione Centrale), with the opening of an additional station in Piazza Municipio (between Università and Toledo stations).

Line 2 Runs from Gianturco, just east of Stazione Centrale, with stops at Piazza Garibaldi (for Stazione Centrale), Piazza Cavour, Montesanto, Piazza Amedeo, Mergellina, Piazza Leopardi, Campi Flegrei, Cavalleggeri d'Aosta, Bagnoli and Pozzuoli.

TAXI

Official taxis are white and have meters; always ensure the meter is running. There are taxi stands at most of the city's main piazzas or you can call one of the following taxi cooperatives:

Consortaxi (☑ 081 22 22)

Consorzio Taxi Napoli (☑ 081 88 88; www.consorziotaxinapoli.it)

Radio Taxi La Partenope (☑ 081 01 01; www.radiotaxilapartenope.it)

The minimum taxi fare is €4.50, of which €3 is the starting fare. The minimum charge increases to €5.50 between 10pm and 7am, on Sundays and on holidays. There is also a baffling range of additional charges, including €1 for a radio taxi call and €0.50 per piece of luggage in the boot.

Official flat rates do exist on some routes, including to/from the airport, Stazione Centrale and the ferry ports. Where available, flat-rate fares must be requested at the beginning of your trip.

From Stazione Centrale, fixed-fare routes include Mergellina (€13.50), seafront hotels (€11.50) and Molo Beverello (€10.50).

See the taxi company websites for a comprehensive list of fares.

BAY OF NAPLES

◎ Sights

Capri

POP 13,400

A stark mass of limestone rock rising sheerly through impossibly blue water, Capri (pronounced *ca*-pri) is the perfect microcosm of Mediterranean appeal – a smooth cocktail of vogueish piazzas and cool cafes, Roman ruins, rugged seascapes and holidaying VIPs. While it's also a popular day-trip destination, consider staying a couple of nights to explore beyond Capri Town and its uphill rival Anacapri. It's here, in Capri's hinterland, that the island really seduces with its overgrown vegetable plots, sun-bleached stucco and indescribably beautiful walking trails.

◉ Capri Town & Around

Whitewashed buildings, labyrinthine laneways, and luxe boutiques and cafes: Capri Town personifies upmarket Mediterranean chic.

Piazza Umberto I   PIAZZA

The heart of Capri Town, this 'flaunt-it-baby' *piazzetta* (little square) seems tailor-made for people-watching and feeling fabulous. While kicking back at the cafes and bars may be expensive, it's an essential Capri experience, especially in the evening, when the main activity in these parts is to style up and scan the candy crowd.

Just off the square, the 17th-century **Chiesa di Santo Stefano** (Piazza Umberto I; ⊙8am-8pm) is known for its well-preserved

---

WORTH A TRIP

PALAZZO REALE DI CASERTA

The one compelling reason to stop at the otherwise nondescript town of Caserta, 30km north of Naples, is to gasp at its colossal, World Heritage-listed **Palazzo Reale** (Map p46; ☑0823 44 80 84; www.reggiadicaserta.beniculturali.it; Viale Douhet 22; adult/reduced €12/6; ⊙palace 8.30am-7pm Wed-Mon, park 8.30am-2hr before sunset Mon-Wed, Giardino Inglese 8.30am-3hr before sunset Mon-Wed). With film credits including *Mission Impossible III* and the interior shots of Queen Amidala's royal residence in *Star Wars: Episode 1 – The Phantom Menace* and *Star Wars: Episode 2 – Attack of the Clones*, this former royal pad is one of the greatest – and last – achievements of Italian baroque architecture.

Known to Italians as the Reggia di Caserta, the *palazzo* (mansions) began life in 1752 after King Charles VII of Bourbon ordered a palace to rival Versailles. Neapolitan Luigi Vanvitelli was commissioned for the job and built a palace bigger than its French rival. With its 1200 rooms, 1790 windows, 34 staircases and a 250m-long facade, it was reputedly the largest building in 18th-century Europe.

Vanvitelli's immense staircase leads up to the royal apartments, richly decorated with tapestries, furniture, crystal and art. The recently restored back rooms of the Throne Room house an extraordinary collection of historic wooden models of the palace, along with architectural drawings and early sketches of the building by Luigi Vanvitelli and his son, Carlo.

The apartments are also home to the Mostra Terrea Motus, an underrated collection of international modern art commissioned after the region's devastating earthquake in 1980.

To clear your head afterwards, explore the elegant landscaped park, which stretches for some 3km to a waterfall and fountain of Diana. Within the park is the famous Giardino Inglese (English Garden), a romantic oasis of intricate pathways, exotic flora, pools and cascades. Bicycle hire (€4) is available on the grounds.

If you're feeling peckish, ditch the uninspiring on-site cafeteria for contemporary cafe **Martucci** (☑0823 32 08 03; Via Roma 9, Caserta; pastries from €0.80, salads from €4; ⊙5am-10.30pm), located 250m east of the palace. The counters here heave with freshly made *panini* (sandwiches), salads, vegetable dishes, baked savouries, pastries and substantial cooked-to-order meals.

Regular trains connect Naples to Caserta (€3.50, 35 to 50 minutes) from Monday to Saturday. Services are reduced and inconvenient on Sunday. Caserta train station is located opposite the palace grounds. If you're driving, follow signs for the Reggia.

Capri

Tyrrhenian Sea

Punta dell'Arcera

Via Grotta Azzurra

Cala del Rio

Cala del Tombosiello

Lido del Faro

Punta Carena

Via Nuova del Faro

Sentiero dei Fortini

Cala Marmolata

Punta del Tuono

Migliera (304m)

ANACAPRI

Piazza Giuseppe Orlandi

Via La Fabbrica

Piazza Vittoria

Via de Tommaso

Piazza Diaz

Via Pagliaro

Via Tuoro

Seggiovia (Funicular)

Via Monte Solaro

Seggiovia del Monte Solaro

Piazzetta Cimitero

Monte Cappello (514m)

Santa Maria a Cetrella

Monte Santa Maria (495m)

Monte Solaro (589m)

Via Migliera

Punta Ventroso

Bagno di Tiberio

Via Provinciale Anacapri

Via Marina Grande

Via Marina Piccola

Via Roma

Torre Saracena

Punta di Mulo

Gulf of Naples (Golfo di Napoli)

See Enlargement

CAPRI TOWN

Via Tiberio

Via Camerelle

Via Tragara

Via Tuoro

Monte Tuoro (261m)

Arco Naturale

Marina di Cuterola

Punta del Capo

Salto di Tiberio

Punta Massullo

Pizzolungo

Scoglio del Monacone

Porto di Tragara

Punta di Tragara

La Fontelina

Isole Faraglioni

Scoglio dell'Unghia Marina

Gulf of Salerno (Golfo di Salerno)

Scoglio delle Sirene

Bagni di Gioia

Tyrrhenian Sea

Enlargement

Piazza Umberto I

Via Serafina

Via Le Botteghe

Via Longano

Via Vittorio Emanuele III

Piazzetta Cerio

1 km
0.5 miles

100 m
0.05 miles

Capri

marble floor (taken from Villa Jovis). Opposite the church, the **Museo Cerio** (⌨ 081 837 66 81; Piazzetta Cerio 5; adult/reduced €2.50/1; ⊙ 10am-1pm Tue-Sat) harbours a library of books and journals (mostly in Italian), and a collection of locally found fossils.

Villa Jovis   RUIN
(Jupiter's Villa; ⌨ 081 837 06 86; Via Amaiuri; adult/reduced €2/1; ⊙ 11am-3pm, closed Tue 1st-15th of month, closed Sun rest of month) A comfortable 2km walk along Via Tiberio, Villa Jovis was the largest and most sumptuous of the island's 12 Roman villas. It was also Tiberius' main Capri residence. Although reduced to ruins, wandering around will give you a good idea of the scale on which Tiberius liked to live.

The vast pleasure complex famously pandered to the emperor's lustful desires, and included imperial quarters and extensive bathing areas set in dense gardens and woodland. His private rooms were on the northern and eastern sides of the complex.

The stairway behind the villa leads to the 330m-high **Salto di Tiberio** (Tiberius' Leap), a sheer cliff from where, as the story goes, Tiberius had out-of-favour subjects hurled into the sea. True or not, the breathtaking views are real enough; if you suffer from vertigo, tread carefully.

A short walk from the villa, down Via Tiberio and Via Matermània, is the **Arco Naturale** – a huge, photogenic rock arch formed by the pounding sea.

Certosa di San Giacomo   MONASTERY
(⌨ 081 837 62 18; Viale Certosa 40; ⊙ 9am-2pm Tue-Sun) **FREE** Generally considered the finest surviving example of Caprese architecture, this picturesque monastery now houses a school, library, temporary exhibition space and a museum with some evocative 17th-century paintings. While the chapel has some soothing 17th-century frescoes, it's the two cloisters that have a real sense of faded glory (the smaller dates to the 14th century, the larger to the 16th century).

To reach here take Via Vittorio Emanuele, to the east of Piazza Umberto I, which meanders down to the monastery.

Giardini di Augusto   GARDEN
(Gardens of Augustus; admission €1; ⊙ 9am-1hr before sunset) Get away from the Capri crowds by heading southwest from the Certosa di San Giacomo monastery where, at the end of Via G Matteotti, you'll come across the unexpected green oasis of the colourful Giardini di Augusto, founded by the Emperor Augustus. You should spend a few minutes contemplating the breathtaking view from here: gaze ahead to the **Isole Faraglioni**, the three dramatic limestone pinnacles that rise vertically out of the sea.

⊚ **Anacapri & Around**

Delve beyond the Villa San Michele di Axel Munthe and the souvenir stores and you'll discover that Capri Town's more subdued sibling is, at heart, the laid-back rural village that it's always been.

★ **Seggiovia del Monte Solaro** VIEW POINT
([☎] 081 837 14 28; single/return €7.50/10; ⊙ 9.30am-4.30pm summer, to 3.30pm winter) Hop onto this *seggiovia* (chairlift) and head up to the summit of **Monte Solaro** (589m), Capri's highest point. The views from the top are utterly unforgettable – on a clear day, you can see the entire Bay of Naples, the Amalfi Coast and the islands of Ischia and Procida.

Villa San Michele di Axel Munthe MUSEUM, GARDEN
([☎] 081 837 14 01; www.villasanmichele.eu; Via Axel Munthe 34; admission €7; ⊙ 9am-6pm summer, reduced hours rest of year) A short walk from Anacapri's Piazza Vittoria awaits the former home of self-aggrandising Swedish doctor Axel Munthe. Other than the collection of Roman sculpture, the villa's winning feature is the beautifully preserved gardens and their inspiring views. Between late June and early August, the gardens play host to classical concerts – check the Axel Munthe Foundation website for program details and reservation information.

Beyond the villa, Via Axel Munthe continues to the 800-step stairway leading down to Capri Town.

🏃 Activities

Beaches BEACH
Come summer, it's hard to resist Capri's turquoise waters. Top swimming spots include **La Fontelina** ([☎] 081 837 08 45; www.fontelina-capri.com), reached along Via Tragara. Access to the private beach will set you back €20 but it's right beside Capri's craggy Faraglioni stacks and is one of the few beaches with direct sunlight until late in the day.

On the west coast, **Lido del Faro** ([☎] 081 837 17 98; www.lidofaro.com) at Punta Carena is another good option; €20 will get you access to the private beach, complete with swimming pool and a pricey but fabulous restaurant. For a free dip, opt for the neighbouring public beach, and grab a decent bite at snack bar Da Antonio. To get here from Anacapri, catch the bus to Faro (every 20 minutes, April to October) and follow the steps down to the beach.

Sercomar DIVING
([☎] 081 837 87 81; www.capriseaservice.com; Via Colombo 64, Marina Grande; ⊙ Apr-Oct; 🚿) Marina Grande is the hub of Capri's thriving watersports business and this outfit is a solid choice for diving fans. Dives start from €100 for a single dive (maximum of three people)

GROTTA AZZURRA

Glowing in an ethereal blue light, the bewitching **Grotta Azzurra** (Blue Grotto; grotto admission €12.50, return boat trip €13.50; ⊙ 9am-1hr before sunset) is Capri's most famous single attraction.

Long known to local fishers, the legendary sea cave was rediscovered by two Germans – writer Augustus Kopisch and painter Ernst Fries – in 1826. Subsequent research, however, revealed that Emperor Tiberius had built a quay in the cave around AD 30, complete with a nymphaeum. Remarkably, you can still see the carved Roman landing stage towards the rear of the grotto.

Measuring 54m by 30m and rising to a height of 15m, the grotto is said to have sunk by up to 20m in prehistoric times, blocking every opening except the 1.3m-high entrance. And this is the key to the magical blue light. Sunlight enters through a small underwater aperture and is refracted through the water; this, combined with the reflection of the light off the white sandy sea floor, produces the vivid blue effect to which the cave owes its name.

The easiest way to visit it is to take a boat tour from Marina Grande. A return trip will cost €26, comprising a return motorboat to the cave, the rowing boat into the cave itself and admission fee; allow a good hour.

The grotto is closed if the sea is too choppy, and swimming in the cave is forbidden, although you can swim outside the entrance – get a bus to Grotta Azzurra, take the stairs down to the right and dive off the small concrete platform. When visiting, keep in mind that the singing 'captains' are included in the price, so don't feel any obligation if they push for a tip.

SOOTHING ISLAND HIKES

Away from the yachts, bikini crowds and glossy boutiques, Capri offers some seriously soul-lifting hikes. Favourite routes include from Arco Naturale to the Belvedere di Tragara (1.2km, 1¼ hours), best tackled in this very direction to avoid a final climb up to Arco Naturale. Another popular route is from Anacapri to Monte Solaro (2km, two hours), the island's highest point. If you don't fancy an upward trek, take the *seggiovia* (chairlift) up and walk down.

Running along the island's oft-overlooked western coast, the Sentiero dei Fortini (Path of the Small Forts; 5.2km, three hours), which connects Punta dell'Arcera near the Grotta Azzurra to Punta Carena, promises more bucolic bliss. For the best effect, start at Punta dell'Arcera so you can end your hike with sunset drinks at Punta Carena. Capri's tourist offices can provide information and maps of the island's various trails.

to €150 for an individual dive. A four-session beginner's course will set you back €350.

Banana Sport BOATING
(☑ 081 837 51 88; Marina Grande; 2hours/day rental €120/220; ⊙ May-Oct) Located on the Marina Grande waterfront, Banana Sport hires out five-person motorised dinghies, allowing you to explore the island's more secluded coves and grottoes.

🛏 Sleeping

Capri's accommodation is top-heavy, with plenty of four- and five-star hotels and fewer budget options. This said, the recent financial downturn has seen many hotels lower their prices in the past couple of years, making the island a little less prohibitive than it used to be. Prices are often cheaper Monday to Thursday and, as a general rule, the further you go from Capri Town, the less you'll pay. Camping is forbidden.

Always book ahead. Hotel space is at a premium during the summer, and many places close in winter, typically between November and March.

Capri Suite GUESTHOUSE €€
(☑ 349 5252881, 335 5280647; www.caprisuite.it; Via Finestrale 9, Anacapri; standard ste €140-190, superior ste €190-260; ❄ 🛜) This striking two-suite guesthouse occupies part of a 17th-century convent in central Anacapri. While low-slung lamps and huge arched windows define the kitchen, traces of frescoes contrast sharply against resin floors, blown-up contemporary photography and designer furniture in the living room. The superior suite comes with chromotherapy soaking tub, right at the foot of your bed.

Villa Eva HOTEL €€
(☑ 081 837 15 49; www.villaeva.com; Via La Fabbrica 8, Anacapri; d €100-140, tr €150-180, apt per person €55-65; ⊙ Easter-Oct; 🛋) Villa Eva is a top 'budget' option, complete with small swimming pool and lush, palm-fringed gardens. Whether it's a stained-glass window or a vintage fireplace, each room is distinct; some come with sea-view terraces. The four- and six-person apartments are ideal for families or groups of friends.

Free wi-fi is available in the pool area. Air-conditioning is optional and charged separately.

Casa Mariantonia BOUTIQUE HOTEL €€
(☑ 081 837 29 23; www.casamariantonia.com; Via Guiseppe Orlandi 80, Anacapri; r €100-260; 🅿 ❄ 🛜 🛋) This fabulous boutique retreat counts Jean-Paul Sartre and Alberto Moravia among its past guests, which may well give you something to muse upon while you're lounging by the fabulous pool. Rooms deliver restrained elegance in soothing hues, and there are private terraces with gorgeous garden views.

Hotel Villa Sarah HOTEL €€
(☑ 081 837 78 17; www.villasarah.it; Via Tiberio 3, Capri Town; s €90-160, d €135-235; ⊙ Easter-Oct; ❄ 🛋) On the road up to Villa Jovis – a 10-minute walk from the centre of Capri Town – Villa Sarah retains a rustic appeal that so many of the island's hotels have long lost. Surrounded by its own fruit-producing gardens and with a small pool, it has 20 airy rooms, all decorated in classical local style with ceramic tiles and old-fashioned furniture. The healthy breakfast includes organic produce.

Hotel La Tosca
PENSION €€

(☑ 081 837 09 89; www.latoscahotel.com; Via Dalmazio Birago 5, Capri Town; s €50-100, d €75-160; ⊙ Apr-Oct; ⊛ 🖀) Away from the glitz of the town centre, this one-star charmer is hidden down a quiet back lane overlooking the Certosa di San Giacomo and the mountains. Rooms are airy and comfortable, with whitewashed walls, striped fabrics and large bathrooms. Several have private terraces, complete with deck chairs and rattan furniture.

★ La Minerva
BOUTIQUE HOTEL €€€

(☑ 081 837 70 67; www.laminervacapri.com; Via Occhio Marino 8, Capri Town; superior d €170-410, deluxe d €230-520; ⊙ mid-Mar–early Nov; ⊛ 🖀 ⊠) This stylish, family-run hotel is highly coveted (book five to six months ahead). All 16 rooms deliver crisp, white-on-white luxury, from silk drapes, plush sofas and 100% linen sheets to heavenly mattresses and your choice of pillows. Deluxe rooms feature jacuzzis and larger terraces. Then there's the gorgeous pool, surrounded by lush greenery and dreamy sea views.

Orsa Maggiore
BOUTIQUE HOTEL €€€

(☑ 081 837 33 51; www.orsamaggiore-capri.com; Via Tuoro 30, Anacapri; d €160-340; ⊙ mid-Apr–mid-Oct; ⊛ @ 🖀 ⊠) If sunset-gazing from a mosaic-lined infinity pool strikes a chord, this airy boutique hotel has your name written all over its whitewashed walls. Umbrian stone floors, wisteria-laced terraces and lush grounds set a suitably chic scene, the hotel's 14 rooms featuring large terraces with chaise longes for sun-kissed R&R.

A small, private spa area (60 minutes, €60 per couple) comes with sauna, Turkish bath, jacuzzi and chromotherapy shower.

🍴 Eating

Traditional food in traditional trattorias is what you'll find on Capri. The island's culinary gift to the world is *insalata caprese,* a salad of fresh tomato, basil and mozzarella bathed in olive oil. Also look out for *caprese* cheese, a cross between mozzarella and ricotta, and *ravioli caprese,* ravioli stuffed with ricotta and herbs.

Many restaurants, like the hotels, close over winter.

Capri Pasta
TAKEAWAY €

(Via Parrocco R Canale 12, Capri Town; mains €8; ⊙ closed Mon) Locals come here for a cheap, tasty takeaway lunch. The just-cooked soul food might include *parmigiana di melanzana* (aubergine parmigiana) and *friarelle* (local broccoli). The house ravioli is legendary and offered fresh or ready-to-eat in dishes like *ravioli fritti* (fried ravioli) stuffed with Caciotta cheese and marjoram.

Salumeria da Aldo
DELI €

(Via Cristoforo Colombo 26, Marina Grande; panini from €3.50) Ignore the restaurant touts and head straight to this honest portside deli, where bespectacled Aldo will make you his legendary *panino alla Caprese* (crusty bread stuffed with silky mozzarella and tomatoes from his own garden). Grab a bottle of Falanghina and you're set for a day at the beach.

★ Da Gelsomina
CAMPANIAN €€

(☑ 081 837 14 99; www.dagelsomina.com; Via Migliera 72, Anacapri; meals €38; ⊙ lunch & dinner Mon-Sun May-Sep, reduced hours rest of year; 🖀) Sublime home-grown produce and wine; sea and vineyard views; a swimming pool for a postprandial dip – it's no wonder you're advised to book three days ahead in the summer. Da Gelsomina ditches culinary clichés for turf classics like *coniglio alla cacciatore* (rabbit with lightly spiced tomato, sage and rosemary) and not-to-be-missed *ravioli caprese,* filled with Cacciotta cheese.

The property also offers five pleasant rooms (doubles €120 to €160) with terraces and sea views. From Anacapri, Da Gelsomina is a 20-minute walk along sleepy Via Migliera. Alternatively, call ahead for a free pick-up from Anacapri.

Pulalli
WINE BAR €€

(☑ 081 837 41 08; Piazza Umberto I 4, Capri Town; meals €25; ⊙ lunch & dinner Wed-Mon Easter-Oct, dinner Tue Aug) Climb the clock-tower steps to the right of Capri Town's tourist office and your reward is a laid-back local hang-out, where fabulous vino meets a discerning selection of cheeses, *salumi* (charcuterie) and more substantial fare like spaghetti with zucchini flowers. Try for a seat on the terrace or, if you're feeling lucky, the coveted table on its own petite balcony.

Buca di Bacco
CAMPANIAN, PIZZERIA €€

(☑ 081 837 07 23; Via Longano 35, Capri Town; pizzas €6.50-12.50, meals €40; ⊙ noon-3pm & 7-11pm) A famous hang-out for artists early last century, this hidden Capri Town treasure is now better known for its solid local cooking, bubbling pizzas and amiable staff. The seafood is especially good, as is the window table with dreamy sea views.

Le Arcate
CAMPANIAN, PIZZERIA €€

(☑081 837 35 88; Via de Tommaso 24, Anacapri; pizzas €7-11, meals €30; ⊙noon-3pm & 7pm-midnight) An unpretentious place with hanging baskets of ivy, sunny yellow tablecloths and well-aged terracotta tiles, Le Arcate specialises in delicious *primi* (first courses) and pizzas. A real show-stopper is the *seppie con verdure all'aceto balsamico* (cuttlefish with vegetables in a balsamic reduction).

 Drinking & Nightlife

The main evening activity is styling up and hanging out, ideally on Capri Town's Piazzetta. There are few nightclubs to speak of and just a few upmarket taverns. Most places open around 10pm (don't expect a crowd until midnight), charging anywhere between €30 and €40 for admission. Many close between November and Easter.

Taverna Anema e Core
CLUB

(☑081 837 64 61; Via Sella Orta 39e, Capri Town; ⊙11.30pm-late daily Jul & Aug, closed Mon & Wed Easter-Jun, Sep & Oct) In Capri Town, this nightlife institution is a hit with permatanned VIPs and holidaying celebs. Dress sharp – you never know who you might stumble across.

Il Celeste
CLUB

(☑081 837 73 08; www.celestecapri.it; Via Camerelle 63, Capri Town; ⊙11.45pm-4am Fri-Sun) A huge hit with the 18-to-25 crowd, Il Celeste channels retro Capri chic with its chintzy chandeliers, candelabras and champagne chesterfields. Dress to impress and groove to house and mainstream dance.

 Shopping

If you're not in the market for a new Rolex or Prada bag, look out for ceramic work, lemon-scented perfume and *limoncello* (lemon liqueur). For perfume don't miss Carthusia I Profumi di Capri (☑081 837 53 35; www.carthusia.it; Via F Serena 28, Capri Town; ⊙9am-6pm); for *limoncello* head up to Anacapri and Limoncello di Capri (☑081 837 29 27; Via Capodimonte 27; ⊙9am-7.30pm).

If you *are* in the market for a new Rolex or Prada bag, head to Via Vittorio Emanuele and Via Camerelle.

ⓘ Information

Tourist office (Marina Grande; ⊙9.15am-1pm & 3-6.15pm Mon-Sat, 9am-3pm Sun Apr-Sep) Each tourist office can provide a free map of the island with town plans of Capri and

Anacapri, and a more detailed one for €1. For hotel listings and other useful information, ask for a free copy of *Capri è*. Branches at Capri Town (☑081 837 06 86; www.capritourism. com; Piazza Umberto I; ⊙8.30am-8.30pm) and Anacapri. (☑081 837 15 24; Via G Orlando 59; ⊙9am-3pm Mon-Sat Apr-Sep).

Capri Island (www.capri.net) Includes listings, itineraries and ferry schedules.

Capri Tourism (www.capritourism.com) Official website of Capri's tourist office.

Farmacia Internazionale (Via Roma 45)

Hospital (☑081 838 12 05; Via Provinciale Anacapri 5)

Police station (☑081 837 42 11; Via Roma 68)

Post office (Via Roma 50; ⊙8am-6.30pm Mon-Fri, 8am-12.30pm Sat) Also a branch in Anacapri (Viale de Tommaso 8)

ⓘ Getting There & Away

See Naples and Sorrento for details of ferries and hydrofoils to the island.

In summer hydrofoils connect with Positano (€17.40 to 19.30, 30 to 40 minutes) and Ischia (€18, one hour).

Note that some companies require you to pay a small supplement for luggage, typically around €2.

ⓘ Getting Around

BUS

Sippic (☑081 837 04 20; Via Roma, Bus Station, Capri Town; €1.80) runs regular buses between Capri Town and Marina Grande, Anacapri and Marina Piccola. It also operates buses from Marina Grande to Anacapri and from Marina Piccola to Anacapri.

Staiano Autotrasporti (☑081 837 24 22; Via Tommaso, Bus Station, Anacapri; €1.80) buses serve the Grotta Azzurra and Faro of Punta Carena.

SCOOTER

Ciro dei Motorini (☑081 837 80 18; www.capriscooter.com; Via Marina Grande 55, Marina Grande; 3/24 hrs €40/65) For scooter hire at Marina Grande, stop here.

FUNICULAR

Funicular (€1.80; ⊙6.30am-12.30am) connects Marina Grande to Capri Town. Like the buses, single tickets cost €1.80.

TAXI

From Marina Grande, a **taxi** (☑in Anacapri 081 837 11 75, in Capri Town 081 837 05 43) costs around €20 to Capri and €25 to Anacapri; from Capri to Anacapri costs about €16.

Ischia

POP 61,100

Sprawling over 46 sq km, Ischia is the biggest and busiest island in the bay. It's a lush concoction of sprawling spa towns, mudwrapped Germans and ancient booty. Also famous for its thermal waters, it has some fine beaches and spectacular scenery.

Most visitors stay on the touristy north coast, but go inland and you'll find a rural landscape of chestnut forests, dusty farms and earthy hillside towns.

◎ Sights

★**Castello Aragonese**   CASTLE

(Castle D'Aragona; ☑081 99 28 34; Rocca del Castello, Ischia Ponte; adult/reduced €10/6; ⊙9am-90min before sunset) Ischia's imposing castle sits on a rocky islet just off Ischia Ponte. A sprawling complex dating largely to the 1400s, when King Alfonso of Aragon gave an older Angevin fortress a makeover, its attractions include an offbeat torture and armoury museum, local art exhibitions, historic church buildings and a macabre burial chamber. And did we mention the breathtaking coastal panoramas?

★**La Mortella**   GARDEN

(☑081 98 62 20; www.lamortella.it; Via F Calese 39, Forio; adult/reduced €12/7; ⊙9am-7pm Tue, Thu, Sat & Sun Apr-early Nov) Over 1000 rare and exotic plants flourish in this veritable Garden of Eden on Ischia's west coast. Designed by Russell Page and inspired by the Moorish gardens of Granada's Alhambra in Spain, the gardens were established by the late British composer Sir William Walton and his Argentinian wife, Susana, who made La Mortella their home in 1949. Classical-music concerts are staged on the premises; check the website.

☆ Activities

Beaches   BEACH

Unlike Capri, Ischia has some great beaches. From chic Sant'Angelo on the south coast, water taxis reach the sandy Spiaggia dei Maronti (one way €5) and the intimate cove of Il Sorgeto (one way €7; ⊙Apr-Oct), with its steamy thermal spring. Sorgeto can also be reached on foot down a poorly signposted path from the village of Panza.

Giardini Poseidon   SPA

(Poseidon Gardens; ☑081 908 71 11; www.giardini poseidonterme.com; Via Mazzella, Spiaggia di Citara; day pass €32; ⊙9am-7pm summer) No, you haven't died and gone to heaven. You're just south of Forio, at this sprawling spa nirvana. Spoil yourself rotten from a wide choice of treatments and facilities, including massages, saunas, jacuzzis and terraced pools spilling down the volcanic cliffside. Waiting at the bottom is your own private beach.

Monte Epomeo   WALKING TRAIL

Lace up those hiking boots and set out on a roughly 2.5km, 50-minute uphill walk from the village of Fontana, which will bring you to the top of Monte Epomeo (788m). Formed by an underwater eruption, it delivers superlative views of the Bay of Naples.

The little church near the summit is the 15th-century Cappella di San Nicola di Bari, which features a pretty maiolica floor.

Ischia Diving   DIVING

(☑081 98 18 52; www.ischiadiving.net; Via Iasolino 106, Ischia Porto; single dive €60) This well-established diving outfit offers some attractively priced dive packages, like five dives (including equipment) for €225.

⌨ Sleeping

Most hotels close in winter and prices normally drop considerably among those that stay open.

Camping Mirage   CAMPGROUND €

(☑081 99 05 51; www.campingmirage.it; Via Maronti 37, Spiaggia dei Maronti, Barano d'Ischia; camping 2 people, car & tent €34.50-41.50; ☒⚄) On one of Ischia's best beaches within walking distance of Sant'Angelo, this shady camping ground offers 50 places, showers, laundry facilities, a bar and a restaurant serving great seafood pasta.

Albergo Macrì   HOTEL €

(☑081 99 26 03; Via Iasolino 78a, Ischia Porto; s €45-65, d €84-110; ☒❋) Down a blind alley near the main port, this place is run by a smiley lady and has a friendly, low-key vibe. While the pine and bamboo furnishings won't snag any design awards, rooms are clean, bright and comfy. All 1st-floor rooms have terraces and the small downstairs bar serves a mean espresso.

Albergo il Monastero   HOTEL €€

(☑081 99 24 35; www.albergoilmonastero.it; Castello Aragonese, Rocca del Castello; s €85, d €120-

IL FOCOLARE: A SLOW FOOD WONDER

Tucked away in the hills above Casamicciola Terme is one restaurant verified food-ies cannot afford to miss – **Il Focolare** (☑ 081 90 29 44; Via Creajo al Crocefisso, Barano d'Ischia; meals €30; ⊙ 12.30-2.45pm Fri-Sun, 7.30-11.45pm, closed Wed Nov-May).

Forget *spaghetti alle vongole* (spaghetti with clams) – this proud Slow Food stalwart celebrates all things turf. Indeed, it's one of the best spots to savour the island's legen-dary *coniglio all'Ischitana* (a claypot-cooked local rabbit with garlic, onion, tomatoes, wild thyme and white wine), a dish that needs to be booked two days in advance.

If you haven't pre-ordered the rabbit, don't fret – the daily menu brims with beauti-ful, seasonal dishes, from *tagliatelle al ragù di cinghiale* (ribbon-shaped pasta with wild boar ragout) to a sublime *antipasto misto,* where you might get anything from *rotolino di zucchini* (fried, bread-crumbed zucchini filled with buffalo mozzarella) to *terrina di parmigiano tartufata con i funghi* (think porcini-mushroom crème brûlée).

To get here, catch bus 16 from Piazza Marina in Casamicciola Terme and ask the driver to let you off at the restaurant (it's the last stop). During the summer high season, the last bus back to town departs at around 12.50am.

170; ⊙ Easter-Oct; ❄) The former monks' cells retain a certain appealing sobriety, with dark-wood furniture, vintage terracotta tiles and no TV (the views are sufficiently prime time). Elsewhere there's a sense of space and style, with vaulted ceilings, plush sofas, a sprinkle of antiques and bold contemporary art by the late owner and artist Gabriele Mattera. The hotel restaurant has an excel-lent reputation.

Hotel Semiramis HOTEL €€
(☑ 081 90 75 11; www.hotelsemiramisischia.it; Spiaggia di Citara, Forio; d €118-156; ⊙ late Apr-Oct; P ❄ 🏠 🛜 🏊) A few minutes' walk from the Po-seidon spa complex, this bright hotel, run by friendly Giovanni and his German wife, channels the tropics with its central pool surrounded by lofty palms. Rooms are large and beautifully tiled in traditional yellow-and-turquoise style. The garden is a lush, glorious oasis of fig trees, vineyards and dis-tant sea views.

🍴 Eating

Seafood aside, Ischia is famed for its rabbit, which is bred on inland farms. Another lo-cal speciality is *rucolino* – a green liquorice-flavoured liqueur made from *rucola* (rocket) leaves.

Montecorvo ITALIAN €€
(☑ 081 99 80 29; www.montecorvo.it; Via Mon-tecorvo 33, Forio; meals €30; ⊙ 12.30-3.30pm & 7.30pm-1am) While the cave-set dining room and junglelike terrace are memorable enough, it's owner Giovanni's imaginative home cooking that steals the show. The an-tipasti see some inspired pairings, whether

it's prawns with orange, or oven-baked sar-dines with mozzarella. Perfect pasta dishes include a zesty *linguine al limone* (linguine with lemon), while the grilled meats are sub-limely succulent.

★ Cantine di Pietratorcia CAMPANIAN €€
(☑ 081 90 82 06; www.pietratorcia.it; Via Provin-ciale Panza 267, Forio; meals €30; ⊙ lunch & dinner Mon-Thu, till late Fri-Sun) Set among tumbling vines and rosemary bushes, this family-run winery is a foodie's nirvana. Tour the 18th-century stone cellars, sip a local drop and graze on rare cheese, including offerings from the Cilento's revered father-and-son team Antonio and Angelo Madaio.

The owners breed their own rabbits in traditional *fosse* (pits), and serve up an ex-traordinary *coniglio all'ischitana* (Ischia-style rabbit with local herbs) if requested in advance. Lunch bookings are obligatory, and it's advisable to book their degustation din-ners too. The winery is closed for lunch from mid-June to mid-September, and closed entirely from mid-November to the end of March.

Ristorante da Ciccio CAMPANIAN €€
(☑ 081 99 16 86; Via Luigi Mazzella 32, Ischia Ponte; meals €25; ⊙ noon-3.30pm & 7.30-11.30pm, closed Tue Dec-Feb) Solid seafood and charming host Carlo make this atmospheric place a winner. Highlights include *tubattone* pasta with mussels and *pecorino* cheese, a zesty mussel soup topped with fried bread and *peperon-cino* (chilli), and a delicious chocolate and almond cake. Tables spill out onto the pave-ment in the summer, from where there's a gorgeous castle view.

ⓘ Information

Ischia online (www.ischiaonline.it) Good all-round website including sights, restaurants and hotels.

Tourist office (www.infoischiaprocida.it; Via Sogliuzzo 72; ⊙ 9am-2pm & 3-8pm Mon-Sat, plus 9am-1pm Sun Jul-Sep)

ⓘ Getting There & Away

Regular hydrofoils and ferries run to/from Naples. You can also catch hydrofoils direct to Capri (€18) and Procida (€8.20).

ⓘ Getting Around

The island's main bus station is in Ischia Porto. There are two principal lines: the Circo Sinistra CS; Left Circle), which circles the island anticlockwise, and the (Circo Destra CD; Right Circle), which travels clockwise. These buses pass through each town and depart every 30 minutes. Buses pass near all hotels and campsites. A single ticket, valid for 90 minutes, costs €1.90; a daily, multiuse ticket is €6; and a two-day ticket is €10. Taxis and microtaxis (scooter-engined three-wheelers) are also available.

Help the island avoid congestion and pollution by not bringing your car. If you want to hire one (or a scooter), there are plenty of rental firms, including **Fratelli del Franco** (☑ 081 99 13 34; www.noleggiodelfranco.it; Via A de Luca 127), which hires out cars (from €30 per day), scooters (around €30) and mountain bikes (around €10 per day). You can't take a rented vehicle off the island.

Procida

POP 10,200

Dig out your paintbox: the Bay of Naples' smallest island (and its best-kept secret) is a soulful blend of hidden lemon groves, weathered fishing folk and pastel-hued houses. August aside – when beach-bound mainlanders flock to its shores – its narrow sun-bleached streets are the domain of the locals.

◉ Sights & Activities

The best way to explore the island – a mere 4 sq km – is on foot or by bike. However, the island's narrow roads can be clogged with cars – one of its few drawbacks.

From panoramic Piazza dei Martiri, the village of **Corricella** tumbles down to its marina in a riot of pinks, yellows and whites. Further south, a steep flight of steps leads

down to **Chiaia** beach, one of the island's most beautiful.

All pink, white and blue, little **Marina di Chiaiolella** has a yacht-stocked marina, old-school eateries and a languid disposition. Nearby, the **Lido** is a popular beach.

Abbazia di San Michele Arcangelo   CHURCH, MUSEUM
(☑ 334 8514028, 334 8514252; associazionemillennium@virgilio.it; Via Terra Murata 89, Terra Murata; donation appreciated; ⊙ 9.45am-12.45pm & 3.30-6pm) This former Benedictine abbey was built in the 11th century and remodelled between the 17th and 19th centuries. While the main church is open to all, it's worth joining one of the regular guided tours to gain access to the pretty barrel-vaulted library and Secret Chapel.

The latter is home to some curious 18th-century coffins, one complete with arm holes for convenient kissing of the deceased's hands. English-language tours should be requested a couple of days in advance.

Procida Diving Centre   DIVING
(☑ 081 896 83 85; www.vacanzeaprocida.it; Via Cristoforo Colombo 6, Marina di Chiaiolella; ⊙ Jun-Sep; ⊛) Conveniently located right on the marina, this outfit runs diving courses and hires out equipment. Prices range from €45 for a single dive to €130 for a snorkelling course, with more advanced open-water diving and rescue courses also on offer.

Blue Dream Yacht Charter Boating   BOATING
(☑ 339 5720874, 081 896 05 79; www.bluedream-charter.com; Via Vittorio Emanuele 14, Marina Grande) If you have grand 'champagne on the deck' aspirations, you can always charter a yacht from here (from €1500 per week). Sleeps six.

✵ Festivals & Events

Procession of the Misteri   RELIGIOUS
Procida's famous Good Friday procession sees a wooden statue of Christ and the Madonna Addolarata, along with life-sized tableaux of plaster and papier-mâché illustrating events leading to Christ's crucifixion, carted across the island.

⨋ Sleeping

★ **Hotel La Vigna**   BOUTIQUE HOTEL €€
(☑ 081 896 04 69; www.albergolavigna.it; Via Principessa Margherita 46; s €75-150, d €90-180, ste €140-230; ❋ @ 🛜) Enjoying a cliffside lo-

cation 1km east of the main port, this 18th-century villa is a delight. Five of the spacious, simply furnished rooms offer direct access to the hotel's soothing garden. Superior rooms (€110 to €200) feature family-friendly mezzanines, while the main perk of the suite is the bedside jacuzzi; perfect for romancing couples.

Casa Sul Mare HOTEL €€
(☑081 896 87 99; www.lacasasulmare.it; Salita Castello 13; r €99-170; 🌐🛜) Overlooking the obscenely picturesque Marina Corricella, friendly Casa Sul Mare offers rooms with exquisite tiled floors and wrought-iron bedsteads. During summer there's a boat service to the nearest beaches.

Casa Giovanni da Procida B&B €€
(☑081 896 03 58; www.casagiovannidaprocida. it; Via Giovanni da Procida 3; d €80-130, €100-145; 🅿🌐🛜) This chic converted farmhouse B&B features split-level minimalist rooms with low-rise beds and contemporary furniture. Bathrooms are small but slick, with huge showerheads and the occasional vaulted ceiling.

✕ Eating

La Conchiglia SEAFOOD €€
(☑081 896 76 02; www.laconchigliaristorante.com; Via Pizzaco 10, Solchiaro; meals €25; ⊙1-3.30pm & 8-9.30pm summer) With lapping turquoise water below and pastel Marina Corricella glowing in the distance, this beachside gem is a top spot to savour a superb *spaghetti alla povera* (spaghetti with *peperoncino*, green capsicum, cherry tomatoes and anchovies). To get here, take the steep steps down from Via Pizzaco or call the restaurant and book a boat from Corricella.

Caracalè SEAFOOD €€
(☑081 896 91 92; Via Marina Corricella 6, Marina Corricella; meals €28; ⊙12.30-3.30pm & 7-11pm, closed Tue Mar-Jun & Sep–mid-Nov) Slap bang on Marina Corricella's cinematic waterfront, Caracalè peddles superb seafood dishes like spaghetti with calamari and artichokes, and succulent grilled swordfish. Menus change twice daily, depending on the morning and afternoon catch.

❶ Information

Procida Holidays (☑081 896 95 94; www. isoladiprocida.it; Via Roma 117; ⊙9am-1pm & 4-8pm Mon-Sat Apr-Oct, closed Sat afternoon Nov-Mar) Can organise accommodation (single/ double from €90/120) and also has a free map of the island.

❶ Getting There & Around

Procida is linked by boat and hydrofoil to Ischia (€8.20), Pozzuoli (€8.20) and Naples.

There is a limited bus service (€1), with four lines radiating out from Marina Grande. Bus L1 connects the port and Marina di Chiaiolella.

Contact **Sprint** (☑339 8659600, 081 896 94 35; www.sprintprocida.com; Via Roma 28; scooters per day €25-30; ⊙8am-1pm & 4-8pm Mon-Sat, 10am-1pm Sun) for scooter and electric-bike hire.

Taxis can be hired for two to three hours for about €35, depending on your bargaining prowess.

SOUTH OF NAPLES

Ercolano & Herculaneum

Ercolano is an uninspiring Neapolitan suburb that's home to one of Italy's best-preserved ancient sites – Herculaneum. A superbly conserved Roman fishing town, Herculaneum is smaller and less daunting than Pompeii, allowing you to visit without that nagging itch that you're bound to miss something.

History

In contrast to modern Ercolano, classical Herculaneum was a peaceful fishing and port town of about 4000 inhabitants, and something of a resort for wealthy Romans and Campanians.

Herculaneum's fate paralleled that of nearby Pompeii. Destroyed by an earthquake in AD 63, it was completely submerged in the AD 79 eruption of Mt Vesuvius. However, as it was much closer to the volcano than Pompeii, it drowned in a 16m-thick sea of mud rather than in the lapilli (burning pumice stone) and ash that rained down on Pompeii. This essentially fossilised the town, ensuring that even delicate items, like furniture and clothing, were remarkably well preserved when uncovered.

The town was rediscovered in 1709, and amateur excavations were carried out intermittently until 1874, with many finds being carted off to Naples to decorate the houses of its well-to-do inhabitants or to end up in museums. Serious archaeological work began again in 1927 and continues to this day, although with much of the ancient site buried beneath modern Ercolano, it's slow going.

◉ Sights

★ Ruins of Herculaneum RUIN

(📞 081 732 43 38; www.pompeiisites.org; Corso Resina 6, Ercolano; adult/reduced €11/5.50, combined ticket incl Pompeii €20/10; ⊘ 8.30am-7.30pm summer, to 5pm winter, last entry 90min before closing; 🚇 Circumvesuviana to Ercolano-Scavi) Unfairly upstaged by Pompeii's ancient offerings, the Ruins of Herculaneum have a wealth of archaeological finds. Indeed, this superbly conserved Roman fishing town of 4000 inhabitants is smaller and easier to navigate than Pompeii, and can be explored with a map and audio guide (€6.50, €10 for two). Archaeological work began again in 1927 and continues to this day.

From the site's main gateway on Corso Resina, head down the wide boulevard, where you'll find the ticket office on the left. Pick up a free map and guide booklet here, then follow the boulevard right to the actual entrance into the ruins themselves.

With Vesuvius erupting above them, thousands of people tried to escape by boat but were suffocated by the volcano's poisonous gases. Indeed, what appears to be a moat around the town is in fact the ancient shoreline. It was here in 1980 that archaeologists discovered some 300 skeletons, the remains of a crowd that had fled to the beach only to be overcome by the terrible heat of clouds surging down from Vesuvius.

➡ Casa d'Argo &
Casa dello Scheletro

As you begin your exploration northeast along Cardo III you'll stumble across Casa d'Argo (Argus House). This noble pad would originally have opened onto Cardo II (as yet unearthed). Onto its porticoed, palm-treed garden open a *triclinium* (dining room) and other residential rooms. Across the street sits the Casa dello Scheletro (House of the Skeleton), a modestly sized house boasting five styles of mosaic flooring, including a design of white arrows at the entrance to guide the most disorientated of guests. In the internal courtyard, don't miss the skylight, complete with the remnants of an ancient security grill. Of the house's mythically themed wall mosaics, only the faded ones are originals; the others now reside in the Museo Archeologico Nazionale (p41).

➡ Terme Maschili

Just across the Decumano Inferiore (one of ancient Herculaneum's main streets), the Terme Maschili (Male Baths) were the men's section of the Terme del Foro (Forum Baths). Note the ancient latrine to the left of the entrance before you step into the *apodyterium* (changing room), complete with bench for waiting patrons and a nifty wall shelf for sandal and toga storage. While those after a bracing soak would pop into the *frigidarium* (cold bath) to the left, the less stoic headed straight into the *tepadarium* (tepid bath) to the right. The sunken mosaic floor here is testament to the seismic activity preceding Mt Vesuvius' catastrophic eruption. Beyond this room lies the *caldarium* (hot bath), as well as an exercise area.

➡ Decumano Massimo

At the end of Cardo III, turn right into the Decumano Massimo. This ancient high street is lined with shops; fragments of advertisements still adorn the walls, such as that to the right of the Casa del Salone Nero. This ancient consumer information listed everything from from the weight of goods to their price.

Further east along Decumano Massimo, a crucifix found in an upstairs room of the Casa del Bicentenario (Bicentenary House) provides possible evidence of a Christian presence in pre-Vesuvius Herculaneum.

➡ Casa di Nettuno e Anfitrite

Turning into Cardo IV from Decumano Massimo, you'll soon hit the Casa di Nettuno e Anfitrite (House of Neptune and Amfitrite), an aristocratic pad taking its name from the extraordinary mosaic in the *nymphaeum* (fountain and bath). The warm colours in which the sea god and his nymph bride are depicted hint at how lavish the original interior must once have been.

A quick walk further southwest along Cardo IV leads you to the women's section of the Terme del Foro, the Terme Femminili. Though smaller than its male equivalent, it boasts finer floor mosaics – note the beautifully executed naked figure of Triton in the *apodyterium* (changing room).

➡ Casa del Tramezzo di Legno

Across the Decumano Inferiore is the Casa del Tramezzo di Legno (House of the Wooden Partition), which unusually features two atria. It's likely that the atria belonged to two separate houses merged together in the 1st century AD. Predictably, the most famous relic here is a wonderfully well-preserved wooden screen, separating the atrium from the *tablinum*, where the owner talked business with his clients. The second room off the left side of the atrium features the remains of an ancient bed.

➡ Casa dell'Atrio a Mosaico

Further southwest on Cardo IV, ancient mansion Casa dell'Atrio a Mosaico (House of the Mosaic Atrium) harbours extensive floor mosaics, although time and nature have left the floor buckled and uneven. Particularly noteworthy is the black-and-white chessboard mosaic in the atrium.

Backtrack up Cardo IV and turn right at Decumano Inferiore. Here you'll find the Casa del Gran Portale (House of the Large Portal), named after the elegant brick Corinthian columns that flank its main entrance. Step inside to admire some well-preserved wall paintings.

➡ Casa dei Cervi

Accessible from Cardo V, the Casa dei Cervi (House of the Stags) is an imposing example of a Roman noble family's house which, before the volcanic mudslide, boasted a seafront address. Constructed around a central courtyard, the two-storey villa contains murals and some beautiful still-life paintings. Waiting for you in the courtyard is a diminutive pair of marble deer assailed by dogs, and an engaging statue of a drunken, peeing Hercules.

➡ Terme Suburbane

Marking the site's southernmost tip is the 1st-century-AD Terme Suburbane (Suburban Baths), one of the best-preserved bath complexes in existence, with deep pools, stucco friezes and bas-reliefs looking down upon marble seats and floors. This is also one of the best places to observe the soaring volcanic deposits that literally smothered the ancient coastline.

MAV   MUSEUM

(Museo Archeologico Virtuale; ☑ 081 1980 6511; www.museomav.com; Via IV Novembre 44; adult/reduced €7.50/6, optional 3D documentary €4; ⊘ 9am-4.30pm Tue-Fri, to 5.30pm Sat & Sun; ☒ Circumvesuviana to Ercolano-Scavi) Using high-tech holograms and computer-generated footage, this 'virtual archaeological museum' brings ruins like Pompei's forum and Capri's Villa Jovis back to virtual life. Especially fun for kids, it's on the main street linking Ercolano-Scavi train station to the Ruins of Herculaneum.

✖ Eating

★ Viva Lo Re   CAMPANIAN €€

(☑ 081 739 02 07; www.vivalore.it; Corso Resina 261, Ercolano; meals €27; ⊘ noon-4pm & 8.30-late Tue-Sat, lunch Sun; ☒ Circumvesuviana to Ercolano-Scavi) Stylish Viva Lo Re (Long Live the King) mixes vintage prints and bookshelves with superb wines, gracious service and some of Campania's finest revamped dishes. Start with the artful antipasto – 'tastings' might include *polpettina di baccalà* (salted cod patty) or *crocchetta di taleggio con porcino* (Taleggio and porcini croquette). End with the *tris*, a decadent trio of desserts.

ⓘ Information

Tourist office (☑ 081 788 12 74; Via IV Novembre 82; ⊘ 8am-6pm Mon-Sat) You'll pass this office on your right as you walk from the train station to the excavations.

ⓘ Getting There & Away

The best way to get to Ercolano is by Circumvesuviana train (get off at Ercolano-Scavi station and walk 500m downhill to the ruins – follow the signs for the *scavi* down the main street, Via IV Novembre. Trains run regularly to/from Naples (€2.20), Pompeii (€1.60) and Sorrento (€2.20).

By car take the A3 from Naples, exit at Ercolano Portico and follow the signs to car parks near the site's entrance.

Mt Vesuvius

Towering (at 1281m) darkly over Naples and its environs, Mt Vesuvius (Vesuvio, 1281m), is the only active volcano on the European mainland. Since it exploded into history in AD 79, burying Pompeii and Herculaneum and pushing the coastline out several kilometres, it has erupted more than 30 times. The most devastating of these was in 1631, the most recent in 1944.

Another full-scale eruption would be catastrophic. Some 600,000 people live within 7km of the crater and, despite incentives to relocate, few are willing to go.

Established in 1995, **Parco Nazionale del Vesuvio** (☑ 081 239 5653; adult/reduced €10/8; ⊘ 9am-7pm Jul & Aug, to 5pm Apr-Jun & Sep, to 4pm Mar & Oct, to 3pm Nov-Feb, ticket office closes 1hr before the crater) attracts about 400,000 visitors annually. From a car park at the summit, an 860m path leads up to the volcano's **crater** (admission incl tour €8; ⊘ 9am-6pm Jul & Aug, to 5pm Apr-Jun & Sep, to 4pm Mar & Oct, to 3pm Nov-Feb). It's not a strenuous walk, but it's more comfortable in trainers than in sandals or flip-flops.

You'd also do well to take sunglasses – useful against swirling ash – and a sweater, as it can be chilly up top, even in summer.

Shuttle-bus operator **Vesuvio Express** (☑ 081 739 36 66; www.vesuvioexpress.it; Piazzale Stazione Circumvesuviana, Ercolano) runs services from Ercolano to Mt Vesuvius, departing from Piazza Stazione Circumvesuviana, right outside Ercolano-Scavi train station. Buses depart every 40 minutes from 9.30am to 4pm daily, with a journey time of 20 minutes each way. Return tickets (which include entry to the volcano summit) are €18.

From Pompeii, **Busvia del Vesuvio** (☑ 340 9352616; www.busviadelvesuvio.com; Via Villa dei Misteri, Pompeii) runs a shuttle service from outside Pompeii-Villa dei Misteri train station (hourly from 9am to 3pm) to its bus terminal in nearby Boscoreale. From here, it's a 25-minute journey up the national park on a 4WD-style bus. Return tickets (including entry to the volcano summit) cost €22.

If you're keen to explore the national park **Naples Trips & Tours** (☑ 349 7155270; www.naplestripsandtours.com) runs a daily horse-riding tour of the park (weather permitting) for €50 and running between three to four hours. It includes transfers to/from Naples or Ercolano-Scavi train station.

If travelling by car, exit the A3 at Ercolano Portico and follow signs for the Parco Nazionale del Vesuvio. Note that when weather conditions are bad the summit path is shut and bus departures are suspended.

Pompeii

POP 25,500

A stark reminder of the malign forces that lie deep inside Vesuvius, Pompeii (Pompei in Italian) is Europe's most compelling archaeological site. Each year about 2.5 million people pour in to wander the ghostly shell of what was once a thriving commercial centre.

Its appeal goes beyond tourism, though. From an archaeological point of view, it's priceless. Much of the value lies in the fact that it wasn't simply blown away by Vesuvius: rather it was buried under a layer of lapilli, as Pliny the Younger describes in his celebrated account of the eruption. The result is a remarkably well-preserved slice of ancient life, where visitors can walk down Roman streets and snoop around millennia-old abodes and businesses (including a brothel).

History

The eruption of Vesuvius wasn't the first disaster to strike the Roman port of Pompeii. In AD 63 a massive earthquake hit the city, causing widespread damage and the evacuation of much of the 20,000-strong population. Many had not returned when Vesuvius blew its top on 24 August AD 79, burying the city under a layer of lapilli and killing some 2000 men, women and children.

The origins of Pompeii are uncertain, but it seems likely that it was founded in the 7th century BC by the Campanian Oscans. Over the next seven centuries the city fell to the ancient Greeks and the Samnites before becoming a Roman colony in 80 BC. After its tragic demise, Pompeii receded from the public eye until 1594, when the architect Domenico Fontana stumbled across the ruins while digging a canal. However, short of recording the find, he took no further action. Exploration proper began in 1748 under the Bourbon king Charles VII and continued into the 19th century. In the early days many of the more spectacular mosaics were siphoned off to decorate Charles' palace in Portici; thankfully, though, most were subsequently moved up to Naples, where they now sit in the Museo Archeologico Nazionale (p41).

◉ Sights

★ **Ruins of Pompeii**   RUIN
(☑ 081 857 53 47; www.pompeiisites.org; entrances at Porta Marina & Piazza Anfiteatro; adult/reduced €11/5.50, combined ticket incl Herculaneum €20/10; ⊙ 8.30am-7.30pm summer, to 5pm winter, last entry 90min before closing) Of Pompeii's original 66 hectares, 44 have now been excavated. Of course that doesn't mean you'll have unhindered access to every inch of the Unesco-listed site – expect to come across areas cordoned off for no apparent reason, a noticeable lack of clear signs and the odd stray dog. Audio guides are a sensible investment.

At the time of writing, the Casa dei Vettii was closed for restoration. The Terme Suburbane, just outside the city walls, can be visited on weekends subject to prior booking at www.arethusa.net. It's here that you'll find the erotic frescoes that scandalised the Vatican when they were revealed in 2001. The saucy panels decorate the changing rooms of what was once a private baths complex.

Old Pompeii

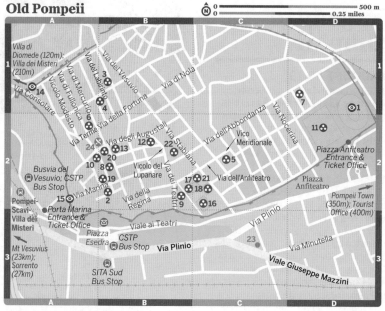

Old Pompeii

➡ **Porta Marina**

The site's main entrance is at **Porta Marina**, the most impressive of the seven gates that punctuated the ancient town walls. A busy passageway now as it was then, it originally connected the town with the nearby harbour, hence the gateway's name. Immediately on the right as you enter the gate is the 1st-century-BC Tempio di Venere (Temple of Venus), formerly one of the town's most opulent temples.

➡ **The Forum**

Continuing northeast along Via Marina you'll hit the grassy **foro** (forum). Flanked by limestone columns, this was the ancient city's main piazza and the buildings surrounding it are testament to its role as the city's hub of civic, commercial, political and religious activity.

At its southwestern end sit the remains of the **basilica**, the 2nd-century-BC seat of the city's law courts and exchange. Their semicircular apses would later influence the design of early Christian churches.

Tragedy in Pompeii

24 AUGUST AD 79

8am Buildings including the **Terme Suburbane** 1 and the **foro** 2 are still undergoing repair after an earthquake in AD 63 caused significant damage to the city. Despite violent earth tremors overnight, residents have little idea of the catastrophe that lies ahead.

Midday Peckish locals pour into the **Thermopolium di Vetutius Placidus** 3 . The lustful slip into the **Lupanare** 4 , and gladiators practise for the evening's planned games at the **anfiteatro** 5 . A massive boom heralds the eruption. Shocked onlookers witness a dark cloud of volcanic matter shoot some 14km above the crater.

3pm–5pm Lapilli (burning pumice stone) rains down on Pompeii. Terrified locals begin to flee; others take shelter. Within two hours, the plume is 25km high and the sky has darkened. Roofs collapse under the weight of the debris, burying those inside.

25 AUGUST AD 79

Midnight Mudflows bury the town of Herculaneum. Lapilli and ash continue to rain down on Pompeii, bursting through buildings and suffocating those taking refuge within.

4am–8am Ash and gas avalanches hit Herculaneum. Subsequent surges smother Pompeii, killing all remaining residents, including those in the **Orto dei Fuggiaschi** 6 . The volcanic 'blanket' will safeguard frescoed treasures like the **Casa del Menandro** 7 and **Villa dei Misteri** 8 for almost two millennia.

TOP TIPS

» Visit in the afternoon
» Allow three hours
» Wear comfortable shoes and a hat
» Bring drinking water
» Don't use flash photography

Terme Suburbane
The *laconicum* (sauna), *caldarium* (hot bath) and large, heated swimming pool weren't the only sources of heat here; scan the walls of this suburban bathhouse for some of the city's raunchiest frescoes.

Villa di Diomede

Casa dei Vettii

Casa del Poeta Tragico

Porta Ercolano

Casa del Fauno

Basilica

Tempio di Apollo

Porta Marina

1

8

2

4

Terme del Foro

Macellum

Teatro Grande

Quadriportico dei Teatri

Porta di Stabia

Teatro Piccolo

Foro
An ancient Times Square of sorts, the forum sits at the intersection of Pompeii's main streets and was closed to traffic in the 1st century AD. The plinths on the southern edge featured statues of the imperial family.

Villa dei Misteri

Home to the world-famous *Dionysiac Frieze* fresco. Other highlights at this villa include *trompe l'oeil* wall decorations in the *cubiculum* (bedroom) and Egyptian-themed artwork in the *tablinum* (reception).

Lupanare

The prostitutes at this brothel were often slaves of Greek or Asian origin. Mattresses once covered the stone beds and the names engraved in the walls are possibly those of the workers and their clients.

Thermopolium di Vetutius Placidus

The counter at this ancient snack bar once held urns filled with hot food. The *lararium* (household shrine) on the back wall depicts Dionysus (the god of wine) and Mercury (the god of profit and commerce).

> **Eyewitness Account**
>
> Pliny the Younger (AD 61–c 112) gives a gripping, first-hand account of the catastrophe in his letters to Tacitus (AD 56–117).

Porta del Vesuvio

Porta di Nola

Casa della Venere in Conchiglia

Porta di Sarno

Grande Palestra

5

3

7

6

Tempio di Iside

Casa del Menandro

This dwelling most likely belonged to the family of Poppaea Sabina, Nero's second wife. A room to the left of the atrium features Trojan War paintings and a polychrome mosaic of pygmies rowing down the Nile.

Orto dei Fuggiaschi

The Garden of the Fugitives showcases the plaster moulds of 13 locals seeking refuge during Vesuvius' eruption – the largest number of victims found in any one area. The huddled bodies make for a moving scene.

Anfiteatro

Magistrates, local senators and the games' sponsors and organisers enjoyed front-row seating at this veteran amphitheatre, home to gladiatorial battles and the odd riot. The parapet circling the stadium featured paintings of combat, victory celebrations and hunting scenes.

LONELY PLANET/GETTY IMAGES ©

1. Parco Archeologico di Baia (p49), Campi Flegrei 2. Ruins of Pompeii (p74) 3. Tempio di Nettuno (p99), Paestum 4. Ancient mosaic in Casa di Nettuno e Anfitrite (p72), Herculaneum

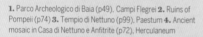

NEIL SETCHFIELD/GETTY IMAGES ©

Historical Riches

Few Italian regions can match Campania's historical legacy. Colonised by the ancient Greeks and loved by the Romans, it's a sun-drenched repository of A-list antiquities, from World Heritage wonders to lesser-known archaeological gems.

Paestum

Great Greek temples never go out of vogue and those at Paestum (p98) are among the greatest outside Greece itself. With the oldest structures stretching back to the 6th century BC, this place makes Rome's Colosseum feel positively modern.

Herculaneum

A bite-sized Pompeii, Herculaneum (p72) is even better preserved than its nearby rival. This is the place to delve into the details, from once-upon-a-time shop advertisements and furniture, to quirky mosaics and even an ancient security device.

Pompeii

Short of stepping into the Tardis, Pompeii (p74) is your best bet for a little time travel. Snap-locked in ash for centuries, its excavated streetscapes offer a tangible, 3D encounter with the ancients and their daily lives.

Subterranean Naples

Eerie aqueducts, mysterious burial crypts and ancient streetscapes: beneath Naples' hyperactive streets lies a wonderland of Graeco-Roman ruins. For a taste, head below the Complesso Monumentale di San Lorenzo Maggiore (p43) or follow the leader on a Napoli Sotterranea (p52) tour.

Campi Flegrei

The Phlegraean Fields simmer with ancient clues. Roam where emperors bathed at the Parco Archeologico di Baia (p49), sneak into a Roman engineering marvel at the Piscina Mirabilis, or spare a thought for doomed martyrs at the Anfiteatro Flavio.

Opposite the basilica, the **Tempio di Apollo** (Temple of Apollo) is the oldest and most important of Pompeii's religious buildings. Most of what you see today, including the striking columned portico, dates to the 2nd century BC, although fragments remain of an earlier version dating to the 6th century BC.

At the forum's northern end is the **Tempio di Giove** (Temple of Jupiter), which has one of two flanking triumphal arches remaining, and the **Granai del Foro** (Forum Granary), now used to store hundreds of amphorae and a number of body casts that were made in the late 19th century by pouring plaster into the hollows left by disintegrated bodies. The **macellum** nearby was once the city's main meat and fish market.

➡ **Lupanare**

From the market head northeast along Via degli Augustali to Vicolo del Lupanare. Halfway down this narrow alley is the **Lupanare**, the city's only dedicated brothel. A tiny two-storey building with five rooms on each floor, its collection of raunchy frescoes was a menu of sorts for its randy clientele.

➡ **Teatro Grande**

Heading back south, Vicolo del Lupanare becomes Via dei Teatri. At the end you'll find the verdant **Foro Triangolare**, which would originally have overlooked the sea and the River Sarno. The main attraction here was, and still is, the 2nd-century-BC Teatro Grande, a 5000-seat theatre carved into the lava mass on which Pompeii was originally built. Behind the stage, the porticoed **Quadriportico dei Teatri** was initially used for the audience to stroll between acts, and later as a barracks for gladiators. Next door, the **Teatro Piccolo** (also known

as the Odeion) was once an indoor theatre renowned for its acoustics, while the pre-Roman **Tempio di Iside** (Temple of Isis) was a popular place of cult worship.

➡ **Casa del Menandro**

Just to the east, Via dell'Anfiteatro (which becomes Vico Meridionale) is where you'll find Casa del Menandro. One of Pompeii's grander homes, its drawcards include an elegant peristyle (colonnaded garden) and a striking mosaic floor in the *caldarium*.

➡ **Terme Stabiane & Casa della Venere in Conchiglia**

As it shoots eastward, Via Marina becomes Via dell'Abbondanza (Street of Abundance). Lined with ancient shops, this was the city's main thoroughfare and where you'll find the **Terme Stabiane**, a typical 2nd-century-BC bath complex. Entering from the vestibule, bathers would stop off in the vaulted *apodyterium* before passing through to the *tepidarium* and *caldarium*. Particularly impressive is the stuccoed vault in the men's changing room, complete with whimsical images of *putti* (winged babies) and nymphs.

Towards the northeastern end of Via dell'Abbondanza, **Casa della Venere in Conchiglia** (House of the Venus Marina) has recovered well from the WWII bomb that damaged it in 1943. Although unexceptional from the outside, it houses a gorgeous peristyle that looks onto a small, manicured garden. And it's here in the garden that you'll find the striking Venus fresco after which the house is named.

➡ **Anfiteatro**

Just southeast of the Casa della Venere in Conchiglia, gladiatorial battles thrilled up to 20,000 spectators at the grassy **anfiteatro**

ⓘ TOURS

You'll almost certainly be approached by a guide outside the *scavi* (excavations) ticket office. Authorised guides wear identification tags and you can expect to pay between €100 and €120 for a two-hour tour, whether you're alone or in a group. Reputable tour operators include **Yellow Sudmarine** (☏ 329 1010328, 334 1047036; www.yellowsudmarine.com) and **Torres Travel** (☏ 081 856 78 02; www.torrestravel.it), both of which offer tours of the ruins, as well as excursions to other regional highlights, including Naples, Capri and the Amalfi Coast.

Yellow Sudmarine also runs cheaper walking tours of Pompeii. Costing €12 per person (excluding entry to the ruins), these two-hour guided walks depart at 11am every Saturday to Thursday (at 3pm on Fridays) from outside the Pompei Scavi-Villa dei Misteri Circumvesuviana train station. Tours should be booked a day ahead, either by email or phone.

(amphitheatre). Built in 70 BC, it's the oldest known Roman amphitheatre in existence. Over the way, lithe ancients kept fit at the **Grande Palestra**, an athletics field with an impressive portico dating to the Augustan period. At its centre lie the remains of a swimming pool.

➡ Casa del Fauno

From the Grande Palestra, backtrack along Via dell'Abbondanza and turn right into Via Stabiana to view some of Pompeii's grandest houses. Turn left into Via della Fortuna and then right down Via del Labirinto to get to Vicolo del Mercurio and the entrance to **Casa del Fauno** (House of the Faun; Via Stabiana), Pompeii's largest private house. Covering an entire *insula* (city block) and boasting two atria at its front end (humbler homes had one), it is named after the delicate bronze statue in the *impluvium* (rainwater pool). It was here that early excavators found Pompeii's greatest mosaics, most of which are now in Naples' Museo Archeologico Nazionale (p41). Valuable on-site remainders include a beautiful, geometrically patterned marble floor.

A couple of blocks away, the **Casa del Poeta Tragico** (House of the Tragic Poet) features one of the world's first 'Beware of the Dog' (*Cave Canem*) warnings. To the north, the currently closed **Casa dei Vettii** on Via di Mercurio is home to a famous depiction of Priapus whose oversized phallus balances on a pair of scales...much to the anxiety of many a male observer.

➡ Villa dei Misteri

From the Casa del Fauna, follow the road west and turn right into Via Consolare, which takes you out of the town through **Porta Ercolano**. Continue past **Villa di Diomede** and you'll come to the 90-room **Villa dei Misteri,** one of the most complete structures left standing in Pompeii. The Dionysiac frieze, the most important fresco still on site, spans the walls of the large dining room. One of the largest paintings from the ancient world, it depicts the initiation of a bride-to-be into the cult of Dionysus, the Greek god of wine. A farm for much of its life, the villa's own vino-making area is still visible at the northern end.

🍽 Sleeping & Eating

There's really no need to stay overnight in Pompeii. The ruins are best visited on a day trip from Naples, Sorrento or Salerno, and once the excavations close for the day, the area around the site becomes decidedly seedy. Most of the restaurants near the ruins are characterless affairs set up for feeding busloads of tourists. Wander down to the modern town and it's a little better, with a few decent restaurants serving excellent local food.

If you'd rather eat at the ruins, the on-site **cafeteria** (Via di Mercurio) peddles the standard choice of *panini*, pizza slices, salads, hot meals and gelato. You'll find it near the Tempio di Giove.

★President 　　　　　　　CAMPANIAN **€€**
(☑081 850 72 45; www.ristorantepresident.it; Piazza Schettini 12; meals €35; ⏲11.40am-3.30pm & 7pm-midnight Tue-Sun, closed Jan; ☒FS to Pompei, ☒Circumvesuviana to Pompei Scavi-Villa dei Misteri) With its dripping chandeliers and gracious service, the President feels like a private dining room in an Audrey Hepburn film. Conducting the charm is owner Paolo Gramaglia, whose passion for local produce sparkles in creations like aubergine *millefoglie* (flaky puff pastry) with Cetara anchovies, mozzarella *filante* (melted mozzarella) and grated *tarallo* (savoury almond biscuit). Treat yourself with a degustation menu (€30 to €50).

ℹ Information

Police station (☑081 856 35 11; Piazza Porta Marina Inferiore)

Pompeii sites (www.pompeiisites.org) Background and practicalities for Pompeii, Herculaneum and other archaeological must-sees.

Post office (Piazza Esedra)

Tourist office (☑081 850 72 55; www.pompeiturismo.it; Via Sacra 1; ⏲8am-3.30pm Mon-Fri, to 1pm Sat)

ℹ Getting There & Away

Circumvesuviana trains run from Pompei Scavi-Villa dei Misteri station to Naples (€2.90, 35 minutes) and Sorrento (€2.20, 30 minutes).

CSTP (☑800 016659; www.cstp.it) bus 4 runs to/from Salerno (€2.20, 90 minutes).

Shuttle buses to Vesuvius depart from outside the Pompei-Scavi-Villa dei Misteri train station.

To get here by car, take the A3 from Naples. Use the Pompeii exit and follow signs to Pompeii Scavi. Car parks (approximately €5 per hour) are clearly marked and vigorously touted.

Sorrento

POP 16,500

On paper, cliff-straddling Sorrento is a place to avoid – a package-holiday centre with few must-see sights, no beach to speak of and a glut of brassy English-style pubs. In reality, it's a strangely appealing place, its laid-back southern Italian charm resisting all attempts to swamp it in graceless development.

Dating to Greek times and known to Romans as Surrentum, it's ideally situated for exploring the surrounding area: to the west, the best of the peninsula's unspoiled countryside and, beyond that, the Amalfi Coast; to the north, Pompeii and the archaeological sites; offshore, the fabled island of Capri.

According to Greek legend, it was in Sorrento's waters that the mythical sirens once lived. Sailors of antiquity were powerless to resist the beautiful song of these charming maidens-cum-monsters, who would lure them and their ships to their doom. Homer's Ulysses escaped by having his oarsmen plug their ears with wax and by strapping himself to his ship's mast as he sailed past.

Sights

Spearing off from Piazza Tasso, Corso Italia (closed to traffic from 7pm to 1am daily during the summer, as well as from 10am to 1pm on Sundays and public holidays) cuts through the *centro storico,* whose narrow streets throng with tourists on summer evenings. An attractive area, it's thick with loud souvenir stores, cafes, churches and restaurants.

Chiesa di San Francesco   CHURCH
(Via San Francesco; ⊗8am-1pm & 2-8pm) The real attraction here is not the church but the beautiful medieval cloister. A harmonious marriage of architectural styles – two sides are lined with 14th-century crossed arches, the other two with round arches supported by octagonal pillars – it is often used to host exhibitions and summer concerts.

Museo Correale   MUSEUM
(☑081 878 18 46; www.museocorreale.it; Via Correale 50; admission €7; ⊗9.30am-6.30pm Tue-Sat, to 1.30pm Sun summer, reduced hours winter) Located to the east of the city centre, this museum is well worth a visit. In addition to a rich assortment of 17th- to 19th-century Neapolitan art and crafts, you'll find Japanese, Chinese and European ceramics, clocks and furniture, as well as Greek and Roman artefacts.

Museo Bottega della Tarsia Lignea   MUSEUM
(☑081 877 19 42; www.museomuta.it; Via San Nicola 28; adult/reduced €8/5; ⊗10am-6.30pm summer, to 5pm winter) Since the 18th century, Sorrento has been famous for its *intarsio* furniture, made with elaborately designed inlaid wood. Some wonderful examples can be found in this museum, housed in an 18th-century palace complete with beautiful frescoes. There's also an interesting collection of paintings, prints and photographs depicting the town and surrounding area in the 19th century.

Duomo   CATHEDRAL
(Corso Italia; ⊗8am-12.30pm & 4.30-8.30pm) To get a feel for Sorrento's history, stroll down Via Pietà from Piazza Tasso and past two medieval palaces en route to the cathedral with its striking exterior fresco, triple-tiered bell tower, four classical columns and elegant maiolica clock. Take note of the striking marble bishop's throne (1573) and the beautiful wooden choir stalls decorated in the local *intarsio* style.

🏃 Activities

Bagni Regina Giovanna   BEACH
(Pollio Felix) Sorrento famously lacks a proper beach, so consider splashing around at Bagni Regina Giovanna, a rocky beach about 2km west of town. Set among the ruins of the Roman Villa Pollio Felix, the water is clean and clear. While you can walk here (follow Via Capo), you'll save your swimming strength by catching the SITA Sud bus or the EAV Bus (Linea A) headed for Massa Lubrense.

Sic Sic   BOATING
(☑081 807 22 83; www.nauticasicsic.com; Marina Piccola; ⊗May-Oct) To seek out the best beaches, rent a boat from this outfit. There's a variety of options, starting at around €50 per hour or €150 per day. It also organises boat excursions.

Tours

City Sightseeing Sorrento   BUS TOUR
(☑081 877 47 07; www.sorrento.city-sightseeing.it; adult/reduced €12/6; ⊗Apr-Oct) A hop-on, hop-off bus tour of Sorrento and the surrounding area. Daily departures are at 9.30am, 11.30am, 1.30pm and 3.30pm from Piazza De Curtis (Circumvesuviana station). English-language commentaries are

Sorrento

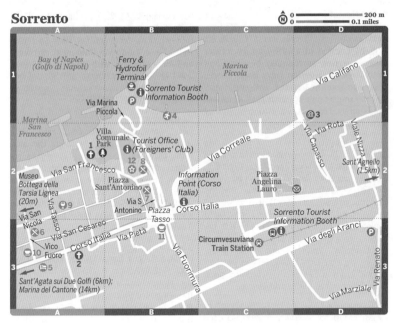

provided, and tickets, available on board, are valid for six hours.

☆ Festivals & Events

Sant'Antonino   RELIGIOUS

(☉14 Feb) The city's patron saint, Sant' Antonino, is remembered annually with processions and huge markets. The saint is credited with having saved Sorrento during WWII when Salerno and Naples were heavily bombed.

Settimana Santa   RELIGIOUS

(Holy Week) Sorrento's Settimana Santa Easter processions are famous throughout Italy. There are two main processions: one at midnight on the Thursday preceding Good Friday, the second on Good Friday.

🛏 Sleeping

Most accommodation is in the town centre or clustered along Via Capo, the coastal road west of the centre. Be sure to book early for the summer season.

Casa Astarita   B&B €

(☏081 877 49 06; www.casastarita.com; Corso Italia 67, Sorrento; d €90-120, tr €110-140; ❄@❷) All six rooms at this pretty B&B combine original structural elements, like niches and

Sorrento

◎ Sights

1 Chiesa di San Francesco	A2
2 Duomo	A3
3 Museo Correale	D1

◎ Activities, Courses & Tours

4 Sic Sic	B1

🛏 Sleeping

5 Casa Astarita	A3

✕ Eating

6 Inn Bufalito	A3
7 La Basilica	B2
8 Ristorante il Buco	B2

◎ Drinking & Nightlife

9 Bollicine	A2
10 Cafè Latino	A3
11 Fauno Bar	B3

◎ Entertainment

12 Teatro Tasso	B2

vaulted ceilings, with the modern comforts of flat-screen TV, fridge and excellent water pressure. Brightly painted doors, tasteful art and antiques complete the eclectic look. Rooms surround a central parlour, where breakfast is served at a large rustic table.

Seven Hostel
HOSTEL €

(📞 081 878 67 58; www.sevenhostel.com; Via Lommella Grande 99, Sant'Agnello; dm/s/d €30/75/80; ❄@🛜) Located in a 19th-century former convent setting surrounded by olive and lemon trees, this design-savvy hostel comes with chic rooftop terraces, live-music gigs and the more down-to-earth perk of an on-site laundry. The rooms are contemporarily furnished and spacious.

Nube d'Argento
CAMPGROUND €

(📞081 878 13 44; www.nubedargento.com; Via Capo 21, Sorrento; camping 2 people, car & tent €35, 2-person bungalows €60-85, 4-person bungalows €90-120; ☉Mar-Dec; @❄🛁) This inviting camping ground is an easy 1km drive west of the Sorrento city centre. Pitches and wooden chalet-style bungalows are spread out beneath a canopy of olive trees – a source of much-needed summer shade – and the facilities are excellent. Youngsters in particular will enjoy the open-air swimming pool, table-tennis table, slides and swings.

La Tonnarella
LUXURY HOTEL €€

(📞081 878 11 53; www.latonnarella.it; Via Capo 31; d €112-140, ste €240-350; ☉Apr-Oct & Christmas; P❄@🛜) La Tonnarella is a dazzling canvas of blue-and-yellow maiolica tiles, antiques, chandeliers and statues. Rooms, most of which have their own balcony or small terrace, continue the sumptuous classical theme with traditional furniture and discreet mod cons. The hotel also has its own private beach, accessible by lift, and a highly regarded terrace restaurant.

Hotel Cristina
HOTEL €€

(📞081 878 35 62; www.hotelcristinasorrento.it; Via Privata Rubinacci 6, Sant'Agnello; s €120, d €120-200, tr €230; ☉Mar-Oct; ❄🛜🛁) Located high above Sant'Agnello, this hotel has superb views, particularly from the swimming pool. The spacious rooms have sea-view balconies and combine inlaid wooden furniture with contemporary flourishes, like Philippe Starck chairs. There's an in-house restaurant and a free shuttle bus to/from Sorrento's Circumvesuviana train station.

✖ Eating

A local speciality to look out for is *gnocchi alla sorrentina* (gnocchi baked in tomato sauce with mozzarella).

Inn Bufalito
CAMPANIAN €€

(📞081 365 69 75; www.innbufalito.it; Vico Fuoro 21; meals €25; ☉noon-midnight summer, reduced hours winter; 🛜🍽) 🌿 A brilliant Slow Food mozzarella bar-restaurant. Head here for moreish local concoctions like Sorrento-style cheese fondue, buffalo-meat carpaccio and local *salsiccia* with broccoli. There's a good choice of vegetarian and gluten-free options, regular cheese tastings, as well as the occasional art exhibition.

La Basilica
ITALIAN, PIZZERIA €€

(Via S Antonino 12; pizzas €6-12, meals €40; ☉noon-midnight) Elegant without the attitude, barrel-vaulted La Basilica serves regional nosh with subtle yet confident twists (think house-made black *scialatielli* pasta with calamari and *pomodorini* or a decadent dark chocolate and whisky tart). For a cheaper feed, dig into the excellent wood-fired pizzas.

Ristorante il Buco
CAMPANIAN €€€

(📞081 878 23 54; Rampa Marina Piccola 5; meals €60; ☉12.30-2.30pm & 7.30-11pm Thu-Tue Feb-Dec) Housed in a monks' former wine cellar, this dress-for-dinner restaurant offers far from monastic-style cuisine. The emphasis is on innovative regional cooking, so expect modern combos like mozzarella and lemon-stuffed ravioli, or zesty risotto with smoked *provola* cheese, green apple and prawns. Reservations recommended.

🍷 Drinking & Nightlife

From wood-panelled wine bars to cocktail-centric cafes, you'll find no shortage of drinking dens in Sorrento.

Cafè Latino
CAFE, BAR

(📞081 878 37 18; Vico Fuoro 4a; ☉10am-1am summer) Think locked-eyes-over-cocktails time. This is the place to impress your partner with cocktails (from €7) on the terrace, surrounded by orange and lemon trees. Sip a Mary Pickford (rum, pineapple, *grenadino* and maraschino) or a glass of chilled white wine. If you can't drag yourselves away, you can also eat here (meals around €30).

Bollicine
WINE BAR

(📞081 878 46 16; Via Accademia 9; ☉7.30pm-2am) The wine list at this unpretentious wine bar with a dark, woody interior includes all the big Italian names and a selection of interesting local labels. If you can't decide what to go for, the amiable bar staff will advise you. There's also a small menu of *panini*, bruschette and one or two pasta dishes.

Fauno Bar CAFE
(☑ 081 878 11 35; Piazza Tasso; ⊙ 7-2am midnight mid-Mar–mid-Jan) On Piazza Tasso, this elegant cafe covers half the square and offers the best people-watching in town. It serves stiff drinks at stiff prices – cocktails start at €7. Snacks, sandwiches, salads and pizzas are also available (from €6).

☆ Entertainment

Teatro Tasso THEATRE
(☑ 081 807 55 25; www.teatrotasso.com; Piazza Sant'Antonino; admission €25; ⊙ 9.30pm summer) The southern Italian equivalent of a London old-world music hall, Teatro Tasso is home to the *Sorrento Musical*, a sentimental 75-minute revue of Neapolitan classics such as 'O Sole Mio' and 'Trona a Sorrent'.

❶ Information

Hospital (☑ 081 533 11 11; Corso Italia 1)
Police station (☑ 081 807 31 11; Via Capasso 11)
Post office (Corso Italia 210)
Sorrento Tour (www.sorrentotour.it) Extensive website with tourist and transport information on Sorrento and environs.

Tourist information For maps and useful information, head to one of Sorrento's tourist information kiosks, located outside the Circumvesuviana train station (Piazza de Curtis, Circumvesuviana station; ⊙ 10am-1pm & 3-7pm summer, to 5pm winter), in town at Corso Italia (⊙ 9am-1pm & 3-10pm) and the Foreigners' Club (Via Luigi De Maio 35; ⊙ 8.30am-4.15pm Mon-Fri), and at the ferry port (Marina Piccola; ⊙ 9am-5pm summer, closed winter).

❶ Getting There & Away

BOAT

Sorrento is the main jumping-off point for Capri and also has good ferry connections to Naples, Ischia and Amalfi coastal towns.
Caremar (p58) Runs ferries to Capri (€13.20, 25 minutes, four daily).
Alilauro (☑ 081 497 22 22; www.alilauro.it) Runs up to five daily hydrofoils between Naples and Sorrento (€12.30, 40 minutes).
Linee Marittime Partenopee (p90) Runs hydrofoils from Sorrento to Capri from April to November (€18.30, 20 minutes, 14 daily).
All ferries and hydrofoils depart from the port at Marina Piccola, where you buy your tickets.

BUS

Curreri (☑ 081 801 54 20; www.curreriviaggi.it) runs six daily services to Sorrento from Naples' Capodichino airport, departing from outside the arrivals hall and arriving in Piazza Tasso.

Buy tickets (€10) for the 75-minute journey on the bus.
SITA Sud (☑ 089 40 51 45; www.sitas-udtrasporti.it) buses serve the Amalfi Coast and Sant'Agata sui Due Golfi. Buses depart from outside the Circumvesuviana train station. Buy tickets at the station bar or from shops bearing the blue SITA sign.

TRAIN

Circumvesuviana (☑ 800 211388; www.eav-campania.it) trains run every 30 minutes between Sorrento and Naples (€4.10), via Pompeii (€2.20) and Ercolano (€2.20).

❶ Getting Around

Local bus Line B runs from Piazza Sant'Antonino to the port at Marina Piccola (€1.30).
Jolly Service & Rent (☑ 081 877 34 50; www.jollyrent.eu; Via degli Aranci 180) has Smart cars from €60 a day and 50cc scooters from €27.
For a **taxi**, call ☑ 081 878 22 04.

West of Sorrento

The countryside west of Sorrento is the very essence of southern Italy. Tortuous roads wind their way through hills covered in olive trees and lemon groves, passing through sleepy villages and tiny fishing ports. There are magnificent views at every turn, the best being from Sant'Agata sui Due Golfi and the high points overlooking Punta Campanella, the westernmost point of the Sorrentine Peninsula.

Sant'Agata sui Due Golfi

Perched high in the hills above Sorrento, sleepy Sant'Agata sui due Golfi commands spectacular views of the Bay of Naples on one side and the Bay of Salerno on the other (hence its name, Saint Agatha on the Two Gulfs). The best viewpoint is the **Convento del Deserto** (☑ 081 878 01 99; Via Deserto; ⊙ gardens 8am-7pm, panoramic lookout 10am-noon & 5-7pm summer, 10am-noon & 3-5pm winter), a Carmelite convent 1.5km uphill from the village centre.

Agriturismo Le Tore (☑ 081 808 06 37; www.letore.com; Via Pontone 43; s €50-80, d €90-120, dinner €25-35; ⊙ Easter-early Nov; Ⓟ @ 🕾 🐾) is a wonderful organic farm with eight barn-like rooms and an apartment that sleeps six (€600 to €1100 per week). A short drive, or a long walk, from the village, the setting is lovely, a rustic farmhouse hidden among fruit trees and olive groves. Request the especially charming Terrazzo room, which comes with a large terrace. Conveniently, the owners also offer a shuttle-bus pick-up from Naples' Capodichino airport or Stazione Centrale, costing around €25 per person one way.

From Sorrento, there's a pretty 3km (approximately one hour) trail up to Sant'Agata. Hourly SITA Sud buses leave from the Circumvesuviana train station.

Marina del Cantone

From Sorrento, follow the coastal road round to Termini. Stop a moment to admire the views before continuing on to Nerano, from where a beautiful hiking trail leads down to the stunning Bay of Ieranto, one of the coast's top swimming spots, and the tranquil, unassuming village of Marina del Cantone.

◉ Sights & Activities

A popular diving destination, the protected waters here are part of an 11-sq-km marine reserve called the Punta Campanella, its underwater grottoes lush with flora and fauna.

Nettuno Diving   DIVING
(☑ 081 808 10 51; www.sorrentodiving.com; Via Vespucci 39; ⊞) Be under the sea with this PADI-certified outfit, which runs various underwater activities. Options include snorkelling excursions, beginner courses and cave dives. Adult rates start at €25 for a day-long outing to the Bay of Ieranto.

🛌 Sleeping & Eating

Villaggio Residence Nettuno   CAMPGROUND, APARTMENTS €
(☑ 081 808 10 51; www.villaggionettuno.it; Via A Vespucci 39; camping 2 people, tent & car per person €15-35, bungalows €35-85, apt €60-250; ☺ Mar-early Nov; P ❋ @ 🛜 ☀) Set among olive groves at the village entrance, Marina's camping ground offers an array of accommodation options, including campsites, mobile homes, and (best of all) apartments in a 16th-century tower for two to five people. It's a friendly, environmentally sound place with excellent facilities and a comprehensive activities list.

Lo Scoglio   ITALIAN €€€
(☑ 081 808 10 26; Marina del Cantone; meals €60; ☺ 12.30-5pm & 7.30-11pm) The only one of the marina's restaurants directly accessible from the sea, Lo Scoglio is a darling of peckish celebrities and VIPs. While meat dishes are available, you'd be sorry to miss the superb seafood. Highlights include a €30 antipasto of raw seafood and *spaghetti al riccio* (spaghetti with sea urchins).

ℹ Getting There & Around

SITA Sud (p85) runs regular bus services between Sorrento and Marina del Cantone (on timetables as Nerano Cantone; €2.50, one hour).

AMALFI COAST

Stretching about 50km along the southern side of the Sorrentine Peninsula, the Amalfi Coast (Costiera Amalfitana) is one of Europe's most breathtaking. Cliffs terraced with scented lemon groves sheer down into sparkling seas; sherbet-hued villas cling precariously to unforgiving slopes while sea and sky merge in one vast blue horizon.

Yet its stunning topography has not always been a blessing. For centuries after the passing of Amalfi's glory days as a maritime superpower (from the 9th to the 12th centuries), the area was poor and its isolated villages were regular victims of foreign incursions, earthquakes and landslides. But it was this very isolation that first drew visitors in the early 1900s, paving the way for the advent of tourism in the latter half of the century. Today the Amalfi Coast is one of Italy's premier tourist destinations, a favourite of cashed-up jet-setters and love-struck couples.

The best time to visit is in spring or early autumn. In summer the coast's single road (SS163) gets very busy and prices are inflated; in winter much of the coast simply shuts down.

ℹ Getting There & Away

BOAT

Boat services to the Amalfi Coast towns are generally limited to the period between April and October.

Alicost (☑ 089 87 14 83; www.alicost.it; Salita Sopramuro 2, Amalfi) operates one daily ferry from Salerno to Amalfi (€7), Positano (€11) and Capri (€20.70) from mid-April to October. On Mondays, Wednesdays, Fridays and Sundays, it also runs two daily hydrofoils between Sorrento and Positano (€15.80) and Amalfi (€16.80).

WALK THE COAST

Rising steeply from the coast, the densely wooded Lattari mountains provide some stunning walking opportunities. An extraordinary network of paths traverses the craggy, precipitous peaks, climbing to remote farmhouses through wild and beautiful valleys. It's tough going, though – long ascents up seemingly endless flights of steps are almost unavoidable.

Probably the best-known walk, the 12km Sentiero degli Dei (Path of the Gods; 5½ to six hours) follows the steep, often rocky paths linking Positano to Praiano. It's a spectacular trail passing through some of the area's least developed countryside. The route is marked by red-and-white stripes daubed on rocks and trees, although some of these have become worn in places and might be difficult to make out. Pick up a map of the walk at local tourist offices, included in a series of three excellent booklets containing the area's most popular hikes, including the equally famed, and lyrically named, Via degli Incanti (Trail of Charms) from Amalfi to Positano.

To the west, the tip of the Sorrentine Peninsula is another hiking hot spot. Some 110km of paths criss-cross the area, linking the spectacular coastline with the rural hinterland. These range from tough all-day treks – such as the 14.1km Alta Via dei Monti Lattari from the Fontanelle hills near Positano down to the Punta Campanella – to shorter walks suitable for the family. Tourist offices throughout the area can provide maps detailing the colour-coded routes. With the exception of the Alta Via dei Monti Lattari (marked in red and white), long routes are shown in red on the map; coast-to-coast trails in blue; paths connecting villages in green; and circular routes in yellow.

If you're intent on trying one of the more demanding routes in the region, invest in a detailed map such as *Monti Lattari, Penisola Sorrentina, Costiera Amalfitana: Carta dei Sentieri* (€9) at 1:30,000 scale by Club Alpino Italiano (CAI). If you prefer a guided hike, there are a number of reliable local guides, including Zia Lucy (www.zialucy.it).

TraVelMar (p93) connects Salerno with Amalfi (€8, six daily) and Positano (€12, six daily) from April to October.

BUS

SITA Sud (p85) operates a frequent, year-round service along the SS163 between Sorrento and Salerno (€3.40), via Amalfi.

CAR & MOTORCYCLE

If driving from the north, exit the A3 autostrada at Vietri sul Mare and follow the SS163 along the coast. From the south leave the A3 at Salerno and head for Vietri sul Mare and the SS163.

TRAIN

From Naples you can take either the Circumvesuviana to Sorrento or a Trenitalia train to Salerno, then continue along the Amalfi Coast, eastwards or westwards, by SITA Sud bus.

Positano

POP 3860

The pearl in the pack, Positano is the coast's most photogenic and expensive town. Its steeply stacked houses are a medley of peaches, pinks and terracottas, and its near-vertical streets (many of which are, in fact, staircases) are lined with voguish shop displays, jewellery stalls, elegant hotels and smart restaurants. Look closely, though, and you'll find reassuring signs of everyday reality – crumbling stucco, streaked paintwork and even, on occasion, a faint whiff of drains.

An early visitor, John Steinbeck wrote in May 1953 in *Harper's Bazaar*: 'Positano bites deep. It is a dream place that isn't quite real when you are there and becomes beckoningly real after you have gone.' More than 60 years on, his words still ring true.

◉ Sights

Chiesa di Santa Maria Assunta CHURCH
(Piazza Flavio Gioia; ⊘8am-noon & 4-9pm) This church is the most famous and – let's face it – only major sight in Positano. Inside, it's a delightfully classical affair, its pillars topped with gilded Ionic capitals and winged cherubs peeking from above every arch. Above the main altar is a 13th-century Byzantine Black Madonna and Child.

Positano

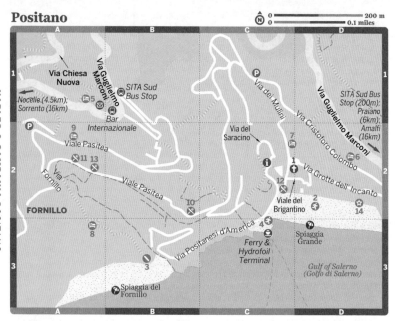

Positano

🏃 Activities

Although Spiaggia Grande is no one's dream beach, with greyish sand covered by legions of brightly coloured umbrellas, the water's clean and the setting is striking. Hiring a chair and umbrella in the fenced-off areas costs around €20 per person per day, but the crowded public areas are free.

Blue Star   BOATING
(☑ 089 81 18 88; www.bluestarpositano.it; Spiaggia Grande; ⊗ 8.30am-9pm summer) Operating out of a kiosk on Spiaggia Grande, Blue Star hires out small motorboats for €70 per hour (€250 for four hours). It also organises excursions to Capri and the Grotta dello Smeraldo (€55).

L'Uomo e il Mare   BOATING
(☑ 089 81 16 13; www.gennaroesalvatore.it; ⊗ 9am-8pm summer) This Italian-English couple offer a range of tours, including Capri and Amalfi day trips (from €55), out of a kiosk near the ferry terminal.

🛏 Sleeping

Most hotels are three-star rated and above and prices are universally high. Cheaper accommodation is more limited and must usually be booked well in advance for summer. Ask at the tourist office about rooms or apartments in private houses.

Hostel Brikette   HOSTEL €
(☑ 089 87 58 57; www.hostel-positano.com; Via Marconi 358; dm €20-26, premium dm €25-40, d

€55-100, apt €60-130; ☺ late Mar-Nov; [✳][@][🛜]) A short walk from the Chiesa Nuova (Bar Internazionale) bus stop, this bright and cheerful hostel offers the cheapest accommodation in town. There are various options: five- to 10-person dorms (single sex and mixed), premium dorms (with private bathroom and panoramic terrace), double rooms and apartments for two to eight people. Extra services include laundry (€10), left-luggage facilities and cheap, delicious home-cooked meals.

Conveniently, the hostel also offers a 'daily hostelling' option, which allows day trippers use of the hostel's facilities (including showers, wi-fi and left-luggage service) for €10.

Pensione Maria Luisa PENSION €

(☏ 089 87 50 23; www.pensionemarialuisa.com; Via Fornillo 42; r €70-85; ☺ Mar-Oct; [@][🛜]) A solid budget choice, Maria Luisa is run by the lovely Carlo, a wonderfully helpful, larger-than-life character. Rooms and bathrooms feature shiny blue tiles and fittings; those with private terraces are well worth the extra €10 for the bay view. Most rooms have fridges and the sunny communal area is another major plus. Breakfast costs an additional €5.

Hotel California HOTEL €€

(☏ 089 87 53 82; www.hotelcaliforniapositano.com; Via Cristoforo Colombo 141; d €160-185; [P][✳][🛜]) While you won't spot the Eagles at this Hotel California, you will find yourself slumbering in a magnificent, pastel-hued 18th-century palace. The rooms in the older part of the house are magnificent, with original friezes adorning the ceilings. The new rooms are spacious and luxuriously decorated, and breakfast is served on a leafy front terrace.

★Hotel Palazzo Murat LUXURY HOTEL €€€

(☏ 089 87 51 77; www.palazzomurat.it; Via dei Mulini 23; r €175-260; ☺ May–mid-Jan; [✳][@][🛜]) Hidden behind an ancient wall from the surge of tourists who pass this pedestrian thoroughfare daily, the Palazzo Murat is a magnificent hotel. Housed within the 18th-century *palazzo* that the one-time King of Naples used as his summer residence, the lush gardens contain banana trees, bottlebrush, Japanese maple and pine trees. Rooms, five in the original part of the building (more expensive), 25 in the newer section, are decorated with sumptuous antiques, original oil paintings and plenty of glossy marble.

Villa Gabrisa BOUTIQUE HOTEL €€€

(☏ 089 81 14 98; www.villagabrisa.it; Via Positea 223; d €220; [✳][🛜]) Tastefully restored, this historical building dates to the 18th century. Rooms exude classic Italian style with painted Tuscan furniture, wrought-iron beds, Murano glass chandeliers, and maiolica and terracotta tiles. While all rooms have fridge and sea-view terrace, some come with bubblelicious jacuzzi. Extras include SKY TV access and on-site restaurant serving regional grub.

✖ Eating

Most restaurants, bars and trattorias, many of which are unashamedly touristy, close over winter, making a brief reappearance for Christmas and New Year.

La Brezza CAFE, BAR €

(☏ 089 87 58 11; Via Regina Giovanna 2; snacks around €6; ☺ 9am-1am; [🛜]) With free wi-fi, web-connected computers (€5 for 30 minutes), and a terrace with beach views, this contemporary, buzzing hangout is the best frontline place for a *panino* or snack. There are regular art exhibitions and a daily 'happy hour' (from 6pm to 8pm), with drinks accompanied by complimentary light eats. Fresh juices and smoothies keep the virtuous hydrated.

★Next2 CAMPANIAN €€

(☏ 089 812 35 16; www.next2.it; Viale Pasitea 242; meals €40; ☺ 6.30-11.30pm) Sleek and refreshingly contemporary, this wine bar-restaurant hybrid gives regional cooking satisfying makeovers. Whenever possible, local and organic ingredients are put to impressive use in creations such as fried ravioli with ricotta and mozzarella on fresh tomatoes, or *parmigiana di pesce bandiera*, a surf variation on the classic aubergine dish. Desserts are wickedly creamy and the alfresco terrace is summertime perfection.

Da Vincenzo CAMPANIAN €€

(☏ 089 87 51 28; Viale Pasitea 172-178; meals €40; ☺ noon-2.30pm & 6-11pm Wed-Mon, 6.30-11pm Tue) Superbly prepared dishes are served here by the third generation of restaurateurs. The emphasis is on fish dishes, which range from the adventurous, like skewers of grilled octopus tentacles with deep-fried artichokes, to seasonal pasta dishes. Enjoy twanging Neapolitan guitarists during the summer months and make room for co-owner Marcella's legendary desserts, considered the best in town. Reservations recommended.

Il Saraceno d'Oro ITALIAN €€

(Viale Pasitea 254; pizzas €6-10, meals €35; ☺ 12.30-3pm & 6.30-11pm daily in summer) A busy, bustling place, the Saracen's blend of

NAPLES & CAMPANIA PRAIANO & FURORE

NOCELLE

A world apart from self-conscious Positano, the tiny, left-alone mountain village of No-celle (450m) affords some of the most spectacular views on the entire coast. A stop on the Sentieri degli Dei hiking route, it's a sleepy, silent place where not much ever happens, much to the delight of its very few residents.

If you can't pull yourself away, consider checking in at **Villa della Quercia** (089 812 34 97; www.villadellaquercia.com; Via Nocelle 5; r €70-75; Apr-Oct;), a former monastery with heavenly views. If peckish, tuck into delicious, regional dishes at **Trattoria Santa Croce** (Via Nocelle 19; Apr-Oct), a reliable low-key nosh spot in the main part of the village.

The easiest way to get here is by local bus from Positano (€1.30, 30 minutes, 17 daily). If you're driving, follow the signs from Positano.

cheery service, uncomplicated food and reasonable prices continues to please the punters. The pizza and pasta choices are good, and the *contorni* (side dishes) excellent (the grilled-vegetable antipasto makes a good choice for vegetarians). The legendary profiteroles in chocolate sauce make for a pleasing epilogue, as does the complimentary end-of-meal glass of *limoncello*.

☆ Entertainment

Generally speaking, Positano's nightlife is genteel, sophisticated and safe.

Music on the Rocks   CLUB
(089 87 58 74; www.musicontherocks.it; Via Grotte dell'Incanto 51; admission €10-30; summer) This is one of the town's few genuine nightspots and one of the best clubs on the coast. Music on the Rocks is dramatically carved into the tower at the eastern end of Spiaggia Grande. Join the flirty, eye-candy crowd and some of the region's top DJs for mainstream house and reliable disco.

ℹ Information

Positano (www.positano.com) A slick website with hotel and restaurant listings, itineraries and transport information.

Post office (Via Marconi 318)

Tourist office (089 87 50 67; Via del Sara-cino 4; 8.30am-7pm Mon-Sat, to 2pm Sun Easter-Oct, 9am-4.30pm Mon-Sat Nov-Easter)

ℹ Getting There & Away

BOAT

Positano has excellent ferry connections to the coastal towns and Capri from April to October.

Alicost (p86) operates one daily service to Amalfi (€7), Salerno (€11) and Capri (€17.40). On

Monday, Wednesday, Friday and Sunday, it also sails once to Sorrento (€15.80).

TraVelMar (p93) runs six daily ferries to Amalfi (€8) and Salerno (€12).

Linee Marittime Partenopee (Map p46; 081 704 19 11; www.consorziolmp.it) runs four daily hydrofoils and four daily ferries to Capri (€18.90).

BUS

SITA Sud (p85) runs frequent buses to/from Amalfi (€2.50, 40 to 50 minutes) and Sorrento (€2.50, one hour). Buses drop you off at one of two main bus stops: coming from Sorrento and the west, opposite Bar Internazionale; arriving from Amalfi and the east, at the top of Via Colombo. When departing, buy bus tickets at Bar Internazionale or, if headed eastwards, from the tobacconist at the bottom of Via Colombo.

ℹ Getting Around

Getting around Positano is largely a matter of walking. If your knees can handle them, there are dozens of narrow alleys and stairways that make walking relatively easy and joyously traffic-free. Otherwise, an orange bus follows the lower ring road every half-hour, passing along Viale Pasitea, Via Colombo and Via Marconi. Buy your ticket on board (€1.60) or at a *tabaccaio* (tobacconist's shop; €1.30). It passes by both SITA Sud bus stops.

Praiano & Furore

An ancient fishing village, Praiano has one of the coast's most popular beaches, Marina di Praia. From the SS163 (next to the Hotel Continental), take the steep path that leads down the side of the cliffs to a tiny inlet with a small stretch of coarse sand and deep-blue water.

The **Centro Sub Costiera Amalfitana** (089 81 21 48; www.centrosub.it; Via Marina di

Praia; dives from €80; 🚣) runs beginner to expert dives exploring the area's coral, marine life and grottoes.

Stunningly set on a cliffside overlooking Marina di Praia, **Hotel Onda Verde** (🖉 089 87 41 43; www.hotelondaverde.com; Via Terramare 3, Praiano; r €110-230; ☺ Apr-Nov; 🌢🛜) is a sound slumber option, its 25 rooms a smart, soothing combo of satin bedheads, Florentine-style furniture, and deckchair-pimped terraces. The hotel restaurant also comes highly recommended, and breakfast and parking are included in the price.

A few kilometres further on, Marina di Furore sits at the bottom of what's known as the fjord of Furore, a giant cleft that cuts through the Lattari mountains. The main village, however, stands 300m above, in the upper Vallone del Furore. A one-horse place that sees few tourists, it breathes a distinctly rural air despite the colourful murals and unlikely modern sculpture.

To get to upper Furore by car follow the SS163 and then the SS366 signposted to Agerola; from Positano, it's 15km. Otherwise, regular SITA Sud buses depart from the bus terminus in Amalfi (€2.50, 25 minutes, at least five daily).

Amalfi

POP 5160

Believe it or not, pretty little Amalfi, with its sun-filled piazzas and small beach, was once a maritime superpower with a population of more than 70,000. For one thing, it's not a big place – you can easily walk from one end to the other in about 20 minutes. For another, there are very few historical buildings of note. The explanation is chilling – most of the old city, and its populace, simply slid into the sea during an earthquake in 1343.

Just around the headland, neighbouring Atrani is a picturesque tangle of whitewashed alleys and arches centred on a lively, lived-in piazza and popular beach.

◎ Sights

Cattedrale di Sant'Andrea   CATHEDRAL
(🖉 089 87 10 59; Piazza del Duomo; ☺ 7.30am-7.30pm) A melange of architectural styles, Amalfi's iconic cathedral makes a striking impression from the top of its sweeping flight of stairs. Between 10am and 5pm (from 12.15pm on Sundays), entrance to the cathedral is through the adjacent Chiostro

del Paradiso, where you have to pay an entrance fee of €3. It's well worth it.

The cathedral dates in part from the early 10th century and its distinctive striped facade has been rebuilt twice, most recently at the end of the 19th century. While the two-toned masonry and 13th-century bell tower are largely Sicilian Arabic-Norman, the interior is predominantly baroque. The lavish **crypt** is home to the reliquary of St Andrew the Apostle. The fresco facing the crypt's altar is by Neapolitan baroque maestro Aniello Falcone.

The pint-sized **Chiostro del Paradiso** was built in 1266 to house the tombs of Amalfi's prominent citizens. From here you enter the **Basilica del Crucifisso** (closed January and February), the town's original 9th-century cathedral, itself built on the remains of an earlier palaeo-Christian temple. It's home to a small but fascinating collection of ecclesial treasures.

Museo della Carta   MUSEUM
(🖉 089 830 45 61; www.museodellacarta.it; Via delle Cartiere 23; admission €4; ☺ 10am-6.30pm) Amalfi's paper museum is housed in a 13th-century paper mill (the oldest in Europe). It lovingly preserves the original paper presses, which are still in full working order, as you'll see during the 15-minute guided tour (three-day advance booking requested for English tour) which explains the original cotton-based paper production and the later wood-pulp manufacturing.

Clued up, you may well be inspired to pick up some of the stationery sold in the gift shop, alongside calligraphy sets and paper pressed with flowers.

Museo Arsenale Amalfi   MUSEUM
(🖉 089 87 11 70; Largo Cesareo Console 3; admission €2; ☺ 10am-1.30pm & 3.30-7pm) Amalfi's other museum of note is home to the *Tavole Amalfitane,* an ancient manuscript draft of Amalfi's maritime code, and other historical documents. Harking back to Amalfi's days as a great maritime republic, the museum is housed in the cavernous Arsenale, once the town's main shipbuilding depot.

🏃 Activities

For all its seafaring history, Amalfi's main beach is not a particularly appealing swimming spot. If you're intent on a dip, think about hiring a boat. You'll find a number of operators along Lungomare dei Cavalieri, charging about €50 for a couple of hours.

Grotta dello Smeraldo GROTTO
(Emerald Grotto; admission €5; ⊙ 9am-4pm summer, to 3pm winter) Four kilometres west of Amalfi, Conca dei Marini is home to one of the coast's most popular sights. Named after the eerie emerald colour that emanates from the water, the Grotta dello Smeraldo is well worth a visit. Stalactites hang down from the 24m-high ceiling, while stalagmites grow up to 10m tall. Each year, on 24 December and 6 January, skin divers from all over Italy make their traditional pilgrimage to the ceramic *presepe* (nativity scene) submerged beneath the water.

SITA Sud buses regularly pass the car park above the cave entrance (from where you take a lift or stairs down to the rowing boats). Alternatively, Coop Sant'Andrea (p93) runs hourly boats from Amalfi (€15 return) between 9.30am and 3.30pm, March to November. Allow 1½ hours for the return trip.

✪ Festivals & Events

Every 24 December and 6 January, divers from all over Italy make a pilgrimage to the ceramic *presepe* (nativity scene) submerged in the Grotta dello Smeraldo.

The **Regatta of the Four Ancient Maritime Republics**, which rotates between Amalfi, Venice, Pisa and Genoa, is held on the first Sunday in June. Amalfi's turn comes round again in 2017.

🛌 Sleeping

A'Scalinatella Hostel HOSTEL €
(☑ 089 87 14 92; www.hostelscalinatella.com; Piazza Umberto I; dm €20-25, s €35-50, d €70-90, all incl breakfast) This bare-bones operation, just round the headland in Atrani, has dorms, rooms and apartments scattered across the village. There is also a laundry available (€7). Doors are locked at 2am.

Hotel Lidomare HOTEL €€
(☑ 089 87 13 32; www.lidomare.it; Largo Duchi Piccolomini 9; s/d €50/120; ❅ 🛜) Family run, this gracious hotel oozes character. Rooms are spacious, with appealingly haphazard decor, vintage tiles and fine antiques. Some rooms have jacuzzi bath-tubs, others have sea views and a balcony, some have both. Breakfast is laid out on top of a grand piano. Highly recommended.

Hotel Centrale HOTEL €€
(☑ 089 87 26 08; www.amalfihotelcentrale.it; Largo Piccolomini 1; s €60-120, d €70-140, tr €90-170, q €100-180; P ❅ @ 🛜) For the money, this is one of the best-value hotels in Amalfi. The entrance is on a tiny little piazza in the *centro storico* but many rooms actually overlook Piazza del Duomo (rooms 21 to 24 are good choices). The bright-green-and-blue tilework gives the place a vibrant fresh look and the views from the rooftop terrace are magnificent.

★ Hotel Luna Convento HOTEL €€€
(☑ 089 87 10 02; www.lunahotel.it; Via Pantaleone Comite 33; s €230-290, d €250-300; P ❅ @ 🛜 ☀) This former convent founded by St Francis in 1222 has been a hotel for some 170 years. Rooms in the original building are former monks' cells, but there's nothing pokey about the bright tiles, balconies and seamless sea views. The newer wing is equally beguiling, with religious frescoes over the bed (to stop any misbehaving). The cloistered courtyard is magnificent.

✕ Eating

Pasticceria Pansa PASTRIES & CAKES €
(Piazza Duomo 40; pastries from €1.50; ⊙ 7.30am-1am summer, to 10.30pm winter) Compromising waistlines since 1830, this vintage pastry peddler is a must for gluttons. Must-tries include the *scorzetta d'arancia* (chocolate-dipped candied orange peels), *torta setteveli* (a multilayered chocolate and hazelnut cake) and the *limoncello*-laced local *delizia al limone*.

Le Arcate CAMPANIAN €€
(☑ 089 87 13 67; www.learcate.net; Largo Orlando Buonocore, Atrani; pizzas from €6, meals €25; ⊙ 12.30-3pm & 7.30-11.30pm Tue-Sun, open Mon Jul & Aug) On a sunny day, it's hard to beat the dreamy location – at the far eastern point of the harbour overlooking the beach – with Atrani's ancient rooftops and church tower behind you. Huge white parasols shade the sprawl of tables, while the dining room is a stone-walled natural cave. Tuck into bubbling pizzas or more substatial dishes like risotto with seafood and grilled swordfish; the food is good, but it's a step down from the setting.

Trattoria Il Mulino ITALIAN €€
(Via delle Cartiere 36; pizzas €6-11, meals €29; ⊙ noon-midnight) A TV-in-the-corner, kids-running-between-the-tables sort of place, this is about as authentic a trattoria-pizzeria as you'll find in Amalfi. There are no culinary acrobatics, just hearty, honest pasta and simple grilled meat, fish and seafood.

The *calamari alla griglia* (grilled calamari) is simple, succulent perfection. You'll find it near the Museo della Carta.

Ristorante La Caravella CAMPANIAN €€€
(089 87 10 29; www.ristorantelacaravella.it; Via Matteo Camera 12; tasting menus €50-120; ⊙ noon-2.30pm & 7.30-11pm Wed-Mon) The regional food here has recently earned the restaurant a Michelin star with dishes that offer nouvelle zap, like black ravioli with cuttlefish ink, scampi and ricotta, or that are unabashedly simple, like the catch of the day served grilled on lemon leaves. Wine aficionados are likely to find something to try on the 15,000-label list. Reservations essential.

❶ Information

Post office (Corso delle Repubbliche Marinare 31) Next door to the tourist office.

Tourist office (www.amalfitouristoffice.it; Corso delle Repubbliche Marinare 27; ⊙ 9am-1pm & 2-6pm Mon-Sat, 9am-1pm Sun, closed Sun Apr, May & Sep, closed Sat & Sun Oct-Mar) Good for bus and ferry timetables.

❶ Getting There & Away

BOAT

Between April and October there are daily sailings to/from Amalfi.

Alicost (p86) operates one daily service to Amalfi (€7), Salerno (€11) and Capri (€19). On Monday, Wednesday, Friday and Sunday, it also sails once to Sorrento (€16.80).

TraVelMar (089 87 29 50; www.travelmar.it) runs ferries to Positano (€8, seven daily) and Salerno (€8, six daily).

Linee Marittime Partenopee (p90) runs three daily hydrofoils and four daily ferries to Capri (€21/20.50).

Coop Sant'Andrea (089 87 29 50; www.coopsantandrea.com; Lungomare dei Cavalieri 1) connects Amalfi to Salerno (€8, six daily) and Positano (€8, seven daily).

BUS

SITA Sud (p85) runs at least 17 daily services from Piazza Flavio Gioia to Sorrento (€3.80, 100 minutes) via Positano (€2.50, 50 minutes). It runs at least 24 daily services to Ravello (€2.50, 25 minutes) and at least nine services to Salerno (€2.50, 1¼ hours).

There are two early-morning connections to Naples (€4.10, two hours), with no services on Sunday, so you're better off catching a bus to Sorrento and then the Circumvesuviana train to Naples.

Buy tickets and check schedules at **Bar Il Giardino delle Palme** (Piazza Flavio Gioia), opposite the bus stop.

Ravello

POP 2460

Sitting high in the hills above Amalfi, refined Ravello is a polished town almost entirely dedicated to tourism. Boasting impeccable bohemian credentials – Wagner, DH Lawrence and Virginia Woolf all lounged here – it's today known for its ravishing gardens and stupendous views, the best in the world according to former resident Gore Vidal.

Most people visit on a day trip from Amalfi – a nerve-tingling 7km drive up the Valle del Dragone – although to best enjoy Ravello's romantic otherworldly atmosphere you'll need to stay overnight.

◎ Sights & Activities

★ **Villa Rufolo** GARDEN
(089 85 76 21; Piazza Duomo; adult/reduced €5/3; ⊙ 9am-sunset) To the south of Ravello's cathedral, a 14th-century tower marks the entrance to this villa, famed for its beautiful cascading gardens. Created by a Scotsman, Scott Neville Reid, in 1853, they are truly magnificent, commanding celestial panoramic views packed with exotic colours, artistically crumbling towers and luxurious blooms.

The villa itself was built in the 13th century for the wealthy Rufolo dynasty and housed several popes, as well as King Robert of Anjou. On seeing the gardens on 26 May 1880, Wagner said he had finally found the enchanted garden of Klingsor (the setting for the second act of the opera *Parsifal*). Today the gardens are used to stage concerts during the town's celebrated festival.

Cathedral CATHEDRAL
(Piazza Duomo; museum admission €3; ⊙ 8.30am-noon & 5.30-8.30pm) Forming the eastern flank of Piazza Duomo, Ravello's cathedral was originally built in 1086 but has since undergone various makeovers. The facade is 16th century, even if the central bronze door, one of only about two dozen in the country, is an 1179 original; the interior is a late-20th-century interpretation of what the original must once have looked like.

Of particular interest is the striking pulpit, supported by six twisting columns set on marble lions and decorated with flamboyant mosaics of peacocks, birds and dancing

NAPLES & CAMPANIA RAVELLO

lions. Note also how the floor is tilted towards the square – a deliberate measure to enhance the perspective effect. To the left of the central nave is the entrance to the cathedral museum and its modest collection of religious artefacts. In the afternoon, entrance to the church is through the side-street Viale Richard Wagner, costing €3 (including museum admission).

Villa Cimbrone   GARDEN

(☑089 85 80 72; Via Santa Chiara 26; adult/reduced €6/3; ☺9am-sunset) If Villa Rufolo's gardens leave you longing for more, the 12th-century Villa Cimbrone has you covered; we're talking vast views from delightfully ramshackle gardens. The best viewpoint is the Belvedere of Infinity, an awe-inspiring terrace lined with classical-inspired statues and busts. You'll find it some 600m south of Piazza Duomo.

✯✯ Festivals & Events

★ Ravello Festival   ARTS

(☑089 85 83 60; www.ravellofestival.com; ☺Jun–mid-Sep) Come summer, the Ravello Festival turns much of the town centre into a stage. Events range from orchestral concerts and chamber music to ballet performances; film screenings and exhibitions are held in atmospheric outdoor venues, most notably the famous overhanging terrace in the Villa Rufolo gardens.

You don't have to come in high summer to catch a concert, however. The town's program of chamber-music concerts runs from April to October. Tickets, bookable by phone or online, start at €25 (plus a €2 booking fee). For further information, contact the **Ravello Concert Society** (www.ravelloarts.org).

🛌 Sleeping

Agriturismo Monte Brusara   AGRITURISMO €

(☑089 85 74 67; www.montebrusara.com; Via Monte Brusara 32; s/d €45/90) An authentic working farm, this mountainside *agriturismo* (farm stay accommodation) is located a tough half-hour walk of about 1.5km from Ravello's centre (call ahead and the owners can arrange to pick you up). It is especially suited to families: children can feed the pony while you sit back and admire the views – or for those who simply want to escape the crowds. The three rooms are comfy but basic and the food is fabulous.

Hotel Villa Amore   PENSION €€

(☑089 85 71 35; www.villaamore.it; Via dei Fusco 5; s/d incl breakfast €80/120; ☺May-Oct; ◉) A welcoming family-run *pensione*, this is the best budget choice in town, with modest, homey rooms and sparkling bathrooms. All rooms have their own balcony and some have bath-tubs. The on-site restaurant (meals around €25) is a further plus.

Hotel Caruso   LUXURY HOTEL €€€

(☑089 85 88 01; www.hotelcaruso.com; Piazza San Giovanni del Toro 2; s €575-720, d €757-976 all incl breakfast; ☺Apr-Nov; 🅿❄🛜🏊) There can be no better place to swim than the Caruso's sensational infinity pool. Seemingly set on the edge of a precipice, its blue waters merge with sea and sky to magical effect. Inside, the sublimely restored 11th-century *palazzo* is no less impressive, with Moorish arches doubling as window frames, 15th-century vaulted ceilings and high-class ceramics. Rooms are suitably mod-conned.

🍴 Eating

Cumpà Cosimo   CAMPANIAN €€

(☑089 85 71 56; Via Roma 44-46; pizzas €7-12, meals €40; ☺12.30-3pm & 7.30pm-midnight) Netta Bottone's rustic cooking is so good that even US celebrity Rosie O'Donnell tried to get her on her show. Netta didn't make it to Hollywood but she stills rules the roost at this historic trattoria. Order the *piatto misto* (mixed plate), which may include Ravello's trademark *crespolini* (cheese and prosciutto-stuffed crepes). Evening options include pizza.

Da Salvatore   CAMPANIAN €€

(☑089 85 72 27; www.salvatoreravello.com; Via della Republicca 2; meals €28; ☺noon-3pm & 7.30-10pm Tue-Sun) Located just before the bus stop and the Albergo Ristorante Garden, Da Salvatore has nothing special by way of decor, but the view more than compensates. Count your lucky stars over creative dishes like tender squid on a bed of pureed chickpeas with spicy *peperoncino*. In the evening, options include top-notch wood-fired pizzas.

ℹ Information

Tourist office (☑089 85 70 96; www.ravellotime. it; Via Roma 18bis; ☺9am-8pm) Has information on the town and a handy map with walking trails.

ℹ Getting There & Away

SITA Sud operates at least 24 buses daily from the eastern side of Piazza Flavio Gioia in Amalfi (€2.50, 25 minutes). By car, turn north about 2km east of Amalfi. Vehicles are not permitted in Ravello's town centre, but there's plenty of space in supervised car parks on the perimeter.

South of Amalfi

From Amalfi to Salerno

The 26km drive to Salerno, though less exciting than the 16km stretch westwards to Positano, is exhilarating and dotted with a series of small towns, each with their own character and each worth a brief look.

Three and a half kilometres east of Amalfi, or a steep 1km-long walk down from Ravello, Minori is a small, workaday town, popular with holidaying Italians. If you're a sweet tooth, make a pit stop at Minori's famous pastry shop, Sal De Riso (☑ 089 85 36 18; www.salderiso.it; Piazza Cantilena 1, Minori; gelati €2, focaccias €3.70, pastries €4; ☉ 7.30am-late summer, reduced hours winter), owned by one of Italy's most revered pastry chefs, Salvatore De Riso. The place also peddles decent focaccia and gelato.

Further along, Maiori is the coast's biggest resort, a brassy place full of large seafront hotels, restaurants and beach clubs.

Just beyond Erchie and its beautiful beach, Cetara is a picturesque tumbledown fishing village with a reputation as a gastronomic highlight. Tuna and anchovies are the local specialities, appearing in various guises at Al Convento (☑ 089 26 10 39; www.alconvento.net; Piazza San Francesco 16, Cetara; meals €25; ☉ 12.30-3pm & 7-11pm summer, closed Wed winter), a sterling seafood restaurant near the small harbour.

Shortly before Salerno, the road passes through Vietri sul Mare, the ceramics capital of Campania. Pop into Ceramica Artistica Solimene (☑ 089 21 02 43; www.solimene.com; Via Madonna degli Angeli 7, Vietri sul Mare; ☉ 9am-7pm Mon-Fri, 10am-1pm & 4-7pm Sat), a vast factory outlet with an extraordinary glass-and-ceramic facade.

Salerno

POP 132,700

Upstaged by the glut of postcard-pretty towns along the Amalfi Coast, Campania's second-largest city is actually a pleasant surprise. A decade of civic determination has turned this major port and transport hub into one of southern Italy's most liveable cities, and its small but buzzing *centro storico* is a vibrant mix of medieval churches, tasty trattorias and good-spirited, bar-hopping locals.

Originally an Etruscan and later a Roman colony, Salerno flourished with the arrival of the Normans in the 11th century. Robert Guiscard made it the capital of his dukedom in 1076 and, under his patronage, the Scuola Medica Salernitana was renowned as one of medieval Europe's greatest medical institutes. More recently, it was left in tatters by the heavy fighting that followed the 1943 landings of the American 5th Army, just south of the city.

◎ Sights

★ Duomo   CATHEDRAL

(Piazza Alfano; ☉ 9.30am-6pm Mon-Sat, 4-6pm Sun) You can't miss the looming presence of Salerno's impressive cathedral, widely considered to be the most beautiful medieval church in Italy. Built by the Normans in the 11th century and later aesthetically remodelled in the 18th century, it sustained severe damage in the 1980 earthquake. It is dedicated to San Matteo (St Matthew), whose remains were reputedly brought to the city in 954 and now lie beneath the main altar in the exquisite vaulted crypt.

Take special note of the magnificent main entrance, the 12th-century Porta dei Leoni, named after the marble lions at the foot of the stairway. It leads through to a beautiful harmonious courtyard, surrounded by graceful arches, overlooked by a 12th-century bell tower.

While the huge bronze doors (similarly guarded by lions) were cast in Constantinople in the 11th century, the three-aisled interior is largely baroque, with only a few traces of the original church. These include parts of the transept and choir floor and the two raised pulpits in front of the choir stalls. Extraordinarily detailed and colourful 13th-century mosaics lace the church.

In the right-hand apse, don't miss the Cappella delle Crociate (Chapel of the Crusades), containing stunning frescoes and more marvellous mosaics. The chapel was so named because crusaders' weapons were blessed here. Under the altar lies the tomb of 11th-century pope Gregory VII.

Museo Virtuale della Scuola Medica Salernitana   MUSEUM

(☑ 089 257 61 26; Via Mercanti 74; adult/reduced €3/1; ☉ 9am-1pm Mon-Sat; ⊞) Slap bang in Salerno's historic centre, this engaging museum deploys 3D and touch-screen technology to explore the teachings and wince-inducing procedures of Salerno's once-famous, now-defunct medical institute. Established around the 9th century,

Salerno

400 m
0.2 miles

Via Dalmazia

Via Nizza

Irno

Piazza
Vittorio
Veneto

Via Torrione

Lungomare Guglielmo Marconi

A3 (Southbound);
Paestum (36km)

Via Volpe

SITA Sud
Buses to
Naples

Piazza
Giuseppe
Mazzini

Piazza della
Concordia

CSTP

Corso Garibaldi

Via Diaz

Piazza
XXIV
Maggio

Corso Vittorio Emanuele II

Via Cilento

Porto Turistico
Ferry & Hydrofoil
Terminal

Via San Benedetto

Tourist
Infopoint

Via Vella

Lungomare Trieste

Via Iannelli

Via Roma

Gulf of Salerno
(Golfo di Salerno)

Piazza Alfano

Via S.Michele

Piazza
Matteotti

Tourist
Office

Via Mercanti

Via Duomo

Duomo

Via del Canali

Vico della
Neve

Piazza
Sedile del
Campo

Piazza
Amendola

Amalfi (26km);
Positano (42km)

Porto Commerciale
Ferry & Hydrofoil
Terminal

Molo
Manfredi

Salerno

the school was the most important centre of medical knowledge in medieval Europe, reaching the height of its prestige in the 11th century. It was closed in the early 19th century.

Museo Pinacoteca Provinciale   MUSEUM
(☑089 258 30 73; Via Mercanti 63; ⊙9am-7.45pm Tue-Sun) **FREE** Art enthusiasts should seek out the Museo Pinacoteca Provinciale, located deep in the heart of the historic quarter. Spread throughout six galleries, this museum houses an interesting art collection dating from the Renaissance right up to the first half of the 20th century.

Among the works are some fine canvases by local boy Andrea Sabatini da Salerno, who was notably influenced by Leonardo da Vinci.

Castello di Arechi   CASTLE
(☑089 296 40 15; www.ilcastellodiarechi.it; Via Benedetto Croce; adult/reduced €3/1.50; ⊙9am-7pm Tue-Sat, to 6.30pm Sun summer, to 5pm Tue-Sun winter) Bus 19 from Piazza XXIV Maggio heads to Salerno's most famous landmark, the forbidding Castello di Arechi, dramatically positioned 263m above the city. Originally a Byzantine fort, it was built by the Lombard duke of Benevento, Arechi II, in the 8th century and subsequently modified by the Normans and Aragonese, most recently in the 16th century. The views of the Gulf of Salerno and Salerno's rooftops are spectacular; you can also visit a permanent collection of ceramics, arms and coins.

🛏 Sleeping

Ostello Ave Gratia Plena   HOSTEL €
(☑089 23 47 76; www.ostellodisalerno.it; Via dei Canali; dm/s/d €16/45/52; @🖥) Housed in a 16th-century convent, Salerno's HI hostel is right in the heart of the *centro storico*. Inside there's a charming central courtyard and a range of bright rooms, from dorms to doubles with private bathroom. The 2am curfew is only for the dorms. The hostel offers bike rental (€2 for the first hour, then €1 per subsequent hour, or €10 per day).

Hotel Plaza   HOTEL €
(☑089 22 44 77; www.plazasalerno.it; Piazza Vittorio Veneto 42; s/d €65/100; 🕸@🖥) A two-minute chug from the train station, the Plaza is convenient, comfortable and fairly charmless (especially the dowdy public areas), but it's not an unfriendly place and the good-sized rooms, with their brown carpet and gleaming bathrooms, are actually pretty good value for money. Those around the back have terraces overlooking the city and, beyond, the mountains.

🍽 Eating

Head to Via Roma and Via Mercanti in the lively medieval centre, where you'll find everything from traditional, family-run trattorias and gelaterie to wine bars, pubs and restaurants.

Cicirinella   CAMPANIAN €€
(☑089 22 65 61; Via Genovesi 28; meals €25; ⊙8pm-midnight daily, plus 1-3pm Sat & Sun) Where weary horses once snoozed, gastronomes now toast, savour and swoon at what is one of Salerno's top eating spots. A handsome combo of white linen, stone walls, and bottled-lined shelves, its open kitchen has a soft spot for seasonal produce and twists on traditional recipes. Highlights include a beautifully presented *antipasto misto* and a sublimely buttery entrecôte. Book ahead Friday and Saturday.

La Cucina di Edoardo   CAMPANIAN €€
(☑089 296 26 67; Vico della Neve 14; meals €30; ⊙12.30-3pm & 7.30-11pm) Snugly tucked away in a *centro storico* side street, Edoardo's Kitchen is one of those scrumptious finds any local *buongustaio* (foodie) will direct you to. The focus is on regional dishes with subtle creative touches – think pistachio-crumbed tuna escalope on a bed of artichoke. Leave room for the *tortino al cioccolato* (chocolate tartlet) and book ahead on weekends.

Pasticceria Pantaleone   PASTRIES & CAKES €
(Via Mercanti 75; pastries from €1.50; ⊙8am-2pm & 4.30-8.30pm, morning only Tue & Sun) Where

better to commit dietary sins than in a deconsecrated church? It's now home to Salerno's finest pastry shop, best known for inventing the *scazzetta,* a pastry of *pan di spagna* sponge, fresh berries and Chantilly cream, soaked in Strega liqueur and finished with a strawberry glacé. Wash down the guilt with a glass of the house liqueur, Elisir, made with aromatic herbs and orange.

Information

Post office (Corso Garibaldi 203)

Tourist office (089 23 14 32; Lungomare Trieste 7; ⊗9am-1pm & 3-7pm Mon-Sat) Main tourist office by the seafront.

Tourist infopoint (089 662 951; Corso Vittorio Emanuele II 193; ⊗9am-1pm & 5-8pm Mon-Fri, 9am-1pm Sat) Inside the Galleria Capitol Cinema shopping centre, has brochures, bus and ferry timetables and accommodation information.

Getting There & Away

BOAT

Between April and October there are daily sailings to/from Salerno.

Alicost (p86) operates one daily service to Amalfi (€7), Positano (€11) and Capri (€20.70).

Linee Marittime Partenopee (p90) runs one daily hydrofoil and three daily ferries to Capri (€23/22.20).

TraVelMar (p93) runs six daily ferries to Amalfi (€8) and Positano (€12).

Departures are from the Porto Turistico, 200m down the pier from Piazza della Concordia. You can buy tickets from the booths by the embarkation point.

Departures for Capri leave from Molo Manfredi at the Porto Commerciale.

BUS

SITA Sud (p85) buses for Amalfi (€2.50, 1¼ hours, at least hourly) depart from **Piazza Vittorio Veneto**, beside the train station, stopping en route at Vietri sul Mare, Cetara, Maiori and Minori. Tickets are available inside the train station.

CSTP (089 48 70 01; www.cstp.it) bus 50 runs from Piazza Vittorio Veneto to Pompeii (€2.20, 70 minutes, 17 daily). For Paestum (€3.40, one hour, hourly) take bus 34 from Piazza della Concordia.

CAR & MOTORCYCLE

Salerno is on the A3 between Naples and Reggio di Calabria, which is toll-free from Salerno southwards.

TRAIN

Salerno is a major stop on southbound routes to Calabria and the Ionian and Adriatic coasts. From the station in Piazza Vittorio Veneto there are regular trains to Naples (IC; €8.50, 35 minutes), Rome (Frecciarossa; €39, two hours) and Reggio di Calabria (IC; €41, 4½ hours).

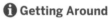 Getting Around

Walking is the most sensible option; from the train station it's a 1.2km walk along Corso Vittorio Emanuele II to the historic centre.

If you want to hire a car there's a **Europcar** (089 258 07 75; www.europcar.com; Via Clemente Mauro 18) agency not far from the train station.

Paestum

Paestum's Unesco-listed temples are among the best-preserved monuments of Magna Graecia, the Greek colony that once covered much of southern Italy. An easy day trip from Salerno or Agropoli, they are one of the region's most iconic sights and absolutely unmissable.

Paestum, or Poseidonia as the city was originally called (in honour of Poseidon, the Greek god of the sea), was founded in the 6th century BC by Greek settlers and fell under Roman control in 273 BC. It became an important trading port and remained so until the fall of the Roman Empire, when periodic outbreaks of malaria and savage Saracen raids led its weakened citizens to abandon the town.

Its temples were rediscovered in the late 18th century by road builders – who proceeded to plough their way right through the ruins.

The **tourist office** (0828 81 10 16; www.infopaestum.it; Via Magna Grecia 887, Paestum; ⊗9am-1pm & 3-5pm Mon-Sun) has information on the area and the Costiera Cilentana.

◎ Sights

Ruins of Paestum   RUIN

(0828 72 26 54; adult/reduced, incl museum €10/5; ⊗8.45am-2hrs before sunset) Tickets to the ruins are sold at the main entry point, near the tourist office, or from the museum, where you can also hire an audio guide (€5).

The first temple you encounter from the main entrance is the 6th-century-BC **Tempio di Cerere** (Temple of Ceres). Originally dedicated to Athena, it served as a Christian church in medieval times.

As you head south, you can pick out the basic outline of the large rectangular forum, the heart of the ancient city. Among the partially standing buildings are the vast domestic housing area and, further south, the amphitheatre; both provide evocative glimpses of daily life here in Roman times.

The Tempio di Nettuno (Temple of Neptune), dating from about 450 BC, is the largest and best preserved of the three temples at Paestum; only parts of its inside walls and roof are missing. Almost next door, the so-called basilica (in fact, a temple to the goddess Hera) is Paestum's oldest surviving monument. Dating from the middle of the 6th century BC, it's a magnificent sight, with nine columns across and 18 along the sides. Ask someone to take your photo next to a column here, it's a good way to appreciate the scale.

Just east of the site, the museum (📞 0828 81 10 23; ⏰ 8.30am-7.30pm, last entry 6.45pm, closed 1st & 3rd Mon of month) houses a collection of fascinating, if weathered, *metopes* (bas-relief friezes). This collection includes 33 of the original 36 *metopes* from the Tempio di Argiva Hera (Temple of Argive Hera), situated 9km north of Paestum, of which virtually nothing else remains. The star exhibit is the 5th-century-BC fresco *Tomba del Truffatore* (Tomb of the Diver), thought to represent the passage from life to death with its depiction of a diver in midair (don't try this at home).

🛏 Sleeping & Eating

★ Casale Giancesare   B&B €
(📞 333 1897737, 0828 72 80 61; www.casale-gian cesare.it; Via Giancesare 8; s €45-90, d €65-120, apt per wk €600-1300; P ❄ @ 🗐 ☂) A 19th-century former farmhouse, this chic, charming, stone-clad B&B is run by the Voza family, who will happily ply you with their homemade wine, *limoncello* and fabulous food. Located 2.5km from Paestum (complimentary pick-up available from Paestum train station), the place is surrounded by vineyards and olive and mulberry trees. There are stunning views, especially from the swimming pool.

Beware of road signs advertising another bed and breakfast, called Residenza Giancesare.

Nonna Scepa   CAMPANIAN €€
(📞 0828 85 10 64; Via Laura 53; meals €35; ⏰ noon-3pm & 7.30-11pm, closed Thu winter; 🚼) There are various restaurants at the site;

however, most serve mediocre food at inflated prices. Instead, seek out the superbly prepared, robust dishes at Nonna Scepa, a family-friendly restaurant that's rapidly gaining a reputation throughout the region for excellence. Dishes are firmly seasonal and, during the summer, concentrate on fresh seafood like the refreshingly simple grilled fish with lemon.

Other popular choices include risotto with zucchini and artichokes, and spaghetti with lobster.

❶ Getting There & Away

The best way to get to Paestum by public transport is to take CSTP (📞 089 48 70 01; www.cstp.it) bus 34 from Piazza della Concordia in Salerno (€3.40, one hour, hourly), or, if approaching from the south, the same bus from Agropoli (€1.30, 15 minutes, hourly).

If you're driving you could take the A3 from Salerno and exit for the SS18 at Battipaglia. Better, and altogether more pleasant, is the Litoranea, the minor road that hugs the coast. From the A3 take the earlier exit for Pontecagnano and follow the signs for Agropoli and Paestum.

COSTIERA CILENTANA

Southeast of the Gulf of Salerno, the coastal plains begin to give way to wilder, jagged cliffs and unspoilt scenery, a taste of what lies further on in the stark hills of Basilicata and the wooded peaks of Calabria. Inland, dark mountains loom over the remote highlands of the Parco Nazionale del Cilento e Vallo di Diano, one of Campania's best-kept secrets.

Several destinations on the Cilento coast are served by the main rail route from Naples to Reggio di Calabria. Check Trenitalia (www.trenitalia.it) for fares and times.

By car take the SS18, which connects Agropoli with Velia via the inland route, or the SS267, which hugs the coast.

Agropoli

POP 20,600

The main town on the southern stretch of the coast, Agropoli makes a good base for Paestum and the beaches to the northwest. Popular with holidaying Italians, it's an otherwise tranquil place with a ramshackle medieval core on a promontory overlooking the sea.

The tourist office (🖋 0974 82 74 14; Piazza della Repubblica 3; ⊙ 10am-1pm & 4-8pm Mon-Sun) can provide you with a city map.

🛏 Sleeping & Eating

Anna
B&B, APARTMENTS €

(🖋 0974 82 37 63; www.bbanna.it; Via S Marco 28-30, Agropoli; s €35-50, d €50-120; 🅿 ✱) Across from Agropoli's sweeping sandy beach, Anna offers bright, spacious rooms with smart striped fabrics and balconies; request a sea view. Sunbeds and bicycles come free, and Anna's downstairs restaurant (pizzas from €3, meals €22) serves gluten-free grub. The friendly owners also offer two simple four-person apartments (€80 to €150) 300m away, both with modern kitchenette and small patio.

Ostello La Lanterna
HOSTEL €

(🖋 0974 83 83 64; lanterna@cilento.it; Via Lanterna 8; dm €13-16, s €17-20, d €32-45, tr €45-54; ⊙ mid-Mar–Oct) Agropoli's friendly Ostello La Lanterna has dorms, doubles and four-bed family rooms, as well as a garden and optional evening meals (€10). The beach is a two-minute walk away.

Il Vecchio Saracino
SEAFOOD €€

(🖋 0974 82 64 15; www.vecchiosaracino.it; Via Granatelle 18, Agropoli; meals €25; ⊙ 8.30pm-midnight daily, also 1-4pm Sun; 🕾) Raise your fork to good-value, whisker-licking seafood at this local institution. Dishes sing with flavour, whether it's the beautifully textured shrimp and artichoke gratin with homemade artichoke conserve, the *paccheri* (large, tube-shaped pasta) with clams and monkfish, or the soul-coaxing Cilento fish soup. Many ingredients and products are proudly homemade, from the salted anchovies to a string of smooth liqueurs.

Parco Nazionale del Cilento e Vallo di Diano

Stretching from the coast up to Campania's highest peak, Monte Cervati (1900m), and beyond to the regional border with Basilicata, the Parco Nazionale del Cilento e Vallo di Diano is Italy's second-largest national park. A little-explored area of barren heights and empty valleys, it's the perfect antidote to the holiday mayhem on the coast.

For further information stop by the tourist office (p698) in Paestum.

◉ Sights & Activities

★ Grotte di Castelcivita
CAVE

(🖋 0828 77 23 97; www.grottedicastelcivita.com; Piazzale N Zonzi, Castelcivita; adult/reduced €10/8; ⊙ standard tours 10.30am, noon, 1.30pm, 3pm Mar-Oct, also 4.30pm & 6pm Apr-Sep, 4hr tours 10am Sat Jun-Oct; 🅿 ♿) Located about 20km northeast of Paestum, the Grotte di Castelcivita complex is where Spartacus is said to have taken refuge following his slave rebellion in 71 BC. The standard one-hour tour winds through a route surrounded by extraordinary stalagmites and stalactites, and a mesmerising play of colours, caused by algae, calcium and iron tinting the naturally sculpted rock shapes.

The longer four-hour tours (€25) take place between June and October, when the water deep within the cave complex has dried up. Hard hats and a certain level of fitness and mobility are required. Visits should be booked a day in advance.

To get here by car take the SS18 from Paestum towards Salerno and follow the signs.

Grotte dell'Angelo
CAVE

(🖋 0975 39 70 37; www.grottedellangelo.sa.it; Pertosa; guided visits adult/reduced €13/10; ⊙ 9am-7pm Apr & May, 10am-7pm Jun-Aug, 10am-6pm Sep, reduced hours rest of year; 🅿 ♿) At the park's eastern edge, this cave system is younger than the Grotta di Castelcivita, dating back a mere 35 million years to the Neolithic period. Used by the Greeks and Romans as places of worship, the caves burrow through the mountains for 2500m, with long underground passages and lofty grottoes filled with a mouthful of stalagmites and stalactites.

By car, take the A3 southbound from Salerno, exit at Petina and follow the SS19 for 9km.

Certosa di San Lorenzo
MONASTERY

(🖋 0975 77 74 45; Padula; adult/reduced €4/2; ⊙ 9am-7pm Wed-Mon) One of southern Europe's largest monasteries, the Certosa di San Lorenzo covers 250,000 sq metres. Begun in the 14th century and modified over time, it was abandoned in the 19th century, then suffered further degradation as a children's holiday home and later a concentration camp. Numerologists can swoon at the following: 320 rooms and halls, 2500m of corridors, galleries and hallways, 300 columns, 500 doors, 550 windows, 13 courtyards, 100 fireplaces, 52 stairways and 41 fountains – it's *huge.*

As you will unlikely have time to see everything here, be sure to visit the highlights, including the vast central courtyard, the magnificent wood-panelled library, sumptuously frescoed chapels and the kitchen with its grandiose fireplace, vibrant maiolica tiles and famous tale: apparently this is where the legendary 1000-egg omelette was made in 1534 for Charles V. Unfortunately, the historic frying pan is not on view – just how big was it, one wonders?

Within the monastery you can also peruse the modest collection of ancient artefacts at the **Museo Archeologico Provinciale della Lucania Occidentale** (⌚0975 7 71 17; ⊘8am-1.15pm & 2-3pm Tue-Sat, 9am-1pm Sun) `FREE`.

For guided hiking opportunities, contact **Gruppo Escursionistico Trekking** (⌚0975 7 25 86; www.getvallodidiano.it; Via Provinciale 29, Silla di Sassano) or **Associazione Trekking Cilento** (⌚0974 84 33 45; www.trekkingcilento.it; Via Cannetiello 6, Agropoli).

🛏 Sleeping & Eating

★**Agriturismo i Moresani**   AGRITURISMO €
(⌚0974 90 20 86; www.imoresani.com; Località Moresani; s €45-55, d €90-110; ⊘Mar-Oct; ✻⚏✈)
Surrounded by rolling hills splashed with vines, pastures and olive trees, this family-run farm puts its homemade *caprino* goat's cheese, wine, olive oil and preserves to good use at its on-site restaurant. Sleep off the feast in one of the warm, rustic rooms on offer, or sign up for the regular horse-riding, cooking and painting courses on offer.

Fattoria Alvaneta   CAMPANIAN €
(⌚0975 7 71 39; www.fattoriaalvaneta.it; Contrada Pantagnoni, Padula; meals €20; ⊘1pm-3pm & 7.30-10.30pm Wed-Mon, also open Tue Aug, closed first week Jul) Farm-to-table feasting awaits at this wonderful hillside *agriturismo*, complete with sweeping views of the Vallo di Diano. Earthy flavours dominate the menu, the farm's home-reared boar, veal and pork shining through in options like *pasta fresca* (fresh egg pasta) with *cinghiale* (boar) and porcini mushrooms.

The creative *antipasto misto* delivers treats like anchovy-laced *zeppole* (fried pizza dough) or *parmigiana di scarola* (escarole parmigiana), a clever adaptation of the classic aubergine version. Young, affable owner Francesco is passionate about the Cilento, and offers on-site accommodation (single/double/triple €35/50/65) and organised tours of the area. If driving from the Certosa, head northeast along Viale Certosa (towards the town centre), turn right into Strada Provinciale 180 and follow the signs for Fattoria Alvaneta.

❶ Getting There & Away

To get the best out of the park and the surrounding region, you will need a car. There is a car-hire company (p98) in Salerno.

Public transport in the area is lacking and frustratingly inconvenient. For a reliable taxi service in the Agropoli area, call **Gennaro Di Giovanni** (⌚338 8743105) or **Raffaello Perez** (⌚333 1324422).

Puglia, Basilicata & Calabria

Includes ➡

Why Go?

Southern Italy is the land of the *mezzogiorno* – the midday sun – which sums up the Mediterranean climate and the languid pace of life. From the heel to the toe of Italy's boot, the landscape reflects the individuality of its people. Basilicata is a crush of mountains and rolling hills with a dazzling stretch of coastline. Calabria is Italy's wildest area with fine beaches and a mountainous landscape with peaks frequently crowned by ruined castles. Puglia is the sophisticate of the south with charming seaside villages along its 800km of coastline, lush flat farmlands, thick forests and olive groves.

The south's violent history of successive invasions and economic hardship has forged a fiercely proud people and influenced its distinctive culture and cuisine. A hotter, edgier place than the urbane north of Italy, this is an area that still feels like it has secret places to explore, although you will need your own wheels (and some Italian) if you plan to seriously sidestep from the beaten track.

Best Places to Eat

➡ Cucina Casareccia (p128)

➡ La Locanda di Federico (p107)

➡ Il Frantoio (p120)

➡ Taverna Al Cantinone (p114)

Best Places to Stay

➡ Sotto le Cummerse (p121)

➡ Palazzo Rollo (p127)

➡ Locanda delle Donne Monache (p147)

➡ Le Monacelle (p143)

➡ Donnaciccina (p159)

When to Go
Bari

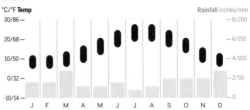

Apr–Jun Spring wildflowers are blooming: a perfect time for hiking in the mountains.

Jul & Aug Summer is beach weather and the best party time for festivals and events.

Sep & Oct No crowds, mild weather and wild mushrooms galore.

PUGLIA

Puglia is comprised of sun-bleached landscapes, silver olive groves, picturesque seascapes, and memorable hilltop and coastal towns. It is a lush, largely flat farming region, skirted by a long coast that alternates between glittering limestone precipices and long sandy beaches. The heel of Italy juts into the Adriatic and Ionian Seas and the waters of both are stunningly beautiful, veering between translucent emerald green and dusky powder blue. Its extensive coastline bears the marks of many conquering invaders: the Normans, the Spanish, the Turks, the Swabians and the Greeks. Yet, despite its diverse influences, Puglia has its own distinct and authentic identity.

In a land where the cuisine is all-important, Puglia's *cucina povera* (peasant cooking) is legendary. Olive oil, grapes, tomatoes, eggplants, artichokes, peppers, salami, mushrooms, olives and fresh seafood strain its table. Although boasting some of Italy's best food and wines, in some places it's rare to hear a foreign voice. But in July and August Puglia becomes a huge party, with *sagre* (festivals, usually involving food), concerts and events, and thousands of Italian tourists heading down here for their annual break.

History

At times Puglia feels and looks Greek – and for good reason. This tangible legacy dates from when the Greeks founded a string of settlements along the Ionian coast in the 8th century BC. A form of Greek dialect (Griko) is still spoken in some towns southeast of Lecce. Historically, the major city was Taras (Taranto), settled by Spartan exiles who dominated until they were defeated by the Romans in 272 BC.

The long coastline made the region vulnerable to conquest. The Normans left their fine Romanesque churches, the Swabians their fortifications and the Spanish their flamboyant baroque buildings. No one, however, knows exactly the origins of the extraordinary 16th-century conical-roofed stone houses, the *trulli,* unique to Puglia.

Apart from invaders and pirates, malaria was long the greatest scourge of the south, forcing many towns to build away from the coast and into the hills. After Mussolini's seizure of power in 1922, the south became the frontline in his 'Battle for Wheat'. This initiative was aimed at making Italy self-sufficient when it came to food, following the sanctions imposed on the country after its conquest of Ethiopia. Puglia is now covered in wheat fields, olive groves and fruit arbours.

PUGLIA ON YOUR PLATE

Puglia is home to Italy's most uncorrupted, brawniest, least known vernacular cuisine. It has evolved from *cucina povera* – literally 'cooking of the poor' or peasant cooking: think of pasta made without eggs and dishes prepared with wild greens gathered from the fields.

Most of Italy's fish is caught off the Puglian coast, 80% of Europe's pasta is produced here and 80% of Italy's olive oil originates in Puglia and Calabria. Tomatoes, broccoli, chicory, fennel, figs, melons, cherries and grapes are all plentiful in season and taste better than anywhere else. Almonds, grown near Ruvo di Puglia, are packed into many traditional cakes and pastries, which used to be eaten only by the privileged.

Like their Greek forebears, the Puglians eat *agnello* (lamb) and *capretto* (kid). *Cavallo* (horse) has only recently galloped to the table while *trippa* (tripe) is another mainstay. Meat is usually roasted or grilled with aromatic herbs or served in tomato-based sauces.

Raw fish (such as anchovies or baby squid) are marinated in olive oil and lemon juice. *Cozze* (mussels) are prepared in multitudinous ways, with garlic and breadcrumbs, or as *riso cozze patata,* baked with rice and potatoes – every area has its variations on this dish.

Bread and pasta are close to the Puglian heart, with per-capita consumption at least double that of the USA. You'll find *orecchiette* (small ear-shaped pasta, often accompanied by a small rod-shaped variety, called *strascinati* or *cavatelli*), served with broccoli or *ragù* (meat sauce), generally topped by the pungent local cheese *ricotta forte*.

Previously known for quantity rather than quality, Puglian wines are now developing apace. The best are produced in Salento (the Salice Salentino is one of the finest reds), in the *trulli* area around Locorotondo (famous for its white wine), around Cisternino (home of the fashionable heavy red Primitivo) and in the plains around Foggia and Lucera.

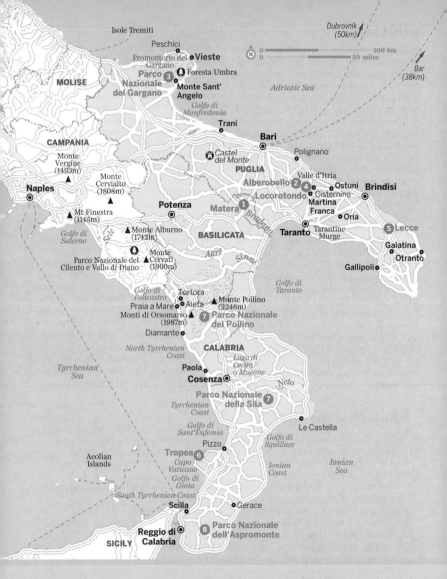

Puglia, Basilicata & Calabria Highlights

1 Marvelling at the *sassi* (cave dwellings) and ancient history of **Matera** (p138).

2 Dipping into the Disney-style scenario of conical *trulli* dwellings in **Alberobello** (p119).

3 Hiking in shady forests and swimming in aqua-blue seas in the **Parco Nazionale del Gargano** (p113).

4 Strolling through the old centre of **Locorotondo** (p121), one of Puglia's prettiest towns.

5 Wondering at ornate baroque facades in **Lecce** (p124).

6 Discovering Calabria's picturesque seaside at **Tropea** (p159).

7 Vanishing into the vast hills of the **Parco Nazionale della Sila** (p151) or the **Parco Nazionale del Pollino** (p153).

8 Driving or trekking into the wilds of the mysterious **Parco Nazionale dell'Aspromonte** (p155).

Bari

POP 320,200

Once regarded as the Bronx of southern Italy, Bari's reputation has gradually improved and the city, Puglia's capital and one of the south's most prosperous, deserves more than a cursory glance. Spruced up and rejuvenated, Bari Vecchia, the historic old town, is an interesting and atmospheric warren of streets. In the evenings the piazzas buzz with trendy restaurants and bars, but there are still parts of the old town that carry a gritty undertone.

ⓘ Dangers & Annoyances

Petty crime can be a problem, so take all of the usual precautions: don't leave anything in your car; don't display money or valuables; and watch out for bag-snatchers on scooters. Be careful in Bari Vecchia's dark streets at night.

◉ Sights

Most sights are in or near atmospheric Bari Vecchia, a medieval labyrinth of tight alleyways and graceful piazzas. It fills a small peninsula between the new port to the west and the old port to the southeast, cramming in 40 churches and more than 120 shrines.

Castello Svevo   CASTLE
(Swabian Castle; ☑ 083 184 00 09; Piazza Federico II di Svevia; admission adult/reduced €2/1; ⊙ 8.30am-7.30pm Thu-Tue) The Normans originally built over the ruins of a Roman fort, then Frederick II built over the Norman castle, incorporating it into his design – the two towers of the Norman structure still stand. The bastions, with corner towers overhanging the moat, were added in the 16th century during Spanish rule, when the castle was a magnificent residence.

Basilica di San Nicola   BASILICA
(www.basilicasannicola.it; Piazza San Nicola; ⊙ 7am-1pm & 4-7pm Mon-Sat, 7am-1pm & 4-9pm Sun) One of the south's first Norman churches, the basilica is a splendid example of Puglian-Romanesque style, built to house the relics of St Nicholas (better known as Father Christmas), which were stolen from Turkey in 1087 by local fishing folk. His remains are said to emanate a miraculous manna liquid with special powers. For this reason – and because he is also the patron saint of prisoners and children – the basilica remains an important place of pilgrimage. The interior is huge and simple with a decorative 17th-century wood-

en ceiling. The magnificent 13th-century ciborium over the altar is Puglia's oldest. The shrine in the crypt, lit by hanging lamps, is beautiful.

Cathedral   CATHEDRAL
(Piazza dell'Odegitria; ⊙ 8am-12.30pm & 4-7.30pm Mon-Fri, 8am-12.30pm & 5-8.30pm Sat & Sun) Built over the original Byzantine church, the 11th-century Romanesque cathedral retains its basilica plan – the plain walls punctuated with deep arcades – and the eastern window is a tangle of plant and animal motifs. Recent excavations (€1; ⊙ 12.30-4pm Sun-Wed, Apr-Oct) have revealed an ancient Christian basilica with a substantial floor mosaic featuring octopus, fish and plant motifs.

Piazza Mercantile   PIAZZA
This beautiful piazza is fronted by the Sedile, the headquarters of Bari's Council of Nobles. In the square's northeast corner is the Colonna della Giustizia (Column of Justice; Piazza Mercantile), where debtors were once tied and whipped.

✦ Festivals

Festa di San Nicola   RELIGIOUS
(⊙ 7-9 May) The Festival of St Nicholas is Bari's biggest annual shindig, celebrating the 11th-century arrival of St Nicholas' relics from Turkey. On the first evening a procession leaves Castello Svevo for the Basilica di San Nicola. The next day there's a deafening fly-past and a fleet of boats carries the statue of St Nicholas along the coast. The evening – and the next – ends with a massive fireworks

---

TOP FIVE HISTORIC CENTRES IN PUGLIA

Locorotondo A blinding white backdrop decked with blood-red geraniums (p121).

Ostuni Narrow streets circle ever upwards to a stunning 15th-century cathedral (p123).

Vieste Whitewashed buildings, intriguing lanes and the sea lapping round the edges (p113).

Martina Franca A wonderfully picturesque townscape of baroque and rococo buildings (p122).

Lecce Fanciful mansions and churches cut from glowing golden sandstone (p124).

Puglia

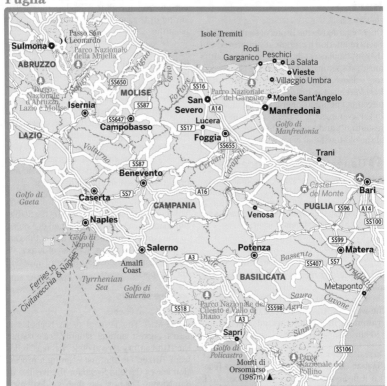

display. It's a jolly, crowded family affair, attended by many Russian visitors who come to view the relics.

🛏 Sleeping

Most hotel accommodation here tends to be bland and overpriced, aimed at business clientele: B&Bs are generally a better option.

Santa Maria del Buon Consiglio B&B $
(✍ 0388 1063436; www.santamariadelbuonconsiglio.com; Via Forno Santa Scolastica 1-3; s €35-70, d €60-100, tr €85-90; ❄ 🛜) A graciously hosted B&B in the heart of old Bari near the port. Rooms have rough-cast stone walls and four-poster beds with drapes.

B&B Casa Pimpolini B&B $
(✍ 080 521 99 38; www.casapimpolini.com; Via Calefati 249; s €45-60, d €70-80; ❄ @) This lovely B&B in the new town is within easy walking distance to shops, restaurants and Bari Vecchia. The rooms are warm and wel-

coming, and the homemade breakfast is a treat. Great value.

Villa Romanazzi Carducci HOTEL $$$
(✍ 080 542 74 00; www.villaromanazzi.com; Via Capruzzi 326; d €79; 🛜) The one hotel in Bari daring to show some flare, the Villa Romanazzi is housed in the pastel pink, 19th-century Villa Rachele. Rooms are a mixture of old and new, although the decor in the villa rooms is more characterful. Add to this an enormous fitness centre, pool and huge verdant park and this is probably Bari's best hotel.

🍴 Eating & Drinking

⭐ **Terranima** PUGLIAN $
(✍ 080 521 97 25; www.terranima.com; Via Putignani 215; meals €8-15; ⏱ 7-11pm Mon-Sat, lunch Sun) Peep through the lace curtains into the cool interior of this rustic trattoria where worn flagstone floors and period furnishings

Map labels: 100 km / 50 miles; Adriatic Sea; Polignano a Mare SS16; Grotte di Castellana; Castellana Grotte; Valle d'Itria; Alberobello; Cisternino SS379; Ostuni; Martina Franca; Riserva Naturale Regionale Orientale; Locorotondo; Brindisi; Oria SS7; Taranto; Tarantine Murge; Lecce; Reserva Marina Porto Cesareo; Galatina; Otranto; Golfo di Taranto; Gallipoli; Santa Maria di Leuca; Ionian Sea

breakfast, lunch and *aperitivi* (predinner drinks with snacks).

★**La Locanda di Federico** PUGLIAN **$$**
(☑080 522 77 05; www.lalocandadifederico.com; Piazza Mercantile 63-64; meals €30; ☺lunch & dinner) With domed ceilings, archways and medieval-style artwork on the walls, this restaurant oozes atmosphere. The menu is typical Puglian, the food delicious and the price reasonable. *Orecchiette con le cime di rape* ('little ears' pasta with turnip tops) is highly recommended.

Barcollo BAR
(☑080 521 38 89; Piazza Mercantile 69/70; cocktails €7; ☺8am-3am) Sit outside on the twinkling square sipping a cocktail and nibbling work-of-art hors d'oeuvres. Incongruously, you'll be gazing at the 'column of justice', to which debtors were once tied and lashed.

🛍 Shopping

Designer shops and the main Italian chains line Via Sparano da Bari, while delis and gourmet food shops are located throughout the city.

Il Salumaio FOOD
(☑080 521 93 45; www.ilsalumaio.it; Via Piccinni 168; ☺8.30am-2pm & 5.30-9.30pm Mon-Sat) Breathe in the delicious scents of fine regional produce at this venerable delicatessen.

Enoteca Vinarius de Pasquale WINE
(☑080 521 31 92; Via Marchese di Montrone 87; ☺8am-2pm & 4-8.30pm Mon-Sat) Stock up on Puglian wines such as Primitivo di Manduria at this gorgeous old shop, founded in 1911.

ℹ Information

From Piazza Aldo Moro, in front of the main train station, streets heading north will take you to Corso Vittorio Emanuele II, which separates the old and new parts of the city.

CTS (☑080 521 88 73; Via Garruba 65-67) Good for student travel and discount flights.
Hospital (☑080 559 11 11; Piazza Cesare)
Morfimare Travel Agency (☑080 578 98 26, booking office 080 578 98 11; www.morfimare.it; Corso de Tullio 36-40) Ferry bookings.
Police Station (☑080 529 11 11; Via Murat 4)
Post Office (Piazza Umberto I 33/8)
Tourist Office (☑080 990 93 41; www.viaggiareinpuglia.it; 1st fl, Piazza Moro 33a; ☺8.30am-1pm & 3-6pm Mon-Fri, 10am-1pm Sat) There is also an information kiosk

make you feel like you're dining in someone's front room. The menu features earthy offerings like *capocollo* (thin slices of lard), potatoes and *cardoncelli* mushrooms, and *sporcamusi* (lemon custard in filo pastry).

Paglionico Vini e Cucina OSTERIA **$**
(☑338 212 03 91; Strada Vallisa 23; meals €10; ☺lunch & dinner) Run by the same family for more than a century, this boisterous *osteria* (casual eatery) chalks up its daily specials of well-prepared and filling Puglian dishes. Grab a seat in the brick-flanked tunnel of a dining room and wait (and wait) to be served by the impressively indefatigable waiter.

Caffè Borghese CAFE **$**
(☑080 524 21 56; Corso Vittorio Emanuele II 22; dishes €6-10; ☺8am-2am Tue-Sun) You'll experience genuine hospitality and friendly service in this small cafe. Its understated charm and simple dishes will have you returning for

Bari

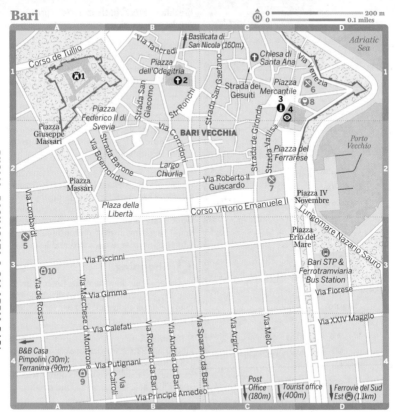

(⊙9am-7pm May-Sep) in front of the train station in Piazza Aldo Moro.

ⓘ Getting There & Away

AIR

Bari's Palese **airport** (www.aeroportidipuglia.it) is served by a host of international and budget airlines, including British Airways, Alitalia and Ryanair.

Pugliairbus (http://pugliairbus.aeroportidipuglia.it) connects the airports of Bari, Brindisi, Taranto and Foggia. It also has a service from Bari airport to Matera (€5, 1¼ hours, three daily), and to Vieste (€20, 3½ hours, four daily May to September).

BOAT

Ferries run from Bari to Albania, Croatia, Greece and Montenegro. All boat companies have offices at the ferry terminal, accessible on bus 20 from the main train station. Fares vary considerably among companies and it's easier to book with a travel agent such as Morfimare (p107).

The main companies and their routes are as follows:

Jadrolinija (www.jadrolinija.hr)

Montenegro Lines (☑382 3031 1164; www.montenegrolines.net) To Bar in Montenegro; Cephalonia, Corfu, Igoumenitsa in Greece; and Durrës in Albania.

Superfast (☑080 528 28 28; www.superfast.com) To Corfu, Igoumenitsa and Patras in Greece. Depart at 7pm or 8pm depending on the route.

Ventouris Ferries (☑for Albania 080 521 27 56, for Greece 080 521 76 99; www.ventouris.gr) Regular ferries to Corfu and Igoumenitsa (Greece) and daily ferries to Durrës (Albania).

BUS

Intercity buses leave from three main locations. From Via Capruzzi, south of the main train station, **SITA** (☑080 579 01 11; www.sitabus.it) covers local destinations. **Ferrovie Appulo-Lucane** (☑080 572 52 29; http://ferrovieappulolucane.it) buses serving Matera (€4.50, 1¼ hours, six daily) also depart from here, as do

Bari

Marozzi (☑ 080 556 24 46; www.marozzivt.
it) buses for Rome (from €33.50, eight hours,
eight daily – note that the overnight bus departs
from Piazza Moro) and other long-distance
destinations.

Buses operated by **Ferrovie del Sud-Est** (FSE;
☑ 080 546 21 11; www.fseonline.it) leave from
Largo Ciaia, south of Piazza Aldo Moro and service the following locations:

Alberobello (€3.90, 1¼ hours, hourly) Continues to **Locorotondo** (€5, 1 hour 35 minutes)
and **Martina Franca** (€5, 1 hour 50 minutes)

Grotte di Castellana (€2.60, one hour, five
daily)

Taranto (€7.50, 1¾ to 2¼ hours, frequent)

TRAIN

A web of train lines spreads out from Bari. Note
that there are fewer services on the weekend.

From the **main train station** (☑ 080 524 43
86) trains go to Puglia and beyond:

Brindisi (from €14, one hour, hourly)

Foggia (from €19, one hour, hourly)

Milan (from €77.50, about eight hours, every
four hours)

Rome (from €50, four hours, every four hours)

Ferrovie Appulo-Lucane serves two main
destinations:

Matera (€4.50, 1½ hours, 12 daily)

Potenza (€9.50, four hours, four daily)

FSE trains leave from the station in Via Oberdan –
cross under the train tracks south of Piazza Luigi
di Savoia and head east along Via Capruzzi for
about 500m. They serve the following towns:

Alberobello €4.50, 1½ hours, hourly

Martina Franca €5, two hours, hourly

Taranto from €7.50, 2½ hours, nine daily

ⓘ Getting Around

Central Bari is compact – a 15-minute walk will
take you from Piazza Aldo Moro to the old town.
For the ferry terminal take bus 20 from Piazza
Moro (€1.50).

Street parking is migraine-inducing. There's
a large parking area (€1) south of the main port
entrance; otherwise, there's a large multistorey
car park between the main train station and the
FSE station. Another car park is on Via Zuppetta
opposite Hotel Adria.

TO/FROM THE AIRPORT

For the airport, take the **Tempesta shuttle bus**
(€4, 30 minutes, hourly) from the main train
station, with pick-ups at Piazza Garibaldi and the
corner of Via Andrea da Bari and Via Calefati. Alternatively, normal city bus 16 covers the same
route and a trip is much cheaper (€1), though
marginally slower (40 minutes). A taxi trip from
the airport to town costs around €24.

Around Bari

The Terra di Bari, or 'land of Bari', surrounding the capital is rich in olive groves and
orchards, and the region has an impressive
architectural history with some magnificent
cathedrals, an extensive network of castles
along its coastline, charming seaside towns
like Trani and Polignano a Mare, and the
mysterious inland Castel del Monte.

Trani

POP 53,900

Known as the 'Pearl of Puglia', beautiful Trani
has a sophisticated feel, particularly in summer when well-heeled visitors pack the array
of marinaside bars. The marina is the place

ⓘ TRAVELLING EAST

Puglia is the main jumping-off point for
onward travel to Greece, Croatia and
Albania. The two main ports are Bari
and Brindisi, from where you catch
ferries to Vlore in Albania, Bar in Montenegro, and Cephalonia, Corfu, Igoumenitsa and Patras in Greece. Fares
from Bari to Greece are generally more
expensive than those from Brindisi.
Taxes are usually from €9 per person
and €12 per car. High season is generally the months of July and August, with
reduced services in low season. Tariffs
can be up to one-third cheaper in low
season.

Driving Tour
Italy's Authentic South

START VIESTE
END MARATEA
LENGTH 650KM TO 700KM; ONE WEEK

Consider a gentle start in lovely, laid-back **1 Vieste** (p113) with its white sandy beaches and medieval backstreets, but set aside half a day to hike or bike in the lush green forests of the **2 Parco Nazionale del Gargano** (p113). Follow the coastal road past dramatic cliffs, salt lakes and flat farming land to **3 Trani** (p109) with its impressive seafront cathedral and picturesque port. The next day, dip into pretty **4 Polignano a Mare** (p112), which has a dramatic location above the pounding surf, before heading to **5 Alberobello** (p119), home to a dense neighbourhood of extraordinary cone-shaped stone homes called *trulli;* consider an overnight *trulli* stay.

Stroll around one of the most picturesque *centro storicos* (historic centres) in southern Italy at **6 Locorotondo** (p121). Hit the road and cruise on to lively baroque **7 Lecce**

(p124), where you can easily chalk up a full day exploring the sights, the shops and the flamboyantly fronted *palazzi* (mansions) and churches, including the Basilica di Santa Croce.

Day five will be one to remember. Nothing can prepare you for Basilicata's **8 Matera** (p138) where the *sassi* (former cave dwellings) are a dramatic reminder of the town's poverty-stricken past. After days of pasta, *fave* beans and *cornetti* (Italian croissants), it's high time you laced up those hiking boots and checked out the trails and activities on offer in the spectacular **9 Parco Nazionale del Pollino** (p153). Finally, wind up the trip and soothe those aching muscles with a dip in the sea at postcard-pretty **10 Maratea** (p146) with its surrounding seaside resorts, medieval village and cosmopolitan harbour offset by a thickly forested and mountainous interior.

to promenade and watch the white yachts and fishing boats in the harbour, while the historic centre, with its medieval churches, glossy limestone streets and faded yet charming *palazzi* (mansions) is an enchanting area to explore. But it's the cathedral, pale against the deep-blue sea, that is the town's most arresting sight.

◉ Sights

Cathedral   CATHEDRAL

(Piazza del Duomo; ⊘ 9am-12.30pm & 3-6.30pm) The dramatic seafront cathedral is dedicated to St Nicholas the Pilgrim, famous for being foolish. The Greek Christian wandered through Puglia, crying '*Kyrie eleison*' (Greek for 'Lord, have mercy'). First thought to be a simpleton, he was revered after his death (aged 19) after several miracles attributed to him occurred.

Construction of the cathedral started in 1097 on the site of a Byzantine church and completed in the 13th century. The magnificent original bronze doors (now displayed inside) were cast by Barisano da Trani, an accomplished 12th-century artisan.

The interior of the cathedral reflects typical Norman simplicity and is lined by colonnades. Near the main altar are the remains of a 12th-century floor mosaic, stylistically similar to that in Otranto. Below the church is the crypt, a forest of ancient columns where the bones of St Nicholas are kept beneath the altar. You can also visit the **campanile** (bell tower; admission €3).

Castle   CASTLE

(☑0883 50 66 03; www.castelloditrani.beniculturali.it; Piazza Manfredi 16; admission €3; ⊘ 8.30am-7.30pm) Two hundred metres north of the cathedral is Trani's other major landmark, the vast, almost modernist Swabian castle built by Frederick II in 1233. Charles V later strengthened the fortifications; it was used as a prison from 1844 to 1974.

Ognissanti Church   CHURCH

(Via Ognissanti; ⊘ hours vary) Built by the Knights Templar in the 12th century, this church is where Norman knights swore allegiance to Bohemond I of Antioch, their leader, before setting off on the First Crusade.

Scolanova Church   CHURCH

(☑0883 48 17 99; Via Scolanova 23; ⊘ hours vary) This church was one of four former synagogues in the ancient Jewish quarter, all of which were converted to churches in the

14th century. Inside is a beautiful Byzantine painting of Madonna dei Martiri.

🛏 Sleeping

★Albergo Lucy   HOTEL **$**

(☑0883 48 10 22; www.albergolucy.com; Piazza Plebiscito 11; d/tr/q from €65/85/105; ❄ 🕙) Located in a restored 17th-century *palazzo* overlooking a leafy square and close to the shimmering port, this family-run place oozes charm. Bike hire and guided tours available. Great value: it doesn't serve breakfast, but there are plenty of cafes a short stroll away.

B&B Centro Storico Trani   B&B **$**

(☑0883 50 61 76; www.bbtrani.it; Via Leopardi 28; s €35-50, d €50-70, tr €70-80, q €85-100, quint €100-125) This simple, old-fashioned B&B inhabits an old backstreet monastery and is run by an elderly couple. It's basic, but the rooms are large and 'Mama' makes a mean *crostata* (jam tart).

Hotel Regia   HOTEL **$$**

(☑0883 58 44 44; www.hotelregia.it; Piazza del Duomo 2; s €120-130, d €130-150; ❄ 🕙) A lone building facing the cathedral, the understated grandeur of 18th-century Palazzo Filisio houses this charming hotel. Rooms are sober and stylish.

🍴 Eating

★Corteinfiore   SEAFOOD **$$**

(☑0883 50 84 02; www.corteinfiore.it; Via Ognissanti 18; meals €30; ⊘ Tue-Sun) Romantic, urbane, refined. The wooden decking, buttercup-yellow tablecloths and marquee-conservatory setting are refreshing. The wines are excellent and the cooking delicious. It also has modern and attractive rooms (from €100) decked out in pale colours.

La Darsena   SEAFOOD **$$**

(☑0883 48 73 33; Via Statuti Marittimi 98; meals €30; ⊘ Tue-Sun) Renowned for its seafood, swish La Darsena is housed in a waterfront *palazzo*. Outside tables overlook the port while inside photos of old Puglia cover the walls beneath a huge wrought-iron dragon chandelier.

❶ Information

From the train station, Via Cavour leads through Piazza della Repubblica to Piazza Plebiscito and the public gardens. Turn left for the harbour and cathedral.

Tourist Office (☑ 0883 58 88 30; www.trani-web.it; 1st fl, Palazzo Palmieri, Piazza Trieste 10; ☺ 8.30am-1.30pm Mon, Wed & Fri, 8:30am-1:30pm & 3.30-5.30pm Tue & Thu) Located 200m south of the cathedral.

❶ Getting There & Away

STP (☑ 0883 49 18 00; www.stpspa.it) has frequent bus services to Bari (€3.90, 45 minutes). Services depart from **Bar Stazione** (Piazza XX Settembre 23), which also has timetables and tickets.

Trani is on the main train line between Bari (€4.40, 40 to 60 minutes, frequent) and Foggia (€9.50, one hour, frequent).

Castel del Monte

You'll see **Castel del Monte** (☑ 0883 56 99 97; www.casteldelmonte.beniculturali.it; adult/reduced €5/2.50; ☺ 9am-6pm Oct-Feb, 10.15am-7.45pm Mar-Sep), an unearthly geometric shape on a hilltop, from miles away. Mysterious and perfectly octagonal, it's one of southern Italy's most talked-about landmarks and a Unesco World Heritage Site.

No one knows why Frederick II built it – there's no nearby town or strategic crossroads. It was not built to defend anything, as it has no moat or drawbridge, no arrow slits and no trapdoors for pouring boiling oil on invaders.

Some theories claim that, according to mid-13th-century beliefs in geometric symbolism, the octagon represented the union of the circle and square, of God-perfection (the infinite) and human-perfection (the finite). The castle was therefore nothing less than a celebration of the relationship between humanity and God.

The castle has eight octagonal towers. Its interconnecting rooms have decorative marble columns and fireplaces, and the doorways and windows are framed in corallite stone. Many of the towers have washing rooms with what are thought to be Europe's first flush loos – Frederick II, like the Arab world he admired, set great store by cleanliness.

It's difficult to reach here by public transport. By car, it's about 35km from Trani.

Polignano a Mare

Dip into this spectacularly positioned small town if you can. Located around 34km south of Bari on the S16 coastal road, Polignano a Mare is built on the edge of a craggy ravine pockmarked with caves. The town is thought to be one of the most important ancient settlements in Puglia and was later inhabited by successive invaders ranging from the Huns to the Normans.

◉ Sights & Activities

On Sunday the *logge* (balconies) are crowded with day trippers from Bari who come here to view the crashing waves, visit the caves and crowd out the *cornetterias* (shops specialising in Italian croissants) in the atmospheric *centro storico*. There are several baroque churches, an imposing Norman monastery and the medieval **Porta Grande**, which was the only access to the historic centre until the 18th century. You can still see the holes that activated the heavy drawbridge and the openings from where boiling oil was poured onto any unwelcome visitors to town.

Several operators organise boat trips to the grottoes, including **Dorino** (☑ 329 6465 904), costing around €20 per person.

⬛ Sleeping & Eating

B&B Santo Stefano   B&B $
(www.santostefano.info; Vico Santo Stefano 9-13; d €69-99; ⬤) Six attractive rooms located in an ancient tower in the old part of Polignano, complete with tufa walls, antique furniture and bright bathrooms.

Antiche Mura   PUGLIAN $$
(☑ 080 424 24 76; www.ristoranteantichemura.it; Via Roma 11; meals €20-35) This delightful little restaurant features a vaulted cavelike interior with lanterns and bells adorning the walls. Unsurprisingly, fish is a speciality, with sea bass, octopus and lobster on the menu.

❶ Getting There & Away

Although there is a twice-daily bus service from Bari, your own car is the best way to reach Polignano.

Promontorio del Gargano

The coast surrounding the promontory seems permanently bathed in a pink-hued, pearly light, providing a painterly contrast to the sea, which softens from intense to powder blue as the evening draws in. It's one of Italy's most beautiful areas, encompassing white limestone cliffs, fairy-tale grottoes, sparkling sea, ancient forests, rare orchids and tangled, fragrant maquis. Once connected to what is now Dalmatia (in Croatia), the 'spur' of the Italian boot has more in common with the land mass across the sea than with the rest of Italy. Creeping urbanisation was halted in 1991 by the creation of the **Parco Nazionale del Gargano**. Aside from its magnificent national park, the Gargano is home to pilgrimage sites and the lovely seaside towns of Vieste and Peschici.

Along the coast you'll spot strange cat's-cradle wood-and-rope arrangements, unique to the area. These are *trabucchi*, ancient fishing traps (possibly Phoenician in origin) from which fishing folk cast their nets, 'walk the plank' and haul in their catch.

Vieste

POP 13,900

Vieste is an attractive whitewashed town jutting off the Gargano's easternmost promontory into the Adriatic Sea. It's the Gargano capital and sits above the area's most spectacular beach, a gleaming wide strip backed by sheer white cliffs and overshadowed by the towering rock monolith, **Scoglio di Pizzomunno**. It's packed in summer and ghostly quiet in winter.

◉ Sights

Vieste is primarily a beach resort, though the steep alleys of the old town make for an atmospheric wander. The **castle** built by Frederick II is occupied by the military and closed to the public.

Chianca Amara   HISTORIC SITE
(Bitter Stone; Via Cimaglia) Vieste's most gruesome sight is this stone where thousands were beheaded when Turks sacked Vieste in the 16th century.

Museo Malacologico   MUSEUM
(☑0884 70 76 88; Via Pola 8; ⊙9.30am-12.30pm & 4-8pm, to 10pm Apr-Oct) **FREE** This impressive shell museum has four rooms of fossils and molluscs, some enormous and all beautifully patterned and coloured.

Cathedral   CATHEDRAL
(Via Duomo) Built by the Normans on the ruins of a Vesta temple, the cathedral is in Puglian-Romanesque style with a fanciful tower that resembles a cardinal's hat. It was rebuilt in 1800.

La Salata   HISTORIC SITE
(adult/child €4/free; ⊙5.30pm & 6.30pm Mon, Wed & Fri Jun; 5.30pm & 6.30pm Mon-Fri Jul & Aug; 4pm & 4.45pm Mon, Wed & Fri Sep; on request Oct-May) This palaeo-Christian graveyard dating from the 4th to 6th centuries AD is 9km out of town. Inside the cave, tier upon tier of narrow tombs are cut into the rock wall; others form shallow niches in the cave floor. Guided tours are essential. Book with **Agenzia Sinergie** (☑338 840 62 15; www.agenziasinergie.com), which can also arrange customised tours of the Gargano.

PUGLIA, BASILICATA & CALABRIA PROMONTORIO DEL GARGANO

CAMPING IN STYLE

If your experience of camping is the scout version of flapping tents, freezing nights and eating cold baked beans out of a tin, you will be delighted at the five-star quality of the typical campsites in this southern region of Italy. They are also prolific, particularly in and around the national parks. In the Gargano region alone there are an astonishing 100 campsites, compared to the relatively modest number of *pensioni* and hotels. If you don't fancy sleeping under canvas (or need a plug for those heated rollers) then consider a bungalow rental.

Virtually all these camping *villaggios* (villages) include well-furnished and equipped bungalows. This means you can really economise on eating out, as well as having the advantages of the campsite facilities, which often include tennis courts, a swimming pool, a children's playground and small supermarket. Bungalows (normally only available for week-long rentals) start from around €200/500 (low/high season) for a two-person bungalow or mobile-home rental. Traditional under-canvas campers can expect to pay a daily rate of approximately €15/25 (winter/summer), which includes camping for two people, tent and car parking space.

Check the following websites for more information and camping listings: www.camping.it; www.camping-italy.net and www.caravanandcampsites.eu.

🏃 Activities

Superb sandy beaches surround the town: in the south are Spiaggia del Castello, Cala San Felice and Cala Sanguinaria; due north, head for the area known as La Salata. Diving is popular around the promontory's rocky coastline, which is filled with marine grottoes.

From May to September fast boats zoom to the Isole Tremiti (p118).

Boat hire and tours can be arranged at the port.

Centro Ormeggi e Sub　　　　BOATING
(☑0884 70 79 83) Offers diving courses and rents out sailing boats and motorboats.

👉 Tours

Agenzia Sol　　　　　　GUIDED TOUR
(☑0884 70 15 58; www.solvieste.it; Via Trepiccioni 5; ⊙9.20am-1.15pm & 5-9pm winter, to midnight summer) Organises hiking, cycling and 4WD tours in the Foresta Umbra; boat tours around the Gargano; and gastronomic tours and small group tours into Puglia. It also sells bus tickets and ferry tickets for the Isole Tremiti.

Leonarda Motobarche　　　　BOAT TOUR
(☑0884 70 13 17; www.motobarcheleonarda.it; per person €13; ⊙Apr-Sep) Boat tours of marine caves.

🛏 Sleeping

★ B&B Rocca sul Mare　　　　B&B $
(☑0884 70 27 19; www.roccasulmare.it; Via Mafrolla 32; per person €25-70; 🐾) In a former convent in the old quarter, this popular and reasonably priced place has charm, with large, comfortable high-ceilinged rooms. There's a vast rooftop terrace with panoramic views and a suite with a steam bath. Simple but tasty meals (€18 for four courses) and bike hire are available; staff also arrange fishing trips and will cook up your catch in the evening. You can arrange to be collected from Bari airport.

Campeggio Capo Vieste　　CAMPGROUND $
(☑0884 70 63 26; www.capovieste.it; Km8; camping 2 people, car & tent €33, 1-bedroom bungalow €77-164; ⊙Mar-Oct; 🐾) This tree-shaded camping ground is right by a sandy beach at La Salata, around 8km from Vieste and accessible by bus. Activities include tennis and a sailing school.

Hotel Seggio　　　　　　HOTEL $$
(☑0884 70 81 23; www.hotelseggio.it; Via Veste 7; d €80-150; ⊙Apr-Oct; P❄@🛜🐾) A butter-coloured *palazzo* in the town's historic centre with steps that spiral down to a pool and sunbathing terrace with a backdrop of the sea. The rooms are modern and plain but it's family run.

🍴 Eating

★ Osteria Al Duomo　　　　OSTERIA $
(☑0884 70 82 43; www.osterialduomo.it; Via Alessandro III 23; meals €25; ⊙lunch & dinner Mar-Nov) Tucked away in a picturesque narrow alley in the heart of the old town, this welcoming *osteria* has a cosy cave interior and outdoor seating under a shady arbour. Homemade pastas with seafood sauces feature prominently.

★ Taverna Al Cantinone　　TRADITIONAL ITALIAN $$
(☑0884 70 77 53; Via Mafrolla 26; meals €25-30; ⊙lunch & dinner Wed-Mon) Run by a charming Italian–Spanish couple who have a passion for cooking; the food is exceptional and exquisitely presented. The menu changes with the seasons.

Enoteca Vesta　　TRADITIONAL ITALIAN $$
(☑0884 70 64 11; www.enotecavesta.it; Via Duomo 14; meals €30-35) You can savour a magnificent selection of Puglian wines to accompany innovative seafood dishes in this restaurant, which is housed in a cool vaulted cave.

ℹ Information

Post Office (Via Vittorio Veneto)
Tourist Office (☑0884 70 88 06; Piazza Kennedy; ⊙8am-8pm Jun-Sep, 8am-1.30pm Mon-Fri & 4-7pm Tue-Thu Oct-May)

ℹ Getting There & Around

BOAT

Vieste's port is to the north of the town, about a five-minute walk from the tourist office. In summer several companies, including **Navigazione Libera del Golfo** (☑0884 70 74 89; www.navlib.it), head to the Isole Tremiti. Tickets can be bought portside and there are several daily boats (€14.50 to €20, 1½ hours).

Several companies also offer tours of the caves that pock the Gargano coast – a three-hour tour costs around €13.

BUS

From Piazzale Manzoni, where intercity buses terminate, a 10-minute walk east along Viale

LUCERA

Lovely Lucera has one of Puglia's most impressive castles and a handsome old town centre with mellow sand-coloured brick- and stonework, and chic shops lining wide, shiny stone streets. Founded by the Romans in the 4th century BC, it was abandoned by the 13th century. Following excommunication by Pope Gregory IX, Frederick II decided to bolster his support base in Puglia by importing 20,000 Sicilian Arabs, simultaneously diminishing the headache Arab bandits were causing him in Sicily. It was an extraordinary move by the Christian monarch, even more so because Frederick allowed Lucera's new Muslim inhabitants the freedom to build mosques and practise their religion a mere 290km from Rome. History, however, was less kind; when the town was taken by the rabidly Christian Angevins in 1269, every Muslim who failed to convert was slaughtered.

Frederick II's enormous castle (⊘9am-2pm year-round & 3-7pm Apr-Sep) FREE, shows just what a big fish Lucera once was in the Puglian pond. Built in 1233, it's 14km northwest of the town on a rocky hillock surrounded by a perfect 1km pentagonal wall, guarded by 24 towers.

On the site of Lucera's Great Mosque, Puglia's only Gothic cathedral (⊘8am-noon & 4-7pm May-Sep, 8am-noon & 5-8pm Oct-Apr) was built in 1301 by Charles II of Anjou. The altar was once the castle banqueting table.

Dominated by a huge rose window, the contemporaneous Gothic Chiesa di San Francesco (⊘8am-noon & 4-7pm) incorporates recycled materials from Lucera's 1st-century-BC Roman amphitheatre (⊘9am-2pm & 3.15-6.45pm Tue-Sun Apr-Sep) FREE. The amphitheatre was built for gladiatorial combat and accommodated up to 18,000 people.

The tourist office (☑0881 52 27 62; ⊘9am-2pm & 3-8pm Tue-Sun Apr-Sep, 9am-2pm Oct-Mar) is near the cathedral.

Ferrovie del Gargano trains run to Lucera from Foggia (€1.50, 20 minutes, three daily) which is on the east coast train line between Bari and Pescara.

PUGLIA, BASILICATA & CALABRIA PROMONTORIO DEL GARGANO

XXIV Maggio, which becomes Corso Fazzini, brings you into the old town and the Marina Piccola's attractive promenade. In summer buses terminate at Via Verdi.

SITA (☑0881 35 20 11; www.sitabus.it) buses run between Vieste and Foggia (€6.50, 2¾ hours, four daily) via Manfredonia. There are also services to Monte Sant'Angelo (€5) via Manfredonia but **Ferrovie del Gargano** (☑0881 58 72 11; www.ferroviedelgargano.com) buses have a direct daily service to Monte Sant'Angelo (€6, two hours) and frequent services to Peschici (€1.70, 35 minutes).

From May to September, **Pugliairbus** (☑080 580 03 58; pugliairbus.aeroportidipuglia.it) runs a service to the Gargano, including Vieste, from Bari airport (€20, 3½ hours, four daily).

Monte Sant'Angelo

POP 13,300 / ELEV 796M

One of Europe's most important pilgrimage sites, this isolated mountaintop has an extraordinary atmosphere. Pilgrims have been coming here for centuries – and so have the hustlers, pushing everything from religious kitsch to parking spaces.

The object of devotion is the Santuario di San Michele. Here, in AD 490, St Michael the Archangel is said to have appeared in a grotto to the bishop of Siponto. He left behind his scarlet cloak and instructions not to consecrate the site as he had already done so.

During the Middle Ages, the sanctuary marked the end of the Route of the Angel, which began in Mont St-Michel (in Normandy) and passed through Rome. In 999 the Holy Roman Emperor Otto III made a pilgrimage to the sanctuary to pray that prophecies about the end of the world in the year 1000 would not be fulfilled. His prayers were answered, the world staggered on and the sanctuary's fame grew.

◉ Sights

The town's serpentine alleys and jumbled houses are perfect for a little aimless ambling. Look out for the different shaped *cappelletti* (chimney stacks) on top of the neat whitewashed houses.

PADRE PIO: SAINT OF THE GARGANO

Pilgrims flock to San Giovanni Rotondo, home to Padre Pio, a humble and pious Capuchin priest 'blessed' with the stigmata and a legendary ability to heal the sick. Pio (1887–1968) was canonised in 2002 and immortalised in the vast numbers of prefabricated statues to be found throughout the Gargano. There's even a statue of Pio beneath the waters off the Isole Tremiti.

The ailing Capuchin priest arrived in San Giovanni Rotondo, then a tiny isolated medieval village, in 1916. As Pio's fame grew, the town too underwent a miraculous transformation. These days, it's a mass of functional hotels and restaurants catering to eight million pilgrims a year. It's all overlooked by the palatial Home for the Relief of Suffering, one of Italy's premier hospitals (established by Pio in 1947).

The Convent of the Minor Capuchin Friars (☑0882 41 71; www.conventosantuariopadrepio.it; Piazza Santa Maria delle Grazie) includes Padre Pio's cell (⊘7am-7pm summer, 7.30am-6.30pm winter), a simple room containing mementoes such as his blood-stained socks. The old church, where he used to say Mass, dates from the 16th century. The spectacular new church, designed by Genovese Renzo Piano (who also designed Paris' Pompidou Centre), resembles a huge futuristic seashell, with an interior of bony vaulting. Padre Pio's body now lies in the geometric perfection of the semicircular crypt.

SITA buses run daily to San Giovanni Rotondo from Monte Sant'Angelo (€2, 50 minutes) and Vieste (€6, 2½ hours).

Santuario di San Michele   GROTTO
(Via Reale Basilica; ⊘7.30am-7.30pm Jul-Sep, 7.30am-12.30pm & 2.30-7pm Apr-Jun & Oct, 7.30am-12:30pm & 2-5pm Nov-Mar) FREE Look for the 17th-century pilgrims' graffiti as you descend the steps. St Michael is said to have left a footprint in stone inside the grotto, so it became customary for pilgrims to carve outlines of their feet and hands. Etched Byzantine bronze and silver doors, cast in Constantinople in 1076, open into the grotto itself. Inside, a 16th-century statue of the archangel covers the site of St Michael's footprint.

Tomba di Rotari   HISTORIC SITE
(admission €1; ⊘10am-1pm & 3-7pm Apr-Oct) A short flight of stairs opposite the Santuario di San Michele leads not to a tomb but to a 12th-century baptistry with a deep sunken basin for total immersion. You enter the baptistry through the facade of the Chiesa di San Pietro with its intricate rose window squirming with serpents – all that remains of the church, destroyed in a 19th-century earthquake. The Romanesque portal of the adjacent 11th-century Chiesa di Santa Maria Maggiore has some fine bas-reliefs.

Castle   HISTORIC SITE
(Largo Roberto Giuscardo 2; admission €2; ⊘9.30am-1pm & 2.30-7pm) At the highest point is this rugged bijou, a Norman castle

with Swabian and Aragonese additions as well as panoramic views.

🛏 Sleeping & Eating

Hotel Michael   HOTEL $
(☑0884 56 55 19; www.hotelmichael.com; Via Basilica 86; s €50-60, d €70-80; 🕸) A small hotel with shuttered windows, located on the main street, across from the Santuario di San Michele, this traditional place has spacious rooms with extremely pink bedspreads. Ask for a room with a view.

Casa li Jalantuúmene   TRATTORIA $$
(☑0884 56 54 84; www.li-jalantuumene.it; Piazza de Galganis 5; meals €40; ⊘lunch Wed-Mon Feb-Dec; 🕸) This renowned restaurant has an entertaining and eccentric chef, Gegè Mangano, and serves excellent fare. It's intimate, there's a select wine list and, in summer, tables spill into the piazza. It has four suites (€130), decorated in traditional Puglian style.

❶ Getting There & Away

Ferrovie del Gargano has a direct service from Vieste (€5.90, two hours, five daily). Buy your tickets from Bar Esperia next to Santuario di San Michele.

SITA (☑0881 35 20 11; www.sitabus.it) buses run from Foggia (€4.60, 1¾ hours, four daily) and Vieste via Manfredonia.

Peschici

POP 4400

Perched above a turquoise sea and tempting beach, Peschici clings to the hilly, wooded coastline. It's a pretty resort area with a tight-knit old walled town of Arabesque whitewashed houses. The small town gets crammed in summer, so book in advance. Boats zip across to the Isole Tremiti (p118) in high season.

Sleeping & Eating

Locanda al Castello B&B $
(☑0884 96 40 38; www.peschicialcastello.it; Via Castello 29; s €35-70, d €70-120; P❋☎) Staying here is like entering a large, welcoming family home. It's by the cliffs with fantastic views. Enjoy hearty home cooking in the restaurant (meals €18).

Baia San Nicola CAMPGROUND $
(☑0884 96 42 31; www.baiasannicola.it; camping €22-37, 2-person bungalow per week €320-620; ☺mid-May–mid-Oct) The best campground in the area, 2km south of Peschici towards Vieste, Baia San Nicola is on a pine-shaded beach, offering camping, bungalows, apartments and myriad amenities.

★Il Trabucco da Mimi SEAFOOD $$
(☑0884 96 25 56; Localita Punta San Nicola; meals €30-40; ☺lunch & dinner Easter-Oct) For the ultimate in fresh fish you can't beat eating in a *trabucco* (the traditional wooden fishing platforms lining the coast). Watch the process in operation – you can even help out – and dine on the catch. The decor is simple and rustic and you'll pay for the experience – but it's worth it.

Porto di Basso SEAFOOD $$
(☑0884 91 53 64; www.portodibasso.it; Via Colombo 38; meals €30-40; ☺Fri-Wed) Superb views of the ocean drop away from the floor-length windows beside the intimate alcove tables in this elegant clifftop restaurant. The menu of fresh local seafood changes daily. Close to the restaurant, two extremely stylish suites with fantastic sea views offer *albergo diffuso*–style accommodation (€110 to €120).

Information

Tourist Office (☑0884 91 53 62; Via Magenta 3; ☺8am-2pm & 5-9pm Mon-Sat summer, 8am-2pm Mon-Fri & 9am-noon & 4-7pm Sat in winter)

Getting There & Away

The bus terminal is beside the sportsground, uphill from the main street, Corso Garibaldi.

Ferrovie del Gargano (p115) buses run frequent daily services between Peschici and Vieste (€1.70, 35 minutes).

From April to September, ferry companies including **MS&G Società di Navigazione** (☑0884 96 27 32; www.msgnavigazioni. it; Corso Umberto I 20) and **Navigare SRL** (☑0884 96 42 34; Corso Garibaldi 30) serve the Isole Tremiti (adult €25 to €30, child €16 to €21, one to 1½ hours).

Foresta Umbra

The 'Forest of Shadows' is the Gargano's enchanted interior – thickets of tall, epic trees interspersed with picnic spots bathed in dappled light. It's the last remnant of Puglia's ancient forests: Aleppo pines, oaks, yews and beech trees shade the mountainous terrain. More than 65 different types of orchid have been discovered here; the wildlife includes roe deer, wild boar, foxes, badgers and the increasingly rare wild cat.

Sights & Activities

Walkers and mountain bikers will find plenty of well-marked trails within the forest's 5790 sq km.

The small visitor centre in the middle of the forest houses a **museum and nature centre** (www.ecogargano.it; admission €1.20; ☺9am-7pm mid-Apr–mid-Oct) with fossils, photographs, and stuffed animals and birds. Half-day guided hikes (per person €10), bike hire (per hour/day €5/25), and walking maps (€2.50) are available.

ALBERGO DIFFUSO

Albergo diffuso doesn't necessarily have a direct translation in English, but the term refers to the Italian hospitality concept that emerged in the 1980s. Designed as a means to revive historic centres in small towns and villages, the concept allows neighbouring apartments and houses to be rented to guests through a centralised hotel-style reception. The aim is to respect the integrity of ancient buildings, so that guest accommodation blends harmoniously into the surrounding streetscape.

Specialist tour operators organise hiking, biking and 4WD excursions in the park. These include Agenzia Sol (p114) and Explora Gargano (☑0884 70 22 37; www.exploragargano.it; Via Santa Maria di Merino 62; hiking & mountain biking half-day from €70, quad tours & jeep safari per day from €50) in Vieste and Soc Cooperative Ecogargano (☑0884 56 54 44; www.ecogargano.it) in Monte Sant'Angelo.

🛏 Sleeping

La Chiusa delle More
B&B $$$

(☑330 54 37 66; www.lachiusadellemore.it; B&B per person €200-240; ☺May-Sep; P❄🛜🏊) La Chiusa delle More offers an escape from the cramped coast. An attractive stone-built *agriturismo* (farm stay), only 1.5km from Peschici, it's set in a huge olive grove, and you can dine on home-grown produce, borrow mountain bikes and enjoy panoramic views from your poolside lounger. Note there is a three-night minimum stay.

Isole Tremiti

POP 500

This beautiful archipelago of three islands, 36km offshore, is a picturesque sight of raggedy cliffs, sandy coves and thick pine woods, surrounded by the glittering dark-blue sea.

Unfortunately the islands are no secret, and in July and August some 100,000 holidaymakers descend on the archipelago. At this time it's noisy, loud and hot. If you want to savour the islands' tranquillity, visit during the shoulder season. In the low season most tourist facilities close down and the few permanent residents resume their quiet and isolated lives.

The islands' main facilities are on San Domino, the largest and lushest island, which was formerly used to grow crops. It's ringed by alternating sandy beaches and limestone cliffs, while the inland is covered in thick maquis flecked with rosemary and foxglove. The centre harbours a nondescript small town with several hotels.

Easily defended, small San Nicola island is the traditional administrative centre – a castlelike cluster of medieval buildings rises up from the rocks. The third island, Capraia, is uninhabited.

Most boats arrive at San Domino. Small boats regularly make the brief crossing to San Nicola (€6 return) in high season –

from October to March a single boat makes the trip after meeting the boat from the mainland.

◉ Sights & Activities

San Domino
ISLAND

Head to San Domino for walks, grottoes and coves. It has a pristine, marvellous coastline and the islands' only sandy beach, Cala delle Arene. Alongside the beach is the small cove Grotta dell'Arene, with calm, clear waters for swimming.

You can also take a boat trip (€12 to €15 from the port) around the island to explore the grottoes: the largest, Grotta del Bue Marino, is 70m long. A tour around all three islands costs €15 to €17. Diving in the translucent sea is another option with Tremiti Diving Center (☑337 64 89 17; www.tremitidivingcenter.com; Via Federico 2). There's an undemanding, but enchanting, walking track around the island, starting at the far end of the village.

San Nicola
ISLAND

Medieval buildings thrust out of San Nicola's rocky shores, the same pale-sand colour as the barren cliffs. In 1010, Benedictine monks founded the Abbazia e Chiesa di Santa Maria here; for the next 700 years the islands were ruled by a series of abbots who accumulated great wealth.

Although the church retains a weather-worn Renaissance portal and a fine 11th-century floor mosaic, its other treasures have been stolen or destroyed throughout its troubled history. The only exceptions are a painted wooden Byzantine crucifix brought to the island in AD 747 and a black Madonna, probably transported here from Constantinople in the Middle Ages.

Capraia
ISLAND

The third of the Isole Tremiti, Capraia, (named after the wild caper plant) is uninhabited. Birdlife is plentiful, with impressive flocks of seagulls. There's no organised transport, but trips can be negotiated with local fishing folk.

🛏 Sleeping & Eating

In summer you'll need to book well ahead and many hotels insist on full board. Camping is forbidden.

La Casa di Gino
B&B $$

(☑0882 46 34 10; www.hotel-gabbiano.com; Piazza Belvedere; r €180; ❄) A tranquil accommodation choice on San Nicola, away from the frenzy of San Domino, this B&B run by the Hotel Gabbiano has stylish white-on-white rooms.

Hotel Gabbiano   HOTEL **$$**
(☑ 0882 46 34 10; www.hotel-gabbiano.com; Piazza Belvedere; s incl breakfast €45-105, d incl breakfast €120-128; ❉ ☎) An established icon on the island and run for more than 30 years by a Neapolitan family, this smart hotel has pastel-coloured rooms with balconies overlooking San Nicola and the sea. It also has a seafood restaurant.

Architiello   SEAFOOD **$$**
(☑ 0882 46 30 54; meals €25; ⊗ Apr-Oct) A class act with a seaview terrace, this specialises in – what else? – fresh fish.

ⓘ Getting There & Away

Boats for the Isole Tremiti depart from several points on the Italian mainland: Manfredonia, Vieste and Peschici in summer, and Termoli in nearby Molise year-round.

Valle d'Itria

Between the Ionian and Adriatic coasts rises the great limestone plateau of the Murgia (473m). It has a strange karst geology: the landscape is riddled with holes and ravines through which small streams and rivers gurgle, creating what is, in effect, a giant sponge. At the heart of the Murgia lies the idyllic Valle d'Itria. Here you will begin to spot curious circular stone-built houses dotting the countryside, their roofs tapering up to a stubby and endearing point. These are *trulli*, Puglia's unique rural architecture. It's unclear why the architecture developed in this way; one popular story says that it was so the dry-stone constructions could be quickly dismantled, to avoid payment of building taxes.

The rolling green valley is criss-crossed by dry-stone walls, vineyards, almond and olive groves, and winding country lanes. This is the part of Puglia most visited by foreign tourists and is the best served for hotels and luxury *masserias* (working farms) or manor farms. Around here are also many of Puglia's self-catering villas; to find them, try websites such as www.tuscanynow.com, www.ownersdirect.co.uk, www.holidayhomesinitaly.co.uk and www.trulliland.com.

Grotte di Castellana

Don't miss these spectacular limestone caves (☑ 080 499 82 11/21; www.grottedicastellana.it; Piazzale Anelli; admission €15; ⊗ 9am-6pm), 40km southeast of Bari and Italy's longest natural subterranean network. The interlinked galleries, first discovered in 1938, contain an incredible range of underground landscapes, with extraordinary stalactite and stalagmite formations – look out for the jellyfish, the bacon and the stocking. The highlight is the Grotta Bianca (White Grotto), an eerie white alabaster cavern hung with stiletto-thin stalactites.

There are two tours in English: a 1km, 50-minute tour that doesn't include the Grotta Bianca (€10, on the half-hour) and a 3km, two-hour tour (€15, on the hour) that does include it. The temperature inside the cave averages 18°C so take a light jacket. Visit, too, the Museo Speleologico Franco Anelli (☑ 080 499 82 30; ⊗ 9.30am-1pm & 3.30-6.30pm mid-Mar–Oct, 10am-1pm Nov–mid-Mar) FREE or the Osservatorio Astronomico Sirio (☑ 080 499 82 13; admission €4), with its telescope and solar filters allowing for maximum solar-system visibility. Guided visits only with advance notification.

The grotto can be reached by rail from Bari on the FSE Bari–Taranto train line but not all trains stop at Grotte di Castellana. However, all services stop at Castellana Grotte (€2.90, 50 minutes, roughly hourly), 2km before the grotto, from where you can catch a local bus (€1.10) to the caves.

Alberobello

POP 11,000
Unesco World Heritage Site Alberobello resembles an urban sprawl – for gnomes. The Zona dei Trulli on the western hill of town is a dense mass of 1500 beehive-shaped houses, white-tipped as if dipped by snow. These dry-stone buildings are made from local limestone; none are older than the 14th century. Inhabitants do not wear pointy hats, but they do sell anything a visitor might want, from miniature *trulli* to woollen shawls.

The town is named after the primitive oak forest Arboris Belli (beautiful trees) that once covered this area. It's an amazing area, but also something of a tourist trap – from May to October busloads of tourists pile into

MASSERIAS: LUXURY ON THE FARM

Masserias are unique to southern Italy. Modelled on the classical Roman villa, these fortified farmhouses – equipped with oil mills, cellars, chapels, storehouses and accommodation for workers and livestock – were built to function as self-sufficient communities. These days, they still produce the bulk of Italy's olive oil, but many have been converted into luxurious hotels, *agriturismi* (farm stay accommodation), holiday apartments or restaurants. Staying in a *masseria* is a unique experience, especially when you can dine on home-grown produce.

The following *masserias* are recommended:

★ Il Frantoio (☎0831 33 02 76; www.trecolline.it; SS16, Km 874; d €140-260, apt €320-350; P @) Stay in a charming, whitewashed farmhouse, where the owners still live and work, producing high-quality organic olive oil. (Or else book yourself in for one of the marathon eight-course lunches; the food is superb.) Armando takes guests for a tour of the farm each evening in his 1949 Fiat. Il Frantoio lies 5km outside Ostuni along the SS16 in the direction of Fasano. You'll see the sign on your left-hand side when you reach the Km 874 sign.

Masseria Torre Coccaro (☎080 482 93 10; www.masseriatorrecoccaro.com; Contrada Coccaro 8; d €284-1365; ❄ @ ☎ ≋) For pure luxury, stay in this superchic yet countrified *masseria*. There's a glorious spa set in a cave, a beach-style swimming pool, cooking courses on offer and a restaurant (meals €90) dishing up home-grown produce.

Masseria Maizza (www.masseriatorremaizza.com; d €290-548, ste €422-1522; ❄ @ ☎ ≋) This farmhouse is located next door to Masseria Torre Coccaro and run by the same people, so you know luxury is assured. The two *masserias* share a balmy beach club (about 4km away) and a neighbouring golf course.

Borgo San Marco (☎080 439 57 57; www.borgosanmarco.it; Contrada Sant'Angelo 33; s €130-140, d €160-230; P ❄ ☎ ≋) Once a *borgo* (medieval town), this *masseria* has 16 rooms, a spa in the orchard and is traditional with a bohemian edge. Nearby are some frescoed rock churches. It's 8km from Ostuni; to get here take the SS379 in the direction of Bari, exiting at the sign that says SC San Marco–Zona Industriale Sud Fasano, then follow the signs. Note that there's a one-week minimum stay in August.

trullo homes, drink in *trullo* bars and shop in *trullo* shops.

If you park in Lago Martellotta, follow the steps up to the Piazza del Popolo where Belvedere Trulli offers fabulous views over the whole higgledy-piggledy picture.

◉ Sights

Rione Monti
HISTORIC QUARTER

Within the old town quarter of Rione Monti more than 1000 trulli cascade down the hillside, most of which are now souvenir shops. The area is surprisingly quiet and atmospheric in the late evening, once the gaudy stalls have been stashed away.

Rione Aia Piccola
HISTORIC QUARTER

To the east, on the other side of Via Indipendenza, is Rione Aia Piccola. This neighbourhood is much less commercialised, with 400 *trulli*, many still used as family dwellings. You can climb up for a rooftop view at many shops, although most do have a strategically located basket for a donation.

Trullo Sovrano
HISTORIC QUARTER

(☎080 432 60 30; Piazza Sacramento; admission €1.50; ⊙10am-6pm) In the modern part of town, the 18th-century Trullo Sovrano is the only two-floor *trullo*, built by a wealthy priest's family. It's a small museum giving something of the atmosphere of *trullo* life, with sweet, rounded rooms that include a re-created bakery, bedroom and kitchen. The souvenir shop here has a wealth of literature on the town and surrounding area, plus Alberobello recipe books.

⌖ Sleeping

It's a unique experience to stay in your own *trullo*, though some people might find Alberobello too touristy to use as a base.

Trullidea TRULLI $$
(📱080 432 38 60; www.trullidea.it; Via Monte San Gabriele 1; 2-person trullo €99-150; 🐕) A series of 15 renovated *trulli* in Alberobello's Trulli Zone, these are quaint, cosy and atmospheric. They're available on a self-catering, B&B, or half- or full-board basis.

Fascino Antico TRULLI $$
(📱080 432 50 89; www.fascinoantico.eu; 1 bed €49-89, 2 bed €59-119, 3 bed €69-139, 4 bed €89-149; 🅿) This lovely *trulli* complex sits just half a kilometre from Alberobello on the SS172 to Locorotondo. Set in a pretty landscaped garden, the rooms are light and comfortable with terracotta tiled floors and kitchenettes. A number of rooms also have bunks and cater for families.

Camping dei Trulli CAMPGROUND $
(📱080 432 36 99; www.campingdeitrulli.com; Via Castellana Grotte; camping 2 people, car & tent €26.50, bungalows per person €25-40, trulli €30-60; 🅿@🅿) This campsite is 1.5km out of town and has some nice tent sites. It has a restaurant, a market, two swimming pools, tennis courts and bicycle hire and you can also rent *trulli* off the grounds.

✗ Eating

Trattoria Amatulli TRATTORIA $
(📱080 432 29 79; Via Garibaldi 13; meals €16; ⊙Tue-Sun) Excellent trattoria with a cheerily cluttered interior papered with photos of smiley diners, plus superb down-to-earth dishes like *orecchiette scure con cacioricotta pomodoro e rucola* ('little ears' pasta with cheese, tomato and rucola). Wash it down with the surprisingly drinkable house wine, costing the lordly sum of €4 a litre.

La Cantina TRADITIONAL ITALIAN $
(📱080 432 34 73; www.ilristorantelacantina.it; cnr Corso Vittorio Emanuele & Vico Lippolis; meals €25; ⊙Wed-Mon) Although tourists have discovered this place, located to the side of a little Doric temple, it has maintained the high standards established back in 1958. There are just seven tables (book ahead), and it serves delicious meals made with fresh seasonal produce.

Il Poeta Contadino TRADITIONAL ITALIAN $$$
(📱080 432 19 17; www.ilpoetacontadino.it; Via Indipendenza 21; meals €65; ⊙Tue-Sun Feb-Dec) Located just outside the main throng, the dining room here has a medieval banqueting feel with its sumptuous decor and chandeliers. Dine on a poetic menu that includes the signature dish, fava bean purée with *cavatelli* (rod-shaped pasta) and seafood.

❶ Information

Tourist Office (📱080 432 51 71; Via Garibaldi; ⊙8am-1pm Mon, Wed & Fri, plus 3-6pm Tue & Thu) Just off the main square. In the Zona dei Trulli there is another tourist information office (📱080 432 28 22; www.prolocoalberobello.it; Monte Nero 1; ⊙9am-7.30pm).

❶ Getting There & Away

Alberobello is easily accessible from Bari (€4.50, 1½ hours, hourly) on the FSE Bari–Taranto train line. From the station, walk straight ahead along Via Mazzini, which becomes Via Garibaldi, to reach Piazza del Popolo.

Locorotondo

POP 14,200

Locorotondo has an extraordinarily beautiful and whisper-quiet pedestrianised *centro storico*, where everything is shimmering white aside from the blood-red geraniums that tumble from the window boxes. Situated on a hilltop on the Murge Plateau, it's a *borghi più belli d'Italia* (www.borghitalia.it) – that is, it's rated as one of the most beautiful towns in Italy. The streets are paved with smooth ivory-coloured stones, with the church of Santa Maria della Graecia as their sunbaked centrepiece.

From Villa Comunale, a public garden, you can enjoy panoramic views of the surrounding valley. You enter the historic quarter directly across from here.

Not only is this deepest *trulli* country, but it's also the liquid heart of the Puglian wine region. Sample some of the local spumante at Cantina del Locorotondo (📱080 431 16 44; www.locorotondodoc.com; Via Madonna della Catena 99; ⊙9am-1pm & 3-7pm).

⬛ Sleeping

⭐**Truddhi** TRULLI $
(📱080 443 13 26; www.trulliresidence.it; Contrada da Trito 292; d €65-80, apt €100-150, per week from €450-741; 🅿) This charming cluster of 10 self-catering *trulli* in the hamlet of Trito near Locorotondo is surrounded by olive groves and vineyards. It's a tranquil place and you can take cooking courses (per day €80) with Mino, a lecturer in gastronomy.

⭐Sotto le Cummerse APARTMENT $$
(📱080 431 32 98; www.sottolecummerse.it; Via Vittorio Veneto 138; apt incl breakfast €82-298; 🅿)

As this is an *albergo diffuso* (difused hotel), you can stay in tastefully furnished apartments scattered throughout the *centro storico*. The apartments are traditional buildings that have been beautifully restored and furnished. Excellent value and a great base for exploring the region.

✕ Eating

★ Quanto Basta
PIZZERIA $

(☑ 080 431 28 55; Via Morelli 12; pizzas €6-7; ◷ dinner Tue-Sun) With its wooden tables, soft lighting and stone floors this old-town pizzeria is cosy and welcoming. The pizzas are delicious and the beer list extensive.

La Taverna del Duca
TRATTORIA $$

(☑ 080 431 30 07; Via Papadotero 3; meals €35; ◷ lunch & dinner, closed Sun night winter) In a narrow side street off Piazza Vittorio Emanuele, this well-regarded trattoria serves local classics such as *orecchiette* with various vegetable sidekicks.

ℹ Information

Tourist Office (☑ 080 431 30 99; www.prolo-colocorotondo.it; Piazza Vittorio Emanuele 27; ◷ 10am-1pm & 3-6pm Mon-Fri, 10am-1pm Sat) Offers free internet access.

ℹ Getting There & Away

Locorotondo is easily accessible via frequent trains from Bari (€5.20, 1½ to two hours) on the FSE Bari–Taranto train line.

Cisternino

POP 12,000

An appealing, whitewashed hilltop town, slow-paced Cisternino has a charming *centro storico* beyond its bland modern outskirts; with its kasbahlike knot of streets, it has been designated as one of the country's *borghi più belli* (most beautiful towns). Beside its 13th-century Chiesa Matrice and Torre Civica there's a pretty communal garden with rural views. If you take Via Basilioni next to the tower you can amble along an elegant route right to the central piazza, Vittorio Emanuele.

Just outside the historic centre, the tourist office (☑ 080 444 66 61; www.pro-lococisternino.it; Via San Quirico 18; ◷ 10.15am-12.15pm & 4.30-7.30pm Mon-Sat) is not always open but can advise on B&Bs in the historic centre.

Cisternino has a grand tradition of *fornello pronto* (ready-to-go roast or grilled meat) and in numerous butchers' shops and trattorias you can select a cut of meat, which is then promptly cooked on the spot. Try it under the whitewashed arches at no-frills but hugely popular Rosticceria L'Antico Borgo (☑ 080 444 64 00; www.rosticceria-lanticoborgo.it; Via Tarantini 9; roast meat €18-28).

Cisternino is accessible by regular trains from Bari (€6, 45 minutes).

Martina Franca

POP 49,800

The old quarter of this town is a picturesque scene of winding alleys, blinding white houses and blood-red geraniums. There are graceful baroque and rococo buildings here too, plus airy piazzas and curlicue ironwork balconies that almost touch above the narrow streets. This town is the highest in the Murgia, and was founded in the 10th century by refugees fleeing the Arab invasion of Taranto. It only started to flourish in the 14th century when Philip of Anjou granted tax exemptions (*franchigie,* hence Franca); the town became so wealthy that a castle and defensive walls complete with 24 solid bastions were built.

◉ Sights & Activities

The beauty of Martina Franca encourages wandering around the *centro storico*'s narrow lanes and alleyways.

Passing under the baroque Arco di Sant'Antonio at the western end of pedestrianised Piazza XX Settembre, you emerge into Piazza Roma, dominated by the imposing, austere 17th-century Palazzo Ducale, built over an ancient castle and now used as municipal offices.

From Piazza Roma, follow the fine Corso Vittorio Emanuele, with baroque town houses, to reach Piazza Plebiscito, the centre's baroque heart. The piazza is overlooked by the 18th-century Basilica di San Martino, its centrepiece city patron, St Martin, swinging a sword and sharing his cloak with a beggar.

Walkers can ask for the *Carta dei Sentieri del Bosco delle Pianelle* (free) from the tourist office, which maps out 10 walks in the nearby Bosco delle Pianelle (around 10km west of town). This lush woodland is part of the larger 12-sq-km Riserva Naturale Regionale Orientata – populated with lofty trees, wild orchids, and a rich and varied bird life with kestrels, owls, buzzards, hoopoe and sparrow hawks.

★ Festivals & Events

Festival della Valle d'Itria   MUSIC
Festival della Valle d'Itria is an annual music festival (late July to early August) featuring international performances of opera, classical and jazz. For information, contact the **Centro Artistico Musicale Paolo Grassi** (☑ 080 480 51 00; www.festivaldellavalleditria.it; ☺ 10am-1pm Mon-Fri) in the Palazzo Ducale.

🛏 Sleeping

B&B San Martino   B&B $
(☑ 080 48 56 01; http://xoomer.virgilio.it/bed-and-breakfast-sanmartino; Via Abate Fighera 32; d €40-120; ✳) A stylish B&B in a historic palace with rooms overlooking gracious Piazza XX Settembre. The apartments have exposed stone walls, shiny parquet floors, wrought-iron beds and small kitchenettes.

Villaggio In   APARTMENT $$
(☑ 080 480 59 11; www.villaggioincasesparse.it; Via Arco Grassi 8; apt per night €75-170, apt per week €335-1030; ✳) These charming arched apartments are located in original *centro storico* homes. The rooms are large, painted in pastel colours and decorated with antiques and country frills. A variety of apartments are on offer, sleeping from two to six people.

🍴 Eating

Il Ritrovo degli Amici   TRADITIONAL ITALIAN $$
(☑ 080 483 92 49; www.ilritrovodegliamici.it; Corso Messapia 8; meals €35; ☺ lunch & dinner Tue-Sat, lunch Sun Mar-Jan) This excellent restaurant with stone walls and vaulting, in a street off Corso Italia, has a convivial atmosphere oiled by the region's spumante. Dishes are traditional, with salamis and sausages as the specialities.

Ciacco   PUGLIAN $$
(☑ 080 480 04 72; Via Conte Ugolino; meals €30; ☺ lunch & dinner Tue-Sun) Dive into the historic centre to find Ciacco, a traditional restaurant with white-clad tables and a cosy fireplace, serving up Puglian cuisine in a modern key. It's tucked down a narrow pedestrian lane a couple of streets in from the Chiesa del Carmine.

La Piazzetta Garibaldi   OSTERIA $$
(☑ 080 430 49 00; Piazza Garibaldi; meals €20-30; ☺ lunch & dinner Thu-Tue) A highly recommended green-shuttered *osteria* in the *centro storico*. Delicious aromas entice you into the cavelike interior and the *cucina tipica* menu doesn't disappoint. Worthy of a long lunch.

ℹ Information

Tourist Office (☑ 080 480 57 02; Piazza Roma 37; ☺ 9am-1pm Mon-Fri, 4.30-7pm Tue & Thu, 9am-12.30pm Sat) The tourist office is within Palazzo Ducale (part of the Bibliotece Comunal).

ℹ Getting There & Around

The FSE train station is downhill from the historic centre. Go right along Viale della Stazione, continuing along Via Alessandro Fighera to Corso Italia; continue to the left along Corso Italia to Piazza XX Settembre. **FSE** (☑ 080 546 21 11) trains run to/from the following destinations:
Bari (€5.20, two hours, hourly)
Lecce (€7.10, two hours, five daily)
Taranto (€2.30, 40 minutes, frequent)

FSE buses run to Alberobello (€1.50, 30 minutes, five per day, Monday to Saturday).

Ostuni

POP 32,500
Ostuni shines like a pearly white tiara, extending across three hills with the magnificent gem of a cathedral as its sparkling centrepiece. It's the end of the *trulli* region and the beginning of the hot, dry Salento. Chic, with some excellent restaurants, stylish bars and swish yet intimate places to stay, it's packed in summer.

◉ Sights

Ostuni is surrounded by olive groves, so this is the place to buy some of the region's DOC 'Collina di Brindisi' olive oil – either delicate, medium or strong – direct from producers.

Cathedral   CATHEDRAL
(Via Cattedrale; admission €1; ☺ 9am-1pm & 3-7pm) Ostuni's dramatic 15th-century cathedral has an unusual Gothic-Romanesque facade with a frilly rose window and an inverted gable.

Museo di Civiltà Preclassiche della Murgia   MUSEUM
(☑ 0831 33 63 83; Via Cattedrale 15; ☺ 10am-1pm Tue-Fri, 10am-1pm & 4-7pm Sat & Sun) **FREE** Located in the Convento delle Monacelle, the museum's most famous exhibit is the 25,000-year-old star of the show: Delia. She was pregnant at the time of her death and her well-preserved skeleton was found in a local cave. Many of the finds here come from the Palaeolithic burial ground, now the **Parco Archeologico e Naturale di Arignano** (☑ 0831 30 39 73), which can be visited by appointment.

🏃 Activities

The surrounding countryside is perfect for cycling.

Ciclovagando　　　　　CYCLING
(☑ 330 985255; www.ciclovagando.com; half/full day €30/40) Organises guided tours. Each tour covers approximately 20km and departs daily from various towns in the district, including Ostuni and Brindisi. For an extra €15 you can sample typical Apulian foods on the tour.

🎊 Festivals & Events

La Cavalcata　　　　　RELIGIOUS
Ostuni's annual feast day is held on 26 August, when processions of horsemen dressed in glittering red-and-white uniforms (resembling Indian grooms on their way to be wed) follow the statue of Sant'Oronzo around town.

🛏 Sleeping

Le Sole Blu　　　　　B&B $
(☑ 0831 30 38 56; www.webalice.it/solebluostuni; Corso Vittorio Emanuele II 16; s €30-40, d €60-80) Located in the 18th-century (rather than medieval) part of town, Le Sole Blu only has one room available: it's large and has a separate entrance, but the bathroom is tiny. However, the two self-catering apartments nearby are excellent value.

★ La Terra　　　　　HOTEL $$
(☑ 0831 33 66 51; www.laterrahotel.it; Via Petrarolo; d €130-170; ⓟ ❋ 🐾) This former 13th-century palace offers atmospheric and stylish accommodation with original niches, dark-wood beams and furniture, and contrasting light stonework and whitewash. The result is a cool contemporary look. The bar is as cavernous as they come – it's tunnelled out of a cave.

🍴 Eating

Osteria Piazzetta Cattedrale　　OSTERIA $$
(☑ 0831 33 50 26; www.piazzettacattedrale.it; Via Arcidiacono Trinchera 7; meals €25-30; ⊙ Wed-Mon; 🐾) Just beyond the arch opposite Ostuni's cathedral is this tiny little hostelry serving up magical food in an atmospheric setting. The menu includes plenty of vegetarian options.

Osteria del Tempo Perso　　OSTERIA $$
(☑ 0831 30 33 20; www.osteriadeltempoperso.com; Gaetano Tanzarella Vitale 47; meals €30; ⊙ Tue-Sun) A sophisticated rustic restaurant in a cavelike former bakery, this laid-back place serves great Puglian food, specialising in roasted meats. To get here, face the cathedral's south wall and turn right through the archway into Largo Giuseppe Spennati, then follow the signs to the restaurant.

Porta Nova　　　MODERN ITALIAN $$
(☑ 0831 33 89 83; www.ristoranteportanova.com; Via G Petrarolo 38; meals €45) This restaurant has a wonderful location on the old city wall. Revel in the rolling views from the terrace or relax in the elegant interior while you feast on top-notch local cuisine, with fish and seafood the speciality.

ℹ Information

Tourist Office (☑ 0831 30 12 68; Corso Mazzini 8; ⊙ 9am-1pm & 5-9pm Mon-Fri, 5.30-8.30pm Sat & Sun) Located off Piazza della Libertà; can organise guided visits of the town in summer and bike rental.

ℹ Getting There & Around

STP buses run to Brindisi (€2.30, 50 minutes, six daily) and to Martina Franca (€2.30, 45 minutes, three daily), leaving from Piazza Italia in the newer part of Ostuni.

Trains run frequently to Brindisi (€4, 25 minutes) and Bari (€9, 50 minutes). A half-hourly local bus covers the 2.5km between the station and town.

Lecce

POP 95,000

Historic Lecce is a beautiful baroque town; it's a glorious architectural confection of palaces and churches intricately sculpted from the soft local sandstone. It is a city full of surprises: one minute you are perusing sleek designer fashions from Milan, the next you are faced with a church – dizzyingly decorated with asparagus column tops, decorative dodos and cavorting gremlins. Swooning 18th-century traveller Thomas Ashe thought it 'the most beautiful city in Italy', but the less-impressed Marchese Grimaldi said the facade of Santa Croce made him think a lunatic was having a nightmare.

Either way, it's a lively, graceful but relaxed university town packed with upmarket boutiques, antique shops, restaurants and bars. Both the Adriatic and Ionian Seas are within easy access and it's a great base from which to explore the Salento.

Lecce

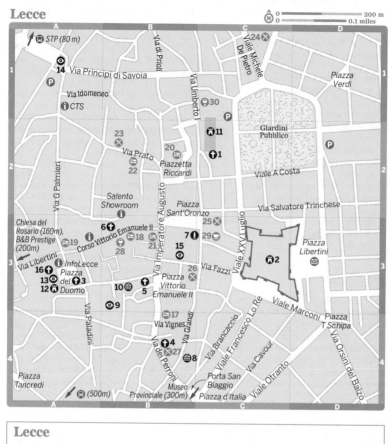

PUGLIA, BASILICATA & CALABRIA LECCE

Lecce

◎ Sights

1	Basilica di Santa Croce	C2
2	Castello di Carlo V	C3
3	Cathedral	A3
4	Chiesa di San Matteo	B4
5	Chiesa di Santa Chiara	B3
6	Chiesa di Sant'Irene	B3
7	Colonna di Sant'Oronzo	B3
8	Museo Faggiano	B4
9	Museo Teatro Romano	B3
10	MUST	B3
11	Palazzo del Governo	C2
12	Palazzo Vescovile	A3
13	Piazza del Duomo	A3
14	Porta Napoli	A1
15	Roman Amphitheatre	B3
16	Seminario	A3

◎ Sleeping

17	Azzurretta B&B	B4

	Centro Storico B&B	(see 17)
18	Palazzo Belli B&B	B3
19	Palazzo Rollo	A3
20	Patria Palace Hotel	B2
21	Risorgimento Resort	B3
22	Suite 68	B2

◎ Eating

23	Alle due Corti	B2
24	Cucina Casareccia	C1
25	Gelateria Natale	C3
26	Mamma Lupa	B3
27	Trattoria di Nonna Tetti	B4

◎ Drinking & Nightlife

28	All'Ombra del Barocco	B3
29	Caffè Alvino	C3
30	Shui 13 Wine Bar	C1

SPIDER MUSIC

In August one of Salento's biggest festivals is a frenzied night of *pizzica* dancing at La Notte della Taranta (www.lanottedellataranta.it) in Melpignano, about 30km south of Lecce. *Pizzica* developed from the ritual *tarantismi*, a dance meant to rid the body of tarantula-bite poison. It's more likely the hysterical dancing was symbolic of a deeper societal psychosis and an outlet for individuals living in bleak, repressed conditions to express their pent-up desires, hopes and unresolved grief. Nowadays, *pizzica* (which can be quite a sensual dance) means 'party', with all-night dances held in various Salento towns throughout summer, leading up to Melpignano's humdinger affair.

◉ Sights

Lecce has more than 40 churches and at least as many *palazzi*, all built or renovated between the 17th and 18th centuries, giving the city an extraordinary cohesion. Two of the main proponents of *barocco leccese* (Lecce baroque – the craziest, most lavish decoration imaginable) were brothers Antonio and Giuseppe Zimbalo, who both had a hand in the fantastical Basilica di Santa Croce.

Basilica di Santa Croce　　　CHURCH
(📞0832 24 19 57; www.basilicasantacroce.eu; Via Umberto I; ◷9am-noon & 5-8pm) It seems that hallucinating stonemasons have been at work on the basilica. Sheep, dodos, cherubs and beasties writhe across the facade, a swirling magnificent allegorical feast. Throughout the 16th and 17th centuries, a team of artists under Giuseppe Zimbalo laboured to work the building up to this pitch. Look for Zimbalo's profile on the facade.

The interior is more conventionally Renaissance and deserves a look, once you've finished gazing outside. Zimbalo also left his mark in the former Convento dei Celestini, just north of the basilica, which is now the Palazzo del Governo, the local government headquarters.

Piazza del Duomo　　　PIAZZA
A baroque feast, Piazza del Duomo is the city's focal point and a sudden open space amid the surrounding enclosed lanes. During times of invasion the inhabitants of Lecce would barricade themselves in the square, which has conveniently narrow entrances. The 12th-century cathedral (◷8.30am-12.30pm & 4-6.30pm) is one of Giuseppe Zimbalo's finest works – he was also responsible for the 68m-high bell tower. The cathedral is unusual in that it has two facades, one on the western end and the other, more ornate, facing the piazza. It's framed by the 15th-century Palazzo Vescovile (Episcopal Palace; Piazza del Duomo) and the 18th-century Seminario (Piazza del Duomo; ◷exhibitions only), designed by Giuseppe Cino.

Museo Faggiano　　　MUSEUM
(📞360 72 24 48; www.museofaggiano.it; Via Grandi 56/58; admission €3; ◷9.30am-1pm & 4-8pm) Breaking the floor to replace sewer pipes led the owner of this private home to the chance discovery of an archaeological treasure trove. Layers of history are revealed beneath the floors and in the walls. Look out for what appears to be the Knights Templar symbol in the rooftop tower.

Museo Provinciale　　　MUSEUM
(📞0832 68 35 03; Via Gallipoli 28; ◷8.30am-7.30pm Mon-Sat, to 1.30pm Sun) FREE The museum stylishly covers 10,000 years of history, from Palaeolithic and Neolithic bits and bobs to a handsome display of Greek and Roman jewels, weaponry and ornaments. The stars of the show are the Messapians, whose jaunty Mycenaean-inspired jugs and bowls date back 2500 years.

Roman Amphitheatre　　　HISTORIC SITE
(Piazza Sant'Oronzo; adult/reduced €2/1; ◷10am-noon & 5-7pm May-Sep) Below the ground level of the piazza is this restored 2nd-century-AD amphitheatre, discovered in 1901 by construction workers. It was excavated in the 1930s to reveal a perfect horseshoe with seating for 15,000.

MUST　　　ART GALLERY
(www.mustlecce.it; Via degli Ammirati 11; admission €3; ◷10am-1.30pm & 2.30-7.30pm) This beautiful conversion of the Monastery of Santa Chiara houses the work of local artists and has a great view of a Roman amphitheatre from the back window. There are plans to expand the remit to cover local history; at present the contemporary art is spread a bit thin.

Colonna di Sant'Oronzo　　　MONUMENT
(Piazza Sant'Oronzo) A statue of Lecce's patron saint perches precariously on a column in the piazza. The column, originally from

Brindisi, marked the end of the Via Appia – the Roman road that stretched from Rome to Brindisi.

Museo Teatro Romano
HISTORIC SITE

(☑0832 27 91 96; Via degli Ammirati; adult/reduced €3/2; ⊙9.30am-1.30pm & 5-7.30pm Mon-Fri, 9.30am-1.30pm Sat) Uncovered in the 1930s, this small Roman theatre has well-preserved russet-coloured Roman mosaics and frescoes.

Castello di Carlo V
CASTLE

(☑0832 24 65 17; ⊙9am-1pm & 5-9pm) **FREE** This 16th-century castle was built around a 12th-century Norman tower to the orders of Charles V and consists of two concentric trapezoidal structures. It's been used as a prison, a court and military headquarters; now you can wander around the baronial spaces and visit the occasional art exhibition.

🍴 Courses

Awaiting Table
COOKING

(www.awaitingtable.com; day/week €195/1995) Silvestro Silvestori's splendid culinary and wine school provides day or weeklong courses with market shopping, tours, tastings, noteworthy lecturers – and lots of hands-on cooking. Book well in advance as courses fill up rapidly.

🛏 Sleeping

★Palazzo Belli B&B
B&B $

(☑380 7758456; www.palazzobelli.it; Corso Vittorio Emanuele II 33; s €50-60, d €70-80; 🛜) A wonderfully central, elegant and well priced op-

tion, located in a fine mansion building near the cathedral. Rooms have marbled floors and wrought-iron beds. Breakfast is served in the nearby All'Ombra del Barocco bar.

★Palazzo Rollo
APARTMENT $

(☑0832 30 71 52; www.palazzorollo.it; Corso Vittorio Emanuele II 14; s €50-60, d €70-90, ste €100-120, apt €70-90; 🅿❄@) Stay in a 17th-century palace – the Rollo family seat for more than 200 years. The three grand B&B suites (with kitchenettes) have high curved ceilings and chandeliers. Downstairs, contemporary-chic studios open onto an ivy-hung courtyard. The rooftop garden has wonderful views.

Azzurretta B&B
GUESTHOUSE $

(☑0832 24 22 11; www.hostelecce.com; Via Vignes 2; s €30-38, d €55-70; 🅿🛜) The friendly brother of the owner of Centro Storico B&B runs this artier version located within the same building; ask for the large double with a balcony, wooden floors and a vaulted ceiling. Massage is available in your room or on the roof terrace. You get a cafe voucher for breakfast. The brothers have a tiny studio flat, which is a little dark but a good option if you're self-catering on a budget.

Suite 68
BOUTIQUE HOTEL $

(☑0832 30 35 06; www.kalekora.it; Via Prato 7-9; s €70-80, d €80-120; ❄@🛜) Strong colours, abstract canvases and vividly patterned rugs in the large, bright rooms give this place a contemporary feel. It's simple and stylish. Bikes available.

LECCE'S NOTABLE CHURCHES

On Corso Vittorio Emanuele, the interior of 17th-century Chiesa di Sant'Irene contains a magnificent pair of mirror-image baroque altarpieces, facing each other across the transept. Other notable baroque churches include the following:

Chiesa di Santa Chiara (Piazza Vittorio Emanuele II; ⊙9.30-11.30am daily, plus 4.30-6.30pm Mon-Sat) A notable baroque church with every niche a swirl of twisting columns and ornate statuary.

Chiesa di San Matteo (Via dei Perroni 29; ⊙7.30-11am & 4-6pm) Located 200m to the south of Chiesa di Santa Chiara; and the last work of Giuseppe Zimbalo.

Chiesa del Rosario (Via Libertini) Instead of the intended dome roof, this church ended up with a quick-fix wooden one following Zimbalo's death before the building was completed.

Chiesa dei SS Nicolò e Cataldo (Via San Nicola; ⊙9am-noon Sep-Apr) The Chiesa dei SS Nicolò e Cataldo, near Porta Napoli, was built by the Normans in 1180. It got caught up in the city's baroque frenzy and was revamped in 1716 by the prolific Giuseppe Cino, who retained the Romanesque rose window and portal.

LECCE IN ONE DAY

Start the day with a cappuccino and *pasticciotto* (custard-filled pastry) at Caffè Alvino on Piazza Sant'Oronzo. All that sugar and froth should be good preparation for the fanciful Basilica di Santa Croce (p126), worth at least an hour of your time.

To get a sense of Lecce's history visit the fascinating Museo Faggiano (p126), then come back to the present with a spot of window-shopping and browsing through the entertaining mix of shops on Corso Vittorio Emanuele II. Be sure to stop for a campari and soda at one of the many bars in town before lunching on typical Puglian fare at firmly traditional Alle due Corti.

Walk off the pasta and beans by heading across town to the excellent Museo Provinciale (p126). Or, for more fancy facades, Lecce's baroque feast of *palazzi*-flanked streets (like Via Palmieri), churches and the cathedral (p126) will keep you happily wandering till dinner-time. Crown your day with a meal at Cucina Casareccia (p128), where you'll feel like one of the family. Stroll back to your hotel via the Basilica di Santa Croce, which is spectacularly lit up at night.

Centro Storico B&B
B&B $

(☎338 5881265; www.bedandbreakfast.lecce.it; Via Vignes 2b; s €35-40, d €70-100; P❄🛜) This friendly and efficient B&B located in a historic palace features big rooms, double-glazed windows and pleasantly old-fashioned decor. The huge rooftop terrace has sun loungers and views; you get a cafe voucher for breakfast, and it also has coffee-and-tea-making facilities.

B&B Prestige
B&B $

(☎349 7751290; www.bbprestige-lecce.it; Giuseppe Libertini 7; s €60-70, d €70-90, tr €100-110; P@🛜) On the corner of Via Santa Maria del Paradiso in the historic centre, the rooms in this lovely B&B are light, airy and beautifully finished. The communal sun-trap terrace has views over San Giovanni Battista church.

Risorgimento Resort
HOTEL $$

(☎0832 24 63 11; www.risorgimentoresort.it; Via Imperatore Augusto 19; d €145-165, ste €190-290; P❄@🛜) A warm welcome awaits at this stylish five-star hotel in the centre of Lecce. The rooms are spacious and refined with high ceilings, modern furniture and contemporary details reflecting the colours of the Salento, and the bathrooms are enormous. There's a restaurant, wine bar and rooftop garden.

Patria Palace Hotel
HOTEL $$

(☎0832 24 51 11; www.patriapalacelecce.com; Piazzetta Riccardi 13; s €106-210, d €165-350; P❄@🛜) This sumptuous hotel is traditionally Italian with large mirrors, dark-wood furniture and wistful murals. The location is wonderful, the bar gloriously art deco with a magnificent carved ceiling, and

the shady roof terrace has views over the Basilica di Santa Croce.

🍴 Eating

Gelateria Natale
GELATO $

(Via Trinchese 7a) Lecce's best ice-cream parlour also has an array of fabulous confectionery.

Mamma Lupa
OSTERIA $

(☎340 7832765; Via Acaja 12; meals €20-25; ⊙lunch Sun-Fri, dinner daily) Looking suitably rustic, this *osteria* serves proper peasant food – such as roast tomatoes, potatoes and artichokes, or horse meatballs – in snug surroundings with just a few tables and a stone-vaulted ceiling.

Trattoria di Nonna Tetti
TRATTORIA $

(☎0832 24 60 36; Piazzetta Regina Maria 28; mains €8-12; ⊙lunch & dinner) A warmly inviting restaurant, popular with all ages and budgets, this trattoria serves a wide choice of traditional dishes. Try the most emblematic Puglian dish here – braised wild chicory with a purée of boiled dried fava beans, along with *contorni* (side dishes) like *patate casarecce* (homemade thinly sliced fries).

★ Cucina Casareccia
TRATTORIA $$

(☎0832 24 51 78; Viale Costadura 19; mains €12; ⊙lunch Tue-Sun, dinner Tue-Sat) Ring the bell to gain entry into a place that feels like a private home, with its patterned cement floor tiles, desk piled high with papers, and charming owner Carmela Perrone. In fact, it's known locally as *le Zie* (the aunts). Here you'll taste the true *cucina povera*, including horse meat done in a *salsa piccante* (spicy sauce). Booking is a must.

Alle due Corti
PUGLIAN $$

(☑ 0832 24 22 23; www.alleduecorti.com; Via Prato 42; mains €12; ☺ lunch & dinner daily, closed winter) For a taste of sunny Salento, check out this no-frills, fiercely traditional restaurant. The seasonal menu is classic Puglian, written in a dialect that even some Italians struggle with. Go for the real deal with a dish of *ciceri e tria* (crisply fried pasta with chickpeas).

Drinking

Via Imperatore Augusto is full of bars, and on a summer's night it feels like one long party. Wander along to find somewhere to settle.

All'Ombra del Barocco
WINE BAR

(www.allombradelbarocco.it; Corte dei Cicala 9; ☺ 8am-1am) This cool restaurant/cafe/wine bar next door to the Liberrima bookshop has a range of teas, cocktails and *aperitivi*. It's open for breakfast and also hosts musical events; the modern cooking is well worth a try. Tables fill the little square outside, an ideal place from which to watch the *passeggiata* (evening stroll).

Caffè Alvino
CAFE

(Piazza Sant'Oronzo; ☺ Wed-Mon) Treat yourself to great coffee and *pasticciotto* (custard-filled pastry) at this iconic chandeliered cafe in Lecce's main square: it has a sumptuous display of cakes.

Shui 13 Wine Bar
WINE BAR

(Via Umberto I 21; ☺ 10am-late summer, 10am-3pm & 6pm-midnight winter) A hip and atmospheric wine bar with candlelit outside tables and a range of Puglian wines.

ⓘ Information

The centre's twin main squares are Piazza Sant'Oronzo and Piazza del Duomo, linked by pedestrianised Corso Vittorio Emanuele II.

CTS (☑ 0832 30 18 62; Via Palmieri 89; ☺ 9am-1pm daily & 4-7.30pm Sun & Mon) Good for student travel.

Hospital (☑ 0832 66 11 11; Via San Cesario) About 2km south of the centre on the Gallipoli road.

InfoLecce (☑ 0832 52 18 77; www.infolecce.it; Piazza del Duomo 2; ☺ 9.30am-1.30pm & 3.30-7.30pm Mon-Sat, from 10am Sun) Independent and helpful tourist information office. Has guided tours and bike rental (per hour/day €3/15).

Police Station (☑ 0832 69 11 11; Viale Otranto 1)

Post Office (Piazza Libertini)

Puglia Blog (www.thepuglia.com) Voted in Italy as the most popular blog on Puglia, this informative site run by Fabio Ingrosso has articles on culture, history, food, wine, accommodation and travel in Puglia.

Salento Showroom (☑ 0832 179 03 57; www.salentotime.it; Via Revina Isabella 22; ☺ 9.30am-1.30pm & 3.30-7.30pm Mon-Sat, from 10am Sun) Independent tourist office that can provide help with accommodation and car hire. Has internet access (per hour €3).

Tourist Office (☑ 0832 24 80 92; www.viaggiareinpuglia.it; Corso Vittorio Emanuele II 24; ☺ 9am-1pm & 4-7pm Mon-Thu, 9am-1pm Fri & Sat)

ⓘ Getting There & Away

BUS

The city bus terminal is located to the north of Porta Napoli.

STP (☑ 0832 35 91 42; www.stplecce.it) Runs buses to Brindisi (€6.30, 35 minutes, nine daily) and throughout Puglia from the **STP bus station** (☑ 800 43 03 46; Viale Porta D'Europa).

FSE (☑ 0832 66 81 11; www.fseonline.it) Runs buses to Gallipoli (€2.60, one hour, four daily) and Otranto (€2.60, 1½ hours, two daily), leaving from Largo Vittime del Terrorismo.

Pugliairbus (http://pugliairbus.aeroportidipuglia.it) Runs to Brindisi airport (€7, 40 minutes, nine daily). **SITA** also has buses to Brindisi airport (€6, 45 minutes, nine daily), leaving from Viale Porte d'Europa.

TRAIN

The train station is 1km southwest of Lecce's historic centre. It runs frequent services to the following destinations:

Bari (from €9, 1½ to two hours)

Bologna (from €82.50, 7½ to 9½ hours)

Brindisi (from €9, 30 minutes)

Naples (from €41, 5½ hours with transfer in Caserta)

Rome (from €66, 5½ to nine hours)

FSE trains head to Otranto, Gallipoli and Martina Franca; the ticket office is located on platform 1.

Brindisi

POP 89,800

Like all ports, Brindisi has its seamy side, but it's also surprisingly slow paced and balmy, particularly the palm-lined Corso Garibaldi linking the port to the train station and the promenade stretching along the interesting seafront.

The town was the end of the ancient Roman road Via Appia, down whose weary length trudged legionnaires and pilgrims, crusaders and traders, all heading to Greece and the Near East. These days little has

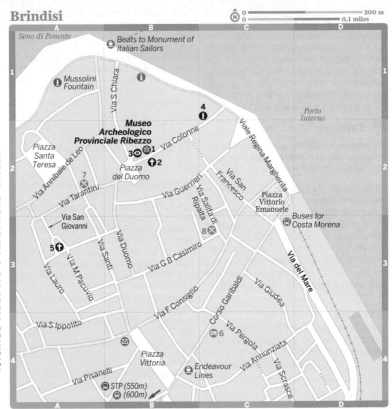

changed except that Brindisi's pilgrims are sun-seekers rather than soul-seekers.

☉ Sights

★ Museo Archeologico Provinciale Ribezzo MUSEUM

(☎ 0831 56 55 08; Piazza del Duomo 8; ☺ 9.30am-1.30pm Tue-Sat & 3.30-6.30pm Tue, Thu & Sat) **FREE** This superb museum covers several floors with well-documented exhibits (in English) including some 3000 bronze sculptures and fragments in Hellenistic Greek style. There are also terracotta figurines from the 7th century, underwater archaeological finds, and Roman statues and heads (not always together).

Chiesa di Santa Maria del Casale CHURCH

(☎ 0831 41 85 45; Via Ruggero de Simone; ☺ 8am-8pm) Located 4km north of town towards the airport, this church was built by Prince Philip of Taranto around 1300. The church

mixes up Puglian Romanesque, Gothic and Byzantine styles, with a Byzantine banquet of interior frescoes. The immense *Last Judgement* on the entrance wall, full of blood and thunder, is the work of Rinaldo di Taranto.

Roman Column MONUMENT

(Via Colonne) The gleaming white column above a sweeping set of sun-whitened stairs leading to the waterfront promenade marks the imperial Via Appia terminus at Brindisi. Originally there were two, but one was presented to the town of Lecce back in 1666 as thanks to Sant'Oronzo for having relieved Brindisi of the plague.

Cathedral CATHEDRAL

(Piazza del Duomo; ☺ 8am-9pm Mon-Fri & Sun, to noon Sat) This 11th-century cathedral was substantially remodelled about 700 years later. You can see how it may have looked from the nearby **Porta dei Cavalieri Templari**, a fan-

Brindisi

ciful portico with pointy arches – all that remains of the Knights Templar's main church.

Tempio di San Giovanni al Sepolcro CHURCH
(Via San Giovanni) The Knights Templar's secondary church is a square brown bulk of Norman stone conforming to the circular plan the Templars so loved.

Monument to Italian Sailors MONUMENT
For a wonderful view of Brindisi's waterfront, take one of the regular boats (return €1.80) on Viale Regina Margherita across the harbour to the monument erected by Mussolini in 1933.

🛏 Sleeping

B&B Federico II APARTMENT $
(☑ 0328 9277735; www.bbfederico2.it; Via Federico II di Svevia 27; s €35-40, d €60-70; 🛜) Positioned near the harbour, these are two simple but attractive apartments arranged around a palm-shaded courtyard. The stand-out factor is the great service, with a warm welcome and a thoughtfully stocked fridge.

Hotel Orientale HOTEL $$
(☑ 0831 56 84 51; www.hotelorientale.it; Corso Garibaldi 40; s/d €75/130; 🅿 ❄ 🛜) This sleek, modern hotel overlooks the long palm-lined *corso*. Rooms are pleasant, the location is good and it has a small fitness centre, private car park and (rare) cooked breakfast option.

🍴 Eating

Trattoria Pantagruele TRATTORIA $$
(☑ 0831 56 06 05; Via Salita di Ripalta 1; meals €30; ☺ lunch & dinner Mon-Fri, dinner Sat) Named after French writer François Rabelais' satirical character, this charming trattoria three blocks from the waterfront serves up excellent fish and grilled meats.

Il Giardino PUGLIAN $$
(☑ 0831 56 40 26; Via Tarantini 14-18; meals €30; ☺ lunch & dinner Tue-Sat, lunch Sun) Established more than 40 years ago in a restored 15th-century *palazzo*, sophisticated Il Giardino serves refined seafood and meat dishes in a delightful garden setting.

❶ Information

The new port is east of town, across the Seno di Levante at Costa Morena, in a bleak industrial wilderness.

The old port is about 1km from the train station along Corso Umberto I, which leads into Corso Garibaldi where there are numerous cafes, shops, ferry companies and travel agencies.
Ferries (www.ferries.gr) Details of ferry fares and timetables to Greek destinations.
Hospital (☑ 0831 53 71 11) Southwest of the centre; take the SS7 for Mesagne.
Post Office (Piazza Vittoria)
Tourist Office (☑ 0831 52 30 72; www.viaggiareinpuglia.it; Viale Regina Margherita 44; ☺ 9am-1pm & 2-8pm Mon-Sat summer, 8.30am-2pm Mon-Sat & 3.30-7pm Mon-Fri winter) Has a wealth of information and brochures on the area. If you are interested in pedal power, pick up *Le Vie Verdi* map with eight bicycling routes in the Brindisi area, ranging from 6km to 30km.

❶ Getting There & Away

AIR
From **Papola Casale** (BDS; www.aeroportidipuglia.it), Brindisi's small airport, there are domestic flights to Rome, Naples and Milan. Airlines include Alitalia, AirOne and easyJet. There are also direct flights from London Stansted with Ryanair.

Major and local car-rental firms are represented at the airport and there are regular SITA buses to Lecce (€6.50, 35 minutes, nine daily) and STP buses to central Brindisi (€1.60, 15 to 30 minutes, every 30 minutes).
Pugliairbus (http://pugliairbus.aeroportidipuglia.it) has services to Bari airport (€8, 1¾ hours) and Lecce (€7, 40 minutes).

BOAT
Ferries, all of which take vehicles, leave Brindisi for Greece and Albania.

Ferry companies have offices at Costa Morena (the newer port); the major ones also have offices in town.

PUGLIA, BASILICATA & CALABRIA BRINDISI

Agoudimos Lines (www.ferries.gr/agoudimos)
To Corfu, Igoumenitsa and Cephalonia in
Greece; to Vlore in Albania.

Endeavour Lines (☎0831 57 38 00; www.
endeavor-lines.com; Via Prov. Le per Lecce 27)
To Igoumenitsa, Patras, Corfu and Cephalonia
in Greece.

Red Star Ferries (☎0831 57 52 89; www.
directferries.co.uk/red_star_ferries.htm) To
Vlore in Albania.

BUS

STP (☎0831 54 92 45) buses go to Ostuni
(€2.90, 50 minutes, six daily) and Lecce (€3.30,
45 minutes, two daily), as well as towns throughout the Salento. Most leave from Via Bastioni
Carlo V, in front of the train station. Ferrovie del
Sud-Est buses serving local towns also leave
from the same place.

TRAIN

The train station has regular services to the
following destinations:

Bari (from €14, one hour)
Lecce (from €9, 30 minutes)
Milan (from €99.50, 8½ to 11 hours)
Rome (from €66, five to seven hours)
Taranto (from €4.50, 1¼ hours)

❶ Getting Around

A free minibus connects the train station and old
ferry terminal with Costa Morena. It departs two
hours before boat departures. You'll need a valid
ferry ticket.

To reach the airport take the STP-run Cotrap
bus from Via Bastoni Carlo V.

Southern & Western Salento

The Penisola Salentina, better known simply
as Salento, is hot, dry and remote, retaining a flavour of its Greek past. It stretches
across Italy's heel from Brindisi to Taranto
and down to Santa Maria di Leuca. Here the
lush greenery of Valle d'Itria gives way to
flat, ochre-coloured fields hazy with wildflowers in spring, and endless olive groves.

Oria

POP 15,400

The multicoloured dome of Oria's cathedral
can be seen for miles around, surrounded by
the narrow streets of this appealing medieval
town. An intriguing, if ghoulish, sight is the
cathedral's **Cripta delle Mummie** (Crypt of
the Mummies), where 11 mummified corpses

of former monks are still preserved. Sur-
mounting the town, the **Frederick II castle**,
built in a triangular shape, has been carefully
restored. It is privately owned.

Dating back to Frederick II's reign, **Il Tor-
neo dei Rioni** is the annual battle between
the town's quarters. It takes the form of a
spectacular *palio* (horse race) and is held
every mid-August.

★**Borgo di Oria** (☎329 2307506; www.
borgodioria.it; apt €50-100; ▣) is a delightful
albergo diffuso run by the charismatic and
well-travelled Francesco Pipino. The self-
catering apartments are large, comfortable
and tastefully furnished. Reception is at Bar
Kenya in Piazza Manfredi.

Waiters in medieval costume welcome
you at **Alle Corte di Hyria** (☎329 6624507; Via
Milizia 146; meals €20-25; ⊙Thu-Tue), an atmospheric restaurant in a stone-walled cavern.

Oria is on the main Trenitalia line and
there are frequent train services from both
Brindisi and Taranto. You can also connect
with Ostuni and change at Francavilla Fontana for Alberobello and Martina Franca.

Galatina

POP 27,300

With a charming historic centre, Galatina –
18km south of Lecce – is at the core of the
Penisola Salentina's Greek past. It is almost
the only place where the ritual *tarantismi*
(Spider Music) is still practised. The taran-
tella folk dance evolved from this ritual, and
each year on the feast day of St Peter and St
Paul (29 June), it is performed at the (now
deconsecrated) church.

⊙ Sights

**Basilica di Santa
Caterina d'Alessandria**   CHURCH
(⊙8am-12.30pm & 4.30-6.45pm Apr-Sep,
8am-12.30pm & 3.45-5.45pm Oct-Mar) Most
people come to Galatina to see the incredible 14th-century Basilica di Santa Caterina
d'Alessandria. Its interior is a kaleidoscope
of fresco. It was built by the Franciscans,
whose patroness was Frenchwoman Marie
d'Enghien de Brienne. Married to Raimondello Orsini del Balzo, the Salentine's wealthiest noble, she had plenty of cash to splash
on interior decoration. The gruesome story
goes that Raimondello (who is buried here)
climbed Mt Sinai to visit relics of Santa Caterina (St Catherine). Kissing the dead saint's
hand, he bit off a finger and brought it back
as a holy relic.

The church is absolutely beautiful, with a pure-white altarpiece set against the frenzy of frescoes. It is not clear who the artists Marie employed really were; they could have been itinerant painters down from Le Marche and Emilia or southerners who'd absorbed the latest Renaissance innovations on trips north. Bring a torch.

🛏 Sleeping

Samadhi   AGRITURISMO
(📞 0836 60 02 84; www.agricolasamadhi.com; Via Stazione 116; per person from €40, per week from €390-995; ❋ 🛜 🏊) Soothe the soul further with a stay at Samadhi, located around 7km east of here in tiny Zollino. It's on a 10-hectare organic farm and the owners are multilingual. As well as ayurvedic treatments and yoga courses, there's a vegan restaurant offering organic meals. Check the website for upcoming retreats and courses.

❶ Getting There & Away

FSE runs frequent trains between Lecce and Galatina (€1.90, 30 minutes), and Zollino (€1.30, 20 minutes).

Otranto

POP 5540

Otranto overlooks a pretty harbour on the turquoise Adriatic coast. In the historic centre, looming golden walls guard narrow car-free lanes, protecting countless little shops selling touristic odds and ends. In July and August it's one of Puglia's most vibrant towns.

Otranto was Italy's main port to the East for 1000 years and suffered a brutal history. There are fanciful tales that King Minos was here and St Peter is supposed to have celebrated the first Western Mass here.

A more definite historical event is the Sack of Otranto in 1480, when 18,000 Turks led by Ahmet Pasha besieged the town. The townsfolk were able to hold the Turks at bay for 15 days before capitulating. Eight hundred survivors were subsequently led up the nearby Minerva hill and beheaded for refusing to convert.

Today the only fright you'll get is the summer crush on Otranto's scenic beaches and in its narrow streets.

◉ Sights

★ Cathedral   CATHEDRAL
(📞 0836 80 27 20; Piazza Basilica; ◔ 8am-noon daily, plus 3-7pm Apr-Sep, 3-5pm Oct-Mar) This ca-

thedral was built by the Normans in the 11th century, though it's been given a few facelifts since. On the floor is a vast 12th-century mosaic of a stupendous tree of life balanced on the back of two elephants. It was created by a young monk called Pantaleone (who had obviously never seen an elephant), whose vision of heaven and hell encompassed an amazing (con)fusion of the classics, religion and plain old superstition, including Adam and Eve, Diana the huntress, Hercules, King Arthur, Alexander the Great, and a menagerie of monkeys, snakes and sea monsters. Don't forget to look up; the cathedral also boasts a beautiful wooden coffered ceiling.

It's amazing that the cathedral survived at all, as the Turks stabled their horses here when they beheaded the martyrs of Otranto on a stone preserved in the altar of the chapel (to the right of the main altar). This **Cappella Mortiri** (Chapel of the Dead) is a ghoulishly fascinating sight, with the skulls and bones of the martyrs arranged in neat patterns in seven tall glass cases.

Castello Aragonese Otranto   CASTLE
(www.castelloaragoneseotranto.it; Piazza Castello; adult/child €2/free; ◔ 10am-1pm & 3-5pm Oct-Mar, 10am-1pm & 3-7pm Apr-May, 10am-1pm & 3-10pm Jun & Sep, 10am-midnight Aug) This squat thick-walled fort, with the Charles V coat of arms above the entrance, has great views from the ramparts. There are some faded original murals and original cannonballs on display.

Chiesa di San Pietro   CHURCH
(Via San Pietro; ◔ 10am-noon & 3-6pm) Vivid Byzantine frescoes decorate the interior of this church, which was being restored at the time of writing. Follow the signs from the castle: if it's closed, ask for the key at the cathedral.

DRAMATIC COASTLINE

For a scenic road trip, the drive south from Otranto to Castro takes you along a wild and beautiful coastline. The coast here is rocky and dramatic, with cliffs falling down into the sparkling, azure sea. When the wind is up you can see why it is largely treeless. Many of the towns here started life as Greek settlements, although there are few monuments to be seen. Further south, the resort town of Santa Maria di Leuca is the tip of Italy's stiletto and the dividing line between the Adriatic and Ionian Seas.

🏃 Activities

There are some great beaches north of Otranto, especially **Baia dei Turchi**, with its translucent blue water. South of Otranto a spectacular rocky coastline makes for an impressive drive down to Castro. To see what goes on underwater, **Scuba Diving Otranto** (☑ 0836 80 27 40; www.scubadiving.it; Via Francesco di Paola 43) offers day or night dives as well as introductory courses and diving courses.

🛏️ Sleeping

⭐ Balconcino d'Oriente   B&B **$**
(☑ 0836 80 15 29; www.balconcinodoriente.com; Via San Francesco da Paola 71; d €60-120, tr €80-150; 🅿️ ❄️) This B&B has an African/Middle Eastern theme throughout with colourful bed linens, African prints, Moroccan lamps and orange colour washes on the walls. The downstairs restaurant serves traditional Italian meals (four courses €50).

⭐ Palazzo Papaleo   HOTEL **$$**
(☑ 0836 80 21 08; www.hotelpalazzopapaleo.com; Via Rondachi 1; r €120-490; 🅿️ ❄️ @ 🛜) 🏊 Located next to the town cathedral, this sumptuous hotel was the first to earn the EU Eco-label in Puglia. Aside from its ecological convictions, the hotel has magnificent rooms with original frescoes, exquisitely carved antique furniture and walls washed in soft greys, ochres and yellows. Soak in the panoramic views while enjoying the rooftop spa. The staff are exceptionally friendly.

Palazzo de Mori   B&B **$$**
(☑ 0836 80 10 88; www.palazzodemori.it; Bastione dei Pelasgi; r €120-150; ⊙ Apr-Oct; ❄️ @) In Otranto's historic centre, this charming B&B serves breakfast on the sun terrace overlooking the port. The rooms are decorated in soothing white-on-white.

🍴 Eating

La Bella Idrusa   PIZZERIA **$**
(☑ 0836 80 14 75; Via Lungomare degli Eroi; pizzas €5; ⊙ dinner Thu-Tue) You can't miss this pizzeria right by the huge Porta Terra in the historic centre. Despite the tourist-trap location, the food is well judged. And it's not just pizzas on offer: it also serves seafood standards.

Laltro Baffo   SEAFOOD **$$**
(☑ 0836 80 16 36; www.laltrobaffo.com; Cenobio Basiliano 23; meals €30-35; ⊙ Tue-Sun) This elegant modern restaurant near the castle – on a side street signed towards the cathedral – dishes

up seafood with a contemporary twist. Try the *polipo alla pignata* (octopus stew).

ℹ️ Information

Tourist Office (☑ 0836 80 14 36; Piazza Castello; ⊙ 9am-1pm & 3-8pm Mon-Fri Jun-Sep, 9am-1pm Mon-Fri Oct-May) Faces the castle.

ℹ️ Getting There & Away

Otranto can be reached from Lecce by FSE train (€2.60, 1½ hours) or bus (€2.60, 1½ hours). **Marozzi** (☑ 0836 80 15 78; www.marozzivt.it) has daily bus services to Rome (€50, 10 hours, three daily). There are no trains on Sunday, so use the replacemenent bus service.

For travel information and reservations, head to **Ellade Viaggi** (☑ 0836 80 15 78; www.elladeviaggi.it; Via del Porto) at the port.

Gallipoli

POP 21,100

Though not as iconic as the Turkish town of the same name, this Gallipoli (meaning 'beautiful town' in Greek) fills an island in the Ionian Sea and is connected by a bridge to the mainland and modern city. It's a picturesque town surrounded by high walls, which were built to protect it against attacks from the sea. An important fishing centre, it feels like a working Italian town, unlike more seasonal coastal places. In the summer bars and restaurants make the most of the island's ramparts, looking out to sea.

◎ Sights & Activities

Gallipoli has some fine beaches, including the **Baia Verde**, just south of town. Nature enthusiasts will want to take a day trip to **Parco Regionale Porto Selvaggio**, about 20km north – a protected area of wild coastline with walking trails amid the trees and diving off the rocky shore.

Cattedrale di Sant'Agata   CATHEDRAL
(Via Antonietta de Pace; ⊙ hours vary) In the centre, on the highest point of the island, is this 17th-century baroque cathedral, lined with paintings by local artists. Zimbalo, who imprinted Lecce with his crazy baroque styles, also worked on the facade.

Frantoio Ipogeo   HISTORIC SITE
(☑ 338 1363063; Via Antonietta de Pace 87; ⊙ 10am-12.30pm & 4-6.30pm Jun-Sep, to midnight Jun & Jul) This is only one of some 35 olive presses buried in the tufa rock below the town. It's here that they pressed Gallipoli's

olive oil, which was then stored in one of the 2000 cisterns carved beneath the old town.

Museo Civico MUSEUM
(☑️0833 26 42 24; Via Antonietta de Pace 108; adult €3; ☺9am-1pm & 4-9pm Mon-Fri, 10am-1pm Sat) Founded in 1878, the museum is a 19th-century time capsule featuring fish heads, ancient sculptures, a 3rd-century-BC sarcophagus and other weird stuff.

Farmacia Provenzana HISTORIC BUILDING
(Via Antonietta de Pace; ☺8.30am-12.30pm & 4.30-8.30pm Sun-Fri) A beautifully decorated pharmacy dating from 1814.

🛌 Sleeping

La Casa del Mare B&B $
(☑️333 4745754; www.lacasadelmare.com; Piazza de Amicis 14; d €60-110; ✳️@🛜) This butter-coloured 16th-century building on a little square in the town centre is a great choice. Helpful and friendly Federico has also restored a flamboyant 18th-century *palazzo* nearby, **Palazzo Flora** (www.palazzoflora. com; Via d'Ospina 19; d €65-120, house €150-300), which sleeps four to six and has fantastic views, especially from the rooftop terrace. During the summer Federico cooks a sumptuous buffet feast for his guests every Friday night (per person €35).

Insula B&B $
(☑️366 3468357; www.bbinsulagallipoli.it; Via Antonietta de Pace 56; s €40-80, d €60-150; ☺Apr-Oct; ✳️@) A magnificent 15th-century building houses this memorable B&B. The five rooms are all different but share the same princely atmosphere with exquisite antiques, vaulted high ceilings and cool pastel paintwork.

Relais Corte Palmieri HOTEL $$
(☑️0833 26 53 18; www.hotelpalazzodelcorso.it; Corte Palmieri 3; s €130-185, d €165-195; ✳️🛜) This cream-coloured, well-kept hotel in the historic centre has elegant rooms accentuated by traditional painted furniture, wrought-iron bedheads and crisp red-and-white linen.

🍴 Eating

Caffè Duomo CAFE $
(Via Antonietta de Pace 72; dessert €9) For good Gallipoli *spumone* (layered ice cream with candied fruit and nuts) and refreshing *granite* (ices made with coffee, fresh fruit or locally grown pistachios and almonds), head to Caffè Duomo.

La Puritate TRATTORIA $$
(☑️0833 26 42 05; Via S Elia 18; meals €40-45; ☺Thu-Tue) A great place for fish in the old town with picture windows and sea views. Follow the excellent antipasti with delicious *primi* (first courses) such as seafood spaghetti, then see what's been caught that day – the swordfish is usually a good bet.

ℹ️ Information

Tourist Office (☑️0833 26 25 29; Via Antonietta de Pace 86; ☺8am-9pm summer, 8am-1pm & 4-9pm Mon-Sat winter) Near the cathedral in the old town.

ℹ️ Getting There & Away

FSE buses and trains head to Lecce (€3.90, one hour, four daily).

Taranto

POP 193,100

According to legend, the city was founded by Taras, son of Poseidon, who arrived on the back of a dolphin (as you do). Less romantically, the city was actually founded in the 7th century BC by exiles from Sparta to become one of the wealthiest and most important colonies of Magna Graecia. The fun finished, however, in the 3rd century BC when the Romans marched in, changed its name to Tarentum and set off a two-millennium decline in fortunes. Its cultural heyday may be over but Taranto still remains an important naval base, second only to La Spezia.

Once a Roman citadel, the collapsing historic medieval centre is gritty and dirty but has a lovely seaside promenade. However, the mainland industrial centre, with Italy's largest steel plant, dominates the skyline.

⊙ Sights

Although Taranto's medieval town centre is rundown and has a gritty undertone, it's gradually being tastefully renovated. It is perched on the small island dividing the Mar Piccolo (Small Sea; an enclosed lagoon) and the Mar Grande (Big Sea). This peculiar geography means that blue sea and sky surround you wherever you go.

Museo Nazionale Archeologico MUSEUM
(☑️099 453 21 12; www.museotaranto.it; Via Cavour 10; adult/child €5/free; ☺8.30am-7.30pm) In the new town is one of Italy's most important archaeological museums, exploring ancient Taras. It houses, among other artefacts, the largest collection of Greek terracotta figures

Taranto

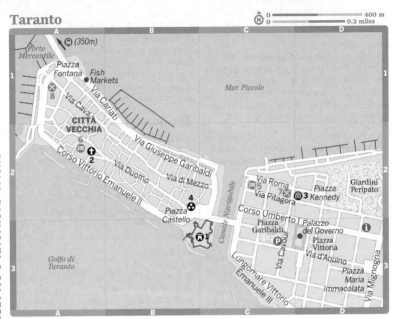

Taranto

◉ Sights
1 Castello Aragonese C3
2 Cathedral A2
3 Museo Nazionale Archeologico D2
4 Temple of Poseidon..............................B2

🛏 Sleeping
5 Europa Hotel..C2
6 Hotel Akropolis.......................................A2

🍴 Eating
7 Trattoria al Gatto Rosso C2
8 Trattoria L'Orologio..............................A1

in the world. Also on exhibit are fine collections of 1st-century-BC glassware, classic black-and-red Attic vases and stunning jewellery such as a 4th-century-BC bronze and terracotta crown.

Cathedral
CATHEDRAL
(Via del Duomo) The 11th-century cathedral is one of Puglia's oldest Romanesque buildings and an extravagant treat. It's dedicated to San Cataldo, an Irish monk who lived and was buried here in the 7th century; the Capella di San Cataldo is a baroque riot of frescoes and polychrome marble inlay.

Castello Aragonese
CASTLE
(📋099 775 34 38; www.castelloaragonesetaranto.
it; Piazza Castello; ⊙by appointment 9am-noon Mon-Fri) Guarding the swing bridge that joins the old and new parts of town, this impressive 15th-century structure was once a prison and is currently occupied by the Italian navy. Opposite are the remaining columns of Taranto's ancient **Temple of Poseidon** (Piazza Castello).

🎉 Festivals & Events

Le Feste di Pasqua
RELIGIOUS
Taranto is famous for its Holy Week celebrations – the biggest in the region – when bearers in Ku Klux Klan–style robes carry icons around the town. There are three processions: the Perdoni, celebrating pilgrims; the Addolorata (lasting 12 hours but covering only 4km); and the Misteri (even slower at 14 hours to cover 2km).

🛏 Sleeping

Hotel Akropolis
HOTEL **$$**
(📋099 470 41 10; www.hotelakropolis.it; Vico Seminario 3; s/d €105/145; 🅿 @ 🛜) A converted medieval *palazzo* in the crumbling old town, this luxurious hotel sits grandly beside the cathedral. There are 13 stylish cream-and-white rooms, original majolica-tiled floors

and tremendous views from the rooftop terrace. The downstairs bar and restaurant is enclosed in stone, wood and glass and has atmospheric curtained alcoves.

Europa Hotel
HOTEL $$
(☑ 099 452 59 94; www.hoteleuropaonline.it; Via Roma 2; s €80-105, d €135-190; ❉ 🗟) On the seafront next to the swing bridge, this hotel has comfortable rooms (some with kitchenettes) overlooking the old town.

🍴 Eating & Drinking

Trattoria L'Orologio
TRATTORIA $
(☑ 099 460 87 36; Via Duca D'Aosta 27; meals €18-25; ☺ lunch & dinner Mon-Fri, lunch Sat) This deeply traditional Tarantine trattoria is known for its seafood, which includes grilled mussels, octopus with lemon and olive oil, and fried prawns and squid.

Trattoria al Gatto Rosso
TRATTORIA $$
(☑ 099 452 98 75; www.ristorantegattorosso.com; Via Cavour 2; meals €30-35; ☺ Tue-Sun) A relaxed and unpretentious trattoria with a real touch of class – heavy tablecloths, deep wine glasses and the like. It is located in the new town and is very popular with discerning business types.

ℹ️ Information

Taranto splits neatly into three. The old town is on a tiny island, lodged between the northwest port and train station and the new city to the southeast. Italy's largest steel plant occupies the city's entire western half. The grid-patterned new city contains the banks, most hotels and restaurants and the **tourist office** (☑ 099 453 23 97; Corso Umberto I 113; ☺ 9am-1pm & 4.30-6.30pm Mon-Fri, 9am-noon Sat).

ℹ️ Getting There & Around

BUS

Buses heading north and west depart from Porto Mercantile. FSE buses go to Bari (€6, 1¾ to 2¼ hours, frequent). Infrequent **SITA** (☑ 899 32 52 04; www.sitabus.it) buses leave for Matera (€5, 1¾ hours, one daily). STP and FSE buses go to Lecce (€6, two hours, four daily).

Marozzi (☑ 080 5799 0111; www.marozzivt.it) has express services serving Rome's Stazione Tiburtina (€43, six hours, three daily). **Autolinee Miccolis** (☑ 099 470 44 51; www.miccolis-spa.it) serves Naples (€23, four hours, three daily) via Potenza (€15, two hours).

The bus **ticket office** (☺ 6am-1pm & 2-7pm) is at Porto Mercantile.

TRAIN

Trenitalia and FSE trains go to the following destinations:
Bari (€7.40, 2½ hours, frequent)
Brindisi (€5.10, 1¼ hours, frequent)
Rome (from €41, 6 to 7½ hours, five daily)

AMAT (☑ 099 452 67 32; www.amat.taranto.it) buses run between the train station and the new city.

BASILICATA

Basilicata has an other-worldly landscape of tremendous mountain ranges, dark forested valleys and villages so melded with the rockface that they seem to have grown there. Its isolated yet strategic location on routes linking ancient Rome to the eastern Byzantine empire has seen it successively invaded, pillaged, plundered, abandoned and neglected.

In the north the landscape is a fertile zone of gentle hills and deep valleys – once covered in thick forests, now cleared and cultivated with wheat, olives and grapes. The purple-hued mountains of the interior are impossibly grand and a wonderful destination for hikers and naturalists, particularly the soaring peaks of the Lucanian Apennines and the Parco Nazionale del Pollino.

On the coast, Maratea is one of Italy's most chic seaside resorts. However, Matera is Basilicata's star attraction, the famous *sassi* (former cave dwellings) of the cave city presiding over a rugged landscape of ravines and caves. Its ancient cave dwellings tell a tale of poverty, hardship and struggle; its history is best immortalised in writer Carlo Levi's superb book *Christ Stopped at Eboli* – a title suggesting Basilicata was beyond the hand of God, a place where pagan magic still existed and thrived.

Today, Basilicata is attracting a slow but steadily increasing trickle of tourists. For those wanting to experience a raw and unspoilt region of Italy, Basilicata's remote atmosphere and wild landscape will appeal.

History

Basilicata spans Italy's instep with slivers of coastline touching the Tyrrhenian and Ionian Seas. It was known to the Greeks and Romans as Lucania (a name still heard today) after the Lucani tribe who lived here as far back as the 5th century BC. The Greeks also prospered, settling along the coastline at Metapontum and Erakleia, but things

Basilicata

started to go wrong under the Romans, when Hannibal, the ferocious Carthaginian general, rampaged through the region.

In the 10th century the Byzantine emperor Basilikòs (976–1025) renamed the area, overthrowing the Saracens in Sicily and the south and reintroducing Christianity. The pattern of war and overthrow continued throughout the Middle Ages as the Normans, Hohenstaufens, Angevins and Bourbons constantly tussled over its strategic location, right up until the 19th century. As talk of the Italian unification began to gain ground, Bourbon-sponsored loyalists took to Basilicata's mountains to oppose political change. Ultimately, they became the much-feared bandits of local lore who make scary appearances in writings from the late 19th and early 20th centuries. In the 1930s Basilicata was used as a kind of open prison for political dissidents – most famously the painter, writer and doctor

Carlo Levi – sent into exile to remote villages by the fascists.

Matera

POP 60,500 / ELEV 405M

Approach Matera from virtually any direction and your first glimpse of its famous *sassi* is sure to stay in your memory forever. Haunting and beautiful, the *sassi* sprawl below the rim of a yawning ravine like a giant nativity scene. The old town is simply unique and warrants at least a day of exploration and aimless wandering. Although many buildings are crumbling and abandoned, others have been restored and transformed into cosy abodes, restaurants and swish cave-hotels. On the cliff top, the new town is a lively place, with its elegant churches, *palazzi* and especially the pedestrianised Piazza Vittorio Veneto.

History

Matera is said to be one of the world's oldest towns, dating back to the Palaeolithic Age and inhabited continuously for around 7000 years. The simple natural grottoes that dotted the gorge were adapted to become homes, and an ingenious system of canals regulated the flow of water and sewage. In the 8th century the caves became home to Benedictine and Basilian monks; the earliest cave paintings date from this period.

The prosperous town became the capital of Basilicata in 1663, a position it held until 1806 when the power moved to Potenza. In the decades that followed, an unsustainable increase in population led to the habitation of unsuitable grottoes – originally intended as animal stalls – even lacking running water. The dreadful conditions fostered a tough and independent spirit: in 1943, Matera became the first Italian city to rise up against German occupation.

By the 1950s more than half of Matera's population lived in the *sassi*, typical caves sheltering families with an average of six children. The infant mortality rate was 50%. In his poetic and moving memoir, *Christ Stopped at Eboli*, Carlo Levi describes how children would beg passers-by for quinine to stave off the deadly malaria. Such publicity finally galvanised the authorities into action and in the late 1950s about 15,000 inhabitants were forcibly relocated to new government housing schemes. In 1993 the *sassi* were declared a Unesco World Heritage Site, and the town is currently gearing up to be the European Capital of Culture in 2019. Ironically, the town's lack of development due to years of misery has transformed it into Basilicata's leading tourist attraction.

⊙ Sights & Activities

There are two *sasso* districts: the more restored, northwest-facing **Sasso Barisano** and the more impoverished, northeast-facing **Sasso Caveoso**. Both are extraordinary, riddled with serpentine alleyways and staircases, and dotted with frescoed *chiese rupestri* (cave churches) created between the 8th and 13th centuries. Today Matera contains some 3000 habitable caves.

The *sassi* are accessible from several points. There's an entrance off Piazza Vittorio Veneto, or take Via delle Beccherie to Piazza del Duomo and follow the tourist itinerary signs to enter either Barisano or Caveoso. Sasso Caveoso is also accessible from Via Ridola.

PUGLIA, BASILICATA & CALABRIA MATERA

WORTH A TRIP

POETIC VENOSA

About 70km north of Potenza, pretty Venosa used to be a thriving Roman colony, owing much of its prosperity to being a stop on the Appian Way. It was also the birthplace of the poet Horace in 65 BC. The main reason to come here is to see the remains of Basilicata's largest monastic complex.

Venosa's main square, Piazza Umberto I, is dominated by a 15th-century Aragonese castle with a small **Museo Archeologico** (☑ 0972 3 60 95; Piazza Umberto I; admission €2.50; ⊙ 9am-8pm Wed-Mon, 2-8pm Tue) that houses finds from Roman Venusia and human bone fragments dating back 300,000 years.

Admission to the museum also gets you into the ruins of the **Roman settlement** (⊙ 9am-1hr before dusk Wed-Mon, 2pm-1hr before dusk Tue) and the graceful later ruins of **Abbazia della Santissima Trinità** (☑ 0972 3 42 11). At the northeastern end of town, the *abbazia* (abbey) was erected above the Roman temple around 1046 by the Benedictines and predates the Norman invasions. Within the complex is a pair of churches, one unfinished. The earlier church contains the tomb of Robert Guiscard, a Norman crusader, and his fearsome half-brother Drogo. The other unfinished church was begun in the 11th century using materials from the neighbouring Roman amphitheatre. A little way south are some Jewish and Christian catacombs.

Hotel Orazio (☑ 0972 3 11 35; www.hotelorazio.it; Vittorio Emanuele II 142; s €45-50, d/t €65/85) is a 17th-century palace complete with antique majolica tiles and marble floors, and is overseen by a pair of grandmotherly ladies.

Venosa can be reached by taking bus S658 north from Potenza and exiting at Barile onto the S93. Buses run Monday to Saturday from Potenza (€3.30, two hours, two daily).

Matera

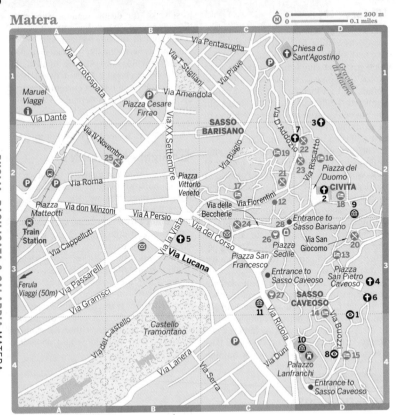

Matera

For a great photograph, head out of town for about 3km on the Taranto-Laterza road and follow signs for the *chiese rupestri*. This takes you up on the Murgia Plateau to the **Belvedere** (Taranto-Laterza Rd), from where you have fantastic views of the plunging ravine and Matera.

Sasso Barisano

Chiesa di Madonna delle Virtù & Chiesa di San Nicola del Greci   CHURCH
(Via Madonna delle Virtù; ⊙10am-7pm Sat & Sun) This monastic complex is one of the most important monuments in Matera and is composed of dozens of caves spread over two floors. **Chiesa Madonna delle Virtù** was built in the 10th or 11th century and restored in the 17th century. Above it, the simple **Chiesa di San Nicola del Greci** is rich in frescoes. The complex was used in 1213 by Benedictine monks of Palestinian origin.

Chiesa San Pietro Barisano   CHURCH
(Piazza San Pietro Barisano; adult/reduced €3/2, joint ticket with Chiesa di Santa Lucia alle Malve & Chiesa di Santa Maria d'Idris €6/4.50) Below the church is an ancient honeycomb of niches where corpses were placed for draining, while at the entrance level are 15th- and 16th-century frescoes. The empty frame of the altarpiece graphically illustrates the town's troubled recent history: the church was plundered when Matera was partially abandoned in the '60s and '70s.

Sasso Caveoso

Chiesa di San Pietro Caveoso   CHURCH
(Piazza San Pietro Caveoso) The only church in the *sassi* not dug into the tufa rock, Chiesa di San Pietro Caveoso was originally built in 1300 and has a 17th-century Romanesque-baroque facade.

Chiesa di Santa Maria d'Idris   CHURCH
(Piazza San Pietro Caveoso; adult/reduced €3/2, joint ticket with Chiesa San Pietro Barisano & Chiesa di Santa Lucia alle Malve €6/4.50; ⊙10am-1pm & 2.30-7pm Tue-Sun Apr-Oct, 10.30am-1.30pm Tue-Sun Nov-Mar) Dug into the Idris rock, this church has an unprepossessing facade, but the narrow corridor communicating with the recessed church of San Giovanni in Monterrone is richly decorated with 12th- to 17th-century frescoes.

Chiesa di Santa Lucia alle Malve   CHURCH
(Via la Vista; adult/reduced €3/2, joint ticket with Chiesa San Pietro Barisano & Chiesa di Santa Maria d'Idris €6/4.50; ⊙10am-1pm & 2.30-7pm Apr-Oct, 10.30am-1.30pm Tue-Sun Nov-Mar) Built in the 8th century to house a Benedictine convent, this church has a number of 12th-century frescoes including an unusual breastfeeding Madonna.

La Raccolta delle Acque   HISTORIC SITE
(☑340 6659107; www.laraccoltadelleacquematera.it; Via Bruno Buozzi 67; adult/child €2.50/1.50; ⊙9.30am-1pm & 2-7pm Apr-Oct, 9.30am-1pm Nov-Mar) Matera's fascinating water-storage system can be better understood when you visit this ancient complex of underground cisterns and canals, which was used to collect rainwater from roofs, streets and houses in the vicinity. The largest cistern is nearly 15m deep and 5m long.

Casa-Grotta di Vico Solitario   HISTORIC SITE
(admission €2) For a glimpse of life in old Matera visit this historic *sasso* off Via Bruno Buozzi. There's a bed in the middle, a loom, a room for manure and a section for a pig and a donkey. You also have access to a couple of neighbouring caves: in one, a black-and-white film depicts gritty prerestoration Matera.

Museo della Scultura Contemporanea   MUSEUM
(MUSMA; ☑366 9357768; www.musma.it; Via San Giacomo; adult/reduced €5/3.50; ⊙10am-2pm Tue-Sun & 4-8pm Sat & Sun Apr-Sep, 10am-2pm Tue-Sun Oct-Mar) Housed in Palazzo Pomarici, MUSMA is a fabulous contemporary

---

EXPLORING THE GORGE

In the picturesque landscape of the Murgia Plateau, the Matera Gravina cuts a rough gouge in the Earth, a 200m-deep canyon pockmarked with abandoned caves and villages. You can hike from the *sassi* (former cave dwellings) into the gorge (steps lead down from the parking place near the Monastero di Santa Lucia) and then up to the Belvedere in one to two hours, but a hike along the canyon rim gives you a better appreciation of the termitelike network of caves that gave birth to the *sassi*. Ferula Viaggi (p144) offers excellent guided hikes into the gorge, as well as a range of hiking and cycling tours throughout Basilicata and Puglia.

MATERA IN...

One Day

Zip out to the **Belvedere** (p141) for a photo-snap of the *sassi* (former cave dwellings) before any heat haze sets in. Back in the *sassi*, approach Sasso Barisano via Via Fiorentini and wind your way along to the monastic complex of **Madonna delle Virtù and San Nicola dei Greci** (p141) with its original frescoes. Then head for more frescoes in the rock churches of Sasso Caveoso, **Santa Maria d'Idris** (p141) and **Santa Lucia alle Malve** (p141). Wander through the *sassi*, imagining life in a cave, stopping to learn about Matera's fascinating system of underground cisterns at **La Raccolta delle Acque** (p141). Early evening, enjoy a *passeggiata* (evening stroll) in and around lively Piazza Vittorio Veneto, followed by dinner at classic **Ristorante Il Cantuccio** (p144).

Two Days

On day two, allow a couple of hours to visit the **Cripta del Peccato Originale**, with its magnificent frescoes. Then either spend the rest of the day hiking in the **gorge** or squeeze in a few museums in town, including the **Museo Nazionale d'Arte Medievale e Moderna della Basilicata**, which showcases Carlo Levi's bold panorama of village life, *Lucania '61*. In the heart of Sasso Caveoso the **Casa-Grotta di Vico Solitario** (p141) may sound a tad contrived but really *does* provide a vivid picture of former living conditions here – both the picturesque and rudimentary aspects. For contemporary sculptures, visit the cave-set **Museo della Scultura Contemporanea** (p141). Finish off with dinner and sunset vistas in a cave at stylish **Baccanti** (p144).

sculpture museum. The setting – deeply recessed caves and frescoed palace rooms – is extraordinary and the works themselves absorbing. You can also book a tour to visit the **Cripta del Peccato Originale** (Crypt of Original Sin), which is located 7km south of Matera and has well-preserved frescoes from the late 8th century. It's known as the Sistine Chapel of the cave churches and the frescoes depict dramatic Old Testament scenes.

The New Town

The focus of the town is Piazza Vittorio Veneto, an excellent, bustling meeting point for a *passeggiata* (evening stroll). It's surrounded by elegant churches and richly adorned *palazzi*, with their backs to the *sassi*; an attempt by the bourgeois to block out the shameful poverty the *sassi* once represented.

Museo Nazionale d'Arte Medievale e Moderna della Basilicata   MUSEUM
(☑ 0835 31 42 35; Palazzo Lanfranchi; adult/reduced €2/1; ⊙9am-8pm Thu-Tue) The stars of the show are Levi's paintings, including the panoramic mural *Lucania '61* depicting peasant life in biblical Technicolor. There's also some centuries-old sacred art from the *sassi*.

Cathedral   CATHEDRAL
(Piazza del Duomo; ⊙closed for renovation) Set high up in town, the subdued, graceful exterior of the 13th-century Puglian-Romanesque cathedral makes the neobaroque excess within all the more of a surprise: ornate capitals, sumptuous chapels and tons of gilding. Pediments mounted on its altars came from the temples at Metaponto. Matera's patron saint, the Madonna della Bruna, is hidden within the older church, **Santa Maria di Costantinopoli**, which can be accessed from the cathedral if it's open.

Museo Nazionale Ridola   MUSEUM
(☑ 0835 31 00 58; Via Ridola 24; adult/reduced €2.50/1.25; ⊙9am-8pm Tue-Sun, 2-8pm Mon) The impressive collection includes local Neolithic finds and some remarkable Greek pottery, such as the *Cratere Mascheroni*, a huge urn more than 1m high.

Tours

There are plenty of official guides for the *sassi* – try www.sassiweb.it. Alternatively, contact the **Cooperativa Amici del Turista** (☑ 0835 33 03 01; www.amicidelturista.it; Via Fiorentini 28-30) or English-speaking guide **Amy Weideman** (☑ 339 2823618; aweideman@libero.it; half-day tour for 2 people €40).

For excellent and informative guided visits, Ferula Viaggi (p144) has tours of the *sassi,* classic tours, underground tours, tours that include tastings or cookery courses, longer trips to the Pollino or into Puglia, and also hiking and cycling tours. Hikes range from short walks to weeklong trips. For a detailed list of walks, see Ferula Viaggi's **Walk Basilicata** (www.walkbasilicata. it). Ferula Viaggi also runs **Bike Basilicata** (www.bikebasilicata.it), which rents bikes and helmets, and supplies a road book and map so you can head off on your own. Guided bike tours include a seven-night 500km odyssey across Puglia and Basilicata.

★☆ Festivals & Events

Sagra della Madonna della Bruna RELIGIOUS
(⊙ 2 Jul) The colourful Procession of Shepherds parades ornately decorated papier-mâché floats around town. The finale is the *assalto al carro,* when the crowd descends on the main cart and tears it to pieces.

Gezziamoci MUSIC
(☑ 0835 33 02 00; www.gezziamociamatera.onyxjazzclub.it; ⊙ Last week of Aug) This jazz festival in the *sassi* and surrounding Murgia park.

🛏 Sleeping

★ **La Dolce Vita B&B** B&B $
(☑ 0835 31 03 24; www.ladolcevitamatera.it; Rione Malve 51; s €40-60, d €60-80; 🕲) This delightful

ecofriendly B&B in Sasso Caveoso has self-contained apartments with solar panels and recycled rainwater for plumbing. They're cool, comfortable and homey. Vincenzo is passionate about Matera and is a mine of information on the *sassi.*

★ **Le Monacelle** HOSTEL, HOTEL $
(☑ 0839 34 40 97; www.lemonacelle.it; Via Riscatto 9-10; dm/s/d €18/55/86; 🕲🕲) Near the *duomo* (cathedral), and incorporating the delightful small Chiesa di San Franceso d'Assisi chapel, this 16th-century building offers simple dorms and elegantly furnished rooms, as well as atmospheric cobbled terraces with stunning *sassi* views. It's warmly welcoming, and the gorge views from the breakfast terrace are a knockout.

Il Vicinato B&B $
(☑ 0835 31 26 72; www.ilvicinato.com; Piazzetta San Pietro Caveoso 7; s/d €60/70; 🕲🕲) This B&B enjoys a great, easy-to-find location. Rooms are decorated in clean modern lines, with views across to Idris rock and the Murgia Plateau. There's a room with a balcony and a small apartment, each with an independent entrance.

Sassi Hotel HOTEL $
(☑ 0835 33 10 09; www.hotelsassi.it; Via San Giovanni Vecchio 89; s/d €70/90, ste incl breakfast €110-160; 🕲🕲) The first hotel in the *sassi*

MATERA IN THE MOVIES

Matera's unique geography makes it wonderfully photogenic: Italian director, writer and intellectual Pier Paolo Pasolini filmed *Il Vangelo Secondo Matteo* (The Gospel According to St Matthew) here in 1964. Not a Christian himself, Pasolini set out on an exploration of the life of Christ using the words of the gospel itself. It is visually and conceptually hugely striking, infused with revolutionary spirit and featuring a cast of nonprofessional actors.

Forty years later, Mel Gibson came to town to make *The Passion of the Christ,* which follows in grueling detail the last 12 hours of Christ's life, from his arrest in the Garden of Gethsemane to his crucifixion at Golgotha; this was filmed at the Belvedere (p141). Mel's three-month stay in Matera was welcomed by the locals, many of whom were cast as extras; **Trattoria Lucana** (☑ 0835 33 61 17; Via Lucana 47; ⊙ Mon-Sat) still serves its homage dish *Fettuccine alla Mel Gibson.*

Film fans might want to follow a visit to Matera with a stay in nearby Bernalda, the ancestral home of film maker Francis Ford Coppola. In what is clearly a labour of love, Coppola has restored a historic mansion in the town to create the upmarket **Palazzo Margherita** (☑ 0835 54 90 60; www.coppolaresorts.com/palazzomargherita; Corso Umberto 64; ste incl breakfast & cooking lessons from €360-€1800, 2-night minimum stay) hotel. The lovely salon upstairs doubles as a screening room where you can watch classic Italian movies from a library compiled by Coppola for guests. And if you're just passing through, have a coffee at the hotel's Cinecittà bar, hung with glamorous black-and-white images of Italian stars and directors. You'll have to ask locals to find the hotel as it has no sign: Coppola prefers it to blend in to this otherwise unstarry little town.

is set in an 18th-century rambling edifice in Sasso Barisano with some rooms in caves and some not. Singles are small but doubles are gracefully furnished. The balconies have superb views of the cathedral.

★ **Hotel in Pietra** BOUTIQUE HOTEL $$
(☑ 0835 34 40 40; www.hotelinpietra.it; Via San Giovanni Vecchio 22; s €70-150, d €85-160, ste €180-230; ❄ @ 🎧) The lobby is set in a former 13th-century chapel complete with soaring arches, while the eight rooms combine soft golden stone with the natural cave interior. Furnishings are Zen-style with low beds, and the bathrooms are super stylish and include vast sunken tubs.

Locanda di San Martino HOTEL $$
(☑ 0835 25 66 00; www.locandadisanmartino.it; Via Fiorentini 71; d €89-200; ❄ 🎧 🏊) A sumptuous hotel where you can swim in a cave – in a subterranean underground swimming pool. The cave accommodation, complete with niches and rustic brick floors, is set around a warren of cobbled paths and courtyards.

Palazzo Viceconte HOTEL $$
(☑ 0835 33 06 99; www.palazzoviceconte.it; Via San Potito 7; d €95-140, ste €139-350; ❄ @) Rooms in this 15th-century *palazzo* near the cathedral have superb views of the *sassi* and gorge. The hotel is elegantly furnished and the rooftop terrace has panoramic views.

✕ Eating

Oi Marì PIZZERIA $
(☑ 0835 34 61 21; Via Fiorentini 66; pizzas from €6.50; ⊙ dinner daily, lunch Sat & Sun) In Sasso Barisano, this lofty and convivial cavern is styled as a Neapolitan pizzeria and has a great cheery atmosphere and excellent substantial pizzas to match, as well as *primi* of the day.

La Talpa TRADITIONAL ITALIAN $
(☑ 0835 33 50 86; Via Fiorentini 167; meals €15-20; ⊙ Wed-Mon) The cavernous dining rooms here are moodily lit and atmospheric. A popular spot for romancing couples.

★ **Ristorante Il Cantuccio** TRATTORIA $$
(☑ 0835 33 20 90; Via delle Becchiere 33; meals €25; ⊙ Tue-Sun) This quaint, homey trattoria near Piazza Vittorio Veneto is as welcoming as its chef and owner, Michael Lella. The menu is seasonal and the dishes traditional and delicious.

Le Botteghe TRATTORIA $$
(☑ 0835 34 40 72; Piazza San Pietro; mains €11.50-16; ⊙ lunch & dinner daily Apr-Sep, closed lunch Tue-Thu Oct-Mar) In Sasso Barisano, this is a classy but informal restaurant in arched whitewashed rooms. Try delicious local specialities like *fusilli mollica e crusco* (pasta and fried bread with local sweet peppers).

Baccanti TRADITIONAL ITALIAN $$$
(☑ 0835 33 37 04; www.baccantiristorante.com; Via Sant'Angelo 58-61; meals €50; ⊙ lunch & dinner Tue-Sat, lunch Sun) As classy as a cave can be. The design is simple glamour against the low arches of the cavern; the dishes are delicate and complex, using local ingredients. And the gorge views are sublime.

🍷 Drinking & Nightlife

L' Arturo Enogastronomia WINE BAR
(Piazza del Sedile 15) A chic little white-painted deli/wine bar towards the *duomo*. Staff will make you up an artisinal sandwich to go with your glass of local *vino*.

Shibuya BAR
(☑ 0835 33 74 09; Vico Purgatorio 12; ⊙ 9am-3am Tue-Sun) This cool little cafe and CD shop is also a bar and has regular DJs; make a beeline for the few outside tables at the top of an ancient alley.

🛍 Shopping

Geppetto CRAFT
(Piazza del Sedile 19; ⊙ 9.30am-1pm & 3.30-8pm) This craft shop stands out amongst the tawdrier outlets selling tufa lamps and tiles. Its speciality is the *cuccù*, a brightly painted ceramic whistle in the shape of a cockerel, which was once prized by Matera's children. The whistles were traditionally considered a symbol of good luck and fertility.

ℹ Information

The maps *Carta Turistica di Matera* and *Matera: Percorsi Turistici* (€1.50), available from various travel agencies, bookstores and hotels around town, describe a number of itineraries through the *sassi* and the gorge.

Basilicata Turistica (www.aptbasilicata.it) Official tourist website with useful information on history, culture, attractions and sights.

Ferula Viaggi (☑ 0835 33 65 72; www.ferulaviaggi.com; Via Cappelluti 34; ⊙ 9am-1.30pm & 3.30-7pm Mon-Sat) Excellent information centre and travel agency. Runs walking tours (www.walkbasilicata.it), cycling tours (www.

bikebasilicata.it), cooking courses and other great tours through Basilicata and Puglia.

Hospital (☑0835 25 31 11; Via Montescaglioso) About 1km southeast of the centre.

Internet Point (☑0835 34 41 66; Via San Biagio 9; per hour €3; ☉10am-1pm & 3.30-8.30pm)

Maruel Viaggi (☑0835 33 31 35; www.maruelviaggi.it; Via Dante; ☉9am-1.30pm & 4-8pm) Private travel agency and information centre with good information on buses. Can organise tours.

Parco Archeologico Storico Naturale delle Chiese Rupestri del Materano (☑0835 33 61 66; www.parcomurgia.it; Via Sette Dolori) For info on the Murgia park.

Police Station (☑0835 37 81; Via Gattini)

Post Office (Via Passerelli; ☉8am-6.30pm Mon-Fri, to 12.30pm Sat)

Sassiweb (www.sassiweb.it) Informative website on Matera.

❶ Getting There & Away

BUS

The **bus station** is north of Piazza Matteotti, near the train station.

Grassani (☑0835 72 14 43; www.grassani.it) Serves Potenza (€5.50, 1½ hours, four daily). Buy tickets on the bus.

Marino (www.marinobus.it) Runs two services daily to Naples (€12, four hours).

Marozzi (☑06 225 21 47; www.marozzivt. it) Runs three daily buses to Rome (€34, 6½ hours). A joint SITA and Marozzi service leaves daily for Siena, Florence and Pisa, via Potenza. Advance booking is essential.

Pugliairbus (☑080 580 03 58; http://pugliairbus.aeroportidipuglia.it) Operates a service to Bari airport (€5, 1¼ hours, four daily).

SITA (☑0835 38 50 07; www.sitabus.it) Goes to Taranto (€5.50, two hours, six daily) and Metaponto (€2.90, one hour, up to five daily) and many small towns in the province. Buy tickets from newspaper kiosks on Piazza Matteotti.

TRAIN

Ferrovie Appulo-Lucane (FAL; ☑0835 33 28 61; http://ferrovieappulolucane.it) runs regular trains (€4.50, 1½ hours, 12 daily) and buses (€4.50, 1½ hours, six daily) to Bari. For Potenza, take a FAL bus to Ferrandina and connect with a Trenitalia train, or head to Altamura to link up with FAL's Bari–Potenza run.

Potenza

POP 68,600 / ELEV 819M

Basilicata's regional capital, Potenza, has been ravaged by earthquakes (the last in 1980) and as the highest town in the land, it

broils in summer and shivers in winter. You may find yourself passing through as it's a major transport hub.

The centre straddles east to west across a high ridge. To the south lie the main Trenitalia and Ferrovie Appulo-Lucane train stations, connected to the centre by buses 1 and 10.

Potenza's few sights are in the old centre, at the top of the hill. To get there, take the elevators from Piazza Vittorio Emanuele II. The ecclesiastical highlight is the cathedral, erected in the 12th century and rebuilt in the 18th. The elegant Via Pretoria, flanked by a boutique or two, makes a pleasant traffic-free stroll, especially during the *passeggiata*.

In central Potenza, Al Convento (☑097 12 55 91; www.alconventopotenza.com; Largo San Michele Arcangelo 21; s/d €40/60; ❉@) is a great accommodation choice housing a mix of polished antiques and design classics.

Grassani (☑0835 72 14 43) has buses to Matera (€5.50, 1½ hours, four daily). SITA (☑0971 50 68 11; www.sitabus.it) has daily buses to Melfi, Venosa and Maratea. Buses leave from Via Appia 185 and also stop near the Scalo Inferiore Trenitalia train station. Liscio (☑097 15 46 73; www.autolineeliscio.it) buses serve various cities including Rome (€24, 4½ hours, three daily).

There are regular train services from Potenza to Foggia (from €6, 2¼ hours), Salerno (from €6, two hours) and Taranto (from €8.50, two hours). For Bari (from €14, three to four hours, three daily), take the Ferrovie Appulo-Lucane (☑0971 41 15 61; ferrovieappulolucane.it) train at Potenza Superiore station.

Appennino Lucano

The Appenino Lucano (Lucanian Apennines) bite Basilicata in half like a row of jagged teeth. Sharply rearing up south of Potenza, they protect the lush Tyrrhenian coast and leave the Ionian shores gasping in the semiarid heat. Careering along its hair-raising roads through the broken spine of mountains can be arduous, but if you're looking for drama, the drive could be the highlight of your trip.

Aliano

The fascists exiled writer and political activist Carlo Levi to this isolated region in 1935.

He lived, and is buried, in the tiny hilltop town of Aliano. Remarkably little seems to have changed since he wrote his dazzling *Christ Stopped at Eboli*, which laid bare the boredom, poverty and hypocrisy of village life. The **Pinacoteca Carlo Levi** (☑ 0835 56 83 15; admission €3; ⊙ 10am-1pm & 4-7.30pm summer, 10am-12.30pm & 3.30-6.30pm Thu-Tue winter) also houses the **Museo Storico di Carlo Levi**, featuring his papers, documents and paintings. Admission to the pinacoteca (art gallery) includes a tour of Levi's house and entry to the museum.

Aliano is accessible by SITA bus (€5.50) from Potenza.

Castelmezzano & Pietrapertosa

The two mountaintop villages of Castelmezzano (elevation 985m) and Pietrapertosa (elevation 1088m), ringed by the Lucanian Dolomites are spectacular. They are Basilicata's highest villages and are often swathed in cloud, making you wonder why anyone would build here – in territory best suited to goats.

Castelmezzano is surely one of Italy's most theatrical villages; the houses huddle along an impossibly narrow ledge that falls away in gorges to the Caperrino river. Pietrapertosa is even more amazing: the Saracen fortress at its pinnacle is difficult to spot as it is carved out of the mountain. You can now 'fly' between these two dramatic settlements courtesy of **Il Volo dell'Angelo** (The Angel Flight; ☑ Pietrapertosa 0971 98 31 10, Castelmezzano 0971 98 60 42; www.volodellangelo. com; per person €35-40, couples €63-72), a heart-in-mouth ride where you are supended, belly down, in a cradle harness, and whizzed via cables across the gorge. The organisers factor in time to explore whichever town you land in before the return cable ride.

You can spend an eerie night in Pietrapertosa at a delightful B&B, **La Casa di Penelope e Cirene** (☑ 0971 98 30 13; Via Garibaldi 32; d from €70). Dine at the authentic Lucano restaurant **Al Becco della Civetta** (☑ 0971 98 62 49; www.beccodellacivetta. it; Vicolo I Maglietta 7; meals €25; ⊙ Wed-Mon) in Castelmezzano, which also offers traditionally furnished, simple whitewashed rooms (double €80).

You'll need your own vehicle to visit Castelmezzano and Pietrapertosa.

Basilicata's Western Coast

Resembling a mini-Amalfi, Basilicata's Tyrrhenian coast is short (about 20km) but sweet. Squeezed between Calabria and Campania's Cilento peninsula, it shares the same beguiling characteristics: hidden coves and pewter sandy beaches backed by majestic coastal cliffs. The SS18 threads a spectacular route along the mountains to the coast's star attraction, the charming seaside settlements of Maratea.

Maratea

POP 5220

Maratea is a charming, if confusing, place at first, being comprised of several distinct localities ranging from a medieval village to a stylish harbour. The setting is lush and dramatic, with a coastal road (narrower even than the infamous Amalfi Coast road!) that dips and winds past the cliffs and pocket-size beaches that line the sparkling Golfo di Policastro. Studded with elegant hotels, Maratea's attraction is no secret and you can expect tailback traffic and fully booked hotels in July and August. Conversely, many hotels and restaurants close from October to March.

◉ Sights & Activities

Your first port of call should be the pretty **Porto di Maratea**, a harbour where sleek yachts and bright-blue fishing boats bob in the water, overlooked by bars and restaurants. Then there's the enchanting 13th-century medieval *borgo* (small town) of **Maratea Inferiore**, with pint-sized piazzas, wriggling alleys and interlocking houses, which offers startling coastal views. Attractive little shops sell ceramics and artisan food.

It's all overlooked by a 21m-high, gleaming white statue of **Christ the Redeemer** – don't miss the roller-coaster road and stupendous views from the statue-mounted summit – below which lie the ruins of **Maratea Superiore**, all that remains of the original 8th-century-BC Greek colony. Another option is the waymarked woodland path, which leaves the village from just beyond the Cappelle dei Cappuccini, and takes you to the statue in 45 minutes; where the path divides near the top, fork right.

The deep green hillsides that encircle this tumbling conurbation offer excellent walking trails and there are a number of easy day trips to the surrounding hamlets of **Acquafredda di Maratea** and **Fiumicello**, with its small sandy beach. The **tourist office** (☑ 0973 87 69 08; Piazza Gesù 40; ☺ 8am-2pm & 5-8pm Mon-Fri, 9am-1pm & 5-8pm Sat & Sun Jul & Aug, 8am-2pm Sep-Jun) is in Fiumicello.

Centro Sub Maratea (☑ 0973 87 00 13; www.marateaproloco.it/it/centro_sub_maratea; Via Santa Caterina 28) offers diving courses and boat tours that include visits to surrounding grottoes and coves.

A worthwhile day trip via car is to pretty **Rivello** (elevation 479m). Perched on a ridge and framed by the southern Apennines, it is a centre for arts and crafts and has long been known for its exquisite working of gold and copper. Rivello's interesting Byzantine history is evident in the tiny tiled cupolas and frescoes of its gorgeous churches.

🛏 Sleeping

B&B Nefer B&B $

(☑ 0973 87 18 28; www.bbnefer.it; Via Cersuta; r €60-90; P ❄ @ 🛜) This friendly B&B, set in the small hamlet of Cersuta 5km northwest of Maratea, has four rooms decorated in sea greens, blues and pinks. Rooms open onto a lush green lawn complete with deckchairs for contemplating the sea view. There's a simple outdoor kitchen area for guest use and a small rocky beach a short walk away.

★ Locanda delle Donne Monache HOTEL $$

(☑ 0973 87 74 87; www.locandamonache.com; Via Mazzei 4; r €130-310; ☺ Apr-Oct; P ❄ @ 🛜 ☀) Overlooking the medieval *borgo*, this exclusive hotel is in a converted 18th-century convent with a suitably lofty setting. It's a hotchpotch of vaulted corridors, terraces and gardens fringed with bougainvillea and lemon trees. The rooms are elegantly decorated in pastel shades, while the Sacello restaurant prepares delicate dishes drawing on the regional flavours of Lucania.

Hotel Villa Cheta Elite HOTEL $$

(☑ 0973 87 81 34; www.villacheta.it; Via Timpone 46; r €140-264; ☺ Apr-Oct; P ❄ 🛜) A charming art nouveau villa at the entrance to the hamlet of Acquafredda, this hotel has a broad terrace with spectacular views, a fabulous restaurant and large rooms decorated with antiques.

✖ Eating

La Caffetteria CAFE $

(Piazza Buraglia; panini from €4; ☺ 7.30am-2am summer, to 10pm winter) The outdoor seating at this delightful cafe in Maratea's central piazza is ideal for dedicated people-watching, and it serves homemade snacks throughout the day.

Taverna Rovita TRADITIONAL ITALIAN $$

(☑ 0973 87 65 88; www.tavernarovitamaratea.it; Via Rovita 13; meals €35; ☺ Mar-Oct) This tavern is just off Maratea Inferiore's main piazza. Rovita is excellent value and specialises in hearty local fare, with Lucanian specialities involving stuffed peppers, game birds, local salami and fine seafood.

Lanterna Rossa SEAFOOD $$

(☑ 0973 87 63 52; meals €40; ☺ daily Jul & Aug, Wed-Mon Feb-Dec) Head for the terrace overlooking the port to dine on exquisite seafood. Highly recommended is the signature dish, *zuppa di pesce* (fish soup).

❶ Getting There & Away

SITA (☑ 0971 50 68 11; www.sitabus.it) operates a comprehensive network of routes including a bus up the coast to Sapri in Campania (€1.80, 50 minutes, six daily). Local buses (€1.10) connect the coastal towns and Maratea train station with Maratea Inferiore, running frequently in summer. InterCity and regional trains on the Rome–Reggio line stop at Maratea train station, below the town.

CALABRIA

Tell a non-Calabrian Italian that you're going to Calabria and you will probably elicit some surprise, inevitably followed by stories of the 'ndrangheta – the Calabrian Mafia – notorious for smuggling and kidnapping wealthy northerners and keeping them hidden in the mountains.

But Calabria contains startling natural beauty and spectacular towns that seem to grow out of the craggy mountaintops. It has three national parks: the Pollino in the north, the Sila in the centre and the Aspromonte in the south. It's around 90% hills, but skirted by some 780km of Italy's finest coast (ignore the bits devoured by unappealing holiday camps). Bergamot grows here, and it's the only place in the world where the plants are of sufficient quality to produce the essential oil used in many perfumes and to flavour Earl Grey tea. As in Puglia, there are hundreds of music and food festivals here year-round, reaching a fever pitch in July and August.

Admittedly, you sometimes feel as if you have stepped into a 1970s postcard, as its towns, destroyed by repeated earthquakes, are often surrounded by brutal breeze-block suburbs. The region has suffered from the unhealthy combination of European and government subsidies (aimed to develop the south) and dark Mafia opportunism. Half-finished houses often mask well-furnished flats where families live happily, untroubled by invasive house taxes.

This is where to head for an adventure into the unknown.

History

Traces of Neanderthal, Palaeolithic and Neolithic life have been found in Calabria, but the region only became internationally important with the arrival of the Greeks in 8th century BC. They founded a colony at what is now Reggio di Calabria. Remnants of this colonisation, which spread along the Ionian coast with Sibari and Crotone as the star settlements, are still visible. However, the fun didn't last for the Greeks and in 202 BC the cities of Magna Graecia all came under Roman control. The Romans did irreparable geological damage destroying the countryside's handsome forests. Navigable rivers became fearsome *fiumare* (torrents) dwindling to wide, dry, drought-stricken riverbeds in high summer.

Calabria's fortified hilltop communities weathered successive invasions by the Normans, Swabians, Aragonese and Bourbons and remained largely undeveloped. Although the 18th-century Napoleonic incursion and the arrival of Garibaldi and Italian unification inspired hope for change, Calabria remained a disappointed, feudal region and, like the rest of the south, was racked by malaria.

A by-product of this tragic history was the growth of banditry and organised crime. Calabria's Mafia, known as the 'ndrangheta (from the Greek for heroism/virtue), inspires fear in the local community, but tourists are rarely the target of its aggression. For many, the only answer has been to get out and, for at least a century, Calabria has seen its young people emigrate in search of work.

Northern Tyrrhenian Coast

The good, the bad and the ugly line the region's western seashore.

The Autostrada del Sole (A3) is one of Italy's great coastal drives. It twists and turns through mountains, past huge swaths of dark-green forest and flashes of cerulean-blue sea. But the Italian penchant for cheap summer resorts has taken its toll here and certain stretches are blighted by shoddy hotels and soulless stacks of flats.

In the low season most places close. In summer many hotels are full, but you should have an easier time with the camping sites.

Praia a Mare

POP 6820

Praia a Mare lies just short of Basilicata, the start of a stretch of wide, pebbly beach that continues south for about 30km to Cirella and Diamante. This flat, leafy grid of a town sits on a wide pale-grey beach, looking out to an intriguing rocky chunk off the coast: the Isola di Dino.

Just off the seafront is the tourist office (☑ 0985 7 25 85; Via Amerigo Vespucci 6; ☉ 8am-1pm), which has information on the Isola di Dino sea caves. Alernatively, expect to pay around €5 for a guided tour from the old boys who operate off the beach.

Autolinee Preite (☑ 0984 41 30 01; www.autoservizipreite.it) operates buses to Cosenza (€5.50, two hours, 10 daily). SITA (☑ 0971 50 68 11; www.sitabus.it) goes north to Maratea and Potenza. Regular trains also pass through for Paola and Reggio di Calabria.

Aieta & Tortora

Precariously perched, otherworldly Aieta and Tortora must have been difficult to reach pre-asphalt. Rocco (☑ 0973 22 943; www.roccobus.it) buses serve both villages, 6km and 12km from Praia respectively. Aieta is higher than Tortora and the journey constitutes much of the reward. When you arrive, walk up to the 16th-century Palazzo Spinello at the end of the road and take a look into the ravine behind it – it's a stunning view.

Diamante

POP 5400

This fashionable seaside town, with its long promenade, is central to Calabria's famous *peperoncino* (chilli) the conversation-stalling spice that so characterises its cuisine. In early September a hugely popular chilli-eating competition takes place. Diamante is also famed for the bright murals that contemporary local and foreign artists have painted on the facades of the old buildings. For the best seafood restaurants head for the seafront at Spiaggia Piccola.

Autolinee Preite (☏ 0984 41 30 01; www.autoservizipreite.it) buses between Cosenza and Praia a Mare stop at Diamante.

Paola

POP 16,900

Paola is worth a stop to see its holy shrine. The large pilgrimage complex is above a sprawling small town where the dress of choice is a tracksuit and the main activity is hanging about on street corners. The 80km of coast south from here to Pizzo is mostly overdeveloped and ugly. Paola is the main train hub for Cosenza, about 25km inland.

Watched over by a crumbling castle, the **Santuario di San Francesco di Paola** (☏ 0982 58 25 18; ☉ 6am-1pm & 2-6pm) FREE is a curious, empty cave with tremendous significance to the devout. The saint lived and died in Paola in the 15th century and the sanctuary that he and his followers carved out of the bare rock has attracted pilgrims for centuries. The cloister is surrounded by naïve wall paintings depicting the saint's truly incredible miracles. The original church contains an ornate reliquary of the saint. Also within the complex is a modern basilica, built to mark the second millennium. Black-clad monks hurry about.

There are several hotels near the station, but you'll be better off staying in towns further north along the coast.

Cosenza

POP 69,800 / ELEV 238M

Cosenza's medieval core is Calabria's best-preserved historic centre, the one piece of history that has managed to escape the earthquakes that have levelled almost everything else in the region. It rises above the confluence of the Crati and Busento rivers, its narrow lanes winding ever upwards to the hilltop castle. Legend states that Alaric, a Visigoth king, was killed and buried at the confluence of the two rivers.

In the past Cosenza was a sophisticated and lively city, but nowadays there's a gritty feel to the old town with its dark, garbage-strewn streets and fading, once-elegant *palazzi*. It's the gateway to La Sila's mountains, home to Calabria's most important university and a major transport hub.

◉ Sights

In the new town, pedestrianised Corso Mazzini provides a pleasant respite from the chaotic traffic and incessant car honking. There are a number of sculptures lining the *corso*, including *Saint George and the Dragon* by Salvador Dalí.

In the old town, head up the winding, charmingly dilapidated Corso Telesio, which has a raw Neapolitan feel to it and is lined with ancient hung-with-washing tenements, antiquated shopfronts plus an instrument maker's and antiquated shoe mender's. The side alleys are a study in urban decay. At the top, the 12th-century **cathedral** (Piazza del Duomo; ☉ 8am-noon & 3-7.30pm) was rebuilt in restrained baroque style in the 18th century. In a chapel off the north aisle is a copy of an exquisite 13th-century Byzantine Madonna.

From the cathedral, you can walk up Via del Seggio through a little medieval quarter before turning right to reach the 13th-century **Convento di San Francesco d'Assisi** (off Via del Seggio). Otherwise head along the *corso* to Piazza XV Marzo, an appealing square fronted by the Palazzo del Governo and the handsome neoclassical **Teatro Rendano** (Piazza XV Marzo).

From Piazza XV Marzo, follow Via Paradiso, then Via Antonio Siniscalchi for the route to the down-at-heel Norman **castle** (Piazza Frederico II), left in disarray by several earthquakes. It's closed for restoration, but the view merits the steep ascent.

⎵ Sleeping

★ **B&B Via dell'Astrologo**　　　　B&B $

(☏ 338 9205394; www.viadellastrologo.com; Via Rutilio Benincasa 16; s €35-40, d €55-80, extra bed €20; ❀) A gem in the historic centre, this small B&B is tastefully decorated with polished wooden floors, white bedspreads, and good-quality artwork. Brothers Mario and

Calabria

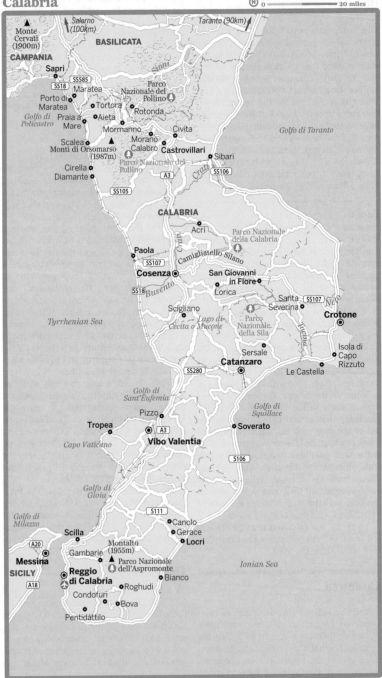

Marco are a mine of information on Cosenza and Calabria in general.

Ostello Re Alarico
HOSTEL $

(☑ 0984 79 25 70; www.ostellorealarico.com; Vico II Giuseppe Marini Serra 10; dm/s/d €16/30/50; ☎) On the opposite side of the river from the *duomo*, this restored palazzo housing doubles and dorms is something of a challenge to find. But the decor is an appealing combination of old (check out the ancient oven) and new. There's a pretty garden, and the young owner is a great enthusiast for the region.

Royal Hotel
HOTEL $$

(☑ 0984 41 21 65; www.hotelroyalsas.it; Via Molinella 24; s/d/t €55/65/75; P ❋ @ ☎) One of the few decent options in town, the Royal is a short stroll from Corso Mazzini. Rooms are impersonal but comfortable. Stay in the new section of the hotel.

✖ Eating

★ Gran Caffè Renzelli
CAFE $

(Corso Telesio 46) This venerable cafe behind the *duomo* has been run by the same family since 1803 when the founder arrived from Naples and began baking gooey cakes and desserts (cakes start at around €1.20). Sink your teeth into *torroncino torrefacto* (a confection of sugar, spices and hazelnuts) or *torta telesio* (made from almonds, cherries, apricot jam and lupins).

Ristorante Calabria Bella
CALABRIAN $

(☑ 0984 79 35 31; www.ristorantecalabriabella.it; Piazza del Duomo; meals €25; ⏱12.30-3pm & 7.15pm-midnight) Traditional Calabrian cuisine, such as *grigliata mista di carne* (mixed grilled meats), is regularly dished up in this cosy restaurant in the old town.

Per... Bacco!!
TRATTORIA $$

(☑ 0984 79 55 69; www.perbaccowinebar.it; Piazza dei Valdesi; meals €25) This smart yet informal restaurant has windows onto the square. Inside are exposed stone walls, vines and heavy beams. The reassuringly brief menu includes a generous and tasty antipasto (€8).

❶ Orientation

The main drag, Corso Mazzini, runs south from Piazza Bilotti (formerly known as Piazza Fera), near the bus station, and intersects Viale Trieste before meeting Piazza dei Bruzi. Head further south and cross the Busento river to reach the old town.

❶ Getting There & Around

AIR

Lamezia Terme airport (Sant'Eufemia Lamezia, SUF; ☑ 0968 41 43 33; www.sacal.it), 63km south of Cosenza, at the junction of the A3 and SS280 motorways, links the region with major Italian cities. The airport is served by Ryanair, easyJet and charters from northern Europe. A shuttle leaves the airport every 20 minutes for the airport train station where there are frequent trains to Cosenza (€4.60, one hour).

BUS

The main **bus station** (☑ 0984 41 31 24) is northeast of Piazza Bilotti. Services leave for Catanzaro (€4.80, 1¾ hours, eight daily) and towns throughout La Sila. **Autolinee Preite** (☑ 0984 41 30 01; www.autoservizipreite.it) has buses heading daily along the north Tyrrhenian coast; **Autolinee Romano** (☑ 0962 2 17 09; www.autolineeromano.com) serves Crotone as well as Rome and Milan.

TRAIN

Stazione Nuova (☑ 0984 2 70 59) is about 2km northeast of the centre. Regular trains go to Reggio di Calabria (from €12, three hours) and Rome (from €45, four to six hours), both usually with a change at Paola, and Naples (from €27, three to four hours), as well as most destinations around the Calabrian coast.

Amaco (☑ 0984 30 80 11; www.amaco.it) bus 27 links the centre and Stazione Nuova, the main train station.

Parco Nazionale della Sila

'La Sila' is a big landscape, where wooded hills create endless rolling views. It's dotted with small villages and cut through with looping roads that make driving a test of your digestion.

It's divided into three areas covering 130 sq km: the Sila Grande, with the highest mountains; the strongly Albanian Sila Greca (to the north); and the Sila Piccola (near Catanzaro), with vast forested hills.

The highest peaks, covered with tall Corsican pines, reach 2000m – high enough for thick snow in winter. This makes it a popular skiing destination. In summer the climate is coolly alpine, spring sees carpets of wildflowers and there's mushroom hunting in autumn. At its peak is the Bosco di Gallopani (Forest of Gallopani). There are several beautiful lakes, the largest of which is Lago di Cecita o Mucone near Camigliatello Silano. There is also plenty of wildlife here,

PARCO NAZIONALE DEL POLLINO

Italy's largest national park, the **Parco Nazionale del Pollino** (Pollino National Park; www.parcopollino.it), straddles Basilicata and Calabria and covers 1960 sq km. It acts like a rocky curtain separating the region from the rest of Italy and has the richest repository of flora and fauna in the south.

The park's most spectacular areas are **Monte Pollino** (2248m), **Monti di Orsomarso** (1987m) and the canyon of the **Gole del Raganello**. The mountains, often snowbound, are blanketed by forests of oak, alder, maple, beech, pine and fir. The park is most famous for its ancient *pino loricato* trees, which can only be found here and in the Balkans. The oldest specimens reach 40m in height.

The park has a varied landscape, from deep river canyons to alpine meadows, and is home to rare stocks of roe deer, wild cats, wolves, birds of prey (including the golden eagle and Egyptian vulture) and the endangered otters, *Lutra lutra*.

Good hiking maps are scarce. The *Carta Excursionistica del Pollino Lucano* (scale 1:50,000), produced by the Basilicata tourist board, is a useful driving map. The large-scale *Parco Nazionale del Pollino* map shows all the main routes and includes some useful information on the park, its flora and fauna and the park communities. Both maps are free and can be found in local tourist offices. You'll need your own vehicle to visit the Pollino.

Basilicata

In Basilicata the park's main centre is **Rotonda** (elevation 626m), which houses the official park office, **Ente Parco Nazionale del Pollino** (0973 66 93 11; Via delle Frecce Tricolori 6; 8am-2pm Mon-Fri, plus 3-5.30pm Mon & Wed). Interesting villages to explore include the unique Albanian villages of **San Paolo Albanese** and **San Costantino Albanese**. These isolated and unspoilt communities fiercely maintain their mountain culture and the Greek liturgy is retained in the main churches. For local handicrafts visit **Terranova di Pollino** for wooden crafts, **Latronico** for alabaster, and **Sant'Arcangelo** for wrought iron.

Asklepios (347 2631462, 0973 66 92 90; www.asklepios.it; Contrada Barone 9; s/d €30/50) has basic accommodation but is the place to stay for walkers as it's run by an English-speaking guide Giuseppe Cosenza who can also arrange mountain-biking and rafting trips.

including the light-grey Apennine wolf, a protected species.

During August, **Sila in Festa** takes place, featuring traditional music. Autumn is mushroom season, when you'll be able to frequent mushroom festivals, including the **Sagra del Fungo** in Camigliatello Silano.

◉ Sights & Activities

La Sila's main town, **San Giovanni in Fiore** (1049m), is named after the founder of its beautiful medieval **abbey**. The town has an attractive old centre, once you've battled through the suffocating suburbs, and is famous for its Armenian-style hand-loomed carpets and tapestry. You can visit the studio and shop of **Domenico Caruso** (0984 99 27 24; www.scuolatappeti.it), but ring ahead.

A popular ski-resort town with 6km of slopes, **Camigliatello Silano** (1272m) looks much better under snow. A few lifts operate on Monte Curcio, about 3km to the south. Around 5.5km of slopes and a 1500m lift can be found near **Lorica** (1370m), on gloriously pretty Lago Arvo – the best place to camp in summer.

Scigliano (620m), in Sila Piccola, is a small hilltop town and has a superb B&B. **Valli Cupe** (334 9174699, 333 8342866; www.vallicupe.it) runs hiking trips in the area around **Sersale** (739m) in the southeast, where there are myriad waterfalls and the dramatic Canyon Valli Cupe. Trips cost only €8 per person per day (Valli Cupe also runs horseriding tours). Specialising in botany, the guides (who speak Italian and French) also visit remote monasteries and churches. Stay in its rustic accommodation in the town.

🛏 Sleeping

★ **B&B Calabria** B&B $
(349 8781894; www.bedandbreakfastcalabria.it; Via Roma 9, Frazione Diano; s/d/t/q €35/60/75/80; Apr-Nov) In the mountains, this B&B has five comfortable rooms, all with separate entrances. Raffaele is a great source of infor-

Otherwise, the chalet-style **Picchio Nero** (☎ 0973 9 31 70; www.picchionero.com; Via Mulino 1; s/d incl breakfast €60/73; **P**) in Terranova di Pollino, with its Austrian-style wooden balconies and recommended restaurant, is a popular hotel for hikers; it's family-run, cosy and friendly, has a small garden and can help arrange excursions.

Two highly recommended restaurants include **Luna Rossa** (☎ 0973 9 32 54; Via Marconi 18; meals €35; ☻ Thu-Tue) in Terranova di Pollino, where creative local specialities are rustled up simply and with real flair in a rustic wood-panelled building providing breathtaking views, and **Da Peppe** (☎ 0973 66 12 51; Corso Garibaldi 13; meals €25-35; ☻ lunch & dinner Tue-Sun) in Rotonda, which uses wonderful local meat and woodland products such as truffles and mushrooms.

Calabria

Civita was founded by Albanian refugees in 1746. Other towns worth visiting are **Castrovillari**, with its well-preserved 15th-century Aragonese castle, and **Morano Calabro** – look up the beautiful MC Escher woodcut of this town. Naturalists should also check out the wildlife museum **Centro Il Nibbio** (☎ 0981 3 07 45; Vico Il Annunziata 11; admission €4; ☻ 10am-1pm & 4-8pm summer, 10am-1pm & 3-6pm winter) in Morano, which explains the Pollino ecosystem.

White-water rafting down the spectacular Lao river is popular in the Calabrian Pollino. **Centro Lao Action Raft** (☎ 0985 2 14 76; www.laoraft.com; Via Lauro 10/12) in Scalea can arrange rafting trips as well as canyoning, trekking and mountain-biking trips. Ferula Viaggi in Matera runs mountain-bike excursions and treks into the Pollino. For guided trips in Calabria visit www.guidapollino.it.

The park has a number of *agriturismi* (farm stay accommodation). Tranquil **Agriturismo Colloreto** (☎ 347 3236914; www.colloreto.it; s/d €28/56), near Morano Calabro, is in a remote rural setting, gorgeous amid rolling hills. Rooms are comfortable and old-fashioned with polished wood and flagstone floors. Also in Calabria, **Locanda di Alia** (☎ 0981 4 63 70; www.alia.it; Via Letticelle 55; s/d €90/120; **P ✳ ✼**) in Castrovillari offers bungalow-style accommodation in a lush green garden; it's famous for an outstanding restaurant, where you can sample delectable local recipes featuring peppers, pork, figs, anise and honey.

PUGLIA, BASILICATA & CALABRIA PARCO NAZIONALE DELLA SILA

mation on the region and can recommend places to eat, visit and go hiking. Rooms have character and clean modern lines and there's a wonderful terrace overlooking endless forested vistas. Mountain bikes available.

Hotel Aquila & Edelweiss　　HOTEL $
(☎ 0984 57 80 44; www.hotelaquilaedelweiss.com; Viale Stazione 15, Camigliatello Silano; s €60-80, d €90-120; **P ✳ @**) This three-star hotel in Camigliatello Silano has a stark and anonymous exterior but it's in a good location and the rooms are cosy and comfortable.

Valli Cupe　　B&B $
(☎ 333 6988835; www.vallicupe.it; Sersale; per person from €20) Valli Cupe can arrange a stay in a charming rustic cottage in Sersale, complete with an open fireplace (good for roasting chestnuts) and a kitchen. All bookings via its website.

Camping del Lago Arvo　　CAMPGROUND $
(☎ 0984 53 70 60; www.campinglagoarvo.it; Lorica; camping 2 people, tent & car €10-14, bungalows €40-

60) Lorica's lakeside is a particularly great place to camp. Try this large comfortable spot, near the Calabrian National Park office.

Park Hotel 108　　HOTEL $$
(☎ 0521 64 81 08; www.hotelpark108.it; Via Nazionale 86, Lorica; r €90-130; **P ☎**) Situated on the hilly banks of Lago Arvo, surrounded by dark-green pines, the rooms here are decorated in classic bland-hotel style – but who cares about decor with views like this!

🛍 Shopping

La Sila's forests yield wondrous wild mushrooms, both edible and poisonous. Sniff around the **Antica Salumeria Campanaro** (Piazza Misasi 5, Camigliatello Silano); it's a temple to all things fungoid, as well as an emporium of fine meats, cheeses, pickles and wines.

ℹ Information

Good-quality information in English is scarce. You can try the national park **visitors centre**

(☑ 0984 53 71 09) at Cupone, 10km from Camigliatello Silano, or the **Pro Loco tourist office** (☑ 0984 57 81 59; Via Roma; ☺ 9.30am-12.30pm & 3.30-6.30pm Wed-Mon) in Camigliatello Silano. A useful internet resource is the official park website (www.parcosila.it). The people who run B&B Calabria in the park are extremely knowledgeable and helpful.

For maps, you can use *Carta del Parco Nazionale della Sila* (€8), which has walking trails (in Italian). The *Sila for 4* is a miniguide in English that outlines a number of walking trails in the park. The booklet is available in tourist offices and from the privately run **New Sila Tourist Service Agency** (☑ 0984 57 81 25; Via Roma 16) – a good source of information on the park.

❶ Getting There & Away

You can reach Camigliatello Silano and San Giovanni in Fiore via regular Ferrovie della Calabria buses along the SS107, which links Cosenza and Crotone.

Ionian Coast

With its flat coastline and wide sandy beaches, the Ionian coast has some fascinating stops from Sibari to Santa Severina, with some of the best beaches on the coast around

Soverato. However, the coast has borne the brunt of some ugly development and is mainly a long, uninterrupted string of resorts, thronged in the summer months and shut down from October to May.

It's worth taking a trip inland to visit Santa Severina, a spectacular mountain-top town, 26km northwest of Crotone. The town is dominated by a Norman castle and is home to a beautiful Byzantine church.

Le Castella

This town is named for its impressive 16th-century Aragonese castle (admission €3; ☺ 9am-midnight summer, 9am-1pm & 3-6pm winter), a vast edifice linked to the mainland by a short causeway. The philosopher Pliny said that Hannibal constructed the first tower. Evidence shows it was begun in the 4th century BC, designed to protect Crotone in the wars against Pyrrhus.

Le Castella is south of a rare protected area (Capo Rizzuto) along this coast, rich not only in nature but also in Greek history. For further information on the park try www.riservamarinacaporizzuto.it.

With around 15 campsites near Isola di Capo Rizzuto to the north, this is the Ionian

---

MAGNA GRAECIA MUSEUMS OF THE IONIAN COAST

In stark contrast to the dramatic Tyrrhenian coast, the Ionian coast is a listless, flat affair dotted with large tourist resorts. However, the Greek ruins at Metaponto and Policoro, with their accompanying museums, bring alive the enormous influence of Magna Graecia in southern Italy.

Metaponto's Greek ruins are a rare site where archaeologists have managed to map the entire ancient urban plan. Settled by Greeks in the 8th and 7th centuries BC, Metapontum's most famous resident was Pythagoras, who founded a school here after being banished from Crotone (in Calabria) in the 6th century BC. After Pythagoras died, his house and school were incorporated into the Temple of Hera. The remains of the temple – 15 columns and sections of pavement – are Metaponto's most impressive sight. They're known as the Tavole Palatine (Palatine Tables; Parco Archeologico), since knights, or paladins, are said to have gathered here before heading to the Crusades. It's 3km north of town, just off the highway; to find it follow the slip road for Taranto onto the SS106.

In town, the Museo Archeologico Nazionale (☑ 0835 74 53 27; Via Aristea 21; admission €2.50; ☺ 9am-8pm Tue-Sun, 2-8pm Mon) houses artefacts from Metapontum and other sites while in the Parco Archeologico FREE, 2km northeast of the train station, are the remains of a Greek theatre and the Doric Tempio di Apollo Licio.

In Policoro, 21km southwest of Matera, the Museo della Siritide (☑ 0835 97 21 54; Via Colombo 8; admission €2.50; ☺ 9am-8pm Wed-Mon, 2-8pm Tue) has a fabulous display of artefacts from 7000 BC through to Lucanian ornaments, Greek mirrors and Roman spears and javelins.

SITA (p145) buses run from Matera to Metaponto (€2.90, one hour, up to five daily) and on to Policoro. Metaponto is on the Taranto–Reggio line; trains connect with Potenza, Salerno and occasionally Naples.

coast's prime camping area. Try **La Fattoria** (☑0962 79 11 65; Via del Faro; camping 2 people, car & tent €23, bungalows €60; ☺Jun-Sep), 1.5km from the sea. Otherwise, **Da Annibale** (☑0962 79 50 04; Via Duomo 35; s/d €50/70; P❉@☎) is a pleasant hotel in town with a splendid fish **restaurant** (meals €30; ☺lunch & dinner).

For expansive sea views dine at bright and airy **Ristorante Micomare** (☑0962 79 50 82; Via Vittoria 7; meals €20-25; ☺lunch & dinner).

Gerace

POP 2830

A spectacular medieval hill town, Gerace is worth a detour for the views alone – on one side the Ionian Sea, on the other dark, interior mountains. About 10km inland from Locri on the SS111, it has Calabria's largest Romanesque **cathedral**. Dating from 1045, later alterations have not robbed it of its majesty.

For a taste of traditional Calabrian cooking, the modest and welcoming **Ristorante a Squella** (☑0964 35 60 86; Viale della Resistenza 8; meals €20) makes for a great lunchtime stop that serves reliably good dishes, specialising in seafood and pizzas. Afterwards you can wander down the road and admire the views.

Further inland is **Canolo**, a small village seemingly untouched by the 20th century. Buses connect Gerace with Locri and also Canolo with Siderno, both of which link to the main coastal railway line.

Parco Nazionale dell'Aspromonte

Most Italians think of the **Parco Nazionale dell'Aspromonte** (www.parcoaspromonte.gov. it) as a hiding place used by Calabrian kidnappers in the 1970s and '80s. It's still rumoured to contain 'ndrangheta strongholds, but as a tourist you're unlikely to encounter any murky business. The national park, Calabria's second largest, is startlingly dramatic, rising sharply inland from Reggio. Its highest peak, **Montalto** (1955m), is dominated by a huge bronze statue of Christ and offers sweeping views across to Sicily.

Subject to frequent mudslides and carved up by torrential rivers, the mountains are nonetheless awesomely beautiful. Underwater rivers keep the peaks covered in coniferous forests and ablaze with flowers in spring. It's wonderful walking country and the park has several colour-coded trails.

Extremes of weather and geography have resulted in some extraordinary villages, such as **Pentidàttilo** and **Roghudi**, clinging limpetlike to the craggy, rearing rocks and now all but deserted. It's worth the drive to explore these eagle-nest villages. Another mountain eyrie with a photogenic ruined castle is **Bova**, perched at 900m above sea level. The drive up the steep, dizzying road to Bova is not for the faint-hearted, but the views are stupendous.

Maps are scarce. Try the **national park office** (☑0965 74 30 60; www.parcoaspromonte. gov.it; Via Aurora; ☺9am-1pm Mon-Fri, 3-5pm Tue & Thu) in **Gambarie**, the Aspromonte's main town and the easiest approach to the park. The roads are good and many activities are organised from here – you can ski and it's also the place to hire a 4WD; ask around in the town.

It's also possible to approach from the south, but the roads aren't as good. The co-operative **Naturaliter** (☑347 3046799; www. naturaliterweb.it), based in Condofuri, is an excellent source of information, and can help arrange walking and donkey treks and place you in B&Bs throughout the region. **Co-operativa San Leo** (☑347 3046799) based in Bova, also provides guided tours and accommodation. In Reggio di Calabria, you can book treks and tours with **Misafumera** (☑0965 67 70 21; www.misafumera.it; Via Nazionale 306d; week-long treks €260-480).

Stay on a bergamot farm at **Azienda Agrituristica Il Bergamotto** (☑347 6012338; Via Amendolea; per person €25) where Ugo Sergi can also arrange excursions. Hiking trails pass nearby so it's a good hiking base. The rooms are simple but it's in a lovely rural location, the views are wonderful and the food is delicious.

To reach Gambarie, take ATAM city bus 127 from Reggio di Calabria (€1, 1½ hours, up to six daily). Most of the roads inland from Reggio eventually hit the SS183 road that runs north to the town.

Reggio di Calabria

POP 185,900

Reggio is the main launching point for ferries to Sicily, which sparkles temptingly across the Strait of Messina. It is also home to the spectacular Bronzi di Riace and has a long, impressive seafront promenade –

PUGLIA, BASILICATA & CALABRIA REGGIO DI CALABRIA

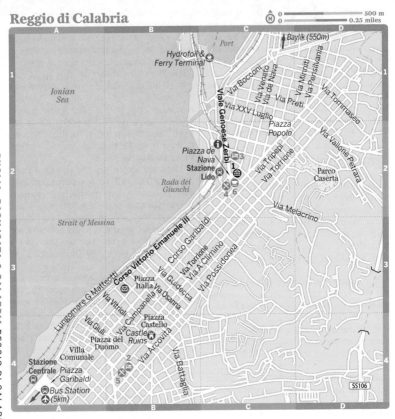

Reggio di Calabria

packed during the *passeggiata*. Otherwise, the city's grid system of dusty streets has the slightly dissolute feel shared by most ports.

Beyond the seafront, the centre gives way to urban sprawl. Ravaged by earth-quakes, the most recent in 1908, this once-proud ancient Greek city has plenty of other woes. As a port and the largest town close to the 'ndrangheta strongholds of Aspromonte, organised crime is a major problem, with the associated corrosive social effect.

On a lighter note, there are plenty of festivals in Reggio – early August sees the Festival dello Stretto (www.festivaldellostretto.it), featuring the traditional music of the south.

⊙ Sights

Museo Nazionale della
Magna Grecia   MUSEUM
(📞0965 81 22 55; www.archeocalabria.benicul-turali.it/; Piazza de Nava 26; adult/child €7/3; ☺ museum closed at the time of writing) The mu-seum's prides are the world's finest exam-ples of ancient Greek sculpture: the Bronzi di Riace, two extraordinary bronze statues

discovered on the seabed near Riace in 1972 by a snorkelling chemist from Rome. Larger than life, they depict the Greek obsession with the body: inscrutable, determined and fierce, their perfect form more godlike than human. The finest of the two has ivory eyes and silver teeth parted in a faint Mona Lisa smile. No one knows who they are – whether man or god – and even their provenance is a mystery. They date from around 450 BC; it's believed they're the work of two artists.

Aside from the bronzes, there are other magnificent ancient exhibits. Look for the 5th-century-BC bronze *Philosopher's Head,* the oldest-known Greek portrait in existence.

While the museum is undergoing extensive renovations, follow the brown 'laboratorio' signs to the Palazzo del Consiglio on Via Portanova where you can see the bronzes for free, albeit lying on their backs on trolleys. Ask to see the video (in English), which tells the gripping story of their discovery and restoration.

🛏 Sleeping

Finding a room should be easy, even in summer, since most visitors pass straight through en route to Sicily.

B&B Casa Blanca   B&B $
(☑347 9459210; www.bbcasablanca.it; Via Arcovito 24; s €50-60, d €70-90; ❈🞸) A little gem in Reggio's heart, this 19th-century *palazzo* has spacious rooms gracefully furnished with romantic white-on-white decor. There's a self-serve breakfast nook, a small breakfast table in each room and two apartments available. Great choice.

Hotel Lido   HOTEL
(☑0965 2 50 01; www.hotellido.rc.it; Via Tre Settembre 6; s/d €60/100; 🞸) A pleasant hotel with modern rooms washed in pastel colours with colourful artwork, Sky TV and the possibility of activities, including nearby windsurfing.

🍴 Eating & Drinking

La Cantina del Macellaio   TRATTORIA $
(☑0965 2 39 32; www.lacantinadelmacellaio.com; Via Arcovito 26; meals €25; ☻dinner daily, lunch Sun) This popular trattoria, recommended by locals, dishes up typical Calabrian cuisine with an emphasis on meat dishes. The wine cellar is extensive and impressive.

Cèsare   GELATERIA $
(Piazza Indipendenza; ☻6am-1am) The most popular gelateria in town is in a green kiosk at the end of the *lungomare* (seafront).

Baylik   SEAFOOD $$
(☑0965 4 86 24; Vico Leone 3; meals €30; ☻lunch daily, dinner Fri-Wed) Worth the slight trek, Baylik is friendly, and the calamari is so fresh your knife glides through it like butter; the spaghetti with clams is another winner.

Caffe Matteotti   CAFE
(www.caffematteotti.it; Corso Vittorio Emanuele 39; ☻7am-2am Tue-Sun) The stylish white tables and chairs on their terrace offer sea views with your *aperitivi*: it's a prime spot for people-watching.

ℹ Information

Walk northeast along Corso Garibaldi for the tourist office, shopping and other services. The *corso* has long been a de facto pedestrian zone during the ritual *passeggiata*.

Hospital (☑0965 39 71 11; Via Melacrino)

Police Station (☑0965 41 11 11; Corso Garibaldi 442)

Post Office (Via Miraglia 14)

Tourist Information Kiosk (Viale Genovese Zerbi; ☻9am-noon & 4-7pm) There are also kiosks at both the Airport (☑0965 64 32 91) and the Stazione Centrale (☑0965 2 71 20).

ℹ Getting There & Away

AIR

Reggio's **airport** (REG; ☑0965 64 05 17; www.aeroportodellostretto.it) is at Ravagnese, about 5km south.

BOAT

Boats for Messina (Sicily) leave from the port (just north of Stazione Lido), where there are three adjacent ferry terminals. In high season there are up to 20 hydrofoils daily; in low season there are as few as two. Some boats continue to the Aeolian Islands.

Services are run by various companies, including **Meridiano** (☑0965 81 04 14; www.meridianolines.it). Prices for cars are €15 one way and for foot passengers €1.50 to €2.80. The crossing takes 20 minutes.

BUS

Most buses terminate at Piazza Garibaldi, in front of the Stazione Centrale. Several different companies operate to towns in Calabria and beyond. Regional trains are more convenient than bus services to Scilla and Tropea.

ATAM (☑ 800 43 33 10; www.atam-rc.it)
Serves the Aspromonte Massif, with bus 127 to
Gambarie (€1.10, 1½ hours, six daily).

Lirosi (☑ 0966 5 79 01) Serves Rome (€48,
eight hours, two daily).

CAR & MOTORCYCLE

The A3 ends at Reggio, via a series of long tunnels. If you are continuing south, the SS106 hugs
the coast round the 'toe', then heads north along
the Ionian Sea.

TRAIN

Trains stop at **Stazione Centrale** (☑ 0965 89 20
21), the main train station at the town's southern
edge, and less frequently at Stazione Lido, near
the museum. There are frequent trains to Milan
(from €140, 9½ to 11½ hours), Rome (from €70,
7½ hours) and Naples (from €55, 4½ to 5½
hours). Regional services run along the coast to
Scilla and Tropea, and also to Catanzaro and less
frequently to Cosenza and Bari.

❶ Getting Around

Orange local buses run by ATAM cover most of
the city. For the port, take bus 13 or 125 from
Piazza Garibaldi outside Stazione Centrale. The
Porto–Aeroporto bus, bus 125, runs from the
port via Piazza Garibaldi to the airport and vice
versa (25 minutes, hourly). Buy your ticket at
ATAM offices, tobacconists or news stands.

Southern Tyrrhenian Coast

North of Reggio, along the coast-hugging
Autostrada del Sole (A3), the scenery rocks
and rolls to become increasingly beautiful
and dramatic, if you ignore the shoddy holiday camps and unattractive developments
that sometimes scar the land. Like the
northern part of the coast, it's mostly quiet
in winter and packed in summer.

Scilla

POP 5160

In Scilla, cream-, ochre- and earth-coloured
houses cling on for dear life to the jagged
promontory, ascending in jumbled ranks
to the hill's summit, which is crowned by
a castle and, just below, the dazzling white
confection of the **Chiesa Arcipretale Maria
Immacolata**. Lively in summer and serene
in low season, the town is split in two by the
tiny port. The fishing district of Scilla Chia-
nalea, to the north, harbours small hotels
and restaurants off narrow lanes, lapped by
the sea. It can only be visited on foot.

Scilla's high point is a rock at the northern
end, said to be the lair of Scylla, the mythical six-headed sea monster who drowned
sailors as they tried to navigate the Strait
of Messina. Swimming and fishing off the
town's glorious white sandy beach is somewhat safer today. Head for Lido Paradiso
from where you can squint up at the castle
while sunbathing on the sand.

◉ Sights

Castello Ruffo   CASTLE
(☑ 0956 70 42 07; admission €1.50; ◷ 8.30am-
7.30pm) An imposing hilltop fortress, the
castle has at times been a lighthouse and a
monastery. It houses a *luntre,* the original
black boat used for swordfishing, and on
which the modern-day *passarelle* is based.

🛏 Sleeping

Le Piccole Grotte   B&B $
(☑ 338 2096727; www.lepiccolegrotte.it; Via Grotte
10; d €90-120; 🕸 🛜) In the picturesque Chi-
analea district, this B&B is housed in a 19th-
century fisher's house beside steps leading
to the crystal-clear sea. Rooms have small
balconies facing the cobbled alleyway or the
sea.

La Locandiera   B&B $
(☑ 0965 75 48 81; www.lalocandiera.org; Via Zagari
27; d €60-100; 🕸 🛜) Run by the same people
who own Le Piccole Grotte, this B&B is
just as picturesque with large, comfortable
rooms and views over the sea.

🍴 Eating & Drinking

Bleu de Toi   SEAFOOD $$
(☑ 0965 79 05 85; www.bleudetoi.it; Via Grotte 40;
meals €30-35; ◷ Wed-Mon) Soak up the Chia-
nalea atmosphere at this little restaurant. It
has a terrace over the water and excellent
seafood dishes, including Scilla's renowned
swordfish.

Dali City Pub   BAR
(Via Porto) On the beach in Scilla town, this
popular bar has a Beatles tribute corner
(appropriately named The Cavern) and has
been going since 1972.

Capo Vaticano

There are spectacular views from this rocky
cape, with its beaches, ravines and limestone
sea cliffs. Birdwatchers' spirits should soar.
Around 7km south of Tropea, Capo Vaticano
has a lighthouse, built in 1885, which is close

to a short footpath from where you can see as far as the Aeolian Islands. Capo Vaticano beach is one of the balmiest along this coast.

Tropea

POP 6780

Tropea, a puzzle of lanes and piazzas, is famed for its captivating prettiness, dramatic position and sunsets the colour of amethyst. It sits on the Promontorio di Tropea, which stretches from Nicotera in the south to Pizzo in the north. The coast alternates between dramatic cliffs and icing-sugar-soft sandy beaches, all edged by translucent sea. Unsurprisingly, hundreds of Italian holidaymakers descend here in summer. If you hear English being spoken it is probably from Americans visiting relatives: enormous numbers left the region for America in the early 20th century.

Despite the mooted theory that Hercules founded the town, it seems this area has been settled as far back as Neolithic times. Tropea has been occupied by the Arabs, Normans, Swabians, Anjous and Aragonese, as well as being attacked by Turkish pirates. Perhaps they were after the town's famous red onions, so sweet they can be turned into marmalade.

◉ Sights

Cathedral   CATHEDRAL
(⊗6.30-11.30am & 4-7pm) The beautiful Norman cathedral has two undetonated WWII bombs near the door: it's believed they didn't explode due to the protection of the town's patron saint, Our Lady of Romania. A Byzantine icon (1330) of the Madonna hangs above the altar – she is also credited with protecting the town from the earthquakes that have pummelled the region.

Santa Maria dell'Isola   CHURCH
The town overlooks Santa Maria dell'Isola, a medieval church with a Renaissance makeover, which sits on its own island, although centuries of silt have joined it to the mainland.

🛏 Sleeping

★ Donnaciccina   B&B $$
(☑0963 6 21 80; www.donnaciccina.com; Via Pelliccia 9; s €40-75, d €80-150; ※@💲) Overlooking the main *corso,* this delightful B&B has retained a tangible sense of history with its carefully selected antiques, canopy beds and terracotta tiled floors. There's also a self-

catering apartment perfectly positioned on the cliff overlooking the sea, and a chatty parrot in reception.

Residence il Barone   B&B $$
(☑0963 60 71 81; www.residenzailbarone.it; Largo Barone; €70-190; ※@💲) This graceful *palazzo* has six suites decorated in masculine neutrals and tobacco browns, with dramatic modern paintings by the owner's brother adding pizazz to the walls. There's a computer in each suite and you can eat breakfast on the small roof terrace with views over the old city and out to sea.

✕ Eating

Al Pinturicchio   TRADITIONAL ITALIAN $
(☑0963 60 34 52; Via Dardona, cnr Largo Duomo; meals €16-22; ⊗dinner) Recommended by the locals, this restaurant in the old town has a romantic ambience, candlelit tables and a menu of imaginative dishes.

Osteria del Pescatore   SEAFOOD $
(☑0963 60 30 18; Via del Monte 7; meals €20-25; ⊗dinner Thu-Tue) Swordfish rates highly on the menu at this simple seafood place tucked away in the backstreets.

ℹ Information

CST Tropea (☑0963 6 11 78; www.csttropea.it; Largo San Michele 7; ⊗9am-1pm & 4-7.30pm Sep-Jun, to 10pm Jul & Aug) Helpful tourist office at the entrance to the old town. Can organize trekking, mountain biking, diving and cultural tours.

Tourist Office (☑0963 6 14 75; Piazza Ercole; ⊗9am-1pm & 4-8pm) In the old town centre.

ℹ Getting There & Away

Trains run to Pizzo (€1.95, 30 minutes, 12 daily), Scilla (€3.70, one hour 20 minutes, every 30 minutes) and Reggio (from €5, two hours, every 30 minutes). **SAV** (☑0963 611 29) buses connect with other towns on the coast.

Pizzo

POP 9240

Stacked high up on a sea cliff, pretty little Pizzo is the place to go for *tartufo,* a death-by-chocolate ice-cream ball, and to see an extraordinary rock-carved grotto church. It's a popular and cheerful tourist stop. Piazza della Repubblica is the epicentre, set high above the sea with great views. Settle here at one of the many gelateria terraces for an ice-cream fix.

Pizzo is located just off the major A3 autostrada; the nearest train station, Vibo Valentia-Pizzo, is located 4km south of town. A bus service connects you to Pizzo.

◉ Sights

Chiesa di Piedigrotta   CAVE
(admission €2.50; ☺9am-1pm & 3-7.30pm) The Chiesa di Piedigrotta is an underground cave full of carved stone statues. It was carved into the tufa rock by Neapolitan shipwreck survivors in the 17th century. Other sculptors added to it and it was eventually turned into a church. Later statues include the less-godly figures of Fidel Castro and John F Kennedy. It's a bizarre, one-of-a-kind mixture of mysticism, mystery and kitsch. Buy tickets at the restaurant above the cave.

Chiesa Matrice di San Giorgio   CHURCH
(Via Marconi) In town, the 16th-century Chiesa Matrice di San Giorgio, with its dressed-up Madonnas, houses the tomb of Joachim Murat, brother of Napoleon and one-time king of Naples. Although he was the architect of enlightened reforms, the locals showed no great concern when Murat was imprisoned and executed here.

Castello Murat   CASTLE
(☑0963 53 25 23; adult/reduced €2.50/1.50; ☺9am-1pm & 3pm-midnight Jun-Sep, 9am-1pm & 3-7pm Oct-May) At the neat little 15th-century Castello Murat, south of Piazza della Repubblica, you can see Murat's cell. His last days and death by firing squad are graphically illustrated by waxworks.

🛏 Sleeping & Eating

Armonia B&B   B&B $
(☑0963 53 33 37; www.casaarmonia.com; Via Armonia 9; s without bathroom €30-60, d without bathroom €40-75; ◉) Run by the charismatic Franco in his 18th-century family home, this B&B has a number of rooms.

Ristorante Pizzeria Don Diego   PIZZERIA $
(☑0963 06 01 07; www.ristorantedondiegopizzo.com; Via M Salomone 243; mains €20) Eat at Ristorante Pizzeria Don Diego, with its spectacular sea views and tasty pizzas.

Sicily

Best Places to Eat

➡ Trattoria Ai Cascinari (p173)

➡ Ti Vitti (p178)

➡ Fattoria delle Torri (p209)

➡ Il Liberty (p208)

Best Places to Stay

➡ Pensione Tranchina (p221)

➡ Villa Athena (p213)

➡ Hotel Signum (p184)

➡ Hotel Villa Belvedere (p190)

Why Go?

More of a sugar-spiked espresso than a milky cappuccino, Sicily rewards visitors with an intense, bittersweet experience. Overloaded with art treasures and natural beauty, under-supplied with infrastructure and continuously struggling against Mafia-driven corruption, Sicily's complexities sometimes seem unfathomable. To really appreciate this place, come with an open mind – and a healthy appetite. Despite the island's perplexing contradictions, one factor remains constant: the uncompromisingly high quality of the cuisine.

After 25 centuries of foreign domination, Sicilians are heirs to an impressive cultural legacy, from the refined architecture of Magna Graecia to the Byzantine splendour and Arab craftsmanship of the island's Norman cathedrals and palaces. This cultural richness is matched by a startlingly diverse landscape that includes bucolic farmland, smouldering volcanoes and kilometres of island-studded aquamarine coastline.

When to Go
Palermo

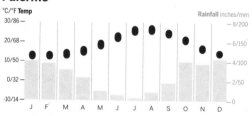

Easter Colourful religious processions and marzipan lambs in every bakery window.

May Wildflowers, dreamy coastal walking and Syracuse's festival of classic drama.

Sep Prime diving off Ustica and other seaside fun without summer prices.

Sicily Highlights

1. Joining the ranks of opera-goers at elegant Teatro Massimo in **Palermo** (p165).

2. Bargaining with the fish vendors at dawn, climbing Europe's most active volcano in the afternoon and enjoying Sicily's nightlife in **Catania** (p192).

3. Marvelling at the majesty of **Segesta** (p222), where a Doric temple sits in splendid isolation on a windswept hillside.

4. Watching international stars perform against the breathtaking backdrop of Mt Etna at the summer performing arts festivals in **Taormina** (p187).

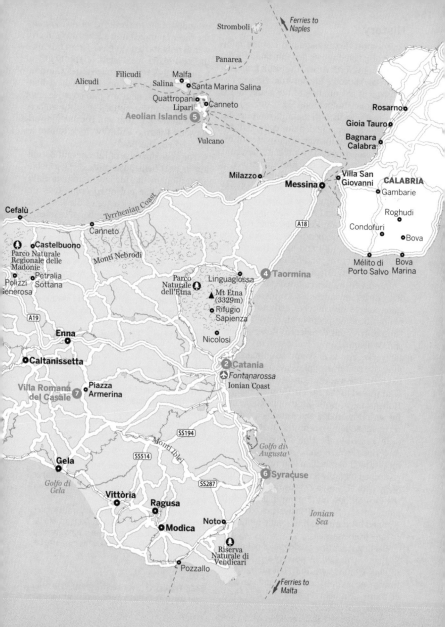

Stromboli

Ferries to
Naples

Panarea

Filicudi   Malfa
Alicudi   Salina
         Santa Marina Salina
         Quattropani
         Lipari   Canneto
Aeolian Islands **5**

Vulcano

Rosarno

Gioia Tauro

Bagnara
Calabra

Milazzo   Villa San
           Giovanni   **CALABRIA**

Messina   Gambarie

Cefalù   *Tyrrhenian Coast*   Roghudi

Canneto   A18   Condofuri   Bova

Castelbuono
Parco Naturale   Monti Nebrodi   Mélito di   Bova
Regionale delle   Porto Salvo Marina
Madonie
Petralia   Parco   Linguaglossa   **4** Taormina
Polizzi   Naturale
Sottana   dell'Etna   ▲ Mt Etna
Generosa   (3329m)
A19   Rifugio
                          Sapienza
Enna
                          Nicolosi
Caltanissetta
                          2 Catania
Villa Romana   Piazza   ☨ Fontanarossa
del Casale **7** Armerina Ionian Coast

                SS194   *Golfo di*
                           Augusta
Gela   SS514
        Golfo di SS287   **6** Syracuse
        Gela
        Vittòria
        Ragusa   *Ionian*
                            Sea
        Modica   Noto

                  Riserva
                  Naturale di
                  Vendicari
        Pozzallo
                  Ferries to
                  Malta

5 Soaking up the sun, watching Stromboli's volcanic fireworks and hiking to your heart's content on the stunningly scenic **Aeolian Islands** (p179).

6 Wandering aimlessly in Ortygia's atmospheric alleys or among the citrus groves, caves and ruins of the vast archaeological park in **Syracuse** (p199).

7 Admiring prancing wild beasts and dancing bikini-clad gymnasts on the newly restored mosaic floors of **Villa Romana del Casale** (p216).

History

Sicily's most deeply ingrained cultural influences originate from its first inhabitants – the Sicani from North Africa, the Siculi from Latium (Italy) and the Elymni from Greece. The subsequent colonisation of the island by the Carthaginians (also from North Africa) and the Greeks, in the 8th and 6th centuries BC respectively, compounded this cultural divide through decades of war when powerful opposing cities struggled to dominate the island.

Although part of the Roman Empire, it was not until the Arab invasions of AD 831 that Sicily truly came into its own. Trade, farming and mining were all fostered under Arab influence and Sicily soon became an enviable prize for European opportunists. The Normans, desperate for a piece of the pie, invaded in 1061 and made Palermo the centre of their expanding empire and the finest city in the Mediterranean.

Impressed by the cultured Arab lifestyle, King Roger squandered vast sums on ostentatious palaces and churches, and encouraged a hedonistic atmosphere in his court. But such prosperity – and decadence (Roger's grandson, William II, even had a harem) – inevitably gave rise to envy and resentment and, after two centuries of pleasure and profit, the Norman line was extinguished and the kingdom passed to the austere German House of Hohenstaufen, with little opposition from the seriously eroded and weakened Norman occupation. In the centuries that followed, Sicily passed to the Holy Roman Emperors, Angevins (French) and Aragonese (Spanish) in a turmoil of rebellion and revolution that continued until the Spanish Bourbons united Sicily with Naples in 1734 as the Kingdom of the Two Sicilies. Little more than a century later, on 11 May 1860, Giuseppe Garibaldi planned his daring and dramatic unification of Italy from Marsala.

Reeling from this catalogue of colonisers, Sicilians struggled in poverty-stricken conditions. Unified with Italy, but no better off, nearly one million men and women emigrated to the USA between 1871 and 1914 before the outbreak of WWI.

Ironically, the Allies (seeking Mafia help in America for the reinvasion of Italy) helped in establishing the Mafia's stranglehold on Sicily. In the absence of suitable administrators, they invited the undesirable *mafioso* (Mafia boss) Don Calógero Vizzini to do the job. When Sicily became a semi-autonomous region in 1948, Mafia control extended right to the heart of politics, and the region plunged into a 50-year silent civil war. It only started to emerge from this after the anti-Mafia maxi-trials of the 1980s, in which Sicily's revered magistrates Giovanni Falcone and Paolo Borsellino hauled hundreds of Mafia members into court, leading to important prosecutions against members of the massive heroin and cocaine network between Palermo and New York, known as the 'pizza connection'.

The assassinations of Falcone and Borsellino in 1992 helped galvanise Sicilian public opposition to the Mafia's inordinate influence, and while organised crime lives on, the thuggery and violence of the 1980s has diminished. A growing number of businesses refuse to pay the extortionate protection money known as the *pizzo*, and there continue to be important arrests, further encouraging those who would speak out against the Mafia. On the political front, two anti-Mafia crusaders were elected to high-profile posts in 2012, Palermo mayor Leoluca Orlando and Sicilian governor Rosario Crocetta.

ℹ Getting There & Away

AIR

An increasing number of airlines fly direct to Sicily's three international airports – Palermo (PMO), Catania (CTA) and Trapani (TPS) – although many still require a transfer in Rome or Milan. **Alitalia** (www.alitalia.com) is the main Italian carrier, while **Ryanair** (☑ 899 55 25 89; www.ryanair.com) is the leading low-cost airline carrier serving Sicily.

BOAT

Regular car and passenger ferries cross the strait between Villa San Giovanni (Calabria) and Messina, while hydrofoils connect Messina with Reggio di Calabria.

Sicily is also accessible by ferry from Naples, Genoa, Civitavecchia, Salerno, Cagliari, Malta and Tunisia. Prices rise between June and September, when advanced bookings may also be required.

BUS

SAIS Trasporti (www.saistrasporti.it) runs long-haul services to Sicily from Rome and Naples.

TRAIN

Direct trains run from Milan, Florence, Rome, Naples and Reggio di Calabria to Messina and on to Palermo, Catania and other provincial capitals – the trains are transported from the mainland by ferry from Villa San Giovanni.

For travellers originating in Rome and points south, InterCity trains cover the distance from mainland Italy to Sicily in the least possible time, without a change of train. If coming from Milan, Bologna or Florence, your fastest option is to take the ultra-high-speed Frecciarossa as far as Naples, then change to an InterCity train for the rest of the journey.

If saving money is your top priority, Espresso or InterCity night trains will still get you to Sicily relatively fast, and won't take such a big bite out of your budget.

ℹ Getting Around

AIR

Regular domestic flights serve the offshore islands of Pantelleria and Lampedusa. Local carriers include Alitalia and Darwin Airline.

BUS

Bus services within Sicily are provided by a variety of companies. Buses are usually faster if your destination involves travel through the island's interior; trains tend to be cheaper (and sometimes faster) on the major coastal routes. In small towns and villages tickets are often sold in bars or on the bus.

CAR & MOTORCYCLE

Having your own vehicle is advantageous in the interior, where public transit is often slow and limited. Roads are generally good and autostradas connect most major cities. There's a cheap and worthwhile toll road running along the Ionian coast. Drive defensively; the Sicilians are some of Italy's most aggressive drivers, with a penchant for overtaking on blind corners, holding a mobile phone in one hand while gesticulating wildly with the other!

TRAIN

The coastal train service is very efficient. Services to towns in the interior tend be infrequent and slow, although if you have the time the routes can be very picturesque. InterCity trains are the fastest and most expensive, while the *regionale* is the slowest.

Sicily Ferry Crossings

ROUTE	COST € (HIGH SEASON ADULT FARE)	DURATION (HOURS)
Genoa-Palermo	90	20
Malta-Pozzallo	120	1¾
Naples-Catania	60	11
Naples-Palermo	52	11
Naples-Trapani	94	7
Reggio di Calabria-Messina	3.50	30min
Tunis-Palermo	62	10

PALERMO

POP 657,000

Palermo is a city of decay and of splendour and – provided you can handle its raw energy, deranged driving and chaos – has plenty of appeal. Unlike Florence or Rome, many of the city's treasures are hidden, rather than scrubbed up for endless streams of tourists.

At one time an Arab emirate and seat of a Norman kingdom, Palermo became Europe's grandest city in the 12th century, then underwent another round of aesthetic transformations during 500 years of Spanish rule. The resulting treasure trove of palaces, castles and churches is a unique architectural fusion of Byzantine, Arab, Norman, Renaissance and baroque gems.

While some of the crumbling *palazzi* (mansions) bombed in WWII are being restored, others remain dilapidated; turned into shabby apartments, the faded glory of their ornate facades is just visible behind strings of brightly coloured washing. The evocative history of the city remains very much part of the daily life of its inhabitants, and the dusty web of backstreet markets in the old quarter has a Middle Eastern feel.

The flip side is the modern city, a mere 15-minute stroll away, parts of which could be neatly jigsawed and slotted into Paris, with a grid system of wide avenues lined by seductive shops and handsome 19th-century apartments.

◉ Sights

Via Maqueda is the main street, running north from the train station, changing names to Via Ruggero Settimo as it passes the landmark Teatro Massimo, then finally widening into leafy Viale della Libertà north of Piazza Castelnuovo, the beginning of the city's modern district.

◉ Around the Quattro Canti

The busy intersection of Corso Vittorio Emanuele and Via Maqueda is known as the Quattro Canti. Forming the civic heart of Palermo, this crossroad divides the historic nucleus into four traditional quarters – Albergheria, Capo, Vucciria and La Kalsa.

La Martorana   CHURCH
(Chiesa di Santa Maria dell'Ammiraglio; Piazza Bellini 3; donation requested; ⊙ 8.30am-1pm & 3.30-5.30pm Mon-Sat, 8.30am-1pm Sun) On the

SICILY PALERMO

SICILY PALERMO

Palermo

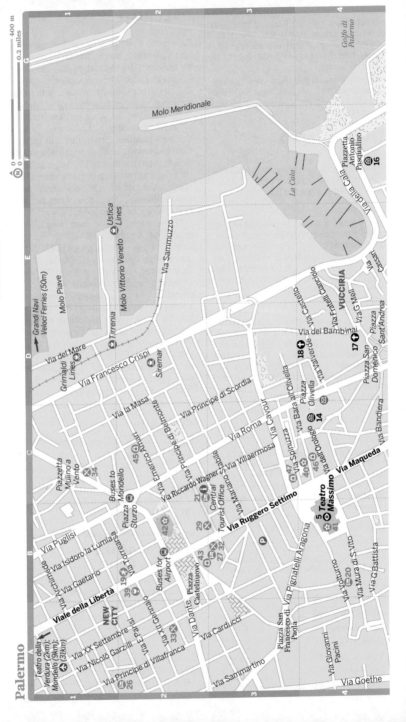

â 0
N 0

0   400 m
0   0.2 miles

G

Golfo di
Palermo

Molo Meridionale

F

La Cala

Piazzetta
Antonio
Pasqualino
16

Grandi Navi
Veloci Ferries (50m)

Molo Piave

Ustica
Lines

Molo Vittorio Veneto

E

Via Sammuzzo

Via G Meli

Via Castello

Via Fratelli Ciaciolo

VUCCIRIA

Via
Cassari

Via del Mare

Tirrenia

Grimaldi
Lines

Via Francesco Crispi

Siremar

D

Via del Bambinai

Via Valverde

Piazza San
Domenico

Piazza
Sant'Andrea

18

17

Via la Masa

Via Principe di Scordia

Via Roma

Via Cavour

Piazza
Olivella

Via Bara all'Olivella

14

Via Bandiera

C

Piazzetta
Mulino a
Vento

34

Buses to
Mondello

Via Emerico Amari

Via Principe di Belmonte

45

Via Riccardo Wagner

Via Villaermosa

Via Mariano Stabile

47

Via Spinuzza

40

46

Via dell'Orologio

Via Maqueda

Piazza
Sturzo

42

21

Central
Tourist Office

Via Ruggero Settimo

5 Teatro
Massimo

41

Via Puglisi

Via Archimede

Via Isidoro la Lumia

Via Gaetario

Via Torrearsa

19

29

43

27 32

P

Via Volturno

Via di S Vito

20

Via Mura di S Vito

Via G Battista

B

Teatro della
Verdura (2km);
Mondello (9km);
(31km)

Viale della Libertà

39

Via XII Gennaio

Buses for
Airport

Piazza
Castelnuovo

Via Dante

33

Via Carducci

Piazza San
Francesco di
Paola

Via Pignatelli Aragona

Via Giovanni
Pacini

**NEW
CITY**

Via XX Settembre

Via E Parisi

Via Nicolò Garzilli

26

Via Principe di Villafranca

Via Sammartino

Via Goethe

A

1

2

3

4

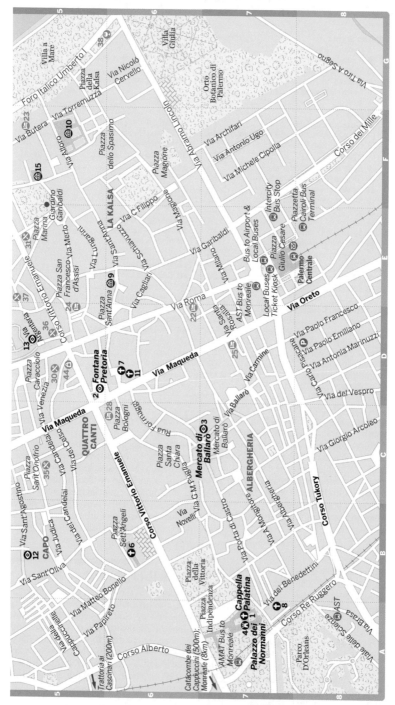

SICILY PALERMO

Palermo

southern side of Piazza Bellini, this luminously beautiful, recently restored 12th-century church was endowed by King Roger's Syrian emir, George of Antioch, and was originally planned as a mosque. Delicate Fatimid pillars support a domed cupola that depicts Christ enthroned amid his archangels. The interior is best appreciated in the morning, when sunlight illuminates magnificent Byzantine mosaics.

**Chiesa Capitolare
di San Cataldo** CHURCH
(Piazza Bellini 3; admission €2.50; ◷9.30am-12.30pm & 3-6pm) This 12th-century church in Arab-Norman style is one of Palermo's most striking buildings. With its dusky-pink bijoux domes, solid square shape, blind arcading and delicate tracery, it illustrates perfectly the synthesis of Arab and Norman architectural styles. The interior, while more austere, is still beautiful, with its inlaid floor and lovely stone-and-brickwork in the arches and domes.

★**Fontana Pretoria** FOUNTAIN
This huge and ornate fountain, with tiered basins and sculptures rippling in concentric circles, forms the centrepiece of Piazza Pretoria, a spacious square just south of the Quattro Canti. The city bought the fountain in 1573; however, the flagrant nudity of the provocative nymphs proved too much for Sicilian church-goers attending Mass next door, and they prudishly dubbed it the Fountain of Shame.

⊙ Albergheria

Southwest of the Quattro Canti is Albergheria, a rather shabby, run-down district once inhabited by Norman court officials, now home to a growing number of immigrants who are attempting to revitalise its dusty backstreets. The top tourist draws here are the Palazzo dei Normanni (Norman Palace) and its exquisite chapel, both at the neighbourhood's far western edge.

★Cappella Palatina   CHAPEL

(Palatine Chapel; adult €8.50, EU citizen 18-25yr €6.50, EU citizen 65+ €5, EU citizen under 18yr free; ☺8.15am-5pm Mon-Sat, 8.15-9.45am & 11.15am-12.15pm Sun) On the middle level of the Norman Palace's three-tiered loggia, this mosaic-clad jewel of a chapel, designed by Roger II in 1130, is Palermo's premier tourist attraction. Gleaming from a painstaking five-year restoration, its aesthetic harmony is further enhanced by the inlaid marble floors and wooden *muqarnas* ceiling, a masterpiece of Arabic-style honeycomb carving that reflects Norman Sicily's cultural complexity.

★Palazzo dei Normanni   PALACE

(Palazzo Reale; Piazza Indipendenza 1; incl Cappella Palatina adult €8.50, youth 18-25yr €6.50, senior 65+ €5, child under 18yr free; ☺8.15am-5pm Fri, Sat & Mon, to 12.15pm Sun) On weekends, when Palermo's venerable Palazzo dei Normanni isn't being used by Sicily's parliament, visitors can take a self-guided tour of several upstairs rooms, including the gorgeous blue Sala Pompeiana, with its Venus & Eros frescoes, the Sala dei Venti, adorned with mosaics of geese, papyrus, lions, leopards and palms, and the Sala di Ruggero II, King Roger's mosaic-decorated bedroom.

Chiesa di San Giovanni degli Eremiti   CHURCH

(☑091 651 50 19; Via dei Benedettini 16; adult/reduced €6/3; ☺9am-6:30pm Tue-Sat, 9am-1pm Sun & Mon) This remarkable, five-domed remnant of Arab-Norman architecture occupies a magical little hillside in the middle of an otherwise rather squalid neighborhood. Surrounded by a garden of citrus trees, palms, cactus and ruined walls, it's built atop a mosque that itself was superimposed on an earlier chapel. The peaceful Norman cloisters outside offer lovely views of the Palazzo Normanno.

★Mercato di Ballarò   MARKET

Snaking for several city blocks east of Palazzo dei Normanni is Palermo's busiest street market, which throbs with activity well into the early evening. It's a fascinating mix of noises, smells and street life, and the cheapest place for everything from Chinese padded bras to fresh produce, fish, meat, olives and cheese – smile nicely and you may get a taste.

☺ Capo

Northwest of Quattro Canti is the Capo neighbourhood, another densely packed web of interconnected streets and blind alleys.

Cattedrale di Palermo   CATHEDRAL

(www.cattedrale.palermo.it; Corso Vittorio Emanuele; Norman tombs & treasury adult/reduced €3/1.50; ☺8am-7pm) A feast of geometric patterns, ziggurat crenulations, majolica cupolas and blind arches, Palermo's cathedral is a prime example of the extraordinary Arab-Norman style unique to Sicily. The interior's most interesting features are the Norman tombs of Roger II and other Sicilian royalty, and the cathedral treasury, home to Constance of Aragon's fabulous gem-encrusted, gold-filigreed 13th-century crown.

Mercato del Capo   MARKET

Capo's street market, running the length of Via Sant'Agostino, is a seething mass of colourful activity during the day, with vendors selling fruit, vegetables, meat, fish, cheese and household goods of every description.

Catacombe dei Cappuccini   CATACOMB

(☑091 652 41 56; Piazza Cappuccini; adult €3, child under 8yr free; ☺9am-1pm & 3-6pm) These catacombs house the mummified bodies and skeletons of some 8000 Palermitans who died between the 17th and 19th centuries. Earthly power, gender, religion and professional status are still rigidly distinguished, with men and women occupying separate corridors, and a first-class section set aside for virgins. From Piazza Independenza, it's a 15-minute walk.

☺ Vucciria

Museo Archeologico Regionale   MUSEUM

(☑091 611 68 05; www.regione.sicilia.it/beni-culturali/salinas; Piazza Olivella 24; ☺8.30am-1.30pm & 3-6.30pm Tue-Fri, 8.30am-1.30pm Sat & Sun) Scheduled to reopen in late 2013 after comprehensive renovations, this splendid, wheelchair-accessible museum displays some of Sicily's most valuable Graeco-Roman artefacts. The museum's crown jewel is the series of decorative friezes from the temples at Selinunte; other treasures include the Hellenistic *Ariete di Bronzo di Siracusa* (Bronze Ram of Syracuse) and the world's largest collection of ancient anchors.

Oratories
CHAPEL

(Tesori della Loggia combined ticket adult/student/child under 6yr €5/4/free; ☺ Tesori della Loggia 9am-1pm Mon-Sat) Vucciria's greatest architectural treasures are its two baroque oratories: **Oratorio del Rosario di Santa Zita** (Via Valverde) and **Oratorio del Rosario di San Domenico** (Via dei Bambinai 2), covered top to bottom with the ornate stuccowork of Giacomo Serpotta (1652–1732). Known collectively as the **Tesori della Loggia**, they can be visited on a single ticket, together with a cluster of nearby churches.

Mercato della Vucciria
MARKET

(Piazza Caracciolo) The market here was once a notorious den of Mafia activity but is a muted affair today compared to the spirited Ballarò and Capo markets.

☺ La Kalsa

Due to its proximity to the port, La Kalsa was subjected to carpet bombing during WWII, leaving it derelict and run down. Mother Teresa considered it akin to the shanty towns of Calcutta and established a mission here. Thankfully, this galvanised embarrassed authorities into action and the quarter is now undergoing extensive restoration.

Galleria Regionale della Sicilia
MUSEUM

(Palazzo Abatellis; ☎ 091 623 00 11; www.regione.sicilia.it/beniculturali/palazzoabatellis; Via Alloro 4; adult/EU 18-25yr/EU under 18yr & over 65yr €8/4/free; ☺ 9am-6pm Tue-Fri, to 1pm Sat & Sun) Housed in the stately 15th-century Palazzo Abatellis, this fine museum features works by Sicilian artists from the Middle Ages to the 18th century. Its greatest treasure is *Triunfo della Morte* (Triumph of Death), a magnificent fresco in which Death is represented as a demonic skeleton mounted on a wasted horse, brandishing a wicked-looking scythe while leaping over his hapless victims.

Galleria d'Arte Moderna
MUSEUM

(☎ 091 843 16 05; www.galleriadartemodernapalermo.it; Via Sant'Anna 21; adult €7, 19-25yr & over 60yr €5, under 19yr free; ☺ 9.30am-6.30pm Tue-Sun) This lovely, wheelchair-accessible museum is housed in a sleekly renovated 15th-century *palazzo* (mansion), which metamorphosed into a convent in the 17th century. Divided over three floors, the wide-ranging collection of 19th- and 20th-century Sicilian art is beautifully displayed. There's a regular program of modern-art exhibitions here, as well as an excellent bookshop and gift shop. English-language audioguides cost €4.

Museo dell'Inquisizione
MUSEUM

(Piazza Marina 61; adult/reduced €5/3; ☺ 10am-6pm) Housed in the basement of the 14th-century Palazzo Chiaromonte Steri, this recently opened museum offers a chilling but fascinating look at the legacy of the Inquisition in Palermo. The honeycomb of former cells has been painstakingly restored to reveal multiple layers of prisoners' graffiti and artwork (religious and otherwise). Excellent guided visits (in English upon request) are available.

Museo Internazionale delle Marionette
MUSEUM

(☎ 091 32 80 60; www.museomarionet tepalermo.it; Piazzetta Antonio Pasqualino 5; adult/reduced €5/3; ☺ 9am-1pm & 2.30-6.30pm Mon-Sat year-round, plus 10am-1pm Sun Sep-May) This whimsical museum houses over 3500 marionettes, puppets, glove puppets and shadow figures from Palermo, Catania and Naples, as well as from further-flung places such as Japan, southeast Asia, Africa, China and India. From October to May, weekly puppet shows (adult/child €6/4) are staged on the museum's top floor in a beautifully decorated traditional theatre complete with a hand-cranked music machine.

☺ New City

North of Piazza Giuseppe Verdi, Palermo elegantly slips into cosmopolitan mode. Here you'll find fabulous neoclassical and art nouveau buildings hailing from the last golden age of Sicilian architecture, along with late-19th-century mansion blocks lining the broad boulevard of Viale della Libertà.

★ Teatro Massimo
OPERA HOUSE

(☎ tour reservations 091 605 32 67; www.teatromassimo.it/servizi/visite.php; Piazza Giuseppe Verdi; guided tours adult/reduced €8/5; ☺ 9.30am-4.30pm Tue-Sun) Palermo's grand neoclassical opera house took over 20 years to complete and has become one of the city's iconic landmarks. The closing scene of *The Godfather: Part III*, with its visually stunning juxtaposition of high culture, crime, drama and death, was filmed here. Guided 25-minute tours are offered in English, Spanish, French and Italian daily except Monday.

Hammam
BATHHOUSE

(☑ 091 32 07 83; www.hammam.pa.it; Via Torrearsa 17d; admission €40; ⊘ women only 2-9pm Mon & Wed, 11am-9pm Fri, couples only 2-8pm Thu, men only 2-8pm Tue, 10am-8pm Sat) For a sybaritic experience, head to this luxurious marble-lined Moorish bathhouse, where you can indulge in a vigorous scrub-down, a steamy sauna and many different types of massages and therapies. There's a one-off charge (€10) for slippers and a hand glove.

★☆ Festivals & Events

Festa di Santa Rosalia
RELIGIOUS

(U Fistinu) In mid-July, Palermo's biggest annual festival celebrates the patron saint of the city, Santa Rosalia, with fireworks, parades and four days of partying.

🛏 Sleeping

Most budget options can be found around Via Maqueda and Via Roma in the vicinity of the train station. Midrange and top-end hotels are concentrated further north. Parking usually costs an extra €10 to €15 per day.

B&B Amélie
B&B €

(☑ 091 33 59 20; www.bb-amelie.it; Via Prinicipe di Belmonte 94; s €40-60, d €60-80, tr €90-100; ❄ @ 🛜) On a pedestrianised New City street a stone's throw from Teatro Politeama, the affable, multilingual Angela has converted her grandmother's spacious 6th-floor flat into a cheery B&B. Rooms are colourfully decorated and the corner triple has a sunny terrace. Angela, a native Palermitan, generously shares her local knowledge and serves a tasty breakfast featuring homemade cakes and jams.

Palazzo Pantaleo
B&B €

(☑ 091 32 54 71; www.palazzopantaleo.it; Via Ruggero Settimo 74h; s/d/ste €80/100/140; P 🛜) Offering unbeatable comfort and a convenient location, Giuseppe Scaccianoce's cheerful B&B occupies the top floor of an old *palazzo* half a block from Piazza Politeama, hidden from the busy street in a quiet courtyard with free parking. The five rooms feature high ceilings, marble, tile or wooden floors, soundproofed windows and modern bathroom fixtures. There's also one spacious suite.

Butera 28
APARTMENT €

(☑ 333 3165432; www.butera28.it; Via Butera 28; apt per day €60-180, per week €380-1150; ❄ 🛜) Delightful owner, Nicoletta, rents 11 comfortable apartments in her elegant *palazzo* near Piazza della Kalsa. Units range in size from 30 to 180 sq m, most sleeping a family of four or more. Four apartments face the sea (number 9 is especially nice), most have laundry facilities, and all have well-equipped kitchens. Nicoletta also offers fabulous **cooking classes** (www.cookingwiththeduchess.com).

Hotel Orientale
HOTEL €

(☑ 091 616 57 27; www.albergoorientale.191.it; Via Maqueda 26; s €30, d €40-50, tr €50-60; ❄ 🛜) The grand marble stairway and arcaded courtyard of this *palazzo*, complete with rusty bicycles, stray cats and strung-up washing, is an evocative introduction to one of Palermo's most atmospherically faded budget hotels. Breakfast is served under the lovely frescoed ceiling in the library. Room 8 overlooks the tail end of the Ballaró market, close enough to hear vendors singing in the morning.

A Casa di Amici
HOSTEL €

(☑ 091 58 48 84; www.acasadiamici.com; Via Volturno 6; dm €19-23, d €65, without bathroom d €40; ❄ @ 🛜) In a renovated 19th-century *palazzo*, this artsy, hostel-type place behind Teatro Massimo has four colourful rooms sleeping two to four, with shared bathrooms and a guest kitchen. Two annexes, including one on Via Dante opened in 2013, offer additional rooms, including one family-friendly unit with private bath and terrace. Multilingual owner Claudia provides helpful maps, information displays, and advice.

B&B Panormus
B&B €

(☑ 091 617 58 26; www.bbpanormus.com; Via Roma 72; s €43-65, d €55-100; ❄ 🛜) A convenient location near the train station, coupled with attractive Liberty-style rooms, make this one of Palermo's most popular B&Bs. Each of the five impeccably clean units has its own private bathroom down the passageway.

Hotel Principe di Villafranca
BOUTIQUE HOTEL €€

(☑ 091 611 85 23; www.principedivillafranca.it; Via Turrisi Colonna 4; d €108-297; P ❄ @ 🛜) Furnished with fine linens and antiques, this sophisticated hotel is just west of Viale della Libertá in one of Palermo's most peaceful, exclusive neighbourhoods. Public spaces include a cosy sitting area with library, fireplace and displays of local designers' work; among the comfortable, high-ceilinged rooms, junior suite 105 stands out, decorated with artwork loaned by Palermo's modern art museum.

Quintocanto Hotel & Spa
HOTEL €€

(☎ 091 58 49 13; www.quintocantohotel.com; Corso Vittoria Emanuele 310; s €125-135, d €145-195, ste €254; ❄@🖥) Housed in a modernised 16th-century *palazzo*, Quintocanto woos visitors with its prime central city location and a wellness centre where guests enjoy free access to the sauna, Turkish bath and whirlpool tub (additional spa services including massages cost extra). Book ahead for rooms 319 and 420, which have terraces with superb views of San Giuseppe Teatini church next door.

Grand Hotel Piazza Borsa
HOTEL €€

(☎ 091 32 00 75; www.piazzaborsa.com; Via dei Cartari 18; s €119-189, d €160-208, ste €350-790; P❄@🖥) Opened in 2010 in Palermo's former stock exchange, this grand four-star encompasses three separate buildings housing 127 rooms. Nicest are the high-ceilinged suites with jaccuzi tubs and windows facing Piazza San Francesco.

 Eating

Sicily's ancient cuisine is a mixture of spicy and sweet flavours, epitomised in the ubiquitous eggplant-based *caponata* and the Palermitan classic *bucatini con le sarde* (hollow tube-shaped noodles with sardines, wild fennel, raisins, pine nuts and breadcrumbs). Cakes, marzipan confections and pastries are all works of art – try the *cannoli* (tubes of pastry filled with sweetened ricotta).

Restaurants rarely start to fill up until 9.30pm. For cheap eats, visit Palermo's markets, wander the tangle of alleys east and south of Teatro Massimo, or spend a Saturday evening snacking with locals at the street food carts in Piazza Caracciolo in the Vucciria district.

Many places close on Sunday, especially in the evening.

★Ferro di Cavallo
TRATTORIA €

(☎ 091 33 18 35; Via Venezia 20; meals €13-17; ☉lunch daily, dinner Wed-Sat) Tables line the pavement and religious portraits beam down upon the bustling mix of tourists and locals at this cheerful little trattoria near the Quattro Canti. Nothing costs more than €7 on the straightforward à la carte menu of Sicilian classics. If you have a sweet tooth save room for one of Palermo's very best *cannoli* (only €1.50).

DON'T MISS

PALERMO'S STREET FOOD

If you were taught that it was bad manners to eat in the street, you can break the rule in good company here. The mystery is simply how Palermo is not the obesity capital of Europe given just how much eating goes on! Palermitans are at it all the time: when they're shopping, commuting, discussing business, romancing...basically at any time of the day. What they're enjoying is the *buffitieri* – little hot snacks prepared at stalls and meant to be eaten on the spot.

Kick off the morning with *pane e panelle*, Palermo's famous chickpea fritter sandwich – great for vegetarians and a welcome change from a sweet custard-filled croissant. You might also want to go for some *crocchè* (potato croquettes, sometimes flavoured with fresh mint), *quaglie* (literally translated as quails, they're actually eggplants cut lengthwise and fanned out to resemble a bird's feathers, then fried) or *sfincione* (a spongy, oily pizza topped with onions and caciocavallo cheese). In summer, locals also enjoy a freshly baked brioche filled with ice cream or *granite* (crushed ice mixed with fresh fruit, almonds, pistachios or coffee).

From 4pm onwards the snacks become decidedly more carnivorous and you may just wish you hadn't read the following translations: how about some barbecued *stigghiola* (goat intestines filled with onions, cheese and parsley), for example? Or a couple of *pani ca meusa* (bread rolls stuffed with sauteed beef spleen). You'll be asked if you want your roll *schietta* (single) or *maritata* (married). If you choose *schietta*, the roll will only have ricotta in it before being dipped into boiling lard; choose *maritata* and you'll get the beef spleen as well.

You'll find street food stalls all over town, especially in Palermo's street markets.

Pizzeria Frida
PIZZERIA €

(www.fridapizzeria.it; Piazza Sant'Onofrio 37-38; pizzas €4.50-11; ⊙7pm-midnight, closed Tue) With pavement seating under umbrella awnings on a low-key Capo piazza, this local favorite makes pizzas in a variety of shapes, including *quadri* (square, picture frame-shaped pizzas) and *vulcanotti* (named after famous volcanoes and looking the part). Toppings include Sicilian specialties like tuna, capers, pistachios, mint, aubergines and ultra-fresh ricotta. Desserts (strawberry tiramisù, almond parfait) are also very tasty.

Zia Pina
TRATTORIA €

(Via Argenteria 67; meals €15-25; ⊙noon-2.30pm) Tucked under a red-and-white-striped awning on a Vucciria backstreet, this highly informal eatery is run by venerable Aunt Pina and a bevy of her brothers. There's no fixed menu, but everything's dependably tasty. Grab a plate full of antipasti, choose your fish from the display up front, and pull up a plastic chair to one of the outdoor tables.

Francu U Vastiddaru
STREET FOOD €

(Corso Vittorio Emanuele 102; sandwiches €1.50-3.50; ⊙8am-late) Palermitan street food doesn't get any better or cheaper than the delicious panini hawked from this hole-in-the-wall sandwich stand just off Piazza Marina. Options range from the classic *panino triplo*, with *panelle* (chickpea fritters), *crochè* (potato croquettes) and eggplant to the owner's trademark *panino vastiddaru* (with roast pork, salami, emmenthal cheese and spiced mushrooms).

I Cuochini
STREET FOOD €

(Via Ruggero Settimo 68; snacks from €0.70; ⊙8.30am-2.30pm Mon-Sat, plus 4.30-7.30pm Sat) Hidden inside a little courtyard off Via Ruggero Settimo, this long-standing Palermitan favourite specialises in low-cost snacks, including delicious *arancinette* (rice balls filled with meat sauce) and divine *panzerotti* (stuffed fried dough pockets). The latter come in countless delectable varieties: ricotta and mint, zucchini blossoms and cheese, mozzarella, cherry tomatoes and anchovies, just to name a few.

Pasticceria Cappello
PASTRIES & CAKES €

(www.pasticceriacappello.it; Via Nicoló Garzilli 10; ⊙7am-9.30pm Thu-Tue) Famous for the *setteveli* (seven-layer chocolate cake) that was invented here – and has long since been copied all over Palermo – this upscale bakery-cafe with its boudoir-style back room creates splendid pastries and desserts of all kinds. Not to be missed is the dreamy *delizia di pistacchio*, a granular pistachio cake topped with creamy icing and a chocolate medallion.

Antico Caffè Spinnato
CAFE €

(☑091 32 92 20; www.spinnato.it; Via Principe di Belmonte 107-15; ⊙7am-1am Sun-Fri, to 2am Sat) At this sophisticated cafe dating back to 1860, Palermitans throng the pavement tables daily to enjoy afternoon piano music, coffee, cocktails, ice cream, sumptuous cakes and snacks.

★Trattoria Il Maestro del Brodo
TRATTORIA €€

(Via Pannieri 7; meals €19-30; ⊙12.30-3.30pm Tue-Sun, 8-11pm Fri & Sat) This no-frills, Slow Food–recommended eatery in the Vucciria offers delicious soups, an array of ultra-fresh seafood, and a sensational antipasto buffet (€8) featuring a dozen-plus homemade delicacies: *sarde a beccafico* (stuffed sardines), eggplant involtini, smoked fish, artichokes with parsley, sun-dried tomatoes, olives and more.

★Trattoria Ai Cascinari
SICILIAN €€

(☑091 651 98 04; Via d'Ossuna 43/45; meals €20-28; ⊙lunch Tue-Sun, dinner Wed-Sat) Friendly service, simple straw chairs and blue-and-white-checked tablecloths set the relaxed tone at this Slow Food–recommended neighbourhood trattoria, 1km north of the Cappella Palatina. Locals pack the labyrinth of back rooms, while waiters circulate non-stop with plates of scrumptious seasonal antipasti and divine main dishes. Save room for homemade ice cream and outstanding desserts from Palermo's beloved Pasticceria Cappello.

Piccolo Napoli
SEAFOOD €€

(☑091 32 04 31; Piazzetta Mulino a Vento 4; meals €25-34; ⊙lunch Mon-Sat, dinner Tue-Sat) Known throughout Palermo for its fresh seafood, this bustling eatery is another hotspot for serious foodies. Nibble on toothsome sesame bread and plump olives while perusing the menu for a pasta dish that catches your fancy, then head to the seafood display (often still wriggling) to choose a second course. The genial owner greets his many regular customers by name.

Drinking & Nightlife

Palermo's liveliest clusters of bars can be found along Via Chiavettieri in the Vuccira neighbourhood (just northwest of Piazza Marina) and in the Champagneria district east of Teatro Massimo, centred on Piazza Olivella, Via Spinuzza, and Via Patania. Higher-end bars and dance venues are concentrated in the newer part of Palermo. In summer, many Palermitans decamp to Mondello by the sea.

 ★ Kursaal Kalhesa   BAR

(✍ 091 616 21 11; www.kursaalkalhesa.it; Foro Italico Umberto I 21; ⊘ noon-3pm & 6pm-1.30am Tue-Sat, noon-1.30am Sun) This bar of choice for the city's avant garde occupies the remnants of a handsome early-19th-century palace next to the 16th-century town gate, Porta dei Greci. Recline on silk-covered divans beneath soaring vaulted ceilings and choose from an extensive list of cocktails and snacks while listening to live music or selections from the in-house DJ.

There's a roaring fire in winter, plus art exhibits, a good program of music and literary events and a bookstore with foreign newspapers. Meals (around €30) are served on the leafy patio upstairs.

Pizzo & Pizzo   WINE BAR

(✍ 091 601 45 44; www.pizzoepizzo.com; Via XII Gennaio 1; ⊘ dinner Mon-Sat) Sure, this sophisticated wine bar is a great place for *aperitivi*, but the buzzing atmosphere and the tempting array of cheeses, cured meats and smoked fish might just convince you to stick around for dinner.

☆ Entertainment

The daily paper *Il Giornale di Sicilia* has a listing of what's on. The tourist office and information booths also have programs and listings. If you can read some Italian, www.balarm.it is another excellent resource.

Teatro Massimo   OPERA

(✍ 091 605 35 80; www.teatromassimo.it; Piazza Giuseppe Verdi) Ernesto Basile's art nouveau masterpiece stages opera, ballet and music concerts. The theatre's program runs from September to June.

Cuticchio Mimmo   PUPPET THEATRE

(✍ 091 32 34 00; www.figlidartecuticchio.com; Via Bara all'Olivella 95; ⊘ 6.30pm Sat & Sun Sep-Jul) This theatre is a charming low-tech choice for children (and adults), staging traditional shows with fabulous handcrafted puppets.

Cantieri Culturali alla Zisa   PERFORMING ARTS

(✍ 091 652 49 42; Via Paolo Gili 4) West of the centre, this newly renovated industrial space has recently emerged as Palermo's trendiest contemporary and experimental arts venue, with frequent live performances and a brand new modern art gallery, ZAC (Zona Arti Contemporanee).

Teatro di Verdura   PERFORMING ARTS

(✍ 091 765 19 63; Viale del Fante 70; ⊘ mid-Jun–Sep) A summer-only program of ballet and music in the lovely gardens of the Villa Castelnuovo, about 6km north of the city centre. There's a delightful open-air bar that opens during shows.

SICILIAN PUPPET THEATRE

Since the 18th century, the Opera dei Pupi (traditional Sicilian puppet theatre) has been enthralling adults and children alike. The shows are a mini theatrical performance with some puppets standing 1.5m high – a completely different breed from the glove puppet popular in the West. These characters are intricately carved from beech, olive or lemon wood with realistic-looking features; flexible joints ensure they have no problem swinging their swords or beheading dragons.

Effectively the soap operas of their day, Sicilian puppet shows expounded the deepest sentiments of life – unrequited love, treachery, thirst for justice and the anger and frustration of the oppressed. The swashbuckling tales centre on the legends of Charlemagne's heroic knights, Orlando and Rinaldo, with an extended cast including the fair Angelica, the treacherous Gano di Magonza and forbidding Saracen warriors. Good puppeteers are judged on the dramatic effect they can create – lots of stamping feet and a gripping running commentary – and on their speed and skill in directing the battle scenes.

Teatro Politeama Garibaldi
PERFORMING ARTS

(Piazza Ruggero Settimo) This grandiose theatre is a popular venue for opera, ballet and classical music, staging afternoon and evening concerts from October through to June. Designed by architect Giuseppe Damiani Almeyda between 1867 and 1874, it features a striking facade resembling a triumphal arch topped by a huge bronze chariot. It's home to Palermo's symphony orchestra, the Orchestra Sinfonica Siciliana (☑ 091 607 25 32; www.orchestrasinfonicasiciliana.it).

Shopping

Via Bara all'Olivella is good for arts and crafts. Check out the puppet workshop of the Cuticchio family, Il Laboratorio Teatrale (Via Bara all'Olivella 48-50; ☺ 10am-1pm & 4-7pm Tue-Sat).

For ceramics and pottery (albeit at higher prices than you'd find in Sicily's hinterland) stop by Le Ceramiche di Caltagirone (www. leceramichedicaltagirone.it; Via Cavour 114; ☺ 9am-1pm & 4-8pm Mon-Sat, 9am-1pm Sun) or Casa Merlo (www.casamerlo.it; Corso Vittorio Emanuele 231; ☺ 9am-1pm & 4-7.30pm Mon-Sat).

For edible souvenirs, visit Gusti di Sicilia (Via Emerico Amari 79; ☺ 8.30am-11pm Mon-Sat, 8.30am-2pm & 6-11pm Sun), an enticing gourmet food emporium, or Bottega dei Sapori e dei Saperi della Legalità (www.liberapalermo.org; Piazza Castelnuovo 13; ☺ 4-8pm Mon, 9.30am-1.30pm & 4-8pm Tue-Sat), a store that sells products grown on lands confiscated from the Mafia.

Information

EMERGENCY
Ambulance (☑ 091 666 55 28, 118)
Police (Questura; ☑ 091 21 01 11, 113; Piazza della Vittoria 8)

MEDICAL SERVICES
Ospedale Civico (☑ 091 666 11 11; www. ospedalecivicopa.org; Via Carmelo Lazzaro) Emergency facilities.

TOURIST INFORMATION
Central tourist office (☑ 091 58 51 72; informazionituristiche@provincia.palermo.it; Via Principe di Belmonte 42; ☺ 8.30am-2pm & 2.30-6pm Mon-Fri) Palermo's provincial tourist office offers maps and brochures as well as the helpful booklet *Un Ospite a Palermo* (www. unospiteapalermo.it), published bi-monthly and containing listings for museums, cultural centres, tour guides and transport companies.

City information booth (Piazza Bellini; 8.30am-1pm & 3-7pm Mon-Sat) The most dependable of Palermo's city-run information booths, next to the churches of San Cataldo and La Martorana. Other booths around the city – at the port, the train station, Piazza Castelnuovo and Piazza Marina – are only intermittently staffed and have unpredictable hours.

Falcone-Borsellino airport information office (☑ 091 59 16 98; in downstairs hall; ☺ 8.30am-7.30pm Mon-Fri, 8.30am-2.30pm Sat)

ℹ Getting There & Away

AIR
Falcone-Borsellino airport (PMO; ☑ 091 702 01 11; www.gesap.it) is at Punta Raisi, 31km west of Palermo.

Alitalia, easyJet, Ryanair and several other airlines operate between major European cities and Palermo. Falcone-Borsellino is also the hub airport for regular domestic flights to the islands of Pantelleria and Lampedusa.

BOAT
The ferry terminal is located just east of the corner of Via Francesco Crispi and Via Emerico Amari.

Grandi Navi Veloci (☑ 010 209 45 91, 091 58 74 04; www.gnv.it; Calata Marinai d'Italia) Runs ferries from Palermo to Civitavecchia (from €73), Genoa (from €90), Naples (from €44) and Tunis (from €72).

Grimaldi Lines (☑ 081 49 64 44, 091 611 36 91; www.grimaldi-lines.com; Via del Mare) Ferries from Palermo to Salerno (from €65).

Siremar (☑ 091 749 31 11; www.siremar.it; Via Francesco Crispi 118) Ferries (€18.35, 2¼ hours) and summer-only hydrofoils (€23.55, 1½ hours) from Palermo to Ustica.

Tirrenia (☑ 091 976 07 73; www.tirrenia. it; Calata Marinai d'Italia) Ferries to Cagliari (from €51, Saturday only) and Naples (from €47).

Ustica Lines (☑ 092 387 38 13; www.usticalines.it) Year-round hydrofoils to Ustica (€22.95, 1½ hours). Summer-only hydrofoils to Lipari (€39.30, four hours) and the other Aeolian Islands.

BUS
Offices for all bus companies are located within a block or two of Palermo Centrale train station. The two main departure points are the brand-new **Piazzetta Cairoli bus terminal** (Piazzetta Cairoli), just south of the train station's eastern entrance, and the **intercity bus stop** on Via Paolo Balsamo, due east of the train station.

AST (Azienda Siciliana Trasporti; ☎091 680 00 32; www.aziendasicilianatrasporti.it; Via Rosario Gregorio 46) Services to southeastern destinations including Ragusa (€13.40, four hours, two to four daily).

Autoservizi Tarantola (☎092 43 10 20) Buses from Palermo to Segesta (one way/return €6.70/10.70, 80 minutes each way, two daily).

Cuffaro (☎091 616 15 10; www.cuffaro.info; Via Paolo Balsamo 13) Services to Agrigento (€8.70, two hours, three to eight daily).

SAIS Autolinee (☎091 616 60 28; www.sai-sautolinee.it; Piazza Cairoli) Buses to Messina (€15.80, 2¾ hours, three to five daily) and Catania (€14.90, 2½ hours, 10 to 14 daily).

SAIS Trasporti (☎091 617 11 41; www.saist-rasporti.it; Via Paolo Balsamo 20) Overnight service to Rome (€48, 12½ hours).

Salemi (☎092 398 11 20; www.autoservizisa-lemi.it) Several buses daily to Marsala (€9.20, 2½ hours), and Trapani's Birgi airport (€10.60, 1¾ to two hours).

Segesta (☎091 616 79 19; www.segesta.it; Piazza Cairoli) Services to Trapani (€9, two hours, at least 10 daily). Also sells Interbus tickets to Syracuse (€12, 3¼ hours, two to three daily).

CAR & MOTORCYCLE

Palermo is accessible on the A20-E90 toll road from Messina and the A19-E932 from Catania via Enna. Trapani and Marsala are also easily accessible from Palermo by motorway (A29), while Agrigento and Palermo are linked by the SS121, a good state road through the island's interior.

Most major auto hire companies are represented at the airport. You'll often save money by booking your rental online before leaving home. Given the city's chaotic traffic and expensive parking, and the excellent public transit from Palermo's airport, you're generally better off postponing rental car pickup until after you leave the city.

TRAIN

From Palermo Centrale station, just south of the centre at the foot of Via Roma, regular trains leave for Messina (from €11.80, 2¾ hours to 3½ hours, hourly), Agrigento (€8.30, two hours, eight to 10 daily) and Cefalù (from €5.15, one hour, hourly). There are also InterCity trains to Reggio di Calabria, Naples and Rome.

For Catania or Syracuse, you're generally better off taking the bus. There's only one direct train to Catania (€12.50, three hours, Monday to Friday early morning); all others require a time-consuming change at Messina.

❶ Getting Around

TO/FROM THE AIRPORT

Prestia e Comandè (☎091 58 63 51; www.prestiaecomande.it) runs a half-hourly bus serv-ice from the airport to the centre of town (one way/return €6.10/11), with stops outside Teatro Politeama Garibaldi (30 minutes) and Palermo Centrale train station (45 minutes). Buses are parked to the right as you exit the airport arrivals hall. Buy tickets on the bus. Return journeys to the airport run with similar frequency, picking up at the same points.

The Trinacria Express train (€5.80, 45 min-utes to 1¼ hours) from the airport (Punta Raisi station) to Palermo takes longer and runs less frequently than the bus.

A taxi from the airport to downtown Palermo costs €45.

BUS

Palermo's orange, white and blue city buses, operated by **AMAT** (☎848 80 08 17; www.amat.pa.it), are frequent but often crowded and slow. The free map handed out at Palermo tourist offices details all the major bus lines; most stop at the train station. Tickets, valid for 90 minutes, cost €1.30 if pre-purchased from *tabacchi* (to-bacconists) or AMAT booths, or €1.70 onboard the bus. A day pass costs €3.50.

Three small buses – Linea Gialla, Linea Verde and Linea Rossa (€0.52 for 24-hour ticket) – op-erate in the narrow streets of the *centro storico* (historic centre) and can be useful if you're mov-ing between tourist sights.

CAR & MOTORCYCLE

Driving is frenetic in the city and best avoided. Use one of the staffed car parks around town (€12 to €20 per day) if your hotel lacks parking.

Around Palermo

Just outside Palermo's city limits, the beach town of Mondello and the dazzling cathe-dral of Monreale are both worthwhile day trips. Just offshore, Ustica makes a great overnight or weekend getaway.

Mondello's long, sandy beach became fashionable in the 19th century, when peo-ple came to the seaside in their carriages, prompting the construction of the huge art nouveau pier that still graces the waterfront. Most of the beaches near the pier are pri-vate (two sun lounges and an umbrella cost €10 to €20); however, there's a wide swath of public beach opposite the centre of town with all the prerequisite pedaloes and jet skis for hire. Given its easygoing seaside feel, Mondello is an excellent base for families. To get here, take bus 806 (€1.30, 30 minutes) from Piazza Sturzo in Palermo.

★**Cattedrale di Monreale** (☎091 640 44 03; Piazza del Duomo; admission to cathedral free, north transept €2, terrace €2; ⌚8.30am-12.45pm & 2.30-5pm Mon-Sat, 8-10am & 2.30-5pm Sun), 8km southwest of Palermo, is considered the finest example of Norman architecture in Sicily, incorporating Norman, Arab, Byzantine and classical elements. Inspired by a vision of the Virgin, it was built by William II in an effort to outdo his grandfather Roger II, who was responsible for the cathedral in Cefalù and the Cappella Palatina in Palermo. The interior, completed in 1184 and executed in shimmering mosaics, depicts 42 Old Testament stories. Outside the cathedral, the **cloister** (adult €6, EU citizen 18-25yr €3, under 18 & over 65yr free; ⌚9am-6.30pm Tue-Sat, 9am-1pm Sun & Mon) is a tranquil courtyard with a tangible oriental feel. Surrounding the perimeter, elegant Romanesque arches are supported by an exquisite array of slender columns alternately decorated with mosaics. To reach Monreale take AMAT bus 389 (€1.30, 35 minutes, half-hourly) from Piazza Indipendenza in Palermo or AST's Monreale bus (one way/return €1.80/2.80, 40 minutes, hourly) from in front of Palermo Centrale train station.

The 8.7-sq-km island of **Ustica** was declared Italy's first marine reserve in 1986. The surrounding waters are a playground of fish and coral, ideal for snorkelling, diving and underwater photography. To enjoy Ustica's wild coastline and dazzling grottoes without the crowds try visiting in June or September. There are numerous dive centres, hotels and restaurants on the island, as well as some nice hiking. To get here from Palermo, take the once-daily car ferry (€18.35, 2½ hours) operated by **Siremar** (☎091 844 90 02; www.siremar.it); or the faster hydrofoils (€23.55, 1½ hours) operated by both Siremar and **Ustica Lines** (☎091 844 90 02; www.usticalines.it). For more details on Ustica, see Lonely Planet's *Sicily* guide.

TYRRHENIAN COAST

The coast between Palermo and Milazzo is studded with popular tourist resorts attracting a steady stream of holidaymakers, particularly between June and September. The best of these is Cefalù, a resort second only to Taormina in popularity. Just inland lie the two massive natural parks of the Madonie and Nebrodi mountains.

Cefalù

POP 14,300

This popular holiday resort wedged between a dramatic mountain peak and a sweeping stretch of sand has the lot: a great beach; a truly lovely historic centre with a grandiose cathedral; and winding medieval streets lined with restaurants and boutiques. Avoid the height of summer when prices soar, beaches are jam-packed and the charm of the place is tainted by bad-tempered drivers trying to find parking.

Sights

★**Duomo di Cefalù** CATHEDRAL
(☎092 192 20 21; Piazza del Duomo; ⌚8am-7pm Apr-Sep, 8am-5pm Oct-Mar) Cefalù's cathedral is one of the jewels in Sicily's Arab-Norman

WORTH A TRIP

CEFALÙ'S BACKYARD PLAYGROUND

Due south of Cefalù, the 40,000-hectare **Parco Naturale Regionale delle Madonie** incorporates some of Sicily's highest peaks, including the imposing Pizzo Carbonara (1979m). The park's wild, wooded slopes are home to wolves, wildcats, eagles and the near-extinct ancient Nebrodi fir trees that have survived since the last ice age. Ideal for hiking, cycling and horse trekking, the park is also home to several handsome mountain towns, including **Castelbuono**, **Petralia Soprana** and **Petralia Sottana**.

The region's distinctive rural cuisine includes roasted lamb and goat, cheeses, grilled mushrooms and aromatic pasta with *sugo* (meat sauce). A great place to sample these specialities is **Nangalarruni** (☎092 167 14 28; www.hostarianangalarruni.it; Via delle Confraternite 10; fixed menus €23-32; ⌚12.30-3pm & 7-10pm, closed Wed in winter) in Castelbuono.

For park information, contact the Ente Parco delle Madonie in Cefalù (p177) or **Petralia Sottana** (☎092 168 40 11; Corso Paolo Agliata 16; ⌚8am-2pm & 3-7pm Mon-Fri, 3-7pm Sat, 10.30am-1pm & 4.30-7pm Sun).

Bus service to the park's main towns is limited; to fully appreciate the Madonie, you're better off hiring a car for a couple of days.

crown, only equalled in magnificence by the Cattedrale di Monreale and Palermo's Cappella Palatina. Filling the central apse, a towering figure of Christ All Powerful is the focal point of the elaborate Byzantine mosaics – Sicily's oldest and best preserved, predating those of Monreale by 20 or 30 years.

La Rocca VIEW POINT

(admission €3; ⊘9am-6.45pm May-Sep, 9am-4.45pm Oct-Apr) Looming over the town, this imposing craggy mass is the site where the Arabs built their citadel, occupying it until the Norman conquest forced them down to the port below. An enormous staircase, the **Salita Saraceno**, winds up through three tiers of city walls, a 30-minute climb. There are stunning views from the ruined 4th-century Tempio di Diana up top.

🏃 Activities

Cefalù's crescent-shaped beach, just west of the medieval centre, is lovely, but in the summer get here early to find a patch for your umbrella and towel. You can escape with a boat tour along the coast during the summer months with several agencies located along Corso Ruggero.

Scooter for Rent SCOOTER RENTAL

(☑092 142 04 96; www.scooterforrent.it; Via Vittorio Emanuele 57; per day/week 50cc Vespa €35/175, mountain bike €10/45) Rents out bicycles (€10 per day) and scooters (from €35 per day).

🛏 Sleeping

Cheap accommodation is generally scarce year-round. Bookings are essential.

B&B Casanova B&B €

(☑092 192 30 65; www.casanovabb.it; Via Porpora 3; s €40-70, d €55-100, q €80-140; ❄️📶) This B&B on the waterfront has rooms of varying size, from a cramped single with one minuscule window to the Ruggero room, a palatial space sleeping up to four, with a vaulted frescoed ceiling, decorative tile floors and French doors offering grand views of Cefalù's medieval centre. All guests share access to a small terrace overlooking the sea.

Hotel Kalura HOTEL €€

(☑092 142 13 54; www.hotel-kalura.com; Via Vincenzo Cavallaro 13; d €89-179; 🅿️❄️@🏊) East of town on a rocky outcrop, this German-run, family-oriented hotel has its own pebbly beach, restaurant and fabulous pool. Most rooms have sea views and the hotel arranges loads of activities, including mountain biking, hiking, canoeing, pedaloes, diving and dance nights. It's a 20-minute walk into town.

La Plumeria HOTEL €€

(☑092 192 58 97; www.laplumeriahotel.it; Corso Ruggero 185; d €129-209; 🅿️❄️📶) Opened in 2010, this hotel's big selling point is its perfect location between the *duomo* and the waterfront, with free parking a few minutes away. Rooms are unexceptional, but clean and well appointed. Room 301 on the top floor is the sweetest of the lot, a cosy eyrie with checkerboard tile floors and a small terrace looking up to the *duomo*.

🍴 Eating & Drinking

There are dozens of restaurants, but the food can be surprisingly mundane and the ubiquitous tourist menus can quickly pall.

★Ti Vitti SICILIAN €€

(www.ristorantetivitti.com; Via Umberto I 34; meals €30-40) At this up-and-coming eatery named after a Sicilian card game, talented young chef Vincenzo Collaro whips up divine pasta, fresh-from-the-market fish dishes and some of the best *cannoli* you'll find anywhere in Sicily. His insistence on using only the freshest ingredients means no swordfish out of season, and special, locally sourced treats such as basilisco mushrooms from the Monte Madonie.

La Botte SICILIAN €€

(☑092 142 43 15; www.labottecefalu.com; Via Veterani 20; meals €30-35; ⊘12.30-2.30pm & 7.30-10.30pm Tue-Sun) This small, family-run restaurant just off Corso Ruggero serves a good choice of antipasti, seasonally driven pasta dishes and seafood-dominated mains. The fixed menu of three fish courses plus a side dish offers good value.

La Galleria SICILIAN, CAFE €€

(☑092 142 02 11; www.lagalleriacefalu.it; Via Mandralisca 23; meals €25-40; ⊘closed Thu year-round & Mon in winter) This is about as hip as Cefalù gets. Functioning as a restaurant, cafe, internet point, bookshop and occasional gallery space, La Galleria has an informal vibe, an internal garden and an innovative menu that mixes standard *primi* and *secondi* with a range of *piatti unici* (€12–15), each designed to be a meal in itself.

ⓘ Information

ATMs are concentrated along Corso Ruggero.

Ente Parco delle Madonie (☑092 192 33 27; www.parcodellemadonie.it; Corso Ruggero 116; ⊙8am-8pm daily May-Sep, 8am-6pm Mon-Sat Oct-Apr) Knowledgeable and friendly staff supply information about the Madonie regional park.

Hospital (☑092 192 01 11; Contrada Pietrapollastra) On the main road out of town in the direction of Palermo.

Police (Questura; ☑092 192 60 11; Via Roma 15)

Tourist office (☑092 142 10 50; strcefalu@regione.sicilia.it; Corso Ruggero 77; ⊙9am-1pm & 3-7.30pm Mon-Sat) English-speaking staff, lots of leaflets and good maps.

ⓘ Getting There & Away

BOAT

SMIV (Società Marittima Italiana Veloce; www.smiv.it) runs daily boat trips between Cefalù and the Aeolian Islands, from May to September. Their 8am boat serves Lipari and Vulcano (one way/return €30/60), returning to Cefalù at 6.45pm. A second boat serves Panarea and Stromboli (one way/return €40/80), leaving at 11am and returning to Cefalù around 11.45pm. Rates include free pick up at any Cefalù hotel. Tickets are available at **Turismez Viaggi** (☑092 142 12 64; www.turismezviaggi.it; Corso Ruggero 83) next door to the tourist office.

TRAIN

The best way of getting to and from Cefalù is by rail. Hourly trains go to Palermo (from €5.15, 45 minutes to 1¼ hours) and virtually every other town on the coast.

AEOLIAN ISLANDS

The Aeolian Islands are a little piece of paradise. Stunning cobalt sea, splendid beaches, some of Italy's best hiking, and an awe-inspiring volcanic landscape are just part of the appeal. The islands also have a fascinating human and mythological history that goes back several millennia; the Aeolians figured prominently in Homer's *Odyssey*, and evidence of the distant past can be seen everywhere, most notably in Lipari's excellent archaeological museum.

The seven islands of Lipari, Vulcano, Salina, Panarea, Stromboli, Alicudi and Filicudi are part of a huge 200km volcanic ridge that runs between the smoking stack of Mt Etna and the threatening mass of Vesuvius above Naples. Collectively, the islands exhibit a unique range of volcanic characteristics, which earned them a place on Unesco's World Heritage list in 2000. The islands are mobbed with visitors in July and August but out of season things remain remarkably tranquil.

ⓘ Getting There & Away

Both **Ustica Lines** (www.usticalines.it) and **Siremar** (www.siremar.it) run hydrofoils year-round from Milazzo, the mainland city closest to the islands (see table, p180). Almost all boats stop first at Vulcano and Lipari. Most then continue onward to the ports of Santa Marina and/or Rinella on Salina island. Beyond Salina, boats either branch off east to Panarea and Stromboli, or west to Filicudi and Alicudi. Frequency of service on all routes increases in the summer.

Both Siremar and **NGI Traghetti** (☑090 928 40 91; www.ngi-spa.it) also run car ferries from Milazzo to the islands; they're slightly cheaper, but slower and less regular than the hydrofoils.

Less frequent year-round services include Ustica Lines hydrofoils from Messina, and Siremar ferries from Naples. In summer only (late June to early September), Ustica Lines also offers a once-daily service from Palermo that makes stops on all seven islands. Boats are sometimes cancelled due to heavy seas.

ⓘ Getting Around

BOAT

Regular hydrofoil and ferry services operate between the islands. Ticket offices with posted timetables can be found close to the docks on all islands.

CAR & SCOOTER

You can take your car to Lipari, Vulcano or Salina by ferry, or garage it on the mainland from €12 per day. The islands are small, with narrow, winding roads. You'll often save money (and headaches) by hiring a scooter on site, or better yet, exploring the islands on foot.

Lipari

POP 11,200 / ELEV 602M

Lipari is the Aeolians' thriving hub, both geographically and functionally, with regular ferry and hydrofoil connections to all other islands. Lipari town, the largest urban centre in the archipelago, is home to the islands' only tourist office and most dependable banking services, along with enough restaurants, bars and year-round residents to offer a bit of cosmopolitan buzz. Meanwhile, the island's rugged shoreline offers excellent opportunities for hiking, boating and swimming.

Lipari has been inhabited for some 6000 years. The island was settled in the 4th millennium BC by Sicily's first known inhabitants, the Stentillenians, who developed a flourishing economy based on obsidian, a glassy volcanic rock. Commerce subsequently attracted the Greeks, who used the islands as ports on the east–west trade route, and pirates such as Barbarossa (or Redbeard), who sacked the city in 1544.

Lipari's two harbours, Marina Lunga (where ferries and hydrofoils dock) and Marina Corta (700m south, used by smaller boats) are linked by a bustling main street, Corso Vittorio Emanuele, flanked by shops, restaurants and bars. Overlooking the colourful snake of day trippers is Lipari's clifftop citadel, surrounded by 16th-century walls.

◉ Sights & Activities

★ Museo Archeologico
Regionale Eoliano   MUSEUM
(✆090 988 01 74; www.regione.sicilia.it/beniculturali/museolipari; Castello di Lipari; adult/18-25yr/EU under 18yr & over 65yr €6/3/free; ⊙9am-1pm & 3-6pm Mon-Sat, 9am-1pm Sun) A must-see for lovers of Mediterranean history, Lipari's archaeological museum boasts one of Europe's finest collections of ancient finds. Especially worthwhile are the Sezione Preistorica, devoted to locally discovered artefacts from the Neolithic and Bronze Ages to the Graeco-Roman era, and the Sezione Classica, whose highlights include ancient shipwreck cargoes and the world's largest collection of Greek theatrical masks.

Other sections worth a quick look are the Sezione Epigrafica (Epigraphic Section), which has a small garden littered with engraved stones and a room of Greek and Roman tombs; and the Sezione Vulcanologica (Vulcanology Section), which illustrates the Aeolians' volcanic geology.

★ Quattrocchi   VIEW POINT
Lipari's best views are from a celebrated view point known as Quattrocchi (Four Eyes), 3km west of town. Climb the main road towards Pianoconte and watch for a sensational coastal panorama unfolding to the south: great, grey cliffs plunge into the sea, while in the distance plumes of sinister smoke rise from the dark heights of neighbouring Vulcano.

★ Spiaggia Valle i Muria   BEACH
This dark, pebbly beach on the southwestern shore, lapped by clean waters and surrounded by dramatic cliffs, is one of Lipari's best swimming and sunbathing spots. The turnoff, about 3km west of Lipari Town, is easily reachable by car, scooter, or local bus; follow the road towards Pianoconte until you see signs. From here, it's a steep 15-minute downhill walk.

Come prepared for the day with water, sunscreen and a picnic lunch. In good weather, Lipari resident Barni serves food and drinks from his rustic cave-like bar on the beach, and also provides boat transfers to and from Marina Corta in Lipari (€5/10 one way/return), a half-hour voyage that offers unforgettable sunset views of Vulcano and the *faraglioni* (rock spires) along Lipari's western shore.

Eastern Beaches   BEACH
On Lipari's eastern shore, sunbathers and swimmers head for Canneto, a few kilometres north of Lipari town, to bask on the pebbly Spiaggia Bianca. Further north are the pumice mines of Pomiciazzo and Porticello, where there's another beach, Spiaggia della Papesca, dusted white by the fine pumice that gives the sea its limpid turquoise colour.

BOATS FROM MILAZZO TO THE AEOLIANS

DESTINATION	COST (€) HYDROFOIL/FERRY	DURATION HYDROFOIL/FERRY
Alicudi	28.70/20.40	3¼/6hr
Filicudi	23.25/17.55	2¾/5hr
Panarea	18.80/13.90	2¼/4½hr
Salina (Rinella)	17.55/13.15	2/3¾hr
Salina (Santa Marina)	19.05/14.65	1¾/3¼hr
Stromboli	21.95/16.75	2¾/6hr
Vulcano	16/12.30	45min/1½hr

Coastal Hikes
WALKING

Lipari's rugged northwestern coastline offers excellent walking opportunities. Most accessible is the pleasant hour-long stroll from Quattropani to Acquacalda along Lipari's north shore, which affords spectacular views of Salina and a distant Stromboli. Take the bus to Quattropani (€1.90), then simply proceed downhill on the main road 5km to Acquacalda, where you can catch the bus (€1.55) back to Lipari.

More strenuous, but equally rewarding in terms of scenery, is the three- to four-hour hike descending steeply from Pianoconte, down past the old Roman baths of Terme di San Calogero to the western shoreline, then skirting the clifftops along a flat stretch before climbing steeply back to the town of Quattropani.

Diving Center La Gorgonia
DIVING

(☑090 981 26 16; www.lagorgoniadiving.it; Salita San Giuseppe) This outfit offers courses, boat transport, equipment hire and general information about scuba diving and snorkelling around Lipari. See the website for a complete price list.

☞ Tours

Numerous agencies in town offer tours to the surrounding islands. Prices vary depending on the season, but typically are around €20 for a tour of Lipari and Vulcano, €45 to visit Filicudi and Alicudi, €45 for a day trip to Panarea and Stromboli, or €80 for a late afternoon trip to Stromboli including a guided hike up the mountain at sunset and a late night return to Lipari.

Da Massimo/Dolce Vita
BOAT TOUR

(☑090 981 30 86; www.damassimo.it; Via Maurolico 2) One of Lipari's best established agencies, well-positioned on a side street between Via Vittorio Emanuele and Via Garibaldi. Specialises in sunset hikes to the top of Stromboli, returning by boat to Lipari the same evening. They also hire boats and dinghies.

🛌 Sleeping

Lipari is the Aeolians' best-equipped base for island-hopping, with plenty of places to stay, eat and drink. Note that prices soar in summer; avoid August if possible.

⭐ Diana Brown
B&B €

(☑090 981 25 84; www.dianabrown.it; Vico Himera 3; s €30-90, d €40-100, tr €50-130; ❄🖭🛜) Tucked down a narrow alley, South African Diana's delightful rooms sport tiled floors, abundant hot water and welcome extras such as kettles, fridges, clothes-drying racks and satellite TV. Darker units downstairs are compensated for by built-in kitchenettes. There's a sunny breakfast terrace and solarium with deck chairs, plus book exchange and laundry service. Optional breakfast costs €5 extra per person.

Enzo Il Negro
GUESTHOUSE €

(☑090 981 31 63; www.enzoilnegro.com; Via Garibaldi 29; s €40-50, d €60-90; ❄🛜) This simple guesthouse near Marina Corta sports spacious, tiled, pine-furnished rooms with fridges. Two panoramic terraces overlook the rooftops, the harbour and the castle walls.

Casajanca
BOUTIQUE HOTEL €€

(☑090 988 02 22; www.casajanca.it; Via Marina Garibaldi 115, Canneto; d €80-200; ❄) A stone's throw from the beach at Canneto, this is a charming little hotel with 10 rooms, all decorated with polished antique furniture and impeccable taste. The dappled courtyard, a relaxing place to enjoy breakfast, boasts an inviting natural thermal pool. Pets are welcome, and transfers from Lipari's port are included in the price.

Hotel Giardino Sul Mare
HOTEL €€

(☑090 981 10 04; www.giardinosulmare.it; Via Maddalena 65; d €80-230; ☉Apr-Oct; ❄🏊) This family-run hotel's top attraction is its superb seaside location, a few blocks south of Marina Corta. The pool terrace on the cliff edge is fabulous, but if you prefer to swim in the sea there's also direct access to a rocky platform below. Most rooms have terraces and high ceilings; they're a bit tired and bland otherwise.

🍴 Eating & Drinking

Fish abound in the waters of the archipelago and include tuna, mullet, cuttlefish and sole, all of which end up on local menus. Try *pasta all'eoliana,* a simple blend of the island's excellent capers with olives, olive oil, anchovies, tomatoes and basil.

Bars are concentrated along Corso Vittorio Emanuele and down by Marina Corta. In peak season everything stays open into the wee hours.

⭐ Le Macine
SICILIAN €€

(☑090 982 23 87; www.lemacine.org; Via Stradale 9, Pianoconte; meals €27-36; ☉12.30-3pm &

7-10pm daily May-Sep, Sat & Sun Oct-Apr) This country restaurant in Pianoconte, 4.5km from Lipari Town, comes into its own in summer, when meals are served on the terrace. Seafood and fresh vegetables star in dishes such as swordfish cakes with artichokes, shrimp-filled ravioli or fish in *ghiotta* sauce (with olive oil, capers, tomatoes, garlic and basil). Reservations are advised, as is the free shuttle service.

Kasbah MODERN SICILIAN, PIZZERIA €€
(☑ 090 981 10 75; Vico Selinunte 41; pizzas €5-9, meals €28-33; ☺ 7-11pm Mar-Oct) Hidden down narrow Vico Selinunte is the new location of this perennial local favorite. Food runs from high-quality wood-fired pizzas to superb pastas, fish dishes and wild cards like stewed lamb with veggies or couscous-crusted anchovy fritters. The casual-chic dining room is all minimalist white decor juxtaposed against grey linen tablecloths and stone walls; out back there's a candlelit garden.

E Pulera MODERN SICILIAN €€€
(☑ 090 981 11 58; www.pulera.it; Via Isabella Conti; meals €35-50; ☺ 7.30-10pm May-Oct) With its serene garden setting, low lighting, artsy tile-topped tables and exquisite food, E Pulera makes an upscale but relaxed choice for a romantic dinner. Start with a carpaccio of tuna with blood oranges and capers, choose from a vast array of Aeolian and Sicilian meat and fish dishes, then finish with *cassata* or *biscotti* with sweet Malvasia wine.

🛍 Shopping

You simply can't leave these islands without a small pot of capers and a bottle of sweet Malvasia wine. You can get both, along with tuna, meats, cheeses and other picnic supplies at **La Formagella** (Via Vittorio Emanuele 250; ☺ 9am-1pm & 4-7pm) or **Fratelli Laise** (www.fratellilaise.com; Via Vittorio Emanuele 118; ☺ 9am-1pm & 4-7pm), both along Lipari's main pedestrian thoroughfare.

ℹ Information

Corso Vittorio Emanuele is lined with ATMs. The other islands have relatively few facilities, so it's best to sort out your finances here before moving on.

Ospedale Civile (☑ 090 988 51 11; Via Sant'Anna) Operates a first-aid service.

Police (☑ 090 981 13 33; Via Marconi)

Tourist office (☑ 090 988 00 95; Via Vittorio Emanuele 202; ☺ 9am-1pm & 4.30-7pm Mon,

Wed & Fri, 9am-1pm Tue & Thu) Lipari's office provides information covering all of the Aeolian Islands.

ℹ Getting There & Around

BOAT

The main port is Marina Lunga, where you'll find a joint **Siremar** (☑ 090 981 12 20; www.siremar.it) and **Ustica Lines** (☑ 090 981 24 48; www.usticalines.it) ticket office at the head of the hydrofoil jetty. Timetable information is displayed here and at the tourist office. Adjacent to the ticket offices is a left-luggage office.

Year-round ferries and hydrofoils serve Milazzo and all the other Aeolian islands; less frequent services include year-round hydrofoils to Messina and ferries to Naples, and summer-only hydrofoil service to Palermo. See the companies' websites for schedules and prices.

BUS

Autobus Guglielmo Urso (☑ 090 981 10 26; www.ursobus.com/orariursobus.pdf) runs frequent buses around the island (€1.55 to €1.90 depending on destination) from the bus stop opposite the Esso petrol station at Marina Lunga. One main route serves the island's eastern shore, from Canneto to Acquacalda, while the other serves the western highland settlements of Quattrocchi, Pianoconte and Quattropani. Multiride booklets (six/10/20 rides €7/10.50/20.50) will save you money if you're here for several days.

CAR, SCOOTER & BICYCLE

Several places around town rent bicycles (€10 per day), scooters (€15 to €40) and cars (€30 to €70), including **Da Luigi** (☑ 090 988 05 40; www.noleggiolipari.it; Marina Lunga) down at the ferry dock.

Vulcano

POP 720 / ELEV 500M

Vulcano is a memorable island, not least because of the vile smell of sulphurous gases. Once you escape the drab and dated tourist centre, Porto di Levante, there's a delightfully tranquil, unspoilt quality to the landscape. Beyond the well-marked trail to the looming Fossa di Vulcano, the landscape gives way to rural simplicity with vineyards, birdsong and a surprising amount of greenery. The island is worshipped by Italians for its therapeutic mud baths and hot springs, and its black beaches and weird steaming landscape make for an interesting day trip.

Boats dock at Porto di Levante. To the right, as you face the island, are the mud baths and the small Vulcanello peninsula, to the left is the volcano. Straight ahead is Porto di Ponente, 700m west, where you will find the Spiaggia Sabbia Nera (Black Sand Beach).

🏃 Activities

⭐ Fossa di Vulcano
WALKING

(admission €3) Vulcano's top attraction is the straightforward, hour-long trek up its 391m volcano (no guide required). Bring a hat, sunscreen and water and follow the signs south along Strada Provinciale, then climb the zigzag gravel track to the crater's edge (290m). From here, circle the rim to the summit for stunning views of the other Aeolians lined up to the north.

Laghetto di Fanghi
MUD BATHS

(admission €2, shower €1, towel €2.60; ⊙7am-11pm summer, 8.30am-5pm winter) Vulcano's harbourside pool of warm coffee-coloured sulphurous gloop has long been prized for its therapeutic qualities. If you don't mind smelling funny for a few days, dive on in, apply some mud to your body and face, wait for the clay mask to dry, rinse off, then head for the hot, bubbling springs in a small natural sea-water pool nearby.

Keep the acidic mud away from your eyes, and wear protective footwear – the springs can get scalding hot!

Beaches
BEACH

At Porto di Ponente, on the far side of the peninsula from the hydrofoil dock, the dramatic black Spiaggia Sabbia Nera curves around a pretty bay; it's one of the archipelago's few sandy beaches. A smaller, quieter black-sand beach, Spiaggia dell'Asina, can be found on the island's southern side near Gelso.

🛏 Sleeping & Eating

Unless you're here for the walking and the mud baths, Vulcano is not a great place for an extended stay; the town is pretty soulless, the hotels are expensive and the sulphurous fumes really do smell.

Casa Arcada
B&B, APARTMENT €

(☑347 649 76 33; www.casaarcada.it; Via Sotto Cratere; B&B per person €27-55, d apt per week €350-790; ❄) This sweet whitewashed complex offers bed and breakfast in five simple rooms with air-con and mini-fridges, along with weekly rental apartments. The communal upstairs terrace affords lovely views

up to the volcano and across the water to Lipari. It's conveniently located at the foot of the volcano, 20m back from the main road between the port and the crater path.

⭐ La Forgia Maurizio
SICILIAN, INDIAN €€

(☑339 137 91 07; Strada Provinciale 45, Porto di Levante; meals €30-40; ⊙noon-3pm & 7-11pm) The owner of this devilishly good restaurant spent 20 winters in Goa, India; Eastern influences sneak into a menu of Sicilian specialities, all prepared and presented with flair. Don't miss the *liquore di kumquat e cardamom,* Maurizio's homemade answer to *limoncello.* The tasting menu is a good deal at €30 including wine and dessert.

ℹ Getting There & Around

BOAT

Vulcano is an intermediate stop between Milazzo and Lipari; both Siremar and Ustica Lines run multiple vessels in both directions throughout the day.

Centro Nautico Baia di Levante (☑339 337 27 95; www.baialevante.it; ⊙Apr-Oct), hire out boats from a shed on the beach to the left of the hydrofoil dock.

Sicily in Kayak (☑329 538 12 29; www.sicilyinkayak.com) offers kayaking tours of Vulcano and the neighbouring islands.

CAR, SCOOTER & BICYCLE

Sprint (☑090 985 22 08; Via Provinciale, Porto di Levante) rent out scooters (per day from €20), bicycles (from €5) and small cars (from €40) from their base well signposted near the hydrofoil dock. Friendly multilingual owners Luigi and Nidra offer tips for exploring the island and also rent out an apartment (€40–70 per night) in Vulcano's tranquil interior.

Salina

POP 2200 / ELEV 962M

In stark contrast to Vulcano's barren landscape, Salina's twin craters of Monte dei Porri and Monte Fossa delle Felci are lushly wooded, a result of the numerous freshwater springs on the island. Wildflowers, thick yellow gorse bushes and serried ranks of grapevines carpet the hillsides in vibrant colours and cool greens, while its high coastal cliffs plunge dramatically towards beaches. The famous Aeolian capers grow plentifully here, as do the grapes used for making Malvasia wine.

Sights & Activities

★Monte Fossa delle Felci HIKING
For jaw-dropping views, climb to the Aeolians' highest point, Monte Fossa delle Felci (962m). The two-hour ascent starts from the **Santuario della Madonna del Terzito**, an imposing 19th-century church at Valdichiesa, in the valley separating the island's two volcanoes. Up top, gorgeous perspectives unfold on the symmetrically arrayed volcanic cones of Monte dei Porri, Filicudi and a distant Alicudi.

★Salus Per Aquam SPA
(Wellness Center; ☎090 984 42 22; www.hotelsignum.it; Via Scalo 15, Malfa; admission €45, treatments extra; ⏲Oct-Mar) Enjoy a revitalising hot-spring soak or a cleansing sweat in a traditional adobe-walled steam house at Hotel Signum's fabulous spa. The complex includes several stylish jacuzzi tubs on a pretty flagstoned patio, and blissful spaces where you can immerse your body in salt crystals, get a massage, or pamper yourself with natural essences of citrus, Malvasia and capers.

Wineries WINERY
Outside Malfa there are numerous wineries where you can try the local Malvasia wine. Signposted off the main road, **Fenech** (☎090 984 40 41; www.fenech.it; Via Fratelli Mirabilo 41) is an acclaimed producer whose 2012 Malvasia won awards at five international competitions. Another important Malvasia is produced at the luxurious Capofaro resort on the 13-acre Tasca d'Almerita estate between Malfa and Santa Marina.

Pollara TOWN
Famously featured in the 1994 film *Il Postino*, sleepy Pollara is sandwiched dramatically between the sea and an extinct volcanic crater on Salina's western edge. Landslide danger blocks pedestrian access to the gorgeous beach, but you can still descend the steep stone steps northwest of town and swim across, or simply admire the spectacular view, backed by volcanic cliffs.

Sleeping

The island remains relatively undisturbed by mass tourism, yet offers some of the Aeolians' finest hotels and restaurants. Accommodation can be found in Salina's three main towns: Santa Marina Salina on the east shore, Malfa on the north shore and Rinella on the south shore, as well as in Lingua, a village adjoining ancient salt ponds 2km south of Santa Marina.

Hotel Mamma Santina BOUTIQUE HOTEL €€
(☎090 984 30 54; www.mammasantina.it; Via Sanità 40, Santa Marina Salina; d €110-250; ⏲Apr-Oct; ❄@🛜≋) A labour of love for its architect owner, this boutique hotel has inviting rooms decorated with pretty tiles in traditional Aeolian designs. Many of the sea-view terraces come equipped with hammocks, and on warm evenings the attached restaurant (meals €35–40) has outdoor seating overlooking the glowing blue pool and landscaped garden.

A Cannata PENSION €€
(☎090 984 31 61; www.acannata.it; Via Umberto, Lingua; r per person incl breakfast €40-90, incl half-board €65-115; 🛜) Near Lingua's waterfront, this long-established family-run place offers three simple rooms above its superb Slow Food–acclaimed restaurant, but its best accommodations are in the cheerful orange and blue annexe down the street, completely remodelled in 2013. Here you'll find 25 spacious units gleaming with hand-painted tiles, many overlooking Lingua's picturesque salt lagoon. Half-board is optional year-round, but highly recommended.

★Hotel Signum BOUTIQUE HOTEL €€€
(☎090 984 42 22; www.hotelsignum.it; Via Scalo 15, Malfa; d €160-500; ❄🛜≋) Hidden in Malfa's hillside lanes and sparkling with recent renovations is this alluring labyrinth of antique-clad rooms, peach-coloured stucco walls and vine-covered terraces with full-on views of Stromboli. The attached wellness centre, a stunning pool and one of the island's best-regarded restaurants make this the perfect place to unwind for a few days in utter comfort.

Capofaro BOUTIQUE HOTEL €€€
(☎090 984 43 30; www.capofaro.it; Via Faro 3, Malfa; d €230-440, ste €370-640; ⏲late Apr-early Oct; ❄@🛜≋) Immerse yourself in luxury at this five-star boutique resort halfway between Santa Marina and Malfa, surrounded by well-tended Malvasia vineyards and a picturesque lighthouse. The 20 rooms all have sharp white decor and terraces looking straight out to smoking Stromboli. Tennis courts, poolside massages, wine tasting, vineyard visits and occasional cooking courses complete this perfect vision of island chic.

✗ Eating

★ **Da Alfredo** SANDWICHES €
(Piazza Marina Garibaldi, Lingua; granite €2.60, sandwiches €8-12) Salina's most atmospheric option for an affordable snack, Alfredo's place is renowned all over Sicily for its *granite:* ices made with coffee, fresh fruit or locally grown pistachios and almonds. It's also worth a visit for its *pane cunzato* – open-faced sandwiches piled high with tuna, ricotta, eggplant, tomatoes, capers and olives; split one with a friend – they're huge!

Al Cappero SICILIAN €
(☑ 090 984 39 68; www.alcappero.it; Pollara; meals €21-25; ⊘ lunch Easter-May, lunch & dinner Jun–mid-Sep) This family-run place in Pollara with a sprawling outdoor terrace specialises in old-fashioned Sicilian home-cooking, including several vegetarian options. It also sells home-grown capers and rents out simple rooms down the street (€20 to €35 per person).

★ **A Cannata** SICILIAN €€
(☑ 090 984 31 61; Via Umberto I 13, Lingua; meals €32; ⊘ 12.30-2.30pm & 7.30-10pm) Delectable home-cooked seafood meals, accompanied by local vegetables, are served in a sun-filled seafront pavilion at this unassuming but exceptional restaurant, run by the same family for nearly four decades. Start with the house speciality, *maccheroni* with eggplant, pine nuts, mozzarella and ricotta, before moving onto a second course of *calamaretti* (baby squid) cooked with Salina's showpiece Malvasia wine.

★ **Ristorante Villa Carla** SICILIAN €€
(☑ 090 980 90 13; Via S Lucia, Leni; meals €30-35; ⊘ 7-10pm Jun-Aug, by arrangement rest of year) At their home in the hills above Rinella, Carla Rando and Carmelo Princiotta serve unforgettable meals featuring specialties such as homemade tagliatelle with pistachio and oranges, or fresh-caught fish grilled in a crust of parsley, basil, mint and citrus zest. Two outdoor terraces framed by roses and cactus offer pretty views across the water to the surrounding islands. Reservations required.

'nni Lausta MODERN SICILIAN €€
(☑ 090 984 34 86; www.isolasalina.com; Via Risorgimento, Santa Marina Salina; meals €25-40; ⊘ noon-11pm Easter-Oct) This stylish modern eatery with its cute lobster logo serves superb food based on fresh local ingredients, with 80% of the produce originating in the property's own garden. The downstairs bar is popular for *aperitivi* and late-night drinking. At lunchtime there's a fixed-price three-course menu including a glass of wine for €25, and takeaway gourmet sandwiches for €5.

ⓘ Information

Banco di Sicilia (Via Risorgimento) ATM on Santa Marina's main pedestrian street.

ⓘ Getting There & Around

BOAT
Hydrofoils and ferries serve Santa Marina Salina and Rinella from Lipari and the other islands. You'll find ticket offices in both ports.

BUS
CITIS (☑ 090 984 41 50; www.trasportisalina.it) runs buses every 90 minutes in low season (more frequently in summer) from Santa Marina Salina to Lingua and Malfa. In Malfa, make connections for Rinella, Pollara, Valdichiesa and Leni. Fares are €1.80 to €2.50 depending on destination. Timetables are posted at the ports and bus stops.

CAR, SCOOTER & BICYCLE
Above Santa Marina Salina's port, **Antonio Bongiorno** (☑ 090 984 34 09; www.rentbongiorno.it; Via Risorgimento 222, Santa Marina Salina) rents bikes (per day from €8), scooters (from €20) and cars (from €50). Several agencies in Rinella offer similar services – look for signs at the ferry dock.

Stromboli

POP 400 / ELEV 924M

Stromboli's perfect triangle of a volcano juts dramatically out of the sea. It's the only island whose smouldering cone is permanently active, attracting a steady stream of visitors like moths to its massive flame. Volcanic activity has scarred and blackened the northwest side of the island, while the eastern side is untamed, ruggedly green and dotted with low-rise whitewashed houses.

The youngest of the Aeolian volcanoes, Stromboli was formed a mere 40,000 years ago and its gases continue to send up an almost constant spray of liquid magma, a process defined by vulcanologists as *attività stromboliana* (Strombolian activity). The most recent major eruptions took place on 27 February 2007 when two new craters opened on the volcano's summit, producing two scalding lava flows down the mountain's western flank. Although seismic activity, including rock falls, continued for several days, fortunately no mass evacuation was deemed necessary. Previously, an eruption in April 2003 showered the village of Ginostra with rocks, and activity in December 2002 produced a tsunami, causing damage to Stromboli town, injuring six people and closing the island to visitors for a few months.

Boats arrive at Porto Scari-San Vincenzo, downhill from the town. Most accommodation, as well as the meeting point for guided hikes up the volcano, is a short walk up the Scalo Scari to Via Roma.

◎ Sights & Activities

★ Stromboli Crater   VOLCANO
For nature lovers, climbing Stromboli is one of Sicily's not-to-be-missed experiences. Since 2005 access has been strictly regulated: you can walk freely to 400m, but need a guide to continue any higher. Organised treks depart daily (between 3.30pm and 6pm, depending on season), timed to reach the summit (924m) at sunset and allowing 45 minutes to observe the crater's fireworks.

The climb itself takes 2½ to three hours, while the descent back to Piazza San Vincenzo is shorter (1½ to two hours). All told, it's a demanding five- to six-hour trek up to the top and back; you'll need to have proper walking shoes, a backpack that allows free movement of both arms, clothing for cold and wet weather, a change of T-shirt, a handkerchief to protect against dust (don't wear contact lenses), a torch/flashlight, one to two litres of water and some food. If you haven't got any of these, Totem Trekking (☑ 090 986 57 52; www.totemtrekkingstromboli. com; Piazza San Vincenzo 4; ☺ 9.30am-1pm & 3.30-7pm) hires out all the necessary equipment, including boots (€6), backpacks (€5), hiking poles (€4), torches (€3) and jackets (€5).

★ Sciara del Fuoco View Point   VIEWPOINT
(Trail of Fire) If you don't fancy climbing to the summit, you can go up to 400m for fabulous panoramas of the Sciara del Fuoco (the blackened laval scar that runs down the mountain's northern flank) and views of the crater's explosions from below. You're allowed to go to the Sciara on your own; bring a torch if you're walking at night.

The explosions usually occur every 20 minutes or so and are preceded by a loud belly-roar as gases force the magma into the air. After each eruption, you can watch

as red-hot rocks tumble down the seemingly endless slope, creating visible splashes as they plop into the sea. For best viewing, come on a on a still night, when the livid red Sciara and exploding cone are dramatically visible.

Arriving here around sunset will allow you to hike one direction in daylight, then stop for pizza and more volcano-gawking at L'Osservatorio on the way back down. Making the trek just before dawn is also a memorable experience, as you'll likely have the whole mountain to yourself.

The trail starts in Piscità, 2km west of Stromboli's port. From here it's about 30 minutes to L'Osservatorio, and another half hour to the view point. Bring plenty of water – the climb gets steep towards the end.

Beaches   BEACH
Stromboli's black sandy beaches are the best in the Aeolian archipelago. The most accessible and popular swimming and sunbathing is at Ficogrande, a strip of rocks and black volcanic sand about a 10-minute walk northwest of the hydrofoil dock. Further-flung black pebble beaches worth exploring are at Piscità to the west and Forgia Vecchia, 300m south of the port.

La Sirenetta Diving   DIVING
(☑ 338 891 96 75, 347 596 14 99; www.lasirenettadiving.it; Via Marina 33; ☺ Jun–mid-Sep) Offers diving courses and accompanied dives.

☞ Tours

Magmatrek (☑ 090 986 57 68; www.magmatrek. it; Via Vittorio Emanuele) has experienced, multilingual vulcanological guides who lead regular treks (maximum group size 20) up to the crater every afternoon (per person €25 plus tax). It can also put together tailor-made treks for individual groups. Other agencies charging identical prices include Il Vulcano a Piedi (☑ 090 98 61 44; www.stromboliguide. it; Via Roma) and Stromboli Adventures (☑ 090 98 62 64; www.stromboliadventures.it; Via Vittorio Emanuele).

Società Navigazione Pippo (☑ 090 98 61 35; pipponav.stromboli@libero.it; Porto Scari) and Antonio Caccetta (☑ 090 98 60 23; Vico Salina 10) are among the numerous boat companies at Porto Scari offering three-hour daytime circuits of the island (€25) and 1½-hour sunset excursions to watch the Sciara del Fuoco from the sea (€20).

🛏 Sleeping & Eating

Over a dozen places offer accommodation, including B&Bs, guesthouses and full-fledged hotels.

⭐ Casa del Sole   GUESTHOUSE €
(☑ 090 98 63 00; www.casadelsolestromboli.it; Via Cincotta; dm €25-30, s €30-50, d €60-100) This cheerful Aeolian-style guesthouse is only 100m from a sweet black-sand beach in Piscità, the tranquil neighbourhood at the west end of town. Dorms, private doubles and a guest kitchen all surround a sunny patio, overhung with vines, fragrant with lemon blossoms, and decorated with the masks and stone carvings of sculptor-owner Tano Russo.

Call for free pickup (low season only) or take a taxi (€10) from the port 2km away.

Albergo Brasile   PENSION €
(☑ 090 98 60 08; www.strombolialbergobrasile. it; Via Soldato Cincotta; d €70-90, half-board per person €70-90; ⊗ Easter-Oct; ❄) This laid-back budget option has cool, white rooms, a pretty entrance courtyard with lemon and olive trees and a multilingual paperback library for guests' reading pleasure. The roof terrace commands views of the sea one side and the volcano the other. Two larger rooms with air-con cost extra. Half-board is compulsory in July and August.

⭐ L'Osservatorio   PIZZERIA €
(☑ 090 98 63 60; pizzas €6.50-10.50; ⊗ 10.30am-late) Sure, you could eat a pizza in town, but come on – you're on Stromboli! Make the 45-minute uphill trek to this pizzeria and you'll be rewarded with exceptional volcano views from the newly expanded panoramic terrace, best after sundown.

La Bottega del Marano   GROCERY, DELI €
(Via Vittorio Emanuele; snacks from €2; ⊗ 8.30am-1pm & 4.30-7.30pm Mon-Sat) The perfect source for volcano-climbing provisions or a self-catering lunch, this reasonably priced neighbourhood grocery, five minutes west of the trekking agency offices, has a well-stocked deli case full of meats, cheeses, olives, artichokes and sun-dried tomatoes, plus shelves full of wine and awesomely tasty mini-focaccias (€2).

Ai Gechi   SEAFOOD €€
(☑ 090 98 62 13; Vico Salina 12, Porto Scari; meals €31-35; ⊗ noon-3pm & 7-11pm Easter–mid-Oct) Follow the trail of painted lizards to this great hideaway, down an alley off Via Roma.

Flanked by a towering cactus, the shaded verandah of a whitewashed Aeolian house serves as the dining area, eclectically decorated with ship lamps and a whale skeleton discovered nearby by the owner. Gorgeous traditional seafood is served with a slightly modern twist, backed by an excellent local wine list.

ℹ Information

Bring enough cash for your stay on Stromboli. Many businesses don't accept credit cards, and the village's lone ATM on Via Roma is sometimes out of service. Internet access is limited and slow.

ℹ Getting There & Away

It takes four hours to reach the island from Lipari by ferry, or 1¼ to two hours by hydrofoil. There's also at least one direct hydrofoil daily from Milazzo (€21.95). Ticket offices for **Ustica Lines** (☑ 090 98 60 03; www.usticalines.it) and **Siremar** (☑ 090 98 60 16; www.siremar.it) are at the port.

IONIAN COAST

Magnificent, overdeveloped, crowded – and exquisitely beautiful – the Ionian coast is Sicily's most popular tourist destination and home to 20% of the island's population. Moneyed entrepreneurs have built their villas and hotels up and down the coastline, eager to bag a spot on Sicily's version of the Amalfi Coast. Above it all towers the muscular peak of Mt Etna (3329m), puffs of smoke billowing from its snow-covered cone.

Taormina

POP 11,100 / ELEV 204M

Spectacularly situated on a terrace of Monte Tauro, with views westwards to Mt Etna, Taormina is a beautiful small town, reminiscent of Capri or an Amalfi coastal resort. Over the centuries, Taormina has seduced an exhaustive line of writers and artists, aristocrats and royalty, and these days it's host to a summer arts festival that packs the town with international visitors.

Perched on its eyrie, Taormina is sophisticated, chic and comfortably cushioned by some serious wealth – very far removed from the banal economic realities of other Sicilian towns. But the charm is not manufactured. The capital of Byzantine Sicily in the 9th century, Taormina is an almost

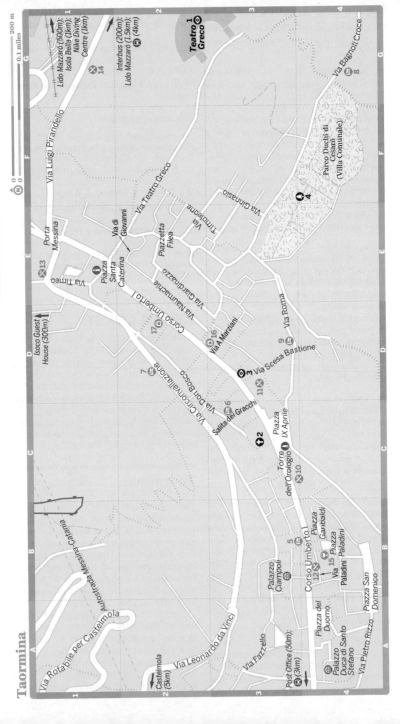

Taormina

Via Rotabile per Castelmola

Autostrada Messina-Catania

Castelmola (5km);

Via Leonardo da Vinci

Via Fazzello

Via Pietro Rizzo

Palazzo Duca di Santo Stefano

Piazza del Duomo

Piazza San Domenico

Palazzo Ciampoli

Corso Umberto I

Via Paladini

Piazza Garibaldi

Piazza Paladini

Post Office (3km);

Torre dell'Orologio

Piazza IX Aprile

Salita dei Gracchi

Via Don Bosco

Via Circonvallazione

Corso Umberto I

Via Scesa Bastione

Via A Marziani

Via Roma

Via Naumachie

Via Giardinazzo

Piazzetta Flea

Via di Giovanni

Via Teatro Greco

Via Timoleone

Via Ginnasio

Via Timeo

Piazza Santa Caterina

Porta Messina

Via Luigi Pirandello

Parco Duchi di Cesarò (Villa Comunale)

Via Bagnoli Croce

Teatro Greco 1

Isoco Guest House (300m)

Lido Mazzarò (500m); Isola Bella (1km); Nike Diving Centre (1km)

Interbus (200m); Lido Mazzarò (1.5km) (4km)

200 m
0.1 miles

Taormina

perfectly preserved medieval town, and if you can tear yourself away from the shopping and sunbathing, it has a wealth of small but perfect tourist sites. Taormina is also a popular resort with gay men.

Be warned that in July and August the town and its surrounding beaches swarm with tourists.

⊙ Sights

A short walk uphill from the bus station brings you to Corso Umberto I (abbreviated as Corso Umberto), a pedestrianised thoroughfare that traverses the length of the medieval town and connects its two historic town gates, Porta Messina and Porta Catania.

★Teatro Greco   AMPHITHEATRE
(⊅094 22 32 20; Via Teatro Greco; adult/reduced/EU under 18yr & over 65yr €10/5/free; ⊙9am-1hr before sunset) Taormina's premier attraction is this horseshoe-shaped theatre, stunningly suspended between sea and sky, with its stage perfectly framing Mt Etna on the southern horizon. Built in the 3rd century BC, it's Sicily's second largest Greek theatre (after Syracuse). In summer it serves as the venue for international arts and film festivals. Visit early in the morning to avoid the crowds.

Corso Umberto   STREET
One of Taormina's chief delights is wandering along its pedestrian-friendly medieval main avenue, lined with antique and jewellery shops, delis and designer boutiques. Midway down, pause to revel in the stunning panoramic views of Mt Etna and the seacoast from Piazza IX Aprile, and pop your head into the charming rococo church, Chiesa San Giuseppe (Piazza IX Aprile; ⊙9am-7pm).

Continue west through the 12th-century clock tower, Torre dell'Orologio, into the Borgo Medievale, Taormina's oldest quarter. A few blocks further along is Piazza del Duomo, home to an ornate baroque fountain depicting a two-legged centaur with the bust of an angel, Taormina's town symbol. Here you'll find the 13th-century cathedral, a survivor of the Renaissance-style remodelling undertaken elsewhere in town by the 15th-century Spanish aristocracy. The Renaissance influence is better illustrated in various palaces along the Corso, including Palazzo Duca di Santo Stefano with its Norman-Gothic windows, Palazzo Corvaja (the tourist office) and Palazzo Ciampoli, now housing the Hotel El Jebel.

Villa Comunale   PARK
(Parco Duchi di Cesarò; Via Bagnoli Croce; ⊙9am-midnight summer, 9am-sunset winter) To escape the crowds, wander down to these stunningly sited public gardens. Created by Englishwoman Florence Trevelyan, they're a lush paradise of tropical plants and delicate flowers. There's also a children's play area.

Castelmola   HILLTOP VILLAGE
For eye-popping views of the coastline, head 5km up Via Leonardo da Vinci to this hilltop village crowned by a ruined castle. The walk will take you around an hour along a well-paved route. Alternatively, Interbus runs an hourly service (one way/return €1.80/2.80) up the hill.

🏃 Activities

Lido Mazzarò   BEACH
Many visitors to Taormina come only for the beach scene. To reach Lido Mazzarò, directly beneath Taormina, take the cable car (Cable Car; one way/return €3/3.50; ⊙9am-8.15pm

SICILY TAORMINA

OFFSHORE ISLANDS

Sicily is an island-lover's paradise, with more than a dozen offshore islands scattered in the seas surrounding the main island. Beyond the major Aeolian Islands of Lipari, Vulcano, Stromboli and Salina covered in this guide, you can detour to the smaller Aeolians: Panarea, Filicudi and Alicudi. Alternatively, cast off from Sicily's western coast to the slow-paced Egadi Islands or the remote, rugged volcanic island of Pantelleria. South of Agrigento, the sand-sprinkled Pelagic Islands of Lampedusa, Linosa and Lampione offer some fantastic beaches. Ustica Lines (www.usticalines.it) and Siremar (www.siremar.it) provide hydrofoil and/or ferry service to all of the islands listed above. For complete information about Ustica, the Egadi Islands and the lesser Aeolian islands, including where to sleep and eat, see Lonely Planet's *Sicily* guide.

Oct-Mar, 9am-1am Apr-Sep). This beach is well serviced with bars and restaurants; private operators charge a fee for umbrellas and deck chairs (discountable at some hotels).

Isola Bella NATURE RESERVE

Southwest of the beach is the minuscule Isola Bella, set in a stunning cove with fishing boats. You can walk here in a few minutes but it's more fun to rent a small boat from Mazzarò and paddle round Capo Sant'Andrea.

Nike Diving Centre DIVING

(☑ 339 196 15 59; www.diveniketaormina.com; single dive incl kite hire from €45) Opposite Isola Bella, this dive centre offers a wide range of courses for children and adults.

Gole dell'Alcantara SWIMMING, WALKING

(www.terralcantara.it/en; admission €8; ⊙ 8am-sunset) Perfect for cooling off on a hot summer day, this series of vertiginous lava gorges with swirling rapids is 20km west of town; take Interbus from Taormina (€5 return, 55 minutes).

✹ Festivals & Events

Taormina FilmFest FILM

(www.taorminafilmfest.it) Hollywood big shots arrive in mid-June for a week of film screenings, premieres and press conferences at the Teatro Greco.

Taormina Arte PERFORMING ARTS

(www.taormina-arte.com) In July and August, this festival features opera, dance, theatre and music concerts from an impressive list of international names.

🛏 Sleeping

Taormina has plenty of luxurious accommodation although some less expensive places can be found. Many hotels offer discounted

parking (from €10) at Taormina's two public parking lots.

★ Isoco Guest House B&B €

(☑ 094 22 36 79; www.isoco.it; Via Salita Branco 2; s €65-120, d €85-120; ⊙ Mar-Nov; P ✻ @) Every room in this welcoming, gay-friendly B&B is dedicated to an artist – from Botticelli to the sculpted buttocks and pant-popping thighs on the walls of the Herb Ritts room. Inviting features include an excellent breakfast, a terrace and sundecks for lounging and an outdoor jacuzzi. German and English spoken.

B&B Le Sibille B&B €

(☑ 349 726 28 62; www.lesibille.net; Corso Umberto 187a; d €60-110, apt per week without breakfast €400-620; ⊙ Apr-Oct; @ 🛜) This B&B wins points for its prime location on Taormina's pedestrian thoroughfare, its rooftop breakfast terrace and its cheerful, artistically tiled self-catering apartments. Light sleepers beware: Corso Umberto can get noisy with holidaymakers!

Hostel Taormina HOSTEL €

(☑ 349 102 61 61, 094 262 55 05; www.hosteltaormina.com; Via Circonvallazione 13; dm €17-23, d €58-80; ✻ @ 🛜) The town's only hostel is open year-round and occupies a house with a roof terrace commanding panoramic sea views. It's small (only 23 beds in three dorms and one private room) and facilities are basic, but manager Francesco is a helpful and friendly guy, beds are comfortable and there's a communal kitchen. No breakfast.

★ Hotel Villa Belvedere HOTEL €€

(☑ 094 22 37 91; www.villabelvedere.it; Via Bagnoli Croce 79; s €70-190, d €80-280, ste €120-450; ⊙ Mar-late Nov; ✻ @ 🛜 ☀) Built in 1902, the jaw-droppingly pretty Villa Belvedere was one of the original grand hotels, well-positioned with fabulous views and luxuriant gardens, which are a particular highlight. There is also a swimming pool with a 100-year-old palm tree rising from a small island in the middle.

Hotel Villa Schuler HOTEL €€

(☑094 22 34 81; www.hotelvillaschuler.com; Via Roma, Piazzetta Bastione; d €150-220; P❄@🛜) Surrounded by shady terraced gardens and with views of Mt Etna, the rose-pink Villa Schuler has been run by the same family for over a century (longer than any other Taormina hotel) and preserves a homely atmosphere. A lovely breakfast is served on the panoramic terrace.

Casa Turchetti B&B €€€

(☑094 262 50 13; www.casaturchetti.com; Salita dei Gracchi 18/20; d €200-250, jr ste €350; ❄🛜) Every detail is perfect in this painstakingly restored former music school, recently converted to a luxurious B&B on a back alley just above Corso Umberto. Vintage furniture and fixtures, handcrafted woodwork, fine homespun sheets and modern bathrooms all contribute to the elegant feel; the spacious rooftop terrace is just icing on the cake.

Eating

Eating out in Taormina goes hand in hand with posing. It's essential to make a reservation at the more exclusive choices. Be aware that Taormina's cafes charge extraordinarily high prices even for coffee.

Granduca PIZZERIA €

(☑094 22 49 83; Corso Umberto 172; pizzas €7-11; ☺dinner) Forget the staid, typically pricey Taormina restaurant upstairs; the best reason to visit Granduca is for pizza on a summer evening, served on the vast downstairs terrace overlooking Mt Etna and the sea – an unbeatable combination of view, quality and price.

La Piazzetta SICILIAN €€

(☑094 262 63 17; Via Paladini 5; meals €25; ☺closed Mon in winter) At this little eatery tucked into the corner of the very picturesque Piazzetta Paladini, enjoy classics such as *pasta alla Norma* (pasta with basil, eggplant, ricotta and tomato) and a variety of fresh fish, accompanied by good local reds and whites.

Tiramisù PIZZERIA, SICILIAN €€

(☑094 22 48 03; Via Cappuccini 1; pizzas €7-14, meals €35; ☺Wed-Mon) This stylish place near Porta Messina makes fabulous meals, from *linguine cozze, menta e zucchine* (pasta with mussels, mint and zucchini) to old favourites like *scaloppine al limone e panna* (veal escalope in lemon cream sauce). When dessert rolls around, don't miss its trademark tiramisù, a perfect ending to any meal here.

Trattoria Da Nino TRATTORIA €€

(☑094 22 12 65; Via Luigi Pirandello 37; meals €27-34; ☺lunch & dinner) Under the same family ownership for 50 years, Nino's place specialises in straightforward, reasonably priced Sicilian home cooking, including an excellent *caponata* plus fresh local fish served grilled, steamed, fried, stewed or rolled up in *involtini* (roulades).

La Giara MODERN SICILIAN €€€

(☑094 22 33 60; Vico la Floresta 1; meals €60) A meal on La Giara's rooftop terrace is a Taormina classic. One of the best-looking restaurants in town, it's got a smooth art deco interior and a piano bar worthy of Bogart in *Casablanca* mood. The menu features modern dishes grounded in island tradition, such as risotto with wild herbs, and squid served in a Marsala reduction. Book ahead.

Drinking & Nightlife

Shatulle BAR

(Piazza Paladini 4; ☺Tue-Sun) One of the best and most popular bars on this intimate square just off Corso Umberto is this hip, gay-friendly spot with outdoor seating, an inviting vibe and a fine selection of cocktails (from €5.50). Piazza Paladini is a perennial favourite with Taormina's young, well-dressed night owls.

Bar Turrisi BAR

(☺9am-2am) High above Taormina, in the hilltop community of Castelmola, this whimsical bar is built on four levels overlooking the church square. Its decor is an eclectic tangle of Sicilian influences, with everything from painted carts to a giant stone *minchia* (you'll need no translation once you see it). Sip a glass of almond wine and enjoy the view.

🔒 Shopping

Taormina is a window-shopper's paradise. The quality in most places is high but don't expect any bargains.

SICILY TAORMINA

Carlo Mirella Panarello CERAMICS

(Via Antonio Marziani) Sicily has a long tradition of producing ceramics and this is a good bet for original designs. The workshop is on Via A Marzani (ring the bell for admission), while around the corner on Corso Umberto I, the shop sells more traditional jewellery, bags and hats.

La Torinese FOOD, WINE

(Corso Umberto 59) This is a fantastic place to stock up on local olive oil, capers, honey and wine. Smash-proof bubble wrapping helps to get everything home in one piece.

ℹ Information

There are plenty of banks with ATMs along Corso Umberto.

Ospedale San Vincenzo (☑ 0942 57 92 97; Contrada Sirina) Downhill and 2km southwest of the centre. Call the same number for an ambulance.

Police station (☑ 094 261 02 01; Corso Umberto 219)

Tourist office (☑ 094 22 32 43; www.gate2taormina.com; Piazza Santa Caterina, off Corso Umberto I; ⊗ 8.30am-2.30pm & 3.30-7pm Mon-Fri year-round, 9am-1pm & 4-6.30pm Sat Apr-Oct) Has helpful multilingual staff and plenty of practical information.

ℹ Getting There & Around

BUS

The bus is the easiest way to reach Taormina.

Interbus (☑ 094 262 53 01; Via Luigi Pirandello) services leave daily for Messina (€4.10, 55 minutes to 1¾ hours, 10 daily Monday to Saturday, two on Sunday) and Catania (€4.90, 1¼ hours, seven to 11 daily), the latter continuing to Catania's Fontanarossa airport (€7.90, 1½ hours).

CAR & SCOOTER

Taormina is on the A18 autostrada and the SS114 between Messina and Catania. Driving near the historic centre is a complete nightmare and Corso Umberto is closed to traffic. The most convenient places to leave your car are the **Porta Catania car park** (per 24hr €15), at the western end of Corso Umberto, or the Lumbi car park north of the centre, connected to Porta Messina (at Corso Umberto's eastern end) by a five-minute walk or a free yellow shuttle bus. Both car parks charge the same rates.

California (☑ 094 22 37 69; www.californiarentcar.com; Via Bagnoli Croce 86; Vespa per day/week €35/224, Fiat Panda €64/300) Rents out cars and scooters, just across from the Villa Comunale.

TRAIN

There are regular trains to and from Messina (€3.95 to €7.50, 40 to 75 minutes, hourly) and Catania (€3.95 to €7.50, 40 to 55 minutes, hourly), but the awkward location of Taormina's station (a steep 4km below town) is a strong disincentive. If you arrive this way, catch a taxi (€15) or an Interbus coach (€1.80, every 30 to 90 minutes) up to town.

Catania

POP 296,000

Catania is a true city of the volcano. Much of it is constructed from the lava that poured down the mountain and engulfed the city in the 1669 eruption in which nearly 12,000 people lost their lives. It is also lava-black in colour, as if a fine dusting of soot permanently covers its elegant buildings, most of which are the work of baroque master Giovanni Vaccarini. He almost single-handedly rebuilt the civic centre into an elegant, modern city of spacious boulevards and set-piece piazzas.

Today Catania is Sicily's second commercial city – a thriving, entrepreneurial centre with a large university and a cosmopolitan urban culture.

◉ Sights

Catania's sights are concentrated within a few blocks of Piazza del Duomo.

Piazza del Duomo SQUARE

A Unesco World Heritage Site, Catania's central square revolves around its grand cathedral, fringed with baroque buildings constructed in the unique local style of contrasting lava and limestone. The piazza's centrepiece is the smiling **Fontana dell'Elefante** (Piazza del Duomo), crowned by a naive black-lava elephant dating from the Roman period and surmounted by an improbable Egyptian obelisk.

At the piazza's southwest corner, the **Fontana dell'Amenano** fountain marks the entrance to Catania's fish market and commemorates the Amenano River, which once ran above ground and on whose banks the Greeks first founded the city of Katáne.

Cattedrale di Sant'Agata CATHEDRAL

(☑ 095 32 00 44; Piazza del Duomo; ⊗ 8am-noon & 4-7pm) Sporting an impressive marble facade with columns from Catania's Roman amphitheatre, this cathedral honours the city's patron, St Agata. The young virgin, whose remains lie sheltered in the cool, vaulted interior, famously resisted the advances of the nefarious Quintian (AD 250) and was horribly mutilated. Her jewel-drenched effigy is ecstatically venerated on 5 February in one of Sicily's largest festivals.

★**La Pescheria** MARKET
(Via Pardo; ⏲7am-2pm) The best show in Catania is this bustling fish market, where vendors raucously hawk their wares in Sicilian dialect, while decapitated swordfish cast sidelong glances at you across silvery heaps of sardines on ice.

Equally colourful is the adjoining **food market**, with carcasses of meat, skinned sheep's heads, strings of sausages, huge wheels of cheese and piles of luscious fruits and vegetables all rolled together in a few noisy, jam-packed alleyways.

★**Graeco-Roman Theatre & Odeon** RUINS
(Via Vittorio Emanuele II 262; adult/reduced incl Casa Liberti €4/2; ⏲9am-1pm & 2.30pm-1hr before sunset Tue-Sun) These twin theatres west of Piazza del Duomo constitute Catania's most impressive Graeco-Roman site. Set in a crumbling residential neighbourhood with laundry atmospherically flapping on the surrounding rooftops, the main theatre with its half-submerged stage is flanked by **Casa Liberti**, an elegantly restored 19th-century *palazzo* that now houses two millennia worth of artefacts discovered during the theatres' excavation. Directly adjacent are the ruins of the smaller Odeon theatre.

★**Teatro Massimo Bellini** OPERA HOUSE
(☎095 730 61 11; www.teatromassimobellini.it; Via Perrotta 12; guided tours €2; ⏲tours 9.30am & 10.30am Tue, Thu & Sat) A few blocks northeast of the *duomo*, this sumptuous, gilt-encrusted opera house forms the centrepiece of Piazza Bellini. Both piazza and opera house were named after composer Vincenzo Bellini, the father of Catania's vibrant modern musical scene.

Museo Belliniano MUSEUM
(☎095 715 05 35; Piazza San Francesco 3; ⏲9am-1pm Mon-Sat) FREE In 1801, renowned opera composer Vincenzo Bellini was born in this house on Piazza San Francesco, now converted into a museum. The collection comprises an interesting array of Bellini memorabilia, including original scores, photographs and the composer's death mask.

Museo Civico MUSEUM
(☎095 34 58 30; Piazza Federico II di Svevia; adult/reduced €6/4.80; ⏲9am-1pm & 3-7pm Mon-Sat, 8.30am-1.30pm Sun) Housed in the grim looking 13th-century Castello Ursino, Catania's civic museum holds the noble Biscari family's collection of paintings, vases, sculpture, coins and other archaeological finds. This foreboding castle once guarded the city from atop a seafront cliff; however, the 1693 earthquake altered the landscape, leaving it completely landlocked.

Villa Bellini PARK
(⏲8am-8pm) Escape the madding crowd and enjoy the fine views of Mt Etna from these lovely gardens along Via Etnea.

Roman Amphitheatre AMPHITHEATRE
The modest ruins of this Roman theatre, below street level in Piazza Stesicoro, are worth a quick look.

Festivals & Events

Festa di Sant'Agata RELIGIOUS
In Catania's biggest religious festival (3 to 5 February), one million Catanians follow the Fercolo (a silver reliquary bust of Saint Agata) along the main street of the city accompanied by spectacular fireworks.

Carnevale di Acireale CARNIVAL
(www.carnevalediacireale.it) Nearby Acireale hosts Sicily's most flamboyant carnival for two weeks in February (sometimes spilling over into late January or early March). Streets in this baroque coastal resort come alive with gargantuan papier mâché puppets, flowery allegorical floats, confetti and fireworks.

Sleeping

Catania is served by a good range of reasonably priced accommodation, making it an excellent base for exploring the Ionian coast and Etna.

★**B&B Crociferi** B&B €
(☎095 715 22 66; www.bbcrociferi.it; Via Crociferi 81; d €75-85, tr €100-110, 4-bed apt €120; ❄📶) Affording easy access to Catania's animated nightlife, this B&B in a beautifully decorated family home makes a wonderful base. Three spacious rooms (each with bathroom across the hall) and two glorious upstairs apartments come with high ceilings, antique tiles, frescoes and artistic accoutrements from the

Catania

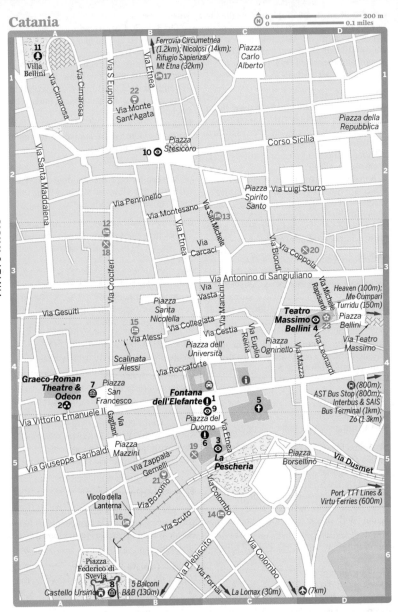

Map labels:

Villa Bellini — 11
Via Cimarosa
Via Cimarosa
Via S. Euplio
Via Etnea
Ferrovia Circumetnea (1.2km); Nicolosi (14km); Rifugio Sapienza/ Mt Etna (32km)
17
Piazza Carlo Alberto
22
Via Monte Sant'Agata
Via Santa Maddalena
Piazza della Repubblica
Piazza Stesicoro — 10
Corso Sicilia
Via Penninello
Piazza Spirito Santo
Via Luigi Sturzo
Via Montesano
Via San Michele
13
12
Via Etnea
Via Carcaci
Via Biondi
Via Coppola
20
18
Via Crociferi
Via Antonino di Sangiuliano
Via Michele Rapisardi
Heaven (100m); Me Cumpari Turridu (150m)
Via Gesuiti
Piazza Santa Nicolella
Via Vasta
Via Mancini
Teatro Massimo Bellini 4
23
Piazza Bellini
15
Via Alessi
Via Collegiata
Via Cestia
Via Euplio Reina
Piazza Ogninello
Via Leonardi
Via Teatro Massimo
Scalinata Alessi
Piazza dell' Università
Via Mazza
Graeco-Roman Theatre & Odeon 2
7
Piazza San Francesco
Via Roccaforte
(800m)
AST Bus Stop (800m); Interbus & SAIS Bus Terminal (1km); Zó (1.3km)
Via Vittorio Emanuele II
Via Gagliani
Fontana dell'Elefante 1
9
5
Piazza del Duomo
6
Piazza Giuseppe Garibaldi
Piazza Mazzini
Via Zappalà-Gemelli
3
19
La Pescheria
Piazza Borsellino
Via Dusmet
21
Vicolo della Lanterna
Via Bozomo
Via Colombo
Port, TTT Lines & Virtu Ferries (600m)
16
Via Scuto
14
Piazza Federico di Svevia
8
Castello Ursino
5 Balconi B&B (130m)
Via Fornai
La Lomax (30m)
(7km)

owners' travels. Things fill up fast, so book ahead. English, German and French spoken.

Palazzu Stidda　　　　APARTMENT €

(☏095 34 88 26; www.palazzu-stidda.com; Vicolo della Lanterna 5; d €70-100, q €120-140; 🛜🏠)

These three delightful apartments in a *palazzo* on a peaceful dead-end alley perfectly blend comfort with whimsy; all are decorated with the owners' artwork, handmade furniture, family heirlooms and finds from local antiques markets. Perfect for fami-

Catania

lies, apartments 2 and 3 each come with a washing machine, kitchen, high chair and stroller. The smaller apartment 1 costs less. French and English spoken.

B&B Faro B&B €
(☑ 349 457 88 56; www.bebfaro.it; Via San Michele 26; s/d/tr €50/80/100; ❋ @) A stylish B&B with five upstairs rooms incorporating polished wood floors, double-glazed windows, modern bathroom fixtures, antique tiles and bold colours. The two suites are especially nice, and during slower periods can be booked for the price of a double. Additional perks include free cable internet and bikes for guests' use. Visiting artists are invited to paint in the studio downstairs.

BAD B&B €
(☑ 095 34 69 03; www.badcatania.com; Via Colombo 24; s €40-55, d €60-80, apt €70-120; ❋ 🕏) An uninhibitedly colourful, modern sense of style prevails at this trendy B&B. All rooms feature local artwork and TVs with DVD players. The two-level upstairs apartment with full kitchen and private terrace is a fab option for self-caterers, especially since the fish and vegetable markets are right around the corner. Staff are happy to suggest cultural goings-on about town.

5 Balconi B&B B&B €
(☑ 095 723 45 34; www.5balconi.it; Via Plebiscito 133; s/d €35/50, with air-con €45/60; ❋ 🕏) You won't find a nicer low-end option than this lovingly remodelled antique *palazzo* in a workaday neighbourhood near Castello Ursino. The friendly owners offer three high-ceilinged rooms with a pair of shared bathrooms, plus a breakfast featuring local organic bread and fresh fruit (delivered to your room upon request). Be advised that the street out front gets lots of traffic.

Il Principe HOTEL €€
(☑ 095 250 03 45; www.ilprincipehotel.com; Via Alessi 24; d €109-189, ste €129-209; ❋ @ 🕏) This newly expanded boutique-style hotel in an 18th-century building features luxurious rooms and two-level suites on one of Catania's busiest nightlife streets (thank goodness for double glazing!). Perks include international cable TV and fluffy bathrobes to wear on your way to the Turkish steam bath. Some rooms have little natural light; check before booking. Special rates available online.

UNA Hotel Palace HOTEL €€
(☑ 095 250 51 11; www.unahotels.it; Via Etnea 218; s €99-125, d €125-175, ste €201-329) This top-end hotel brings a bit of city slick to Catania. Part of an Italy-wide chain, it's got a gleaming white interior, polished service and good rooms. For icing on the cake, check out the views of Mt Etna from the rooftop garden bar, where cocktails and aperitifs are served at sunset. Prices drop significantly in the off-season.

✖ Eating

Popular street snacks in Catania include *arancini* (fried rice balls filled with meat, cheese, tomatoes and/or peas) and *seltz* (fizzy water with fresh-squeezed lemon juice and natural fruit syrup). Don't leave town without trying *pasta alla Norma* (pasta with basil, eggplant and ricotta), a Catania original named after Bellini's opera *Norma*.

Trattoria di De Fiore
TRATTORIA €

(📱095 31 62 83; Via Coppola 24/26; meals €15-25; ☺from 1pm Tue-Sun) This neighbourhood trattoria is presided over by septuagenarian chef Mamma Rosanna, who uses fresh, local ingredients to recreate her great-grandmother's recipes, including superb *pasta alla Norma* and *zeppoline di ricotta* (sweet ricotta fritters dusted with powdered sugar). Service can be excruciatingly slow and they don't always open promptly at 1pm, but food this good is worth the wait.

Locanda Cerami
PIZZERIA €

(📱095 224 67 82; www.locandacerami.com; Via Crociferi 69; pizza €5.50-11; ☺7.30-11pm) On the atmospheric Via Crociferi, this gorgeous pizzeria has an excellent setting – in the summer months, the tables are on the steps of one of the many baroque churches – and some of the most innovative pizzas you'll find anywhere on the island, plus an excellent wine list. Try the *principessa* pizza, with pistachio nuts and aromatic speck.

★ Me Cumpari Turridu
SICILIAN €€

(📱095 715 01 42; Via Ventimiglia 15; meals €35-40; ☺Mon-Sat) Mixing tradition with modernity both in food and decor, this quirky little spot spoils meat eaters with a variety of barbecued meat, as well as fresh pasta dishes such as ricotta and marjoram ravioli in a pork sauce. Vegetarians can opt for the Ustica lentil stew, with broad beans and fennel; there's also a wealth of Sicilian cheeses on offer.

Le Tre Bocche
TRATTORIA €€

(📱095 53 87 38; Via Mario Sangiorgi 7; meals €35-45; ☺Tue-Sun) This fantastic Slow Food–recommended trattoria takes pride in the freshest seafood and fish – so much so, they have a stand at the Pescheria market. Short pastas come with wonderful sauces such as *bottarga* (fish roe) and artichoke, spaghetti is soaked in sea urchins or squid ink, and risottos are mixed with zucchini and king prawns. It's about 800m due north of the train station.

Osteria Antica Marina
SEAFOOD €€

(📱095 34 81 97; Via Pardo 29; meals €35-45; ☺Thu-Tue) This rustic but classy trattoria behind the fish market is *the* place to come for seafood. A variety of tasting menus showcases everything from swordfish to scampi,

cuttlefish to calamari. Decor-wise think solid wooden tables and rough stone walls. Reservations are essential.

🍷 Drinking & Nightlife

Not surprisingly for a busy university town, Catania has a reputation for its effervescent nightlife. Fun streets for bar-hopping include (from west to east) Via Alessi, Via Collegiata, Via Vasta, Via Mancini, Via Montesano, Piazza Spirito Santo and Via Teatro Massimo.

Heaven
BAR

(Via Teatro Massimo 39; ☺9pm-2am) Pedestrianised Via Teatro Massimo heaves late at night as crowds swill outside the many bars. One of the best-known addresses is Heaven, a trendy lounge bar sporting kooky black and white designs and a 12m-long LED-lit bar. Outside, where most people end up, there's seating on massive black leather sofas. DJs up the ante on Wednesday, Friday and Saturday nights.

Agorá Bar
BAR

(www.agorahostel.com; Piazza Curró 6; ☺6pm-late) This atmospheric bar occupies a neon-lit cave 18m below ground, complete with its own subterranean river. The Romans used it as a spa; nowadays a cosmopolitan crowd lingers over late-night drinks.

Energie Cafe
BAR, CAFE

(Via Monte Sant'Agata 10; ☺noon-late) A favourite with Catania's stylish *aperitivo* crowd, this slick urban bar has kaleidoscopic 70s-inspired decor, streetside seating and laid-back jazz-infused tunes. On Sunday afternoons, its mellow 'Fashion Aperitif' happy hour features a rich buffet and live DJ set.

☆ Entertainment

Pick up a copy of *Lapis,* a free bi-weekly program of music, theatre and art available throughout the city, or check the website www.lapisnet.it/catania.

Teatro Massimo Bellini
OPERA HOUSE

(📱095 730 61 11; www.teatromassimobellini.it; Via Perrotta 12; ☺Nov-Jun) Catania's premier theatre is named after the city's most famous son, composer Vincenzo Bellini. Sporting the full red-and-gilt look, it stages a year-round season of opera and an eight-month program of classical music from November to June. Tickets start around €13.

Zò   CULTURAL CENTRE
(☑ 095 53 38 71; www.zoculture.it; Piazzale Asia 6) In the waterfront Le Ciminiere complex, Zò is dedicated to promoting contemporary art and performance. It hosts an eclectic programme of events that ranges from club nights, concerts and film screenings to art exhibitions, dance performances, installations and theatre workshops. Many events are free of charge.

La Lomax   CULTURAL CENTRE
(☑ 095 286 28 12; www.lalomax.it; Via Fornai 44) This multipurpose cultural centre hosts all sorts of events – club nights, folk-music festivals, modern art exhibitions and more. It's near Castello Urbino, hidden on a small street off Via Plebiscito.

ℹ️ Information

Banks with ATMs are concentrated around Piazza del Duomo and along Via Etnea.
Municipal tourist office (☑ 095 742 55 73; www.comune.catania.it; Via Vittorio Emanuele II 172; ⏰ 8.15am-7.15pm Mon-Fri, to 12.15pm Sat)
Ospedale Vittorio Emanuele (☑ 091 743 54 52; Via Plebiscito 628) Has a 24-hour emergency doctor.
Police station (☑ 095 736 71 11; Piazza Santa Nicolella)

ℹ️ Getting There & Away

AIR
Catania's airport, **Fontanarossa** (☑ 095 723 91 11; www.aeroporto.catania.it), is 7km southwest of the city centre. To get there, take the special Alibus 457 (€1, 30 minutes, half hourly from 5am to midnight) from outside the train station.
Etna Transporti/Interbus (☑ 095 53 03 96; www.interbus.it) also runs a regular shuttle from the airport to Taormina (€7.90, 1½ hours, six to 11 daily). All the main car-hire companies are represented at the airport.

BOAT
The ferry terminal is located southwest of the train station along Via VI Aprile.
TTT Lines (☑ 095 34 85 86, 800 91 53 65; www.tttlines.it) runs nightly ferries from Catania to Naples (seat €38 to €60, cabin per person €52 to €165, 11 hours).
Virtu Ferries (☑ 095 53 57 11; www.virtuferries.com) runs direct ferries from Pozzallo (south of Catania) to Malta (1¾ hours) Friday through Wednesday from May through September; Thursday service is added from mid-July to August. Fares vary depending on length of stay in Malta (same-day return €80 to €132, open return €108 to €157 depending on season). Coach

transfer between Catania and Pozzallo (€7 each way) adds 2½ hours to the journey.

BUS
All intercity buses terminate in the area just north of Catania's train station. AST buses leave from Piazza Giovanni XXIII; buy tickets at Bar Terminal on the west side of the square. Interbus/Etna and SAIS leave from a terminal one block further north, with their ticket offices diagonally across the street on Via d'Amico.
Interbus (☑ 095 53 03 96; www.interbus.it; Via d'Amico 187) runs buses to:
Piazza Armerina (€8.90, 1¾ hours, two to four daily)
Ragusa (€8.30, two hours, five to 12 daily)
Syracuse (€6, 1¼ hours to 1½ hours, hourly Monday to Friday, fewer on weekends)
Taormina (€4.90, 1¼ to 1¾ hours, eight to 17 daily)
SAIS Trasporti (☑ 095 53 61 68; www.saistrasporti.it; Via d'Amico 181) goes to:
Agrigento (€12.40, three hours, nine to 14 daily)
Rome (€49, 11 hours) Overnight service.
Its sister company **SAIS Autolinee** (www.saisautolinee.it) also runs services to:
Messina (€8.10, 1½ hours, hourly Monday to Saturday, 12 on Sunday)
Palermo (€14.90, 2¾ hours, hourly Monday to Saturday, 10 on Sunday)
AST (☑ 095 723 05 35; www.aziendasicilianatrasporti.it) runs to many smaller towns around Catania, inclusing Nicolosi (€2.50, 50 to 80 minutes, hourly) at the foot of Mt Etna.

CAR & MOTORCYCLE
Catania is easily reached from Messina on the A18 autostrada and from Palermo on the A19. From the autostrada, signs for the centre of Catania will bring you to Via Etnea.

TRAIN
From Catania Centrale station on Piazza Papa Giovanni XXIII there are frequent trains.
Agrigento (€10.40 to €14.50, 3¾ hours)
Messina (€7 to €10.50, 1¾ hours, hourly)
Palermo (€12.50 to to €15.30, three to 5¾ hours, one direct daily)
Syracuse (€6.35 to €9.50, 1¼ hours, nine daily)
The private Ferrovia Circumetnea train circles Mt Etna, stopping at towns and villages on the volcano's slopes.

ℹ️ Getting Around

Several useful **AMT city buses** (☑ 095 751 96 11; www.amt.ct.it) terminate in front of the train station, including buses 1-4 and 4-7 (both running hourly from the station to Via Etnea) and Alibus 457 (station to airport every 30 minutes). A

90-minute ticket costs €1. From mid-June to mid-September, a special service (bus D-Est) runs from Piazza Raffaello Sanzio to the local beaches.

For drivers, some words of warning: there are complicated one-way systems around the city and the centre is pedestrianised, which means parking is scarce.

Catania's one-line metro currently has only six stops, all on the periphery of town. For tourists, it's mainly useful as a way to get from the central train station to the Circumetnea train that goes around Mt Etna. Tickets cost €1.

For a taxi, call **Radio Taxi Catania** (☑ 095 33 09 66).

Mt Etna

ELEV 3329M

Dominating the landscape of eastern Sicily and visible from the moon (if you happen to be there), Mt Etna is Europe's largest volcano and one of the world's most active. Eruptions occur frequently, both from the volcano's four summit craters and from its slopes, which are littered with fissures and old craters. The volcano's most devastating eruptions occurred in 1669 and lasted 122 days. Lava poured down Etna's southern slope, engulfing much of Catania and dramatically altering the landscape. More recently, in 2002, lava flows from Mt Etna caused an explosion in Sapienza, destroying two buildings and temporarily halting the cable-car service. Less destructive eruptions have continued to occur regularly over the past decade, with 2013 seeing several dramatic instances of lava fountaining – vertical jets of lava spewing from the mountain's southeast crater. Locals understandably keep a close eye on the smouldering peak.

The volcano is surrounded by the huge Parco dell'Etna, the largest unspoilt wilderness remaining in Sicily. The park encompasses a remarkable variety of environments, from the severe, almost surreal, summit to deserts of lava and alpine forests.

◉ Sights & Activities

The southern approach to Mt Etna presents the easier ascent to the craters. The AST bus from Catania drops you off at Rifugio Sapienza (1923m) from where a cable car (☑ 095 91 41 41; www.funiviaetna.com; one way/return €14.50/27, incl bus & guide €51; ☺ 9am-4.30pm) runs up the mountain to 2500m. From the upper cable-car station it's a 3½-to four-hour return trip up the winding track to the authorised crater zone (2920m).

Make sure you leave enough time to get up and down before the last cable car leaves at 4.45pm. Or, you can pay the extra €24 for a guided 4WD tour to take you up from the cable car to the crater zone.

An alternative ascent is from Piano Provenzano (1800m) on Etna's northern flank. This area was severely damaged during the 2002 eruptions, as still evidenced by the bleached skeletons of the surrounding pine trees. To reach Piano Provenzano you'll need a car, as there's no public transport beyond Linguaglossa, 16km away.

☞ Tours

Several companies offer private excursions up the mountain.

Volcano Trek   WALKING TOUR
(☑ 333 209 66 04; www.volcanotrek.com) Run by expert geologists.

Gruppo Guide Alpine Etna Sud WALKING TOUR
(☑ 095 791 47 55; www.etnaguide.com) The official guide service on Etna's southern flank, with an office just below Rifugio Sapienza.

Gruppo Guide Alpine Etna Nord   WALKING TOUR
(☑ 095 777 45 02; www.guidetnanord.com) Offers similar service from Linguaglossa on Etna's northern flank.

STAR   DRIVING TOUR
(☑ 347 495 70 91; www.funiviaetna.com/star_etna_nord.html; €40) Between May and October, STAR runs 4WD excursions to the summit from Piano Provenzano.

☷ Sleeping & Eating

There's plenty of B&B accommodation around Mt Etna, particularly in the small, pretty town of Nicolosi. Contact Nicolosi's tourist information office for a full list.

Agriturismo San Marco   AGRITURISMO €
(☑ 389 423 72 94; www.agriturismosanmarco.com; per person B&B/half-board/full board €35/53/68; ☷☷) This delightful *agriturismo* – near Rovittello, on Etna's northern flank – is a bit off the beaten track, but the bucolic setting, rustic rooms and superb country cooking more than compensate. There's also a swimming pool and kids' play area complete with swing and slides. Call ahead for directions.

Rifugio Sapienza   MOUNTAIN CHALET €€
(☑ 095 91 53 21; www.rifugiosapienza.com; Piazzale Funivia; per person B&B/half-board/full board

€55/75/90) As close to the summit as you can get, this place adjacent to the cable car offers comfortable accommodation with a good restaurant.

ℹ Information

Catania's downtown tourist office provides information about Etna, as do several offices on the mountain itself.

Etna Sud Tourist Office (☑095 91 63 56; ☺9am-4pm) Near the summit at Rifugio Sapienza.

Parco dell'Etna (☑095 82 11 11; www.par-coetna.ct.it; Via del Convento 45; ☺9am-2pm & 4-7.30pm) In Nicolosi, on Etna's southern side.

Proloco Linguaglossa (☑095 64 30 94; www.prolocolinguaglossa.it; Piazza Annunziata 5; ☺9am-1pm & 4-7pm Mon-Sat, 9am-noon Sun) In Linguaglossa, on Etna's northern side.

ℹ Getting There & Away

BUS

AST (☑095 723 05 35; www.aziendasicilianatrasporti.it) runs daily buses from Catania to Rifugio Sapienza (one way/return €3.40/5.60, one hour). Buses leave from the car park opposite Catania's train station at 8.15am, travelling via Nicolosi, and return at 4.30pm.

TRAIN

You can circle Etna on the private **Ferrovia Circumetnea** (FCE; ☑095 54 12 50; www.circumetnea.it; Via Caronda 352a) train line. Catch the metro from Catania's main train station to the FCE station at Via Caronda (metro stop Borgo) or take bus 429 or 432 going up Via Etnea and ask to be let off at the Borgo metro stop.

The train follows a 114km trail around the base of the volcano, providing fabulous views. It also passes through many of Etna's unique towns such as Adrano, Bronte and Randazzo. See the website for fares and timetables.

SYRACUSE & THE SOUTHEAST

Home to Sicily's most beafitul baroque towns and Magna Graecia's most magnificent ancient city, the southeast is one of Sicily's most compelling destinations. The classical charms of Syracuse are reason enough to visit, but once you leave the city behind you'll find an evocative checkerboard of river valleys and stone-walled citrus groves dotted with handsome towns. Shattered by a devastating earthquake in 1693, the towns of Noto, Ragusa and Modica are the superstars here, rebuilt in the ornate and much-lauded

Sicilian baroque style that lends the region a cohesive aesthetic appeal. Writer Gesualdo Bufalino described the southeast as an 'island within an island' and, certainly, this pocket of Sicily has a remote, genteel air – a legacy of its glorious Greek heritage.

Syracuse

POP 124,000

A dense tapestry of overlapping cultures and civilisations, Syracuse is one of Sicily's most appealing cities. Settled by colonists from Corinth in 734 BC, this was considered to be the most beautiful city of the ancient world, rivalling Athens in power and prestige. Under the demagogue Dionysius the Elder, the city reached its zenith, attracting luminaries such as Livy, Plato, Aeschylus and Archimedes, and cultivating the sophisticated urban culture that was to see the birth of comic Greek theatre.

As the sun set on Ancient Greece, Syracuse became a Roman colony and was looted of its treasures. While modern-day Syracuse lacks the drama of Palermo and the energy of Catania, the ancient island neighbourhood of Ortygia continues to seduce visitors with its atmospheric squares, narrow alleyways and lovely waterfront, while the Parco Archaeologico della Neapolis, 2km across town, remains one of Sicily's great classical treasures.

◉ Sights

◉ Ortygia

★ Duomo CATHEDRAL

(Map p202; Piazza del Duomo; ☺8am-7pm) Built on the skeleton of a 5th-century BC Greek temple whose Doric columns are still visible underneath, Syracuse's cathedral was converted into a church when the island was evangelised by St Paul. Its most striking feature is the columned facade (1728–53), added by Andrea Palma after the church was damaged in the 1693 earthquake.

The original temple, dedicated to Athena, was renowned throughout the Mediterranean, in part thanks to Cicero, who visited Ortygia in the 1st century BC. Its roof was crowned by a golden statue of Athena that served as a beacon to sailors at sea (nowadays replaced by a statue of the Virgin Mary). In the baptistry, look out for a 13th-century Norman font, adorned by seven bronze lions.

SICILY SYRACUSE

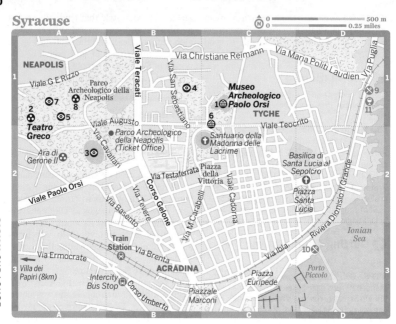

Syracuse

★Fontana Aretusa   FOUNTAIN
(Map p202) At this ancient spring, fresh water still bubbles up as it did 2500 years ago
when this was Ortygia's main water supply.
According to legend, the goddess Artemis
transformed her beautiful handmaiden Aretusa into the spring to protect her from the
river god Alpheus. Now populated by ducks,
grey mullet and papyrus plants, it's a popular summer evening hangout.

Galleria Regionale
di Palazzo Bellomo   ART GALLERY
(Map p202; ☎ 093 16 95 11; www.regione.sicilia.
it/beniculturali/palazzobellomo; Via Capodieci 16;
adult/reduced €8/4; ☉ 9am-7pm Tue-Sat, 9am-1pm
Sun) Housed in a 13th-century Catalan-Gothic
palace, this art museum's eclectic collection

ranges from early Byzantine and Norman
stonework to 19th-century Caltagirone ceramics; in between, there's a good range of
medieval religious paintings and sculpture.

Castello Maniace   CASTLE
(Map p202; adult/reduced €4/2; ☉ 9am-6.30pm
Wed-Sat, 9am-1.30pm Tue & Sun) Guarding the
island's southern tip, Ortygia's 13th-century
castle is a lovely place to wander, gaze out
over the water and contemplate Syracuse's
past glories. It also hosts occasional rotating
exhibitions.

La Giudecca   NEIGHBOURHOOD
Simply walking through Ortygia's tangled
maze of alleys is an atmospheric experience, especially down the narrow lanes of
Via Maestranza, the heart of the old guild

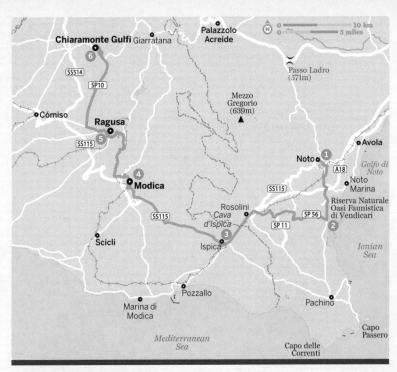

🏃 Driving Tour
Baroque Towns

DISTANCE 71KM
DURATION TWO DAYS

A land of remote rocky gorges, sweeping views and silent valleys, Sicily's southeastern corner is home to the 'baroque triangle', an area of Unesco-listed hilltop towns famous for their lavish baroque architecture. This tour takes in some of the finest baroque towns in Sicily, all within easy driving distance of each other.

Just over 35km south of Syracuse, **① Noto** is home to what is arguably Sicily's most beautiful street – Corso Vittorio Emanuele, a pedestrianised boulevard lined with golden baroque *palazzi*. From Noto, head 12km south along the SP19 to the **② Riserva Naturale Oasi Faunistica di Vendicari**, a coastal preserve whose trails, wetlands and beaches are prime territory for walking, birdwatching and swimming. Next, head 23km southwest along the SP56, SP11 and SS115 to **③ Ispica**, a hilltop town overlooking a huge canyon, the Cava d'Ispica,

riddled with prehistoric tombs. Continuing up the SS115 for a further 18km brings you to **④ Modica**, a bustling town set in a deep rocky gorge. There's excellent accommodation here and a wealth of great restaurants, so this makes a good place to overnight. The best of the baroque sights are up in Modica Alta, the high part of town, but make sure you have energy left for the *passeggiata* (evening stroll) on Corso Umberto I and dinner at Osteria dei Sapori Perduti.

Next morning, a short, winding, up-and-down drive through rock-littered hilltops leads to **⑤ Ragusa**, one of Sicily's nine provincial capitals. The town is divided in two – it's Ragusa Ibla that you want, a claustrophobic warren of grey stone houses and elegant *palazzi* that opens up onto Piazza Duomo, a superb example of 18th-century town planning. Although you can eat well in Ragusa, consider lunching in **⑥ Chiaramonte Gulfi**, a tranquil hilltop town some 20km to the north along the SP10, famous for its olive oil and delicious pork.

Ortygia

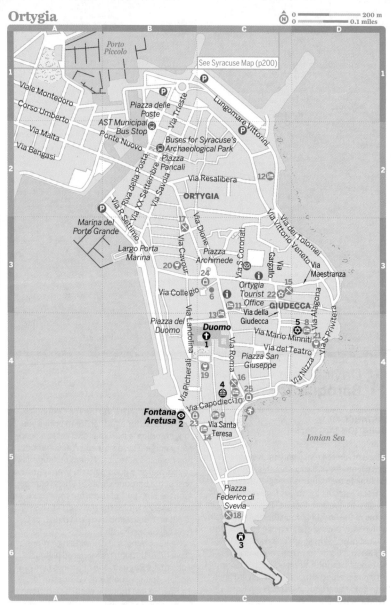

quarter, and the crumbling Jewish ghetto of **Via della Giudecca**.

At the hotel Alla Giudecca (p205) you can visit an ancient Jewish **miqwe** (ritual bath; Map p202; ☎ 093 12 22 55; Via Alagona 52; hourly tours €5; ⏱11am & noon daily, 4pm, 5pm & 6pm Mon-Sat) some 20m below ground level. Blocked up in 1492 when the Jewish community was expelled from Ortygia, the baths were rediscovered during renovation work.

Ortygia

SICILY SYRACUSE

◉ Mainland Syracuse

**Parco Archeologico
della Neapolis**   ARCHAEOLOGICAL SITE
(Map p200; ☑ 093 16 50 68; Viale Paradiso; adult/
reduced €10/free-€5; ☺ 9am-6pm Apr-Oct, 9am-
4pm Nov-Mar) For the classicist, Syracuse's
real attraction is this archaeological park,
with its pearly white, 5th-century BC **Teatro Greco** (Map p200; Parco Archeologico della
Neapolis), hewn out of the rock above the
city. This theatre saw the last tragedies of
Aeschylus (including *The Persians*), which
were first performed here in his presence.
In summer it is brought to life again with
an annual season of classical theatre.

Just beside the theatre is the mysterious **Latomia del Paradiso** (Map p200;
Parco Archeologico della Neapolis), a precipitous limestone quarry where stone for the
ancient city was extracted. Riddled with
catacombs and surrounded by citrus and
magnolia trees, this is also where the 7000
survivors of the war between Syracuse and
Athens in 413 BC were imprisoned. The
Orecchio di Dionisio (Ear of Dionysius; Map
p200; Parco Archeologico della Neapolis, Latomia
del Paradiso), a grotto 23m by 3m deep, was
named by Caravaggio after the tyrant, who
is said to have used the almost perfect
acoustics of the quarry to eavesdrop on his
prisoners.

Nearer the park's entrance you'll find the
2nd-century AD **Anfiteatro Romano** (Map
p200), originally used for gladiatorial combats and horse races, and the 3rd-century
BC Ara di Gerone II, a monolithic sacrificial
altar to Heron II where up to 450 oxen could
be killed at one time.

To reach the park, take bus 1, 3 or 12 from
Ortygia's Piazza Pancali and get off at the
corner of Corso Gelone and Viale Teocrito.
Alternatively, the walk from Ortygia will
take about 30 minutes. If driving, you can
park along Viale Augusto (tickets available
at the nearby souvenir kiosks).

★ **Museo Archeologico
Paolo Orsi**   MUSEUM
(Map p200; ☑ 093 146 40 22; Viale Teocrito; adult/
reduced €8/4; ☺ 9am-6pm Tue-Sat, 9am-1pm Sun)
In the grounds of Villa Landolina, about
500m east of the archaeological park, the
wheelchair-accessible museum contains one
of Sicily's largest, best organised and most
interesting archaeological collections. Allow
plenty of time to get through the museum's
four distinct sectors; serious archaeology
buffs may even want to consider splitting
their visit into two days.

Museo del Papiro   MUSEUM
(Map p200; ☑ 093 16 16 16; www.museodelpapiro.
it; Viale Teocrito 66; ☺ 9am-1pm Tue-Sun) **FREE**
This small museum includes papyrus documents and products, boats and an English-
language film about the history of papyrus.
The plant grows in abundance around the

Ciane River, near Syracuse, and was used to make paper in the 18th century.

Catacombe di
San Giovanni
CATACOMB

(Map p200) A block north of the archaeological museum, this vast labyrinth of 10,000 underground tombs dates back to Roman times. A 30-minute guided tour ushers visitors through the catacombs as well as the atmospheric ruins of the Basilica di San Giovanni, Syracuse's earliest cathedral.

🏃 Activities

In midsummer, when Ortygia steams like a cauldron, people flock to the beaches south of town at **Arenella** (take bus 23 from Piazza della Posta) and **Fontane Bianche** (bus 21 or 22). There's also great sunbathing (for a fee) and diving off the rocks – but no sand – adjacent to Bar Zen (p206), 2km north of Ortygia.

Lido Maniace
BEACH

(Map p202; www.lidomaniace.it; 2 people €10) If you want something glam (though also a bit squashed) rent a pew on Syracuse's tiny Lido Maniace – a rocky platform of sun beds and shade where you can dip into the water. Otherwise, swim off one of the wooden platforms near the Giudecca.

🍵 Courses

Biblios Cafe
LANGUAGE

(Map p202; ☑ 093 12 14 91; www.biblios-cafe.it; Via del Consiglio Reginale 11) This well-loved cafe-cum-bookshop organises a whole range of cultural activities, including visits to local vineyards, art classes and language courses. The Italian lessons, which emphasise everyday conversational language, can be organised on an individual or group basis, from one hour to four weeks.

🎭 Festivals & Events

Ciclo di Rappresentazioni
Classiche
PERFORMING ARTS

(Festival of Greek Theatre; www.indafondazione.org) Syracuse boasts the only school of classical Greek drama outside Athens, and in May and June it hosts live performances of Greek plays (in Italian) at the Teatro Greco, attracting Italy's finest performers. Tickets (€28 to €64) are available online, from the Via Cavour office in Ortygia or at the ticket booth outside the theatre.

Festa di Santa Lucia
RELIGIOUS

On 13 December a procession carrying the enormous silver statue of the city's patron saint wends its way from the cathedral to Piazza Santa Lucia, accompanied by fireworks.

🛏 Sleeping

Stay on Ortygia for atmosphere. Cheaper accommodation is located around the train station.

★ B&B dei Viaggiatori,
Viandanti e Sognatori
B&B €

(Map p202; ☑ 093 12 47 81; www.bedandbreakfast-sicily.it; Via Roma 156, Ortygia; s €35-50, d €55-70, tr €75-80; ❄ 🖗) Decorated with verve and boasting a prime location in Ortygia, this B&B in an old *palazzo* at the end of Via Roma has a lovely bohemian feel, with books and pieces of antique furniture juxtaposed against bright walls. The sunny roof terrace with sweeping sea views makes a perfect breakfast spot. The owners also manage the nearby **B&B L'Acanto** (Map p202; ☑ 093 146 11 29; www.bebsicily.com; Via Roma 15; s €35-50, d €55-70, tr €75-85, q €100).

B&B Aretusa
APARTMENTS €

(Map p202; ☑ 093 148 34 84; www.aretusavacanze.com; Vicolo Zuccalà 1; d €59-90, tr €70-120, q €105-147; 🅿 ❄ @ 🖗) This great budget option, elbowed into a tiny pedestrian street in a 17th-century building, has large rooms and apartments with kitchenettes, computers, wi-fi, satellite TV and small balconies from where you can shake hands with your neighbour across the way.

Palazzo del Sale
B&B €

(Map p202; ☑ 093 16 59 58; www.palazzodelsale.com; Via Santa Teresa 25, Ortygia; s €75-95, d €90-115, d with terrace €100-125; ❄ @ 🖗) The six rooms at this designer B&B are hot property in summer, so book ahead. All are well sized, with high ceilings and good beds. Coffee and tea are always available in the comfortable communal lounge. The owners also operate a second property right on the beach near Porto Piccolo (www.giuggiulena.it).

★ Hotel Gutkowski
HOTEL €€

(Map p202; ☑ 0931 46 58 61; www.guthotel.it; Lungomare Vittorini 26; s €60-80, d €75-130; ❄ @ 🖗) Book ahead for one of the sea-view rooms at this calmly stylish hotel on the Ortygia waterfront, at the edge of the Giudecca neighbourhood. Rooms are divided between two buildings, both with pretty tiled floors and a minimalist mix of vintage and industrial details. There's a nice sun terrace with sea views, and a cosy lounge area with fireplace.

Alla Giudecca
HOTEL €€

(Map p202; ☑ 093 12 22 55; www.allagiudecca.it; Via Alagona 52; s €60-100, d €80-120; ❄ @ 🛜) Located in the old Jewish quarter, this charming hotel boasts 23 suites with warm terracotta-tiled floors, exposed wood beams and lashings of heavy white linen. The communal areas are a warren of vaulted rooms full of museum-quality antiques and enormous tapestries, and feature cosy sofas gathered around huge fireplaces.

Villa dei Papiri
AGRITURISMO €€

(☑ 093 172 13 21; www.villadeipapiri.it; Contrada Cozzo Pantano; d €50-132, 2-person ste €105-154, 4-person ste €140-208; 🅿 ❄ @ 🛜) Immersed in an Eden of orange groves and papyrus reeds 8km outside Syracuse, this lovely *agriturismo* sits next to the Fonte Ciana spring immortalised in Ovid's *Metamorphosis*. Eight family suites are housed in a beautifully converted 19th-century farmhouse, with double rooms dotted around the lush grounds. Breakfast is served in a baronial stone-walled hall.

Hotel Roma
HOTEL €€

(Map p202; ☑ 093 146 56 26; www.hotelroma-siracusa.it; Via Roma 66; s €75-105, d €105-149; 🅿 ❄ @ 🛜) Within steps of Piazza del Duomo, this *palazzo* has rooms with parquet floors, oriental rugs, wood-beam ceilings and tasteful art work, plus free bike use, a gym and a sauna.

✗ Eating

Ortygia is the best place to eat. Its narrow lanes are chock-full of trattorias, restaurants, cafes and bars, and while some are obvious tourist traps, there are plenty of quality options in the mix. Most places specialise in seafood.

Sicilia in Tavola
SICILIAN €

(Map p202; ☑ 392 461 08 89; Via Cavour 28; pasta €7-12; ☺ Tue-Sun) One of several popular eateries on Via Cavour, this snug hole-in-the-wall trattoria has built a strong local reputation on the back of its homemade pasta and fresh seafood. To taste for yourself try the prawn ravioli, which is served with small cherry tomatoes and chopped mint, or the delicious *fettuccine allo scoglio* (with seafood sauce).

Red Moon
SEAFOOD €

(Map p200; ☑ 093 16 03 56; Riva Porto Lachio 36; meals €25; ☺ lunch & dinner Thu-Tue) Serving some of Syracuse's best seafood under its tented octagonal roof, this reasonably priced family-run place on the mainland makes a pleasant refuge from Ortygia's well-worn tourist track. Start with *spaghetti ai ricci* (spaghetti with sea urchin roe), move on to *fritto misto* (fried shrimp and squid) or grilled fish, then finish with a refreshing lemon sorbet.

★ Le Vin De L'Assasin Bistrot
MEDITERRANEAN €€

(Map p202; ☑ 093 16 61 59; Via Roma 15; meals €30-45; ☺ dinner Tue-Sun, lunch Sun) At this stylish, high-ceilinged Ortygia eatery run by the Parisian-trained Saro, chalkboard offerings include French classics such as *quiche lorraine* and *croque monsieur*, Breton oysters, salads with impeccable vinaigrette dressing, a host of meat and fish mains, and a splendid *millefoglie* of eggplant and sweet red peppers. It's a perfect late-night stop for wine by the glass or homemade, over-the-top chocolatey desserts.

Taberna Sveva
SICILIAN €€

(Map p202; ☑ 093 12 46 63; Piazza Federico di Svevia; meals €25-35; ☺ Thu-Tue) Away from the tourist maelstrom, the charming eatery is tucked away in a quiet corner of Ortygia. On warm summer evenings the outdoor terrace is the place to sit, with al fresco tables on a tranquil cobbled square in front of Syracuse's 13th-century castle. The food is traditional Sicilian; expect plenty of tuna and swordfish and some wonderful pastas.

Jonico-a Rutta 'e Ciauli
SICILIAN €€

(Map p200; ☑ 093 16 55 40; Riviera Dionisio il Grande 194; pizza €4-7, meals €25-35; ☺ Wed-Mon Jun-Sep) It's a long and not particularly enticing hike to this seafront restaurant, but once you're there you'll appreciate the effort. Inside it's all exposed brickwork and rusty farm tools; outside on the terrace it's pure bliss, with the sun in your face, a cooling sea breeze and dreamy views. Not surprisingly, fish features heavily on the menu.

★ Don Camillo
MODERN SICILIAN €€€

(Map p202; ☑ 093 16 71 33; www.ristorantedon-camillosiracusa.it; Via Maestranza 96; meals €55; ☺ lunch & dinner Mon-Sat) This elegant restaurant with top-notch service is full of classy surprises: 'black' king prawns in a thick almond cream soup, red snapper with fig and lemon, *tagliata di tonno* (grilled and sliced tuna) with a red pepper 'marmalade' and blood-orange ice cream for dessert. Slow Food recommended.

 Drinking & Nightlife

Syracuse is a vibrant university town, which means plenty of life on the streets after nightfall.

Bar San Rocco   BAR
(Map p202; Piazzetta San Rocco; ☺5pm-late) Head to San Rocco, the smoothest of several bars on Piazzetta San Rocco, for early evening *aperitivi* (complete with bountiful bar snacks) and late-night cocktails. Inside, it's a narrow, stone-vaulted affair, but the main action is outside on the vivacious piazzetta where summer crowds gather until the early hours. Occasional live music and DJ sets fuel the laid-back vibe.

Bar Zen   BAR
(Map p200; ☺9am-midnight mid-Jun–Sep) At this seaside bar affiliated with Jonico restaurant, you can plunge off the rocks and sunbathe all day, then retire to the outdoor deck for evening drinks and live music.

Il Blu   WINE BAR
(Map p202; Via Nizza; ☺6pm-late) A superb wine bar with a cosy front porch near the waterfront, this is a great place to take in the sun between dips in the sea.

Café Giufá   MUSIC
(Map p202; ☑093 146 53 95; Via Cavour 25; ☺closed Mon in winter) A fun bar that spreads onto the tiny square at the back, the Giufá has some good DJs who like reggae, jungle and dub beats.

☆ Entertainment

Piccolo Teatro dei Pupi   PUPPET THEATRE
(Map p202; ☑093 146 55 40; www.pupari.com; Via della Giudecca 17) Syracuse's thriving puppet theatre hosts regular performances; see the website for a calendar. You can also buy puppets at its workshop next door.

🔒 Shopping

Browsing Ortygia's quirky boutiques is great fun.

Untitled   CLOTHING
(Map p202; ☑093 16 45 74; www.untitled-trend-wear.com; Via Serafino Privitera 39; ☺10.30am-2.30pm & 4.30-8.30pm) With pieces by Italian and international designers, this boutique

has clothes to die for and prices to give you a heart attack.

Massimo Izzo   JEWELLERY
(Map p202; www.massimoizzo.com; Piazza Archimede 25; ☺4.30-8.30pm Mon, 9am-1pm & 4.30-8.30pm Tue-Sat) The flamboyant jewellery of Messina-born Massimo Izzo features bold idiosyncratic designs made with Sciacca coral, gold and precious stones, inspired by the sea, theatre and classical antiquity.

Galleria Bellomo   ARTISANAL
(Map p202; www.bellomogallery.com; Via Capodieci 15; ☺10.30am-1.30pm & 4.30-8pm Mon-Sat) This gallery near Fontana Aretusa specialises in papyrus products, including greeting cards, bookmarks and writing paper and watercolour landscapes.

ℹ Information

Ortygia tourist office (Map p202; ☑093 146 42 55; Via Maestranza 33; ☺8am-2pm & 2.30-5.30pm Mon-Fri, 8am-2pm Sat) English-speaking staff and lots of good information.

Ospedale Umberto I (☑093 172 40 33; Via Testaferrata 1)

Police station (☑093 16 51 76; Piazza S Giuseppe)

Tourist office (Map p202; ☑0800 05 55 00; infoturismo@provsr.it; Via Roma 31; ☺8am-8pm Mon-Sat, 9.15am-6.45pm Sun) English-speaking staff, city maps and other useful information.

ℹ Getting There & Away

Syracuse's train and bus stations are a block apart from each other, halfway between Ortygia and the archaeological park.

BUS
Long-distance buses operate from the bus stop along Corso Umberto, just east of Syracuse's train station.

Interbus (☑093 16 67 10; www.interbus.it) runs buses to Catania (€6, 1½ hours, 15 daily Monday to Saturday, eight on Sunday) and its airport, Noto (€3.40, 55 minutes, two to four daily) and Palermo (€12, 3¼ hours, three daily).

AST (☑093 146 27 11; www.aziendasicilianatrasporti.it) offers services to Piazza Armerina (€8.80, four hours, one daily) and Ragusa (€6.90, 2¼ hours, four daily Monday to Saturday, two Sunday).

CAR & MOTORCYCLE
The modern A18 and SS114 highways connect Syracuse with Catania and points north, while the SS115 runs south to Noto and Modica. Arriv-

ing by car, exit onto the eastbound SS124 and follow signs to Syracuse and Ortygia.

Traffic on Ortygia is restricted; you're better off parking and walking once you arrive on the island. The large Talete parking garage on Ortygia's north side is a bargain – free between 5am and 9pm, and only €1 for overnight parking.

TRAIN

From Syracuse's **train station** (Via Francesco Crispi), several trains depart daily for Messina (InterCity/regional train €18.50/9.70, 2½ to 3¼ hours) via Catania (€9.50/6.35, 1¼ hours). Some go on to Rome, Turin and Milan as well as other long-distance destinations. For Palermo, the bus is a better option. There are also local trains from Syracuse to Noto (€3.45, 30 minutes) and Ragusa (€7.65, 2¼ hours).

❶ Getting Around

For travel between the bus and train stations and Ortygia, catch the free AST shuttle bus 20 (every 20 to 60 minutes). To reach Parco Archeologico della Neapolis from Ortygia, take AST city bus 1, 3 or 12 (two-hour ticket €1.10), departing from Ortygia's Piazza Pancali.

Noto

POP 23,800 / ELEV 160M

Flattened by the devastating earthquake of 1693, Noto was grandly rebuilt by its nobles into the finest baroque town in Sicily. Now a Unesco World Heritage Site, the town is especially impressive in the early evening, when its golden-hued sandstone buildings seem to glow with a soft inner light, and at night when illuminations accentuate the beauty of its intricately carved facades. The baroque masterpiece is the work of Rosario Gagliardi and his assistant, Vincenzo Sinatra, local architects who also worked in Ragusa and Modica.

◉ Sights

Two piazzas break up the long Corso Vittorio Emanuele: Piazza dell'Immacolata to the east and Piazza XVI Maggio to the west. The latter is overlooked by the beautiful Chiesa di San Domenico and the adjacent Dominican monastery, both designed by Rosario Gagliardi. On the same square, Noto's elegant 19th-century Teatro Comunale is worth a look. For sweeping views of Noto's baroque splendour, climb to the rooftop terrace at **Chiesa di Santa Chiara** (Corso Vittorio Emanuele; admission €2; ⊙ 9.30am-1pm & 3-7pm) or the *campanile* (bell tower) of **Chiesa di**

San Carlo al Corso (Corso Vittorio Emanuele; admission €2; ⊙ 9am-12.30pm & 4-7pm).

★**Cattedrale di San Nicolò**   CATHEDRAL
(www.cattedralenoto.it; Piazza Municipio; ⊙ 9am-1pm & 3-8pm) Pride of place in Noto goes to the renovated San Nicolò Cathedral. On 16 March 1996 the town was horrified when the roof and dome of the cathedral collapsed during a thunderstorm – luckily it was 10.30pm and the cathedral was empty. In 2007 the cathedral reopened, scrubbed of centuries of dust and dirt and once again gleaming in its peachy glow.

Piazza Municipio   SQUARE
In the centre of Noto's most graceful square is the Cattedrale di San Nicolò, surrounded by elegant town houses such as Palazzo Landolina, once home to Noto's oldest noble family, and Palazzo Ducezio (Town Hall), best known for its Sala degli Specchi (Hall of Mirrors).

Palazzo Nicolaci di Villadorata   PALACE
(📞 320 556 80 38; www.palazzonicolaci.it; Via Nicolaci; adult/reduced €4/2; ⊙ 10am-1pm & 3-7.30pm) In the Palazzo Villadorata, the wrought-iron balconies are supported by a swirling pantomime of grotesque figures. Although empty of furnishings, the richly brocaded walls and frescoed ceilings of the *palazzo* give an idea of the sumptuous lifestyle of Sicilian nobles, as brought to life in the Giuseppe Tomasi di Lampedusa novel *Il Gattopardo* (The Leopard).

★ᛉ Festivals & Events

Noto's colourful two-week-long flower festival, Infiorata, is celebrated in mid- to late May with parades, historical re-enactments and a public art project in which artists decorate the length of Via Corrada Nicolaci with designs made entirely of flower petals.

⊨ Sleeping

B&Bs are plentiful in Noto; the tourist office keeps a detailed list.

Ostello Il Castello   HOSTEL €
(📞 320 838 88 69; www.ostellodinoto.it; Via Fratelli Bandiera 1; dm €17, d without bathroom €45) Directly uphill from the centre, this old-school hostel with eight- to 16-bed dorms commands fabulous views over the *duomo* and offers great value for money, despite the paltry breakfast.

La Corte del Sole
RURAL INN €€

(☑320 82 02 10; www.lacortedelsole.it; Contrada Bucachemi; per person €55-126; P ✳ @ 🛜 ≋) A few kilometres downhill from Noto, overlooking the Vendicari bird sanctuary, is this lovely rural retreat set around a central courtyard. The best of the 34 ceramic-clad, wood-beamed rooms overlook the pool. Other amenities include an in-house restaurant, a lovely breakfast area built around an ancient olive-oil press, bike hire, cooking courses and a shuttle bus to the nearby beach.

Hotel della Ferla
HOTEL €€

(☑093 157 60 07; www.hoteldellaferla.it; Via Gramsci; s €48-78, d €84-120; P ✳ 🛜) This friendly family-run hotel in a residential area near the train station offers large, bright rooms with pine furnishings and small balconies, plus free parking.

✕ Eating

The people of Noto are serious about their food, so take time to enjoy a meal and follow it up with a visit to one of the town's excellent ice-cream shops.

★ Caffè Sicilia
GELATO €

(☑093 183 50 13; Corso Vittorio Emanuele 125; desserts from €2; ☺8am-10pm Tue-Sun) Dating from 1892 and especially renowned for its granite, this beloved place vies with its next-door neighbour, Dolceria Corrado Costanzo, for the honours of Noto's best dessert shop. Frozen desserts are made with the freshest seasonal ingredients (wild strawberries in springtime, for example) while the delicious torrone (nougat) bursts with the flavours of local honey and almonds.

★ Il Liberty
MODERN SICILIAN €€

(☑093 157 32 26; www.illiberty.com; Via Cavour 40; meals €27-35; ☺noon-2.30pm & 7.30-10pm Tue-Sun) Step into the atmospheric vaulted dining room and sample chef Giuseppe Angelino's contemporary spin on Sicilian cookery. An excellent local wine list supplements the inspired menu, which moves from superb appetisers like millefoglie – wafer-thin layers of crusty cheese and ground pistachios layered with minty sweet-and-sour vegetables – straight through to desserts like warm cinnamon-ricotta cake with homemade orange compote.

★ Trattoria Crocifisso
RISTORANTE €

(☑093 157 11 51; www.ristorantecrocifisso.it; Via Principe Umberto 48; meals €30-35; ☺1-2.15pm & 8-11pm Thu-Tue) High up the many stairs of Noto Alta, this Slow Food–acclaimed trattoria with an extensive wine list is a Noto favourite. The rustic antipasto is rich in creamy aubergine, fried fennel, olives, cheeses and so on, and this is a great place to taste a Sicilian classic, in season - macco di fave (broadbean puree) with ricotta and toasted breadcrumbs.

Ristorante Il Cantuccio
MODERN SICILIAN €€

(☑093 183 74 64; www.ristoranteilcantuccio.it; Via Cavour 12; meals €30-35; ☺dinner Tue-Sun, lunch Sun) Chef Valentina presents a seasonally changing menu that combines familiar Sicilian ingredients in exciting new ways. Try her exquisite gnocchi al pesto del Cantuccio (ricotta-potato dumplings with basil, parsley, mint, capers, almonds and cherry tomatoes), then move on to memorable main courses such as lemon-stuffed bass with orange-fennel salad.

❶ Information

Tourist office (☑093 157 37 79; www.comune.noto.sr.it; Piazza XVI Maggio; ☺9am-1pm & 3-8pm) An excellent and busy information office with multilingual staff and free maps.

❶ Getting There & Around

BUS
From Largo Pantheon just east of Noto's historic centre, AST and Interbus serve Catania (€8.10, 1½ to 2¾ hours) and Syracuse (€3.40, 55 minutes).

TRAIN
There's frequent service to Syracuse (€3.45, 30 minutes, eight daily except Sunday), but Noto's station is inconveniently located 1km downhill from the centre.

Modica

POP 54,700 / ELEV 296M

A powerhouse in Grecian times, Modica may have lost its pre-eminent position to Ragusa, but it remains a superbly atmospheric town with its ancient medieval buildings climbing steeply up either side of a deep gorge.

The multilayered town is divided into Modica Alta (Upper Modica) and Modica Bassa (Lower Modica). A devastating flood in 1902 resulted in the wide avenues of Corso Umberto and Via Giarrantana (the river was dammed and diverted), which remain the main axes of the town, lined by palazzi and tiled stone houses.

● Sights

Aside from simply wandering the streets and absorbing the atmosphere, a visit to the extraordinary Chiesa di San Giorgio (⊙9am-noon & 4-7pm) is a highlight. This church, Gagliardi's masterpiece, is a vision of pure rococo splendour, a butter-coloured confection perched on a majestic 250-step staircase. Its counterpoint in Modica Bassa is the Cattedrale di San Pietro (Corso Umberto I), another impressive church atop a rippling staircase lined with life-sized statues of the Apostles.

⊨ Sleeping

Modica's quality-to-price ratio tends to be excellent, making this a top destination for discerning travellers.

★Villa Quartarella   AGRITURISMO €
(☑360 65 48 29; www.quartarella.com; Contrada Quartarella; s €40, d €75-80) Spacious rooms and welcoming hosts set the tone at this converted villa in the countryside south of Modica. Owners Francesco and Francesca are generous in sharing their love and encyclopaedic knowledge of local history, flora and fauna and can suggest multiple itineraries in the surrounding area. The delicious, ample breakfasts include everything from home-raised eggs to intriguing Modican sweets.

B&B Il Cavaliere   B&B €
(☑093 294 72 19; www.palazzoilcavaliere.it; Corso Umberto I 259; s €39-59, d €65-80, ste €95-130; ❄🛜) Stay in aristocratic style at this classy B&B in a 19th-century *palazzo*, just down from the bus station on Modica's main strip. Standard rooms have less character than the beautiful front suite and the large, high-ceilinged common rooms, which retain original tiled floors and frescoed ceilings. The elegant breakfast room has lovely views of San Giorgio church.

Hotel Relais Modica   HOTEL €
(☑093 275 44 51; www.hotelrelaismodica.it; Via Campailla; d €85-110; ❄@) Guests are assured of a warm welcome at this inviting old-school hotel. Housed in a converted *palazzo* just off Corso Umberto I, it's an attractive hostelry with 10 bright, cheery rooms, each slightly different but all spacious and quietly elegant. There's free internet in reception and satellite TV in the rooms.

✕ Eating

Dolceria Bonajuto   CHOCOLATE €
(☑093 294 12 25; www.bonajuto.it; Corso Umberto I 159; ⊙9am-1.30pm Mon-Sat, 4.30-8.30pm daily) Sicily's oldest chocolate factory is the perfect place to taste Modica's famous chocolate. Flavoured with cinnamon, vanilla, orange peel and even hot peppers, it's a legacy of the town's Spanish overlords who imported cocoa from their South American colonies.

Taverna Nicastro   SICILIAN €
(☑093 294 58 84; Via S Antonino 28; meals €14-20; ⊙dinner Tue-Sat) With over 60 years of history and a long-standing Slow Food recommendation, this is one of the upper town's most authentic and atmospheric restaurants, and a bargain to boot. The carnivore-friendly menu includes grilled meat, boiled veal, lamb stew and pasta specialities such as ricotta ravioli with pork *ragù* (meat sauce).

Fattoria delle Torri   SEAFOOD €€
(☑093 275 12 86; Vico Napolitano 14, Modica Alta; meals from €35; ⊙closed Sun evening & Mon) This is one of Modica's smartest restaurants. Housed in an elegant 18th-century *palazzo*, it has a beautiful dining area with tables set under stone arches, and bay windows looking onto a small internal garden. The seafood is particularly gorgeous, especially when combined with a crisp, dry white wine such as Cerasuolo di Vittoria.

La Locanda del Colonnello   SICILIAN €€
(☑093 275 24 23; Vico Biscari 6; meals €25-30; ⊙lunch & dinner Wed-Mon) This is a fantastic place to try Sicilian specialities with an original twist – like *macco di fave* (broad bean mash) with roasted octopus. For something more traditional, try the ravioli stuffed with ricotta and marjoram in a pork sauce, or the roast lamb with potatoes. Finish with a smooth *gelo di limone* (lemon jelly).

ℹ Information

Tourist office (☑093 275 96 34; www.comune.modica.rg.it; Corso Umberto I 141; ⊙9am-1pm & 3.30-7.30pm Mon-Sat, 10am-1pm Sun) Can supply the odd map or list, but no English is spoken.

ℹ Getting There & Away

BUS

Frequent buses run Monday to Saturday from Piazzale Falcone-Borsellino at the top of Corso Umberto I to Syracuse (€6), Noto (€3.90) and

SICILY MODICA

Ragusa (€2.40); on Sunday, service is limited to two buses in each direction.

TRAIN

From Modica's station, 600m southwest of the centre, there are three trains daily (one on Sunday) to Syracuse (€7, 1¾ hours) and six (one on Sunday) to Ragusa (€2.25, 25 minutes).

Ragusa

POP 72,800 / ELEV 502M

Like a grand old dame, Ragusa is a dignified and well-aged provincial town. Like every other town in the region, Ragusa collapsed after the 1693 earthquake; a new town called Ragusa Superiore was built on a high plateau above the original settlement. But the old aristocracy were loath to leave their tottering *palazzi* and rebuilt Ragusa Ibla on the original site. The two towns were only merged in 1927.

Ragusa Ibla remains the heart and soul of the town, and has all the best restaurants and the majority of sights. A sinuous bus ride or some very steep and scenic steps connect the lower town to its modern sister up the hill.

◉ Sights

Grand churches and *palazzi* line the twisting, narrow streets of Ragusa Ibla, interspersed with *gelaterie* and delightful piazzas where the local youth stroll and the elderly gather on benches. Palm-planted Piazza del Duomo, the centre of town, is dominated by the 18th-century **Cattedrale di San Giorgio** (Piazza Duomo; ⊙10am-12.30pm & 4-6.30pm), with its magnificent neoclassical dome and stained-glass windows.

At the eastern end of the old town is the **Giardino Ibleo** (⊙8am-8pm), a pleasant public garden laid out in the 19th century that is perfect for a picnic lunch.

⸺ Sleeping

L'Orto Sul Tetto   B&B €
(☑093 224 77 85; www.lortosultetto.it; Via Tenente Distefano 56; s €45-60, d €70-110; 🕸🛜) This sweet little B&B behind Ragusa's *duomo* offers an intimate experience, with just three rooms and a lovely roof terrace where breakfast is served.

Locanda Don Serafino   INN €€
(☑093 222 00 65; www.locandadonserafino.it; Via XI Febbraio 15; s €80-138, d €90-168; 🕸⌨) This historic inn near the *duomo* has beautiful rooms, some with original vaulted stone ceilings, plus a well-regarded restaurant nearby. For €9 extra, guests get access to the Lido Azzurro beach at Marina di Ragusa, 25km away.

Caelum Hyblae   B&B €€
(☑093 222 04 02; www.bbcaelumhyblae.it; Salita Specula 11, Ragusa Ibla; d €100-120) With its book-lined reception and crisp white decor, this stylish, family-run B&B exudes quiet sophistication. Each of the seven rooms has views over the cathedral and while they're not the biggest, they're immaculately turned out with unadorned walls, pristine beds and functional modern furniture.

✖ Eating

Quattro Gatti   SICILIAN €
(☑093 224 56 12; Via Valverde 95; meals €18; ⊙dinner, closed Mon Oct-May & Sun Jun-Sep) This Sicilian-Slovak eatery near the Giardini Iblei serves an amazing four-course fixed-price menu bursting with fresh, local flavours. The antipasti spread is especially memorable, as are the seasonally changing specials scribbled on the blackboard up front. Slovak-inspired offerings such as goulash and apple strudel round out a menu of Sicilian classics.

Gelati DiVini   GELATO €
(☑093 222 89 89; www.gelatidivini.it; Piazza Duomo 20; ice cream from €2; ⊙10am-midnight) This exceptional *gelateria* makes wine-flavoured ice creams like marsala and muscat, plus unconventional offerings including rose, fennel, wild mint and the surprisingly tasty *gocce verdi*, made with local olive oil.

La Rusticana   TRATTORIA €€
(☑093 222 79 81; Corso XXV Aprile 68; meals €25; ⊙Wed-Mon) Fans of the *Montalbano* TV series will want to eat here, as this is where scenes set in the fictional Trattoria San Calogero were filmed. In reality, it's a cheerful, boisterous trattoria whose generous portions and relaxed vine-covered terrace ensure a loyal clientele. The food is defiantly *casareccia* (home-style), so expect no-frills pastas and uncomplicated cuts of grilled meat. Slow Food recommended.

Ristorante Duomo   MODERN SICILIAN €€€
(☑093 265 12 65; Via Capitano Bocchieri 31; meals €90-100, tasting menus €135-140) This is generally regarded as one of Sicily's best restaurants. Behind the stained-glass door, small rooms are outfitted like private parlours, ensuring a suitably romantic ambience for Chef Ciccio Sultano's refined creations.

These combine ingredients in imaginative, unconventional ways while making constant use of classic Sicilian ingredients such as pistachios, fennel, almonds and Nero d'Avola wine. Book ahead.

ℹ️ Information

Tourist office (☎ 093 268 47 80; Piazza della Repubblica; ⏰ 10am-1pm & 3.30-6.30pm) At the western edge of the lower town.

ℹ️ Getting There & Around

BUS

Long-distance and municipal buses share a terminal on Via Zama in the upper town. Buy tickets at the Interbus/Etna kiosk in the main lot or at cafes around the corner. **Interbus** (www.interbus.it) runs to Catania (€8.30, two hours, five to 12 daily). **AST** (☎ 093 268 18 18; www.aziendasicilianatrasporti.it) serves Syracuse (€6.90, three hours, eight daily Monday to Saturday, two on Sunday) via Modica (€2.40, 30 minutes) and Noto (€4.80, 2¼ hours).

City bus 33 (€1.10) runs hourly between the bus terminal and the lower town of Ragusa Ibla. From the train station, bus 11 (bus 1 on Sundays) makes a similar circuit.

TRAIN

From the station in the upper town, there are two trains to Syracuse (€7.65, 2¼ hours) via Noto (€5.75, 1½ hours) Monday to Saturday.

CENTRAL SICILY & THE MEDITERRANEAN COAST

Central Sicily is a land of vast panoramas, undulating fields, severe mountain ridges and hilltop towns not yet sanitised for tourists. Moving towards the Mediterranean, the perspective changes, as ancient temples jostle for position with modern high-rise apartments outside Agrigento, Sicily's most lauded classical site and also one of its busier modern cities.

Agrigento

POP 59,100 / ELEV 230M

Agrigento does not make a good first impression. Seen from a distance, the modern city's rows of unsightly apartment blocks loom incongruously on the hillside, distracting attention from the splendid Valley of the Temples below, where the ancient Greeks once built their great city of Akragas. Never

fear: once you get down among the ruins, their monumental grace becomes apparent, and it's easy to understand how this remarkable complex of temples became Sicily's preeminent travel destination, first put on the tourist map by Goethe in the 18th century.

Three kilometres uphill from the temples, Agrigento's medieval core is a pleasant place to pass the evening after a day exploring the ruins. The intercity bus and train stations are both in the upper town, within a few blocks of Via Atenea, the main street of the medieval city.

👁️ Sights

👁️ Valle dei Templi

⭐ **Valley of the Temples (Valle dei Templi)** ARCHAEOLOGICAL SITE (☎ 092 262 16 11; www.parcovalledeitempli.it; adult/EU under 18yr & over 65yr/EU 18-25yr incl Quartiere Ellenistico-Romano €10/free/5, incl Museo Archeologico €13.50/free/7) One of southern Europe's most compelling archaeological sites, the 1300-hectare Parco Valle dei Templi encompasses the ruins of the ancient city of Akragas. The highlight is the stunning Tempio della Concordia, one of the best-preserved Greek temples in existence and one of a series built on a ridge to act as beacons for homecoming sailors.

Three kilometres south of Agrigento, the park is divided into two distinct zones, separated by the main SS118 road. There are two ticket offices, one at the park's eastern edge and another at Piazza Alexander Hardcastle between the eastern and western zones. The car park is by the eastern entrance.

⭐ **Museo Archeologico** MUSEUM (☎ 092 24 01 11; Contrada San Nicola; admission incl Valley of the Temples adult/reduced €13.50/7; ⏰ 9am-7pm Tue-Sat, 9am-1pm Sun & Mon) North of the temples, this wheelchair-accessible museum is one of Sicily's finest, with a huge collection of clearly labelled artefacts from the excavated site. Especially noteworthy are the dazzling displays of Greek painted ceramics and the aweinspiring reconstructed *telamone*, a colossal statue recovered from the nearby Tempio di Giove.

👁️ Medieval Agrigento

Roaming the town's lively, winding streets is relaxing after a day among the temples.

Agrigento

Agrigento

Chiesa di Santa Maria dei Greci   CHURCH
(Salita Santa Maria dei Greci; ⊙9am-12.30pm & 4-6pm Mon-Sat) This 11th-century Norman church is built on the site of a 5th-century BC temple to Athena. Glass floor panels reveal the temple's foundations, while a narrow passageway left of the church allows you to see the ancient Greek columns.

Monastero del Santo Spirito   CONVENT
This hillside convent was founded by Cistercian nuns at the end of the 13th century. Ring the buzzer at the door marked No 8, and their modern-day counterparts will sell you a tray of delicious cakes and pastries (€11), including *dolci di mandorla* (almond pastries)*, cuscusu* (almond and pistachio 'couscous') and – at Christmas time – *bucellati* (rolled sweet dough with figs).

☞ Tours

The tourist office maintains a list of multilingual guides. The official rate is €140 for a half-day tour, although discounts can be negotiated.

✹ Festivals & Events

Sagra del Mandorlo in Fiore   CULTURE
A huge folk festival held on the first Sunday in February, when the Valley of the Temples is cloaked in almond blossom.

🛏 Sleeping

Camere a Sud   B&B €
(☑349 638 44 24; www.camereasud.it; Via Ficani 6; r €60-70; ❈@🤶) A lovely B&B in the centre of Agrigento, Camere a Sud has three guest rooms decorated with style and taste – traditional decor and contemporary textiles are

matched with bright colours and modern art. The sumptuous breakfast is served on the terrace in the warmer months.

PortAtenea B&B €

(☑349 093 74 92; www.portatenea.com; cnr Via Atenea & Via C Battisti; s €35-45, d €55-70; ❋🔊) Five minutes from the train and bus stations at the entrance to Agrigento's main pedestrian thoroughfare, this B&B wins points for its large roof terrace overlooking the Valley of the Temples. The three double rooms and two triples are spacious and well appointed, with hairdryers and cheerful decor.

★Villa Athena LUXURY HOTEL €€€

(☑092 259 62 88; www.hotelvillaathena.it; Via Passeggiata Archeologica 33; s €130-190, d €150-350, ste €240-890; ▣❋@🔊☀) With the Tempio della Concordia lit up in the near distance and palm trees lending an exotic Arabian-nights feel, the views from this historic five-star are magnificent. Housed in an aristocratic 18th-century villa, the hotel's interior, gleaming after a recent makeover, is a picture of white, ceramic cool.

The Villa Suite, with two cavernous rooms floored in antique tiles, a freestanding jacuzzi tub and a vast terrace looking straight at the temples, vies for the title of coolest hotel room in Sicily.

✖️ Eating

Trattoria Concordia TRATTORIA €

(☑092 22 26 68; Via Porcello 8; meals €18-30; ☺lunch & dinner) Tucked up a side alley, this rustic trattoria with exposed stone and stucco walls specialises in grilled fish along with traditional Sicilian *primi* like *casarecce con pesce spada, melanzane e menta* (pasta with swordfish, eggplant and mint).

★Kalòs MODERN SICILIAN €€

(☑092 22 63 89; www.ristorantekalos.it; Piazzetta San Calogero; meals €30-40; ☺lunch & dinner) Food is excellent at this smart restaurant with a couple of cute tables on the tiny balcony. Feast on *primi* such as fettucine with prawns and artichokes or pasta *all'agrigentina*, with fresh tomatoes, basil and pistachio; follow with *secondi* such as grilled lamb chops and citrus shrimp; and for dessert perhaps almond *semifreddo* or pear tart with chocolate and hazelnuts.

L'Ambasciata di Sicilia SICILIAN €€

(☑092 22 05 26; Via Giambertoni 2; meals €22-33; ☺Mon-Sat) At the 'Sicilian Embassy', they do everything they can to improve foreign relations, plying tourists with tasty plates of traditional Sicilian fare and good seafood. Order an octopus and it arrives so fresh it feels as if it's staring you in the eyes. Try to get a table on the small outdoor terrace, which has splendid views.

🍷 Drinking & Nightlife

QOC BAR

(☑092 22 71 07; www.qoc.me; Via Cesare Battisti 8; ☺Tue-Sun) A great place to hang out among young *agrigentini*, this trendy spot just off Via Atenea bills itself as an 'Outfit, Restaurant, Bar', but it does 'bar' best, with good, themed *aperitivi* and late-night cocktails. There's a nice-looking restaurant upstairs and a fixed-menu lunch (€10), although food is only average.

☆ Entertainment

Teatro Pirandello THEATRE

(☑092 22 50 19; www.teatroluigipirandello.it; Piazza Pirandello; tickets €18-23) This city-run theatre is Sicily's third largest, after Palermo's Teatro Massimo and Catania's Teatro Massimo Bellini. Works by local hero Luigi Pirandello figure prominently in the program, which runs from November to April.

ℹ️ Information

There are banks on Piazza Vittorio Emanuele I and Via Atenea.

Ospedale San Giovanni di Dio (☑092 244 21 11; Contrada da Consolida) North of the centre.

Police station (☑112; Piazzale Aldo Moro 2)

Tourist information point (Train Station; ☺8am-8pm Mon-Fri, 8am-2pm Sat)

Tourist office (☑800 236 837; www.comune. agrigento.it; Piazzale Aldo Moro 1; ☺8am-2pm Mon-Fri, 8am-1pm Sat) Inside the Provincia building, offers information on the city and province.

ℹ️ Getting There & Away

BUS

The intercity bus station and ticket booths are located on Piazza Rosselli. **Autoservizi Camilleri** (☑092 247 18 86; www.camilleriargentoelattuca. it) runs buses to Palermo (€8.70, two hours) five times Monday to Saturday and once on Sunday; **Cuffaro** (☑091 616 15 10; www.cuffaro.info) offers more frequent Palermo services – three to eight departures daily. **SAL** (Società Autolinee Licata; www.autolineesal.it) also offers direct service to Palermo's Falcone-Borsellino airport (€12.10, 2½ hours, four Monday to Saturday). **Lumia** (☑092 22 04 14; www.autolineelumia.it)

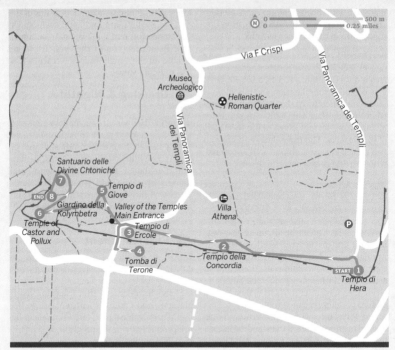

Archaeological Walking Tour
Valley of the Temples

LENGTH THREE HOURS

Begin your exploration in the so-called Eastern Zone, home to Agrigento's best-preserved temples. From the eastern ticket office, a short walk leads to the 5th-century BC ❶ **Tempio di Hera** (Temple of Hera, aka Juno), perched on the ridgetop. Though partly destroyed by an earthquake, the colonnade remains largely intact as does a long sacrificial altar. Traces of red are the result of fire damage likely dating to the Carthaginian invasion of 406 BC.

Next descend past a gnarled 800-year-old olive tree and a series of Byzantine tombs to the ❷ **Tempio della Concordia**. This remarkable edifice, the model for Unesco's logo, has survived almost entirely intact since its construction in 430 BC, partly thanks to its conversion into a Christian basilica in the 6th century, partly due to the shock-absorbing, earthquake-dampening qualities of the soft clay underlying its hard rock foundation.

Further downhill, the ❸ **Tempio di Ercole** (Temple of Hercules), is Agrigento's oldest, dat-

ing from the end of the 6th century BC. Down from the main temples, the miniature ❹ **Tomba di Terone** (Tomb of Theron) dates to 75 BC.

Now cross the road to the Western Zone, stopping first at the ❺ **Tempio di Giove** (Temple of Olympian Zeus). This would have been the world's largest Doric temple had its construction not been interrupted by the Carthaginian sacking of Akragas. A later earthquake reduced it to the crumbled ruin you see today. Lying flat on his back amid the rubble is an 8m-tall *telamon* (a sculpted figure of a man with arms raised), originally intended to support the temple's weight. It's actually a copy; the original is in Agrigento's archeological museum.

Take a brief look at the ruined 5th-century BC ❻ **Temple of Castor and Pollux**, and the 6th-century BC complex of altars and small buildings known as the ❼ **Santuario delle Divine Chtoniche** (Sanctuary of the Chthonic Deities), before ending your visit in the ❽ **Giardino della Kolymbetra**, a lush garden in a natural cleft near the sanctuary, with more than 300 (labelled) species of plants and some welcome picnic tables.

has departures to Trapani and its Birgi Airport (€11.80, three to four hours, three daily Monday to Saturday, one on Sunday); and **SAIS** (☑ 092 22 93 24; www.saistrasporti.it) runs buses to Catania (€12.40, three hours, 10 to 15 daily).

CAR & MOTORCYCLE

The SS189 links Agrigento with Palermo, while the SS115 runs along the coast, northwest towards Trapani and southeast to Syracuse.

Driving in the medieval town is near impossible due to all the pedestrianised streets. There's metered parking at the train station and free parking along Via Esseneto just below.

TRAIN

From Agrigento Centrale station (Piazza Marconi), direct trains run regularly to Palermo (€8.30, 2¼ hours, seven to 10 daily). Service to Catania (€10.40 to €14.50, four hours) is less frequent and usually requires a change of trains. For other destinations, you're better off taking the bus.

❶ Getting Around

TUA (Trasporti Urbani Agrigento; ☑ 092 241 20 24) buses run down to the Valley of the Temples from the Piazza Rosselli bus station, stopping in front of the train station en route. Take bus 1, 2 or 3 (€1.10 with pre-purchased ticket, €1.65 on board) and get off at either the museum or the Piazzale dei Templi. Bus 1 continues to Porto Empedocle and bus 2 continues to San Leone. The Linea Verde (Green Line) bus runs hourly from the train station to the cathedral.

WESTERN SICILY

Directly across the water from North Africa and still retaining vestiges of the Arab, Phoenician and Greek cultures that once prevailed here, western Sicily has a bit of the Wild West about it. There's plenty to stir the senses, from Trapani's savoury fish couscous, to the dazzling views from hilltop Erice, to the wild coastal beauty of Riserva Naturale dello Zingaro.

Marsala

POP 82,300

Best known for its sweet dessert wines, Marsala is an elegant town of stately baroque buildings within a perfect square of walls.

The city was originally founded by Phoenician escapees from the Roman onslaught at nearby Mozia. Not wanting to risk a second attack, they fortified their new home with 7m-thick walls, ensuring that it was the last Punic settlement to fall to the Romans. In AD 830 it was conquered by the Arabs, who gave it its current name, Marsa Allah (Port of God).

It was here in 1860 that Giuseppe Garibaldi, leader of the movement for Italian unification, landed in his rickety old boats with his 1000-strong army – a claim to fame that finds its way into every tourist brochure.

⊙ Sights & Activities

For a taste of local life, take a stroll at sunset around pretty Piazza della Repubblica, heart of the historic centre.

Cantine Florio WINERY
(☑ 092 378 11 11; www.duca.it/cantineflorio; Via Vincenzo Florio 1; tours €10; ⊙ wine shop 9am-1pm & 3.30-6pm Mon-Fri, 9.30am-1pm Sat, English-language tours 3.30pm Mon-Fri & 10.30am Sat year-round, plus 11am Mon-Fri Apr-Oct) These venerable wine cellars just east of town open their doors to visitors to explain the Marsala-making process and the fascinating history of local viticulture. Afterwards visitors can sample the goods in Florio's spiffy new tasting room. Take bus 16 from Piazza del Popolo.

Museo Archeologico
Baglio Anselmi MUSEUM
(☑ 092 395 25 35; Lungomare Boeo; adult €4, EU citizen 18-25yr or over 65yr €2; ⊙ 9am-8pm Tue-Sun, 9am-1.30pm Mon) Marsala's finest treasure is the partially reconstructed remains of a Carthaginian *liburna* (warship) sunk off the Egadi Islands during the First Punic War. Displayed alongside objects from its cargo, the ship's bare bones provide the only remaining physical evidence of the Phoenicians' seafaring superiority in the 3rd century BC and offer a glimpse of a civilisation extinguished by the Romans.

Whitaker Museum MUSEUM
(☑ 092 371 25 98; adult/child €9/5; ⊙ 9.30am-1.30pm & 2.30-6.30pm Mar-Sep) On the island of Mozia, 10km north of Marsala, this museum displays archaeologist Joseph Whitaker's unique collection of Phoenician artefacts, assembled over decades. The museum's greatest treasure (on loan to the Getty Museum in Los Angeles at research time) is *Il Giovinetto di Mozia,* a marble statue of a young man in a pleated robe, suggesting Carthaginian influences.

SICILY MARSALA

WORTH A TRIP

SICILY'S BEST-PRESERVED ROMAN MOSAICS

Near the town of Piazza Armerina in central Sicily is the stunning 3rd-century Roman **Villa Romana del Casale** ([☎] 093 568 00 36; www.villaromanadelcasale.it; adult/reduced €10/5; [☉] 9am-6pm summer, 9am-4pm winter), a Unesco World Heritage Site and one of the few remaining sites of Roman Sicily. This sumptuous hunting lodge is thought to have belonged to Diocletian's co-emperor Marcus Aurelius Maximianus. Buried under mud in a 12th-century flood, it remained hidden for 700 years before its magnificent floor mosaics were discovered in the 1950s. Visit out of season or early in the day to avoid the hordes of tourists.

The mosaics cover almost the entire floor (3500 sq metres) of the villa and are considered unique for their narrative style, the range of subject matter and variety of colour – many are clearly influenced by African themes. Along the eastern end of the internal courtyard is the wonderful **Corridor of the Great Hunt**, vividly depicting chariots, rhinos, cheetahs, lions and the voluptuously beautiful Queen of Sheba. Across the corridor is a series of apartments, where floor illustrations reproduce scenes from Homer. But perhaps the most captivating of the mosaics is the so-called **Room of the Ten Girls in Bikinis**, with depictions of sporty girls in scanty bikinis throwing a discus, using weights and throwing a ball; they would blend in well on a Malibu beach. These most famous of Piazza Armerina's mosaics were fully reopened to the public in 2013 after years of painstaking restoration and are among Sicily's greatest classical treasures.

Travelling by car from Piazza Armerina, follow signs south of town to the SP15, then continue 5km to reach the villa.

Getting here without a car is more challenging. Buses operated by Interbus (p803) from Catania (€8.90, 1¾ hours) or **SAIS** ([☎] 093 568 01 19; www.saisautolinee.it) from Enna (€3.40, 40 minutes) run to Piazza Armerina; from here catch a local bus (€0.70, 30 minutes, summer only) or a taxi (€20) the remaining 5km.

🛏 Sleeping & Eating

Marsala has few hotels within the historic centre.

★ **Il Profumo del Sale**   B&B €
([☎] 092 3189 0472; www.ilprofumodelsale.it; Via Vaccari 8; s €35, d €50-60; [❄]) A dream B&B in every imaginable sense, Profumo del Sale has a perfect city centre location and three attractive rooms – including a palatial front unit with cathedral views from its small balcony – all enhanced by welcoming touches like almond cookies and fine soaps. Sophisticated owner Celsa is full of great tips about Marsala and the local area.

Hotel Carmine   HOTEL €€
([☎] 092 371 19 07; www.hotelcarmine.it; Piazza Carmine 16; s €70-105, d €100-130; [P][❄][@][❄]) This lovely hotel in a 16th-century monastery has elegant rooms (especially rooms 7 and 30), with original blue-and-gold majolica tiles, stone walls, antique furniture and lofty beamed ceilings. Enjoy your cornflakes in the baronial-style breakfast room with its historic frescoes and over-the-top chandelier, or sip your drink by the roaring fireplace in winter. Modern perks include a rooftop solarium.

★ **San Lorenzo Osteria**   SICILIAN €€
(SLO; [☎] 092 371 25 93; Via Garraffa 60; meals €25-35; [☉] closed Tue; [❄]) With roots as a wedding catering business, this stylish eatery opened to universal acclaim in 2012. It's a class act all around – from the ever-changing menu of market-fresh seafood scrawled daily on the blackboard to the interior's sleek modern lines to the gorgeous presentation of the food. The stellar wine list features some local choices you won't find elsewhere.

Il Gallo e l'Innamorata   SICILIAN €€
([☎] 092 3195 4446; www.osteriailgalloelinnamorata.com; Via Bilardello 18; meals €25-30; [☉] closed Tue) Warm orange walls and arched stone doorways lend an artsy, convivial atmosphere to this Slow Food–acclaimed eatery. The à la carte menu is short and sweet, featuring a few well-chosen dishes each day, including the classic *scaloppine al Marsala* (veal cooked with Marsala wine and lemon).

ⓘ Information

Tourist office (☑092 399 33 38, 092 371 40 97; ufficioturistico.proloco@comune.marsala. tp.it; Via XI Maggio 100; ◉8.30am-1.30pm & 3-8pm Mon-Sat) Spacious office with comfy couches right off the main square; provides a wide range of maps and brochures.

ⓘ Getting There & Away

From Marsala, bus operators include **Lumia** (www.autolineelumia.it) to Agrigento (€9.90, 2½ hours, one to three daily); and **Salemi** (☑092 398 11 20; www.autoservizisalemi.it) to Palermo (€9.20, 2½ hours, at least nine daily).

The train is the best way to get to Trapani (€3.45, 30 minutes, 10 daily, five on Sunday).

Selinunte

The ruins of Selinunte are the most impressively sited in Sicily. The huge city was built in 628 BC on a promontory overlooking the sea, and over two and a half centuries became one of the richest and most powerful in the world. It was destroyed by the Carthaginians in 409 BC and finally fell to the Romans in about 350 BC, at which time it went into rapid decline and disappeared from historical accounts.

The city's past is so remote that the names of the various temples have been forgotten and they are now identified by the letters A to G, M and O. The most impressive, **Temple E**, has been partially rebuilt, its columns pieced together from their fragments with part of its tympanum. Many of the carvings, particularly from **Temple C**, are now in the archaeological museum in Palermo. Their quality is on a par with the Parthenon marbles and clearly demonstrates the high cultural levels reached by many Greek colonies in Sicily.

The ticket office and entrance to the ruins (☑092 44 62 51; www.selinunte.net; adult €6, EU citizen 18-25yr €3, under 18yr or over 65yr free; ◉9am-6pm summer, 9am-4pm winter) is located near the eastern temples. Try to visit in spring when the surroundings are ablaze with wildflowers.

For overnight stays, **Sicilia Cuore Mio** (☑092 44 60 77; www.siciliacuoremio.it; Via della Cittadella 44; d €68-95; 🛜🅿) is a lovely B&B with an upstairs terrace overlooking both the ruins and the sea. Guests enjoy breakfast (including homemade jams, *cannoli*, and more) on a shady patio bordered by olive trees. Escape the touristy and mediocre res-

taurants near the ruins by heading for **Lido Zabbara** (☑092 44 61 94; Via Pigafetta; buffet per person €12), a beachfront place in nearby Marinella di Selinunte with good grilled fish and a varied buffet, or drive 15km east to **Da Vittorio** (☑092 57 83 81; www.ristorante vittorio. it; meals €28-45) in Porto Palo, another great place to enjoy seafood, sunset and the sound of lapping waves.

Selinunte is midway between Agrigento and Trapani, about 10km south of the junction of the A29 and SS115 near Castelvetrano. **Autoservizi Salemi** (☑092 48 18 26; www. autoservizisalemi.it) runs five to seven buses daily from Selinunte to Castelvetrano (€2, 25 to 35 minutes), where you can make onward bus connections to Agrigento (€8.30, two hours), or train connections to Marsala (€3.95, 35 to 55 minutes), Trapani (€5.75, 1¼ hours) and Palermo (€7.65, 2½ hours).

Trapani

POP 70,600

The lively port city of Trapani makes a convenient base for exploring Sicily's western tip. Its historic centre is filled with atmospheric pedestrian streets and some lovely churches and baroque buildings, although the heavily developed outskirts are rather bleak. The surrounding countryside is beautiful, ranging from the watery vastness of the coastal salt ponds to the rugged mountainous shoreline north of town.

Once situated at the heart of a powerful trading network that stretched from Carthage to Venice, Trapani's sickle-shaped spit of land hugs the precious harbour, nowadays busy with a steady stream of tourists and traffic to and from Tunisia, Pantelleria and the Egadi Islands.

◎ Sights

The narrow network of streets in Trapani's historic centre remains a Moorish labyrinth, although it takes much of its character from the fabulous 18th-century baroque of the Spanish period – a catalogue of examples can be found down the pedestrianised **Via Garibaldi**. The best time to walk down here is in the early evening (around 7pm) when the *passeggiata* is in full swing.

Trapani's other main street is Corso Vittorio Emanuele, punctuated by the huge **Cattedrale di San Lorenzo** (Corso Vittorio Emanuele; ◉8am-4pm), with its baroque facade and stuccoed interior. Facing off the

Trapani

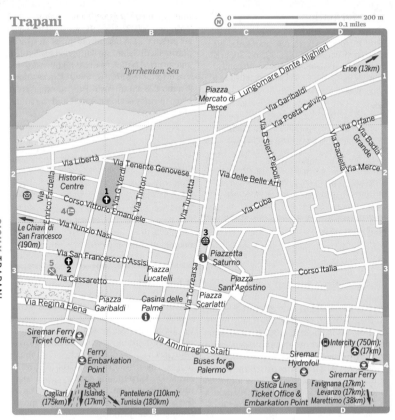

Tyrrhenian Sea

Erice (13km)

Lungomare Dante Alighieri

Piazza
Mercato di
Pesce

Via Garibaldi

Via Poeta Calvino

Via Orfane

Via Badia Grande

Via Libertà

Via Tenente Genovese

Via B Sieri Pepoli

Via delle Belle Arti

Via Badiella

Via Merce

Historic
Centre

Via Enrico Fardella

Corso Vittorio Emanuele

Via G Verdi

Via Tintori

Via Turretta

Via Cuba

Le Chiavi di
San Francesco
(190m)

Via Nunzio Nasi

Piazzetta
Saturno

Corso Italia

Via San Francesco D'Assisi

Piazza
Lucatelli

Via Torrearsa

Piazza
Sant'Agostino

Via Cassaretto

Via Regina Elena

Piazza
Garibaldi

Casina delle
Palme

Piazza
Scarlatti

Piazza
Saturno

Siremar Ferry
Ticket Office

Via Ammiraglio Staiti

Ferry
Embarkation
Point

Buses for
Palermo

Siremar
Hydrofoil

Intercity (750m);
(17km)

Siremar Ferry

Cagliari
(175km)

Egadi
Islands
(17km)

Pantelleria (110km);
Tunisia (180km)

Ustica Lines
Ticket Office &
Embarkation Point

Favignana (17km);
Levanzo (17km);
Marettimo (38km)

east end of the corso is another baroque confection, the **Palazzo Senatorio** (cnr Corso Vittorio Emanuele & Via Torrearsa).

Chiesa del Purgatorio   CHURCH
(☑ 092 356 28 82; Via San Francesco d'Assisi; voluntary donation requested; ☻ 7.30am-noon & 4-7pm Mon-Sat, 10am-noon & 4-7pm Sun) Just off the corso in the heart of the city, this church houses the impressive 18th-century *Misteri,* 20 life-sized wooden effigies depicting the story of Christ's Passion, which take centre stage during the city's dramatic Easter Week processions. Explanatory panels in English, Italian, French and German help visitors to understand the story behind each figure.

Museo Nazionale Pepoli   MUSEUM
(☑ 092 355 32 69; Via Conte Pepoli 200; adult €6, EU citizen under 18yr or over 65yr free, EU citizen 18-25yr €3; ☻ 9am-1.30pm & 2.30-7.30pm Tue-Sat, 9am-12.30pm Sun; tours hourly 9am-noon & 2.30-6.30pm) In a former Carmelite monastery,

this museum houses the collection of Conte Pepoli, who devoted his life to salvaging Trapani's local arts and crafts, most notably the garish coral carvings – once all the rage in Europe before Trapani's offshore coral banks were decimated. The museum also has a good collection of Gagini sculptures, silverwork, archaeological artefacts and religious art. It's 12km east of town.

Egadi Islands   ISLANDS
The islands of Levanzo, Favignana and Marettimo make a pleasant day trip from Trapani. For centuries the lucrative tuna industry formed the basis of the islands' economy, but overfishing of the surrounding waters means that the Egadi survives primarily on income from tourists who come to cycle, dive or simply enjoy the relaxed pace of life.

The best range of meals and accommodation can be found on **Favignana**, while the islands' single greatest tourist attraction is **Grotta del Genovese** (☑ 339 741

88 00, 092 392 40 32; www.grottadelgenovese.it; guided cave tour €10, incl transport one way/round trip €16/22.50; ☉tours 10.30am daily, extra tour 2.30pm or 3pm Jul & Aug) on **Levanzo**, a cave decorated with Mesolithic and Neolithic art work, including a famous image of a prehistoric tuna. To really get away from it all, head to **Marettimo**, whose main attractions are the lovely whitewashed port and the surrounding network of walking trails. **Siremar** (☑092 354 54 55; www.siremar.it; Via Ammiraglio Staiti) and **Ustica Lines** (☑092 387 38 13; www.usticalines.it; Via Ammiraglio Staiti) run year-round hydrofoil services to the islands from Trapani and Marsala.

🎉 Festivals & Events

I Misteri   RELIGIOUS
(www.processionemisteritp.it) Sicily's most venerated Easter procession is a four-day festival of extraordinary religious fervour. Nightly processions, bearing life-sized wooden effigies, make their way through the old quarter to a specially erected chapel in Piazza Lucatelli. The high point is on Good Friday when the celebrations reach fever pitch.

Couscous Fest   FOOD
(www.couscousfest.it) In San Vito Lo Capo, 40km north of Trapani, this late-September festival celebrates Sicilian multiculturalism with world music concerts and international couscous cook offs.

🛏 Sleeping

The most convenient – and nicest – place to stay is in Trapani's pedestrianised historic centre, just north of the port.

Ai Lumi B&B   B&B €
(☑092 354 09 22; www.ailumi.it; Corso Vittorio Emanuele 71; s €40-70, d €70-100, tr €90-125, q €100-150; ▣⬤) Housed in an 18th-century *palazzo,* this centrally located B&B offers 13 rooms of varying size. Best are the spacious apartments (numbers 33, 34 and 35), with kitchenettes and balconies overlooking Trapani's most elegant pedestrian street. Upstairs apartment 23 is also lovely, with a private balcony reached by a spiral staircase. Guests get discounts at the hotel's atmospheric restaurant next door.

Le Chiavi di San Francesco   HOTEL €
(☑092 343 80 13; www.lechiavidisanfrancesco. com; Via Tartaglia 18; d €80-110, ste €140; ▣⬤) Opposite the Chiesa di San Francesco, this popular hotel has 16 rooms featuring cheerful colour schemes and small but clean bathrooms. Angle for one of the superior rooms up front, which offer more space, better light and optional kitchen facilities.

✴ Eating

Sicily's Arab heritage and Trapani's unique position on the sea route to Tunisia have made couscous ('*cuscus*' or '*kuscus*' as they sometimes spell it around here) a local speciality.

La Rinascente   PASTRIES & CAKES €
(☑092 32 37 67; Via Gatti 3; cannoli €1.80; ☉9am-1pm & 3-7pm, closed Sun afternoon & Wed) When you enter this bakery through the side door, you'll feel like you've barged into someone's kitchen – and you have! Thankfully, owner Giovanni Costadura's broad smile will quickly put you at ease, coupled with some of the best *cannoli* on the planet, which you can watch being created on the spot.

★Al Solito Posto   SICILIAN €€
(☑092 32 45 45; www.trattoria-alsolitoposto.com; Via Orlandini 30; meals €20-35; ☉closed Sun & 15-31 Aug) A 15-minute walk east of the centre, this wildly popular trattoria is a well-deserved wearer of the Slow Food badge. From superb *primi* (try the trademark *busiate con pesto alla trapanese*) to super-fresh seafood *secondi* (don't miss the local tuna in May and June) to the creamy-crunchy homemade *cannoli,* everything is top-notch.

★Osteria La Bettolaccia   SICILIAN €€
(☑092 32 16 95; www.labettolaccia.it; Via Enrico Fardella 25; meals €30-45; ☉closed Sat & Sun lunch all year, plus Sun dinner Nov-Easter) An unwaveringly authentic, Slow Food favourite, this centrally located eatery just two blocks from the ferry terminal is the perfect place to try *cous cous con zuppa di mare* (couscous with mixed seafood in a spicy fish sauce, with tomatoes, garlic and parsley). In response to its great popularity, the dining

PANTELLERIA

Halfway between Trapani and Tunisia, this volcanic outcrop is Sicily's largest offshore island. Buffeted year-round by winds, Pantelleria is characterised by jagged lava stone, low-slung caper bushes, dwarf vines, steaming fumaroles and mudbaths. There are no true beaches, but Pantelleria's gorgeous, secluded coves – including Cala Tramontana, Cala Levante and Balata dei Turchi – are perfect for snorkelling, diving and boat excursions.

The island has excellent hiking trails, along the coast and in the high vineyard country of Piana di Ghirlanda. Near Mursia on the west coast, there are signposted but poorly maintained remnants of sesi (Bronze Age funerary monuments). Throughout the island you'll also find Pantelleria's famous dammusi (houses with thick, whitewashed walls and shallow cupolas). The island's exotic and remote atmosphere has long made it popular with celebrities, including Truman Capote, Sting, Madonna and Giorgio Armani.

Darwin (p220) offers regular flights to Pantelleria from Palermo and Trapani, and Siremar (www.siremar.it) runs one ferry daily to/from Trapani (€34, six hours). For further information about Pantelleria see www.pantelleria.com.

room was expanded in 2013, but it's still wise to book ahead.

❶ Information

The city centre has several banks with ATMs.

Ospedale Sant'Antonio Abate (☏ 092 380 91 11; Via Cosenza 82)

Police station (☏ 092 359 81 11; Piazza Vittoria Veneto)

Tourist office (☏ 092 354 45 33; point@ stradadelvinoericedoc.it; Piazzetta Saturno; ☺9am-1pm & 4-7pm Mon-Sat) Trapani's tourist office offers city maps, bike sightseeing tours, bike rental (€8 per day), tour guides and information about wineries along the Strada del Vino Erice DOC. The subsidiary Casina delle Palme (Piazza Garibaldi; ☺9am-1pm & 4-7pm Mon-Sat) branch is opposite the ferry terminal in Piazza Garibaldi.

❶ Getting There & Around

For bus, plane and ferry tickets, try **Egatours** (☏ 092 32 17 54; www.egatourviaggi.it; Via Ammiraglio Staiti 13), a travel agency located opposite the port.

AIR

Trapani's small **Vincenzo Florio Airport** (TPS; Birgi Airport; www.airgest.it) is 17km south of town at Birgi. **Ryanair** (www.ryanair.com) offers direct flights to London Luton and a dozen other European cities; **Air One** (flyairone.com) serves cities on the Italian mainland, while **Darwin** (www.darwinairline.com) goes to the Mediterranean island of Pantelleria. AST buses connect the airport with downtown Trapani (€4.70, 45 minutes, hourly) and Marsala (€2.50, 45 minutes, four daily).

BOAT

Ferry ticket offices are inside Trapani's ferry terminal, opposite Piazza Garibaldi.

For Ustica Lines and Siremar hydrofoils, the ticket office and embarkation point is 150m further east along Via Ammiraglio Staiti.

Grimaldi Lines (www.grimaldi-ferries.com) runs weekly services to Tunisia (deck/cabin from €60/85, 8½ hours) and Civitavecchia (€120, 14½ hours).

Tirrenia (www.tirrenia.it) runs a weekly service to Cagliari (deck/cabin from €40/160, 12 hours).

Ustica Lines (☏ 092 387 38 13; www.usticalines. it) and **Siremar** (☏092 354 54 55; www.siremar.it) both operate hydrofoils year-round to the Egadi Islands. Ustica Lines also offers summer-only Saturday morning services to Ustica (€28, 2½ hours) and Naples (€94, seven hours), while Siremar and **Traghetti delle Isole** (www. traghettidelleisole.it) offer nightly ferry service to Pantelleria (€34, six hours).

BUS

Intercity buses arrive and depart from the terminal 1km east of the centre (just southeast of the train station).

Segesta (☏ 092 32 84 04; www.segesta.it) runs express buses to Palermo (€9, two hours, hourly). Board at the bus stop across the street from Egatours or at the bus station.

Lumia (☏ 092 32 17 54; www.autolineelumia. it) buses serve Agrigento (€11.80, 2¾ to 3½ hours, one to three daily).

Two free city buses (No 1 and 2) operated by **ATM** (☏ 092 355 95 75; www.atmtrapani.it) do circular trips through Trapani, connecting the bus station, the train station and the port.

CAR & MOTORCYCLE

To bypass Trapani's vast suburbs and avoid the narrow streets of the city centre, follow signs from the A29 autostrada directly to the port, where you'll find abundant paid parking along the broad waterside avenue Via Ammiraglio Staiti, within walking distance of most attractions.

TRAIN

From Trapani's station on Piazza Umberto I, there are rail links to Palermo (€8, 2¼ to 3½ hours, three to four direct trains daily) and Marsala (€3.45, 30 minutes, 10 Monday to Saturday, four on Sunday).

Erice

POP 28,800 / ELEV 751M

One of Italy's most spectacular hill towns, Erice combines medieval charm with astounding 360-degree views. Erice sits on the legendary Mt Eryx (750m); on a clear day, you can see Cape Bon in Tunisia. Wander the medieval tangle of streets interspersed by churches, forts and tiny cobbled piazzas. The town has a seductive history as a centre for the cult of Venus. Settled by the mysterious Elymians, Erice was an obvious abode for the goddess of love, and the town followed its peculiar ritual of sacred prostitution, with the prostitutes themselves accommodated in the Temple of Venus. Despite countless invasions, the temple remained intact – no guesses why.

Erice's tourist infrastructure is excellent. Posted throughout town, you'll find bilingual (Italian–English) informational displays along with town maps displaying suggested walking routes.

⊙ Sights

The best views can be had from Giardino del Balio, which overlooks the turrets and wooded hillsides south to Trapani's salt-pans, the Egadi Islands and the sea. Looking north, there are equally staggering views of San Vito Lo Capo's rugged headlands.

Castello di Venere   CASTLE
(www.comune.erice.tp.it/minisitocastello; Via Castello di Venere; adult €3, 8-14yr or over 65yr €1.50, child under 8yr free; ⊙10am-6pm daily Apr-Oct, 10am-4pm Sat & holidays Nov-Mar) Erice's Norman castle was built in the 12th and 13th centuries over the Temple of Venus, which had long been a site of worship for the ancient Elymians. The views from up top, extending to San Vito Lo Capo on one side and the Saline di Trapani on the other, are spectacular.

SICILY ERICE

WORTH A TRIP

SICILY'S OLDEST NATURE RESERVE

Saved from development and road projects by local protests, the tranquil Riserva Naturale dello Zingaro (☑092 43 51 08; www.riservazingaro.it; adult €3, child 8-14yr €2, under 8yr or over 65yr free; ⊙7am-7.30pm Apr-Sep, 8am-4pm Oct-Mar) is the star attraction on the Golfo di Castellammare, halfway between Palermo and Trapani. Founded in 1981, this was Sicily's first nature reserve. Zingaro's wild coastline is a haven for the rare Bonelli's eagle along with 40 other species of bird. Mediterranean flora dusts the hillsides with wild carob and bright yellow euphorbia, and hidden coves, such as Capreria and Marinella Bays, provide tranquil swimming spots. The main entrance to the park is 2km north of the village of Scopello. Several walking trails are detailed on maps available free at the entrance or downloadable from the park website. The main 7km trail along the coast passes by the visitor centre and five museums documenting everything from local flora and fauna to traditional fishing methods.

Once home to tuna fishers, Scopello now mainly hosts tourists, although outside of peak summer season it retains some of its sleepy village atmosphere. Its port, 1km below town, has a picturesque beach backed by a rust-red *tonnara* (tuna-processing plant) and dramatic *faraglioni* (rock towers) rising from the water.

★Pensione Tranchina (☑092 454 10 99; www.pensionetranchina.com; Via Diaz 7; B&B per person €36-46, half-board per person €55-72; ❋⊛) is the nicest of several places to stay and eat clustered around the cobblestoned courtyard at Scopello's village centre. Friendly hosts Marisin and Salvatore offer comfortable rooms, a roaring fire on chilly evenings and delicious home-cooked meals featuring local fish and home-grown fruit and olive oil.

Erice Monuments Circuit CHURCH

(admission €5; ⊙ 10am-6pm Apr-Jun & Oct, 10am-8pm Jul & Aug, 10am-7pm Sep, 10am-12.30pm Nov-Feb, 10am-4pm Mar) A single ticket grants admission to Erice's five major ecclesiastical attractions: the 14th-century cathedral's treasury and 28m-high campanile (climb to the top for great views), San Martino's wood sculptures, San Giuliano's Gruppa Misteri (Good Friday group sculptures) and San Giovanni's marble sculptures. Buy your ticket at any of the churches.

🛏 Sleeping & Eating

Hotels, many with their own restaurants, are scattered along Via Vittorio Emanuele, Erice's main street. After the tourists have left, the town assumes a beguiling medieval air.

Erice has a tradition of *dolci ericini* (Erice sweets) made by the local nuns. There are numerous pastry shops in town, the most famous being Maria Grammatico (☑ 092 386 93 90; www.mariagrammatico.it; Via Vittorio Emanuele 14; ⊙ 9am-10pm May, Jun & Sep, to 1am Jul & Aug, to 7pm Oct-Apr), revered for its *frutta martorana* (marzipan fruit) and almond pastries.

Hotel Elimo HOTEL €€

(☑ 092 386 93 77; www.hotelelimo.it; Via Vittorio Emanuele 23; s €80-110, d €90-130, ste €150-170; 🅿@🛜) Communal spaces at this atmospheric historic house are filled with tiled beams, marble fireplaces, intriguing art, knick-knacks and antiques. The bedrooms are more mainstream, although many (along with the hotel terrace and restaurant) have breathtaking vistas south and west towards the Saline di Trapani, the Egadi Islands, and the shimmering sea.

ℹ Information

The main **tourist office** (☑ 092 350 23 22; strerice@regione.sicilia.it; Porta Trapani; ⊙ 10.30am-1.30pm & 3.30-5.30pm Tue-Sat, 10.30am-1.30pm Sun, 2.30-5.30pm Mon) is adjacent to Porta Trapani (Erice's Old Town gate); there's a subsidiary branch in the **town centre** (☑ 092 386 93 88; strerice@regione.

sicilia.it; Via Tommaso Guarrasi 1; ⊙ 10.30am-1.30pm Tue-Sun).

ℹ Getting There & Away

Regular AST buses run to and from Trapani (€2.80, 45 minutes). Connecting Erice and Trapani there is a **funicular** (Funivia; ☑ 092 356 93 06; www.funiviaerice.it; one way/return €5.50/9; ⊙ 1-8pm Mon, 8.10am-8pm Tue-Fri, 10am-10pm Sat, 10am-8pm Sun) situated opposite the car park at the foot of Erice's Via Vittorio Emanuele. This drops you in Trapani near the corner of Via Manzoni and Via Capua and you'll need to catch AST bus 21 or 23 (€1) westbound to get to the centre of Trapani.

Segesta

ELEV 304M

Set on the edge of a deep canyon in the midst of wild, desolate mountains, the 5th-century BC ruins of Segesta (☑ 092 495 23 56; adult €6, EU citizen 18-25yr €3, EU citizen under 18yr or over 65yr free; ⊙ 9am-4pm Oct-Mar, 9am-6pm Apr-Sep) are a magical site. On windy days the 36 giant columns of its magnificent temple are said to act like an organ, producing mysterious notes.

The city, founded by the ancient Elymians, was in constant conflict with Selinunte in the south, whose destruction it sought with dogged determination and singular success. Time, however, has done to Segesta what violence inflicted on Selinunte; little remains now, save the theatre and the never-completed Doric temple, the latter dating from around 430 BC and remarkably well preserved. A shuttle bus (€1.50) runs every 30 minutes from the temple entrance 1.5km uphill to the theatre.

Tarantola (☑ 092 43 10 20; www.tarantola-bus.com) runs three buses daily from Trapani (one way/return €3.80/6.20, 35 to 50 minutes), plus two daily buses from Via Balsamo near Palermo's train station (one way/return €6.70/10.70, 1¼ hours). Alternatively, catch a train from Trapani (€3.45, 30 minutes, one or two daily) to Segesta Tempio station, turn left under the double underpass, then climb 1.5km (20 minutes) to the site.

Understand Southern Italy

Southern Italy Today

Singing about his native city in his song 'Napule è', musician Pino Daniele muses: *'Napule è nu sole amaro'* (Naples is a bitter sun). This irony could easily encompass the whole of Italy's Mezzogiorno (land of the midday sun). A region justifiably famous for its cultural cachet, celebrity-graced coastlines and gregarious locals, southern Italy is also one of the European Union's 'problem children'. In the face of soaring unemployment and suffocating corruption, a growing number of *meridionali* (southern Italians) are questioning their region's future.

Best on Film

Il Postino (*The Postman;* Michael Radford; 1994) Exiled poet Pablo Neruda brings poetry and passion to a drowsy southern Italian isle and a misfit postman.

Matrimonio all'italiana (*Marriage, Italian-Style;* Vittorio De Sica; 1964) Sophia Loren and Marcello Mastroianni join forces in this comedy about a cynical businessman and his shrewd Neapolitan mistress.

Cinema Paradiso (Giuseppe Tornatore; 1988) A bittersweet tale about a director who returns to Sicily and rediscovers his true loves: the girl next door and the movies.

Best in Print

The Italians (Luigi Barzini; 1964) A revealing look at Italian culture beyond the well-worn clichés.

Christ Stopped at Eboli (Carlo Levi; 1945) Bittersweet recollections from a writer exiled by Fascists to a mountain village in Basilicata.

Midnight in Sicily (Peter Robb; 1996) A disturbing yet fascinating portrait of postwar Sicily.

The Silent Duchess (Dacia Maraini; 1992) A feminist-flavoured historical novel set in 18th-century Palermo.

Wanted: Work

While Italy's economic woes continue to fuel anxiety throughout the country, it's a headache that pounds strongest in the south. National unemployment may have reached a record high of 12.2% in mid-2013 but in southern Italy the rate was a significantly higher 20.1%. The number of jobless youth in Italy's south is more than double that of the country's wealthier north. And while the rate of NEET (Not in Education, Employment or Training) youths aged between 15 and 29 currently exceeds 20% nationwide, it peaks at a staggering 45% in the southern regions.

For a growing number of locals, the toxic cocktail of high unemployment and taxes, red tape and rampant cronyism is proving too much to take. Between 2011 and 2012 alone, the number of Italians emigrating to greener economic pastures rose 30%, from 60,000 to 79,000. The increase has been especially sharp for those aged between 20 and 40, desperate to forge careers in the more robust economies of northern Europe, Britain and beyond. Dubbed the 'lost generation', they are part of the so-called 'brain drain' – an exodus of highly qualified Italian graduates and professionals bidding the *bel paese* (beautiful country) a bitter-sweet *arrivederci*.

Migrant Challenges

While Italy's unemployment crisis may be weighing heavily on the Italians, it's an even greater burden for the country's immigrants. Figures released by the Consiglio Nazionale dell'Economia e del Lavoro (CNEL; National Council of Economy and Labour) showed the number of unemployed foreigners in Italy increased from 220,000 in 2008 to 385,000 in 2013. By mid-2013, the overall jobless rate for immigrants had reached 14.1%. According to the CNEL, it's a situation expected only to worsen as the number of job seekers grows.

Immigrants who do have jobs often have their own obstacles to tackle. Wage disparity between Italians and non-Italians is widening. While the average Italian takes home €1,304 a month, their immigrant counterparts take home an average of €968. The common practice of finding employment through personal contacts and acquaintances often works against migrant workers. Many end up on the black market, leaving them vulnerable to exploitation from unscrupulous employees.

Italy is becoming increasingly multicultural. Migrants made up 7.9% of Italy's population in 2012 – a three-fold increase from 2002. According to the CNEL, the country would face zero demographic growth and accelerated ageing without migrants. Despite this, not all Italians are putting out their welcome mats. In 2010, the shooting of an immigrant worker in the town of Rosarno, Calabria, sparked Italy's worst race riots in years. And in 2013, Senate vice-president and Lega Nord politician Roberto Calderoli compared Integration Minister Cecile Kyenge, Italy's first black minister, to an orang-utan, sparking international condemnation.

Fighting the 'ndrangheta

It may still be kicking, but Calabria's the 'ndrangheta (an organised crime syndicate) has been suffering its own series of headaches. The July 2013 arrest of drug-dealing heavyweight Roberto Pannunzi in Bogotá, Colombia, delivered a severe blow to the organisation. It was the Rome-born fugitive who had reputedly forged the ties between the 'ndrangheta and Colombia's Medellín cartels, which transformed the former into Italy's richest crime organisation. Weeks after Pannunzi's arrest, a major crackdown on mafia-linked contract-rigging led to the further arrest of 38 people. Among them was the mayor of the Calabrian town of Scalea, Pasquale Basile, who was accused of mediating between rival mafia clans and awarding municipal contracts to 'ndrangheta-run firms. The operation also seized a bountiful booty of mafia assets, including bank accounts, luxury cars and yachts. Three years earlier, an even larger crackdown led to the arrest of 300 alleged 'ndrangheta members across the country on charges ranging from extortion and drugs trafficking to murder.

Despite the lengthening string of arrests, tackling the country's most ruthless mafia body remains a long, arduous war. In a confidential cable dated from 2008 and released by Wikileaks in 2013, a US diplomat claimed that if it weren't a part of Italy, Calabria would be considered a 'failed state', due to the 'ndrangheta's stranglehold on the economy and all aspects of life.

POPULATION: **17.4 MILLION**

AREA: **83,733 SQ KM**

HIGHEST POINT: **MT ETNA**

NUMBER OF UNESCO WORLD HERITAGE SITES: **14**

AVERAGE CUPS OF COFFEE PER PERSON PER YEAR: **600**

. . . .

if Italy were 100 people

92 would be Italian
4 would be Albanian or Eastern European
1 would be North African
3 would be from elsewhere

. . . .

belief systems
(% of population)

87 — Roman Catholic
4 — Other Christians
1.5 — Mulism
3.5 — Other religions

. . . .

population per sq km

NAPLES   LOS ANGELES   ITALY

♦ ≈ 201 people

History

Italy's south is frequently dismissed by northerners as the land of *terroni* (peasants) – the backward sibling to Italy's savvy north. Yet the south is terribly ancient, its history tracing back some 8000 years; writer Carlo Levi, exiled here, called it 'that other world... which no-one may enter without a magic key'. Magical it may be, but there has been plenty to regret during its long history – including invasions, feudalism, and a centuries-long scourge of malaria that stunted the south's development. Venture into these parts and expect to have your preconceptions of modern Italy challenged.

The Early Years

Italy's south has been busy for a very long time. The first inhabitant we know of is the 'Altamura Man' who is currently wedged in the karst cave of Lamalunga, Puglia, slowly becoming part of the crystal concretions that surround him. He's about 130,000 years old.

Fast forward to around 7000 BC, when the Messapians, an Illyrian-speaking people from the Balkans, were settling down in the Salento and around Foggia. Alongside them were other long-gone tribes such as the Daunii in the Gargano, the Peucetians around Taranto and the Lucanians in Basilicata, who were starting to develop the first settled towns in the region – by 1700 BC there is evidence that they were beginning to trade with the Mycenaeans from mainland Greece and the Minoans in Crete.

The first evidence of an organised settlement on Sicily belongs to the Stentillenians, who came from the Middle East and settled on the island's eastern shores sometime between 4000 and 3000 BC. But it was the settlers from the middle of the second millennium BC who radically defined the island's character and whose early presence helps us understand Sicily's complexities. Thucydides (c 460–404 BC) records three major tribes: the Sicanians, who originated either in Spain or North Africa and settled in the north and west (giving these areas their Eastern flavour); the Elymians from Greece, who settled in the south; and the Siculians (or Sikels), who came from the Calabrian peninsula and spread out along the Ionian Coast.

Graeco-Roman Greats

Pompeii & Herculaneum, Campania (p74)

Paestum, Campania (p98)

Selinunte, Sicily (p217)

Segesta, Sicily (p222)

Valley of the Temples, Agrigento, Sicily (p211)

TIMELINE	c 200,000– 9000 BC	3000– 1000 BC	750–600 BC
	As long ago as 700,000 BC, Palaeolithic humans like the 'Altamura Man' lived precarious lives in caves. Painted caves like the Grotta dei Cervi bear testimony to this period.	The Bronze Age reaches Italy courtesy of the Mycenaeans of Eastern Europe. The use of copper and bronze marks a leap in sophistication, and is accompanied by a more complex social organisation.	The Greeks begin establishing cities all over southern Italy and Sicily, including Naxos and Syracuse in Sicily, and Cumae, Sybaris, Croton, Metaponto, Eraklea and Taras in southern Italy.

Magna Graecia

Following the earlier lead of the Elymians, the Chalcidians landed on Sicily's Ionian Coast in 735 BC and founded a small settlement at Naxos. They were followed a year later by the Corinthians, who built their colony on the southeastern island of Ortygia, calling it Syracoussai (Syracuse). The Chalcidians went further south from their own fort and founded a second town called Katane (Catania) in 729 BC, and the two carried on stitching towns and settlements together until three-quarters of the island was in Hellenic hands.

On the mainland, the Greeks' major city was Taras, which dominated the growing region now known as Magna Graecia (Greater Greece). They exploited the opportunities offered by its harbour, trading with Greece, the Near East and the rich colonies in Sicily to build up a substantial network of commerce. Their lucrative business in luxury goods soon made them rich and powerful and by the 4th century BC, the population had swelled to 300,000 and city life was cultured and civilised.

Although only a few monuments survive, among them the ambitious temples of Paestum in Campania and Selinunte in Sicily, the Greek era was a true golden age for the south. Art, sculpture, poetry, drama, philosophy, mathematics and science were all part of the cultural life of Magna Graecia's cities. Exiled from Crotone (Calabria), Pythagoras spent years in Metapontum and Taras; Empedocles, Zeno and Stesichorus were all home-grown talents.

But despite their shared Greekness, these city-states' deeply ingrained rivalries and parochial politics undermined their civic achievements, ultimately leading to damaging conflicts like the Peloponnesian War (431–399 BC), fought by the Athenians against the Peloponnesian League (led by Sparta). Although Syracuse fought successfully against the attacking Athenian forces, the rest of Sicily was in a constant state of civil war. In 409 BC this provided the perfect opportunity for the powerful city-state of Carthage (in modern-day Tunisia) to seek revenge for its humiliation in 480 BC, when Carthaginian mercenaries, commanded by Hamilcar, were defeated by the crafty Greek tyrant Gelon. Led by Hamilcar's bitter but brilliant nephew Hannibal, the Carthaginians wreaked havoc in the Sicilian countryside, completely destroying Selinunte, Himera, Agrigento and Gela. The Syracusans were eventually forced to surrender everything except the city of Syracuse itself to Carthage.

During the 4th century, the mainland Greek colonies came under increasing pressure from other powers with expansionist ambitions. The Etruscans began to move south towards the major port of Cumae

Get to grips with the history, peoples and wars of Ancient Greece by logging on to www.ancient greece.com, which gives easy, potted histories of all the key characters and places.

264–146 BC	280 BC–AD 109	AD 79
The Punic Wars rage between the Romans and the Carthaginians. In 216 BC Hannibal inflicts defeat on the Romans at Cannae, but the Romans go on to ultimately defeat the Carthaginians in 146 BC.	The Romans built the Via Appia and then the Via Appia Traiana, which covered 540km and enabled travellers to make the journey from Rome to Brindisi in just 14 days.	Mt Vesuvius showers molten rock and ash upon Pompeii and Herculaneum. Pliny the Younger later describes the eruption in letters; the towns are only rediscovered in the 18th century.

➡ Cast of Pompeii victim

in Campania and then the Samnites and Sabines started to capture the highlands of the Appenines in Basilicata. Unable to unite and beat off the growing threat, the Greeks had little choice but to make a Faustian pact with the Romans, long-standing admirers of the Greeks and seemingly the perfect allies. It was a partnership that was to cost them dearly; by 270 BC the whole of southern Italy was under Roman control.

Eastern Influences

Roman control of southern Italy was to set the tone for centuries to come. While they turned the Bay of Naples into a holiday hot spot for emperors and built the Via Appia (280–264 BC) and later the Via Appia Traiana (AD 109) – the first superhighway to the south from Rome – the Romans also stripped the southern landscape of its trees, creating just the right conditions for the malarial scourge that the region would face centuries later. They parcelled up the land into huge *latifondi* (estates) that they distributed among a handful of wealthy Romans, who established a damaging agricultural monoculture of wheat to feed the Roman army. Local peasants, meanwhile, were denied even the most basic rights of citizenship.

Despite the Romans' attempts at Latinising the region, this period actually had the effect of reinforcing Eastern influences on the south. As it was, the Romans admired and emulated Greek culture, the locals in cities like Neapolis (modern-day Naples) continued to speak Greek, and the Via Appia made Puglia the gateway to the East. In AD 245 when Diocletian came to power, he decided that the empire was simply too vast for good governance and split it in two. When Constantine came to power in AD 306, the groundwork was already established for an Eastern (Byzantine) Empire and a Western Empire – in AD 324 he officially declared Constantinople the capital of Nova Roma.

With southern Italy's proximity to the Balkans and the Near East, Puglia and Basilicata were exposed to a new wave of Eastern influence, bringing with it a brand-new set of Christian beliefs. These new ideas reached Sicily in AD 535, when the Byzantine general Belisarius landed an army on the island's shores. Despite falling to the Visigoths in AD 470 after more than 700 years of Roman occupation, the island's population was still largely Greek, both in language and custom. The Byzantines were eager to use Sicily as a launching pad for the retaking of the lands owned by the combined forces of Arabs, Berbers and Spanish Muslims, collectively known as the Saracens, but their dreams were not to be realised.

In AD 827 the Saracen army landed at Mazara del Vallo, in Sicily. Palermo fell in AD 831, followed by Syracuse in AD 878. Under them,

---

It is commonly said that there is less Italian blood running through modern Sicilian veins than there is Phoenician, Greek, Arabic, Norman, Spanish or French.

Messages could be shot around the Roman Empire in days or weeks. At wayside inns, despatch riders would have a meal and change mounts. The Romans even devised a type of odometer, a cogwheel that engaged with the wheel of a chariot or other vehicle.

300–337 ⟩	476 ⟩	827–965 ⟩	1059 ⟩
After a series of false starts, the Roman Empire is divided into an Eastern and Western half just east of Rome. In 330 Constantine moves the imperial capital to Byzantium and refounds it as Constantinople.	The last western Emperor, Romulus Augustulus, is deposed. Goths, Ostrogoths and Byzantines tussle over the spoils of the empire.	A Saracen army lands at Mazaradel Vallo in Sicily in 827. The island is united under Arab rule and Palermo becomes the second-largest city in the world after Constantinople.	Pope Nicholas II and Norman mercenary Robert Guiscard sign a concordat at Melfi, making Robert the duke of Apulia and Calabria. Robert agrees to rid southern Italy of Saracens and Byzantines.

IMPERIAL INSANITY

Bribes? *Bunga bunga* parties? Spare a thought for the ancient Romans, who suffered their fair share of eccentric leaders. We salute some of the empire's wackiest, most ruthless and downright kinkiest rulers.

Tiberius (ruled AD 14–37) With a steady governing hand but prone to depression, Tiberius had a difficult relationship with the Senate and withdrew in his later years to Capri, where, they say, he devoted himself to drinking, orgies and fits of paranoia.

Gaius (Caligula; ruled AD 37–41) 'Little Shoes' made grand-uncle Tiberius look tame. Sex – including with his sisters – and gratuitous, cruel violence were high on his agenda. He emptied the state's coffers and suggested making a horse consul before being assassinated.

Nero (ruled AD 54–68) Augustus' last descendant, Nero had his pushy stage mother murdered, his first wife's veins slashed, his second wife kicked to death, and his third wife's ex-husband killed. The people accused him of playing the fiddle while Rome burned to the ground in AD 64.

Diocletian (ruled AD 284–305) Dalmatian-born Diocletian had little time for the growing cult of Christianity. He ordered the burning of churches and sacred scriptures, and had Christians thrown to wild beasts in a grisly public spectacle. One of them was Naples' patron saint, San Gennaro, slaughtered in Pozzuoli's Anfiteatro Flavio.

churches were converted to mosques and Arabic was implemented as the common language. At the same time, much-needed land reforms were introduced and trade, agriculture and mining were fostered. New crops were introduced, including citrus trees, date palms and sugar cane, and a system of water supply and irrigation was developed. Palermo was chosen as the capital of the new emirate and, over the next 200 years, it became one of the most splendid cities in the Arab world.

The Arabs introduced spaghetti to Sicily; 'strings of pasta' were documented by the Arab geographer Al-Idrissi in Palermo in 1150.

Pilgrims & Crusaders

Ever since Puglia and Basilicata's colonisation by the Greeks, multifarious myths had established themselves in the region – many were related to the presence of therapeutic waters and the practice called *incubatio,* a rite whereby one had to sleep close to a holy place to receive revelations from a deity. In its early days, the cult of the Archangel Michael was mainly a cult of healing forces based on the saint's revelations. It started to gain currency in the early 5th century but it wasn't until the arrival of the Lombards in the 7th century that it really began to take off.

1130	1215	1224	1270–1500
Norman invader Roger II is crowned king of Sicily, a century after the Normans landed in southern Italy; a united southern Italian kingdom is created.	Frederick II is crowned Holy Roman Emperor in Aachen where he symbolically re-inters Charlemagne's body in a silver and gold reliquary. He takes the cross and vows of a crusader.	The Università degli Studi di Napoli Federico II is founded in Naples. The oldest state university in the world, its alumni include Catholic theologian and philosopher Thomas Aquinas.	The French Angevins and Spanish Aragonese spend the best part of two centuries fighting over southern Italy. Instability, warfare, the Black Death and overtaxation strangle the region's economic development.

Sweeping down from the north, the Lombards found in St Michael a mirror image of their own pagan deity, Wodan. In Michael, they saw similar characteristics: the image of a medieval warrior, a leader of celestial armies. There is little doubt that their devotion to the saint was instrumental in their easy conversion to Catholicism, as they repeatedly restored and enlarged the Monte Sant'Angelo shrine, making it the most important centre of the cult in the western world. Soon the trail of pilgrims along the Via Traiana became so great that the road was nicknamed the Via Sacra Langobardorum (Holy Road of the Lombards), and dozens of churches, hostels and monasteries were built to accommodate the pilgrims along the way.

Another group of pilgrims in this region were the Normans. A French tribe, they arrived in southern Italy in the 10th century, initially en route from Jerusalem, and later as mercenaries attracted by the money to be made fighting for the rival principalities and against the Saracens in Sicily. By 1053, after six years of mercenary activity, Robert Guiscard (c 1015–85), the Norman conquistador, had comprehensively defeated the combined forces of the Calabrian Byzantines, the Lombards and the papal forces at the Battle of Civitate. Having established his supremacy, Robert turned his attentions to expanding the territories under his control. To achieve this, he had to negotiate with the Vatican. In return for being invested with the titles of Duke of Apulia and Calabria in 1059, Robert agreed to chase the Saracens out of Sicily and restore Christianity to the island. He delegated this task – and promised the island – to his younger brother Roger I (1031–1101), who landed his troops at Messina in 1061, capturing the port by surprise. In 1064, Roger tried to make good on his promise and take Palermo but was repulsed by a well-organised Saracen army; it wasn't until Robert arrived in 1072 with substantial reinforcements that the city fell into Norman hands. Impressed by the island's cultured Arab lifestyle, Roger shamelessly borrowed and improved on it, spending vast amounts of money on palaces and churches and encouraging a cosmopolitan atmosphere in his court.

By 1130 most of southern Italy, including Sicily, was in Norman hands and it was only a question of time before the prosperous duchy of Naples gave in to the inevitable. It did so in 1139 – the Kingdom of the Two Sicilies was thus complete.

The Wonder of the World

Frederick II, king of Sicily and Holy Roman Emperor, presided over one of the most glamorous periods of southern history. The fact that

---

Best Places for Arab-Norman Flavour

Cappella Palatina, Palazzo dei Normanni, Palermo (p169)

Chiesa Capitolare di San Cataldo, Palermo (p168)

Cattedrale di Palermo, Palermo (p169)

Duomo, Cefalù (p177)

Kingdom in the Sun is John Julius Norwich's wonderful romp through the Norman invasions of the south, leading to their spectacular takeover of Sicily.

1516	1600	1647	1714
Holy Roman Emperor Charles V of Spain inherits southern Italy. The region is strategically important to Spain in its battle with France. Charles invests in defences in cities like Lecce.	Naples is Europe's biggest city, boasting a population of over 300,000. Among its growing number of residents is renegade artist Caravaggio, who arrives in 1606.	Gross mismanagement causes the southern Italian economy to collapse. In Naples, the Masaniello Revolt breaks out over heavy taxes. Revolt spreads to the provinces and peasant militias rule the countryside.	The end of the War of the Spanish Succession forces the withdrawal of Spanish forces from Lombardy. The Spanish Bourbon family establishes an independent Kingdom of the Two Sicilies.

he came to wield such power and wear Charlemagne's crown at all is one of those unexpected quirks of history.

He inadvertently inherited the crown of Sicily and the south from his mother Constance (the posthumous daughter of Roger I) in 1208 after William II died childless; the crown to the Holy Roman Empire came to him through his father, Henry VI, the son of Frederick Barbarossa. The union of the two crowns in 1220 meant that Frederick II would rule over lands covering Germany, Austria, the Netherlands, Poland, the Czech Republic, Slovakia, southern France, southern Italy, the Kingdom of Sicily and the remnants of the Byzantine world.

It was a union that caused the popes much discomfort. While they wanted and needed an emperor who would play the role of temporal sword, Frederick's wide-reaching kingdom all but encircled the Papal

BORN TO FIGHT

In the late 10th century, Norman fighters began to earn a reputation across Europe as fierce and tough mercenaries. As inheritance customs left younger sons disadvantaged, younger brothers were expected to seek their fortunes elsewhere which they did with remarkable success.

According to one legend, Norman involvement in southern Italy began in 1013 at the shrine of St Michael at Monte Sant'Angelo, when Latin rebel Meles, chaffing under Byzantine authority, invited the Normans to serve him as mercenaries. By 1030 what had begun as an offer of service in return for booty became a series of unusually successful attempts at wresting control from local warlords.

In the forefront of the Italian conquests were the brothers Hauteville: the eldest William 'Bras de Fer' (Iron Arm; c 1009–46), who controlled Puglia, and Robert Guiscard (the Cunning; c 1015–85), who rampaged over Calabria and southern Campania. By 1053, after six years of incessant fighting, Robert had defeated the combined forces of the Calabrian Byzantines, the Lombards and the papal forces at Civitate.

Up to this point the Normans (as mercenaries) had fought both for and against the papacy as their needs had required. But Robert's relationship with the Vatican underwent a radical transformation following the Great Schism of 1054, which resulted in a complete break between the Byzantine and Latin churches. In their turn, the popes saw in the Normans a powerful potential ally, and so in 1059 Pope Nicholas II and Robert signed a concordat at Melfi, which invested Robert with the titles of Duke of Apulia (including Basilicata) and Calabria. In return Robert agreed to chase the Byzantines and Saracens out of southern Italy and Sicily and restore the southern kingdom to papal rule.

Little would the pope suspect that Roger would go on to develop a territorial monarchy and become a ruler who saw himself as detached from the higher jurisdiction of both Western and Eastern Emperor – or even the pope himself.

1737

Naples' original Teatro San Carlo is built in a swift eight months. Designed by Giovanni Antonio Medrano, it was rebuilt in 1816 after a devastating fire.

1752

Work commences on the Palazzo Reale in Caserta, north of Naples. Commissioned by Charles VII of Bourbon and designed by Luigi Vanvitelli, the palace would outsize Versailles.

RICHARD I'ANSON/GETTY IMAGES ©

➡ Teatro San Carlo (p56)

States, and his belief in the absolute power of monarchy gave them grave cause for concern.

Like Charlemagne before him, Frederick controlled a kingdom so vast that he could realistically dream of reviving the fallen Roman Empire, and dream he did. Under his rule, Sicily was transformed into a centralised state playing a key commercial and cultural role in European affairs, and Palermo gained a reputation as the continent's most important city; most of the northern Italian city-states were brought to heel. In 1225 Frederick married Jolanda of Brienne and gained the title of king of Jerusalem, making him the first Roman emperor to bear that title. In 1228 the Crusade he launched was not only nearly bloodless but it saw the return of the shrines of Jerusalem, Nazareth and Bethlehem to the Christian fold.

As well as being a talented statesman, Frederick was also a cultured man, and many of his biographers see him as the precursor to the Renaissance prince. Few other medieval monarchs corresponded with the sages of Judaism and Islam; he also spoke six languages and was fascinated by science, nature and architecture. He even wrote a scholarly treatise on falconry during one of the long, boring sieges of Faenza, and Dante once called him the father of Italian poetry.

Steven Runciman's *Fall of Constantinople 1453* provides a classic account of this bloody episode in Crusading history. It manages to be academically sound and highly entertaining at the same time.

Yet despite his brilliance, Frederick's vision for an international empire was incompatible with the ambitions of the papacy and he struggled throughout his reign to remain on good terms with increasingly aggressive popes. Finally, in 1243, Pope Innocent IV proclaimed him deposed, characterising him as a 'friend of Babylon's sultan' and a heretic. At the same time, the northern Italian provinces were straining against his centralised control and years of war and strategising were finally taking their toll. Only in Puglia, his favourite province throughout his reign, did Frederick remain undisputed master.

In December 1250, after suffering a bout of dysentery, he died suddenly in Castel Fiorentino near Lucera. His heirs, Conrad and Manfred, did not long survive him; Conrad died of malaria four years later in Lavello in Basilicata, and Manfred was defeated at the Battle of Benevento in 1266 by Charles of Anjou, the pope's pretender to the throne. Two years later another battle took the life of Manfred's 15-year-old nephew and heir, Conradin, who was publicly beheaded in Naples.

By 1270 the brilliant Hohenstaufen period was officially over. And while Frederick's reign marked a major stage in the transformation of Europe from a community of Latin Christians under the rule of two competing powers (pope and emperor) to a Europe of nation states, he had failed to leave any physical legacies. The following ruling family, the Angevins, did not make the same mistake: Naples' Castel Nuovo

1798–99	1805	1814–15	1848
Napoleon invades Italy and occupies Rome. Ferdinand I sends an army to evict him, but his troops flee. The French counter-attack and take Naples, establishing the Parthenopean Republic.	Napoleon is proclaimed king of the newly constituted Kingdom of Italy, comprising most of the northern half of the country. A year later, he also retakes the Kingdom of Naples.	After Napoleon's fall, the Congress of Vienna is held to re-establish the balance of power in Europe. The result for Italy is largely a return of the old occupying powers.	European revolts spark rebellion in Italy. The Bourbons are expelled from Sicily but retake it in a rain of fire that earns Ferdinand II the epithet 'Re Bomba' (King Bomb).

(built by Charles of Anjou in 1279) and Castel Sant'Elmo (constructed by Robert of Anjou in the early 14th century) remain two of the city's iconic landmarks.

Sicily's Slide from Glory

Under the Angevins, who succeeded the German Hohenstaufens, Sicily was weighed down by onerous taxes, religious persecution was the order of the day and Norman fiefdoms were removed and given to French aristocrats. On Easter Monday 1282, the city of Palermo exploded in rebellion. Incited by the alleged rape of a local girl by a gang of French troops, peasants lynched every French soldier they could get their hands on. The revolt spread to the countryside and was supported by the Sicilian nobility, who had formed an alliance with Peter of Aragon. Peter landed at Trapani with a large army and was proclaimed king. For the next 20 years, the Aragonese and the Angevins were engaged in the War of the Sicilian Vespers – a war that was eventually won by the Spanish.

By the end of the 14th century, Sicily had been thoroughly marginalised. The eastern Mediterranean was sealed off by the Ottoman Turks, while the Italian mainland was off limits on account of Sicily's political ties with Spain. As a result, the Renaissance passed the island by, reinforcing the oppressive effects of poverty and ignorance. Even Spain lost interest in its colony, choosing to rule through viceroys. By the end of the 15th century, the viceroy's court was a den of corruption, and the most influential body on the island became the Catholic Church (whose archbishops and bishops were mostly Spanish). The church exercised draconian powers through a network of Holy Office tribunals, otherwise known as the Inquisition.

Reeling under the weight of state oppression, ordinary Sicilians demanded reform. Unfortunately, their Spanish monarchs were preoccupied by the wars of the Spanish succession and Sicily was subsequently passed around for decades from European power to European power like an unwanted Christmas present. Eventually the Spanish reclaimed the island in 1734, this time under the Bourbon king Charles III of Sicily (r 1734–59).

The Bourbon Paradox

Assessment of Bourbon rule in southern Italy is a controversial topic. Many historians consider it a period of exploitation and stagnation. Others, more recently, have started to re-evaluate the Kingdom of the Two Sicilies, pointing out the raft of positive reforms Charles III implemented. These included abolishing many noble and clerical privileges, curtailing the legal rights of landowners within their fiefs and restrict-

Edward Gibbon's *History of the Decline and Fall of the Roman Empire* is the acknowledged classic work on the subject of the empire's darker days. Try the abridged single-volume version.

Between January and August of 1656, the bubonic plague wiped out about half of Naples' 300,000 inhabitants and much of the economy. The city would take almost two centuries to reach its pre-plague headcount again.

1860	1861	1880–1915	1889
In the name of Italian unity, Giuseppe Garibaldi lands with 1000 men, known as the Red Shirts, in Sicily. He takes the island and moves into southern Italy.	By the end of the 1859–61 Franco-Austrian War, Vittorio Emanuele II controls Lombardy, Sardinia, Sicily, southern Italy and parts of central Italy, and is proclaimed king of a newly united Italy.	People vote with their feet; millions of impoverished southerners embark on ships for the New World, causing a massive haemorrhage of the most able-bodied and hardworking southern male youths.	Raffaele Esposito invents 'pizza margherita' in honour of Queen Margherita, who takes her first bite of the Neapolitan staple on a royal visit to the city.

ing ecclesiastical jurisdiction at a time when the Church was reputed to own almost a third of the land within the kingdom.

Naples had already begun prospering under the rule of Spanish viceroy Don Pedro de Toledo (1532–53), whose building boom attracted some of Italy's greatest artistic talent. Under Charles, the city became one of the great capital cities of Europe, attracting hundreds of aristocratic travellers. On top of this, Charles was a great patron of architecture and the arts. During his reign Pompeii and Herculaneum (both destroyed in the AD 79 eruption of Mt Vesuvius) were discovered and the Archaeological Museum in Naples was founded. He was responsible for the building of the Teatro San Carlo, the largest opera house in Europe, and he also built the huge palaces of Capodimonte and Caserta. Some subsequent Bourbon monarchs also made positive contributions, such as Ferdinand II (1830–59), who laid the foundations for modern industry, developing the southern harbours, creating a merchant fleet, building the first Italian railway line, constructing road systems, including the dramatic Amalfi Coast drive.

But while Charles might rightfully claim a place among southern Italy's outstanding rulers, later Bourbon princes were some of the most eccentric and pleasure-seeking monarchs in Europe. Charles' son, Ferdinand I (1751–1825), was venal and poorly educated. He spent his time hunting and fishing, and he delighted in the company of the *lazzaroni,* the Neapolitan underclass. He much preferred to leave the business of government to his wife, the ambitious and treacherous Archduchess Maria Carolina of Austria, whose main aim was to free southern Italy from Spanish influence and secure a rapprochement with Austria and Great Britain. Her chosen administrator was the English expatriate Sir John Acton, who replaced the long-serving Tanucci, a move that was to mire court politics in damaging corruption and espionage.

When the French Revolution broke out in 1789 Maria Carolina was initially sympathetic to the movement, but after her sister, Marie Antoinette, was beheaded by the revolutionaries she became a fanatic Francophobe. The following French invasion of Italy in 1799, and the crowning of Napoleon as king in 1800, jolted the south out of its Bourbon slumbers. Although Napoleonic rule was to last only 14 years, this brief flirtation with republicanism awakened hopes of an independent Italian nation. Returning to his beloved Naples in 1815, Ferdinand, who was once so at ease with his subjects, was now terrified of popular revolution and became determined to exert his absolute authority. Changes that had been made by the Bonapartist regime were reversed, causing widespread discontent. Revolutionary

For a wide-ranging general site on Italian history, check out www.arcaini.com. It covers, in potted form, everything from prehistory to the postwar period, and includes a brief chronology.

History of the Italian People, by Giuliano Procacci, is one of the best general histories of the country in any language. It covers the period from the early Middle Ages until 1948.

1908

On the morning of 28 December, Messina and Reggio di Calabria are struck by a 7.5-magnitude earthquake and a 13m-high tsunami. More than 80,000 lives are lost.

1915

Italy enters WWI on the side of the Allies to win Italian territories still in Austrian hands after Austria's offer to cede some of the territories is deemed insufficient.

1919

Former socialist journalist Benito Mussolini forms a right-wing militant group, the *Fasci Italiani di Combattimento* (Italian Combat Fasces), precursor to his Fascist Party.

LEEMAGE/GETTY IMAGES ©

➡ Portrait of Benito Mussolini

agitators sprang up everywhere, and the countryside, now full of discharged soldiers, became more lawless than ever.

Yet there was no putting the genie back in the box. The heavy-handed tactics of Ferdinand II only exacerbated the situation, and in 1848 Sicily experienced a violent revolt that saw the expulsion of the Bourbons from the island. Although the revolt was crushed, Ferdinand's response was so heavy-handed that he earned himself the nickname 'Re Bomba' (King Bomb) after his army mercilessly shelled Messina. From such a promising beginning, the last decades of Bourbon rule were so oppressive that they were almost universally hated throughout liberal Europe. The seeds had well and truly been sown for the Risorgimento (Resurgence), which would finally see the whole peninsula united into a modern nation state.

The Kingdom of Death

Although not commonly acknowledged, the widespread presence of malaria in the Italian peninsula during the 19th and 20th centuries is one of the most significant factors in the social and economic development (or lack of it) of the modern nation. An endemic as well as an epidemic disease, malaria was so enmeshed in Italian rural society that it was widely regarded as the Italian national disease. Even the word itself comes from the Italian *mal aria* (bad air), as it was originally thought that the disease was caused by a poisoning of the air as wet earth dried out during the heat of summer.

The scale of the problem came to light in the decades following Italian unification in 1861. Out of 69 provinces only two were found to be free of malaria; and in a population of 25 million people, at least 11 million were permanently at risk of the disease. Most famously, Giuseppe Garibaldi, one of the founding fathers of modern Italy, lost both his wife, Anita, and a large number of his troops to the disease. Thus stricken, Garibaldi urged the newly united nation to place the fight against malaria high on its list of priorities.

In the dawning era of global competition, Italian farming was dangerously backward. As a predominantly grain-producing economy, it was tragically ironic that all of Italy's most fertile land was in precisely the zones – coastal plains and river valleys – where malaria was most intense. To survive, farm workers had no choice but to expose themselves to the disease. Unfortunately, disease in turn entailed suffering, days of absence and low productivity.

More significantly, although malaria ravaged the whole peninsula, it was particularly an affliction of the south, as well as the provinces of Rome and Grosseto in the centre. Of all the provinces, six were especially afflicted – Abruzzi, Basilicata, Calabria, Lazio, Puglia and

The exodus of southern Italians to North and South America between 1880 and WWI is one of the great mass movements of a population in modern times. By 1927, 20% of the Italian population had emigrated.

1922	1927	1934	1940
Mussolini and his Fascists stage a march on Rome in October. Doubting the army's loyalty, a fearful King Vittorio Emanuele III entrusts Mussolini with the formation of a government.	A study released by the Italian government puts the number of Italian citizens living abroad at around 9.2 million. Southern Italians make up over 60% of the Italian diaspora.	Screen siren Sophia Loren is born, and spends her childhood living in Pozzuoli and Naples. Her break would come in 1951, as an extra in Mervyn LeRoy's film *Quo Vadis*.	Italy enters WWII on Nazi Germany's side, invading Greece in October. Greek forces counter-attack and enter southern Albania. Germany saves Italy in April 1941 by over-running Yugoslavia and Greece.

Sardinia – earning the south the lugubrious epithet 'the kingdom of death'. Giovanni Battista Grassi (the man who discovered that mosquitos transmit malaria) estimated that the danger of infection in the south was 10 times greater than in northern Italy.

No issue illustrates the divide between the north and south of the country quite so vividly as the malaria crisis. The World Health Organisation defines malaria in the modern world as a disease of poverty that distorts and 'slows a country's economic growth'. In the case of the Italian south, malaria was a significant factor in the underdevelopment of the region at a critical time in its history. Malarial fever thrives on exploitative working conditions, substandard housing and diet, illiteracy, war and ecological degradation, all of which Italy's south had certainly had its fair share of by the early 20th century. As late as 1918, the Ministry of Agriculture reported that 'malaria is the key to all the economic problems of the South'. Against this background of regional inequality, the fever became an important metaphor deployed by *meridionalisti* (southern spokesmen) such as Giustino Fortunato (1848–1932) and Francesco Nitti (1868–1953) to describe the plight of the south and to demand redress. Nitti attributed the entirety of southern backwardness to this single factor.

Between 1900 and 1907, the Italian parliament passed a series of laws establishing a national campaign – the first of its kind in the world – to eradicate or at least control the disease. But it was to take the best part of half a century to bring malaria under control, as two world wars and the Fascist seizure of power in 1922 were to overwhelm domestic policies, causing the program to stall and then collapse entirely amid military defeat and occupation.

Final victory against the disease was only achieved following the end of WWII, when the government was able to re-establish public-health infrastructures and implement a five-year plan which included the use of a new pesticide, DDT, to eradicate malaria. The designation of 'malarial zone' was only officially lifted from the entire peninsula in 1969.

Between 1944 and 1946 the German Wehrmacht systematically sabotaged the pumping systems that drained Italy's marshes and confiscated quinine from the Department of Health. The ensuing malaria epidemic proved as deadly as any WWI ground offensive.

The Southern Question

The unification of Italy meant sudden and dramatic changes for all the southern provinces. The huge upsurge in *brigantaggio* (banditry) and social unrest throughout the last decades of the 19th century is often attributed to widespread disillusionment about the unification project. Though remembered as a leading figure in the push towards unification, it was never the intention of 19th-century Italian statesman Camillo Benso, Count of Cavour, to unify the whole country. Even

1943	1944	1946	1950
King Vittorio Emanuele III sacks Mussolini. He is replaced by Marshall Badoglio, who surrenders after Allied landings in southern Italy. German forces free Mussolini.	Mt Vesuvius explodes into action on 18 March. The eruption is captured on film by United States Army Air Forces personnel stationed nearby.	Italians vote in a national referendum in June to abolish the monarchy (by about 12.7 million votes to 10.7 million) and create a republic. The south is the only region to vote against the republic.	The *Cassa per il Mezzogiorno* is established to help fund public works and infrastructure in the south. Poor management and corruption sees at least one third of the money squandered.

HISTORY ON SCREEN

Il Gattopardo (The Leopard; Luchino Visconti; 1963) A Sicilian aristocrat grapples with the political and social changes heralded by the 19th century Risorgimento (reunification).

Le quattro giornate di Napoli (The Four Days of Naples; Nanni Loy; 1962) Neapolitan courage shines through in this film about the famous popular uprisings against the Nazis in September 1943.

Il resto di niente (The Remains of Nothing; Antonietta De Lillo; 2003) Eleonora Pimental de Fonesca, heroine of the ill-fated Neapolitan revolution of 1799, is the protagonist in this tale.

Salvatore Giuliano (Francesco Rosi; 1963) A neorealist classic about the murder of Sicily's very own modern Robin Hood.

later during his premiership, Cavour favoured an expanded Piedmont rather than a united Italy.

For southerners, it was difficult to see the benefits of being part of this new nation state. Naples was stripped of its capital-city status; the new government carried away huge cash reserves from the rich southern Italian banks; taxes went up and factories closed as new tariff policies, dictated by northern interests, caused a steep decline in the southern economy. Culturally, southerners were also made to feel inferior; to be southern or 'Bourbon' was to be backward, vulgar and uncivilised.

After WWI the south fared a little better, experiencing some slow progress in infrastructure projects like the construction of the Puglian aqueduct, the extension of the railways and the improvement of civic centres including Bari and Taranto. But Mussolini's 'Battle for Wheat' – the drive to make Italy self-sufficient in food – compounded many of the south's problems. It destroyed even more valuable pastureland by turning it over to the monoculture of wheat, while reinforcing the parlous state of the southern peasantry, who remained uneducated, disenfranchised, landless and at high risk of malaria. To escape such a hopeless future, many of them packed their bags and migrated to North America, northern Europe and Australia, starting a trend that was to become one of the main features of post-WWII Italy.

The south was the only region to vote against the 1946 referendum that established the Italian Republic. In Naples, 80% voted to keep the monarchy. Still, change moved on apace. After the wreckage of

Denis Mack Smith produced one of the most penetrating works on Mussolini in his biography, *Mussolini*. It explores the life and career of the Italian dictator and his influence on Adolf Hitler.

1950s–60s	1980	1999	2003
Soaring unemployment causes another mass migration of about two million people from the south to the factories of northern Italy, Europe and Australia.	At 7.34pm on 25 November, a 6.8 Richter scale earthquake strikes Campania. The quake kills almost 3000 people and causes widespread damage; the city of Naples also suffers damage.	Brindisi becomes a strategic base for the Office of the UN and the World Food Organisation. The disused military airport's hangars are converted into storage space for humanitarian aid.	Sicilian *mafioso* Salvatore 'Totò' Riina is arrested in Palermo. Nicknamed 'The Beast', the 'boss of bosses' had ordered the bombing death of antimafia magistrates Giovanni Falcone and Paolo Borsellino.

WWII was cleared – especially that caused by Allied air raids in Sicily and Naples – the *Cassa per il Mezzogiorno* reconstruction fund was established to bring the south into the 20th century with massive, cheap housing schemes and big industrial projects like the steel plant in Taranto and the Fiat factory in Basilicata. The scheme was eventually scrapped by the central government in 1992 amid allegations of misappropriated funds.

In the same year, the huge *Tangentopoli* (Bribesville) scandal – the institutionalisation of kickbacks and bribes, which had been the country's modus operandi since WWII – made headline news. Although it was largely focused on the industrial north of Italy, the repercussions of the widespread investigation (known as *Mani Pulite,* or Clean Hands) were inevitably felt in southern regions like Sicily and Campania, where politics, business and organised crime had been long-time bedfellows.

Contemporary Tribulations

The 21st century has so far proven tumultuous for southern Italy. The so-called 'Scampia feud' of late 2004 and early 2005 – a deadly turf battle fought out by rival Camorra clans in Naples – saw an estimated 47 people gunned down in four months alone. In 2008 a Camorra death squad shot seven men in Castel Volturno, northwest of Naples. Six of the dead were West African migrants; the incident was seen as a warning to Nigerian criminal clans who were attempting to muscle in on the city's lucrative drugs market.

In 2011, Italy replaced Greece as the main EU entry point for illegal immigrants. According to Frontex, the EU borders agency, 32,906 illegal immigrants reached Italian shores in the first quarter of 2011 alone, mostly Tunisians and Libyans escaping political upheaval. Of these, two-thirds landed on Lampedusa, a tiny island wedged between Sicily and Tunisia. The seemingly endless waves of refugees, both arriving alive and drowned at sea, provoked distress and frustration for residents, many of whom rely on tourism for their livelihood.

Italy's ongoing financial crisis hasn't helped to lift southern morale either. The closure or relocation of factories to wealthier northern regions has merely accelerated the Mezzogiorno's already dire economic reality. Between 2007 and 2012, nearly 150,000 jobs were lost in the south, with more than 1.3 million residents heading north in search of work. In cities like Naples, scenes of shoppers collecting scraps left by market vendors have become increasingly common. In the cultural sector, several high-profile museums have cut staff, building maintenance and access to various galleries.

The Nazis took Naples in 1943, but were quickly forced out during the *quattro giornate di Napoli* (four days of Naples), a series of popular uprisings between 26 and 30 September. This paved the way for the Allies to enter the city on 1 October.

2003	2004–05	2005	2010
The Campania government launches Progetto Vesuvia in an attempt to clear Mt Vesuvius' heavily populated lower slopes. The €30,000 offered to relocate is rejected by most in the danger zone.	Tension between rival Camorra clans explodes on the streets of suburban Naples. In only four months, almost 50 people are gunned down in retribution attacks.	Nichi Vendola, representing the Communist Refoundation Party, is elected president of Puglia. He is the first gay communist to be elected president of a southern Italian region.	Local youths in Rosarno, Calabria, shoot air rifles at African migrants returning from work in January. About 2000 migrants subsequently clash with locals in two days of violent rioting.

Adding further bitterness to the maelstrom of unemployment, high taxes and a seemingly perpetual recession is Italy's ongoing political instability. Inconclusive elections in February 2013 led to lengthy post-electoral negotiations. From these, Enrico Letta, a member of the Partito Democratico (PD), was named prime minister, forming an unlikely (and unwieldy) left-right coalition with Silvio Berlusconi's Freedom Party and centrists led by former prime minister Mario Monti.

The growing disillusionment felt by many Italians led to 25% of the votes going to burgeoining Five Star Movement, a grassroots organisation demanding greater environmentalism, access to water, sustainable transport, Internet connectivity, and development. Despite its initial success, this new kid on the political block would itself become a victim of uncertainty. Local elections in May 2013 revealed a sharp drop in support for the party, a shift many blamed on the Five Star Movement's stubborn refusal to negotiate with the centre-left during the February election crisis.

Although much has happened since it was written, Paul Ginsborg's *A History of Contemporary Italy: Society and Politics 1943-1988* remains one of the single most readable and insightful books on postwar Italy.

2011	2011	2013	2013
Thousands of boat people fleeing the revolutionary chaos in northern Africa land on the island of Lampedusa. Italy grants 30,000 refugees temporary visas, creating tension with France.	Berlusconi is forced to quit as Prime Minister, and economist Mario Monti is put in charge, heading a government of technocrats. Young, antimafia prosecutor Luigi de Magistris becomes mayor of Naples.	On 4 March, Naples' much-loved Città della Scienza museum is destroyed in an arson attack. The crime is widely blamed on the Camorra, with the mayor of Naples' tweeting 'Naples is under attack'.	After an inconclusive election, Enrico Letta is named Prime Minister of a shaky left-right coalition. The Five Star Movement wins 25% of the votes but refuses to enter any pacts with the other parties.

The Southern Way of Life

The Mezzogiorno (land of the midday sun) is more than its haunting ruins, poetic coastlines and peeling *palazzi* (mansions). Its true protagonists are the *meridionali* (southern Italians), whose character and nuances echo a long, nail-biting history of dizzying highs and testing lows. To understand the southern psyche is to understand the complexities and contradictions that have moulded Italy's most misunderstood half.

Through Southern Eyes

A one-man 'Abbott & Costello', Antonio de Curtis (1898–1967), aka Totò, famously depicted the Neapolitan *furbizia* (cunning). Appearing in more than 100 films, including *Miseria e Nobiltà* (Misery & Nobility; 1954), his roles as a hustler living on nothing but his quick wits would guarantee him cult status in Naples.

Alessio is a 30-something Sicilian expat. Born into a close-knit family near Catania, he studied physics in Florence before moving to Bonn to complete a PhD in astrophysics...and to start a career as a culinary consultant. Every Easter and Christmas, he makes the 2276km journey back home to catch up with family and friends, and to sink his teeth into a steaming *arancino* (a deep-fried, stuffed rice ball; his favourite Italian snack). Alessio's story is not unusual in a part of Italy so bittersweetly defined by emigration, nostalgia and tradition. Alessio muses: 'A deep part of my personality and feelings are based in the south. Even though I am happy and grateful for what I have obtained abroad, I often feel homesick. The bucolic life spent enjoying the sun with family and friends, eating, drinking and singing, Sicilian hills in the background, is an image that haunts me. I think this is true for many expats.'

Perhaps even more uniquely southern is the love/hate dynamic underlying this relationship. As Alessio explains: 'In Germany, there's a sense of personal civic responsibility. In southern Italy, suspicion of strangers has stifled this collective feeling from developing. The other obstacle is a stubborn sense of pride. 'Too often in the south, doing something that's civic minded – like picking rubbish off the street or not using your car to help reduce pollution – leaves you open to mockery from others, who see your action as a sign of weakness.' There is regret in Alessio's voice: 'It's frustrating to think that a society so rich in culture and traditions, so warm-hearted, could do much more for itself if it only learned to trust and cooperate.'

Yet, things are changing. Both the internet and travel are helping to shape a generation more aware of, and open to, foreign ideas. Online communities are allowing people once socially or ideologically isolated to connect with others, to share experiences and develop new ways of tackling old problems. Alessio is hopeful: 'Words like "integration" and "openness" are becoming more meaningful in the south. Slowly, people are becoming more aware of the common ground they share. With this awareness, we can hopefully build a brighter, collectively minded future.'

Dreams & Diasporas

Emigration to Immigration

Alessio's move abroad echoes that of millions of *meridionali* (southern Italians). Severe economic problems in the south following Italy's unification and after each of the world wars led to massive emigration as

LIFE IN A SOUTHERN TOWN

It's just 4.30am and the first of the town's bars open for farmers and insomniacs. The barman serves his first *caffè* of the day. He likes his job, but earns a modest €800 per month.

By 8am the barber's bicycle is outside his shop. He'll stay open until 11am – he's past retirement age but keeps the shop going. He'd like to talk but he hasn't got time today; he's going to see his son in the north.

At 9am the main road is blocked with cars. Locals are commuting from one end of the town to the other. Youths with big sunglasses and high-maintenance hair (and that's just the men) pop into the bar for a cappuccino before heading to the beach.

At 9.15am a car drives slowly around the streets, making its recorded announcement through a rooftop megaphone, 'blade sharpening, kitchen gas repairs'. There's a queue at the shop selling mozzarella (the *burrata* – cheese made from mozzarella and cream – sells out quickly). In fields outside the town, brightly dressed workers – all women – are toiling, picking tomatoes.

An Albanian woman hurries on her way to the shops. She's looking after an elderly resident in his museum-like home. The €500 she earns each month goes further at home, but it's lonely work.

At 11am the church bell tolls in remembrance for a local gentleman. His death is announced, like the others in town, by black-bordered notices plastered around the town centre.

At 1pm shopkeepers shut for lunch. The main street is deserted. Houses are shuttered. Lunchtime is sacred.

The town begins to stir at 5pm. Shops reopen and *nonni* (grandfathers) pedal slowly down the main street. The sun has moved, so they transfer their allegiance to the bar on the opposite side of the street.

As evening settles, dressed-up denizens hit the seafront for their ritual *passeggiata* (evening stroll), bumping into friends and relatives, checking out the talent and stopping for gelato. After midnight, the town settles in for the night...*Buona notte*.

people searched for a better life in northern Italy, northern Europe, North and South America, and Australia. Between 1880 and 1910, more than 1.5 million Sicilians alone left for the US, and in 1900 the island was the world's main area of emigration. In Campania, a staggering 2.7 million people left the motherland between 1876 and 1976.

Today, huge numbers of young southerners – often the most highly educated – continue to move abroad. This brain-drain epidemic is fuelled by a scandalously high youth unemployment rate – 38.4% in early 2013. Adding insult to injury is Italy's entrenched system of patronage and nepotism, which commonly makes landing a job more about who you know than what you know. According to Alessio, the standard of education available is another contributing factor: 'There's a common belief that southern universities aren't the best, so parents who can afford it send their kids north or overseas to complete their studies. Some return after completing their master's degree but many get accustomed to the freedom and opportunities found in the bigger cities and tend to stay.'

Yet, southern Italy has itself become a destination for people searching for a better life. Political and economic upheavals in the 1980s brought new arrivals from central Europe, Latin America and North Africa, including from Italy's former colonies in Tunisia, Somalia and Ethiopia. More recently, waves of Chinese, Filipino and Sri Lankan immigrants have given Italian streetscapes an Asian twist.

From a purely economic angle, these new arrivals are vital for the country's economic health. Without immigrant workers to fill the gaps left in the labour market by pickier locals, Italy would be sorely lacking in

Today, people of Italian origin account for more than 40% of the population in Argentina and Uruguay, more than 15% in Brazil, more than 5% in Switzerland, the US and Venezuela, and more than 4% in Australia and Canada.

tomato sauce and shoes. From hotel maids on the Amalfi Coast to fruit pickers on Calabrian farms, it is often immigrants who take the low-paid service jobs that keep Italy's economy afloat. Unfortunately, their vulnerability has sometimes led to exploitation, with several reported cases of farmhands being paid below-minimum wages for back-breaking work.

The North/South Divide

In his film *Ricomincio da tre* (I'm Starting from Three; 1980), acting great Massimo Troisi comically tackles the problems faced by southern Italians forced to head north for work. The reverse scenario is tackled in the more recent comedy *Benvenuti al Sud* (Welcome to the South; 2010), in which a northern Italian postmaster is posted to a small southern Italian town, bullet-proof vest and prejudices in tow. Slapstick aside, both films reveal Italy's very real north/south divide. While the north is celebrated for its fashion empires and moneyed metropolises, Italy's south is a PR nightmare of high unemployment, crumbling infrastructure and Mafia arrests. At a deep semantic level, the word *meridionale* (southern Italian) continues to conjure a string of unflattering words and images.

From the Industrial Revolution to the 1960s, millions of southern Italians fled to the industrialised northern cities for factory jobs. As the saying goes, '*Ogni vero Milanese ha un nonno Pugliese*' (Every true Milanese has a Pugliese grandparent). For many of these domestic migrants, the welcome north of Rome was anything but warm. Disparagingly nicknamed *terroni* (peasants), many faced discrimination on a daily basis, from everyone from landlords to baristas. While such overt discrimination is now practically nonexistent, historical prejudices linger. Many northerners resent their taxes being used to 'subsidise' the 'lazy', 'corrupt' south – a sentiment well exploited by the right-wing, Milan-based Lega Nord (Northern League) party.

Yet negative attitudes can work both ways. Many southerners view their northern compatriots as just a little *freddi* (cold) and uptight. As Raffaella, a 30-something employee at Lecce University, comments: 'Many friends of mine are desperate to return after a few years spent in northern Italy or abroad. They find life too isolated and anonymous. People don't know their neighbours.' Her friend, Deborah, a business consultant, agrees: 'People who live in the south are different from those living in the north. Here, family and friends are important; more important than work.'

THE OLD PROVERBIAL

They might be old clichés, but proverbs can be quite the cultural revelation. Here are six of the south's well-worn best:

➡ *Cu si marita, sta cuntentu nu jornu, Cu' ammazza nu porcu, sta cuntentu n'annu* (Sicilian). Whoever gets married remains happy for a day, whoever butchers a pig remains happy for a year.

➡ *Aprili fa li ciuri e li biddizzi, l'onuri l'avi lu misi ri maju* (Sicilian). April makes the flowers and the beauty, but May gets all the credit.

➡ *A chi troppo s'acàla 'o culo se vede* (Neapolitan). He who bows too low bares his arse.

➡ *Cu va 'n Palermu e 'un viri Murriali, sinni parti sceccu e tonna armali* (Sicilian). Whoever goes to Palermo and doesn't see Monreale goes there a jackass and returns a fool.

➡ *Quannu la pulice se vitte a la farina, disse ca era capu mulinaru* (Pugliese). When the flea found itself in the flour, it said it was the master miller.

➡ *Lu mericu piatusu fa a chiaja virminusa* (Sicilian). A compassionate doctor makes the wound infected.

The Southern Psyche

Beautiful Family, Beautiful Image

Family is the bedrock of southern Italian life, and loyalty to family and friends is usually non-negotiable. As Luigi Barzini (1908–84), author of *The Italians,* noted, 'A happy private life helps tolerate an appalling public life.' This chasm between the private arena and the public one is a noticeable aspect of the southern mentality, and has evolved over years of intrusive foreign domination. Some locals mightn't think twice about littering their street, but step inside their home and you'll get floors clean enough to eat from. After all, you'd never want someone dropping in and thinking you're a *zingaro* (gypsy), right?

Maintaining a *bella figura* (beautiful image) is very important to the average southerner, and how you and your family appear to the outside world is a matter of honour, respectability and pride. As Alessio explains: 'In the south, you are better than your neighbour if you own more and better things. This mentality is rooted in the past, when you really did need to own lots of things to attain certain social roles and ultimately sustain your family.' Yet *fare bella figura* (making a good impression) goes beyond a well-kept house; it extends to dressing well, behaving modestly, performing religious and social duties and fulfilling all essential family obligations. In the context of the extended family, where gossip is rife, a good image protects one's privacy.

It's Not What You Know...

In Europe's most ancient, entrenched bureaucracy, strong family ties are essential to getting things done. Putting in a good word for your son, niece or grandchild isn't just a nice gesture, but an essential career boost. As a Ministry of Labour study recently revealed, most people in Italy still find employment through personal connections. For better or worse, *clientelismo* (nepotism) is as much a part of the Italian lexicon as *caffè* (coffee) and *tasse* (taxes). Just ask former Prime Minister Silvio Berlusconi, who in 2009 chose a *Grande Fratello* (Big Brother) contestant, a soap-opera starlet, a TV costume-drama actress and a Miss Italy contestant to represent Italy as members of the European Union parliament. In a case of art imitating life, Massimiliano Bruno's film *Viva L'Italia* (2012) features a crooked, well-connected senator who secures jobs for his three children, among them a talentless TV actress with a speech impediment. The Italian film industry itself came under attack in 2012 when newspaper *Il Fatto Quotidiano* accused several members of the Italian Academy (which votes for the prestigious David di Donatello film awards) of having conflicts of interest. As the satirist Beppe Severgnini wryly comments in his book *La Bella Figura: A Field Guide to the Italian Mind,* 'If you want to lose an Italian friend or kill off a conversation, all you have to say is "On the subject of conflicts of interest..." If your interlocutor hasn't disappeared, he or she will smile condescendingly.'

A Woman's Place

'In Sicily, women are more dangerous than shotguns', said Fabrizio (Angelo Infanti) in *The Godfather.* 'A woman at the window is a woman to be shunned', proclaimed the writer Giovanni Verga in the 19th century. And 'Women are too stupid to be involved in the complex world of finance', decided a judge when faced with a female Mafia suspect in the 1990s. As in many places in the Mediterranean, a woman's position in southern Italy has always been a difficult one. In the domestic sphere, a mother and wife commands the utmost respect within the home. She is considered the moral and emotional compass for her family. As Alessio reveals: 'The mother is the spine of a family, hence southern men are often called

Any self-respecting Italian bookshelf features one or more Roman rhetoricians. To *fare la bella figura* (make a good impression) among academics, trot out a phrase from Cicero or Horace (Horatio), such as 'Where there is life there is hope' or 'Whatever advice you give, be brief'.

John Turturro's film *Passione* (2010) is a *Buena Vista Social Club*–style exploration of Naples' rich and eclectic musical traditions. Spanning everything from folk songs to contemporary tunes, it offers a fascinating insight into the city's complex soul.

mammoni (mummy's boys). The mum is always the mum, an omnipresent role model and the nightmare of newly wedded wives.'

But times are also changing. According to Luca, a young Pugliese: 'It's only two generations ago that men and women were almost segregated. Women only used to go out on Saturdays, and they had separate beaches for men and women.' His father Marcello adds: 'When my father met my mother, he saw her walking along the street and tried to speak to her. Her brother said to him: "You speak to me first." When he was permitted to visit, my aunt sat between them and my grandmother was a chaperone.'

Turkish-Italian director Ferzan Özpetek explores the clash of southern tradition and modernity in his film *Mine vaganti* (Loose Cannons; 2010), a situation comedy about two gay brothers and their conservative Pugliese family.

These days, more and more unmarried southern women live with their partners, especially in the cities. Improvements in educational opportunities and more liberal attitudes mean that the number of women with successful careers is growing. According to a 2012 report released by the Organisation for Economic Co-operation and Development (OECD), entry rates into higher education for women in Italy were 57% in 2010, compared to 42% for men. Overall, women make up around 59% of all university-level first-degree graduates in Italy, as well as constituting 52% of advanced research qualifications (doctorates) awarded in the country – one of the highest percentages among OECD countries.

Despite this, true gender equality remains an unattained goal. The World Economic Forum's 2012 Global Gender Gap Report ranked Italy 80th worldwide in terms of overall gender equality, sliding from 74th position in 2011. It ranked 101st in female economic participation and opportunity, 65th in educational attainment, and 71st in political empowerment.

The Sacred & the Profane

While almost 80% of Italians identify as Catholics, only around 15% of Italy's population regularly attends Sunday mass. Recent church scandals and shifting attitudes on issues such as gay rights mean that Italians are questioning the church's moral authority like never before. That said, *La Famiglia Cristiana* (The Christian Family) remains Italy's most popular weekly magazine and the church remains stronger in southern Italy than in the north. Indeed, even the more cosmopolitan, secular sections of southern society maintain an air of respect for the church. The church continues to exert considerable influence on public policy and political parties, especially those of the center- and far-right, and religious festivals and traditions continue to play a major role in southern Italian life. Every town has its own saint's day, celebrated with music, special events, food and wine. Indeed, these religious festivals are one of the best ways to experience the culture of the south. Cream of the crop is Easter, with lavish week-long events to mark Holy Week. People pay handsomely for the privilege and prestige of carrying the various back-breaking decorations around the town – the processions are usually solemnly, excruciatingly slow.

Pilgrimages and a belief in miracles remain a central part of the religious experience. You will see representations of Padre Pio – the Gargano saint who was canonised for his role in several miraculous recoveries – in churches, village squares, pizzerias and private homes everywhere. Around eight million pilgrims visit his shrine every year. Three times a year, thousands cram into Naples' Duomo to witness their patron saint San Gennaro's blood miraculously liquefy in the phial that contains it. When the blood liquefies, the city is considered safe from disaster. Another one of Naples' holy helpers is Giuseppe Moscati (1880–1927), a doctor who dedicated his life to serving the city's poor. According to the faithful, the medic continues to heal from up above; a dedicated chapel

CALCIO: THE OTHER RELIGION

Catholicism may be Italy's official faith, but its true religion is *calcio* (football). On any given weekend from September through to May, you'll find millions of *tifosi* (football fans) at the *stadio* (stadium), glued to the TV, or checking the score on their mobile phone. In Naples' Piazzetta Nilo, you'll even find an altar to Argentine football star Diego Maradona, who elevated the city's Napoli team to its most successful era in the 1980s and early 1990s.

It's no coincidence that in Italian *tifoso* means both 'football fan' and 'typhus patient'. When the ball ricochets off the post and slips fatefully through the goalie's hands, when half the stadium is swearing while the other half is euphorically shouting 'Goooooooooooooooool!!', 'fever pitch' is the term that comes to mind.

Indeed, nothing quite stirs Italian blood like a good (or a bad) game. Nine months after Neapolitan Fabio Cannavaro led Italy to victory in the 2006 World Cup, hospitals in northern Italy reported a baby boom. In February the following year, rioting at a Palermo–Catania match in Catania left one policeman dead and around 100 injured. Blamed on the Ultras (a minority group of hardcore football fans), the violence shocked both Italy and the world, leading to a temporary ban of all matches in Italy, and increased stadium security.

Yet, the same game that divides also unites. You might be a Juventus-loathing Bari supporter on any given day, but when national team *Azzurri* (the Blues) bag the World Cup, you are nothing but a heart-on-your-sleeve *italiano*. In his book *The 100 Things Everyone Needs to Know About Italy,* Australian journalist David Dale writes that Italy's 1982 World Cup win 'finally united twenty regions which, until then, had barely acknowledged that they were part of the one country'.

inside the city's Chiesa del Gesù Nuovo heaves with *ex-voti* (including golden syringes) offered in thanks for miraculous recoveries.

And yet, the line between the sacred and the profane remains a fine one in the south. In *Christ Stopped at Eboli,* his book about his stay in rural Basilicata in the 1930s, writer-painter-doctor Carlo Levi wrote: 'The air over this desolate land and among the peasant huts is filled with spirits. Not all of them are mischievous and capricious gnomes or evil demons. There are also good spirits in the guise of guardian angels.'

While the mystical, half-pagan world Levi describes may no longer be recognisable, ancient pagan influences live on in daily southern life. Here, curse-deterring amulets are as plentiful as crucifix pendants, the most famous of which is the iconic, horn-shaped *corno*. Adorning everything from necklines to rear-view mirrors, this lucky charm's evil-busting powers are said to lie in its representation of the bull and its sexual vigour. A rarer, but by no means extinct, custom is that of Naples' 'o Scartellat. Usually an elderly man, he'll occasionally be spotted him burning incense through the city's older neighbourhoods, clearing the streets of bad vibes and inviting good fortune. The title itself is Neapolitan for 'hunchback', as the task was once the domain of posture-challenged figures. According to Neapolitan lore, touching a hunchback's hump brings good luck...which beats some of the other options, among them stepping in dog poop and having wine spilt on you accidentally.

Italy's culture of corruption and *calcio* (football) is captured in *The Dark Heart of Italy,* in which English expat author Tobias Jones wryly observes, 'Footballers or referees are forgiven nothing; politicians are forgiven everything'.

The Mafia

To many outside Italy, 'Mafia' means Sicily's Cosa Nostra, seared into popular culture thanks to Francis Ford Coppola's classic film, *The Godfather*. In reality, Cosa Nostra has three other major partners in crime: Campania's Camorra, Calabria's 'ndrangheta and Puglia's Sacra Corona Unita. Apt at everything from loan sharking to trafficking narcotics, arms and people, these four criminal networks produce a staggering annual turnover estimated at around €10.5 billion.

Origins

In 2011, police seized an adult tiger from the estate of murdered Sacra Corona Unita boss Lucio Vetrugno. Kept in a cage for 16 years, the giant feline had come in handy for intimidating Vetrugno's enemies. The tiger was subsequently transferred to an animal park in Bologna.

The concept of 'the *mafioso*' dates back to the late 15th century, when Sicily's rent-collecting *gabellotti* (bailiffs) employed small gangs of armed peasants to help them solve 'problems'. Soon robbing large estates, the bandits struck fear and admiration into the peasantry, who were happy to support efforts to destabilise the feudal system. They became willing accomplices, protecting the outlaws, and although it was another 400 years before crime became 'organised', the 16th and 17th centuries witnessed a substantial increase in the activities of brigand bands. The peasants' loyalty to their own people resulted in the name Cosa Nostra (Our Thing). The early Mafia's way of protecting itself from prosecution was to become the modern Mafia's most important weapon: the code of silence, or *omertà*.

In the 1860s, a band of Sicilians exiled to Calabria began forming their own organised gangs, planting the seeds for the 'ndrangheta. For almost a century, these gangs remained a local menace, known for extortion, racketeering and rural banditry. But it was the murder of a local godfather in 1975 that sparked a bloody gang war, transforming the organisation and creating a rebellious faction infamous for holding northern Italian businessmen to ransom. With its profits invested in narcotics, the 'ndrangheta went on to transform itself into Italy's most powerful Mafia entity.

The powerful Camorra reputedly emerged from the criminal gangs operating among the poor in late 18th-century Naples. The organisation had its first big break after the failed revolution of 1848. Desperate to overthrow Ferdinand II, pro-constitutional liberals turned to *camorristi*

MAFIA MOVIES

Gomorra (Matteo Garrone; 2009) A shocking, award-winning exposé on the Camorra, based on Roberto Saviano's best-selling book.

The Godfather Trilogy (Francis Ford Coppola; 1972–90) Marlon Brando plays an old-school mobster in this Oscar-winning saga.

Il camorrista (The Camorrista; Giuseppe Tornatore; 1986) Camorra battles and betrayals inspired by real-life *capo* (boss) Raffaele 'Il Professore' Cutolo.

Mi manda Picone (Picone Sent Me; Nanni Loy; 1983) A cult comedy about a small-time hustler embroiled in Naples' seedy underworld.

In nome della legge (In the Name of the Law; Pietro Germi; 1949) A young judge is sent to a Mafia-riddled Sicilian town in this neorealist film, cowritten by Federico Fellini.

to help garner the support of the masses, and the Camorra's political influence was sealed. Dealt a serious blow by Mussolini, the organisation would get its second wind from the invading Allied forces of 1943, which turned to the flourishing underworld as the best way to get things done. The black market thrived and the Camorra slowly began to spread its roots again.

In the 1970s, the Camorra gave birth to the Sacra Corona Unita (Sacred United Crown), created by Camorra boss Raffaele Cutolo to gain access to Puglia's seaports. Originally named the Nuova Grande Camorra Pugliese, it gained its current name in the early 1980s after its Pugliese members cut ties with Campania and strengthened their bond with Eastern Europe's criminal networks.

The Value of Vice

Today's Mafia means business, its revenues matching those of some of Italy's biggest corporations. This is a far cry from the days of roguish characters bullying shopkeepers into paying the *pizzo* (protection money). As journalist Roberto Saviano writes in his Camorra exposè *Gomorra*: 'Only beggar Camorra clans inept at business and desperate to survive still practice the kind of monthly extortions seen in Nanni Loy's film *Mi manda Picone*'.

The top money-spinner is drugs, and king of that trade is the 'ndrangheta. The Calabrian mafia is the main player in Transatlantic cocaine trafficking, overseeing its shipment from Latin America to Europe via West Africa in a business worth a staggering €43 million a year.

Another trafficked 'product' is people, with an estimated 5000 refugees smuggled annually into Puglia alone. Many illegal African arrivals are hired out as farmhands by their Mafia handlers, demanding a percentage of the labourers' below-minimum wages. Most workers receive no more than €25 for up to two weeks' work on southern farms.

Italy's ongoing financial woes have proven another boon. With liquidity in short supply, a growing number of hard-pressed companies have turned to dirty money. Mafia-affiliated loan sharks commonly offer cash with an average interest rate of 10%. In Naples alone, an estimated 50% of shops are run with Camorra money. Mafia profits are also reinvested in legitimate real estate, credit markets and businesses, from wind farms in Sicily to property in London and Sydney. Critics call this 'the Invisible Mafia'.

Backlash of the Brave

Despite the Mafia's ever-expanding reach, the war against it marches on. In August 2013, authorities finally caught up with fugitive Sicilian *mafioso* Domenico Rancadore in suburban London. On the run since 1993, the reputed head of the Cosa Nostra in Trabia had reinvented himself as a mild-mannered house husband by the name of Marc Skinner. In July 2013, the capture of 'ndrangheta boss Roberto Pannunzi in Bogota, Colombia, made the news. Considered Europe's most wanted drug trafficker, the crime lord reputedly imported two tons of cocaine from Colombia to Europe every month. In April 2013 Italian authorities made their biggest confiscation of Mafia assets in history, seizing assets worth €1.3 billion.

The assassination of Sicilian anti-Mafia judges Giovanni Falcone and Paolo Borsellino in 1992 sparked particularly intense anti-Mafia sentiment throughout Italy. In 1994, Paolo Borsellino's sister Rita cofounded the group Libera (www.libera.it), whose member organisations were permitted to transform properties seized from the Mafia into agricultural cooperatives, *agriturismi* (farm stay accommodation) and other legitimate enterprises. Equally encouraging has been the establishment of Addiopizzo (www.addiopizzo.org), a Sicilian organisation encouraging consumers to support businesses that have said 'no' to Mafia extortion.

THE MAFIA THE VALUE OF VICE

The Camorra's weekly drug trade rates range from €100 for lookouts to €1000 for those willing to hide the drugs at home. On the tough streets of Naples' poorest neighbourhoods, the lure of quick cash proves irresistible for many, with kids as young as 12 recruited by local clans.

Arrested in 2009, Ugo Gabriele broke the mould like no other. Beefy and cunning, the then 27 year old would go down in history as Italy's first cross-dressing mobster. In between managing prostitution and drug rackets for Naples' Scissionisti clan, 'Kitty' found time to shape his eyebrows, dab on the lipstick and dye his hair platinum blonde.

The Southern Table

If you live to eat well, you've come to the right place. Blessed with sun, mineral-rich soils and the salty goodness of the Mediterranean, southern Italy was always destined for culinary fame. Waves of migration have flavoured the pot – the Greeks supplied the olives, the Arabs brought the pine nuts, aubergines (eggplants), almonds, raisins and honey, and the Spanish came with tomatoes. The end result is a larder bursting with buxom vegetables, glistening fish, spicy meats and decadent sweets. Peckish? Read on for a crash course in southern gluttony.

The Simple Things

Tomatoes were not introduced to Italy until the 16th century, brought from the Americas. The word 'pommidoro' literally means 'golden apple'.

Picture it: wood-fired bread drizzled in extra virgin olive oil, sprinkled with ripe *pomodori* (tomatoes) and fragrant *basilico* (basil). The flavours explode in your mouth. From the chargrilled crunch of the bread to the sweetness of the tomatoes, it's a perfect symphony of textures and flavours.

In many ways, *pane e pomodoro* (bread and tomatoes) captures the very soul of the southern Italian kitchen. Down here, fresh produce is the secret and simplicity is the key. Order grilled fish and chances are you'll get exactly that. No rich, overbearing sauces...just grilled fish with a wedge of lemon on the side. After all, it's the freshness of the fish you should be savouring, right?

This less-is-more approach is a testament to the south's impoverished past. Pasta made without eggs, bread made from hard durum wheat and wild greens scavenged from the countryside are all delicious, but their consumption was driven by necessity. The tradition of *sopratavola* (raw vegetables such as fennel or chicory eaten after a meal) arose because people could not afford fruit. That of *sottaceti* (vegetables cooked in vinegar and preserved in jars with olive oil) is part of the waste not, want not philosophy.

In modern times, the simple goodness of this *cucina povera* (poor man's cuisine) has made it the darling of health-conscious foodies.

Regional Focus

In reality, southern Italian cuisine encompasses the culinary traditions of five regions: Campania, Puglia, Basilicata, Calabria and Sicily. They might share similarities, but they are all distinctly unique. So raise your fork to the following appetite-piquing regional fortes.

Campania
Perfect Pizza

It was in Naples that the city's most famous *pizzaiolo,* Raffaele Esposito, invented the classic pizza margherita. Esposito was summoned to fire up a treat for a peckish King Umberto I and his wife Queen Margherita on a royal visit in 1889. Determined to impress the Italian royals, Esposito based his creation of tomato, mozzarella and basil on the red, white and green flag of the newly unified Italy. The resulting topping met with the queen's approval and was subsequently named in her honour.

Pizza purists claim that you really can't top Esposito's classic combo when made by a true Neapolitan *pizzaiolo* (pizza chef). Not everyone is in accordance and Italians are often split between those who favour the thin-crust Roman variant, and those who go for the thicker Neapolitan version. Whatever your choice, the fact remains that the pizza they make in Naples is nothing short of superb. It's also a brilliant cheap feed – giant discs of bubbling perfection usually start from €3.

According to the official Associazione Verace Pizza Napoletana (Real Neapolitan Pizza Association), genuine Neapolitan pizza dough must be made using highly refined type 00 wheat flour (a small dash of type 0 is permitted), compressed or natural yeast, salt, and water with a pH level between 6 and 7. While a slow-speed mixer can be used for kneading the dough, only hands are allowed to form the *disco di pasta* (pizza base), which should not be thicker than 3mm. The pizza itself should be cooked at 485°C (905°F) in a double-domed, wood-fired oven using oak, ash, beech or maple timber.

The Cult of Caffè

According to the Neapolitans, it's the local water that makes their coffee stronger and better than any other in Italy. While the magic formula is up for debate, there's no doubting that Naples brews the country's thickest, richest, most unforgettable espresso. Indeed, coffee plays a venerable role in Neapolitan cultural identity. Celebrated Neapolitan folk songs include *'O cafè* (Oh, coffee) and *A tazza 'e cafè* (The Cup of Coffee), while Italian design company Alessi pays tribute to the city's distinctive, stovetop coffee maker with its own *Caffettiera napoletana* (Neapolitan coffee maker), designed by prolific Neapolitan artist Riccardo Dalisi.

New-World coffee capitals like Melbourne and Portland might innovate with single origin beans, lighter roasts, latte art and new brewing technologies, but in Naples, tradition holds sway. Locals still favour the Arabica and Robusta blends that deliver a dense crema, higher caffeine jolt, longer shelf life and, crucially, a price point everyone can afford. While the city's most famous *torrefazioni* (roasters) include Kimbo and Moreno, its most locally loved and respected brand remains San Passalacqua.

Whichever you choose, chances are you'll be savouring it standing up. In Naples, as in the rest of Italy, drinking coffee at a bar is usually a moment to pause, but rarely linger. It's a standing-up sniff, swirl and gulp, and an exchanged *buongiorno* or *buona sera* with the barista, and a hop back onto the street. But don't be fooled – the speed with which it's consumed does not diminish the importance of quality.

Don't believe the hype about espresso: one diminutive cup packs less of a caffeine wallop than a large cup of French-pressed or American-brewed coffee, and leaves drinkers less jittery.

Magnificent Mozzarella

So you think the cow's milk mozzarella served in Capri's *insalata caprese* (a salad made of mozzarella, tomato, basil and olive oil) is tasty? Try Campania's porcelain-white *mozzarella di bufala* (buffalo-milk mozzarella) and you'll move onto an entirely different level of deliciousness. Made on the plains surrounding Caserta and Paestum, it's best eaten when freshly made that morning – the delicate, sweet flavour and luscious texture is nothing short of a revelation. You'll find it served in *trattorias* (informal restaurants) and restaurants across the region. Sorrento even has a dedicated mozzarella eatery, Inn Bufalito. Bought fresh from *latterie* (dairies), it comes lukewarm in a plastic bag filled with a slightly cloudy liquid, the run-off from the mozzarella making. Fresh mozzarella should have an elastic consistency; a tight, smooth surface; and no yellowish marks or spots. Sliced, it should appear grainy, layered, and seeping pearls of milky whey.

While the most common form is round and fresh, *mozzarella di bufala* also comes in a twisted plait form *(treccia),* as well as smoked *(affumicata).* The most decadent variation is *burrata,* a mozzarella filled with a wickedly buttery cream. *Burrata* itself was invented in the neighbouring region of Puglia; the swampy fields around Foggia are famed for their buffalo-milk goodness.

As for that irresistible taste, it's the high fat content and buffalo milk protein that give *mozzarella di bufala* the distinctive, pungent flavour so often absent in the versions sold abroad.

Fifty years ago, Italy's *Domus* magazine dispatched journalists nationwide to collect Italy's best regional recipes. The result is Italy's food bible, *The Silver Spoon,* now available in English from Phaidon (2005).

Puglia, Basilicata & Calabria
Italy's Busiest Virgin

Campania and Sicily may produce some impressive olive oils, but southern Italy's *olio* (oil) heavyweight is Puglia. The region produces around 40% of Italy's olive oil, much of it from the region's north. Indeed, Puglia is home to an estimated 50 to 60 million olive trees, and some of these gnarled, silver-green icons are said to be thousands of years old.

While Pugliese oil is usually made up of two particular types of olives – faintly bitter coratina (from Corato) and sweet, fat ogliarola (from around Cima di Bitonto) – there is no shortage of common olive varieties. Among these are cellina di nardò, frantoio, leccino, peranzana, garganica, rotondella, cima di bitonto and cima di mola. The European Union itself formally recognises four Denomination of Origin of Production (DOP) areas in Puglia in order to protect the unique characteristics of each terroir: Collina di Brindisi DOP, Dauno DOP, Terra d'Otranto DOP and Terra di Bari DOP. Sweet fruitiness characterises the oils from Collina di Brindisi, while Dauno DOP oils are noted for their aromatic, well-rounded nature. Ancient growing regions define both the Terra di Bari DOP and Terra d'Otranto DOP oils, the former known for their clear colour and almond notes, the latter for their darker green hue and fresh herb aroma.

Antonio Carluccio's *Southern Italian Feast: More Than 100 Recipes Inspired by the Flavour of Southern Italy,* is a splendid collection to inspire you to get cooking.

Whatever the origin, the best oil is made from olives that are picked and rushed to the mill, as olives that are left for too long after harvesting quickly become acidic. Pugliese farmers traditionally harvest the easy way: by letting the olives drop into nets, rather than paying for labour-intensive harvesting by hand. This means the olives are too acidic and the oil has to be refined, often taken north to mix with higher quality, costlier oils. That said, more and more places in the south produce stunning oils at low prices; you can buy it at local farms such as the organic Il Frantoio.

The Beauty of Bread

Puglia's celebrated olive oils are a fine match for the region's equally lauded *pane* (bread). Indeed, eating a meal in Puglia or neighbouring Basilicata without bread is like playing tennis without a racquet – it is considered essential for wiping up the sauce (a practise fondly called *fare scarpetta,* 'to make a little shoe'). Puglia's wood-fired variety is the stuff of legend, usually made from hard durum wheat (also used in pasta), with a russet-brown crust, an eggy-golden interior and a distinctively fine flavour. The best comes from Altamura, where it's thrice-risen, getting even better with time.

For an excellent food and travel portal, visit www.deliciousitaly.com, which also lists courses and wine tours.

Many of Puglia's and Basilicata's recipes call for breadcrumbs, among them summery spaghetti with oven-roasted tomatoes, breadcrumbs and garlic, and fusilli pasta with tomato, breadcrumbs and *crusco* (a dried, sweet pepper unique to Basilicata). Across in Calabria, breadcrumbs and pasta meet in classics like spaghetti with anchovies and chilli. The breadcrumbs themselves are made from stale bread – in Italian, it's called *pane rafferme* (firmed-up bread), which is a much more glass-half-full way of looking at it.

Another southwest staple is *friselli,* dried bagel-shaped rolls born out of practicality, ideal for labourers on the move. Douse them in water to soften and then dress with tomatoes, olive oil and oregano. Just leave a little room for bagel-shaped *taralli,* hard little savoury biscuits that make for a tasty snack. In Bari they're traditionally plain, in Taranto they're sprinkled with fennel seeds, and in Lecce they're sexed-up with a touch of chilli.

Sicily
To Market, To Market

Only Naples' Mercato di Porta Nolana can rival the sheer theatricality and gut-rumbling brilliance of Sicily's *mercati* (markets). Loud, crowded and exhilarating, these alfresco larders are a technicolor testament to the importance of fresh produce in daily life. Watch the hard-to-please hagglers bullying vendors into giving them precisely what they want to understand that quality really matters here. It's these people, the *nonne* (grandmothers) and *casalinghe* (homemakers), who keep the region's culinary traditions alive.

Two of the most atmospheric markets are Palermo's Mercato del Capo and Catania's La Pescheria, featuring souk-like laneways crammed with glistening tuna and swordfish, swaying sausages and tubs of olives and pungent cheeses. Look out for pistachios from Bronte; almonds from Noto; and *caciocavallo,* one of southern Italy's most renowned cheeses. Don't panic: despite the name 'horse cheese', it's made from cow's milk. It has a distinctive gourd-shaped, pale-mustard exterior, and the name is thought to have arisen either because it was once made from mare's milk, or because it would be hung from the horse's back when transported. Freshly made, it tastes *dolce* (sweet); after two month's aging, it's *piccante* (spicy) or *affumicato* (smoked).

Another must for cheese aficionados is sheep's-milk *pecorino;* the most distinctive Sicilian *pecorini* come from the Madonie and Nebrodi Mountains.

La Dolce Vita

From *gelso di melone* (watermelon jelly) and *buccellati* (little pies filled with minced fruit), to *biscotti regina* (sesame-coated biscuits) and *cassatelle* (pouches of dough stuffed with sweetened ricotta and chocolate), Sicilians have a way with sugar that verges on the pornographic. Down

> The average Italian adult consumes around 42 litres of wine per annum – a sobering figure compared with the 100 litres consumed on average back in the 1950s. Somewhat surprisingly, the world's top consumers of wine live in the Vatican City (54.78 litres per person).

THE BIG FORK MANIFESTO

The year was 1987. McDonald's had just begun their expansion into Italy, and lunch outside the bun seemed to be fading into fond memory. Enter Carlo Petrini and a handful of other journalists from the small Piedmontese town of Bra, in northern Italy. Determined to buck the trend, these *neoforchettoni* ('big forks', or foodies) created a manifesto. Published in the like-minded culinary magazine *Gambero Rosso*, the manifesto declared that a meal should be judged not by its speed, but by the pure pleasure it offers.

The organisation they founded would soon become known worldwide as Slow Food. Its mission: to reconnect artisanal producers with enthusiastic, educated consumers. The movement has taken root, with more than 100,000 members in 150 countries – not to mention Slow Food *agriturismi* (farm stay accommodation), restaurants, farms, wineries, cheesemakers and revitalised farmers' markets across Italy.

While traditions in the south remain stronger than in Italy's north, the Slow Food Movement does its bit to prevent their disappearance and to promote interest in food, taste and the way things are produced. For more information, see www.slowfoodpuglia.it (in Italian), or you can look up the main website at www.slowfood.com (in English).

here, *pasticcerie* (pastry shops) are culinary sex shops, leading taste buds into temptation. Ditch the guilt, you're not alone – Sicilians normally migrate from restaurant tables to the nearest pastry shop for a coffee and cake at the bar.

It was the Saracens who first brought sugar cane to Sicily, a novelty that helped kindle the island's passion for sweets. Sicily's legendary *cassata* (a coma-inducing concoction of sponge cake, ricotta, marzipan, chocolate and candied fruit) comes from the Arabic word *qas'ah* (a reference to the terracotta bowl used to shape the cake), while *cannolo* (a pastry shell with a sweet ricotta filling) originates from *canna* (cane, as in sugar cane).

The Arabs also kickstarted the Sicilian mania for all things icy, including *granita* (flavoured crushed ice), *gelato* (ice cream) and *semifreddo* (literally 'semifrozen'; a cold, creamy dessert). The origins of ice cream lie in the Arab *sarbat* (sherbet), a concoction of sweet fruit syrups chilled with iced water, later developed into *granita* (where crushed ice was mixed with anything from fruit juice to coffee and almond milk) and *cremolata* (fruit syrups chilled with iced milk), the forerunner to *gelato*.

Homemade *gelato* (*gelato artiginale*) is sold at cafes and bars across the island, and is truly delicious. *Granite* are sometimes topped with fresh whipped cream, or you could try it like a Sicilian – first thing in the morning in a brioche. Favourite flavours include *caffè* (coffee) and *mandorla* (almond), though *limone* (lemon) is especially invigorating in summer.

> While it's perfectly normal to order 'a biscotti' or 'a cannoli' back home in Sydney or New York, these are actually plural forms in Italian; use the singular form *'un biscotto'* or *'un cannolo'* when in Italy – unless, of course, you're seriously famished.

Southern Staples

Pasta: Fuel of the South

In the 1954 cult film *Un americano a Roma* (An American in Rome), a US-obsessed Alberto Sordi snubs a plate of pasta in favour of an unappetising 'American-style' concoction. It only takes a few mouthfuls before Sordi thinks better of it, plunging into the pasta with unbridled passion. It's hard not to follow Sordi's lead.

A standard *primo* (first course) on menus across the south, pasta is not only delicious, it's often a filling meal in itself. Your waiter will understand and there is usually no pressure to order a *secondo* (second course). The south's knack for pasta dishes is hardly surprising given that it was here that pasta first hit Italy, introduced to Sicily by Arab merchants in the Middle Ages. It was a perfect match. Southern Italy's sunny, windy disposition was just right for producing *pasta secca* (dry pasta), while the foodstuff's affordability and easy storage made it handy in the face of hardship. It's no coincidence that *pasta fresca* (fresh pasta) has, traditionally, been more prevalent in Italy's more affluent north.

Arriving from Sicily, *pasta secca* took off in a big way in Campania, especially after the 1840 opening of Italy's first pasta plant in Torre Annunziata, a town on the Bay of Naples. Not that Torre Annunziata was Campania's first pasta-making hub. Some 30km southeast of Naples, the small town of Gragnano has been making pasta since the 17th century. Gragnano's main street was specifically built along the sun's axis so that the pasta put out to dry by the town's *pastifici* (pasta factories) would reap a full day's sunshine. To this day, *pasta di Gragnano* enjoys an air of exclusivity.

And while *pasta secca* may be the dominant form of pasta on southern plates, the Mezzogiorno is not without its fresh pasta icons. The most famous is arguably Puglia's *orecchiette* (meaning 'little ears'), best savoured in dishes such as *orecchiette con cime di rapa* (with turnip tops) and *orecchiette con pomodori e ricotta forte* (with tomato sauce and strong ricotta).

> Puglia produces around 80% of Europe's pasta, and per-capita consumption of bread and pasta is at least double that of the USA. It's also said that there are 50 million olive trees in Puglia, equivalent to the Italian population, and the region is the sixth-biggest wine-making region in the world.

Eat Your Greens...Purples, Reds & Yellows

Vegetables across the world must loathe their southern Italian counterparts. Not only do they often look more beautiful, they're prepared with a know-how that turns them into culinary protagonists. Take the humble *melanzana* (aubergine/eggplant), glammed up in the punchy *melanzane ripiene al forno* (baked aubergine stuffed with olives, capers and tomatoes) and decadent *parmigiana melanzane* (batter-fried aubergine layered with parmesan, mozzarella, ham and tomato sauce). Another version, simply named *parmigiana*, does the same for *carciofi* (globe artichokes). Campania's *pomodoro San Marzano* (San Marzano plum tomato) is one of the world's most lauded tomatoes. Grown in the shadow of Mt Vesuvius, its low acidity and intense, sweet flavour makes a perfect *conserva di pomodoro* (tomato concentrate). It's this sauce that adorns so many of Naples' signature pasta dishes, including the colourfully named *spaghetti alla puttanesca* (whore's spaghetti).

The word *melanzane* (aubergine/ eggplant) comes from 'mela insane', meaning crazy apple. In Latin it was called *solanum insanum* as it was thought to cause madness.

THE SOUTHERN TABLE SOUTHERN STAPLES

FESTIVE FAVOURITES

In Italy, culinary indulgence is the epicentre of any celebration and major holidays are defined by their specialities. Lent is heralded by *Carnevale* (Carnival), a time for *sanguinaccio* ('blood pudding' made with dark chocolate and cinnamon), *chiacchiere* (fried biscuits sprinkled with icing sugar) and Sicily's *mpagnuccata* (deep-fried dough tossed in soft caramel).

If you're in southern Italy around 19 March (St Joseph's Feast Day), expect to eat *zeppole* (fritters topped with lemon-scented cream, sour cherries and dusting sugar) in Naples and Bari, and *crispelle di riso* (citrus-scented rice fritters dipped in honey) in Sicily.

Lent specialities like the Sicilian *quaresimali* (hard, light almond biscuits) give way to Easter binging with the obligatory lamb, *colomba* (dove-shaped cake) and *uove di pasqua* (foil-wrapped chocolate eggs with toy surprises inside). The dominant ingredient at this time of year is egg, also used to make traditional regional specialities like Naples' legendary *pastiera* (a shortcrust pastry tart filled with ricotta, cream, candied fruits and cereals flavoured with orange water).

If you're in Palermo around late October, before the festival of Ognissanti (All Souls' Day), you will see plenty of stalls selling the famous *frutti della Martorana,* named after the church that first began producing them. These marzipan biscuits, shaped to resemble fruits (or whatever takes the creator's fancy), are part of a Sicilian tradition that dates back to the Middle Ages.

Come Christmas, it's time for stuffed pasta, seafood dishes and national staples like Milan's *panettone* (yeasty, golden cake studded with raisins and dried fruit), Verona's simpler, raisin-free *pandoro* (star-shaped cake dusted with vanilla-flavoured icing sugar) and Siena's *panforte* (chewy, flat cake made with candied fruits, nuts, chocolate, honey and spices). It's at this time that Neapolitans throw caution (and scales) to the wind with *raffioli* (sponge and marzipan biscuits), *struffoli* (tiny fried pastry balls dipped in honey and sprinkled with colourful candied sugar) and *pasta di mandorla* (marzipan), while their Sicilian cousins toast to the season with *cucciddatu* (ring-shaped cake made with dried figs, nuts, honey, vanilla, cloves, cinnamon and citrus fruits). The Sicilians stop there, though, further expanding waistlines with yuletide *buccellati* (dough rings stuffed with minced figs, raisins, almonds, candied fruit and orange peel, especially popular around Christmas).

Of course, it's not all about religion. Some Italian holidays dispense with the spiritual premise and are all about the food. During spring, summer and early autumn, towns across Italy celebrate *sagre,* the festivals of local foods in season. You'll find a *sagra della melanzana* (aubergine/eggplant) in Campania, *del pomodoro* (tomatoes) in Sicily and *della cipolla* (onion) in Puglia (wouldn't want to be downwind of that one). For a list of *sagre,* check out www.prodottitipici.com/sagre.

Ironically, southern Italy's sophisticated flair with vegetables is firmly rooted in centuries of deprivation and misery. The food of the poor, the so-called *mangiafoglie* (leaf eaters), was largely based on the *verdure* (vegetables) grown under the nourishing southern sun, from artichokes and courgettes (zucchini), to tomatoes and peppers. Hardship and sunshine helped develop celebrated antipasto staples like *zucchine fritte* (pan-fried courgettes) and *peperoni sotto aceto* (marinated pickled peppers), as well as celebrated Sicilian dishes like *peperonata in agridolce* (a stew of red, green and yellow peppers, onions, pine nuts, raisins and capers). Onions feel the love in Puglia's moreish *calzone pugliese* (onion pie), while legumes see the light in the region's broad bean and chicory puree; 'a dish to die for' according to celebrity chef/restaurateur/food writer Antonio Carluccio.

The Vine Revival

Winemaking in the south dates back to the Phoenicians. The Greeks introduced Campania to its now-famous Greco (Greek) grape, and dubbed the south 'Enotria' (Wineland). Yet, despite this ancient viticulture, oenophiles had often dismissed local *vini* (wines) as little more than 'here for a good time, not a long time' drops. A case in point is wine critic Burton Anderson, who in his 1990 *Wine Atlas of Italy* wrote that Campania's noteworthy winemakers could be 'counted on one's fingers'.

Anderson would need a few more hands these days. In little more than two decades, southern Italy has transformed itself into one of the world's hottest in-the-know wine regions, with renewed pride in native varieties and stricter, more modern winemaking practices.

Campania

Campanian producers such as Feudi di San Gregorio, Mastroberardino, Terredora di Paolo and Mustilli have returned to their roots, cultivating ancient grape varieties like the red Aglianico (thought to be the oldest cultivated grape in Italy) and the whites Falanghino, Fiano and Greco (all were growing long before Mt Vesuvius erupted in AD 79). Taurasi, a full-bodied Aglianico wine, sometimes known as the Barolo of the south, is one of southern Italy's finest labels. One of only three in the region to carry Italy's top quality rating, DOCG (*Denominazione di Origine Controllata e Garantita;* Controlled and Guaranteed Denomination of Origin), it goes perfectly with barbequed and boiled meats. The other two wines boasting the DOCG honour are the fresh, fragrant Fiano di Avellino and the dry, bright Greco di Tufo, both seafood-friendly whites from the Avellino area.

Campania's other wine-producing areas include the Campi Flegrei (home to spicy Piedirosso and tangy Falanghina vines), Ischia (whose wines were the first to receive Denominazione di Origine Controllata status) and the Cilento, home to the Cilento bianco (Cilento white) and to the Aglianico Paestum. Mt Vesuvius' most famous drop is the dry Lacryma Christi (Tears of Christ), a blend of locally grown Falanghina, Piedirosso and Coda di Volpe grapes.

Puglia & Basilicata

The different characteristics of these regions' wines reflect their diverse topography and terroir. In Puglia, there are vast, flat acreages of vines, while Basilicata's vineyards tend to be steep and volcanic.

It's the Pugliese reds that gain most plaudits. The main grapes grown are the Primitivo (a clone of the Zindanfel grape), Negroamaro, Nero di Troia and Malvasia. The best Primitivi are found around Manduria, while Negroamaro reaches its peak in the Salento, particularly around Salice,

In Matera, Ferula Viaggi is an excellent agency offering food-themed tours and tastings, where you can, for example, see mozzarella being made and taste local wines.

The annual *Italian Wines,* produced by the Gambero Rosso, is considered to be the bible of Italian vino, offering plenty of information about southern wines and wineries. You can buy it online at www.gambero rosso.it.

Guagnano and Copertino. The two grapes are often blended to derive the best from the sweetness of Primitivo and the slightly bitter, wilder edge of Negroamaro.

Almost all Puglia reds work perfectly with pasta, pizza, meats and cheeses. Puglia whites have less cachet; however, those grown on the Murge, particularly Locorotondo and Martina, are good, clean, fresh-tasting wines, while those from Gravina are a little weightier. They are all excellent with fish.

In Basilicata, the red wine of choice is made from the Aglianico grape, the best being produced in the Vulture region. It is the volcanic terroir that makes these wines so unique and splendid. Basilicata, like Puglia, has seen a renaissance in recent years with much inward investment, such as that of oenologist Donato d'Angelo at his eponymous winery at Rionero in Vulture.

Sicily

Sicily is the second-largest wine-producing region in Italy, yet few Sicilian wines are well known beyond the island.

The most common varietal is Nero d'Avola, a robust red similar to Syrah or Shiraz. Vintages are produced by numerous Sicilian wineries, including Planeta, which has four estates around the island; Donnafugata in Western Sicily; Azienda Agricola COS near Mount Etna; and Azienda Agricola G Milazzo near Agrigento. Try Planeta's Plumbago and Santa Cecilia labels, Donnafugata's Mille e una Notte, COS' Nero di Lupo and Milazzo's Maria Costanza and Terre della Baronia Rosso.

Local Cabernet Sauvignons are less common but are also worth sampling; the version produced by Tasca d'Almerita at its Regaleali estate in Caltanissetta province is particularly highly regarded (the estate also produces an excellent Nero d'Avola under its Rosso del Conte label).

The Sangiovese-like Nerello Mascalese and Nerello Cappuccio are used in the popular Etna Rosso, a dark-fruited, medium-bodied wine that goes perfectly with lamb and goat-milk cheeses.

There is only one Sicilian DOCG, Cerasuolo di Vittoria, a blend of Nero d'Avola and Frappato grapes.

While Sicily's *vini rossi* (red wines) are good, the region's real forte are its *bianchi* (whites), including those produced at Abbazia Santa Anastasia near Castelbuono, and Fazio Wines near Erice, Tasca d'Almerita and Passopisciaro. Common white varietals include Carricante, Chardonnay, Grillo, Inzolia, Cataratto, Inzolia, Cataratto, Grecanico and Corinto. Look out for Tasca d'Almerita's Nozze d'Oro Inzolia blend, Fazio's Catarratto Chardonnay, Abbazia Santa Anastasia's chardonnay blends, and Passopisciaro's Guardiola Chardonnay.

Equally impressive are Sicily's dessert wines. Top billing goes to Marsala's sweet wine; the best labels are Florio and Pellegrino. Italy's most famous Moscato (Muscat) is the Passito di Pantelleria from the island of the same name. Deep amber in colour, its taste is an extraordinary mélange of apricots and vanilla.

Although some producers find these official Italian classifications unduly costly and creatively constraining, the DOCG *(Denominazione di Origine Controllata e Garantita)* and DOC *(Denominazione di Origine Controllata)* designations are awarded to wines that meet regional quality-control standards.

THE SOUTHERN TABLE THE VINE REVIVAL

Art & Architecture

Southern Italy is Western Europe's cultural attic – a dusty repository filled to the rafters with ancient temples and statues, exotic mosaics, brooding castles, vainglorious frescoes and innovative installations. It's an overwhelming heap, so why not start with the undisputed highlights?

Art

Classical Splendour

Click on to www.exibart.com for up-to-date listings of art exhibitions throughout Italy, as well as exhibition reviews, articles and interviews.

The Greeks had settled many parts of Sicily and southern Italy as early as the 8th century BC, naming it Magna Graecia (Greater Greece) and building great cities such as Syracuse and Taranto. These cities were famous for their magnificent temples, many of which were decorated with sculptures modelled on, or inspired by, masterpieces by Praxiteles, Lysippus and Phidias.

The Greek colonisers were equally deft at ceramics, adorning vases with painted scenes from daily life, mythology and Greek theatre. Some of the most vivid examples are the 4th-century-BC phylax vases, with larger-than-life characters and costumes that depict scenes from phylax plays, a type of ancient southern-Italian farce.

In art, as in so many other realms, the Romans looked to the Greeks for examples of best practice, and sculpture, architecture and painting flourished during their reign. Yet the art produced in Rome was different in many ways from the Greek art that influenced it. Essentially secular, it focused less on harmony and balance and more on accurate representation, mainly in the form of sculptural portraits. Innumerable versions of Pompey, Titus and Augustus all show a similar visage, proving that the artists were seeking verisimilitude in their representations, and not just glorification.

Wealthy Roman citizens also dabbled in the arts, building palatial villas and adorning them with statues looted from the Greek world or copied from Hellenic originals. You'll find many fine examples of both in Syracuse's Museo Archeologico Paolo Orsi, including the celebrated *Venere Anadiomene,* a 1st century Roman copy depicting a voluptuous goddess of love. Status-conscious Romans didn't stop there, lavishing floors with mosaics and walls with vivid frescoes. Outstanding mosaics live on at Sicily's Villa Romana del Casale, Pompeii, Herculaneum and Naples' Museo Archeologico Nazionale. Pompeii itself claims the world's largest ancient wall fresco, hidden inside the Villa dei Misteri.

EH Gombrich's seminal work *The Story of Art,* first published in 1950, gives a wonderful overview of the history of Italian art.

The Glitter of Byzantine

In 330, Emperor Constantine, a convert to Christianity, made the ancient city of Byzantium his capital and renamed it Constantinople. The city became the great cultural and artistic centre of Christianity and it remained so up to the time of the Renaissance, though its influence on the art of that period was never as fundamental as the art of ancient Rome.

Artistically, the Byzantine period was notable for its extraordinary mosaic work and – to a lesser extent – its painting. Its art was influenced by the decoration of the Roman catacombs and the early Christian churches, as well as by the Oriental Greek style, with its love of rich decoration and luminous colour.

As a major transit point on the route between Constantinople and Rome, Puglia and Basilicata were heavily exposed to Byzantine's Eastern aesthetics. Indeed, the art that most encapsulates these regions are the 10th- and 11th-century Byzantine frescoes, hidden away in locked chapels dotted across the territory. There is an incredible concentration in Matera, Basilicata, the most fantastic of which is the monastic complex of Chiesa di Madonna delle Virtù & Chiesa di San Nicola del Greci. In Puglia, the town of Mottola is home to the Cripta di San Nicola (known as the Sistine Chapel of the south), while in Brindisi, the Chiesa di Santa Maria del Casale serves up a dazzling array of exotic tiling.

In Sicily, Byzantine, Norman and Saracen influences fused to create a distinct regional style showcased in the mosaic-encrusted splendour of Palermo's Cappella Palatina inside the Palazzo dei Normanni, not to mention the cathedrals of Monreale and Cefalù.

ART & ARCHITECTURE ART

Giotto & the 'Rebirth' of Italian Art

Italy's Byzantine painters were apt with light and shade, but it would take Florentine painter Giotto di Bondone (c 1266-1337) to break the spell of conservatism and venture into a new world of naturalism. Best known for his frescoes in Padua and Assisi, faded fragments of his work also survive in Naples' Castel Nuovo and Basilica di Santa Chiara.

Giotto and the painters of the Sienese School introduced many innovations in art: the exploration of perspective and proportion, a new interest in realistic portraiture, and the beginnings of a new tradition of land-

---

STARS OF NEAPOLITAN BAROQUE

Michelangelo Merisi da Caravaggio (1573–1610) Bridging Mannerism and the baroque, Caravaggio injected raw emotion and foreboding shadow into his art. Two of his greatest works are *La sette opere di Misericordia* (Seven Acts of Mercy; 1607) and *Flagellazione* (Flagellation; 1607-10), hanging in Naples' Pio Monte della Misericordia and Museo Nazionale di Capodimonte respectively.

Giuseppe de Ribera (1591–1652) Though Spanish born, most of this bullying painter's finest work was created in southern Italy, including his dramatic *St Jerome* (1626) and *Apollo and Marsyas* (c 1637), both in the Museo Nazionale di Capodimonte.

Cosimo Fanzago (1591–1678) This revered sculptor, decorator and architect cut marble into the most whimsical forms, producing luscious, inlaid spectacles. Naples' Certosa di San Martino aside, his beautiful high altar in Naples' Chiesa di San Domenico Maggiore is not to be missed.

Mattia Preti (1613–99) Dubbed 'Il Cavaliere Calabrese' (The Calabrian Knight), Preti infused thunderous, apocalyptic scenes with a deep, affecting humanity. Seek out his *Feast of Absalom* (c 1670) in the Museo Nazionale di Capodimonte.

Luca Giordano (1632–1705) Affectionately nicknamed Luca *fa presto* (Luca does it quickly) for his dexterous ways with a brush. Fabulous frescoes aside, his canvassed creations include *Apollo and Marsyas* (c 1660) in the Museo Nazionale di Capodimonte.

Francesco Solimena (1657–1747) Lavish and grandiose compositions define this icon's work. One of his best is the operatic fresco *Expulsion of Eliodoro from the Temple* (1725) in Naples' Chiesa del Gesù Nuovo.

Giuseppe Sanmartino (1720–93) Arguably the finest sculptor of his time, Sanmartino's ability to breathe life into his creations won him a legion of fans, including the bizarre alchemist prince, Raimondo di Sangro. Don't miss his *Cristo Velato* (Veiled Christ) in di Sangro's Cappella Sansevero, Naples.

scape painting. The influx of eastern scholars fleeing Constantinople in the wake of its fall to the Ottoman Turkish Muslims in 1453 prompted a renewed interest in classical learning and humanist philosophy. Coupled with the increasingly ambitious, competitive nature of northern Italy's city states, these developments would culminate in the Renaissance.

Centred in Florence in the 15th century, and Rome and Venice in the 16th century, the Renaissance was slower to catch on in southern Italy, which was caught up in the power struggles between its French and Spanish rulers. One of the south's few Renaissance masters was Antonello da Messina (1430–79), whose luminous works include *The Virgin Annunciate* (1474–77) in Palermo's Galleria Regionale della Sicilia and *The Annunciation* (1474) in Syracuse's Galleria Regionale di Palazzo Bellomo.

Bad Boys & the Baroque

With the advent of the baroque, it was the south's time to shine. Under 17th-century Spanish rule, Naples was transformed into Europe's largest city. Swelling crowds and counter-Reformation fervour sparked a building boom, with taller-than-ever *palazzi* (mansions) and showcase churches sprouting up across the city. Ready to adorn these new landmarks was a brash, arrogant and fiery league of artists, ditching Renaissance restraint for baroque exuberance.

The main influence on 17th-century Neapolitan art was the Milanese-born artist Caravaggio (1573–1610). A controversial character, he escaped to Naples in 1606 after killing a man in Rome; although he only stayed for a year, his impact on the city's artistic scene was huge. Caravaggio's dramatic depiction of light and shade, his supreme draughtsmanship and his naturalist style had an electrifying effect on the city's younger artists. One look at his *Flagellazione* (Flagellation; 1607–10) in Naples' Museo Nazionale di Capodimonte or his *La sette opere di Misericordia* (Seven Acts of Mercy; c 1607) in the Pio Monte della Misericordia and you'll understand why.

One of Caravaggio's greatest fans was artist Giuseppe de Ribera (1591–1652), whose combination of shadow, colour and gloomy naturalism is

In *M: The Man Who Became Caravaggio*, Peter Robb gives a passionate personal assessment of the artist's paintings and a colourful account of Caravaggio's life, arguing he was murdered for having sex with the pageboy of a high-ranking Maltese aristocrat.

CONTEMPORARY MOVEMENTS

Of the many movements that shaped Italy's 20th-century art scene, few match the radical innovation of Arte Povera (Poor Art). Emerging from the economic and political instability of the 1960s, its artists aimed to blur the boundary between art and life. Using everyday materials and mediums ranging from painting and photography to installations, they created works that put the viewer at the centre, triggering personal memories and associations. The movement would ultimately pave the way for contemporary installation art. Its leading practitioners included Mario Merz (1925–2003), Luciano Fabro (1936–2007) and Giovanni Anselmo (b 1934), the latter's sculptures inspired by the geological forces of Stromboli. Another icon of the scene is the Greek-born Jannis Kounellis (b 1936), whose brooding installations often focus on the disintegration of culture in the modern world. Naples' MADRE contains a fine collection of Kounellis' creations, as well as other Arte Povera works. Among the wittiest is Michelangelo Pistoletti's *Venere degli stracci* (Venus of the Rags), in which a Greek goddess contemplates a pile of modern hand-me-downs.

Reacting against Arte Povera's conceptual tendencies was the 'Transavanguardia' movement of the late 1970s and 1980s, which refocussed attention on painting and sculpture in a traditional (primarily figurative) sense. Among its leading artists are Mimmo Paladino (b 1948) and Francesco Clemente (b 1952). Both of these Campanian artists are represented in Naples' Novecento a Napoli, a museum dedicated to 20th-century southern Italian art.

brilliantly executed in his masterpiece, *Pietà* (1637), which is hanging in Naples' Certosa di San Martino. Merciless to the extreme, Lo Spagnoletto (The Little Spaniard, as Ribera was known) reputedly won a commission for the Cappella del Tesoro in Naples' Duomo by poisoning his rival Domenichino (1581–1641), as well as wounding the assistant of a second competitor, Guido Reni (1575–1642). The Duomo was adorned with the frescoes of a number of rising stars, among them Giovanni Lanfranco (1582–1647) and Luca Giordano (1632–1705).

A fledgling apprentice to Ribera, Naples-born Giordano found great inspiration in the brushstrokes of Mattia Preti (1613–99). By the second half of the 17th century, Giordano had become the single most important artist in Naples. His finest fresco, the *Triumph of Judith,* decorates the treasury ceiling of the Certosa di San Martino's church.

Architecture

Ancient Legacies

One word describes the buildings of ancient southern Italy: monumental. The Greeks invented the architectural orders (Doric, Ionic and Corinthian) and used them to great effect in once-mighty cities like Akragas (modern-day Agrigento), Catania and Syracuse. More than two millennia later, the soaring temples of Segesta, Selinunte, the Valley of the Temples and Paestum confirm not only the ancient Greeks' power, but also their penchant for harmonious proportion. This skill is also underscored in their sweeping theatres, the finest of which still stand in Syracuse, Taormina and Segesta.

Having learned a few valuable lessons from the Greeks, the Romans refined architecture to such a degree that their building techniques, designs and mastery of harmonious proportion underpin most of the world's architecture and urban design to this day. In Brindisi, a brilliant white column marks one end of the Via Appia – the ancient cross-country road connecting Rome to the east coast. In Pozzuoli, they erected the Anfiteatro Flavio, the empire's third-largest arena and the very spot where Roman authorities had planned to feed San Gennaro to hungry bears. (In the end, they opted to behead the Christian at the nearby Solfatara Crater.)

Medieval Fusion

Following on from Byzantine architecture and its mosaic-encrusted churches was Romanesque, a style that found four regional forms in Italy: Lombard, Pisan, Florentine and Sicilian Norman. All displayed an emphasis on width and the horizontal lines of a building rather than height, and featured church groupings with *campaniles* (bell towers) and baptisteries that were separate to the church. Surfacing in the 11th century, the Sicilian Norman style encompassed an exotic mix of Norman, Saracen and Byzantine influences, from marble columns to Islamic-inspired pointed arches to glass tesserae detailing. Clearly visible in the two-toned masonry and 13th-century bell tower of Amalfi's Cattedrale di Sant'Andrea, one of the greatest examples of the form is the cathedral of Monreale, just outside Palermo.

With the 12th and 13th centuries came the Gothic aesthetic, though the Italians didn't embrace this style as enthusiastically as the French, Germans and Spanish did. Its flying buttresses, grotesque gargoyles and over-the-top decorations were just too far from the classical ideal that was (and still is) bred in Italian bones. This said, the Gothic style did leave its mark in southern Italy, albeit in the muted version encapsulated by Naples' Chiesa di San Lorenzo Maggiore and Chiesa di San Domenico Maggiore, Palermo's Palazzo Bellomo and Lucera's cathedral. The south's

One of the few well-known female artists of the Italian Renaissance was Artemisia Gentileschi (1593–1652), whose style is reminiscent of Caravaggio's. One of her most famous paintings, *Judith and Holofernes,* is in Naples' Museo Nazionale di Capodimonte.

ART & ARCHITECTURE ARCHITECTURE

most striking Gothic icon, however, is Puglia's Castel del Monte; its Italianate windows, Islamic floor mosaics and Roman triumphal entrance attests to the south's flair for absorbing foreign influence.

Baroque: the Golden Age

Just as Renaissance restraint redefined Italy's north, the wild theatricality of 17th- and 18th-century baroque revamped the south. Encouraging the makeover was the Catholic Church, for whom baroque's awe-inducing qualities were the perfect weapon against the Reformation and its less-is-more philosophy. Deploying swirls of frescoes, gilt and polychromatic marble, churches like Naples' Chiesa del Gesù Nuovo and Chiesa di San Gregorio Armeno turned Catholicism into a no-holds-barred extravaganza.

Inlaid marble would become a dominant special effect, adorning everything from tombs and altars, to floors and entire chapel walls. The form's undisputed master was Cosimo Fanzago (1591–1678), an occasionally violent sculptor whose masterpieces include Naples' Certosa di San Martino's church, a mesmerising kaleidoscope of colours, patterns and precision.

In Puglia's Salento region, *barocco leccese* (Lecce baroque) saw the style reach extraordinary new heights. Local limestone was carved into lavish decorative detail around porticoes, windows, balconies and loggias, themselves crowned with human and zoomorphic figures as well as a riot of gargoyles, flora, fruit, columns and cornices. The leading exponents of the style were Gabriele Riccardi (1524–82) and Francesco Antonio Zimbalo (1567–1631), but it was Francesco's grandson Giuseppe Zimbalo (1620–1710), nicknamed Lo Zingarello (The Little Gypsy), who was its most exuberant disciple. Among his greatest designs is the upper facade of Lecce's Basilica di Santa Croce.

It would take an earthquake in 1632 to seal Sicily's baroque legacy. Faced with destruction, ambitious architects set to work rebuilding the towns and cities of the island's southeast, among them Noto, Modica and Ragusa. Grid-patterned streets were laid and spacious piazzas were lined with confident, curvaceous buildings. The result was a highly idiosyncratic *barocco siciliano* (Sicilian baroque), best known for its cheeky stone *putti* (cherubs), wrought-iron balustrades and grand external staircases. Equally unique was the use of dramatic, centrally placed church belfries, often shooting straight above the central pediment. Two of the finest examples are Ragusa's Cattedrale di San Giorgio and Modica's Chiesa di San Giorgio, both designed by the prolific Rosario Gagliardi (1698–1762).

Sicily's most celebrated baroque architect, however, was Giovanni Battista Vaccarini (1702–68). Trained in Rome, Vaccarini dedicated three decade of his life to rebuilding earthquake-stricken Catania, using the region's volcanic black rock to dramatic effect in the Piazza del Duomo. His reputation led him to join forces with Neapolitan starchitect Luigi Vanvitelli (1700–73) in the creation of Italy's epic baroque epilogue, the Palazzo Reale in Caserta, Campania.

For a Blast of Baroque

··························

Lecce, Puglia (p124)

··························

Noto, Sicily (p207)

··························

Catania, Sicily (p192)

··························

Naples, Campania (p39)

Survival Guide

Directory A–Z

Accommodation

Accommodation in Italy's south is ever improving and increasingly varied. Hotels and *pensioni* (guesthouses) make up the bulk of the offerings, covering everything from cheap sleeps near the train station to trendy art hotels and five-star retreats with ocean views. Youth hostels, camping grounds and an ever-increasing number of B&Bs are a boon for the euro-economisers, while *agriturismi* (farm stays) and *masserie* (southern Italian farms or estates) allow you to live out your bucolic Italian fantasies. Capturing the imagination still more are the options to spend the night in everything from castles to convents and monasteries.

Where applicable, our accommodation reviews list minimum to maximum high-season rates. Where indicated, half-board means breakfast and either lunch or dinner; full board is breakfast, lunch and dinner.

Some hotels, in particular the lower-end places, barely alter their prices throughout the year. In low season there's no harm in bargaining for a discount, especially if you intend to stay for several days.

Hotels usually require that reservations be confirmed with a credit-card number. No-shows will be docked a night's accommodation.

The high season is during July and August, though prices peak again around Easter and Christmas. It's essential to book in advance during these periods. Conversely, prices drop between 30% and 50% in low season. In the winter months (November to Easter) many places, particularly on the coast, completely shut down. In the cities and larger towns accommodation tends to remain open all year. The relative lack of visitors in these down periods means you should have little trouble getting a room in those places that do stay open.

Agriturismi, Masserie & B&Bs

An *agriturismo* (*agriturismi* in the plural) is accommodation on a working farm, where you'll usually be able to sample the produce. Traditionally families simply rented out rooms in their farmhouses; it's still possible to find this type of lodging, although many *agriturismi* have now evolved into sophisticated accommodation.

There are several Italian guidebook directories devoted solely to *agriturismi*, or try www.agriturismo.it or www.agriturismo.net (also good for self-catering apartments and villas).

Unique to southern Italy, *masserie* are large farms or estates, usually built around a fortified watchtower, with plenty of surrounding accommodation to house workers and livestock. Many have been converted into luxurious hotels, *agriturismi*, or holiday apartments. A *masseria* isn't necessarily old: sometimes new buildings built around similar principles are called *masserie*.

B&Bs are a burgeoning sector of the southern accommodation market and can be found in both urban and rural settings. Options include everything from restored farmhouses, city *palazzi* and seaside bungalows to rooms in family houses. Tariffs per person cover a wide range, from about €30 to €100. For more information, contact **Bed & Breakfast Italia** (www.bbitalia.it).

Camping

Italians go camping with gusto and most facilities in Campania, Puglia, Calabria and Sicily (less so in Basilicata, where camping options are few and far between) include swimming pools, restaurants and supermarkets. With hotel prices shooting up in July and August, camping grounds can be a great option, especially since many have enviable seaside locations.

Charges often vary according to the season, peaking in July and August, when accommodation should be booked well in advance. Typical high-season prices range from €10 to €20 per adult, free to €12 for children and from €5 to €25 for a site.

Many camping grounds offer the alternative of bungalows or even simple, self-contained flats. In high season, some only offer deals for stays of a week or longer.

Most camping grounds operate only in high season, which is roughly April to October (in many cases June to September only).

Lists of camping grounds are available from local tourist offices or online – try www.campeggi.com, www.camping.it or www.italcamping.it.

Major bookshops also sell the annual *Campeggi e Villaggi turistici* (Camping and Holiday Villages, €14.90), a list of Italian, Corsican, French, Spanish and Croatian camp grounds published by Touring Club Italiano (TCI).

BOOK YOUR STAY ONLINE

For more accommodation reviews by Lonely Planet authors, check out http://lonelyplanet.com/hotels/. You'll find independent reviews, as well as recommendations on the best places to stay. Best of all, you can book online.

Convents & Monasteries

Some convents and monasteries let out cells or rooms as a modest revenue-making exercise and happily take in tourists, while others only take in pilgrims or people on a spiritual retreat. Many impose a fairly early curfew, but prices tend to be quite reasonable.

A useful, if slightly ageing, publication is Eileen Barish's *The Guide to Lodging in Italy's Monasteries*. A more recent book on the same subject is Charles M Shelton's *Beds and Blessings in Italy: A Guide to Religious Hospitality*.

MonasteryStays.com (www.monasterystays.com) A well-organised online booking centre for monastery and convent stays.

In Italy Online (www.initaly.com/agri/convents.htm) Well worth a look for monastery and convent accommodations in Abruzzo, Emilia-Romagna, Lazio, Liguria, Lombardy, Puglia, Sardinia, Sicily, Tuscany, Umbria and the Veneto. You pay US$6 to access the online newsletter with addresses.

Chiesa di Santa Susana (www.santasusanna.org/comingToRome/convents.html) This American Catholic church in Rome has a list of convent and monastery accommodation options around the country on its website. Note that some places are just residential accommodation run by religious orders and not necessarily big on monastic atmosphere. The church doesn't handle bookings; to request a spot, you'll need to contact each individual institution directly.

Hostels

Ostelli per la gioventù (youth hostels) are run by the **Associazione Italiana Alberghi per la Gioventù** (AIG; www.aighostels.com), affiliated with **Hostelling International** (HI; www.hihostels.com). A valid HI card is required in all associated youth hostels in Italy. You can buy one in your home country or direct at many hostels.

A full list of Italian hostels, with details of prices, locations and so on, is available online or from hostels throughout the country. Nightly rates in basic dorms vary from around €16 to €30, which usually includes

---

OFFBEAT ACCOMMODATION

Looking for something out of the ordinary? Southern Italy offers a number of sleeping options that you won't find anywhere else in the world.

➡ In Naples, spend a regal night or two in the aristocratic *palazzo* of a powerful Bourbon bishop. Now the **Decumani Hotel de Charme** (☑081 551 81 88; www.decumani.it; Via San Giovanni Maggiore Pignatelli 15; s €99-124, d €99-164; ❄ @ ☎; ☐R2 to Via Mezzocannone), it comes complete with a sumptuous baroque salon.

➡ Down near Italy's heel, rent a *trullo*, one of the characteristic whitewashed conical houses of southern Puglia (p103).

➡ On the island of Pantelleria (p220), halfway between Sicily and Africa, sleep in a *dammuso* (traditional house with thick, whitewashed walls and a shallow cupola).

a buffet breakfast. You can often get lunch or dinner for an extra €10 or so. Many hostels also offer singles/doubles (for around €30/50) and family rooms.

A growing contingent of independent hostels offer some great alternatives to HI hostels. Many are barely distinguishable from budget hotels, with some offering sleek design and in-house perks like trendy bars and live music. One of many hostel websites is www.hostelworld.com.

Hotels & Pensioni

There is often very little difference between a *pensione* (guesthouse) and an *albergo* (hotel). However, a *pensione* will generally be of one- to three-star quality and is traditionally a family-run operation, while an *albergo* can sometimes be awarded up to five stars. *Locande* (inns) previously fell into much the same category as *pensioni*, but the term has become trendy in some parts and reveals little about the quality of a place. *Affittacamere* are rooms for rent in private houses. They are generally simple affairs.

Quality can vary enormously and the official star system gives only limited clues. One-star hotels and *pensioni* tend to be basic and usually do not offer private bathrooms. Two-star places are similar but rooms will generally have a private bathroom. At three-star establishments you can usually assume reasonable standards. Four- and five-star hotels offer facilities such as room service, laundry and dry-cleaning.

Prices are highest in major tourist destinations. A *camera singola* (single room) costs from around €30. A *camera doppia* (twin beds) or *camera matrimoniale* (double room with a double bed) will cost from around €50.

Tourist offices usually have booklets with local accommodation listings. Many hotels are also signing up with (steadily proliferating) online accommodation-booking services. You could start your search at any of the following:

Alberghi in Italia (www.alberghi-in-italia.it)

All Hotels in Italy (www.hotelsitalyonline.com)

Hotels web.it (www.hotelsweb.it)

In Italia (www.initalia.it)

Travel to Italy (www.travel-to-italy.com)

Customs Regulations

There are no duty-free sales within the EU. Visitors coming into Italy from non-EU countries can import the following items duty free:

Spirits	1L (or 2L wine)
Perfume	50g
Eau de Toilette	250ml
Cigarettes	200
Other Goods	up to €175

Anything over these limits must be declared on arrival and the appropriate duty paid. On leaving the EU, non-EU citizens can reclaim any Value Added Tax (VAT) on expensive purchases.

Discount Cards

Many sights offer free admission to people under 18 and over 65 years; visitors aged between 18 and 25 also often get a discount, though this often only apply to EU citizens. In Naples and Campania, consider buying a **Campania Artecard** (www.campaniaartecard.it), which offers free public transport and free or reduced admission to many museums and archaeological sites.

YOUTH, STUDENT & TEACHER CARDS

The European Youth Card offers thousands of discounts on Italian hotels, museums, restaurants, shops and clubs, while a student, teacher or youth travel card can save you money on flights to Italy. All cards listed below are available from the **Centro Turistico Studentesco e Giovanile** (CTS; www.cts.it), a youth travel agency with branches throughout southern Italy. The bottom three cards listed below are available worldwide from student unions, hostelling organisations and youth travel agencies such as STA Travel (www.statravel.com).

CARD	WEBSITE	COST	ELIGIBILITY
European Youth Card (Carta Giovani)	www.europeanyouthcard.org	€11	under 30 years
International Student Identity Card (ISIC)	www.isic.org	US$25, UK£9, €13	full-time student
International Teacher Identity Card (ITIC)	www.isic.org	US$25, UK£9, €18	full-time teacher
International Youth Travel Card (IYTC)	www.isic.org	US$25, UK£9, €13	under 26 years

Electricity

Electricity in Italy conforms to the European standard of 220V to 230V. Wall outlets typically accommodate plugs with two or three round pins.

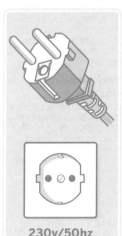

230v/50hz

230v/50hz

Embassies & Consulates

Most countries have an embassy in Rome, where passport enquiries should

be addressed. South of the capital, you'll find some honorary consulates in several major cities.

Australian Embassy (☑06 85 27 21; www.italy.embassy.gov. au; Via Antonio Bosio 5, Rome)

Canadian Embassy (☑06 85444 2911; www.canadainter national.gc.ca/italy-italie; Via Zara 30, Rome)

Canadian Honorary Consulate (☑081 40 13 38; Via Carducci 29, Naples)

French Embassy (☑06 68 60 11; www.ambafrance-it.org; Piazza Farnese 67, Rome)

French Consulate (☑081 598 07 11; www.ambafrance-it.org; Via Francesco Crispi 86, Naples)

German Embassy (☑06 49 21 31; www.rom.diplo.de; Via San Martino della Battaglia 4, Rome)

German Consulate (☑081 248 85 11; www.neapel.diplo.de; Via Francesco Crispi 69, Naples)

German Honorary Consulate (☑080 524 40 59; Via Michele Garruba 125, Bari)

German Honorary Consulate (☑091 982 08 08; Via Principe di Villafranca, 33, Palermo)

Irish Embassy (☑06 585 23 81; www.ambasciata-irlanda.it; Villa Spada, Via Giacomo Medici 1, Rome)

Japanese Embassy (☑06 48 79 91; www.it.emb-japan.go.jp; Via Quintino Sella 60, Rome)

Netherlands Embassy (☑06 3228 6001; www.olanda. it; Via Michele Mercati 8, Rome)

Netherlands Consulate (☑081 551 30 03; www.olanda. it; Via A Depretis 114 , Naples)

Netherlands Consulate (☑080 556 92 22; www.olanda. it; Viale Ennio Quinto 2-I, Bari)

Netherlands Consulate (☑091 630 60 05; www.olanda. it; Via Trapani 1d , Palermo)

New Zealand Embassy (☑06 853 75 01; www.nz embassy.com/italy; Via Clitunno 44, Rome)

Swiss Embassy (☑06 80 95 71; www.eda.admin.ch/roma; Via Barnaba Oriani 61, Rome)

Swiss Consulate (☑080 524 96 97; Piazza Luigi di Savoia Duca degli Abruzzi 41a, Bari)

UK Embassy (☑06 4220 0001; www. ukinitaly.fco.gov.uk; Via XX Settembre 80a, Rome)

UK Consulate (☑081 423 89 11; Via dei Mille 40, Naples)

UK Consulate (☑080 554 36 68; www.ukinitaly.fco.gov.uk; Via Dalmazia 127, Bari)

UK Consulate (☑091 32 64 12; www.ukinitaly.fco.gov.uk; Via Cavour 117, Palermo)

US Embassy (☑06 4 67 41; www.italy.usembassy.gov; Via Vittorio Veneto 121, Rome)

US Consulate (☑081 583 81 11; www.italy.usembassy. gov; Piazza della Repubblica, Naples)

US Consulate (☑091 30 58 57; www.italy.usembassy.gov; Via Vaccarini 1, Palermo)

Food

For information about eating in southern Italy, see Eat & Drink Like a Local (p28) and The Southern Table (p248).

EATING PRICE RANGES

In restaurant reviews, 'meals' refers to two courses, a glass of house wine, and *coperto* (cover charge) for one person. Reviews are listed according to three budget categories as follows:

€ less than €25

€€ €25–€45

€€€ more than €45

Gay & Lesbian Travellers

Although homosexuality is legal in Italy, attitudes in the south remain largely conservative and overt displays of affection by homosexual couples could attract consternation and unpleasant responses.

You'll find gay scenes in Naples, Catania and Taormina (the latter mostly in the summer), and to a lesser extent in Palermo and Bari.

Resources include:

Arcigay (www.arcigay.it) Bologna-based national organisation for the LGBTI community.

Arcigay Napoli (www.arcigaynapoli.org) Website for Naples' main LGBTI organisation, listing special events as well as gay and gay-friendly venues in town.

Gay.it (www.gay.it) Website featuring LGBTI news, feature articles and gossip.

Gay Friendly Italy.com (www.gayfriendlyitaly.com) English-language site produced by Gay.it, featuring information on everything from hotels and events to LGBTI politics and rights.

Pride (www.prideonline.it) National monthly magazine of art, music, politics and gay culture.

Health

Recommended Vaccinations

No vaccinations are required to travel to Italy. The World Health Organization (WHO), however, recommends that all travellers should be covered for diphtheria, tetanus, measles, mumps, rubella and polio, as well as hepatitis B.

Health Insurance

If you're an EU citizen (or from Switzerland, Norway or Iceland), a European Health Insurance Card (EHIC) covers you for most medical care in public hospitals free of charge, but not for emergency repatriation home or non-emergencies. The card is available from health centres and, depending on your country, online. For more information, see http://ec.europa.eu/social/.

Citizens from other countries should find out if there is a reciprocal arrangement for free medical care between their country and Italy (Australia, for instance, has such an agreement; carry your Medicare card).

If you do need health insurance, make sure you get a policy that covers you for the worst possible scenario, such as an accident requiring an emergency flight home. Find out in advance if your insurance plan will make payments directly to providers or reimburse you later for overseas health expenditures.

Availability of Health Care

Good health care is readily available throughout southern Italy, although public hospitals tend to be less impressive the further south you travel. Pharmacists can give you valuable advice and sell over-the-counter medication for minor illnesses. They can also advise you when more specialised help is required and point you in the right direction. In major cities you are likely to find English-speaking doctors or a translator service available.

Pharmacies generally keep the same hours as other shops, closing in the evenings and on Sundays. However, a handful remain open on a rotation basis (*farmacie di turno*) for emergency purposes. These are usually listed in newspapers. Closed pharmacies display a list of the nearest ones open.

If you need an ambulance anywhere in Italy, call ☏118. For emergency treatment, head straight to the *pronto soccorso* (casualty) section of a public hospital, where you can also get emergency dental treatment.

Environmental Hazards

Italian beaches are occasionally inundated with jellyfish. Their stings are painful, but not dangerous. Dousing them in vinegar will deactivate any stingers that have not fired. Calamine lotion, antihistamines and analgesics may reduce the reaction and relieve pain.

Italy's only dangerous snake, the viper, is found throughout Puglia and Basilicata. To minimise the possibility of being bitten, always wear boots, socks and long trousers when walking through undergrowth where snakes may be present. Don't put your hands into holes and crevices, and be careful when collecting firewood.

Viper bites do not cause instantaneous death and an antivenom is widely available in pharmacies. Keep the victim calm and still, wrap the bitten limb tightly, as you would for a sprained ankle, and attach a splint to immobilise it.

Always check all over your body if you have been walking through a potentially

---

TRAVEL HEALTH WEBSITES

It's always a good idea to consult your government's travel health website before departure.

Australia www.smartraveller.gov.au

Canada travel.gc.ca/travelling/health-safety

UK www.gov.uk/foreign-travel-advice

USA travel.state.gov

tick-infested area as ticks can cause skin infections and other more serious diseases such as Lyme disease and tick-borne encephalitis.

If a tick is found attached, press down around the tick's head with tweezers, grab the head and gently pull upwards. Avoid pulling the rear of the body as this may squeeze the tick's gut contents through the attached mouth into the skin, increasing the risk of infection and disease.

Lyme disease begins with the spreading of a rash at the site of the bite, accompanied by fever, headache, extreme fatigue, aching joints and muscles, and severe neck stiffness. If untreated, symptoms usually disappear, but disorders of the nervous system, heart and joints can develop later. Treatment works best early in the illness: medical help should be sought. Symptoms of tick-borne encephalitis include blotches around the bite, which is sometimes pale in the middle, and headaches, stiffness and other flu-like symptoms (as well as extreme tiredness) appearing a week or two after the bite. Again, medical help must be sought.

Leishmaniasis is a group of parasitic diseases transmitted by sandflies and found in coastal parts of Puglia. Cutaneous leishmaniasis affects the skin and causes ulceration and disfigurement; visceral leishmaniasis affects the internal organs. Avoiding sandfly bites by covering up and using repellent is the best precaution.

Insurance

A travel-insurance policy to cover theft, loss and medical problems is a good idea. It may also cover you for cancellation or delays to your travel arrangements. Paying for your ticket with a credit card can often provide limited travel accident insurance and you may be able to reclaim the payment if the operator doesn't deliver. Ask your credit-card company what it will cover.

Worldwide travel insurance is available at www.lonelyplanet.com/travel-insurance. You can buy, extend and claim online anytime – even if you're already on the road.

Internet Access

→ Internet access in the south has improved in the past couple of years, with an increasing number of hotels, B&Bs, hostels and even some *agriturismi* now offering free wi-fi. On the downside, public wi-fi hotspots and internet cafes remain thin on the ground and signal strength is variable. You'll still have to pay for access at many top-end hotels (upwards of €10 per day) and at internet cafes (€2 to €6 per hour).

→ Some internet cafes will request identification before allowing you to use their facilities.

Legal Matters

Despite Mafia notoriety, southern Italy is relatively safe and the average tourist will only have a brush with the law if robbed by a bag-snatcher or pickpocket.

Police

If you run into trouble in Italy, you're likely to end up dealing with the *polizia statale* (state police) or the *carabinieri* (military police). The former wear powder blue trousers with a fuchsia stripe and a navy blue jacket, the latter wear black uniforms with a red stripe and drive dark blue cars with a red stripe. The following table outlines Italian police organisations and their jurisdictions.

Polizia statale (state police)	thefts, visa extensions and permits
Carabinieri (military police)	general crime, public order and drug enforcement (often overlapping with the *polizia statale*)
Vigili urbani (local traffic police)	parking tickets, towed cars
Guardia di finanza	tax evasion, drug smuggling
Guardia forestale (aka *corpo forestale*)	environmental protection

Drugs & Alcohol

→ Under Italy's tough drug laws, possession of any controlled substances, including cannabis, can get you into hot water. Those caught in possession of 5g of cannabis can be considered traffickers and prosecuted as such. The same applies to tiny amounts of other drugs. Those caught with amounts below this threshold can be subject to minor penalties.

→ The legal limit for blood-alcohol level is 0.05% and random breath tests do occur.

Your Rights

→ You should be given verbal and written notice of the charges laid against you within 24 hours by the arresting officers.

→ You have no right to a phone call upon arrest.

→ The prosecutor must apply to a magistrate for you to be held in preventive custody awaiting trial (depending on the seriousness of the offence) within 48 hours of arrest.

→ You have the right not to respond to questions without the presence of a lawyer. If the magistrate orders preventive custody, you have the right to then contest this within the following 10 days.

Maps

The city maps in Lonely Planet guides, combined with the good, free local maps available at most Italian tourist offices, will be sufficient for many travellers. For more specialised maps, browse the good selection at the national bookshop chain Feltrinelli, or consult the websites below.

Touring Club Italiano (TCI; www.touringclub.com) Italy's largest map publisher operates shops around Italy and publishes decent 1:500,000 and 1:200,000 maps of Italy (€11.90 and €19.90 respectively), plus a series of 15 regional maps at 1:200,000 (€7.90 each) and an exhaustive series of walking guides with maps, co-published with the Club Alpino Italiano (CAI).

Stanfords (www.stanfords.co.uk) Excellent UK-based shop that stocks many useful maps.

Omni Resources (www.omnimap.com) US-based online retailer with an impressive selection of Italian maps.

Money

Italy's currency is the euro. The seven euro notes come in denominations of €500, €200, €100, €50, €20, €10 and €5. The eight euro coins are in denominations of €2 and €1, and 50, 20, 10, five, two and one cents.

For exchange rates and on-the-road costs, see p14.

Credit & Debit Cards

➡ ATMs (called 'Bancomats') are widely available throughout southern Italy and are the best way to obtain local currency. International credit and debit cards can be used in any ATM displaying the appropriate sign.

➡ Visa and MasterCard are among the most widely recognised cards, but others like Cirrus and Maestro are also well covered. Only some banks give cash advances over the counter, so you're better off using ATMs.

➡ Cards are also good for payment in most hotels, restaurants, shops, supermarkets and tollbooths.

➡ Check any charges with your bank. Most banks now build a fee of around 2.75% into every transaction. In addition, ATM withdrawals can attract a further fee, usually around 1.5%.

➡ If your card is lost, stolen or swallowed by an ATM, you can telephone toll free to have an immediate stop put on its use:

Amex (☏800 928391)
Diners Club (☏800 393939)
MasterCard (☏800 870866)
Visa (☏800 819014)

Moneychangers

You can change money in banks, at the post office or in

OPENING HOURS

➡ We have listed high-season opening hours for each review; hours will generally decrease in the shoulder or low seasons. In coastal resort areas, many hotels and restaurants close during the winter, reopening around Easter.

➡ 'Summer' hours generally refer to the period from April to September or October. 'Winter' hours generally refer to the period from October or November to March.

➡ The opening hours of museums, galleries and archaeological sites vary enormously. As a rule, museums close on Monday, but from June to September many sights open daily.

BUSINESS TYPE	STANDARD HOURS	NOTES
Banks	8.30am–1.30pm & 3.30–4.30pm Mon–Fri	Exchange offices usually keep longer hours
Central post offices	8am–7pm Mon–Fri, 8.30am–noon Sat	
Smaller branch post offices	8am–2pm Mon–Fri, 8.30am–noon Sat	
Restaurants	noon–2.30pm & 7.30–11pm or midnight	Kitchen often shuts an hour earlier; most places close at least one day a week
Cafes	7.30am–8pm	
Bars, pubs & clubs	10pm–4am	May open earlier if they have eateries on the premises; things don't really get started until after midnight
Shops	9am–1pm & 3.30–7.30pm (or 4–8pm) Mon–Sat	In larger cities, department stores and supermarkets may stay open at lunchtime or on Sundays

PRACTICALITIES

⇒ **Weights & Measurements** Use the metric system for weights and measures.

⇒ **Smoking** Banned in closed public spaces, though some locals continue to flaunt the law.

⇒ **Newspapers** If your Italian is up to it, try the following newspapers: *Corriere della Sera,* the country's leading daily, and its southern spin-off *Corriere del Mezzogiorno;* or *La Repubblica,* a centre-left daily with a flow of Mafia conspiracies and Vatican scoops.

⇒ **Radio** Tune into state-owned Italian RAI-1, RAI-2 and RAI-3 (www.rai.it), which broadcast all over Italy and abroad. The regions' plethora of contemporary music stations include Radio Kiss Kiss (www.kisskiss.it).

⇒ **TV** Channels include state-run RAI-1, RAI-2 and RAI-3 (www.rai.it) and the main commercial stations (mostly run by Silvio Berlusconi's Mediaset company): Canale 5 (www.canale5.mediaset.it), Italia 1 (www.italia1.mediaset.it), Rete 4 (www.rete4.mediaset.it) and La 7 (www.la7.it).

a *cambio* (exchange office). Post offices and banks tend to offer the best rates; exchange offices keep longer hours, but watch for high commissions and inferior rates.

Taxes & Refunds

A value-added tax of 22%, known as IVA *(Imposta di Valore Aggiunto),* is slapped onto just about everything in Italy. If you are a non-EU resident and spend more than €155 (€154.94 to be more precise!) on a purchase, you can claim a refund when you leave. The refund only applies to purchases from affiliated retail outlets that display a 'tax free for tourists' (or similar) sign. You have to complete a form at the point of sale, then have it stamped by Italian customs as you leave. At major airports you can then get an immediate cash refund; otherwise, it will be refunded to your credit card. For information, visit **Tax Refund for Tourists** (www.taxrefund.it) or pick up a pamphlet on the scheme from participating stores.

Tipping

Tipping is not generally expected or demanded in Italy as it is in some other countries. This said, a discretionary tip for good service is appreciated in some circumstances. Use the following table as a guide.

PLACE	SUGGESTED TIP
Restaurant	10–15%
Bar	Loose change if at the bar, 10% for table service
Porter, maid, room service	€2
Taxi	Round up to the nearest euro

Post

Poste Italiane (☏80 31 60; www.poste.it), Italy's postal system, is reasonably reliable. *Francobolli* (stamps) are available at post offices and authorised tobacconists (look for the big white-on-black 'T' sign). Since letters often need to be weighed, what you get at the tobacconist for international airmail will occasionally be an approximation of the proper rate. Tobacconists keep regular shop hours.

Postal Rates & Services

The cost of sending a letter by *via aerea* (airmail) depends on its weight, size and where it is being sent. Most people use *posta prioritaria* (priority mail), Italy's most efficient mail service, guaranteed to deliver letters sent to Europe within three days and to the rest of the world within four to nine days. Letters up to 20g cost €0.85 within Europe, €2 to Africa, Asia and North and South America and €2.50 to Australia and New Zealand. Letters weighing 21g to 50g cost €2.60 within Europe, €3.50 to Africa, Asia and the Americas, and €4.50 to Australia and New Zealand.

Public Holidays

Most Italians take their annual holiday in August, with the busiest period occurring around August 15, known locally as Ferragosto. This means that many businesses and shops close for at least a part of that month. It also means that southern Italy's islands and coastal resorts become incredibly lively (and crowded). Settimana Santa (Easter week) is another busy holiday period for Italians.

National public holidays include the following:

New Year's Day (Capodanno) 1 January

Epiphany (Epifania) 6 January

Easter Monday (Pasquetta) March/April

Liberation Day (Giorno della Liberazione) 25 April

Labour Day (Festa del Lavoro) 1 May

Republic Day (Festa della Repubblica) 2 June

Feast of the Assumption (Ferragosto) 15 August

All Saints' Day (Ognissanti) 1 November

Feast of the Immaculate Conception (Immaculata Concezione) 8 December

Christmas Day (Natale) 25 December

Boxing Day (Festa di Santo Stefano) 26 December

Safe Travel

Despite mafia notoriety, southern Italy is not a dangerous place and the biggest threat you will face is from faceless pickpockets and bag-snatchers. The following tips will help ensure a safe and happy stay:

➡ Leave valuables in your hotel room and never leave them in your car.

➡ If carrying a bag or camera, wear the strap across your body and away from the road – moped thieves can swipe a bag and be gone in seconds.

➡ Be vigilant for pickpockets in crowded areas, including at train stations and ferry terminals, on buses and in markets (especially those in Naples, Palermo and Catania).

➡ Never buy electronics, including mobile phones, from market vendors – one common scam sees the boxes filled with bricks.

➡ Always report thefts to the police within 24 hours, and ask for a statement, otherwise your travel insurance company won't pay out.

Telephone

Directory Enquiries

National and international phone numbers can be requested at ☑1254 (or online at 1254.virgilio.it).

Domestic Calls

➡ Italian telephone area codes all begin with ☑0 and consist of up to four digits. The area code is followed by a number of anything from four to eight digits. The area code is an integral part of the telephone number and must always be dialled, even when calling from next door.

➡ Mobile-phone numbers begin with a three-digit prefix such as ☑330.

➡ Toll-free (free-phone) numbers are known as *numeri verdi* and usually start with ☑800.

➡ Nongeographical numbers start with ☑840, 841, 848, 892, 899, 163, 166 or 199.

➡ Some six-digit national rate numbers are also in use (such as those for Alitalia, rail and postal information).

➡ As elsewhere in Europe, Italians choose from a host of providers of phone plans and rates, making it difficult to make generalisations about costs.

International Calls

➡ The cheapest options for calling internationally are free or low-cost computer programs/smartphone apps such as Skype and Viber.

➡ Cut-rate call centres, found in all of the main cities, are also a cheaper option. You simply place your call from a private booth inside the centre and pay for it when you've finished.

➡ International calling cards, sold at newsstands and tobacconists, also offer cheaper call rates. They can be used at public telephones. Dial ☑00 to get out of Italy, then the relevant country and area codes, followed by the telephone number.

➡ To call Italy from abroad, dial the international access number (☑011 in the United States, ☑00 from most other countries), Italy's country code (☑39) and the area code of the location you want, including the leading ☑0.

Mobile Phones

➡ Italy uses GSM 900/1800, compatible with the rest of Europe and Australia but not with North American GSM 1900 or the totally different Japanese system.

➡ Most modern smartphones are multiband, meaning that they are compatible with a variety of international networks. Before bringing your own phone to Italy, however, check with your service provider to make sure it is compatible, and beware of calls being routed internationally (which will make it very expensive for a 'local' call).

➡ Unlocking your phone for use with an Italian SIM card is often the cheapest option, but always check with your home mobile-service provider first to ascertain whether your handset will allow the use of another SIM card.

➡ You can get a temporary or prepaid account from most phone company stores in Italy if you already own a GSM, multiband cellular phone (take your passport). Activating a local prepaid SIM card can cost as little as €10 (sometimes with €10 worth of calls on the card). Pay-as-you-go SIM cards are also readily available at telephone and electronics stores throughout Italy. Alternatively, you can buy or lease an inexpensive Italian phone for the duration of your trip.

➡ You can easily top up your Italian account with recharge cards *(ricariche)*, available from most tobacconists, as well as from some bars, supermarkets and banks.

➡ Of the main mobile phone companies, TIM (Telecom Italia Mobile), Wind and Vodafone have the densest networks of outlets across the country.

Payphones & Phonecards

Telecom Italia is the largest telecommunications organisation in Italy. You'll find Telecom payphones throughout the country, on the streets, in train stations and in Telecom offices. Most payphones only accept *carte/schede telefoniche* (phonecards), although some also accept credit cards. Telecom offers a wide range of prepaid cards for both domestic and international use; for a full list, see www.telecomitalia.it/telefono/carte-telefoniche. You can buy phonecards (most commonly €3 or €5) at post offices, tobacconists and newsstands.

Time

➡ Italy is one hour ahead of GMT. When it is noon in London, it is 1pm in Italy.

➡ Daylight savings time, when clocks are moved forward one hour, starts on the last Sunday in March. Clocks are put back an hour on the last Sunday in October.

➡ Italy operates on a 24-hour clock.

Tourist Information

The quality of tourist offices varies dramatically. One office might have enthusiastic staff, another might be indifferent. Most offices offer a plethora of brochures, maps and leaflets, even if they're uninterested in helping in any other way. Outside major cities and international tourist areas, it's fairly unusual for the staff to speak English.

Four tiers of tourist office exist: local, provincial, regional and national.

Local & Provincial Tourist Offices

Despite their different (and sometimes elaborate) names, provincial and local offices offer similar services and we collectively refer to them with the term 'tourist office'. All deal directly with the public, and most will respond to written and telephone requests for information. Staff can usually provide a city map, lists of hotels and information on the major sights. In larger towns and major tourist areas, staff usually have a working knowledge of at least one other language, generally English but also possibly French and German.

Main offices are generally open Monday to Friday; some also open on weekends, especially in urban areas or during peak summer season. Affiliated information booths (at train stations and airports, for example) may keep slightly different hours.

The main local and provincial tourist office categories are summarised below.

Azienda di Promozione Turistica (APT) This main provincial tourist office offers information on the town and its surrounding province.

Azienda Autonoma di Soggiorno e Turismo (AAST) These local tourist offices in larger towns and cities of the south provide town-specific information only (bus routes, museum opening times, etc).

Pro Loco These local tourist offices in smaller towns and villages offer services similar to AAST.

Regional Tourist Authorities

Regional offices are generally more concerned with planning, budgeting, marketing and promotion than with offering a public information service, so don't expect too much. However, they still maintain some useful websites, as listed below. In some cases you'll need to look for the Tourism or Turismo link within the regional site.

Basilicata (www.aptbasilicata.it)

Calabria (www.turiscalabria.it)

Campania (www.incampania.com)

Puglia (www.viaggiareinpuglia.it)

Sicily (www.regione.sicilia.it/turismo)

Tourist Offices Abroad

The **Italian National Tourist Office** (ENIT; www.enit.it) maintains offices in 23 cities on five continents. Contact information for all offices can be found on the website.

Travellers with Disabilities

Southern Italy is not easygoing for disabled travellers. Cobbled streets, hair-raising traffic, blocked pavements and tiny lifts make life very difficult for wheelchair users, and those with sight or hearing difficulties. The Italian National Tourist Office in your country may be able to provide advice on Italian associations for the disabled and information on what help is available.

Italy's national rail company, Trenitalia, offers a national helpline for disabled passengers at ☏ 199 303 060 (6.45am to 9.30pm daily).

For more information and help, try the following organisations:

Accessible Italy (www.accessibleitaly.com) A San Marino–based company that specialises in holiday services for disabled travellers, ranging from tours to the hiring of adapted transport to romantic Italian weddings. This is the best first port of call.

Cooperative Integrate Onlus (CO.IN; www.coinsociale.it) This Rome-based organisation provides information on the capital (including transport and access) and is happy to share its contacts throughout Italy.

Visas

➡ European citizens whose country is part of the Schengen Treaty may enter Italy with nothing more than a valid identity card or passport.

➡ Residents of 28 non-EU countries – including Australia, Brazil, Canada, Israel, Japan, New Zealand and the USA – do not require visas for tourist visits of up to 90 days (this list varies for those wanting to travel to the UK and Ireland).

➡ All non-EU and non-Schengen nationals entering Italy for more than 90 days, or for any reason other than tourism (such as study or work) may need a specific visa. Visit www.esteri.it/visti/home_eng.asp or contact an Italian consulate for details.

➡ You should also have your passport stamped on entry as, without a stamp, you could encounter problems when trying to obtain a residence permit *(permesso di soggiorno)*. If you enter the EU via another member state, get your passport stamped there.

➡ EU citizens do not require any permits to live or work in Italy but, after three months' residence, they are supposed to register themselves at the municipal registry office where they live and offer proof of work or sufficient funds to support themselves.

➡ Non-EU foreign citizens with five years' continuous legal residence may apply for permanent residence.

Study Visas

Non-EU citizens who want to study at a university or language school in Italy must have a study visa. These can be obtained from your nearest Italian embassy or consulate. You will normally need to show confirmation of your enrolment, proof of payment of fees and adequate funds to support yourself. The visa covers only the period of the enrolment. This type of visa is renewable within Italy but, again, only with confirmation of ongoing enrolment and proof that you are able to support yourself (bank statements are preferred).

Volunteering

Concordia International Volunteer Projects (www.concordiavolunteers.org.uk) Short-term community-based projects covering the environment, archaeology and the arts. You might find yourself working as a volunteer on a restoration project or in a nature reserve.

World Wide Opportunities on Organic Farms (www.wwoof.it) For a membership fee of €25 this organisation provides a list of farms looking for volunteer workers.

Women Travellers

The most common source of discomfort for solo women travellers in southern Italy is harassment. Local men are rarely shy about staring at women and this can be disconcerting, especially if the staring is accompanied by the occasional *'ciao bella'*. In many places, local Lotharios will try it on with exasperating insistence, which can be flattering or a pain. Foreign women are particular objects of male attention. Usually, the best response to undesired advances is to ignore them. If that doesn't work, politely tell your interlocutors you're waiting for your *marito* (husband) or *fidanzato* (boyfriend) and, if necessary, walk away. Avoid becoming aggressive as this may result in an unpleasant confrontation. If all else fails, approach the nearest member of the police.

Watch out for men with wandering hands on crowded buses. Either keep your back to the wall or make a loud fuss if someone starts fondling your behind. A loud *'Che schifo!'* (How disgusting!) will usually do the trick. If a more serious incident occurs, report it to the police, who are then required to press charges.

Transport

GETTING THERE & AWAY

A plethora of airlines link Italy to the rest of the world, and an extensive network of intra-European and domestic flights provide easy access to many southern Italian destinations. Good rail and/or bus services connect most of southern Italy's major cities and towns, while car and passenger ferries operate to ports throughout the Mediterranean.

Flights, tours and rail tickets can be booked online at www.lonelyplanet.com/bookings.

Entering the Country

European Union and Swiss citizens can travel to Italy with their national identity card alone. All other nationalities must have a valid passport and may be required to fill out a landing card (at airports).

By law you should have your passport or ID card with you at all times. You'll need one of these for police registration every time you check into accommodation.

Air

Airlines & Airports

A number of international airlines compete with the country's national carrier, **Alitalia** (www.alitalia.com), amongst them Italy's **Meridiana fly** (✆89 29 28; www.meridiana.it) and **Air One** (✆89 24 44; www.flyairone.com), as well as cut-rate big guns **Ryanair** (www.ryanair.com) and **EasyJet** (www.easyjet.com).

Italy's main intercontinental gateways are Rome's **Leonardo da Vinci Airport** (Fiumicino, FCO; www.adr.it) and Milan's **Malpensa Airport** (✆02 232323; www.sea-aeroportimilano.it). Both are served by non-stop flights from around the world. Ven-

ice's **Marco Polo Airport** (✆041 260 92 60; www.veniceairport.it; Viale Galileo Galilei 30/1, Tessera) is also served by a handful of intercontinental flights.

Most direct flights into southern Italy are domestic or intra-European, so you may need to change at Rome, Milan or Venice if arriving from outside Europe.

Handy airports in southern Italy include the following:

Capodichino Airport, Naples (www.gesac.it) Connections include London (Gatwick), Paris and Berlin. Airlines include Alitalia, British Airways, Lufthansa and easyJet. Seasonal connections to New York (JFK).

Karol Wojtyła Airport, Bari (BRI; www.aeroportidipuglia.it) Flights include London (Gatwick and Stansted), Paris (Charles de Gaulle and Beauvais), Berlin, Cologne, Munich and Prague. Airlines include Alitalia, British Airways, easyJet, Ryanair, Germanwings and Wizzair.

CLIMATE CHANGE & TRAVEL

Every form of transport that relies on carbon-based fuel generates CO_2, the main cause of human-induced climate change. Modern travel is dependent on aeroplanes, which might use less fuel per kilometre per person than most cars but travel much greater distances. The altitude at which aircraft emit gases (including CO_2) and particles also contributes to their climate change impact. Many websites offer 'carbon calculators' that allow people to estimate the carbon emissions generated by their journey and, for those who wish to do so, to offset the impact of the greenhouse gases emitted with contributions to portfolios of climate-friendly initiatives throughout the world. Lonely Planet offsets the carbon footprint of all staff and author travel.

Papoila Airport, Brindisi (BDS; www.aeroportidipuglia. it) Destinations include London (Stansted), Paris (Orly and Beauvais), Geneva, Eindhoven, Zurich, Munich and Barcelona (Girona). Airlines include Alitalia, AirOne, easyJet, Germanwings, Ryanair and Air Berlin.

Lamezia Terme Airport, Cosenza (Sant'Eufemia Lamezia, SUF; ☎0968 41 43 33; www.sacal.it) Destinations include London (Gatwick and Stansted), Zurich and Brussels, with seasonal routes including Berlin, Tel Aviv and Toronto. Airlines include Ryanair, Germanwings and Air Transat.

Falcone-Borsellino Airport, Palermo (PMO; Punta Raisi Airport; www.gesap.it) European connections include London (Gatwick and Stansted), Marseilles, Madrid, Vienna, Munich, Cologne and Amsterdam. There are also inter-continental flights to Tunis and New York (seasonal), and regular domestic flights to the islands of Pantelleria and Lampedusa.

Fontanarossa Airport, Catania (CTA; www.aeroporto. catania.it) Destinations include London (Gatwick), Paris (Charles de Gaulle and Orly), Amsterdam, Copenhagen, Geneva, Zurich, Berlin, Cologne and Barcelona. Airlines include Alitalia, Air Berlin, Lufthansa, easyJet and Germanwings.

Vincenzo Florio Airport, Trapani (TPS; Birgi Airport; www.airgest.it) Ryanair operates direct flights to several European destinations, including London (Luton), Paris (Beauvais), Barcelona (Girona), Malta and Stockholm (Skavsta). Darwin Airline serves Pantelleria.

Tickets

The internet is the easiest way of locating and booking reasonably priced seats.

Full-time students and those aged under 26 may qualify for discounted fares at agencies such as STA Travel (www.statravel.com). Many of these fares require a valid International Student Identity Card (ISIC).

Land

Reaching southern Italy overland involves travelling the entire length of the country, which can either be an enormous drain on your time or, if you have plenty to spare, a wonderful way of seeing Italy. Buses are usually the cheapest option, but services are less frequent and less comfortable than the train.

Border Crossings

The main points of entry to Italy are: the Mont Blanc Tunnel from France at Chamonix; the Grand St Bernard, Gotthard and Lötschberg Base tunnels from Switzerland; and the Brenner Pass from Austria. All are open year-round. Mountain passes are often closed in winter and sometimes even in autumn and spring, making the tunnels a more reliable option. Make sure you have snow chains if driving in winter.

Regular trains on two western lines connect Italy with France (one along the coast and the other from Turin into the French Alps). Trains from Milan head north into Switzerland and on towards the Benelux countries. Further east, two main lines head for the main cities in central and eastern Europe. Those crossing the Brenner Pass go to Innsbruck, Stuttgart and Munich. Those crossing at Tarvisio proceed to Vienna, Salzburg and Prague. The main international train line to Slovenia crosses near Trieste.

Bus

Buses are the cheapest overland option to Italy, but services are less frequent, less comfortable and significantly slower than the train.

Eurolines (www.eurolines. com) A consortium of coach companies with offices throughout Europe. Italy-bound buses head to Milan, Venice, Florence and Rome, from where Italian train and bus services continue south.

Marozzi (www.marozzivt.it) Offers daily services from Rome to Bari, Brindisi, Otranto and Matera.

Miccolis (www.miccolis-spa. it) Runs daily services from Naples to Potenza, Taranto, Brindisi and Lecce.

Marino (www.marinobus.it) Runs daily services from Naples to Bari and Matera.

Liscio (☎0971 5 46 73; www. autolineeliscio.it) Connects Potenza to Rome, Naples, Salerno, Florence, Siena and Perugia. Also connects Rome to Matera.

Lirosi (www.lirosilinee.com) Runs services from Rome to Reggio di Calabria.

SAIS (www.saistrasporti.it) Operates long-haul services to Sicily from Rome and Naples.

Car & Motorcycle
CONTINENTAL EUROPE

➡ When driving in Europe, always carry proof of vehicle ownership and third-party insurance. If driving an EU-registered vehicle, your home country insurance is sufficient. Ask your insurer for a European Accident Statement (EAS) form, which can simplify matters in the event of an accident.

➡ A European breakdown assistance policy is a good investment and can

---

BUS PASSES

Eurolines (www.eurolines-pass.com) offers a low-season bus pass valid for 15/30 days that costs €215/320 (reduced €185/250). This pass allows unlimited travel between 51 European cities, including Milan, Venice, Florence and Rome. Fares increase to €355/465 (reduced €300/385) in midsummer.

be obtained through the **Automobile Club d'Italia** (ACI; from non-Italian phone number ☎800 116800, roadside assistance ☎803 116; www.aci.it).

➡ Every vehicle travelling across an international border should display a nationality plate of its country of registration.

➡ There is an excellent network of autostradas (motorways/freeways) in Italy, represented by a white A followed by a number on a green background. The main north–south link is the Autostrada del Sole, from Milan to Reggio di Calabria (called the A1 from Milan to Rome, the A2 from Rome to Naples and the A3 from Naples to Reggio di Calabria).

➡ There's a toll to use most of Italy's autostradas. You can pay by cash or credit card as you leave the autostrada; to avoid lengthy queues, buy a prepaid Viacard charge card from ACI offices, motorway petrol stations and roadside Autogrill stores, and some banks, in denominations of €25, €50 or €75. These cards are valid throughout Italy. For information on road tolls and passes, or to pay any unpaid toll fees, click onto **Autostrade per Italia** (www.autostrade.it).

➡ Italy's scenic roads are tailor-made for motorcycle touring, and motorcyclists swarm into the country every summer. With a bike you rarely have to book ahead for ferries and can enter restricted-traffic areas in cities. Crash helmets and a motorcycle licence are compulsory. Unless you're touring, it is probably easier to rent a bike once you are at your destination.

UNITED KINGDOM
You can take your car across to France by ferry or via the Channel Tunnel on **Euro-tunnel** (www.eurotunnel.com). The latter runs four crossings (35 minutes) an hour be-

tween Folkestone and Calais in the high season.

For breakdown assistance, both the **AA** (☎in UK 0800 072 3279; www.theaa.com/breakdown-cover) and the **RAC** (☎in UK 0800 015 6000; www.rac.co.uk/euro-breakdown) offer comprehensive cover in Europe.

Train

➡ The comprehensive European Rail Timetable (UK£14.99), updated monthly, is available from **Thomas Cook Publishing** (www.thomascookpublishing.com).

➡ It is always advisable, and sometimes compulsory, to book seats on international trains to and from Italy. Some of the main international services include transport for private cars. Consider taking long journeys overnight as the supplemental fare for a sleeper costs substantially less than Italian hotels.

➡ Within Italy, direct trains run from Milan, Florence and Rome to Naples, Reggio di Calabria and to Messina, Sicily. Trains to Sicily are transported from the mainland by ferry from Villa San Giovanni, just north of Reggio di Calabria. From Messina, services continue on to Palermo, Catania and other provincial Sicilian capitals.

➡ From both Rome and Milan, high-velocity Freccia trains run to Bari (Puglia). Those travelling from Milan will usually need to change trains in Bologna. Trains to Basilicata usually require at least one change along Italy's main north–south route. The handiest place is Salerno, southeast of Naples.

UNITED KINGDOM
The passenger train **Eurostar** (☎08705 186 186; www.eurostar.com) travels between London and Paris, or London and Brussels. Alternatively, you can get a train ticket that

includes crossing the Channel by ferry.

For the latest fare information on journeys to Italy, including the Eurostar, contact the **Rail Europe Travel Centre** (www.raileurope.co.uk) or **International Rail** (www.internationalrail.com).

Sea

Multiple ferry companies connect southern Italy with countries throughout the Mediterranean. Many routes only operate in summer, when ticket prices also rise. During this period, all routes are busy and you need to book several weeks in advance. Fares to Greece are generally more expensive from Bari than those available from Brindisi, although unless you're planning on travelling in the Salento, Bari is the more convenient port of arrival and also has better onward links for bus and train travel. Prices for vehicles vary according to their size.

The helpful website www.traghettionline.com (in Italian) covers all the ferry companies in the Mediterranean. Another useful resource for ferries from Italy to Greece is www.ferries.gr.

International ferry companies serving southern Italy include the following:

Adria Ferries (www.adriaferries.com)

Agoudimos Lines (www.agoudimos-lines.com)

Blue Star Ferries (www.bluestarferries.com)

Grandi Navi Veloci (www.gnv.it)

Grimaldi (www.grimaldi-lines.com)

Jadrolinija (www.jadrolinija.hr)

Montenegro Lines (www.montenegrolines.net)

SNAV (www.snav.it)

Ventouris (www.ventouris.gr)

Virtu Ferries (www.virtuferries.com)

GETTING AROUND

Unless you're a masochist, avoid driving in larger centres such as Naples, Bari, Lecce, Palermo and Catania, where anarchic traffic and parking restrictions will quickly turn your holiday sour. Beyond these urban centres, however, having your own car is the easiest way to get around Italy's south. Buses and trains will get you to most of the main destinations, but they are run by a plethora of private companies, which makes buying tickets and finding bus stops a bit of a pain. Furthermore, the rail network in Salento is still of the narrow-gauge variety, so trains chug along at a snail's pace.

Your own vehicle will give you the most freedom to stray off the main routes and discover out-of-the-way towns and beaches. This is particularly the case in the Parco Nazionale del Cilento e Vallo di Diano in Campania, the Pollino National Park in Basilicata, the Salento in Puglia and throughout much of rural Sicily.

This said, it's also worth considering the downside of driving. Aside from the negative environmental impact, petrol prices are notoriously high, less-travelled roads are often poorly maintained, and popular routes (including Campania's Amalfi Coast, the SS16 connecting Bari and the Salento in Puglia, and Sicily's Ionian and Tyrrhenian coastal routes) can be heavily trafficked during holiday periods and throughout the summer.

Air

The privatised national airline, Alitalia, is the main domestic carrier. Cut-rate competitors within Italy include **Meridiana fly** (☑89 29 28; www.meridiana.it), **Air One** (☑89 24 44; www.flyairone.com), **Ryanair** (www.ryanair.com) and **EasyJet** (www.easyjet.com). A useful search engine for comparing multiple carriers' fares and purchasing low-cost domestic flights is **AZfly** (www.azfly.it).

Airport taxes are factored into the price of your ticket.

Bicycle

Cycling may be more popular in northern Italy, but it can be just as rewarding south of Rome. Cyclo-trekking is particularly popular in the Murgia and the Promontorio del Gargano in Puglia. Cycling is also very popular in the Salentine cities of Lecce, Galatina, Gallipoli and Otranto, with more challenging itineraries in Basilicata's Parco Nazionale del Pollino and on Sicily's hilly terrain.

Avoid hitting the pedal in large cities like Naples and Palermo, where unruly traffic makes cycling a veritable death wish. Cycling along the Amalfi Coast is another bad idea (think blind corners and sheer drops). Bikes are prohibited on the autostradas.

Bikes can be wheeled onto any domestic train displaying the bicycle logo. Simply purchase a separate bicycle ticket, valid for 24 hours (€3.50). Certain international trains, listed on Trenitalia's 'In treno con la bici' page, also allow transport of assembled bicycles for €12. Bikes dismantled and stored in a bag can be taken for free, even on night trains. Most ferries also allow free bicycle passage.

Bikes are available for hire in most towns. Rental costs for a city bike start from around €20 per day; mountain bikes are a bit more.

If you fancy seeing the south on a saddle, the following reputable organisations offer advice and/or guided tours:

Cyclists' Touring Club (www.ctc.org.uk) This UK organisation can help you plan your tour or organise a guided tour. Membership costs £41 (£25 for seniors, £16 for under-18s).

Puglia in Bici (www.pugliainbici.com) A very good organisation offering bike rental and tailor-made itineraries throughout Puglia.

INTERNATIONAL FERRY ROUTES TO/FROM SOUTHERN ITALY

COUNTRY	FROM	TO	COMPANY
Albania	Durrës	Bari	Ventouris, Adria Ferries
Albania	Vlore	Brindisi	Agoudimos Lines
Croatia	Dubrovnik	Bari	Jadrolinija
Greece	Cephalonia, Corfu, Igoumenitsa, Patras, Zante	Brindisi	Agoudimos Lines
Greece	Corfu, Igoumenitsa, Patras	Bari	Blue Star Ferries, Superfast
Malta	Valletta	Pozzallo, Catania	Virtu Ferries
Montenegro	Bar	Bari	Montenegro Lines
Tunisia	Tunis	Palermo	GNV
Tunisia	Tunis	Palermo, Salerno, Trapani	Grimaldi

Gargano Bike Holidays
(www.garganobike.com)
Specialises in cultural and scenic mountain bike tours exploring the Gargano on half-day to weekly trips.

Boat

Domestic *navi* (large ferries) service Campania and Sicily, while *traghetti* (smaller ferries) and *aliscafi* (hydrofoils) service the Bay of Naples, the Amalfi Coast, the Isole Tremiti in Puglia, and the Aeolian Islands in Sicily. Most services are pared back between October and Easter, and some are suspended altogether during this period. Most ferries carry vehicles; hydrofoils do not.

Ferries for Sicily leave from Naples, as well as from Villa San Giovanni and Reggio di Calabria. The main points of arrival in Sicily are Palermo, Catania, Trapani and Messina.

The comprehensive Italian website **Traghettionline** (www.traghettionline.com) includes links to multiple Italian ferry companies, allowing you to compare prices and buy tickets.

On overnight ferries, travellers can book a two- to four-person cabin or a *poltrona*, which is an airline-type armchair. Deck class (which allows you to sit/sleep in lounge areas or on deck) is only available on some ferries.

Bus

Numerous companies provide bus services in southern Italy, from meandering local routes to fast and reliable intercity connections. Buses are usually priced competitively with the trains and are often the only way to get to smaller towns. If your destination is not on a main train line (trains tend to be cheaper on major routes), buses are usually a faster way to get around – this is

especially true for the Salento in Puglia, Basilicata and for inland Calabria and Sicily.

Services are provided by a variety of companies. While these can be frequent on weekdays, they are reduced considerably on Sundays and holidays – runs between smaller towns often fall to one or none. Keep this in mind if you depend on buses as it is easy to get stuck in smaller places, especially at the weekends.

It's usually possible to get bus timetables *(orari)* from local tourist offices and the bus companies' websites. In larger cities most of the intercity bus companies have ticket offices or sell tickets through agencies. In villages and even some good-size towns, tickets are sold in bars – just ask for *biglietti per il pullman* – or on the bus itself.

Advance booking, while not generally required, is a good idea in the high season for overnight or long-haul trips.

Car & Motorcycle

Italy boasts an extensive privatised network of autostradas, represented on road signs by a white 'A' followed by a number on a green background. The main north–south link is the Autostrada del Sole (the 'Motorway of the Sun'), which extends from Milan to Reggio di Calabria (called the A1 from Milan to Rome, the A2 from Rome to Naples, and the A3 from Naples to Reggio di Calabria). The east–west A16 links Naples to Canosa di Puglia. From here, it becomes the A14, shooting southeast to Bari and continuing south to Taranto. From Bari, the SS16 is the main arterial route to the Salento; in summer this can be heavily trafficked.

There are tolls on most motorways, payable by cash or credit card as you exit. For information on traffic

conditions, tolls and driving distances, see www.autostrade.it.

There are several additional road categories, listed below in descending order of importance.

Strade statali (state highways) Represented on maps by 'S' or 'SS'. They vary from toll-free, four-lane highways to two-lane main roads. The latter can be extremely slow, especially in mountainous regions.

Strade regionali (regional highways connecting small villages) Coded SR or R.

Strade provinciali (provincial highways) Coded SP or P.

Strade locali (local roads) Often not even paved or mapped.

Automobile Associations

The **Automobile Club d'Italia** (ACI; ☑from non-Italian phone account 800 116800, roadside assistance 803116; www.aci.it) is a driver's best resource in Italy. For 24-hour roadside emergency service, dial ☑80 31 16 (or ☑800 116800 if calling with a non-Italian mobile phone number). Foreigners do not have to join but instead pay a per-incident fee.

Driving Licence

All driving licences from EU member states are fully recognised throughout Europe. In practice, many non-EU licences (such as Australian, Canadian, New Zealand and US licences) are also accepted by car-hire outfits in Italy. Travellers from other countries will need to obtain an International Driving Permit (IDP) through their national automobile association.

Fuel & Spare Parts

Italy's petrol prices are among the highest in Europe and vary from one service station *(benzinaio, stazione di servizio)* to another. At the time of research, lead-free gasoline *(senza piombo;* 95 octane) was averaging €1.79

per litre, with diesel (*gasolio*) costing €1.69 per litre.

Spare parts are available at many garages or via the 24-hour ACI motorist assistance number ☑80 31 16.

Hire

CARS

➡ Pre-booking a car via the internet often costs less than hiring a car in Italy. Online booking agency **Rentalcars. com** (www.rentalcars. com) compares the rates of numerous car-rental companies.

➡ Renters must generally be aged 25 or over, with a credit card and home country driving licence or an International Driving Permit.

➡ Consider hiring a small car, which will reduce your fuel expense and help you negotiate narrow city lanes and tight parking spaces.

➡ Check with your credit-card company to see if it offers a Collision Damage Waiver, which covers you for additional damage if you use that card to pay for the car.

➡ All the major car-hire outlets have offices at the airports. Multinational car rental agencies include the following:

Auto Europe (www.auto europe.com)

Avis (www.avis.com)

Budget (www.budget.com)

Europcar (www.europcar.com)

Hertz (www.hertz.it)

Maggiore (www.maggiore.it)

MOTORCYCLES

➡ Agencies throughout Italy rent motorbikes, ranging from small Vespas to larger touring bikes. Prices start at around €35/150 per day/ week for a 50cc scooter, or upwards of €80/400 per day/week for a 650cc motorcycle.

➡ A licence is not required to ride a scooter under 50cc but you must be aged 14 or over and you cannot carry passengers or ride on an autostrada. To ride a motorcycle or scooter up to 125cc, you must be aged 16 or over and have a licence (a car licence will suffice). For motorcycles over 125cc you will need a motorcycle licence.

➡ Do not venture onto the autostrada with a bike of less than 150cc.

Road Rules

Before getting behind the wheel, it's worth acquainting yourself with the country's road rules. Here are some of the most essential:

➡ Cars drive on the right side of the road and overtake on the left.

➡ Seat belt use (front and rear) is mandatory.

➡ Give way to cars entering an intersection from a road on your right, unless otherwise indicated.

➡ In the event of a breakdown, a warning triangle is compulsory, as is the use of an approved yellow or orange safety vest if you leave your vehicle. Recommended accessories include a first-aid kit, spare-bulb kit and fire extinguisher.

➡ Italy's blood-alcohol limit is 0.05%. Random breath tests take place and penalties can be severe.

➡ Some cities, including Naples, ban non-residents from driving in the *centro storico* (historic centre). Fines can be steep.

➡ Speed limits for cars are 130km/h to 150km/h on autostradas; 110km/h on other main highways; 90km/h on minor, non-urban roads; 50km/h in built-up areas.

➡ The speed limit for mopeds is 40km/h.

➡ Speeding fines follow EU standards and are proportionate with the number of kilometres that you are caught driving over

the limit, reaching up to €3119 including suspension of your driving licence.

➡ Helmets are required on all two-wheeled transport.

➡ Motorbikes can enter most restricted traffic areas in Italian cities, and traffic police generally turn a blind eye to motorcycles or scooters parked on footpaths.

➡ Headlights are compulsory day and night for all vehicles on autostradas, and are advisable for motorcycles, even on smaller roads.

Local Transport

Bus & Underground Trains

Every city or town of any size has an efficient *urbano* (urban) and *extraurbano* (suburban) system of buses. Services are generally limited on Sundays and holidays. Naples and Catania also have a metro system.

Purchase bus and metro tickets before boarding. You must validate bus tickets on-board and metro tickets at the station turnstile. Tickets can be bought from a *tabaccaio* (tobacconist), newsstands, ticket booths or dispensing machines at bus stations and in underground stations, and usually cost around €1 to €1.50. Some southern Italian cities offer good-value 24-hour or daily tourist tickets.

Taxi

You can catch a taxi at the ranks outside most train and bus stations, or simply telephone for a radio taxi. Note that radio taxi meters start running from when you've called rather than when you're picked up.

Charges vary somewhat from one region to another. Most short city journeys cost between €10 and €15. Generally, no more than four people are allowed in one taxi.

Train

Trains in Italy are relatively cheap compared with other European countries, and the better train categories are fast and comfortable.

Trenitalia (☑89 20 21; www.trenitalia.com) is the partially privatised, state train system that runs most services. Its privately owned competitor **Italo** (☑06 07 08; www.italotreno.it) runs high-velocity trains on two lines, one between Turin and Salerno, and one between Venice and Naples.

Italy operates several types of trains:

Regionale/Interregionale Slow and cheap, stopping at all or most stations.

InterCity (IC) Faster services operating between major cities.

Alta Velocità (AV) State-of-the-art, high-velocity trains, including Frecciarossa, Frecciargento, Frecciabianca and Italo trains. Speeds of up to 300km/hr and connections to the major Italian cities. More expensive than Inter-City express trains, but journey times cut by almost half.

As with the bus services, there are a number of private train lines operating throughout Italy's south, including the following:

Circumvesuviana (www.eav campania.it) Links Naples and Sorrento, stopping at Ercolano (Herculaneum) and Pompeii.

Ferrovia Cumana (www.eav campania.it) Connects Naples

to the Campi Flegrei to the west. Stops include Pozzuoli.

Ferrotramviaria (www. ferrovienordbarese.it) Services towns in Puglia's Terra di Bari, including Bitonto, Ruvo di Puglia, Andria and Barletta. Replacement bus service operates Sundays.

Ferrovie Appulo Lucane (FAL; www.fal-srl.it) Links Bari province with Basilicata, including stops at Altamura, Matera, Gravina in Puglia and Potenza. Replacement buses on Sundays.

Ferrovie del Sud-Est (www. fseonline.it) The main network covering Puglia's Murgia towns and the Salento, servicing tourist hotspots like Castellana Grotte, Alberobello, Martina Franca, Lecce, Gallipoli and Otranto. Replacement buses on Sundays.

Train Routes

Train Journey Durations:
Naples–Sorrento (1hr 5min)
Naples–Bari (3hr 50min)
Naples–Palermo (9hr 5min)
Bari–Brindisi (1hr)
Bari–Lecce (1hr 20min)
Reggio di Calabria–Catania (3hr 30min)

Principal Train Lines
Local Train Lines
Private Train Lines

Ferrovia Circumetnea

(www.circumetnea.it) A 114km line connecting the towns around the base of Mt Etna in Sicily. No service on Sundays.

Classes & Costs

Prices vary according to the class of service, time of travel and how far in advance you book. Most Italian trains have 1st- and 2nd-class seating; a 1st-class ticket typically costs from a third to a half more than the 2nd-class ticket.

Travel on Trenitalia's InterCity and Alta Velocità (Frecciarossa, Frecciargento, Frecciabianca) trains means paying a supplement, determined by the distance you are travelling and included in the ticket price. If you have a standard ticket for a slower train and end up hopping on an IC train, you'll have to pay the difference on board. (You can only board an Alta Velocità train if you have a booking, so the problem does not arise in those cases.)

Validate train tickets in the yellow machines (usually found at the head of rail platforms) just before boarding. Failure to do so usually results in fines.

Reservations

Reservations are obligatory on Alta Velocità trains. Otherwise they're not required on other train lines and, outside of peak holiday periods, you should be fine without them. You can make reservations online, at railway station counters, travel agents and – when they haven't broken down – at the automated machines sprinkled around most stations.

Language

Standard Italian is taught and spoken throughout Italy. Regional dialects are an important part of identity in many parts of the country, but you'll have no trouble being understood anywhere if you stick to standard Italian, which we've also used in this chapter.

The sounds used in spoken Italian can all be found in English. If you read our coloured pronunciation guides as if they were English, you'll be understood. The stressed syllables are indicated with italics. Note that ai is pronounced as in 'aisle', ay as in 'say', ow as in 'how', dz as the 'ds' in 'lids', and that r is a strong and rolled sound. Keep in mind that Italian consonants can have a stronger, emphatic pronunciation – if the consonant is written as a double letter, it should be pronounced a little stronger, eg *sonno* *son*·no (sleep) versus *sono* *so*·no (I am).

BASICS

Italian has two words for 'you' – use the polite form *Lei* lay if you're talking to strangers, officials or people older than you. With people familiar to you or younger than you, you can use the informal form *tu* too.

In Italian, all nouns and adjectives are either masculine or feminine, and so are the articles *il/la* eel/la (the) and *un/una* oon/*oo*·na (a) that go with the nouns.

In this chapter the polite/informal and masculine/feminine options are included where necessary, separated with a slash and indicated with 'pol/inf' and 'm/f'.

WANT MORE?

For in-depth language information and handy phrases, check out Lonely Planet's *Italian Phrasebook*. You'll find it at **shop.lonelyplanet.com**, or you can buy Lonely Planet's iPhone phrasebooks at the Apple App Store.

Hello.	*Buongiorno.*	bwon·*jor*·no
Goodbye.	*Arrivederci.*	a·ree·ve·*der*·chee
Yes./No.	*Sì./No.*	see/no
Excuse me.	*Mi scusi.* (pol)	mee skoo·zee
	Scusami. (inf)	skoo·za·mee
Sorry.	*Mi dispiace.*	mee dees·*pya*·che
Please.	*Per favore.*	per fa·*vo*·re
Thank you.	*Grazie.*	*gra*·tsye
You're welcome.	*Prego.*	*pre*·go

How are you?
Come sta/stai? (pol/inf)   ko·me sta/stai

Fine. And you?
Bene. E Lei/tu? (pol/inf)   be·ne e lay/too

What's your name?
Come si chiama? pol   ko·me see *kya*·ma
Come ti chiami? inf   ko·me tee *kya*·mee

My name is ...
Mi chiamo ...   mee *kya*·mo ...

Do you speak English?
Parla/Parli   *pär*·la/*par*·lee
inglese? (pol/inf)   een·*gle*·ze

I don't understand.
Non capisco.   non ka·*pee*·sko

ACCOMMODATION

Do you have a ... room?	*Avete una camera ...?*	a·*ve*·te *oo*·na *ka*·me·ra ...
double	*doppia con letto matri-moniale*	*do*·pya kon *le*·to ma·tree·mo·*nya*·le
single	*singola*	*seen*·go·la
How much is it per ...?	*Quanto costa per ...?*	*kwan*·to *kos*·ta per ...
night	*una notte*	*oo*·na *no*·te
person	*persona*	per·*so*·na

Is breakfast included?
La colazione è compresa?
la ko·la·*tsyo*·ne e kom·*pre*·sa

air-con	*aria condizionata*	a·rya kon·dee·tsyo·*na*·ta
bathroom	*bagno*	*ba*·nyo
campsite	*campeggio*	kam·*pe*·jo
guesthouse	*pensione*	pen·*syo*·ne
hotel	*albergo*	al·*ber*·go
youth hostel	*ostello della gioventù*	os·*te*·lo de·la jo·ven·*too*
window	*finestra*	fee·*nes*·tra

DIRECTIONS

Where's ...?
Dov'è ...?
do·*ve* ...

What's the address?
Qual'è l'indirizzo?
kwa·*le* leen·dee·*ree*·tso

Could you please write it down?
Può scriverlo, per favore?
pwo *skree*·ver·lo per fa·*vo*·re

Can you show me (on the map)?
Può mostrarmi (sulla pianta)?
pwo mos·*trar*·mee (soo·la *pyan*·ta)

at the corner	*all'angolo*	a·*lan*·go·lo
at the traffic lights	*al semaforo*	al se·*ma*·fo·ro
behind	*dietro*	*dye*·tro
far	*lontano*	lon·*ta*·no
in front of	*davanti a*	da·*van*·tee a
left	*a sinistra*	a see·*nee*·stra
near	*vicino*	vee·*chee*·no
next to	*accanto a*	a·*kan*·to a
opposite	*di fronte a*	dee *fron*·te a
right	*a destra*	a *de*·stra
straight ahead	*sempre diritto*	*sem*·pre dee·*ree*·to

EATING & DRINKING

What would you recommend?
Cosa mi consiglia?
ko·za mee kon·*see*·lya

What's in that dish?
Quali ingredienti ci sono in questo piatto?
kwa·li een·gre·*dyen*·tee chee *so*·no een *kwe*·sto *pya*·to

What's the local speciality?
Qual'è la specialità di questa regione?
kwa·*le* la spe·cha·lee·*ta* dee *kwe*·sta re·*jo*·ne

That was delicious!
Era squisito!
e·ra skwee·*zee*·to

KEY PATTERNS

To get by in Italian, mix and match these simple patterns with words of your choice:

When's (the next flight)?
A che ora è (il prossimo volo)?
a ke o·ra e (eel *pro*·see·mo *vo*·lo)

Where's (the station)?
Dov'è (la stazione)?
do·*ve* (la sta·*tsyo*·ne)

I'm looking for (a hotel).
Sto cercando (un albergo).
sto cher·*kan*·do (oon al·*ber*·go)

Do you have (a map)?
Ha (una pianta)?
a (oo·na *pyan*·ta)

Is there (a toilet)?
C'è (un gabinetto)?
che (oon ga·bee·*ne*·to)

I'd like (a coffee).
Vorrei (un caffè).
vo·*ray* (oon ka·fe)

I'd like to (hire a car).
Vorrei (noleggiare una macchina).
vo·*ray* (no·le·ja·re oo·na ma·kee·na)

Can I (enter)?
Posso (entrare)?
po·so (en·*tra*·re)

Could you please (help me)?
Può (aiutarmi), per favore?
pwo (a·yoo·*tar*·mee) per fa·*vo*·re

Do I have to (book a seat)?
Devo (prenotare un posto)?
de·vo (pre·no·*ta*·re oon po·sto)

Cheers!
Salute!
sa·*loo*·te

Please bring the bill.
Mi porta il conto, per favore?
mee *por*·ta eel *kon*·to per fa·*vo*·re

I'd like to reserve a table for ...	*Vorrei prenotare un tavolo per ...*	vo·*ray* pre·no·*ta*·re oon *ta*·vo·lo per ...
(eight) o'clock	*le (otto)*	le (o·to)
(two) people	*(due) persone*	(doo·e) per·*so*·ne

I don't eat ...	*Non mangio ...*	non *man*·jo ...
eggs	*uova*	*wo*·va
fish	*pesce*	*pe*·she
nuts	*noci*	*no*·chee

Key Words

bar	*locale*	lo·*ka*·le
bottle	*bottiglia*	bo·*tee*·lya

breakfast	prima colazione	pree·ma ko·la·tsyo·ne
cafe	bar	bar
cold	freddo	fre·do
dinner	cena	che·na
drink list	lista delle bevande	lee·sta de·le be·van·de
fork	forchetta	for·ke·ta
glass	bicchiere	bee·kye·re
grocery store	alimentari	a·lee·men·ta·ree
hot	caldo	kal·do
knife	coltello	kol·te·lo
lunch	pranzo	pran·dzo
market	mercato	mer·ka·to
menu	menù	me·noo
plate	piatto	pya·to
restaurant	ristorante	ree·sto·ran·te
spicy	piccante	pee·kan·te
spoon	cucchiaio	koo·kya·yo
vegetarian (food)	vegetariano	ve·je·ta·rya·no
with	con	kon
without	senza	sen·tsa

Meat & Fish

beef	manzo	man·dzo
chicken	pollo	po·lo
duck	anatra	a·na·tra
fish	pesce	pe·she
herring	aringa	a·reen·ga
lamb	agnello	a·nye·lo
lobster	aragosta	a·ra·gos·ta
meat	carne	kar·ne
mussels	cozze	ko·tse
oysters	ostriche	o·stree·ke
pork	maiale	ma·ya·le
prawn	gambero	gam·be·ro
salmon	salmone	sal·mo·ne
scallops	capasante	ka·pa·san·te
seafood	frutti di mare	froo·tee dee ma·re
shrimp	gambero	gam·be·ro
squid	calamari	ka·la·ma·ree
trout	trota	tro·ta
tuna	tonno	to·no
turkey	tacchino	ta·kee·no
veal	vitello	vee·te·lo

Fruit & Vegetables

apple	mela	me·la
beans	fagioli	fa·jo·lee
cabbage	cavolo	ka·vo·lo
capsicum	peperone	pe·pe·ro·ne
carrot	carota	ka·ro·ta
cauliflower	cavolfiore	ka·vol·fyo·re
cucumber	cetriolo	che·tree·o·lo
fruit	frutta	froo·ta
grapes	uva	oo·va
lemon	limone	lee·mo·ne
lentils	lenticchie	len·tee·kye
mushroom	funghi	foon·gee
nuts	noci	no·chee
onions	cipolle	chee·po·le
orange	arancia	a·ran·cha
peach	pesca	pe·ska
peas	piselli	pee·ze·lee
pineapple	ananas	a·na·nas
plum	prugna	proo·nya
potatoes	patate	pa·ta·te
spinach	spinaci	spee·na·chee
tomatoes	pomodori	po·mo·do·ree
vegetables	verdura	ver·doo·ra

Other

bread	pane	pa·ne
butter	burro	boo·ro
cheese	formaggio	for·ma·jo
eggs	uova	wo·va
honey	miele	mye·le
ice	ghiaccio	gya·cho
jam	marmellata	mar·me·la·ta
noodles	pasta	pas·ta

SIGNS

Entrata/Ingresso	Entrance
Uscita	Exit
Aperto	Open
Chiuso	Closed
Informazioni	Information
Proibito/Vietato	Prohibited
Gabinetti/Servizi	Toilets
Uomini	Men
Donne	Women

oil	olio	o·lyo
pepper	pepe	pe·pe
rice	riso	ree·zo
salt	sale	sa·le
soup	minestra	mee·nes·tra
soy sauce	salsa di soia	sal·sa dee so·ya
sugar	zucchero	tsoo·ke·ro
vinegar	aceto	a·che·to

Drinks

beer	birra	bee·ra
coffee	caffè	ka·fe
(orange) juice	succo (d'arancia)	soo·ko (da·ran·cha)
milk	latte	la·te
red wine	vino rosso	vee·no ro·so
soft drink	bibita	bee·bee·ta
tea	tè	te
(mineral) water	acqua (minerale)	a·kwa (mee·ne·ra·le)
white wine	vino bianco	vee·no byan·ko

EMERGENCIES

Help!
Aiuto! a·yoo·to

Leave me alone!
Lasciami in pace! la·sha·mee een pa·che

I'm lost.
Mi sono perso/a. (m/f) mee so·no per·so/a

There's been an accident.
C'è stato un incidente. che sta·to oon een·chee·den·te

Call the police!
Chiami la polizia! kya·mee la po·lee·tsee·a

Call a doctor!
Chiami un medico! kya·mee oon me·dee·ko

Where are the toilets?
Dove sono i gabinetti? do·ve so·no ee ga·bee·ne·tee

I'm sick.
Mi sento male. mee sen·to ma·le

QUESTION WORDS

How?	Come?	ko·me
What?	Che cosa?	ke ko·za
When?	Quando?	kwan·do
Where?	Dove?	do·ve
Who?	Chi?	kee
Why?	Perché?	per·ke

It hurts here.
Mi fa male qui. mee fa ma·le kwee

I'm allergic to ...
Sono allergico/a a ... (m/f) so·no a·ler·jee·ko/a a ...

SHOPPING & SERVICES

I'd like to buy ...
Vorrei comprare ... vo·ray kom·pra·re ...

I'm just looking.
Sto solo guardando. sto so·lo gwar·dan·do

Can I look at it?
Posso dare un'occhiata? po·so da·re oo·no·kya·ta

How much is this?
Quanto costa questo? kwan·to kos·ta kwe·sto

It's too expensive.
È troppo caro/a. (m/f) e tro·po ka·ro/a

Can you lower the price?
Può farmi lo sconto? pwo far·mee lo skon·to

There's a mistake in the bill.
C'è un errore nel conto. che oo·ne·ro·re nel kon·to

ATM	Bancomat	ban·ko·mat
post office	ufficio postale	oo·fee·cho pos·ta·le
tourist office	ufficio del turismo	oo·fee·cho del too·reez·mo

TIME & DATES

What time is it?	Che ora è?	ke o·ra e
It's one o'clock.	È l'una.	e loo·na
It's (two) o'clock.	Sono le (due).	so·no le (doo·e)
Half past (one).	(L'una) e mezza.	(loo·na) e me·dza

in the morning	di mattina	dee ma·tee·na
in the afternoon	di pomeriggio	dee po·me·ree·jo
in the evening	di sera	dee se·ra

yesterday	ieri	ye·ree
today	oggi	o·jee
tomorrow	domani	do·ma·nee

Monday	lunedì	loo·ne·dee
Tuesday	martedì	mar·te·dee
Wednesday	mercoledì	mer·ko·le·dee
Thursday	giovedì	jo·ve·dee
Friday	venerdì	ve·ner·dee
Saturday	sabato	sa·ba·to
Sunday	domenica	do·me·nee·ka

January	*gennaio*	je·*na*·yo
February	*febbraio*	fe·*bra*·yo
March	*marzo*	*mar*·tso
April	*aprile*	a·*pree*·le
May	*maggio*	*ma*·jo
June	*giugno*	*joo*·nyo
July	*luglio*	*loo*·lyo
August	*agosto*	a·*gos*·to
September	*settembre*	se·*tem*·bre
October	*ottobre*	o·*to*·bre
November	*novembre*	no·*vem*·bre
December	*dicembre*	dee·*chem*·bre

NUMBERS

1	*uno*	*oo*·no
2	*due*	*doo*·e
3	*tre*	tre
4	*quattro*	*kwa*·tro
5	*cinque*	*cheen*·kwe
6	*sei*	say
7	*sette*	*se*·te
8	*otto*	*o*·to
9	*nove*	*no*·ve
10	*dieci*	*dye*·chee
20	*venti*	*ven*·tee
30	*trenta*	*tren*·ta
40	*quaranta*	kwa·*ran*·ta
50	*cinquanta*	cheen·*kwan*·ta
60	*sessanta*	se·*san*·ta
70	*settanta*	se·*tan*·ta
80	*ottanta*	o·*tan*·ta
90	*novanta*	no·*van*·ta
100	*cento*	*chen*·to
1000	*mille*	*mee*·lel

TRANSPORT

Public Transport

At what time does the ... leave/arrive?	*A che ora parte/ arriva ...?*	a ke o·ra *par*·te/ a·*ree*·va ...
boat	*la nave*	la *na*·ve
bus	*l'autobus*	*low*·to·boos
ferry	*il traghetto*	eel tra·*ge*·to
metro	*la metro- politana*	la me·tro- po·lee·*ta*·na
plane	*l'aereo*	la·e·re·o
train	*il treno*	eel *tre*·no
... ticket	*un biglietto ...*	oon bee·*lye*·to
one-way	*di sola andata*	dee *so*·la an·*da*·ta
return	*di andata e ritorno*	dee an·*da*·ta e ree·*tor*·no
bus stop	*fermata dell'autobus*	fer·*ma*·ta del *ow*·to·boos
platform	*binario*	bee·*na*·ryo
ticket office	*biglietteria*	bee·lye·te·*ree*·a
timetable	*orario*	o·*ra*·ryo
train station	*stazione ferroviaria*	sta·*tsyo*·ne fe·ro·*vyar*·ya

Does it stop at ...?
Si ferma a ...?   see *fer*·ma a ...

Please tell me when we get to ...
Mi dica per favore quando arriviamo a ...   mee *dee*·ka per fa·*vo*·re kwan·do a·ree·*vya*·mo a ...

I want to get off here.
Voglio scendere qui.   *vo*·lyo *shen*·de·re kwee

Driving & Cycling

I'd like to hire a/an ...	*Vorrei noleggiare un/una ... (m/f)*	vo·*ray* no·le·*ja*·re oon/*oo*·na ...
4WD	*fuoristrada (m)*	fwo·ree·*stra*·da
bicycle	*bicicletta (f)*	bee·chee·*kle*·ta
car	*macchina (f)*	*ma*·kee·na
motorbike	*moto (f)*	*mo*·to
bicycle pump	*pompa della bicicletta*	*pom*·pa de·la bee·chee·*kle*·ta
child seat	*seggiolino*	se·jo·*lee*·no
helmet	*casco*	*kas*·ko
mechanic	*meccanico*	me·*ka*·nee·ko
petrol/gas	*benzina*	ben·*dzee*·na
service station	*stazione di servizio*	sta·*tsyo*·ne dee ser·*vee*·tsyo

Is this the road to ...?
Questa strada porta a ...?   *kwe*·sta *stra*·da *por*·ta a ...

Can I park here?
Posso parcheggiare qui?   po·so par·ke·*ja*·re kwee

The car/motorbike has broken down (at ...).
La macchina/moto si è guastata (a ...).   la *ma*·kee·na/*mo*·to see e gwas·*ta*·ta (a ...)

I have a flat tyre.
Ho una gomma bucata.   o *oo*·na *go*·ma boo·*ka*·ta

GLOSSARY

(m) indicates masculine gender, (f) feminine gender and (pl) plural

abbazia – abbey

agriturismo – tourist accommodation on farms; farm stay

(pizza) al taglio – (pizza) by the slice

albergo – hotel

alimentari – grocery shop; delicatessen

anfiteatro – amphitheatre

aperitivo – before-evening-meal drink and snack

APT – Azienda di Promozione Turistica; local town or city tourist office

autostrada – motorway; highway

battistero – baptistry

biblioteca – library

biglietto – ticket

borgo – archaic name for a small town, village or town sector (often dating to Middle Ages)

camera – room

campo – field

cappella – chapel

carabinieri – police with military and civil duties

Carnevale – carnival period between Epiphany and Lent

casa – house

castello – castle

cattedrale – cathedral

centro storico – historic centre

certosa – monastery belonging to or founded by Carthusian monks

chiesa – church

chiostro – cloister; covered walkway, usually enclosed by columns, around a quadrangle

cima – summit

città – city

città alta – upper town

città bassa – lower town

colonna – column

comune – equivalent to a municipality or county; a town or city council; historically, a self-governing town or city

contrada – district

corso – boulevard

duomo – cathedral

enoteca – wine bar

espresso – short black coffee

ferrovia – railway

festa – feast day; holiday

fontana – fountain

foro – forum

funivia – cable car

gelateria – ice-cream shop

giardino – garden

golfo – gulf

grotta – cave

isola – island

lago – lake

largo – small square

lido – beach

locanda – inn; small hotel

lungomare – seafront road/ promenade

mar, mare – sea

masseria – working farm

mausoleo – mausoleum; stately and magnificent tomb

mercato – market

monte – mountain

necropoli – ancient name for cemetery or burial site

nord – north

osteria – simple, trattoria-style restaurant, usually with a bar

palazzo – mansion; palace; large building of any type, including an apartment block

palio – contest

parco – park

passeggiata – traditional evening stroll

pasticceria – cake/pastry shop

pensione – guesthouse

piazza – square

piazzale – large open square

pietà – literally 'pity' or 'compassion'; sculpture, drawing or painting of the dead Christ supported by the Madonna

pinacoteca – art gallery

ponte – bridge

porta – gate; door

porto – port

reale – royal

rifugio – mountain hut

ristorante – restaurant

rocca – fortress

sala – room; hall

salumeria – delicatessen

santuario – sanctuary; 1. the part of a church above the altar; 2. an especially holy place in a temple (antiquity)

sassi – literally 'stones'; stone houses built in two ravines in Matera, Basilicata

scalinata – staircase

scavi – excavations

spiaggia – beach

stazione – station

stazione marittima – ferry terminal

strada – street; road

sud – south

superstrada – expressway; highway with divided lanes

tartufo – truffle

tavola calda – literally 'hot table'; pre-prepared meat, pasta and vegetable selection, often self-service

teatro – theatre

tempietto – small temple

tempio – temple

terme – thermal baths

tesoro – treasury

torre – tower

trattoria – simple restaurant

Trenitalia – Italian State Railways; also known as Ferrovie dello Stato (FS)

trullo – conical house

via – street; road

viale – avenue

vico – alley; alleyway

villa – town house; country house; also the park surrounding the house

Behind the Scenes

SEND US YOUR FEEDBACK

We love to hear from travellers – your comments keep us on our toes and help make our books better. Our well-travelled team reads every word on what you loved or loathed about this book. Although we cannot reply individually to postal submissions, we always guarantee that your feedback goes straight to the appropriate authors, in time for the next edition. Each person who sends us information is thanked in the next edition – the most useful submissions are rewarded with a selection of digital PDF chapters.

Visit **lonelyplanet.com/contact** to submit your updates and suggestions or to ask for help. Our award-winning website also features inspirational travel stories, news and discussions.

Note: We may edit, reproduce and incorporate your comments in Lonely Planet products such as guidebooks, websites and digital products, so let us know if you don't want your comments reproduced or your name acknowledged. For a copy of our privacy policy visit lonelyplanet.com/privacy.

OUR READERS

Many thanks to the travellers who used the last edition and wrote to us with helpful hints, useful advice and interesting anecdotes:

Alison Jones, Carol Buchman, Caroline Laurent, Christophe de Metsenaere, Cinzia Rascazzo, Margaret Wilson, Michael DeLuzio

AUTHOR THANKS

Cristian Bonetto

First and foremost, an epic thank you to my hawk-eyed coauthors, who bring to this guide the absolute best southern Italy has to offer. On the ground, an equally epic *grazie* to my 'Re e Regina di Napoli', as well as to the incredibly generous Lorenzo Andrei, Vincenzo Mattiucci, Joe Brizzi, Andrea Maglio, Giancarlo Di Maio, Susy Galeone, Voza family, Luca Coda, Harriet Driver and Valentina Vellusi.

Gregor Clark

Grazie mille to all of the kind-hearted Italians who helped make this trip so memorable, especially Angela and Nicoletta in Palermo, the Tagliavia family in Polizzi Generosa, Francesca in Stromboli, Marisin and Salvatore in Scopello, Stefano in Milazzo and Diana in Lipari. Thanks to Gurty Spam for joining me on the Aeolians and helping me renew my Stromboli obsession. Finally, big hugs to Gaen, Meigan and Chloe, who always make returning home the happiest part of the trip.

Helena Smith

Thanks to everyone who helped with advice, good food and hospitality along the way.

ACKNOWLEDGMENTS

Climate Map Data Climate map data adapted from Peel MC, Finlayson BL & McMahon TA (2007) 'Updated World Map of the Köppen-Geiger Climate Classification', *Hydrology and Earth System Sciences*, 11, 1633¬44.

Illustration pp76-7 by Javier Martinez Zarracina.

Cover photograph: Promontorio del Gargano, Puglia. Massimo Ripani, 4Corners.

THIS BOOK

This 2nd edition of Lonely Planet's *Southern Italy* guidebook was researched and written by Cristian Bonetto, Gregor Clark and Helena Smith. The previous edition was written by Cristian Bonetto, Gregor Clark and Olivia Pozzan. This guidebook was commissioned in Lonely Planet's London office, and produced by the following:

Commissioning Editor Joe Bindloss

Coordinating Editors Briohny Hooper, Samantha Forge

Senior Cartographer Valentina Kremenchutskaya

Book Designer Katherine Marsh

Managing Editor Angela Tinson

Cover Research Naomi Parker

Language Content Branislava Vladisavljevic

Thanks to Sasha Baskett, Elin Berglund, Ryan Evans, Larissa Frost, Liz Heynes, Genesys India, Jouve India, Indra Kilfoyle, Annelies Mertens, Wayne Murphy, Darren O'Connell, Trent Paton, Dianne Schallmeiner, John Taufa, Gerard Walker, Juan Winata

Index

NOTES